THE PENGUIN BOOK OF

WOMEN'S HUMOR

❧ ❧

*Edited with an Introduction
by Regina Barreca*

PENGUIN BOOKS

PENGUIN BOOKS
Published by the Penguin Group
Penguin Books USA Inc., 375 Hudson Street,
New York, New York 10014, U.S.A.
Penguin Books Ltd, 27 Wrights Lane,
London W8 5TZ, England
Penguin Books Australia Ltd, Ringwood,
Victoria, Australia
Penguin Books Canada Ltd, 10 Alcorn Avenue,
Toronto, Ontario, Canada M4V 3B2
Penguin Books (N.Z.) Ltd, 182–190 Wairau Road,
Auckland 10, New Zealand

Penguin Books Ltd, Registered Offices:
Harmondsworth, Middlesex, England

First published in Penguin Books 1996

3 5 7 9 10 8 6 4

Pages 651–658 constitute an extension of this copyright page.

LIBRARY OF CONGRESS CATALOGING IN PUBLICATION DATA
The Penguin book of women's humor / edited with an introduction by
Regina Barreca.
p. cm.
Includes index.
ISBN 0 14 017.294 7 (pbk.)
1. Women—Humor. 2. Women—Literary collections. I. Barreca,
Regina.
PN6231.W6P46 1996
808.87—dc20 96–9009

Printed in the United States of America
Set in Adobe Bembo

In memory of Diane Cleaver, who knew by heart
that while life is no joke,
it is nevertheless
remarkably funny.

Acknowledgments

⊱⊰

I COULD grow old thanking people for their help with this collection: literally hundreds of friends, colleagues, students, audience members, and readers mailed, faxed, phoned, told, and invented stories for this book. I'm enormously and gleefully grateful, and hope that I've done them justice in repeating the punchlines. I'd particularly like to thank the following for their lifesaving suggestions and contributions: colleague and research assistant Julie Nash (who knows that this book is pretty much her godchild), editor Michael Millman and assistant editor Kristine Puopolo at Penguin (with particular applause reserved for Kris's efforts in securing that most elusive of prizes—copyright permissions—and for her work above, beyond, below, and between the lines of duty), production editor Barbara Campo, Carole DeSanti at Dutton (who got me started in the first place), as well as Professor Nancy Walker at Vanderbilt University, whose ground-breaking work on women's comedy remains the finest discussion of gender and humor anyone can read. The following remarkable gang also deserve all the applause and pastry I can send their way: Rose Quiello, Allison Hild, Valerie Smith-Matteson, Sandy Cohen, Allison Kane, Casey Leadingham, Kim Schliecher-Derechin, Stephanie Smith, Margaret Mitchell, Lauren Robinson, Jennifer Berman, Nicole Hollander, Libby Reid, Bonnie Januszewski-Ytuarte, Pam Katz, Brenda Gross, Esther Cohen, Lee Jacobus, John Glavin, Bob Sullivan, Mary Anne Yanulis, Fay Weldon, Chris Francis, Nancy Lager, Lynette Lager, Deborah Morse, Faith Middleton, Blanche Boyd, Roxanne Coady, Jane Kim, Suzy Staubach, Jim Kincaid, Nan Graham, Richard Caccavale, humor colleagues Susan Horowitz, Barbara Levy, and Audrey Bilger, the Research Foundation at the University of Connecticut, the faculty and staff of the English Department (particularly the Pizza Night crowd), as well as the patient and knowledgeable staff at UConn's interlibrary loan office. My thanks go to my family—Hugo Sr., Hugo Jr., Wendy, Tim, and Matthew—and especially to my husband, Michael Meyer, whose sense of humor has kept me going when the laughter is most difficult to hear. Finally, this book is dedicated to the memory of Diane Cleaver, a feisty, funny woman who inspired us all.

Contents

❧ ❧

Topical Index

WOMEN'S HUMOR

Introduction

THE CREATION and enjoyment of humor have traditionally been considered masculine privileges, sort of like writing in the snow or running for public office.

Better to keep the ladies away from such matters so that their pretty little lives could remain the unsullied, innocent, delightful romps men assumed to be the easy lot of feminine existence. Keep the ladies ladylike; keep them away from the dangers of politics, sex, and humor.

There are problems with this arrangement. Even if we ignore thousands of years of history littered with such "ladylike" events as witch-hunts, death in childbirth, and the systematic oppression of women in the workplace, women's lives have hardly resembled the tableau of simple domestic bliss we were purported to inhabit. Women's lives have always been full of sex and politics: even when we were not expected to participate in—(let alone enjoy controlling) these events, women never did escape their impact on our lives.

Much women's humor, while not explicitly political, nevertheless raises questions concerning the accepted wisdom of the system. Actress and comedian Pam Stone, for example, reflects on the problems of the euphemisms surrounding women's lives.

> I had a girlfriend who told me she was in the hospital for female problems. I said, "Get real! What does that mean?" She says, "You know, *female* problems." I said, "What? You can't parallel park? You can't get credit?"

When it *is* explicitly political, women's humor often satirizes the social forces designed to keep women in "their place," a phrase that has become synonymous with keeping women quietly bound by cultural stereotypes. In "An Anti-Suffrage Monologue," turn-of-the-century writer Marie Jenney Howe parodies the absurd voice of one of the early antifeminists, whose neoconservative daughters buy *The Total Woman* and learn to wear Saran Wrap to the front door in order to appear sexy to their husbands. (A friend of mine suggested that if she opened the door wrapped in Saran, her husband would mistake her for one big leftover and put her in the microwave.)

In this crafty parody of an antisuffragette attitude, Howe writes:

> Woman must remain woman. If man goes over and tries to be like woman, if woman goes over and tries to be like man, it will become so very confusing and so difficult to explain to our children. Let us take a practical example. If a woman puts on a man's coat and trousers, takes a man's cane and hat and cigar, and goes out on the street, what will happen to her? She will be arrested and thrown into jail. Then why not stay at home?

The parody remains an effective bit of humor because the argument against women taking part in the working of the world makes as much sense today as it did a hundred years ago, which to say that it makes no sense at all.

It should come as no surprise, then, that women's lives have always been filled with humor. Women's humor emerges as a tool for survival in the social and professional jungles, and as a weapon against the absurdities of injustice. The one thing it has never been is a fluffy concoction of adorably sweet sensibilities. Comedian Judy Tenuta's reminiscences about her childhood are hardly constructed of the stuff making up most poignant epiphanies: "Once I was riding my bike and my mom was waving to me from the window. She said, 'Judy, soon your body will change.' I said, 'I know—puberty.' She said, 'No, that Good Humor truck.'"

It's a risk for women to use humor (even good humor) because their "femininity" might be (read: will inevitably be) called into question. Comedy writer Anne Beatts faced this directly when she admitted, "I'm often accused of 'going too far,' but I recognize that behind my desire to shock is an even stronger desire to evade the 'feminine' stereotype: 'You say women are afraid of mice? I'll show you! I'll *eat* the mouse!'"

Women's humor is about life, death, sex, work, families, politics, social custom, and shoes. (There is a great disparity between the number of witty remarks concerning shoes made by women and those made by men. There are a few other differences, too.)

Unlike writing in the snow or running for public office, humor takes intelligence, courage, insight, and a sense of irreverence not necessarily associated with good spelling or even good penmanship. The pages that follow prove that women did not suddenly get funny in the '90s any more than women suddenly got ambitious in the '70s or sexually aware in the '60s or intelligent in the 1890s. In the late eighteenth century Jane Austen was, with her characteristic and perfectly aimed irony, examining the appeal of congenital ignorance in women. Of the heroine of *Northanger Abbey*, Austen writes:

> She was heartily ashamed of her ignorance. A misplaced shame. Where people wish to attach, they should always be ignorant. To come with a well-informed mind, is to come with an inability of administering to the vanity of others, which a sensible person would always wish to avoid. A woman especially, if she should have the misfortune of knowing anything, should conceal it as well as she can.

Clearly Austen is not concerned with concealing her own devastating wit. Austen is a troublemaker, like all the best female humorists.

Her letters reveal a woman who did not suffer fools gladly. Writing to her various relations and friends, she reveals a character shockingly different from the modest and frail creature she is often assigned. "I do not want people to be very agreeable," quips Austen, "as it saves me the trouble of liking them a great deal." Even less nurturing, perhaps, is her commentary on the demise of an acquaintance: "Only think of Mrs. Holder's being dead! Poor woman, she has done the only thing in the world she could possibly do to make one cease to abuse her." Sweet Jane Austen was hardly an angel painting on a tiny piece of ivory; she was instead a scintillating, scathing, and delightful satirist so expert at her craft that those whose metaphoric throats were being slit hardly had time to see the knife. Who'd have expected her to be so handy with the cutting remark?

Women have always come fully equipped with an appreciation for and a need to exercise a variety of talents, humor being one among many. But it is true that women's humor has only lately been brought to the front of the line, shuffled up from the crowded background, to receive its much deserved attention, laughter, and applause. Where did they come from, these fast-talking, wisecracking, brilliantly satiric, funny women? From where did they inherit their ability to repeal the restrictions proclaiming that Good girls cannot be funny (a rule as tight and unnatural as a girdle but far more difficult to shed)?

The appearance of literally hundreds of new women performance artists and comics, in addition to the popular success of dozens of women who have established themselves as leaders in a difficult profession, is only the most visible indicator of the waves of women's comic sense. We can also point to floods of material by rediscovered old and newly discovered recent authors, poets, playwrights, educators, politicians, performers, cartoonists, writers of humor, and scholars of women's comedy. Important, too, is the need to recognize humor in the works of so-called serious writers, those who produce the literature we reluctantly read in school as well as the books we eagerly buy in a shop. To highlight the humor of writers such as Emily Brontë, George Eliot, Emily Dickinson, Edith Wharton, and Zora Neale Hurston is not to discover a lost treasure (these women were never lost) but merely to draw attention to the fact that not only are they smart and good, but they're also funny. There is a long-standing community of women producing humor, and there is a substantial body of work as evidence.

Despite this rich history, I was not immune to sly remarks from certain erstwhile friends indicating an alarmingly widespread belief that a collection of women's comedy would make for a short book. I knew this would not be a problem. If anything, this book would have been twice as long had I not been prevented from including even more material by a desire to save our forests—and the refusal of certain publishers to grant permission to reprint.

My difficulty was not in finding material but in sorting it. At first it seemed that simple chronology would offer the best solution. But might it not be unnerving to have a whole battalion of iambic pentameter greeting the happy reader casually picking the volume off a bookstore shelf while sipping cappuccino? It also would mean that all stories about birth-control devices, cars, VCRs, and right-wing antifeminists would end up huddled together and some folks might assume causal relationships among these enterprises. (That there might in fact be a connection between birth-control devices and VCRs could well be true—it remains difficult to program both successfully—but that is the subject of another book.)

Theme, perhaps, could be the organizing force? But how to sort through the complex interweaving of subjects that make up one of the most significant aspects of feminine humor? How to file Carol Leifer's remark, "I got divorced recently. It was a mixed marriage. I'm human, he was Klingon." Under divorce? Mixed marriage? *Star Trek*? How about choosing a label for Jill Ruckelshaus's observation, "It occurred to me when I was thirteen and wearing white gloves and Mary Janes and going to dancing school, that no one should have to dance backward all their lives." Politics? (Ruckelshaus was, after all, mayor of Ottawa.) Girlhood? Shoes? What about Erma Bombeck's experience of dealing with the customs of conferencing? "I was so opposed to nametags that once when a woman slapped a gummed label over my left bosom that said, 'Hello! My name is Erma!' I leaned over and said, 'Now, what shall we name the other one?' " One could wax lyrical on the possibilities of developing a title to fit that remark. No; the only way to go was alphabetical order—and to cheat by using an index that bows to the necessity of subjects but hides them in small print.

Erma Bombeck's assertion that "a lot of people think I write humor. . . . As an observer of the human condition all I do is question it. I rarely find it funny" dovetails neatly with a similar disclaimer made by Charlotte Lennox in the mid-eighteenth century: "When actions are a censure upon themselves, the reciter will always be considered as a satirist." Pulitzer Prize–winning playwright Wendy Wasserstein offers her own reasons for giving voice to her irreverent wit: "When I speak up, it's not because I have any particular answers; rather, I have a desire to puncture the pretentiousness of those who seem so certain they do." And novelist Margaret Drabble points out:

> One of the ways to avoid being a butt or a laughingstock yourself is to make people laugh—not as in the pious old cliché "*with* you rather than at you"; no they had to laugh at you, but they had to laugh because *you made them*, because you were funny . . . there was nothing, literally, nothing, that couldn't be turned into a joke. In fact, the more horrible and discreditable the subject matter, the better the joke.

Women's humor, however, is not only about telling jokes; it is about telling stories, and about retelling stories that might once have been painful but can be redeemed through humor. For example, in Ann E. Imbrie's otherwise serious nonfiction work on the death of a childhood friend, we nevertheless see moments highlighting the humorous absurdities of the world experienced by young women coming of age:

Learning about sex was a little bit like learning grammar. Every teacher you had assumed some other teacher taught you the year before, or the year before that, as if none of them wanted to talk about it, as if grammar was a bunch of dirty words. A massive silence surrounded dangling participles and infinitive clauses, and you learned to fear making mistakes you didn't know how to avoid.

When comedian Ellen Cleghorn comments on the state of the judicial system, she sounds more like a woman speaking to a friend over coffee than our stereotype of a stand-up comic rolling out the usual predigested patter:

When this judge let a rapist go because the woman had been wearing a miniskirt and so was "asking for it" I thought, ladies, what we all should do is this: next time we see an ugly guy on the street, shoot him. After all, he knew he was ugly when he left the house. He was asking for it.

For many years, it was true that women tended to make jokes of their own in rooms of their own, or in the hidden corners of rooms they were actually permitted to inhabit, such as the kitchen. Jokes about the kitchen did not always involve adorable remarks about the quantity of flour needed for muffins, however. Phyllis Diller, for one, maintained: "If your husband wants to lick the beaters on the mixer, shut them off before you give them to him." Diller's reflections on her housekeeping also resemble the less-than-Martha-Stewart-would-suggest attitude prevalent among women humorists. "Our house has gone past the 'lived in' look," explains Diller. "It has more a 'no survivors' look." Poet Marge Piercy suggests in her brilliant work "What's That Smell in the Kitchen?" that burning dinner is not incompetence but war. Not particularly regarded as a domestic humorist, even Fran Lebowitz wryly notes, "Cheese that is required by law to append the word *food* to its title does not go well with red wine or fruit," thereby adding her remarks to the coven in the kitchen.

Not surprisingly, the laughter emanating from these corners can sometimes make men nervous. Nervous-making, too, is that in many cases when a group of women are laughing together and a man joins the group innocently asking "What's so funny?" the inevitable collective response is "Oh, nothing."

Now, this might have been the nicest guy in world who walked by and asked this question, but he might well take the chorus's answer seriously, walking away thinking that women's laughter is a cyclical thing, based on the moon, tides, or estrogen levels and having little to do with a witty vision of the world at large. The laughing women, meanwhile, have resigned themselves to abandoning the very idea of an explanation, assuming their humor could not be properly understood without a lecture on three thousand years of cultural history to give the fellow an adequate perspective on feminine existence. Rightly or wrongly, they think that he won't "get it" and that they will look foolish.

Often, but not always, the women will be right: he won't understand what they're laughing at any more than they will understand his passionate devotion to the Three Stooges. (There is a chromosomal link between masculinity and the Stooges; show Larry, Moe, and Curly at the Olympic Games and we can do away with genetic testing: if you laugh, you play on the men's teams.) Molly Ivins, political columnist supreme and best-selling "arthur," as she terms it, has noticed

> a surprising number of men are alarmed by the thought of a witty woman. They think of women's wit as sarcastic, cutting, "ball-busting." . . . Margaret Atwood, the Canadian novelist, once asked a group of women at a university why they felt threatened by men. The women said they were afraid of being beaten, raped, or killed by men. She then asked a group of men why they felt threatened by women. They said they were afraid women would laugh at them.

This leads to another big concern when dealing with humor, especially humor designed by and often for a particular group: What translates and what gets lost in translation? What's the appropriate response to the baffled, deer-in-the-headlights blankness of someone who says, "But this isn't funny"? One can always be a little sharp and suggest that the individual in question lighten up and work on developing a sense of humor, but that is not really a sufficient or kind answer. Better to offer the possibility that, although tastes differ, there is strong backing for regarding the specific piece as humorous. Many of the selections that follow reflect a personal, although hardly an eccentric, taste, but it is to be hoped that they will also help all of us come up with smart and snappy answers to life's questions.

If it's true that we can't always come up with the perfect answer, then maybe we should set up as possible heroines those women who have. My vote goes to Liz Carpenter. The story goes: after working for the Johnson administraton at the White House, Carpenter wrote a book about her experiences in Washington. The book did pretty well. One evening she met Arthur Schlesinger, Jr., at a cocktail party. He came over to her and smiled and said, "I liked your book, Liz. Who wrote it for you?" Now, clearly this was meant as his little joke. If she had stammered and blushed, he would have won the point. He could then say, "See, you just can't joke around with these women." Instead, Carpenter rejoined, "I'm glad you like it, Arthur. Who read it to you?"

Now, joking at the joker's expense is equivalent to going out to dinner with a con artist who expects to stick you with the bill and refusing to be his victim—whether that means calling him on his game or walking out before he does. When we find ourselves in this sort of situation, someone else has begun a game they expect to win at our expense. We are allowed to prevent this from happening. We are allowed to *joke back*.

The trouble is, most of us have been brought up to be so concerned with putting the welfare of others before our own that we can't let ourselves triumph with a great comeback. Most of the women I know laugh at Carpenter's line but then catch themselves staring at the following concerns: What if Arthur Schlesinger is secretly illiterate? What if his father is dyslexic? What if his kid uses "Hooked on Phonics"? Then we'd feel like we should volunteer for the Literacy Action committee three evenings a week.

This is a misplaced anxiety. Jokers do not worry about the victim's response. This doesn't mean we have to become vicious versions of the worst male stereotypes, but it neatly illustrates the expectation embedded in our culture that you can say what you want to a woman because she's not going to talk back.

It really is okay to answer back. Tallulah Bankhead did. Seeing a lover who did not acknowledge her in public, she went up to him and said, "What's the matter, darling, don't you recognize me with my clothes on?" When Judy Holliday was being chased around by a casting director, she took out her "falsies" and handed them to her eager suitor saying, "I believe it's these you're after."

When Liz Winstead replies to the question "Why aren't you married?" with the retort "I think, therefore I'm single," we want to applaud. The same goes for Carrie Snow's argument that women should find female physicians because "going to a male gynecologist is like going to a mechanic who doesn't own his own car." In response to Pat Buchanan's speech at the 1992 Republican national convention, where women's reproductive rights were considered the handmaidens of witch-craft, Brett Butler suggested that we could not condemn Buchanan's speech "because, after all, it was much better in the original German." When Diane Ford talks about farting, belching, and scratching, she says her boyfriend complains that these activities aren't ladylike. "I tell him that neither is a blow job but he doesn't complain about that." Women's humor is not for the fainthearted or the easily shocked.

For too long women have been told to smile in front of men but never to laugh in front of them except to giggle at a joke *they* told. Faking a laugh is like faking an orgasm: we've been taught to believe it's preferable to pretend pleasure than to say "That one didn't do it for me." And we have certainly been taught not to say the most dangerous of lines: "That one didn't do it for me, but let me suggest something that might." To imply that women have forms of pleasure different from men's is still heretical.

There is a tradition of women's comedy informed by and speaking to the experience of being a female in a world where that experience is devalued. In Jane Wagner and Lily Tomlin's brilliant *Search for Signs of Intelligent Life in the Universe*, we hear a monologue summing up the plight of the woman who asks her doctor for help:

> "You're sure, doctor? Pre*men*strual syndrome? I mean, I'm get-ting divorced. My mother's getting divorced. I'm raising twin boys. I have a lot of job pressure—I've got to find one. The ERA didn't pass, not long ago I lost a very dear friend, and . . . and . . . my husband is involved . . . not just involved but in love, I'm afraid . . . with this woman . . . who is quite a bit younger than I am. And you think it's my *period* and *not* my life?"

Sometimes we try so hard to be happy that we can't possibly have a good time, which makes it especially necessary to be in touch with the irony of the everyday. Having a sense of humor about troubled times is like having a sense of humor about sex or death; humor allows you to have perspective on an otherwise potentially overwhelming prospect. "We live in a Great Nation," writes Molly Ivins, "but those who at-tempt to struggle through it unarmed with a sense of humor are apt to wind up in my Aunt Eula's Fort Worth Home for the Terminally Literal-Minded, gibbering like some demented neoconservative about the Decline of Civilization." Not only does humor allow for the ele-vation and exploration, rather than denigration, of feelings and ideas; at its best it also encourages us, as Ivins does, to "keep fightin' for freedom and justice, beloveds, but don't you forget to have fun doin' it."

Humor doesn't dismiss a subject but, rather, often opens that subject up for discussion, especially when the subject is one that is not considered "fit" for public discussion. Humor can be a shortcut, an eye-opener—the sort of thing people used to use alcohol for—to get to the truth of the matter. The best humor allows for opinion and rebuttal. It also allows for joy, compassion, and a new way of looking at a very old world.

Seeing humor as a way of making our feelings and responses available to others without terrifying our listeners can free us to take ourselves less gloomily, although not less seriously. The women in this book do not trade in their fatalism just to be funny. When we can frame a difficult matter with humor, we can often reach someone who would otherwise withdraw. Humor is a show both of strength and of vulnerability: you are willing to make the first move but you are trusting in the response of your listener.

Making a generously funny comment, pointing to the absurdity of a situation, turning embarrassment or unease into something to be shared instead of repressed is risky, but it is also often exactly what is needed. Angels can fly, someone once told me, because they take themselves lightly. The women quoted here are no angels, as Mae West once put it (and as Charlotte Brontë's Jane Eyre had put it long before Mae West), but in taking themselves and life lightly, they soar until the world, un-balanced and absurd as it is, can be seen from a perspective infinitely instructive, irreverent, and enlightening.

Anonymous*

꙳ ꙳

The Advantages of Being a Woman Artist

Working without the pressure of success.
Not having to be in shows with men.
Having an escape from the art world in your 4 free-lance jobs.
Knowing your career might pick up after you're eighty.
Being reassured that whatever kind of art you make it will be labeled
   feminine.
Not being stuck in a tenured teaching position.
Seeing your ideas live on in the work of others.
Having the opportunity to choose between career and motherhood.
Not having to choke on those big cigars or paint in Italian suits.
Having more time to work after your mate dumps you for someone
   younger.
Being included in revised versions of art history.
Not having to undergo the embarrassment of being called a genius.
Getting your picture in the art magazines wearing a gorilla suit.

Anonymous

꙳ ꙳

Feminism

"Mother, what is a Feminist?"
"A Feminist, my daughter,
Is any woman now who cares

* From a poster distributed by the Guerrilla Girls.

To think about her own affairs
As men don't think she oughter."

Anonymous

~≈ ≈~

FROM *A Poster Distributed by the NUS*
Women's Campaign

Because woman's work is never done and is underpaid or unpaid or
boring or repetitious and we're the first to get the sack and what we
look like is more important than what we do and if we get raped it's
our fault—for lots and lots of other reasons we are part of the women's
liberation movement.

Mary Alcock (1742–1798)

~≈ ≈~

A Receipt for Writing a Novel

Would you a favourite novel make,
Try hard your reader's heart to break,
For who is pleased, if not tormented?
(Novels for that were first invented.)
'Gainst nature, reason, sense, combine
To carry on your bold design,
And those ingredients I shall mention,
Compounded with your own invention,
I'm sure will answer my intention.
Of love take first a due proportion—
It serves to keep the heart in motion:
Of jealousy a powerful zest,
Of all tormenting passions best;
Of horror mix a copious share,
And duels you must never spare;

Hysteric fits at least a score,
Or, if you find occasion, more;
But fainting-fits you need not measure,
The fair ones have them at their pleasure;
Of sighs and groans take no account,
But throw them in to vast amount;
A frantic fever you may add,
Most authors make their lovers mad;
Rack well your hero's nerves and heart,
And let your heroine take her part;
Her fine blue eyes were made to weep,
Nor should she ever taste of sleep;
Ply her with terrors day or night,
And keep her always in a fright,
But in a carriage when you get her,
Be sure you fairly overset her;
If she will break her bones—why let her.
Again, if e'er she walks abroad,
Of course you bring some wicked lord,
Who with three ruffians snaps his prey,
And to a castle speeds away;
There, close confined in haunted tower,
You leave your captive in his power,
Till dead with horror and dismay,
She scales the walls and flies away.

Now you contrive the lovers' meeting,
To set your reader's heart a-beating,
But ere they've had a moment's leisure,
Be sure to interrupt their pleasure;
Provide yourself with fresh alarms
To tear 'em from each other's arms;
No matter by what fate they're parted,
So that you keep them broken-hearted.

A cruel father some prepare
To drag her by her flaxen hair;
Some raise a storm, and some a ghost,
Take either, which may please you most.
But this you must with care observe,
That when you've wound up every nerve
With expectation, hope and fear,

Hero and heroine must disappear.
Some fill one book, some two without 'em,
And ne'er concern their heads about 'em:
This greatly rests the writer's brain,
For any story, that gives pain,
You now throw in—no matter what,
However foreign to the plot;
So it but serves to swell the book,
You foist it in with desperate hook—
A masquerade, a murdered peer,
His throat just cut from ear to ear—
A rake turned hermit—a fond maid
Run mad, by some false loon betrayed—
These stores supply the female pen,
Which writes them o'er and o'er again,
And readers likewise may be found
To circulate them round and round.

Now, at your fable's close, devise
Some grand event to give surprise—
Suppose your hero knows no mother—
Suppose he proves the heroine's brother—
This at one stroke dissolves each tie,
Far as from east to west they fly:
At length, when every woe's expended,
And your last volume's nearly ended,
Clear the mistake, and introduce
Some tattling nurse to cut the noose;
The spell is broke—again they meet
Expiring at each other's feet;
Their friends lie breathless on the floor—
You drop your pen; you can no more—
And ere your reader can recover,
They're married—and your history's over.

Louisa May Alcott (1832-1888)

FROM *Work*

CHRISTIE

"Aunt Betsey, there's going to be a new Declaration of Independence."

"Bless and save us, what do you mean, child?" And the startled old lady precipitated a pie into the oven with destructive haste.

"I mean that, being of age, I'm going to take care of myself, and not be a burden any longer. Uncle wishes me out of the way; thinks I ought to go, and, sooner or later, will tell me so. I don't intend to wait for that, but, like the people in fairy tales, travel away into the world and seek my fortune. I know I can find it."

Christie emphasized her speech by energetic demonstrations in the bread-trough, kneading the dough as if it was her destiny, and she was shaping it to suit herself; while Aunt Betsey stood listening, with uplifted pie-fork, and as much astonishment as her placid face was capable of expressing. As the girl paused, with a decided thump, the old lady exclaimed:

"What crazy idee you got into your head now?"

"A very sane and sensible one that's got to be worked out, so please listen to it, ma'am. I've had it a good while, I've thought it over thoroughly, and I'm sure it's the right thing for me to do. I'm old enough to take care of myself; and if I'd been a boy, I should have been told to do it long ago. I hate to be dependent; and now there's no need of it, I can't bear it any longer. If you were poor, I wouldn't leave you; for I never forget how kind *you* have been to me. But Uncle doesn't love or understand me; I *am* a burden to him, and I must go where I can take care of myself. I can't be happy till I do, for there's nothing here for me. I'm sick of this dull town, where the one idea is eat, drink, and get rich; I don't find any friends to help me as I want to be helped, or any work that I can do well; so let me go, Aunty, and find my place, wherever it is."

"But I do need you, deary; and you mustn't think Uncle don't like you. He does, only he don't show it; and when your odd ways fret him, he ain't pleasant, I know. I don't see why you can't be contented; I've lived here all my days, and never found the place lonesome, or the folks unneighborly." And Aunt Betsey looked perplexed by the new idea.

"You and I are very different, ma'am. There was more yeast put into my composition, I guess; and, after standing quiet in a warm corner so long, I begin to ferment, and ought to be kneaded up in time, so that I may turn out a wholesome loaf. You can't do this; so let me go where it can be done, else I shall turn sour and good for nothing. Does that make the matter any clearer?" And Christie's serious face relaxed into a smile as her aunt's eye went from her to the nicely moulded loaf offered as an illustration.

"I see what you mean, Kitty; but I never thought on't before. You be better riz than me; though, let me tell you, too much emptins makes bread poor stuff, like baker's trash; and too much workin' up makes it hard and dry. Now fly 'round, for the big oven is most het, and this cake takes a sight of time in the mixin'."

"You haven't said I might go, Aunty," began the girl, after a long pause devoted by the old lady to the preparation of some compound which seemed to require great nicety of measurement in its ingredients; for when she replied, Aunt Betsey curiously interlarded her speech with audible directions to herself from the receipt-book before her.

"I ain't no right to keep you, dear, ef you choose to take (a pinch of salt). I'm sorry you ain't happy, and think you might be ef you'd only (beat six eggs, yolks and whites together). But ef you can't, and feel that you need (two cups of sugar), only speak to Uncle, and ef he says (a squeeze of fresh lemon), go, my dear, and take my blessin' with you (not forgettin' to cover with a piece of paper)."

Christie's laugh echoed through the kitchen; and the old lady smiled benignly, quite unconscious of the cause of the girl's merriment.

"I shall ask Uncle to-night, and I know he won't object. Then I shall write to see if Mrs. Flint has a room for me, where I can stay till I get something to do. There is plenty of work in the world, and I'm not afraid of it; so you'll soon hear good news of me. Don't look sad, for you know I never could forget *you*, even if I should become the greatest lady in the land." And Christie left the prints of two floury but affectionate hands on the old lady's shoulders, as she kissed the wrinkled face that had never worn a frown to her.

Full of hopeful fancies, Christie salted the pans and buttered the dough in pleasant forgetfulness of all mundane affairs, and the ludicrous dismay of Aunt Betsey, who followed her about rectifying her mistakes, and watching over her as if this sudden absence of mind had roused suspicions of her sanity.

"Uncle, I want to go away, and get my own living, if you please," was Christie's abrupt beginning, as they sat round the evening fire.

"Hey! what's that?" said Uncle Enos, rousing from the doze he was enjoying, with a candle in perilous proximity to his newspaper and his nose.

Christie repeated her request, and was much relieved, when, after a meditative stare, the old man briefly answered:

"Wal, go ahead."

"I was afraid you might think it rash or silly, sir."

"I think it's the best thing you could do; and I like your good sense in pupposin' on't."

"Then I may really go?"

"Soon's ever you like. Don't pester me about it till you're ready; then I'll give you a little suthing to start off with." And Uncle Enos returned to "The Farmer's Friend," as if cattle were more interesting than kindred.

•

A Wail

UTTERED AT THE WOMEN'S CLUB
God bless you, merry ladies;
    May nothing you dismay,
As you sit here at ease and hark
    Unto my doleful lay.
Get out your pocket-handkerchiefs,
    Give o'er your jokes and songs,
Forget awhile your Woman's Rights,
    And pity authors' wrongs.

There is a town of high repute,
    Where saints and sages dwell
Who in these latter days are forced
    To bid sweet peace farewell.
For all the men are demigods,
    So rumor doth declare,
And all the women are De Staels,
    And genius fills the air.

So eager pilgrims penetrate
    To their most private nooks,

Storm their back doors in search of news,
    And interview their cooks.
Worship at every victim's shrine,
    See haloes round their hats,
Embalm the chickenweed from their yards,
    And photograph their cats.

There's Emerson, the poet wise,
    That much enduring man
No washing-day is sacred now,
    Spring cleaning's never o'er.
Their doorsteps are the stranger's camp,
    Their trees bear many a name,
Artists their very night-caps sketch,
    And this—and this is fame!

Deluded world! your Mecca is
    A sand-bank glorified.
The river that you seek and sing
    Has "skeeters" but no tide.
The gods raise "garden sarce" and milk,
    And in those classic shades
Dwell nineteen chronic invalids,
    And forty-two old maids.

Some April shall the world behold
    Embattled authors stand,
With steel pens of the sharpest tip
    In every inky hand.
Their bridge will be a bridge of sighs,
    Their motto "Privacy,"
Their bullets like that Luther flung
    When bidding Satan flee.

Their monument of ruined books,
    Of precious wasted days,
Of tempers tried, distracted brains
    That might have won fresh bays.
And round this sad memorial
    Oh, chant for requiem,
"Here lie our martyred geniuses,
    Concord has conquered them."

FROM *Jo's Boys*

JO'S LAST SCRAPE

The March family had enjoyed a great many surprises in the course of their varied career, but the greatest of all was when the Ugly Duckling turned out to be, not a swan, but a golden goose, whose literary eggs found such an unexpected market that in ten years Jo's wildest and most cherished dream actually came true. How or why it happened she never clearly understood, but all of a sudden she found herself famous in a small way, and, better still, with a snug little fortune in her pocket to clear away the obstacles of the present and assure the future of her boys.

It began during a bad year when everything went wrong at Plumfield; times were hard, the school dwindled, Jo overworked herself and had a long illness; Laurie and Amy were abroad, and the Bhaers too proud to ask help even of those as near and dear as this generous pair. Confined to her room, Jo got desperate over the state of affairs, till she fell back upon the long-disused pen as the only thing she could do to help fill up the gaps in the income. A book for girls being wanted by a certain publisher, she hastily scribbled a little story describing a few scenes and adventures in the lives of herself and sisters,—though boys were more in her line,—and with very slight hopes of success sent it out to seek its fortune.

Things always went by contraries with Jo. Her first book, labored over for years, and launched full of the high hopes and ambitious dreams of youth, foundered on its voyage, though the wreck continued to float long afterward, to the profit of the publisher at least. The hastily written story, sent away with no thought beyond the few dollars it might bring, sailed with a fair wind and a wise pilot at the helm straight into public favor, and came home heavily laden with an unexpected cargo of gold and glory.

A more astonished woman probably never existed than Josephine Bhaer when her little ship came into port with flags flying, cannon that had been silent before now looming gayly, and, better than all, many kind faces rejoicing with her, many friendly hands grasping hers with cordial congratulations. After that it was plain sailing, and she merely had to load her ships and send them off on prosperous trips, to bring home stores of comfort for all she loved and labored for.

The fame she never did quite accept; for it takes very little fire to make a great deal of smoke nowadays, and notoriety is not real glory. The fortune she could not doubt, and gratefully received; though it was not half so large a one as a generous world reported it to be. The tide having turned continued to rise, and floated the family comfortably into a snug harbor where the older members could rest secure from storms, and whence the younger ones could launch their boats for the voyage of life.

All manner of happiness, peace, and plenty came in those years to bless the patient waiters, hopeful workers, and devout believers in the wisdom and justice of Him who sends disappointment, poverty, and sorry to try the love of human hearts and make success the sweeter when it comes. The world saw the prosperity, and kind souls rejoiced over the improved fortunes of the family; but the success Jo valued most, the happiness that nothing could change or take away, few knew much about.

It was the power of making her mother's last years happy and serene; to see the burden of care laid down forever, the weary hands at rest, the dear face untroubled by any anxiety, and the tender heart free to pour itself out in the wise charity which was its delight. As a girl, Jo's favorite plan had been a room where Marmee could sit in peace and enjoy herself after her hard, heroic life. Now the dream had become a happy fact, and Marmee sat in her pleasant chamber with every comfort and luxury about her, loving daughters to wait on her as infirmities increased, a faithful mate to lean upon, and grandchildren to brighten the twilight of life with their dutiful affection. A very precious time to all, for she rejoiced as only mothers can in the good fortunes of their children. She had lived to reap the harvest she sowed; had seen prayers answered, hopes blossom, good gifts bear fruit, peace and prosperity bless the home she had made; and then, like some brave, patient angel, whose work was done, turned her face heavenward, glad to rest.

This was the sweet and sacred side of the change; but it had its droll and thorny one, as all things have in this curious world of ours. After the first surprise, incredulity, and joy, which came to Jo, with the ingratitude of human nature, she soon tired of renown, and began to resent her loss of liberty. For suddenly the admiring public took possession of her and all her affairs, past, present, and to come. Strangers demanded to look at her, question, advise, warn, congratulate, and drive her out of her wits by well-meant but very wearisome attentions. If she declined to open her heart to them, they reproached her; if she refused to endow pet charities, relieve private wants, or sympathize with every ill and trial known to humanity, she was called hard-hearted, selfish, and haughty; if she found it impossible to answer the piles of letters sent her, she was neglectful of her duty to the admiring public; and if she preferred the privacy of home to the pedestal upon which she was requested to pose, "the airs of literary people" were freely criticised.

She did her best for the children, they being the public for whom she wrote, and labored stoutly to supply the demand always in the mouths of voracious youth,—"More stories, more right away!" Her family objected to this devotion at their expense, and her health suffered; but for a time she gratefully offered herself up on the altar of juvenile literature, feeling that she owed a good deal to the little friends in whose sight she had found favor after twenty years of effort.

But a time came when her patience gave out, and wearying of being a lion, she became a bear in nature as in name, and retiring to her den, growled awfully when ordered out. Her family enjoyed the fun, and had small sympathy with her trials, but Jo came to consider it the worst scrape of her life; for liberty had always been her dearest possession, and it seemed to be fast going from her. Living in a lantern soon loses its charms, and she was too old, too tired, and too busy to like it. She felt that she had done all that could reasonably be required of her when autographs, photographs, and autobiographical sketches had been sown broadcast over the land; when artists had taken her home in all its aspects, and reporters had taken her in the grim one she always assumed on these trying occasions; when a series of enthusiastic boarding-schools had ravaged her grounds for trophies, and a steady stream of amiable pilgrims had worn her doorsteps with their respectful feet; when servants left after a week's trial of the bell that rang all day; when her husband was forced to guard her at meals, and the boys to cover her retreat out of back windows on certain occasions when enterprising guests walked in unannounced at unfortunate moments.

A sketch of one day may perhaps explain the state of things, offer some excuse for the unhappy woman, and give a hint to the autograph-fiend now rampant in the land; for it is a true tale.

"There ought to be a law to protect unfortunate authors," said Mrs. Jo one morning soon after Emil's arrival, when the mail brought to her an unusually large and varied assortment of letters. "To me it is a more vital subject than international copyright; for time is money, peace is health, and I lose both with no return but less respect for my fellow-creatures and a wild desire to fly into the wilderness, since I cannot shut my doors even in free America."

"Lion-hunters are awful when in search of their prey. If they could change places for a while it would do them good; and they'd see what bores they were when they 'do themselves the honor of calling to express their admiration of our charming work,' " quoted Ted, with a bow to his parent, now frowning over twelve requests for autographs.

"I have made up my mind on one point," said Mrs. Jo with great firmness. "I will *not* answer this kind of letter. I've sent at least six to this boy, and he probably sells them. This girl writes from a seminary, and if I send her one all the other girls will at once write for more. All begin by saying they know they intrude, and that I am of course annoyed by these requests; but they venture to ask because I like boys, or they like the books, or it is only one. Emerson and Whittier put these things in the waste-paper basket; and though only a literary nursery-maid who provides moral pap for the young, I will follow their illustrious example; for I shall have no time to eat or sleep if I try to satisfy these dear unreasonable children;" and Mrs. Jo swept away the entire batch with a sigh of relief.

"I'll open the others and let you eat your breakfast in peace, *liebe Mutter*," said Rob, who often acted as her secretary. "Here's one from the South;" and breaking an imposing seal, he read:—

Madam,—As it has pleased Heaven to bless your efforts with a large fortune, I feel no hesitation in asking you to supply funds to purchase a new communion-service for our church. To whatever denomination you belong, you will of course respond with liberality to such a request.

Respectfully yours,
Mrs. X. Y. Zavier

"Send a civil refusal, dear. All I have to give must go to feed and clothe the poor at my gates. That is my thank-offering for success. Go on," answered his mother, with a grateful glance about her happy home.

"A literary youth of eighteen proposes that you put your name to a novel he has written; and after the first edition your name is to be taken off and his put on. There's a cool proposal for you. I guess you won't agree to that, in spite of your soft-heartedness towards most of the young scribblers."

"Could n't be done. Tell him so kindly, and don't let him send the manuscript. I have seven on hand now, and barely time to read my own," said Mrs. Jo, pensively fishing a small letter out of the slop-bowl and opening it with care, because the down-hill address suggested that a child wrote it.

"I will answer this myself. A little sick girl wants a book, and she shall have it, but I can't write sequels to all the rest to please her. I should never come to an end if I tried to suit these voracious little Oliver Twists, clamoring for more. What next, Robin?"

"This is short and sweet."

Dear Mrs. Bhaer,—I am now going to give you my opinion of your works. I have read them all many times, and call them first-rate. Please go ahead.

> Your admirer,
> Billy Babcock.

"Now that is what I like. Billy is a man of sense and a critic worth having, since he has read my works many times before expressing his opinion. He asks for no answer, so send my thanks and regards."

"Here's a lady in England with seven girls, and she wishes to know your views upon education. Also what careers they shall follow,—the oldest being twelve. Don't wonder she's worried," laughed Rob.

"I'll try to answer it. But as I have no girls, my opinion is n't worth much and will probably shock her, as I shall tell her to let them run and play and build up good, stout bodies before she talks about careers. They will soon show what they want, if they are let alone, and not all run in the same mould."

"Here's a fellow who wants to know what sort of a girl he shall marry, and if you know of any like those in your stories."

"Give him Nan's address, and see what he'll get," proposed Ted, privately resolving to do it himself if possible.

"This is from a lady who wants you to adopt her child and lend her money to study art abroad for a few years. Better take it, and try your hand at a girl, mother."

"No, thank you, I will keep to my own line of business. What is that blotted one? It looks rather awful, to judge by the ink," asked Mrs. Jo, who beguiled her daily task trying to guess from the outside what was inside her many letters. This proved to be a poem from an insane admirer, to judge by its incoherent style.

To J. M. B.

"Oh, were I a heliotrope,
  I would play poet,
And blow a breeze of fragrance
  To you; and none should know it.

"Your form like the stately elm
  When Phœbus gilds the morning ray;
Your cheeks like the ocean bed
  That blooms a rose in May.

> *"Your words are wise and bright,*
>   *I bequeath them to you a legacy given;*
> *And when your spirit takes its flight,*
>   *May it bloom a flower in heaven.*
>
> *"My tongue in flattering language spoke,*
> *And sweeter silence never broke*
> *In busiest street or loneliest glen.*
> *I take you with the flashes of any pen.*
>
> *"Consider the lilies, how they grow;*
>   *They toil not, yet are fair,*
> *Gems and flowers and Solomon's seal.*
>   *The geranium of the world is J. M. Bhaer.*
>   *"James."*

While the boys shouted over this effusion,—which is a true one,—their mother read several liberal offers from budding magazines for her to edit them gratis; one long letter from a young girl inconsolable because her favorite hero died, and "would dear Mrs. Bhaer rewrite the tale, and make it end good?" another from an irate boy denied an autograph, who darkly foretold financial ruin and loss of favor if she did not send him and all other fellows who asked autographs, photographs, and autobiographical sketches; a minister wished to know her religion; and an undecided maiden asked which of her two lovers she should marry. These samples will suffice to show a few of the claims made on a busy woman's time, and make my readers pardon Mrs. Jo if she did not carefully reply to all.

"That job is done. Now I will dust a bit, and then go to my work. I'm all behindhand, and serials can't wait; so deny me to everybody, Mary. I won't see Queen Victoria if she comes to-day." And Mrs. Bhaer threw down her napkin as if defying all creation.

"I hope the day will go well with thee, my dearest," answered her husband, who had been busy with his own voluminous correspondence. "I will dine at college with Professor Plock, who is to visit us to-day. The *Jünglings* can lunch on Parnassus; so thou shalt have a quiet time." And smoothing the worried lines out of her forehead with his good-by kiss, the excellent man marched away, both pockets full of books, an old umbrella in one hand, and a bag of stones for the geology class in the other.

"If all literary women had such thoughtful angels for husbands, they would live longer and write more. Perhaps that would n't be a blessing to the world though, as most of us write too much now," said Mrs. Jo, waving her feather duster to her spouse, who responded with flourishes of the umbrella as he went down the avenue.

Rob started for school at the same time, looking so much like him with his books and bag and square shoulders and steady air that his mother laughed as she turned away, saying heartily. "Bless both my dear professors, for better creatures never lived!"

Emil was already gone to his ship in the city; but Ted lingered to steal the address he wanted, ravage the sugar-bowl, and talk with "Mum;" for the two had great larks together.

Mrs. Jo always arranged her own parlor, refilled her vases, and gave the little touches that left it cool and neat for the day. Going to draw down the curtain, she beheld an artist sketching on the lawn, and groaned as she hastily retired to the back window to shake her duster.

At that moment the bell rang and the sound of wheels was heard in the road.

"I'll go; Mary lets 'em in;" and Ted smoothed his hair as he made for the hall.

"Can't see any one. Give me a chance to fly upstairs," whispered Mrs. Jo, preparing to escape. But before she could do so, a man appeared at the door with a card in his hand. Ted met him with a stern air, and his mother dodged behind the window-curtain to bide her time for escape.

"I am doing a series of articles for the 'Saturday Tattler,' and I called Mrs. Bhaer the first of all," began the new-comer in the insinuating tone of his tribe, while his quick eyes were taking in all they could, experience having taught him to make the most of his time, as his visits were usually short ones.

"Mrs. Bhaer never sees reporters, sir,"

"But a few moments will be all I ask," said the man, edging his way further in.

"You can't see her, for she is out," replied Teddy, as a backward glance showed him that his unhappy parent had vanished,—through the window, he supposed, as she sometimes did when hard bestead.

"Very sorry. I'll call again. Is this her study? Charming room!" And the intruder fell back on the parlor, bound to see something and bag a fact if he died in the attempt.

"It is not," said Teddy, gently but firmly backing him down the hall, devoutly hoping that his mother had escaped round the corner of the house.

"If you could tell me Mrs. Bhaer's age and birthplace, date of marriage, and number of children, I should be much obliged," continued the unabashed visitor as he tripped over the door-mat.

"She is about sixty, born in Nova Zembla, married just forty years ago to-day, and has eleven daughters. Anything else, sir?" And Ted's sober face was such a funny contrast to his ridiculous reply that the reporter owned himself routed, and retired laughing just as a lady followed by three beaming girls came up the steps.

"We are all the way from Oshkosh, and couldn't go home without seein' dear Aunt Jo. My girls just admire her works, and lot on gettin' a sight of her. I know it's early; but we are goin' to see Holmes and Longfeller, and the rest of the celebrities, so we ran out here fust thing. Mrs. Erastus Kingsbury Parmalee, of Oshkosh, tell her. We don't mind waitin'; we can look round a spell if she ain't ready to see folks yet."

All this was uttered with such rapidity that Ted could only stand gazing at the buxom damsels, who fixed their six blue eyes upon him so beseechingly that his native gallantry made it impossible to deny them a civil reply at least.

"Mrs. Bhaer is not visible to-day,—out just now, I believe; but you can see the house and grounds if you like," he murmured, falling back as the four pressed in gazing rapturously about them.

"Oh, thank you! Sweet, pretty place I'm sure! That's where she writes, ain't it? Do tell me if that's her picture! Looks just as I imagined her!"

With these remarks the ladies paused before a fine engraving of the Hon. Mrs. Norton, with a pen in her hand and a rapt expression of countenance, likewise a diadem and pearl necklace.

Keeping his gravity with an effort, Teddy pointed to a very bad portrait of Mrs. Jo, which hung behind the door, and afforded her much amusement, it was so dismal, in spite of a curious effect of light upon the end of the nose and cheeks as red as the chair she sat in.

"This was taken for my mother; but it is not very good," he said, enjoying the struggles of the girls not to look dismayed at the sad difference between the real and the ideal. The youngest, aged twelve, could not conceal her disappointment, and turned away, feeling as so many of us have felt when we discover that our idols are very ordinary men and women.

"I thought she'd be about sixteen and have her hair braided in two tails down her back. I don't care about seeing her now," said the honest child walking off to the hall door, leaving her mother to apologize, and her sisters to declare that the bad portrait was "perfectly lovely, so speaking and poetic, you know, 'specially about the brow."

"Come, girls, we must be goin', if we want to get through to-day. You can leave your albums and have them sent when Mrs. Bhaer has written a sentiment in 'em. We are a thousand times obliged. Give our best love to your ma, and tell her we are so sorry not to see her."

Just as Mrs. Erastus Kingsbury Parmalee uttered the words her eye fell upon a middle-aged woman in a large checked apron, with a handkerchief tied over her head, busily dusting an end room which looked like a study.

"One peep at her sanctum since she is out," cried the enthusiastic lady, and swept across the hall with her flock before Teddy could warn his mother, whose retreat had been cut off by the artist in front, the reporter at the back part of the house,—for he had n't gone,—and the ladies in the hall.

"They've got her!" thought Teddy, in comical dismay. "No use for her to play housemaid since they've seen the portrait."

Mrs. Jo did her best, and being a good actress, would have escaped if the fatal picture had not betrayed her. Mrs. Parmalee paused at the desk, and regardless of the meerschaum that lay there, the man's slippers close by, and a pile of letters directed to "Prof. F. Bhaer," she clasped her hands, exclaiming impressively, "Girls, this is the spot where she wrote those sweet, those moral tales which have thrilled us to the soul! Could I—ah, could I take one morsel of paper, an old pen, a postage stamp even, as a memento of this gifted woman?"

"Yes'm, help yourselves," replied the maid, moving away with a glance at the boy whose eyes were now full of the merriment he could not suppress.

The oldest girl saw it, guessed the truth, and a quick look at the woman in the apron confirmed her suspicion. Touching her mother, she whispered, "Ma, it's Mrs. Bhaer herself. I know it is."

"No? yes? it is! Well, I do declare, how nice that is!" And hastily pursuing the unhappy woman, who was making for the door, Mrs. Parmalee cried eagerly, "Don't mind us! I know you're busy, but just let me take your hand and then we'll go."

Giving herself up for lost, Mrs. Jo turned and presented her hand like a tea-tray, submitting to have it heartily shaken, as the matron said, with somewhat alarming hospitality,—

"If ever you come to Oshkosh, your feet won't be allowed to touch the pavement; for you'll be borne in the arms of the populace, we shall be so dreadful glad to see you."

Mentally resolving never to visit that effusive town, Jo responded as cordially as she could; and having written her name in the albums, provided each visitor with a memento, and kissed them all round, they at last departed, to call on "Longfeller, Holmes, and the rest,"—who were all out, it is devoutly to be hoped.

"You villain, why didn't you give me a chance to whip away? Oh, my dear, what fibs you told that man! I hope we shall be forgiven our sins in this line, but I don't know what *is* to become of us if we don't dodge. So many against one isn't fair play." And Mrs. Jo hung up her apron in the hall closet, with a groan at the trials of her lot.

"More people coming up the avenue! Better dodge while the coast is clear! I'll head them off!" cried Teddy, looking back from the steps, as he was departing to school.

Mrs. Jo flew upstairs, having locked her door, calmly viewed a young ladies' seminary camp on the lawn, and being denied the house, proceed to enjoy themselves by picking the flowers, doing up their hair, eating lunch, and freely expressing their opinion of the place and its possessors before they went.

A few hours of quiet followed, and she was just settling down to a long afternoon of hard work, when Rob came home to tell her that the Young Men's Christian Union would visit the college, and two or three of the fellows whom she knew wanted to pay their respects to her on the way.

"It is going to rain, so they won't come, I dare say; but father thought you'd like to be ready, in case they do call. You always see the boys, you know, though you harden your heart to the poor girls," said Rob, who had heard from his brother about the morning visitations.

"Boys don't gush, so I can stand it. The last time I let in a party of girls, one fell into my arms and said, 'Darling, love me!' I wanted to shake her," answered Mrs. Jo, wiping her pen with energy.

"You may be sure the fellows won't do it, but they *will* want autographs, so you'd better be prepared with a few dozen," said Rob, laying out a quire of note-paper, being a hospitable youth and sympathizing with those who admired his mother.

"They can't outdo the girls. At X College I really believe I wrote three hundred during the day I was there, and I left a pile of cards and albums on my table when I came away. It is one of the most absurd and tiresome manias that ever afflicted the world."

Nevertheless Mrs. Jo wrote her name a dozen times, put on her black silk, and resigned herself to the impending call, praying for rain, however, as she returned to her work.

The shower came, and feeling quite secure, she rumpled up her hair, took off her cuffs, and hurried to finish her chapter; for thirty pages a day was her task, and she liked to have it well done before evening. Josie had brought some flowers for the vases, and was just putting the last touches when she saw several umbrellas bobbing down the hill.

"They are coming, Aunty! I see uncle hurrying across the field to receive them," she called at the stairfoot.

"Keep an eye on them, and let me know when they enter the avenue. It will take but a minute to tidy up and run down," answered Mrs. Jo, scribbling away for dear life, because serials wait for no man, not even the whole Christian Union *en masse*.

"There are more than two or three. I see half a dozen at least," called sister Ann from the hall door. "Not a dozen, I do believe, Aunty, look out; they are all coming! What *shall* we do?" And Josie quailed at the idea of facing the black throng rapidly approaching.

"Mercy on us, there are hundreds! Run and put a tub in the back entry for their umbrellas to drip into. Tell them to go down the hall and leave them, and pile their hats on the table; the tree won't hold them all. No use to get mats; my poor carpets!" And down went Mrs. Jo to prepare for the invasion, while Josie and the maids flew about dismayed at the prospect of so many muddy boots.

On they came, a long line of umbrellas, with splashed legs and flushed faces underneath; for the gentlemen had been having a good time all over the town, undisturbed by the rain. Professor Bhaer met them at the gate, and was making a little speech of welcome, when Mrs. Jo, touched by their bedraggled state, appeared at the door, beckoning them. Leaving their host to orate bareheaded in the wet, the young men hastened up the steps, merry, warm, and eager, clutching off their hats as they came, and struggling with their umbrellas, as the order was passed to march in and stack arms.

Tramp, tramp, tramp, down the hall went seventy-five pairs of boots; soon seventy-five umbrellas dripped sociably in the hospitable tub, while their owners swarmed all over the lower part of the house; and seventy-five hearty hands were shaken by the hostess without a murmur, though some were wet, some very warm, and nearly all bore trophies of the day's ramble. One impetuous party flourished a small turtle as he made his compliments; another had a load of sticks cut from noted spots; and all begged for some memento of Plumfield. A pile of cards mysteriously appeared on the table, with a written request for autographs; and despite her morning vow, Mrs. Jo wrote every one, while her husband and the boys did the honors of the house.

Josie fled to the back parlor, but was discovered by exploring youths, and mortally insulted by one of them, who innocently inquired

if she was Mr. Bhaer. The reception did not last long, and the end was
better than the beginning; for the rain ceased, and a rainbow shone
beautifully over them as the good fellows stood upon the lawn singing
sweetly for a farewell. A happy omen, that bow of promise arched over
the young heads, as if Heaven smiled upon their union, and showed
them that above the muddy earth and rainy skies the blessed sun still
shone for all.

Three cheers, and then away they went, leaving a pleasant recollection of their visit to amuse the family as they scraped the mud off the
carpets with shovels and emptied the tub half-full of water.

"Nice, honest, hard-working fellows, and I don't begrudge my half-
hour at all; but I *must* finish, so don't let any one disturb me till tea-
time," said Mrs. Jo, leaving Mary to shut up the house; for papa and
the boys had gone off with the guests, and Josie had run home to tell
her mother about the fun at Aunt Jo's.

Peace reigned for an hour, then the bell rang and Mary came giggling up to say, "A queer kind of a lady wants to know if she can catch
a grasshopper in the garden."

"A what?" cried Mrs. Jo, dropping her pen with a blot; for of all
the odd requests ever made, this was the oddest.

"A grasshopper ma'am. I said you was busy, and asked what she
wanted, and she says she, 'I've got grasshoppers from the grounds of
several famous folks, and I want one from Plumfield to add to my collection. Did you ever?" And Mary giggled again at the idea.

"Tell her to take all there are and welcome. I shall be glad to get
rid of them; always bouncing in my face and getting in my dress,"
laughed Mrs. Jo.

Mary retired, to return in a moment nearly speechless with merriment.

"She's much obliged, ma'am, and she'd like an old gown or a pair
of stockings of yours to put in a rug she's making. Got a vest of Emerson's she says, and a pair of Mr. Holmes's trousers, and a dress of Mrs.
Stowe's. She must be crazy!"

"Give her that old red shawl, then I shall make a gay show among
the great ones in that astonishing rug. Yes, they are all lunatics, these
lion-hunters; but this seems to be a harmless maniac, for she does n't
take my time and gives me a good laugh," said Mrs. Jo, returning to
her work after a glance from the window, which showed her a tall, thin
lady in rusty black, skipping wildly to and fro on the lawn in pursuit of
the lively insect she wanted.

Maria Allen (c. 1750-?)

~⁓⁑⁓~

FROM *A Letter to Frances Burney*

I like your Plan immensely of Extirpating that vile race of beings call'd man but I (who you know am clever (VERREE) clever) have thought of an improvement in the sistim suppose we were to Cut of [sic] their *prominent members* and by that means render them Harmless innofencive Little Creatures; We might have such charming *vocal* Music Every house might be Qualified to get up an opera and Piccinis Music would be still more in vogue than it is & we might make such usefull Animals of them in other Respects Consider Well this scheme.

Lisa Alther (1944-   )

~⁓⁑⁓~

FROM *Kinflicks*

Groggy with two in-flight martinis, Ginny huddled by the DC-7's emergency exit. When she'd picked up her ticket for this flight, she'd made a brave joke to the clerk about someone's wanting to hijack a plane bound between Stark's Bog, Vermont, and Hullsport, Tennessee. The clerk had replied without looking up, "Believe me, honey, no one in their right mind would want anything to do with those planes they send to Tennessee." To be aware of death was one thing, she mused; to accept it, another. All her life, awash with shame, she had secretly rejoiced over each plane crash as it was reported in the papers because it meant They'd missed her again.

She grabbed the plastic card from the nubby green seat-back pocket and studied the operaticn of the plane's emergency exits, deployment procedures for the inflatable slide. It occurred to her that if use of the

emergency exits was required, she'd be frozen by panic and trampled by
all her frenzied fellow passengers as they tried to get past her and out
the escape hatch. It also occurred to her that perhaps the reason every
person in the plane didn't struggle to sit by an emergency exit, as she
did, was that they knew something she didn't: that the likelihood of
needing to clamber out the exit to safety was more than offset by the
likelihood of the exit's flying open in midflight and sucking those near
it into the troposphere.

But she knew that this pattern of blindly seeking out emergency
exits was already too set in her to be thwarted with ease. Just as some
people's eyes, due to early experience with The Breast, were irresistibly
drawn to bosoms throughout their lives, so were hers riveted by neon
signs saying EXIT. At the Saturday morning cowboy serials as a child,
she had been required by the Major to sit right next to the exit sign in
case the theater should catch fire. He told her about a Boston theater
fire when he was young in which a crazy man had carved his way with
a Bowie knife through the hysterical crowds to an exit. Ever since, she'd
been unable to watch a movie or listen to a lecture or ride in a plane
without the comforting glow of an exit sign next to her, like a nightlight
in a small child's bedroom.

Nevertheless, on this particular flight, she first realized that the
emergency exit, the escape lines coiled in the window casings, the yellow
oxygen masks being playfully manipulated by the shapely stewardesses,
were all totems designed to distract passengers from the fact that if the
plane crashed, they'd all had it—splat! As eager as she was to deny the
possibility of personal extinction while negotiating the hostile skies of
United Air Lines, even Ginny was only faintly comforted by the presence
of her seat cushion flotation device. She knew full well that the Blue
Ridge Mountains of Virginia were below her should the engines falter
and the plane flutter down like a winged bird. The sea was swelling
some three hundred miles to the east. She tried to picture herself,
stranded in a mountain crevice, afloat on her ritual seat cushion above
a sea of gore and gasoline and in-flight martinis.

In the crush of the waiting room prior to boarding, Ginny had
inspected with the intensity of the Ancient Mariner the visages of all her
fellow passenger-victims: Were these the kind of people she'd want to
be adrift with in a life raft? She could never decide how Fate worked
it: Did planes stay aloft because of the absence of actively wicked people
on board to be disposed of? Or was the opposite the case: Did planes
falter and fall because of the absence of people sufficiently worthy to
redeem the flight, people who had to be kept alive to perform crucial

missions? Whichever was the case, Ginny had closely studied her companions in folly, looking for both damning and redeeming personality types and laying odds on a mid-air collision. With relief, she'd discovered three small babies.

Her fellow travelers had also scrutinized *her* upon boarding this winged silver coffin, Ginny reflected. In fact, one plump woman in a hideous Indian print caftan had studied her so closely that Ginny was sure the woman *knew* that she was the one who'd broken the macrobiotic recipe chain letter earlier that week. Which of the assembled Vermont housewives, they all must have wondered as they found their seats, would be the one to demand six thousand books of S & H Green Stamps and a parachute for a descent into a redemption center at a Paramus, New Jersey, shopping mall? Whose tote bag contained the bomb, nestled in a hollowed-out gift wheel of Vermont cheddar cheese, or submerged in a take-out container of spaghetti sauce? Ginny had often thought that she should carry such a bomb aboard her plane flights herself, because the likelihood of there being *two* bomb-toting psychopaths on the same flight was so infinitesimal as to be an impossibility. It was the mentality that fostered the arms race: Better to be done in by the bomb that she herself, in a last act of existential freedom, could detonate.

•

In this case the chaperones were the highway patrolmen, not long ago students at Hullsport High themselves, but gone over now to the enemy. Taking their revenge on us for their no longer being young and unfettered by families, they liked nothing better than to ticket someone for driving in the wrong direction around the church circle. Their formerly athletic bodies gone to flab under their khaki shirts, they now cruised for a living and delighted in breaking up back-seat tussles on dark dirt roads.

•

The next thing I knew, I was holding his stiff cock in one hand as he lurched back and forth in front of me. I felt as though I were an animal trainer trying to lead a recalcitrant baby elephant by the trunk.

•

I wrote Clem lots of lonely letters. He wrote me lots of identical lonely letters. We could have saved enough money in postage to have financed an elopement by writing lonely letters to ourselves.

Margaret Atwood (1939-)

FROM *Their Attitudes Differ*

II

I approach this love
like a biologist
pulling on my rubber
gloves & white labcoat

You flee from it
like an escaped political
prisoner, and no wonder

III

A truth should exist,
it should not be used
like this. If I love you

is that a fact or a weapon?

FROM *She considers evading him*

I can change my-
self more easily
than I can change you

They eat out

In restaurants we argue
over which of us will pay for your funeral

though the real question is
whether or not I will make you immortal.

At the moment only I
can do it and so

I raise the magic fork
over the plate of beef fried rice

and plunge it into your heart.
There is a faint pop, a sizzle

and through your own split head
you rise up glowing:

the ceiling opens
a voice sings Love Is A Many

Splendoured Thing
you hang suspended above the city

in blue tights and a red cape,
your eyes flashing in unison.

The other diners regard you
some with awe, some only with boredom:

they cannot decide if you are a new weapon
or only a new advertisement.

As for me, I continue eating;
I liked you better the way you were,
but you were always ambitious.

•

Aging Female Poet Sits on the Balcony

The front lawn is littered with young men
who want me to pay attention to them
not to their bodies and their freshly-
washed cotton skins, not to their enticing
motifs of bulb and root, but
to their poems. In the back yard
on the other hand are the older men
who want me to pay attention to their
bodies. Ah men,
why do you want
all this attention?

I can write poems for myself, make
love to a doorknob if absolutely
necessary. What do you have to offer me
I can't find otherwise
except humiliation? Which I no longer
need. I gather
dust, for practice, my attention
wanders like a household pet
once leashed, now
out on the prowl, an animal
neither dog nor cat, unique
and hairy, snuffling
among the damp leaves at the foot
of the hedge, among the afterbloom
of irises which melt like blue and purple
ice back into air; hunting for something
lost, something to eat or love, among
the twists of earth,
among the glorious bearclaw sunsets, evidence
of the red life that is leaking
out of me into time, which become
each night more final.

●

FROM *Letters, Towards & Away*

I don't wear gratitude
well. Or hats.

What would I do with
veils and silly feathers
or a cloth rose
growing from the top of my head?

What should I do with this
peculiar furred emotion?

You make them
turn and turn, according to
the closed rules of your games
but there is no joy in it.

●

FROM *Lady Oracle*

If you could cry silently people felt sorry for you. As it was I snorted, my eyes turned the color and shape of cooked tomatoes, my nose ran, I clenched my fists, I moaned, I was embarrassing, finally I was amusing, a figure of fun. The grief was always real but it came out as a burlesque of grief, an overblown imitation.

•

. . . hair in the female was regarded as more important than either talent or the lack of it.

•

I was regarded as a good typist; at my high school typing was regarded as a female secondary sex characteristic, like breasts.

•

My mother's two categories; nice men did things for you, bad men did things to you.

•

"For nurses, nurse novels may be too much like life," I said.

"Nurses do not read the nurse novels. They are read by women who wish mistakenly to be a nurse. In any case, if the nurses wish to avoid the problems of their life, they must write spy stories, that is all. What is gravy for the goose will be misplaced on the gander, such is fate."

•

How could I be sleeping with this peculiar man. . . . Surely only true love could justify my lack of taste.

•

"I guess you're a publishing success," he said. "What's it like to be a successful bad writer?"

I was beginning to feel angry. "Why don't you publish and find out?" I said.

Jane Austen (1775–1817)

✦

FROM *The Letters of Jane Austen*

Charles Powlett gave a dance on Thursday, to the great disturbance of all his neighbors, of course, who, you know, take a most lively interest in the state of his finances, and live in hopes of his being soon ruined.

•

I do not want people to be very agreeable, as it saves me the trouble of liking them a great deal.

•

You express so little anxiety about my being murdered under Ash Park Copse by Mrs. Hulbert's servant, that I have a great mind not to tell you whether I was or not, and shall only say that I did not return home that night or the next, as Martha kindly made room for me in her bed, which was the shut-up one in the new nursery.

•

It was a pleasant evening; Charles found it remarkably so, but I cannot tell why, unless the absence of Miss Terry, towards whom his conscience reproaches him with being now perfectly indifferent, was a relief to him. There were only twelve dances, of which I danced nine, and was merely prevented from dancing the rest by the want of a partner.

•

I give you joy of our new nephew, and hope if he ever comes to be hanged it will not be till we are too old to care about it.

•

Only think of Mrs. Holder's being dead! Poor woman, she has done the only thing in the world she could possibly do to make one cease to abuse her.

•

Composition seems to me impossible with a head full of joints of mutton and doses of rhubarb.

•

FROM *Northanger Abbey*

Her love of dirt gave way to an inclination for finery, and she grew clean as she grew smart. . . .

•

But from fifteen to seventeen she was in training for a heroine; she read all such works as heroines must read to supply their memories with those quotations which are so serviceable and so soothing in the vicissitudes of their eventful lives.

•

. . .—for I will not adopt that ungenerous and impolitic custom so common with novel writers, of degrading by their contemptuous censure the very performances, to the number of which they are themselves adding—joining with their greatest enemies in bestowing the harshest epithets on such works, and scarcely ever permitting them to be read by their own heroine, who, if she accidentally take up a novel, is sure to turn over its insipid pages with disgust. Alas! if the heroine of one novel be not patronized by the heroine of another, from whom can she expect protection and regard? I cannot approve of it. Let us leave it to the Reviewers to abuse such effusions of fancy at their leisure, and over every new novel to talk in threadbare strains of the trash with which the press now groans. Let us not desert one another; we are an injured body. Although our productions have afforded more extensive and un-affected pleasure than those of any other literary corporation in the world, no species of composition has been so much decried. From pride, ignorance, or fashion, our foes are almost as many as our readers. And while the abilities of the nine-hundredth abridger of the History of England, or of the man who collects and publishes in a volume some dozen lines of Milton, Pope, and Prior, with a paper from the *Spectator*, and a chapter from Sterne, are eulogized by a thousand pens,—there seems almost a general wish of decrying the capacity and undervaluing the labour of the novelist, and of slighting the performances which have only genius, wit, and taste to recommend them. "I am no novel reader—I seldom look into novels—Do not imagine that I often read novels—it is really very well for a novel."—Such is the common cant.—"And what are you reading, Miss—?" "Oh! it is only a novel!" replies the young lady; while she lays down her book with affected indifference, or momentary shame.—"It is only *Cecilia*, or *Camilla*, or *Belinda*," or, in short, only some work in which the greatest powers of the mind are displayed, in which the most thorough knowledge of human nature, the happiest delineation of its varieties, the liveliest effusions of wit and humour are conveyed to the world in the best chosen language. Now, had the same young lady been engaged with a volume of the *Spectator*, instead of such a work, how proudly would she have produced the book, and told its name; though the chances must be against her being occupied by any part of that voluminous publication, of which either the matter or manner would not disgust a young person of taste: the substance of its papers so often consisting in the statement of improbable circumstances, unnatural characters, and topics of conversation, which no longer concern any one living; and their language, too, frequently so coarse as to give no very favourable idea of the age that could endure it.

•

"I consider a country dance as an emblem of marriage. Fidelity and complaisance are the principal duties of both; and those men who do not chuse to dance or marry themselves, have no business with the partners or wives of their neighbours."

•

"And such is your definition of matrimony and dancing. Taken in that light certainly, their resemblance is not striking; but I think I could place them in such a view.—You will allow, that in both, man has the advantage of choice, woman only the power of refusal; that in both, it is an engagement between man and woman, formed for the advantage of each; and that when once entered into, they belong exclusively to each other til the moment of its dissolution; that it is their duty, each to endeavour to give the other no cause for wishing that he or she had bestowed themselves elsewhere, and their best interest to keep their own imaginations from wandering towards the perfections of their neighbours, or fancying that they should have been better off with any one else. You will allow all this?"

•

"I can read poetry and plays, and things of that sort, and do not dislike travels. But history, real solemn history, I cannot be interested in. Can you?"

•

"The quarrels of popes and kings, with wars or pestilences, in every page; the men all so good for nothing, and hardly any women at all— it is very tiresome: and yet I often think it odd that it should be so dull, for a great deal of it must be invention. The speeches that are put into the heroes' mouths, their thoughts and designs—the chief of all this must be invention, and invention is what delights me in other books."

•

She was heartily ashamed of her ignorance. A misplaced shame. Where people wish to attach, they should always be ignorant. To come with a well-informed mind, is to come with an inability of administering to the vanity of others, which a sensible person would always wish to avoid. A woman especially, if she have the misfortune of knowing any thing, should conceal it as well as she can.

The advantages of natural folly in a beautiful girl have been already set forth by the capital pen of a sister author;—and to her treatment of the subject I will only add in justice to men, that though to the larger and more trifling part of the sex, imbecility in females is a great enhancement of their personal charms, there is a portion of them too reasonable and too well informed themselves to desire any thing more in a woman than ignorance.

•

The anxieties of common life began soon to succeed to the alarms of romance.

•

FROM *Sense and Sensibility*

He was not an ill-disposed young man, unless to be rather cold hearted, and rather selfish, is to be ill-disposed. . . .

•

Sir John was loud in his admiration at the end of every song, and as loud in his conversation with the others while every song lasted.

•

Mrs. Jennings was a widow, with an ample jointure. She had only two daughters, both of whom she had lived to see respectably married, and she had now therefore nothing to do but to marry all the rest of the world.

•

His temper might perhaps be a little soured by finding, like any others of his sex, that through some unaccountable bias in favour of beauty, he was the husband of a very silly woman. . . .

•

Elinor was pleased that he had called; and still more pleased that she had missed him.

•

The parties stood thus:

The two mothers, though each really convinced that her own son was the tallest, politely decided in favour of the other.

The two grandmothers, with not less partiality, but more sincerity, were equally earnest in support of their own descendant.

Lucy, who was hardly less anxious to please one parent than the other, thought the boys were both remarkably tall for their age, and could not conceive that there could be the smallest difference in the world between them, and Miss Steele, with yet greater address gave it, as fast as she could, in favour of each.

Elinor, having once delivered her opinion on William's side, by which she offended Mrs. Ferrars and Fanny still more, did not see the necessity of enforcing it by any farther assertion; and Marianne, when called on for hers, offended them all, by declaring that she had no opinion to give, as she had never thought about it.

.

Because they neither flattered herself nor her children, she could not believe them good-natured; and because they were fond of reading, she fancied them satirical: perhaps without exactly knowing what it was to be satirical; but that did not signify. It was censure in common use, and easily given.

.

Mr. Palmer maintained the common, but unfatherly opinion among his sex, of all infants being alike; and though she could plainly perceive at different times, the most striking resemblance between this baby and every one of his relations on both sides, there was no convincing his father of it; no persuading him to believe that it was not exactly like every other baby of the same age. . . .

.

Elinor agreed to it all, for she did not think he deserved the compliment of rational opposition.

.

Mrs. Dashwood was surprised only for a moment at seeing him; for his coming to Barton was, in her opinion, of all things the most natural. Her joy and expression of regard long outlived her wonder. He received the kindest welcome from her; and shyness, coldness, reserve could not stand against such a reception. They had begun to fail him before he entered the house, and they were quite overcome by the captivating manners of Mrs. Dashwood. Indeed a man could not very well be in love with either of her daughters, without extending the passion to her; and Elinor had the satisfaction of seeing him soon become more like himself. His affections seemed to reanimate towards them all, and his interest in their welfare again became perceptible. He was not in spirits however; he praised their house, admired its prospects, was attentive, and kind; but still he was not in spirits. The whole family perceived it, and Mrs. Dashwood, attributing it to some want of liberality in his mother, sat down to table indignant against all selfish parents.

"What are Mrs. Ferrars's views for you at present, Edward?" said she, when dinner was over and they had drawn round the fire. "Are you still to be a great orator in spite of yourself?"

"No. I hope my mother is now convinced that I have no more talents than inclination for a public life!"

"But how is your fame to be established? For famous you must be to satisfy all your family; and with no inclination for expense, no affection for strangers, no profession, and no assurance, you may find it a difficult matter."

"I shall not attempt it. I have no wish to be distinguished; and I have every reason to hope I never shall. Thank Heaven! I cannot be forced into genius and eloquence."

"You have no ambition, I well know. Your wishes are all moderate."

"As moderate as those of the rest of the world, I believe. I wish as well as every body else to be perfectly happy; but like every body else it must be in my own way. Greatness will not make me so."

"Strange if it would!" cried Marianne. "What have wealth or grandeur to do with happiness?"

"Grandeur has but little," said Elinor, "but wealth has much to do with it."

"Elinor, for shame!" said Marianne; "money can only give happiness where there is nothing else to give it. Beyond a competence, it can afford no real satisfaction, as far as mere self is concerned."

"Perhaps," said Elinor, smiling, "we may come to the same point. *Your* competence and *my* wealth are very much alike, I dare say; and without them, as the world goes now, we shall both agree that every kind of external comfort must be wanting. Your ideas are only more noble than mine. Come, what is your competence?"

"About eighteen hundred or two thousand a-year; not more than *that*."

Elinor laughed. "*Two* thousand a-year! *One* is my wealth! I guessed how it would end."

"And yet two thousand a-year is a very moderate income," said Marianne. "A family cannot well be maintained on a smaller. I am sure I am not extravagant in my demands. A proper establishment of servants, a carriage, perhaps two, and hunters, cannot be supported on less."

Elinor smiled again, to hear her sister describing so accurately their future expenses at Combe Magna.

"Hunters!" repeated Edward—"But why must you have hunters? Every body does not hunt."

Marianne coloured as she replied, "But most people do."

"I wish," said Margaret, striking out a novel thought, "that somebody would give us all a large fortune apiece!"

"Oh, that they would!" cried Marianne, her eyes sparkling with animation, and her cheeks glowing with the delight of each imaginary happiness.

"We are all unanimous in that wish, I suppose," said Elinor, "in spite of the insufficiency of wealth."

•

FROM *Pride and Prejudice*

"Happiness in marriage is entirely a matter of chance. If the dispositions of the parties are ever so well known to each other, or ever so similar before-hand, it does not advance their felicity in the least. They always continue to grow sufficiently unlike afterwards to have their share of vexation; and it is better to know as little as possible of the defects of the person with whom you are to pass your life."

•

. . . Sir William thus began.

"What a charming amusement for young people this is, Mr. Darcy — There is nothing like dancing after all. — I consider it as one of the first refinements of polished societies."

"Certainly, Sir; — and it has the advantage also of being in vogue among the less polished societies of the world. — Every savage can dance."

•

. . . her mother attended her to the door with many cheerful prognostics of a bad day. Her hopes were answered; Jane had not been gone long before it rained hard.

•

Without thinking highly either of men or of matrimony, marriage had always been her object; it was the only honourable provision for well-educated young women of small fortune, and however uncertain of giving happiness, must be their pleasantest preservative from want.

•

"Indeed, Mr. Bennett," said she, "it is very hard to think that Charlotte Lucas should ever be mistress of this house, that I should be forced to make way for her, and live to see her take my place in it!"

"My dear, do not give way to such gloomy thoughts. Let us hope for better things. Let us flatter ourselves that I may be the survivor."

•

"Now be sincere; did you admire me for my impertinence?"

"You may as well call it impertinence at once. It was very little less. The fact is, that you were sick of civility, of deference, of officious attention. You were disgusted with the women who were always speaking and looking, and thinking for your approbation alone. I roused, and interested you, because I was so unlike them."

•

. . . Mr. Collins made his declaration in form. Having resolved to do it without loss of time, as his leave of absence extended only to the following Saturday, and having no feelings of diffidence to make it distressing to himself even at the moment, he set about it in a very orderly manner, with all the observances which he supposed a regular part of the business. On finding Mrs. Bennet, Elizabeth, and one of the younger girls together, soon after breakfast, he addressed the mother in these words.

"May I hope, Madam, for your interest with your fair daughter Elizabeth, when I solicit for the honour of a private audience with her in the course of this morning?"

Before Elizabeth had time for any thing but a blush of surprise, Mrs. Bennet instantly answered.

"Oh dear! — Yes — certainly. — I am sure Lizzy will be very happy — I am sure she can have no objection. — Come, Kitty, I want you up stairs." And gathering her work together, she was hastening away, when Elizabeth called out.

"Dear Ma'am, do not go. — I beg you will not go. — Mr. Collins must excuse me. — He can have nothing to say to me that any body need not hear. I am going away myself."

"No, no, nonsense, Lizzy. — I desire you will stay where you are." — And upon Elizabeth's seeming really, with vexed and embarrassed looks, about to escape, she added, "Lizzy, I *insist* upon your staying and hearing Mr. Collins."

Elizabeth would not oppose such an injunction—and a moment's consideration making her also sensible that it would be wisest to get it over as soon and as quietly as possible, she sat down again, and tried to conceal by incessant employment the feelings which were divided between distress and diversion. Mrs. Bennet and Kitty walked off, and as soon as they were gone Mr. Collins began.

"Believe me, my dear Miss Elizabeth, that your modesty, so far from doing you any disservice, rather adds to your other perfections.

You would have been less amiable in my eyes had there *not* been this little unwillingness; but allow me to assure you that I have your respected mother's permission for this address. You can hardly doubt the purport of my discourse, however your natural delicacy may lead you to dissemble; my attentions have been too marked to be mistaken. Almost as soon as I entered the house I singled you out as the companion of my future life. But before I am run away with by my feelings on this subject, perhaps it will be advisable for me to state my reasons for marrying— and moreover for coming into Hertfordshire with the design of selecting a wife, as I certainly did."

The idea of Mr. Collins, with all his solemn composure, being run away with by his feelings, made Elizabeth so near laughing that she could not use the short pause he allowed in any attempt to stop him farther, and he continued:

"My reasons for marrying are, first, that I think it a right thing for every clergyman in easy circumstances (like myself) to set the example of matrimony in his parish. Secondly, that I am convinced it will add very greatly to my happiness; and thirdly—which perhaps I ought to have mentioned earlier, that it is the particular advice and recommendation of the very noble lady whom I have the honour of calling patroness. Twice has she condescended to give me her opinion (unasked too!) on this subject: and it was but the very Saturday night before I left Hunsford—between our pools at quadrille, while Mrs. Jenkinson was arranging Miss de Bourgh's foot-stool, that she said, 'Mr. Collins, you must marry. A cleryman like you must marry.—Chuse properly, chuse a gentlewoman for my sake; and for your own, let her be an active, useful sort of person, not brought up high, but able to make a small income go a good way. This is my advice. Find such a woman as soon as you can, bring her to Hunsford, and I will visit her." Allow me, by the way, to observe, my fair cousin, that I do not reckon the notice and kindness of Lady Catherine de Bourgh as among the least of the advantages in my power to offer. You will find her manners beyond any thing I can describe; and your wit and vivacity I think must be acceptable to her, especially when tempered with the silence and respect which her rank will inevitably excite. Thus much for my general intention in favour of matrimony; it remains to be told why my views were directed to Longbourn instead of my own neighbourhood, where I assure you there are many amiable young women. But the fact is, that being, as I am, to inherit this estate after the death of your honoured father, (who, however, may live many years longer), I could not satisfy myself without resolving to chuse a wife from among his daughters, that the loss to them might be as little as possible, when the melancholy event takes place—which, however, as I have already said, may not be for several years. This has been my motive, my fair cousin, and I flatter myself it will not sink me in your esteem. And now nothing remains for me but to assure you in the most animated language of the violence of my affection. To fortune I am perfectly indifferent, and shall make no demand of that nature on your father, since I am well aware that it could not be complied with; and that one thousand pounds in the 4 per cents. which will not be yours till after your mother's decease, is all that you may ever be entitled to. On that head, therefore, I shall be uniformly silent; and you may assure yourself that no ungenerous reproach shall ever pass my lips when we are married."

It was absolutely necessary to interrupt him now.

"You are too hasty, Sir," she cried. "You forget that I have made no answer. Let me do it without farther loss of time. Accept my thanks for the compliment you are paying me. I am very sensible of the honour of your proposals, but it is impossible for me to do otherwise than decline them."

"I am not now to learn," replied Mr. Collins, with a formal wave of the hand, "that it is usual with young ladies to reject the addresses of the man whom they secretly mean to accept, when he first applies for their favour; and that sometimes the refusal is repeated a second or even a third time. I am therefore by no means discouraged by what you have just said, and shall hope to lead you to the altar ere long."

"Upon my word, Sir," cried Elizabeth, "your hope is rather an extraordinary one after my declaration. I do assure you that I am not one of those young ladies (if such young ladies there are) who are so daring as to risk their happiness on the chance of being asked a second time. I am perfectly serious in my refusal.—You could not make *me* happy, and I am convinced that I am the last woman in the world who would make *you* so.—Nay, were your friend Lady Catherine to know me, I am persuaded she would find me in every respect ill qualified for the situation."

"Were it certain that Lady Catherine would think so," said Mr. Collins very gravely—"but I cannot imagine that her ladyship would at all disapprove of you. And you may be certain that when I have the honour of seeing her again I shall speak in the highest terms of your modesty, economy, and other amiable qualifications."

"Indeed, Mr. Collins, all praise of me will be unnecessary. You must give me leave to judge for myself, and pay me the compliment of believing what I say. I wish you very happy and very rich, and by refusing your hand, do all in my power to prevent your being otherwise. In making me the offer, you must have satisfied the delicacy of your feelings with regard to my family, and may take possession of Longbourn estate whenever it falls, without any self-reproach. This matter may be considered, therefore, as finally settled." And rising as she thus spoke, she would have quitted the room, had not Mr. Collins thus addressed her.

"When I do myself the honour of speaking to you next in this subject I shall hope to receive a more favourable answer than you have now given me; though I am far from accusing you of cruelty at present, because I know it to be the established custom of your sex to reject a man on the first application, and perhaps you have even now said as much to encourage my suit as would be consistent with the true delicacy of the female character."

"Really, Mr. Collins," cried Elizabeth with some warmth, "you puzzle me exceedingly. If what I have hitherto said can appear to you in the form of encouragement, I know not how to express my refusal in such a way as may convince you of its being one."

"You must give me leave to flatter myself, my dear cousin, that your refusal of my addresses is merely words of course. My reasons for believing it are briefly these:—It does not appear to me that my hand is unworthy your acceptance or that the establishment I can offer would be any other than highly desirable. My situation in life, my connections with the family of De Bourgh, and my relationship to your own, are circumstances highly in my favour; and you should take it into farther consideration that in spite of your manifold attractions, it is by no means certain that another offer of marriage may ever be made you. Your portion is unhappily so small that it will in all likelihood undo the effects of your loveliness and amiable qualifications. As I must therefore conclude that you are not serious in your rejection of me, I shall chuse to attribute it to your wish of increasing my love by suspense, according to the usual practice of elegant females."

"I do assure you, Sir, that I have no pretension whatever to that kind of elegance which consists in tormenting a respectable man. I would rather be paid the compliment of being believed. I thank you again and again for the honour you have done me in your proposals, but to accept them is absolutely impossible. My feelings in every respect forbid it. Can I speak plainer? Do not consider me now as an elegant female intending to plague you, but as a rational creature speaking the truth from her heart."

"You are uniformly charming!" cried he, with an air of awkward gallantry; "and I am persuaded that when sanctioned by the express authority of both your excellent parents, my proposals will not fail of being acceptable."

To such perseverance in wilful self-deception Elizabeth would make no reply, and immediately and in silence withdrew; determined, if he persisted in considering her repeated refusals as flattering encouragement, to apply to her father, whose negative might be uttered in such a manner as must be decisive, and whose behaviour at least could not be mistaken for the affectation and coquetry of an elegant female.

•

"Mr. Darcy is not to be laughed at!" cried Elizabeth. "That is an uncommon advantage, and uncommon I hope it will continue, for it would be a great loss to me to have many such acquaintance. I dearly love a laugh."

"Miss Bingley," said he, "has given me credit for more than can be. The wisest and the best of men, nay, the wisest and best of their actions, may be rendered ridiculous by a person whose first object in life is a joke."

"Certainly," replied Elizabeth—"there are such people, but I hope I am not one of *them*. I hope I never ridicule what is wise or good. Follies and nonsense, whims and inconsistencies *do* divert me, I own, and I laugh at them whenever I can.—But these, I suppose, are precisely what you are without."

"Perhaps that is not possible for any one. But it has been the study of my life to avoid those weaknesses which often expose a strong understanding to ridicule."

"Such as vanity and pride."

"Yes, vanity is a weakness indeed. But pride—where there is a real superiority of mind, pride will be always under good regulation."

Elizabeth turned away to hide a smile.

"Your examination of Mr. Darcy is over, I presume," said Miss Bingley;—"and pray what is the result?"

"I am perfectly convinced by it that Mr. Darcy has no defect. He owns it himself without disguise."

"No"—said Darcy, "I have made no pretension. I have faults enough, but they are not, I hope, of understanding. My temper I dare not vouch for.—It is I believe too little yielding—certainly too little for the convenience of the world. I cannot forget the follies and vices of others so soon as I ought, nor their offences against myself. My feelings are not puffed about with every attempt to move them. My temper would perhaps be called resentful.—My good opinion once lost is lost for ever."

"*That* is a failing indeed!"—cried Elizabeth. "Implacable resentment is a shade in a character. But you have chosen your fault well.—I really cannot *laugh* at it. You are safe from me."

•

Mr. Bennet treated the matter differently. "So, Lizzy," said he one day, "your sister is crossed in love I find. I congratulate her. Next to being married, a girl likes to be crossed in love a little now and then. It is something to think of, and gives her a sort of distinction among her companions. When is your turn to come? You will hardly bear to be long outdone by Jane. Now is your time. Here are officers enough at Meryton to disappoint all the young ladies in the country. Let Wickham be *your* man. He is a pleasant fellow, and would jilt you creditably."

"Thank you, Sir, but a less agreeable man would satisfy me. We must not all expect Jane's good fortune."

"True," said Mr. Bennet, "but it is a comfort to think that, whatever of that kind may befal you, you have an affectionate mother who will always make the most of it."

Sheila Ballantyne (contemporary)

～ぺ ҙ～

FROM *Norma Jean, the Termite Queen*

"How do I know all this? Because I'm crazy. You can always trust the information given you by people who are crazy: They have access to truth not available through regular channels."

•

When a man wishes to regain the advantage in an argument with his wife, he . . . raises his voice higher than the prevailing conversation; but not so high that it could be defined as screaming. . . .

In simple terms, what this maneuver seeks to accomplish is to convince the wife that she has overstepped the boundaries governing the argument, which were defined earlier, and in secret, by the husband; and to arouse her inherent guilt and shame for having behaved with less control than he. . . .

He must begin to make statements—always addressed *to* or *about* his wife—which gradually increase in their degree of incoherence and the intensity of abusiveress. It is helpful to include references to: her weight; the fact that her facial expression is hard, ugly, unfeminine (do not be diverted by the logic of the situation, i.e., that this is so because she is angry and fighting; your objective is to *exploit* this fact in a way that will distract her and prevent her from using it as a legitimate defense.)

•

Norma Jean finishes packing the lunches, writing the names on each little bio-degradable bag. Well, you've got two choices: you can use plastic to wrap them, which is not bio-degradable, and fouls the environment; or you can use paper bags, which are bio-degradable, but which cause deforestation. Those are the choices. Unless you want to tie a salami around their necks.

Tallulah Bankhead (1902-1968)

❧ ❦

One-liner and Anecdotes

"What's the matter, darling, don't you recognize me with my clothes on?" (to a lover who doesn't acknowledge her at a party)

•

A young woman paying a visit to the lavatory was amazed to hear Tallulah's unmistakable gravelly tones coming from the neighboring cubicle.

"Say, there's no paper in here, do you have any in there with you?"

Receiving a negative reply she tried again, "Well, do you have any Kleenex on you?"

Again, the reply was negative.

"Not even some cotton wool or a piece of wrapping paper?"

A long pause followed the third negative, then there was the sound of a purse opening and a resigned voice came through the partition, "Would you have two fives for a ten?"

Mary Barber (1690–1757)

The Conclusion of a Letter
to the Rev. Mr. C——

'Tis time to conclude, for I make it a rule
To leave off all writing, when Con. comes from school.
He dislikes what I've written, and says I had better
To send what he calls a poetical letter.

  To this I replied, "You are out of your wits;
A letter in verse would put him in fits;
He thinks it a crime in a woman to read—
Then what would he say should your counsel succeed?
'I pity poor Barber, his wife's so romantic:
A letter in rhyme!—Why the woman is frantic!
This reading the poets has quite turned her head;
On my life, she should have a dark room and straw bed.
I often heard say that St. Patrick took care
No poisonous creature should live in this air:
He only regarded the body, I find,
But Plato considered who poisoned the mind.
Would they'd follow his precepts, who sit at the helm,
And drive poetasters from out of the realm!

  'Her husband has surely a terrible life;
There's nothing I dread like a verse-writing wife:
Defend me, ye powers, from that fatal curse,
Which must heighten the plagues of *for better for worse*!

  'May I have a wife that will dust her own floor,
And not the fine minx recommended by More.

(That he was a dotard is granted, I hope,
Who died for asserting the rights of the Pope.)
If ever I marry, I'll choose me a spouse,
That shall *serve* and *obey*, as she's bound by her vows;

That shall, when I'm dressing, attend like a valet;
Then go to the kitchen, and study my palate.
She has wisdom enough, that keeps out of the dirt,
And can make a good pudding, and cut out a shirt.
What good's in a dame that will pore on a book?
No—give me the wife that shall save me a cook.' "

   Thus far I had written—then turned to my son,
To give him advice, ere my letter was done.
"My son, should you marry, look out for a wife
That's fitted to lighten the labours of life.
Be sure, wed a woman you thoroughly know,
And shun, above all things, a *housewifely shrew*,
That would fly to your study, with fire in her looks,
And ask what you got by your poring on books,
Think dressing of dinner the height of all science,
And to peace and good humour bid open defiance.

   "Avoid the fine lady, whose beauty's her care;
Who sets a high price on her shape, and her air;
who in dress, and in visits, employs the whole day,
And longs for the evening, to sit down to play.

   "Choose a woman of wisdom, as well as good breeding,
With a turn, or at least no aversion, to reading:
In the care of her person, exact and refined;
Yet still, let her principal care be her mind:
Who can, when her family cares give her leisure,
Without the dear cards, pass an evening with pleasure,
In forming her children to virtue and knowledge,
Nor trust, for that care, to a school, or a college:
By learning made humble, not thence taking airs
To despise or neglect her domestic affairs:
Nor think her less fitted for doing her duty,
By knowing its reasons, its use, and its beauty.

   "When you gain her affection, take care to preserve it,
Lest others persuade her you do not deserve it.
Still study to heighten the joys of her life;
Nor treat her the worse for her being your wife.
If in judgement she errs, set her right, without pride:
'Tis the province of insolent fools to deride.
A husband's first praise is a Friend and Protector:

Then change not these titles for Tyrant and Hector.
Let your person be neat, unaffectedly clean,
Though alone with your wife the whole day you remain.
Choose books, for her study, to fashion her mind,
To emulate those who excelled of her kind.
Be religion the principal care of your life,
As you hope to be blest in your children and wife;
So you, in your marriage, shall gain its true end.
And find, in your wife, a Companion and Friend."

•

To Mrs. Frances-Arabella Kelly

Today, as at my glass I stood,
To set my head-clothes and my hood,
I saw my grizzled locks with dread,
And called to mind the Gorgon's head.

Thought I, whate'ver the poets say,
Medusa's hair was only grey:
Though Ovid, who the story told,
Was too well-bred to call her old;
But, what amounted to the same,
He made her an immortal dame.

Yet now, whene'er a matron sage
Hath felt the rugged hand of age,
You hear our witty coxcombs cry,
"Rot that old witch—she'll never die";
Though, had they but a little reading,
Ovid would teach them better breeding.

I fancy now I hear you say,
"Grant heaven my locks may ne'er be grey!
Why am I told this frightful story,
To beauty a *memento mori*?"

And, as along the room you pass,
Casting your eye upon the glass,
"Surely," say you, "this lovely face
Will never suffer such disgrace:
The bloom, that on my cheek appears,
Will never be impaired by years.

Her envy, now I plainly see,
Makes her inscribe those lines to me.
These beldames, who were born before me,
Are grieved to see the men adore me:
Their snaky locks freeze up the blood;
My tresses fire the purple flood.

   "Unnumbered slaves around me wait,
And from my eyes expect their fate.
I own of conquest I am vain,
Though I despise the slaves I gain.
Heaven gave me charms, and destined me
For universal tyranny."

Djuna Barnes (1892–1982)

FROM *Nightwood*

. . . skill is never so amazing as when it seems inappropriate.

•

"You know what man really desires?" inquired the doctor, grinning into the immobile face of the Baron. "One of two things: to find someone who is so stupid that he can lie to her, or to love someone so much that she can lie to him."

•

The Catholic is the girl that you love so much that she can lie to you, and the Protestant is the girl that loves you so much that you can lie to her, and pretend a lot that you do not feel.

•

"One cup poured into another makes different waters; tears shed by one eye would blind if wept into another's eye. The breast we strike in joy is not the breast we strike in pain; any man's smile would be consternation on another's mouth. Rear up, eternal river, here comes grief! Man has no foothold that is not also a bargain. So be it! Laughing I came into Pacific Street, and laughing I'm going out of it; laughter is the pauper's money."

•

To men she sent books by the dozen; the general feeling was that she was a well-read woman, though she had read perhaps ten books in her life.

Lynda Barry (1956–   )

~❦ ❦~

FROM *Down the Street*

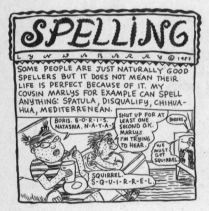

LOVE ADVENTURE

L Y N D A · "I'M A HOG FOR YOU" · B A R R Y © 1987

THERE WERE THESE VERY POPULAR BUSHES IN OUR NEIGHBORHOOD WHERE PRACTICALLY EVERYONE ON THE PLANET GOT THEIR FIRST KISS. ME AND DEENA SAID WE GOT OURS THERE TOO BY SOMEBODY'S COUSIN FROM IDAHO BUT IT WAS A LIE. WE HAD NEVER KISSED NO ONE.

NO ONE'S EVER GONNA KISS US MAN. AND NOBODY EVEN BELIEVES US ABOUT THAT GUY FROM IDAHO EITHER. WHO'D EVER KISS A GUY FROM IDAHO?

AT LEAST WE'RE NOT SLUTS.

SO?

WE TRIED TO COPY THE SENSUOUS LOOKS THAT MAKE A MAN HYPNOTISED AS SEEN ON T.V. AND IN OUR OPINION WE GOT THOSE LOCKS PERFECTED.

WHEN I FINALLY GOT MY FIRST KISS AND DEENA GOT HERS WE COULD NOT HELP BUT FEEL A CERTAIN ELEMENT OF DISAPPOINTMENT. WE COULD NOT EXPLAIN EXACTLY WHERE THIS FEELING CAME FROM AND NEITHER DID WE KNOW THAT WE WOULD SPEND THE NEXT TWENTY YEARS TRYING TO FIND OUT.

WELL HOW COME AFTER THEY KISSED US THEY START ACTING LIKE THEY DON'T EVEN LIKE US ANYMORE?

BECAUSE GUYS ARE STUPID.

THEN HOW COME WE STILL LIKE THEM?

DON'T KNOW YET.

WE TRIED THEM OUT AT PARTIES BUT AS IT TURNED OUT THE GUYS OUR AGE WERE NOT AS SOPHISTICATED AS WE WERE.

YOU GUYS BEEN AT THE AQUARIUM OR SOMETHING?

I DON'T GET IT.

IS THIS SOME KIND OF DARE?

How to DRAW GIRLS

L Y N D A · 12 STITCHES · B A R R Y © 1988

WITH YOUR HOST

MARLYS

OK. THE FIRST NUMBER ONE THING IN DRAWING GIRLS IS PRACTICE YOUR EYES! GET THEM MATCHING OR YOUR DRAWING WILL LOOK LIKE THERE'S A MENTAL PROBLEM!"

EYEBALL GOES IN THE MIDDLE PUT 'EM ON THE LINES

EYEBROWS

DON'T FORGET CURLY EYELASHES IT MAKES THE EYES BEAUTIFUL!

KEEP ON DOING IT UNTIL YOU GET IT PERFECT BUT DON'T JUST WASTE PAPER!

NUMBER TWO: THE MOUTH AND NOSE IS EASY! FIRST DRAW THE SHAPE OF HER HEAD IN A "U". THEN YOU JUST ADD ON THE KIND OF MOUTH AND NOSE YOU WANT DEPENDING ON HER PERSONALITY!

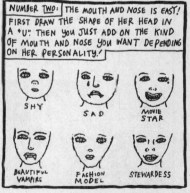

SHY

SAD

MOVIE STAR

BEAUTIFUL VAMPIRE

FASHION MODEL

STEWARDESS

NUMBER THREE: WHAT ABOUT HER HAIR? THERES A LOT OF HAIR-DOS FOR HER TO HAVE! THERES A LOT OF STYLES!

PEEK-A-BOO   A BEAUTY PAGEANT   INDIAN PRINCESS

A FRANCE LADY   A GORGEOUS FLIP   RATTED BUBBLE

NUMBER FOUR: THE HARDEST PART: YOU HAVE TO DRAW HER WHOLE BODY AND THIS IS WHERE YOU CAN WRECK EVERYTHING SO BE CAREFUL! MY SECRET IS: DRAW A LONG BEAUTIFUL DRESS AND HER HOLDING FLOWERS AND DON'T FORGET SOME ELEGANT ACCESSORIES!

A CROWN ALWAYS LOOKS LOVELY

PUT IN BIRDS →

DRAW ON A WATCH

DECORATE THE DRESS PLEASE

FLOWERS CAN HIDE HANDS THATS TOO HARD TO DRAW

← HER PURSE ITS IMPORTANT

DRAW A TREE HERE AND SHE CAN LOOK LIKE SHES IN THE FOREST

SHOES CAN STICK OUT

THE END BY MARLYS

JUMP SHOT
BY LYNDA BOLD SOUL SISTER BARRY © 1988

THE TEENAGER NAME OF RICHARD COMES OUT LATE SOME NIGHTS TO SHOOT BASKETS ON OUR CORNER. YOU CAN WATCH HIM FROM MY BEDROOM WINDOW.

YOU CAN LAY ON THE BED AND HEAR THE BALL, THE PING PING OF IT AGAINST THE STREET BOUNCING. YOU CAN HEAR HIM WALK IT THEN RUN IT AND DO HIS PERFECT HOOK SHOT.

BOUNCE, BOUNCE, BOUNCE, STOP. THE FAST NO-SOUND OF HIS FEET IN THE AIR, THE BALL FLYING UP, PAUSE, THEN <u>WHAM-WHAM</u> AGAINST THE BACKBOARD, A HIGH BOUNCE OFF THE RIM, HIM WHISPERING SON OF A BITCH.

HIM JUMPING UP ON THE CORNER, HIM JUMPING HIGH AND TURNING IN THE AIR UNDER A STREET LIGHT WITH A THOUSAND MILLION BUGS FLYING AROUND IT GOING WILD, WILD, WILD.

Anne Beatts (1947-)

~☙ ❧~

FROM *Can a Woman Get a Laugh'
and a Man Too?*

Real girls weren't funny. Real girls were pretty and fluffy and could do
the splits in cheerleader tryouts. Real girls didn't crack jokes. Did you
ever hear Sandra Dee crack a joke? Annette Funicello didn't even laugh;
she just put her hands on her hips and got mad at Ricky or Tommy or
Eddie or whoever was carrying her surfboard, so that they could tell her
how cute she was when she was mad.

•

I'm often accused of "going too far," but I recognize that behind my
desire to shock is an even stronger desire to evade the "feminine" stereotype: "You say women are afraid of mice? I'll show you! I'll *eat* the
mouse!"

•

Interview

. . . we were working on a sketch and came up with a line that we
thought was wonderful: "Tell Granny Loopner only twenty-eight more
cloves and her pomander ball will be finished." We tried this line out
on one of the male writers and he just shrugged his shoulders. We said,
"Do you know what a pomander ball is?" "No." So then we said, "Do
you know what cloves are?" and he said, "Do you mean garlic cloves?"
So we went around and asked three different men, "What are cloves?"
and none of them knew. Finally, we asked Lorne Michaels, the producer, and he said, "Well, it's a spice, right?" I guess that's why he's the
producer.

I can still remember feeling a little indentation in my thumb from
pressing those goddamn cloves into the orange. And you finally get one
in and the clove part falls off and you have to use another one. It's a
big production. But I'm faced with the question of, "Can we put that

line over? Will there be enough women in the room who will know?" There's a reluctance to use it.

•

They never say, "Do you know what a carburetor is?" Never. Okay, pomander ball I could understand their not knowing. But cloves? Haven't they ever eaten baked ham? They've never noticed, they've never baked a ham, they've never hung around the kitchen on Easter while mother put cloves in the ham. There is a women's culture that men just don't know about. So when they say "Hey, that joke's not funny," it's sometimes because they don't understand the vocabulary. They don't understand what the joke is based on.

•

Right. As a woman doing humor on issues relating to women, I do have a position, I know what it is, right away. I don't have to say, "Well, let's see, who's the asshole here? Whom am I going to make fun of? The Israelis or the Arabs—which ones are the more stupid?" I can say, "I see what the issue is. Obviously, it's wrong for the woman in the ring around the collar commercials to be foundering in the depths of misery because her husband has a ring around his collar. Why doesn't he wash his own goddamn shirt?" I have strong feelings and a strong position and I know where the humor is coming from.

Joy Behar (contemporary)

❧ ❦

One-liners

"Sure I want a man in my life," says Behar, "but not in my house. I want him to hook up the VCR and leave. Why should I want him in the house?"

•

"When I got married, I said to my therapist, 'I want to do something creative.' He said, 'Why don't you have a baby?' I hope he's dead now."

•

It's important for a woman's point of view to be heard. People say to me, "Do you speak as a woman?" No, I speak as a man. Of course I speak as a woman! What a stupid question that is. I'm a female. What?

Am I supposed to speak as if I had a schlong? (That's Italian for "facial hair.")

Aphra Behn (1649-1689)

~❦ ❦~

FROM *The Rover*

Enter Blunt *and* Lucetta *with a light.*

LUCETTA: Now we are safe and free; no fears of the coming home of my old jealous husband, which made me a little thoughtful when you came in first—but now love is all the business of my soul.

BLUNT: I am transported!—pox on't, that I had but some fine things to say to her, such as lovers use,—I was a fool not to learn of Fred a little by heart before I came—something I must say—

[Aside.

'Sheartlikins, sweet soul! I am not used to compliment, but I'm an honest gentleman, and thy humble servant.

LUCETTA: I have nothing to pay for so great a favor, but such a love as cannot but be great, since at first sight of that sweet face and shape, it made me your absolute captive.

BLUNT: Kind heart! how prettily she talks! Egad, I'll show her husband a Spanish trick; send him out of the world and marry her: she's damnably in love with me, and will ne'er mind settlements, and so there's that saved.

[Aside.

LUCETTA: Well Sir, I'll go and undress me, and be with you instantly.

BLUNT: Make haste then, for adsheartlikins, dear soul, thou canst not guess at the pain of a longing lover, when his joys are drawn within the compass of a few minutes.

LUCETTA: You speak my sense, and I'll make haste to prove it.

[Exit.

BLUNT: 'Tis a rare girl! and this one night's enjoyment with her will be worth all the days I ever passed in Essex.—would she would go with me into England; though to say truth there's

plenty of whores already.—But a pox on 'em, they are such
mercenary—prodigal whores, that they want such a one as
this, that's free and generous, to give 'em good examples—
Why, what a house she has, how rich and fine!

SANCHO: Sir, my lady has sent me to conduct you to her chamber.

                                                          [*Enter* Sancho.

BLUNT: Sir, I shall be proud to follow—here's one of her servants
            too! 'Sheartlikins, by this garb and gravity, he might be a
            Justice of Peace in Essex, and is but a pimp here.

                                                              [*Exeunt.

The scene changes to a chamber with an alcove bed in it, a table, etc.
Lucetta *in bed. Enter* Sancho *and* Blunt, *who takes the candle of*
Sancho *at the door.*

SANCHO: Sir, my commission reaches no farther.

                                                          [*Exit* Sancho.

BLUNT: Sir, I'll excuse your compliment—what, in bed, my sweet
            mistress?

LUCETTA: You see, I still outdo you in kindness.

BLUNT: And thou shalt see what haste I'll make to quit scores—oh
            the luckiest rogue!

                                                 [*He undresses himself.*

LUCETTA: Should you be false or cruel now!—

BLUNT: False! 'Sheartlikins, what dost thou take me for? . . . an
            insensible heathen—a pox of thy old jealous husband; and
            he were dead, egad, sweet soul, it should be none of my
            fault if I did not marry thee.

LUCETTA: It never should be mine.

BLUNT: Good soul! I'm the fortunatest dog!

LUCETTA: Are you not undressed yet?

BLUNT: As much as my impatience will permit.

                               [*Goes towards the bed in his shirt, drawers, etc.*

LUCETTA: Hold, sir, put out the light, it may betray us else.

BLUNT: Anything, I need no other light, but that of thine eyes!—
            'Sheartlikens, there I think I had it. [*Puts out the candle, the
            bed descends, he gropes about to find it.*]—Why—why—where
            am I got? what, not yet?—where are you, sweetest?—ah,
            the rogue's silent now—a pretty love-trick this—how she'll
            laugh at me anon!—you need not, my dear rogue! You
            need not!—I'm all on fire already—come, come, now call
            me in pity.—Sure I'm enchanted! I have been round the

chamber, and can find neither woman, nor bed—I locked the door, I'm sure she cannot go that way—or if she could, the bed could not.—Enough, enough, my pretty wanton, do not carry the jest too far—[*Lights on a trap, and is let down.*] Ha, betrayed! Dogs! Rogues! Pimps!—help! help!

Enter Lucetta, Philippo, *and* Sancho *with a light.*

PHILIPPO: Ha, ha, he's dispatched finely.

LUCETTA: Now, sir, had I been coy, we had missed of this booty.

PHILIPPO: Nay, when I saw 'twas a substantial fool, I was mollified; but when you dote upon a serenading coxcomb, upon a face, fine clothes, and a lute, it makes me rage.

LUCETTA: You know I was never guilty of that folly, my dear Philippo, but with yourself—but come, let's see what we have got by this.

PHILIPPO: A rich coat!—sword and hat—these breeches too—are well lined!—see here, a gold watch!—a purse—ha!—gold!—at least two hundred pistoles!—a bunch of diamond rings! and one with the family arms!—a gold box!—with a medal of his king! and his lady mother's picture!—these were sacred relics, believe me!—see, the waistband of his breeches have a mine of gold!—old Queen Bess's, we have a quarrel to her ever since eighty-eight, and may therefore justify the theft, the Inquisition might have committed it.

LUCETTA: —See, a bracelet of bowed gold! these his sisters tied about his arm at parting—but well—for all this, I fear his being a stranger, may make a noise and hinder our trade with them hereafter.

PHILIPPO: That's our security; he is not only a stranger to us, but to the country too—the common shore into which he is descended, thou knowest conducts him into another street, which this light will hinder him from ever finding again— he knows neither your name, nor that of the street where your house is, nay, nor the way to his own lodgings.

LUCETTA: And art not thou an unmerciful rogue! not to afford him one night for all this? . . .

PHILIPPO: Blame me not, Lucetta, to keep as much of thee as I can to myself—come, that thought makes me wanton!—let's to bed!—Sancho, lock up these.

This is the fleece which fools do bear,
Designed for witty men to shear.

[*Exeunt.*

The scene changes, and discovers Blunt, *creeping out of a common shore, his face, etc. all dirty.*

BLUNT: Oh Lord!   [*Climbing up.*
I am got out at last, and (which is a miracle) without a clue—and now to damning and cursing!—but if that would ease me, where shall I begin! with my fortune, myself, or the quean that cozened me!—what a dog was I to believe in woman! oh coxcomb!—ignorant conceited coxcomb! to fancy she could be enamoured with my person! at first sight enamoured!—oh, I'm a cursed puppy! 'tis plain, fool was writ upon my forehead! she perceived it!—saw the Essex calf there—for what allurements could there be in this countenance! which I can endure, because I'm acquainted with it—oh, dull silly dog! to be thus soothed into a cozening! had I been drunk, I might fondly have credited the young quean!—but as I was in my right wits, to be thus cheated, confirms it: I am a dull believing English country fop—but my comrades! death and the devil! there's the worst of all—then a ballad will be sung tomorrow on the Prado, to a lousy tune of the enchanted 'squire, and the annihilated damsel—but Fred that rogue! and the colonel, will abuse me beyond all Christian patience—had she left me my clothes, I have a bill of exchange at home, would have saved my credit—but now all hope is taken from me— well, I'll home (if I can find the way) with this consolation, that I am not the first kind believing coxcomb; but there are, gallants, many such good natures amongst ye.
          And tho you've better arts to hide your follies,
          Adsheartlikins, y'are all as errant cullies.   [*Exit.*

•

FROM *An Epistle to the Reader,* *Prefixed to* The Dutch Lover

Good, Sweet, Honey, Sugar-Candied Reader,

Which I think is more than anyone has called you yet, I must have a word or two with you before you do advance into the treatise; but 'tis not to beg your pardon for diverting you from your affairs by such an idle pamphlet as this is, for I presume you have not much to do and therefore are to be obliged to me for keeping you from worse employment, and if you have a better you may get you gone about your business: but if you will misspend your time, pray lay the fault upon yourself; for I have dealt pretty fairly in the matter, told you in the title page what you are to expect within. Indeed, had I hung a sign of the Immortality of the Soul, of the Mystery of Godliness, or of Ecclesiastical Policy, and then had treated you with Indiscerptibility and Essential Spissitude (words which, though I am no competent judge of, for want of languages, yet I fancy strongly ought to mean just nothing) with a company of apocryphal midnight tales culled out of the choicest insignificant authors.

•

. . . as for comedy, the finest folks you meet with there are still unfitter for your imitation, for though within a leaf or two of the prologue, you are told that they are people of wit, good humor, good manners, and all that: yet if the authors did not kindly add their proper names, you'd never know them by their characters; for whatsoe'er's the matter, it hath happened so spitefully in several plays, which have been pretty well received of late, that even those persons that were meant to be the ingenious censors of the play, have either proved the most debauched or most unwitty people in the company: nor is this error very lamentable, since as I take it comedy was never meant, either for a converting or a conforming ordinance. In short, I think a play the best divertissement that wise men have: but I do also think them nothing so who do discourse as formally about the rules of it, as if 'twere the grand affair of human life. This being my opinion of plays, I studied only to make this as entertaining as I could, which whether I have been successful in, my gentle reader, you may for your shilling judge.

•

. . . there comes me into the pit, a long, lither, phlegmatic, white, ill-favored, wretched fop, an officer in masquerade newly transported with a scarf and feather out of France, a sorry animal that has nought else to shield it from the uttermost contempt of all mankind, but that respect which we afford to rats and toads, which though we do not well allow to live, yet when considered as a part of God's creation, we make honorable mention of them. A thing, reader—but no more of such a smelt: this thing, I tell ye, opening that which serves it for a mouth, out issued such a noise as this to those that sat about it, that they were to expect a woeful play, God damn him, for it was a woman's. Now how this came about I am not sure, but I suppose he brought it piping hot from some who had with him the reputation of a villainous wit: for creatures of his size of sense talk, without all imagination, such scraps as they pick up from other folks. I would not for a world be taken arguing with such a property as this; but if I thought there were a man of any tolerable parts, who could upon mature deliberation distinguish well his right hand from his left, and justly state the difference between the number of sixteen and two, yet had this prejudice upon him; I would take a little pains to make him know how much he errs. For waiving the examination why women having equal education with men were not as capable of knowledge of whatsoever sort as well as they, I'll only say as I have touched before, that plays have no great room for that which is men's great advantage over women, that is learning.

Jennifer Berman (contemporary)

FROM *Adult Children of Normal Parents*

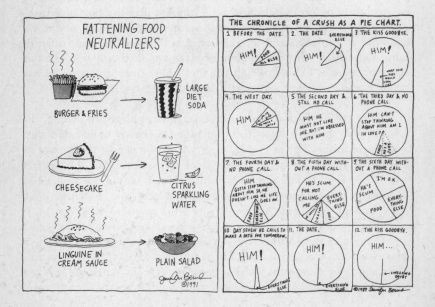

Shirley Temple Black (1928–)

One-liner

"I stopped believing in Santa Claus at an early age. Mother took me to see him in a department store and he asked me for my autograph."

Naomi Bliven (1925–)

One-liner

"Behind almost every woman you ever heard of stands a man who let her down."

Erma Bombeck (1927-   )

⊰ ❧ ⊱

FROM *Just Wait till You Have Children of Your Own!*

Dialogue between a mother who was told having a daughter drive would be a blessing and a daughter who up until now believed everything a mother did she did out of love

MOTHER: I'm not a well woman, Debbie. You know that. After the last baby, fifteen years ago, the doctor said I would experience periods of tension and depression. I am tense and depressed now. What are you doing?

DEBBIE: Putting the key in the switch.

MOTHER: DON'T TOUCH A THING IN THIS CAR UNTIL I TELL YOU TO. First, I want you to relax. You cannot drive a car when your hands are gripped around the door handle and the whites of the knuckles are showing.

DEBBIE: You're the one clutching the door handle.

MOTHER: That's what I said. Just relax and put all the anxieties about driving out of your mind. Forget that behind the wheel of this car you are a potential killer. That you are maneuvering a ton of hard, cold steel which you can wrap around a telephone pole just by closing your eyes to sneeze. Are you relaxed?

DEBBIE: I think so.

MOTHER: All right now. Let's go over the check list. Do you have flares in your trunk for when you get a flat tire?

DEBBIE: Yes.

MOTHER: Do you have a dime so you can call AAA when the motor stops dead on you?

DEBBIE: Yes.

MOTHER: Do you have your license so you can show it to the nice officer when he stops you for violating something?

DEBBIE: Yes, Mother.

MOTHER: All right then. Just turn the key and at the same time step on the accelerator.

DEBBIE: Aren't you going to fasten your seat belt?

MOTHER: Are you crazy? I may want to leave in a hurry. Let's get on with it. Just gently touch the accelerator.

DEBBIE: Like this?

MOTHER: HOLD IT! STOP THE CAR! Let us get one thing straight. The radio has to be off. There is not room in this car for Dionne Warwick, you and me. One of us has to go. You're driving. It can't be you. I'm supervising. It can't be me. Dionne is singing. She is expendable. Now, just relax and push on the accelerator. Any idiot can drive. I do it every day. Just ease along, unwind, hang loose and don't think about the drunk over the hill waiting to slam into you. What are you doing?

DEBBIE: Stopping the car.

MOTHER: What for?

DEBBIE: There's a stop sign.

MOTHER: Why are you stopping back here? That stop sign is forty feet away, for crying out loud. Pull up. Pull up. Give it a little gas. Go ahead. NO, WAIT! Do you realize you almost sent me sailing through the windshield?

DEBBIE: I guess I'm not used to the brakes yet. I'm sorry.

MOTHER: I know. So was Sylvia's daughter. Remember I told you about her? Her MOTHER was teaching her how to drive. She took off so fast she gave her mother a whiplash. I think she's out of traction now. Her daughter is wonderful, though. Never complains when she has to drive her mother to the doctor or adjust her braces. Now then, where were we? It looks all right. Just sneak out and . . . YOU'RE TOO CLOSE TO MY SIDE OF THE ROAD. We're all tensed up. Maybe if we pulled over to the curb here and relaxed a bit. You're doing fine. It's just that you lack experience. Like, when you meet a car you have to remember that anything on his side of the line belongs to him. We can't be greedy, can we? Are you relaxed? Good. Just put your hand out and enter the stream of traffic. Not too fast now.

DEBBIE: But . . .

MOTHER: If they want to go over twenty-five miles an hour, let 'em pass. The cemeteries are full of drivers who passed.

DEBBIE: Do you suppose you could show me how to park?
MOTHER: To what?
DEBBIE: To park.
MOTHER: There's nothing to it. You just go to the shopping center
            and make a small right angle and there you are. When your
            tires bump the concrete island, stop.
DEBBIE: No, I mean parallel park between two other cars. One in
            front and one in back.
MOTHER: Where did you hear talk like that? You're driving ten
            minutes and already you want to get cute with it. It sounds
            like a wonderful way to get your fenders dented, missy.
DEBBIE: Our Driver's Ed teacher says that's part of the test.
MOTHER: So the Driver's Ed teacher is smarter than your mother.
            Then why isn't he sitting here getting stomach cramps?
            That's the trouble with teachers today. No guts. I think
            we're getting tired, Debbie. I have a headache and an acid
            stomach. Let's head for home. There's a pamphlet I want
            you to read on "Highway Statistics Compiled on a Labor
            Day Weekend by the New Jersey Highway Patrol."

*Dialogue between a daddy who was instructed to check out the driving
ability of his wife's reckless daughter and daddy's little girl*

DEBBIE: You don't mind if I play the radio, do you, Daddy?
DADDY: Ummmmmmmm.
DEBBIE: Want me to go over the check list?
DADDY: Neh.
DEBBIE: Could I also dispense with "Mother, may I?" every time I
            shift gears?
DADDY: Sure.
DEBBIE: Want to test me on the "Highway Statistics Compiled on
            a Labor Day Weekend by the New Jersey Highway Patrol"?
DADDY: No. You're doing fine, dear. Wake me when we get home.
            Szzzzzzzzzzzzz.

*Dialogue between a father who regards his car as a mistress and a son
who is moving in on his territory*

FATHER: Do you know how long it took me to get a car of my own?
RALPH: You were twenty-eight years old.
FATHER: I was twenty-eight years old, boy, before I sat behind the
            wheel of my first car. Got my first pair of long trousers that
            same year. And I apprecia . . . I wish to heavens you'd stop
            making those noises.

•

"Why don't you grow up?"

If I said it to them once I said it a million times. Is it my imagination or have I spent a lifetime shutting refrigerator doors, emptying nose tissue from pants pockets before washing, writing checks for milk, picking up wet towels and finding library books in the clothes hamper?

Mr. Matterling said, "Parenting is loving." (What did he know? He was my old Child Psychology teacher who didn't have any children. He only had twenty-two guppies and two catfish to clean the bowl.) How I wish that for one day I could teach Mr. Matterling's class. How I would like to tell him it's more than loving. More than clean gravel. More than eating the ones you don't like.

Parenting is frustration that you have to see to believe. Would I have ever imagined there would be whole days when I didn't have time to comb my hair? Mornings after a slumber party when I looked like Margaret Mead with a migraine? Could I have ever comprehended that something so simple, so beautiful and so uncomplicated as a child could drive you to shout, "We are a family and you're a part of this family and by God, you're going to spend a Friday night with us having a good time if we have to chain you to the bed!"

And a plaintive voice within me sighed, "Why don't you grow up?"

Parenting is fearful, Mr. Matterling. You don't know how fearful until you sit next to your son on his maiden voyage behind the wheel of your car and hear him say, "My Driver's Ed teacher says I've only got one problem and that's every time I meet a car I pass over the center line."

And you worry. I worried when they stayed home. ("Suppose I get stuck with my son and have to feed him on my Social Security check?") I worried when they were gone. ("If the stuffed animal is missing from her bed, that's it. She's eloped!")

I worried when they talked to me. ("Mary Edith started taking WHAT?") I worried when they didn't talk to me. ("This is your mother and what do you mean Mother who?")

I worried when they dated a lot. ("They're not meditating in the Christian Science reading room until 2 A.M., Ed.") I worried when they didn't date. ("Maybe we should try a sixteenth of an inch padding.")

I worried when their grades were bad. ("He won't be able to get into karate school with those marks.") I worried when their grades were good. ("So swing a little. You wanta spend the rest of your life reading William F. Buckley and basting your acne?")

I worried when they got a job. ("She looks so tired, and besides it could bring back her asthma attacks.") I worried when they didn't get a job. ("Mark my word, he'll take after your brother, Wesley, who didn't get a paper route until he was thirty-three.")

And a tired voice within me persisted, "Why don't you grow up?"

Parenting is pain, Mr. Matterling. And disappointment. The first time I leaned over to kiss my son good night and he turned his back to the wall and said, "See ya." The first time I sat in the pouring rain for four quarters (and a thirty-minute half-time Salute to Railroads) and got chewed out for being the only mother there with an umbrella.

The first time they hit me with, "I'm not going to Grandma's. It's boring." The first time they ignored me on Mother's Day and explained coldly, "It's your fault. You didn't give us our allowance this week."

The first time they left the house and forgot to say, "Good-bye."

And the anger and the resentment came, Mr. Matterling. You forgot that part. The nights when I Freudianly set the table for two. The days when I felt like a live-in domestic. Days when I felt like sending Betty Friedan a cigar and the kids to my favorite charity. (Or my unfavorite charity.) Days when I beat myself to death with my own inadequacies. What kind of kids am I raising who would let a hamster die from starvation? What kind of kids would snicker during the playing of "The Star-Spangled Banner"? What kind of kids would tell you with a straight face they inherited a world less than perfect? What kind of kids would have a water fight in church . . . WITH HOLY WATER YET!?

"Grow up, won't you?"

And the days of compassion. These were the most agonizing of all. When the tenderness I felt for my children swelled so that I thought I would burst if I didn't cradle them in my arms.

This half child, half adult groping miserably to weigh life's inconsistencies, hypocrisy, instant independence, advice, rules and responsibilities.

The blind date that never showed. The captaincy that went to a best friend. The college reject, the drill team have-nots, the class office also-rans, the honors that went to someone else. And they turned to me for the answer.

And the phone was ringing. I was worming the dog. My husband had to be picked up in ten minutes. There was cake in the oven, a brush salesman at the door and I mumbled some tired chestnut about Abe Lincoln and his thousand failures but how late in life he won the big prize. And then, almost sanctimoniously, I admonished, "That's part of growing up and why don't you?"

And there were joys. Moments of closeness . . . an awkward hug;

a look in the semidarkness as you turned off the test pattern as they slept. The pride of seeing them stand up when older people entered the room and saying, "Yes, sir" and "No, ma'am" without your holding a cue card in front of them. The strange, warm feeling of seeing them pick up a baby and seeing a wistfulness in their faces that I have never seen before. And I said to myself . . . softly this time, "Why don't you grow up?"

I shall never forgive Mr. Matterling for not warning me of the times of panic. It's not time yet. It can't be. I'm not finished. I had all the teaching and the discipline and the socks to pick up and the buttons to sew on, and those lousy meal worms to feed the lizard every day . . . there was no time for loving. That's what it's all about, isn't it? Did they ever know I smiled? Did they ever understand my tears? Did I talk too much? Did I say too little? Did I ever look at them and really see them? Do I know them at all? Or was it all a lifetime of "Why don't you grow ups"?

I walk through the house and mechanically shut a refrigerator door that is already shut. I stoop to retrieve a towel that has not fallen to the floor but hangs neatly on the towel rack. From habit, I smooth out a spread that is already free of wrinkles. I answer a phone that has not rung and with a subtlety that fools no one, I hide the cake for dinner in the oven.

And I shout, "WHY DON'T YOU GROW UP!"

And the silence where once had abounded frustration, fear, disappointment, resentment, compassion, joy and love echoes, "I did."

Elayne Boosler (1953–   )

~❧ ❧~

FROM Punchline—*I Don't Get It*

In the movie *Punchline*, Tom Hanks is a medical student afraid of blood and Sally Field is a New Jersey housewife with three kids. Naturally, they become stand-up comics. . . .

Real comedy can't be learned; it comes from a need for justice. The best who stand up, stand up for something.

Great comics leave something wonderful behind when they leave the stage. Mr. Hanks's character is a self-described "hate stylist" whose crowning performance is a heartfelt diatribe against *debutantes*, of all things. It does not make the heart soar. And if this character is afraid of blood, he's really in the wrong business now.

Comedy is a blood sport. It flays the truth and spurts twisted logic. In America, people become comics because we don't have bullfighting.

Is it harder for women in comedy? It is after films like this. The housewife is introduced by the club owner as a woman with a chronic yeast infection, yet this purported natural wit says nothing in response. She does an apologetic routine that's a crude and embarrassed foray into cheap vibrator jokes and reverse sexism. In life, material like this gets booed off the stage. But the film's character—a complaining, asexual "comedienne" holding down the stereotype—wins the bake-off. And that's misleading, because comedy is very, very sexy when it's done right.

Elizabeth Bowen (1899–1973)

❧ ❧

FROM *Collected Impressions*

THE MULBERRY TREE
If any one said "You are always so such-and-such" one felt one had formed a new intimacy and made one's mark. . . . It seemed fatal not to be at least one thing to excess, and if I could not be outstandingly good at a thing I preferred to be outstandingly bad at it. Personality came out in patches, like damp through a wall.

•

OUT OF A BOOK
No, it is not only our fate but our business to lose innocence, and once we have lost that it is futile to attempt a picnic in Eden.

•

Pink May

"Yes, it was funny," she said, "about the ghost. It used to come into my bedroom when I was dressing for dinner—when I was dressing to go out."

"You were frightened?"

"I was in such a hurry; there never was any time. When you have to get dressed in such a hell of a hurry any extra thing is just one thing more. And the room at the times I'm talking about used to be full of daylight—sunset. It had two french windows, and they were on a level with the tops of may trees out in the square. Then may was in flower that month, and it was pink. In that sticky sunshine you have in the evenings the may looked sort of theatrical. It used to be part of my feeling of going out." She paused, then said, "That was the month of my life."

"What month?"

"The month we were in that house. I told you, it was a furnished house that we took. With rents the way they are now, it cost less than a flat. They say a house is more trouble, but this was no trouble, because we treated it like a flat, you see. I mean, we were practically never in. I didn't try for a servant because I know there aren't any. When Neville got up in the mornings he percolated the coffee; a char came in to do the cleaning when I'd left for the depot, and we fixed with the caretaker next door to look after the boiler, so the baths were hot. And the beds were comfortable, too. The people who really lived there did themselves well."

"You never met them?"

"No, never—why should we? We'd fixed everything through an agent, the way one does. I've an idea the man was soldiering somewhere, and she'd gone off to be near him somewhere in the country. They can't have had any children, any more than we have—it was one of those small houses, just for two."

"Pretty?"

"Y-yes," she said. "It was chintzy. It was one of those oldish houses made over new inside. But you know how it is about other people's belongings—you can't ever quite use them, and they seem to watch you the whole time. Not that there was any question of settling down—how could we, when we were both out all day? And at the beginning of June we moved out again."

"Because of the . . .?"

"Oh no," she said quickly. "Not that reason, at all." She lighted a cigarette, took two puffs and appeared to deliberate. "But what I'm telling you *now* is about the ghost."

"Go on."

"I was going on. As I say, it used to be funny, dressing away at top speed at the top of an empty house, with the sunsets blazing away outside. It seems to me that all those evenings were fine. I used to take taxis back from the depot: you must pay money these days if you want time, and a bath and a change from the skin up was essential—you don't know how one feels after packing parcels all day! I couldn't do like some of the girls I worked with and go straight from the depot on to a date. I can't go and meet someone unless I'm feeling special. So I used to hare home. Neville was never in."

"I'd been going to say . . ."

"No, Neville worked till all hours, or at least he had to hang round in case something else should come in. So he used to dine at his club on the way back. Most of the food would be off by the time he got there. It was partly that made him nervy, I dare say."

"But you weren't nervy?"

"I tell you," she said, "I was happy. Madly happy—perhaps in rather a nervy way. Whatever you are these days, you are rather more so. That's one thing I've discovered about this war."

"You were happy . . ."

"I had my reasons—which don't come into the story."

After two or three minutes of rapid smoking she leaned forward to stub out her cigarette. "Where was I?" she said, in a different tone.

"Dressing . . ."

"Well, first thing when I got in I always went across and opened my bedroom windows, because it seemed to me the room smelled of the char. So I always did that before I turned on my bath. The glare on the trees used to make me blink, and the thick sort of throaty smell of the may came in. I was never certain if I liked it or not, but it somehow made me feel like after a drink. Whatever happens tomorrow, I've got tonight. You know the feeling? Then I turned on my bath. The bathroom was the other room on that floor, and a door led through to it from one side of the bed. I used to have my bath with that door ajar, to let light in. The bathroom black-out took so long to undo.

"While the bath ran in I used to potter about and begin to put out what I meant to wear, and cold-cream off my old make-up, and so on. I say 'potter' because you cannot hurry a bath. I also don't mind telling you that I whistled. Well, what's the harm in *somebody's* being happy? Simply thinking things over won't win this war. Looking back at that month, I whistled most of the time. The way they used to look at me, at the depot! The queer thing is, though, I remember whistling but I can't remember when I happened to stop. But I must *have* stopped, because it was then I heard."

"Heard?"

She lit up again, with a slight frown. "What was it I heard first, that first time? I suppose, the silence. So I must have stopped whistling, mustn't I? I was lying there in my bath, with the door open behind me, when the silence suddenly made me sit right up. Then I said to myself, 'My girl, there's nothing queer about *that*. What else would you expect to hear, in an empty house?' All the same, it made me heave the other way round in my bath, in order to keep one eye on the door. After a minute I heard what wasn't a silence—which immediately made me think that Neville had come in early, and I don't mind telling you I said 'Damn.' "

"*Oh?*"

"It's a bore being asked where one is going, though it's no bother to say where one has been. If Neville *was* in he'd be certain to search the house, so I put a good face on things and yelled 'Hoi.' But he didn't answer, because it wasn't him."

"*?*"

"No, it wasn't. And whatever was in my bedroom must have been in my bedroom for some time. I thought, 'A wind has come up and got into that damned chintz.' Any draught always fidgets me; somehow it gets me down. So I got out of my bath and wrapped the big towel round me and went through to shut the windows in my room. But I was surprised when I caught sight of the may trees—all their branches were standing perfectly still. That seemed queer. At the same time, the door I'd come through from the bathroom blew shut, and the lid fell off one of my jars of face cream on to the dressing-table, which had a glass top.

"No, I didn't see what it was. The point was, whatever it was saw me.

"That first time, the whole thing was so slight. If it had been only that one evening, I dare say I shouldn't have thought of it again. Things only get a hold on you when they go on happening. But I always have been funny in one way—I especially don't like being watched. You might not think so from my demeanour, but I don't really like being criticized. I don't think I get my knife into other people: why should they get their knife into me? I don't like it when my ear begins to burn.

"I went to put the lid back on the jar of cream and switch the lights on into the mirror, which being between the two windows never got the sort of light you would want. I thought I looked odd in the mirror—rattled. I said to myself, 'Now what have I done to *someone?*' but except for Neville I literally couldn't think. Anyway, there was no time—when I picked up my wristwatch I said, 'God!' So I flew round, dressing. Or rather, I flew round as much as one could with something or somebody getting in the way. That's all I remember about that *first* time, I think. Oh yes, I did notice that the veil on my white hat wasn't all that it ought to be. When I had put that hat out before my bath the whole affair had looked as crisp as a marguerite—a marguerite that has only opened today.

"You know how it is when a good deal hangs on an evening— you simply can't afford to be not in form. So I gave myself a good shake on the way downstairs. 'Snap out of that!' I said. 'You've got personality. You can carry a speck or two on the veil.'

"Once I got to the restaurant—once I'd met him—the whole thing went out of my mind. I was in twice as good form as I'd ever been. And the turn events took . . .

"It was about a week later that I had to face it. I was up against something. The more the rest of my life got better and better, the more that one time of each evening got worse and worse. Or rather, it wanted to. But I wasn't going to let it. With everything else quite perfect— well, would *you* have? There's something exciting, I mean, some sort of a challenge about knowing someone's *trying* to get you down. And when that someone's another woman you soon get a line on her technique. She was jealous, that was what was the matter with her.

"Because, at all other times the room was simply a room. There wasn't any objection to me and Neville. When I used to slip home he was always asleep. I could switch all the lights on and kick my shoes off and open and shut the cupboards—he lay like the dead. He *was* abnormally done in, I suppose. And the room was simply a room in somebody else's house. And the mornings, when he used to roll out of bed and slip-slop down to make the coffee, without speaking, exactly like someone walking in his sleep, the room was no more than a room in which you've just woken up. The may outside looked pink-pearl in the early sunshine, and there were some regular birds who sang. Nice. While I waited for Neville to bring the coffee I used to like to lie there and think my thoughts.

"If he was awake at all before he had left the house, he and I exchanged a few perfectly friendly words. I had *no* feeling of anything blowing up. If I let him form the impression that I'd been spending the evenings at movies with girl friends I'd begun to make at the depot, then going back to their flats to mix Ovaltine—well, that seemed to me the considerate thing to do. If he'd even been more *interested* in my life—but he wasn't interested in anything but his work. I never picked on him about that—I must say, I do know when a war's a war. Only men are so different. You see, this other man worked just as hard but *was* interested in me. He said he found me so restful. Neville never said that. In fact, all the month we were in that house, I can't remember anything Neville said at all.

"No, what *she* couldn't bear was my going out, like I did. She was either a puritan, with some chip on her shoulder, or else she'd once taken a knock. I incline to that last idea—though I can't say why.

"No, I can't say why. I have never at all been a subtle person. I don't know whether that's a pity or not. I must say I don't care for subtle people—my instinct would be to give a person like that a miss. And on the whole I should say I'd succeeded in doing so. But that, you see, was where her advantage came in. You can't give a . . . well, I couldn't give *her* a miss. She was there. And she aimed at encircling me.

"I think maybe she had a poltergeist that she brought along with her. The little things that happened to my belongings . . . Each evening I dressed in that room I lost five minutes—I mean, each evening it took me five minutes longer to dress. But all that was really below her plane. That was just one start at getting me down before she opened up with her real technique. The really subtle thing was the way her attitude changed. That first time (as I've told you) I felt her disliking me—well, really 'dislike' was to put it mildly. But after an evening or two she was through with that. She conveyed the impression that she had got me taped and was simply so damned sorry for me. She was sorry about every garment I put on, and my hats were more than she was able to bear. She was sorry about the way I did up my face—she used to be right at my elbow when I got out my make-up, absolutely silent with despair. She was sorry I should never again see thirty, and sorry I should kid myself about that . . . I mean to say, she started pitying me.

"Do you see what I mean when I say her attitude could have been quite infectious?

"And that wasn't all she was sorry for me about. I mean, there are certain things that a woman who's been happy keeps putting out of her mind. (I mean, when she's being happy about a man.) And other things you keep putting out of your mind if your husband is *not* the man you are being happy about. There's a certain amount you don't ask yourself, and a certain amount that you might as well not remember. Now those were exactly the things she kept bringing up. She liked to bring those up better than anything.

"What I don't know is, and what I still don't know—*why* do all that to a person who's being happy? To a person who's living the top month of her life, with the may in flower and everything? What had I

ever done to her? She was dead—I suppose? . . . Yes, I see now, she
must have taken a knock."

"*What makes you think that?*"

"I know now how a knock feels."

"*Oh . . . ?*"

"Don't look at me such a funny way. I haven't changed, have I?
You wouldn't have noticed anything? . . . I expect it's simply this time
of year: August's rather a tiring month. And things end without warning,
before you know where you are. I hope the war will be over by next
spring; I do want to be abroad, if I'm able to. Somewhere where there's
nothing but pines or palms. I don't want to see London pink may in
flower again—*ever*."

"*Won't Neville . . . ?*"

"Neville? Oh, didn't you really realize? Didn't I . . . ? He, I,
we've—I mean, we're living apart." She rose and took the full, fuming
ash-tray across to another table, and hesitated, then brought an empty
tray back. "Since we left that house," she said. "I told you we left that
house. That was why. We broke up.

"It was the *other* thing that went wrong," she said. "If I'd still kept
my head with Neville, he and I needn't ever—I mean, one's marriage
is something . . . I'd thought I'd always be married, whatever else happened. I ought to have realized Neville was in a nervy state. Like a fool
I spilled over to Neville; I lost my head. But by that time I hadn't
any control left. When the one thing you've lived for has crashed
to bits . . .

"Crashed was the word. And yet I see now, really, that things had
been weakening for some time. At the time I didn't see, any more than
I noticed the may was fading out in the square—till one morning the
weather changed and I noticed the may was brown. All the happiness
stopped like my stopping whistling—but at what particular moment I'm
never sure.

"The beginnings of the end of it were so small. Like my being a
bit more unpunctual every evening we met. That made us keep losing
our table at restaurants—you know how the restaurants are these days.
Then I somehow got the idea that none of my clothes were becoming;
I began to think he was eyeing my hats unkindly, and that made me
fidget and look my worst. Then I got an idiot thing about any girl that
he spoke of—I didn't like anyone being younger than me. Then, at
what had once been our most perfect moments, I began to ask myelf if
I *was* really happy, till I said to him—which was fatal—'Is there so much
in this?' . . . I should have seen more red lights—when, for instance, he

said, 'You know, *you're* getting nervy.' And he quite often used to say 'Tired?' in rather a tired way. I used to say, it was just getting dressed in a rush. But the fact is, a man hates the idea of a woman rushing. One night I know I did crack: I said, 'Hell, I've got a ghost in my room!' He put me straight into a taxi and sent me—not took me—home.

"I did see him several times after that. So his letter—his letter was a complete surprise . . . The joke was, I really had been out with a girl that evening I came in, late, to find his letter.

"If Neville had not been there when I got the letter, Neville and I might still—I suppose—be married. On the other hand—there are always two ways to see things—if Neville had *not* been there I should have gone mad . . . So now," she said, with a change of tone, "I'm living in an hotel. Till I see how things turn out. Till the war is over, or something. It isn't really so bad, and I'm out all day. Look, I'll give you my address and telephone number. It's been wonderful seeing you, darling. You promise we'll meet again? I do really need to keep in touch with my friends. And *you* don't so often meet someone who's seen a ghost!"

"But look, did you ever see it?"

"Well, not exactly. No, I can't say I *saw* it."

"You mean, you simply heard it?"

"Well, not exactly that . . ."

"You saw things move?"

"Well, I never turned around in time. I . . .

"If you don't understand—I'm sorry I ever told you the story! Not a ghost—when it ruined my whole life! Don't you see, can't you see there must have been *something?* Left to oneself, one doesn't ruin one's life!"

•

The Unromantic Princess

When the Princess was born the Queen, who knew what was usual, invited two Fairy Godmothers to her christening. Unfortunately, they arrived in a workaday mood, and full of modern ideas about girls. So that the gifts they gave the Princess were as follows: one gave her Punctuality; the other, Commonsense. This had not been the Queen's idea at all, and she was grievously disappointed. Besides being so dull, the two Fairy Godmothers were a nuisance throughout the christening party. They would not sit down to lunch, but moved about restlessly, nibbling moth-wing sandwiches out of their reticules. They cast a gloom on the party, where all the other guests were in gold, silver or mother o' pearl brocade, with their severe poke bonnets tied under their chins and sensible boots that had tramped miles in Fairyland. Their motto was: "One should never fly when one could walk." They gave the guests several quite unasked-for home truths, and everyone found them tiresome old bodies. Everyone blamed the Queen for not being more exclusive. She felt wretched, and stole away to her baby's cradle. "My poor darling, you *shall* be lovely," she said. The Princess gurgled and blinked, but did not look quite happy.

At the ceremony, the Princess had been christened Angelica. She had a whole string of other names, but they did not count; she was *called* Princess Angelica—this had seemed to the Queen a safe name: if she grew up beautiful it would suit her beautifully; if she were simply good it should do as well. After the christening, the poor Queen began to watch her daughter anxiously. "When I have another baby, I shall pointedly *not* ask those wretched Fairies," she said. But she had no other baby, so Princess Angelica grew very important. Before she could walk, her terrible Punctuality began to make itself felt throughout the palace. If anyone were late anywhere she would yell: as for her Commonsense, it was impossible to appease her with rattles or fluffy jumping toys.

Unhappily for the Princess, these two gifts she had been given did not take up the whole of her character. She had a soft heart, was dreamy and loved beautiful things. When her Commonsense eye drove her mother away from her cradle, she would be found weeping because her mother had gone. The third time she ever walked, she tottered up to a mirror, and the royal nurse saw her taking a good look at herself. But what she saw in the mirror made her crinkle her face up. She was a fine baby, chubby and rosy, a model to all the baby girls in the land. But what the poor Princess had been looking for had been curls.

Her hair never would curl. It was soft and fine, but nothing would make it anything but straight. The first time she drove out in the royal coach with the Queen, all the mothers in the crowd nudged their pretty, curly children and said: "You learn to be good, like Princess Angelica!" the Princess heard, and tears rolled down her face. "There," said the mothers, "she's crying because you are so naughty!" The first two inventions to be called after her were *The Princess Angelica Alarm Clock*, and *The Princess Angelica Children's Self-Help Guild*. The Queen's heart bled for her poor little girl.

When the Princess was seven the Queen died of a fever, and the King became very melancholy and old. He relied more and more on

Princess Angelica's advice and used to talk to her about matters of state. He used to send for her to sit with him in the evenings, so that she often sat up far too late. Punctuality told her this was long after bedtime, and Commonsense that she would be pasty and cross-feeling next day. But she sat patiently on in her black frock, doing what she could for her beautiful mother's sake.

The Princess read geography, history and natural history to satisfy her Commonsense. But to please her dreamy side she read fairy tales. She read fairy tales, but these were very discouraging. They were nearly always about princesses of dazzling beauty, who though shut up in towers, transformed into cats or swooped off with by dragons were always rescued by a beautiful Third Son. The Third Son always turned out to be somebody they could marry, but they fell in love as soon as their eyes met. He had generally loved her first, or heard of her dazzling beauty, though, disguised as a miller, a bear or a minstrel, he had had no opportunity of speaking to her. The Princess saw that it should be very romantic to be a Princess at all. But then she went back to look at her own face in the mirror: a nice little good snub face, edged with straight brown hair. "Will anyone marry me?" she said to her nurse one day. "Oh, yes, indeed," said her nurse, "someone will have to. And much honoured they'll be."

When the year of mourning for the Queen's death was over, the King thought he would give a party to cheer up the Princess. He asked all the children of all the important people, and kindly had galleries built round the walls of the royal garden so that the children of unimportant people could come and look on. The day was very fine: the sun shone, the birds sang, the fountains flung rainbows into the air, even the royal goldfish swam more merrily in the marble-edged pools. The rose-trees had been kept for a week under large glass shades, so as to bring all the roses out at once. Princess Angelica, in a white satin dress, stood by the centre fountain receiving her guests. A small pearl crown was fastened with tight elastic underneath her slippery brown hair. All the children of the important people were very proper and shy: they shook hands, curtsied, then stood round in a circle staring at her. Yes, the scene was gay, but the party was not. As this was the Princess's first party, she did not realise how dull it was being till she looked up at the galleries and saw the merry faces of the unimportant children, who were having a good deal of fun, licking ice-cream out of cones and pointing at what they saw in a rude but natural way. She noticed, particularly, one little boy with red curls, in a yellow shirt. He had finished not only his own cone of ice-cream but one he had pinched from the little boy on his right: now he was leaning his elbows on the rail of the gallery and looking down in a serious, dreamy way. He looked about twelve. The Princess thought at once: "He must be a Third Son."

But, oh dear! Down here, the important children danced a quadrille rather creakily on the lawn. Then they played catch with hollow golden balls. When the Princess missed a catch, which she did once or twice from nervousness, they all murmured "Too bad." They were so much afraid of not doing everything up to time that they had all borrowed their mother's or father's wrist-watches, which they kept looking at. They were all so afraid of saying something not sensible that they could not speak at all. The Princess's heart sank. She *saw* this was very dull, and felt all the children up there must be pitying her. She did not know that they only saw the fountains, the roses and the flashing gold balls, heard the loud tunes the band played with great pleasure and envied the Princess's pearl crown and quilted satin dress. She glanced up again and again at the proud, dreamy red-haired boy with his elbow sticking out through a hole in his shirt. "He *knows* he is in disguise," thought Princess Angelica.

Suddenly, the important children all gaped. The Princess, who had been holding a golden ball in her hands, stopped, smiled up, and suddenly threw the ball at a gallery. The red-haired boy, unfolding his arms in a flash, caught the ball with one hand. All the children in the galleries shot up with excitement. The boy held the ball, looking down at the garden and smiling. Then he threw it back. But not, oh, not to the Princess! He threw it to one important little girl whose long flaxen curls bobbed beautifully on her emerald velvet dress. The Princess's heart broke. She pushed her crown back, pretending not to notice. She thought: "I have behaved with absolute commonsense. If one recognises a Third Son in disguise, one should do something about him. I was quite right."

The important girl with flaxen curls missed the ball disdainfully and let it roll on to an important boy.

But the palace guards, who had been watching the galleries carefully to see the unimportant children did not misbehave, noticed the incident. What the red-haired boy had done was a shocking breach of manners. To have a gold ball thrown to you by a princess is an honour: you should throw it back to *her*, having first bowed three times. To throw the ball to anyone else is treason. The captain of the guard said: "He has insulted the Princess." So the guard went quietly round the gallery and arrested the red-haired boy. The Princess saw him being dragged out. Soon after, the trumpets sounded for tea.

Next day the red-haired boy was brought for trial into the palace courtyard. The King said he was sorry, but the Princess would have to be there. He would have been glad to have let the matter drop, but all the courtiers were furious and kept him up to it. The flaxen-haired important little girl had to be there as a witness. The poor Princess could not fail to be up to time: as it happened the King's procession was late, so she sat on her small throne looking round the empty court till the trumpets sounded and the procession appeared: the prisoner was then brought in by another door. The flaxen-haired girl looked down her nose disdainfully. The boy with the red curls looked scornful, indifferent. Standing between his two guards he gazed round the courtyard and all the people in it: his eyes once met the Princess's with a flicker.

The heralds sounded their trumpets and the trial began. To two long rolling speeches made by people in wigs the poor Princess was far too anxious to listen. The boy was being accused of treason, but he did not seem to be listening either. The King sat listening sadly; he had never thought the party he gave for his daughter could end in such a way: his wish all along had been to make the Princess and everyone else happy. He suddenly put up his hand to make the long speech stop, leaned forward and said to the boy kindly:

"Didn't you *know* you were rude to the Princess?"

The boy, looking up at the King, said: "No, Your Majesty."

"But didn't you think?"

"No, Your Majesty. Why should I?"

The King, who always thought for rather too long before he could do anything, looked perplexed.

"I didn't think," said the boy. "I just threw the ball."

The King cleared his throat and said: "But why do you think the Princess threw the ball to you?"

"I don't know," said the boy. "I suppose she wanted to."

"Did you not see she was doing you an honour?"

"Well, no," said the boy. "I thought it was just fun."

"Fun or no fun," said the King, "why didn't you throw it back to her?"

The boy looked puzzled. "I couldn't, he said; "I had thrown it back to that girl." He glanced at the blonde little girl, who was looking less pretty to-day in plain grey cloth.

"Now listen," went on the King. "By the law of the land you are threatened with a very serious punishment. People have been beheaded for treason, you know. Your only chance is to tell us why you did what you did. Why did you throw the ball to that young lady instead of to the Princess?"

The boy looked amazed—perhaps that such a long question should have such a simple answer as he was going to give.

"Because her dress was so pretty."

There was a sensation in court. The ladies present could not help being pleased by the reply: they whispered among themselves and said how poetic the boy was. A man in a wig got up and, shaking his finger sternly, said: "But the Princess's dress was exceedingly beautiful."

"But I like emerald green better than white."

There was another buzz. The King, holding up his hand for silence, said: "You seem to be speaking the truth; nobody could invent this. I have one other question to ask: Are you sorry for what you have done?"

"Yes, I was at once," said the boy, "because the Princess looked so fearfully disappointed. If I could have had the ball back I would have thrown it to her. She had a nicer face than anyone else there. The young lady in green has a dull face. When I saw how she opens her mouth when she's trying to catch things, and how butter-fingered she was, I was sorry at once. Then the guard arrested me. But I am sorry still."

The blonde little girl went into hysterics, and had to be carried screaming out of the court. (What the boy said about her having a dull face stuck to her all her life and she never married.)

The King said: "Will you tell the Princess you are sorry?"

The boy turned to the Princess's throne. Bowing, he said in a cold voice: "I am sorry I hurt Your Royal Highness's feelings."

Everyone who was present turned to look at the Princess. She said in a small sad voice: "Oh, that is quite all right."

The King announced: "I command that this charge of treason be withdrawn."

The guards took their hands from the boy's shoulders: he bowed to both thrones, turned, and walked out of the court.

The next dress the Princess had made was emerald green, and everybody pretended not to know why. On her small white pony, followed by her governess on a black mare and four palace guards on chargers, she rode through the streets every day. People used to set their clocks by her, for she always followed the same route, through the poorer parts of the town where she thought she was most likely to meet the boy. She bowed to right and left, trying not to look anxious. For weeks she was unlucky; she thought he must have left town. Then one day she saw him lying on the steps of a fountain, quite idle, sunning himself like a dog. She pulled up her pony, her governess reined in her mare, the four chargers were pulled back on their haunches.

The boy stood up and bowed.

"Thank you," she said, "for what you so kindly said about my face."

"Oh, it's quite true," said the boy; "I have often thought about you."

"Have you?" said the Princess.

"Yes; so many people have so much nonsense about them, but there seems to be no nonsense about you."

"Oh," said the Princess.

"Yes," said the boy warmly, "I have written a poem." He fished about in his pocket and brought out a piece of paper, very crumpled and grey.

The Princess read:—

> "Dear kind Princess in white
> I did not mean, indeed, to ruin your delight.
> The roses were so red, the fountains were so bright
> That when you threw the ball
> I did not think at all.
>
> "You did not understand
> What made me lose my head. The goldfish and the band.
> The sunshine was so bright, the trumpets were so grand
> That when you looked at me
> I did not even see.
>
> "When you stood still in white
> She ran about in green, the green was oh so bright,
> But she was oh so wrong and you were oh so right.
> I did not see you till,
> Too late, you stood so still.
>
> "You must not be so sad.
> I cannot bear to see the sorry smile you had.
> The fountains are so small, the music is so bad,
> The roses wither, when
> I think I hurt you then."

"May I keep it?" said the Princess.

The boy looked doubtful. "Yes, all right," he said. "I think I remember it."

"I am wearing green to-day," said the Princess timidly.

"So I see," said the boy. "But I think white suits you better."

He bowed, and the Princess rode on, tucking the poem carefully into her pocket.

When she got back to the palace, they all saw an extraordinary thing had happened. *The Princess was ten minutes late for lunch.* When she saw the clock, something seemed to slip or come unhooked inside her character: she did not know whether she were sorry or glad. As luck would have it, her two Fairy Godmothers had arrived for lunch. They had not been back since the christening, but, both being on their way from a committee in Fairyland, had happened to find themselves in the air above the palace and, as they had forgotten their sandwiches, thought they would drop in. They may not have known how unpopular they were with the King ever since they had made his dear Queen so unhappy at the Princess's christening. If they had known it might not have stopped them: fairies are not sensitive. So here they sat in the hall with their reticules, waiting for the Princess to come home.

"I am sorry," said the Princess, "I'm afraid I am late."

"What!" said the Fairy who had given her Punctuality.

"I am late," repeated the Princess.

"Well, no gift I gave has *ever* not worked before!"

"It has not worked to-day."

"Why?" said the Fairy who had given her Commonsense.

"I stopped to talk to a boy."

"Is he a member of the Princess Angelica Children's Self-Help Guild?"

"No. He writes poetry."

"And you stopped to *talk!* Then where was your Commonsense?"

"I don't know," said the Princess with a happy smile.

"Miserable child," said the two Fairies in chorus, "you prove yourself unworthy of our two great gifts."

"Well, I didn't ask for them," said the Princess politely but firmly. "And they have stopped work of their own accord to-day."

The Fairies looked at each other. "We will take them away," they said in one terrible voice. "You shall have instead what has brought many Princesses to bad ends: Good Looks and a Sense of the Ridiculous. Some day you will be sorry."

The Princess tried to quail. But even before the Fairies had finished speaking, she had a curious sensation in the tips of her hair: it began violently curling. In two minutes, it was in little tight clusters, like brown silk rosebuds, all over her head. Her eyes, opened wide in surprise, turned from grey to the brightest blue, and a pair of lovely dimples appeared in her smiling cheeks. At the same time, the sight of the two Fairy Godmothers sitting side by side in the hall, looking at her triumphantly and balefully, made her burst out into fits of hysterical laughter. "There, you *see*," said the Fairies. "Your bad end is beginning." They rose, spread their musty brown wings and flew off down the hall, through the arch and away over the palace to look for lunch somewhere else. The pages standing out in the courtyard saw their reticules, sensible boots and tight poke bonnets disappear in the sky, and thought they looked as ugly as a couple of crows.

The Princess did not come to a bad end. Fairy Godmothers may do much to spoil (or, if they are nicer than hers, to improve) your chances, but they cannot really interfere with the nice character you have inherited from your father and mother and the right way you are brought up. Curls, bright blue eyes and dimples did not make the Princess's face less kind and good. She exercised her Sense of the Ridiculous by making her father turn out a good many silly courtiers who had been making the palace fussy, prim and dull. She preferred amusing people, but, if you look closely at it, only nice people stay amusing for long, so the new appointments she saw to worked very well. Her advice became still more valuable to the King her father, and while all the countries round them were having revolutions, he continued to reign. As for her good looks—which increased as she grew older—everybody fell in love with her: this pleased and excited her so much that for some years she, quite naturally, forgot the red-haired boy. But one day she turned up his poem in the pocket of her out-grown emerald green dress. She showed it to the King, who said: "By the way, that reminds me: we have no court poet. How would it be . . ." So they arranged a poetry competition, which the red-haired boy, who was now nearly grown-up, won. So he came to court, in discreet black clothes, and walked about, refusing to show his poetry and looking critically at the Princess: he did not dare to presume on their former meeting.

One day the Princess, who was now grown-up, passing him in a passage, said: "Why do you look so cross?"

The red-haired young man said: "This appointment leads to nothing; I want to be important. I am a Third Son, and I ought to have more luck."

The Princess started. "Third Son?" she said. "Whose?"

"I have no idea," he said. "I only know that."

"What would you like best to do?" she said.

"Marry you," said he. "I do not think curls and dimples suit you, but there is still no nonsense about you and you have the nice good face that I always liked. Marry you, yes, and then take charge of this country. The court is all very well, but everything outside it ought to be run on much more modern lines. The unpunctuality nowadays is appalling, and the laws should be overhauled from a commonsense point of view. If I have to write any more poetry, I shall go mad."

The Princess sighed. She thought of all the nice princes who came from miles away to tell her she was perfect. But, unfortunately, she always laughed at them.

"Very well," she said, "I will ask my father."

The King said: "There is nothing I should like better. Times are changing. But I thought that young man was here to write poetry. Are *you* not disappointed?"

"No," said the Princess.

The Princess's children did not have Fairy Godmothers.

•

FROM *The Death of the Heart*

He looks impressive, silly, intensely moral, and as though he would like to denounce himself. She would never let him denounce himself, and this was rather like taking somebody's toys away.

•

She walked about with the rather fated expression you see in photographs of girls who have subsequently been murdered, but nothing had so far happened to her.

•

Arts and crafts had succeeded Sturm and Drang.

•

A romantic man often feels more uplifted with two women than with one: his love seems to hit the ideal mark somewhere between two different faces.

•

The ironical thing is that everyone else gets their knives into us bourgeoisie on the assumption we're having a good time.

•

"The whole of Shakespeare is about me. All the others, of course, feel that too, which is why they are all dead nuts on Shakespeare."

•

She had yet to learn how often intimacies between women go backwards, beginning with revelations and ending up in small talk without loss of esteem.

•

"No, don't kiss me now."
    "Why not now?"
    "Because I don't want you to."
    "You mean," he said, "that I didn't once when you did?"

•

". . . there are no half measures. We either have dinner or telephone the police. . . ."

•

FROM *The Heat of the Day*

She had found all men to be one way funny like Tom—no sooner were their lips unstuck from your own than they began again to utter morality.

•

"But isn't much to be learned from the lessons of history, Connie?"

•

"Also in my experience one thing you don't learn from is anything anyway set up to be a lesson; what you are to know you pick up as you go along."

•

FROM *The Little Girls*

". . . I happened to know there was that drawer full of I don't know how many pair of long, long gloves, folded up and beautifully put away. So then I lifted the gloves up, to stow my sugar mice underneath, and there was the pistol or revolver. That was how, as I told you, I knew there was one.".

•

FROM *The Hotel*

"You know, women's lives are sensational. . . ."

"Well, I suppose it's inconsistent of me," said Mrs. Kerr. "I'm not a Feminist, but I do like being a woman."

•

What, I should like to know, is the use of speaking ninety-nine languages, if one has nothing to say?

•

"I do think men are pathetic, don't you? If only they were more interesting."

"I should have said they were interesting."

"You wouldn't if you'd had as many as I have," said Veronica gloomily. "I do envy you being so fearfully clever, Sydney: it's kept you young for your age. I dare say I thought men were interesting when I was about seventeen. Now I can see they're all exactly the same."

•

"Isn't it funny that for everybody there seems to be just one age at which they are really themselves? I mean, there are women you meet who were obviously born to be twenty (and pretty at that) and who seem to have lost their way since, and men you do wish you'd known when they were, say thirty, or twenty-four, or feel sorry you mayn't come across them when they're forty or fifty-five, and children like that horrid little Cordelia who are simply shaping up to be pale, sarcastic women of twenty-nine, who won't, once they're that, ever grow older."

•

FROM *To the North*

. . . she had asked Mrs. Patrick, the housekeeper, if it would be suitable for a young girl of her age to go out all alone for a ride in a bus. (Pauline had been told what happens in London and warned, especially, to avoid hospital nurses.) Mrs. Patrick, with hospital nurses also in mind, said it depended entirely upon the character of the bus. Taking thought, she had recommended the No. 11. The No. 11 is an entirely moral bus. Springing from Shepherd's Bush, against which one has seldom heard anything, it enjoys some innocent bohemianism in Chelsea. . . .

Except for the Strand, the No. 11 route, Mrs. Patrick considered, had the quality of Sunday afternoon literature; from it Pauline could derive nothing but edification.

•

At her confirmation classes they had worked their way through the Commandments: at the seventh, an evening had been devoted to impure curiosity. She had been offered, and had accepted, a very delicate book and still could not think of anything without blushing.

So that now flowers made her blush, rabbits made her blush excessively; she could no longer eat an egg. Only minerals seemed to bear contemplation . . .

•

Gerda Bligh was not really a fool, she was an honest girl of about Emmeline's age, with a tendency to hysteria. Having read a good many novels about marriage, not to speak of some scientific books, she now knew not only why she was unhappy but exactly how unhappy she could still be.

•

FROM *Eva Trout*

Iseult Smith's abandonment of a star career for an obscure marriage puzzled those for whom it was hearsay only—but the reason leaped to the eye: the marriage was founded on a cerebral young woman's first physical passion.

•

FROM *The House in Paris*

With no banal reassuring grown-ups present, with grown-up intervention taken away, there is no limit to the terror strange children feel of each other, a terror life obscures but never ceases to justify. There is no end to the violations committed by children on children, quietly talking alone.

•

We do not consider him ripe for direct sex-instruction yet, though my husband is working towards this through botany and mythology.

We are educating him on broad undenominational lines such as God is Love.

•

. . . there must be something she wanted; and that therefore she was no lady.

•

"Humour is being satisfied you are right, irony, being satisfied that they should think you wrong. Humorous people know there is nothing they need dread. English good-natured jokes seem to me terrible; they are full of jokes about mortification—the dentist, social ambition, love."

"I think that humour is English courage," she said.

"Ostrich courage," said Max.

Blanche McCrary Boyd (1945–)

FROM *The Revolution of Little Girls*

In the bathroom I confronted the most serious obstacle to the loss of my virginity: Under my skirt I was wearing a panty girdle. I hadn't really meant to wear the girdle, but when I was dressing I kept hearing my mother's voice saying, *Any woman looks better in a girdle,* so I'd put it on experimentally, and it felt so secure, so bracing, that I'd left it on. Now I didn't know what to do about it. I considered taking it off, but it was too bulky for the pocket of my trenchcoat.

What I did have in the pocket of my trenchcoat was a Norform vaginal suppository that Darlene had given me to insert "just before intercourse." It was supposed to lubricate me, a word that made me feel like a car. But when was "just before intercourse"? After I peed, I inserted the suppository and pulled the girdle back into place, feeling deeply relieved. The girdle meant I couldn't make love, but the suppository meant I sincerely wanted to.

•

Sexually, I began to experiment. I read the sex scenes in *Peyton Place* and drifted into them like hypnosis, my old teddy bear clutched tight between my legs. I felt bad about my teddy bear, who was not holding up well under this assault, but as long as I didn't touch myself, I was sure I couldn't be doing anything wrong. Then, one afternoon when it was too hot in the apartment to wear a lot of clothes, my wildness overcame my scruples. I bled and it wasn't my period. As the word *masturbation* occurred to me, I realized I had deflowered myself.

•

[My English teacher] Mr. Endicott . . . went back to his desk and took up reading *Our Town* again.

It's hard to explain what happened next. The class was so tense and unnerved that we began to listen desperately to the play. Dr. Gibbs was chastising his son George for not doing his chores and leaving his mother to chop wood. *Our Town* was set in 1900, but I didn't think that could account for all the differences from Plaxton that I was noticing. My father had died in an automobile accident; Reggie's father was a butcher at Mack's Meats; Cliff's father was our town doctor and, as everyone knew, he beat his son—that's where the scars on Cliff's back came from.

When Dr. Gibbs got disgruntled because Mrs. Gibbs was staying too long at choir practice, I began to giggle. The women on the way home from choir practice had stopped on the corner to gossip about the town drunk: "Really," one of them said, "it's the worst scandal that ever was in this town!"

I was trying to stop giggling when Mrs. Gibbs arrived home and Dr. Gibbs complained, "You're late enough," and Mrs. Gibbs replied, "Now, Frank, don't be grouchy. Come out and smell my heliotrope in the moonlight."

I started to laugh out loud. I didn't know what heliotrope was, and this remark struck me as hilariously off-color.

Mr. Endicott stopped reading. I put my head down on the desk but I knew he was looking at me. "Try to get hold of yourself, Ellen." The pleasant sarcasm was back in his voice.

But this laughter was like nothing that had ever happened to me. My face felt hot, and my new contact lenses were floating off my eyes. I gripped the edges of my desk as Mr. Endicott continued to read.

A few minutes later Mr. Webb, Dr. Gibbs's neighbor, went up to his daughter's room to see why she wasn't in bed. "I just can't sleep yet, Papa," she said. "The moonlight's so *won*-derful. And the smell of Mrs. Gibbs's heliotrope. Can you smell it?"

A howling noise escaped me. I began to pound helplessly on my desk.

"My dear," Mr. Endicott said, "heliotrope is a flower."

I stood up, squinting to hold my lenses in place. I could hardly breathe, much less speak. The laughter was brutalizing me with its terrible release, and I was no longer sure if I was laughing or crying.

Now Mr. Endicott sounded concerned. "Do you want to go home, my dear?"

I pulled my books against my chest, nodding.

"Go by the office."

I struggled down the hallway, still laughing, my face soaked with tears. In the principal's office I couldn't speak so I wrote a note to the secretary and pushed it across her desk: GOING HOME. CAN'T STOP LAUGHING.

•

After my freshman year at Duke University, I went to summer school at Harvard. Because of the Boston Strangler, my mother didn't want me to go. "I just hate to *think* of you like that, with your face all purple and your tongue hanging out. Why can't you be a normal girl and get a tan?"

The dean at Duke probably wouldn't have wanted me to go to Harvard either. At Duke I was viewed as a troublemaker, partly because of hypnosis.

In high school I had learned how to hypnotize people by accident. "Look deep into my eyes," I said to my sister Marie one night, when we'd been watching an evil hypnotist in a B movie on television. I said this with great conviction, and Marie looked at me as if it were a joke. Then something peculiar happened: she seemed to drift toward my eyes. "I'm going to count to five," I whispered, "and when I get to five you'll be in a deep trance." I whispered because I was afraid. There was a current between us as certain as the electricity in a doorbell I'd once touched.

Marie's eyelids fluttered. As I counted to five, her eyes closed. "Can you bark?" I asked.

"Yes," she said.

"Will you do it?"

"Yes."

"Be a dog, then. Bark."

Her eyes remained closed, but Marie's lips pulled back from her teeth, and she began to make little yipping noises. I recognized our neighbor's chihuahua.

I counted backward from five and Marie woke up. "I don't think we ought to tell Momma or Aunt Doodles about this," I said.

During my senior year in high school I developed a different technique, no longer hypnotizing through eye contact, which scared me too much, but with a lighted cigarette in a semidark room. Making people bark remained my favorite trick. Sometimes I told them what kind of dog to be, and other times I allowed them to choose—German shepherd, Lhasa apso, whatever. I knew I shouldn't be doing hypnosis, especially at parties, but at Duke it made me popular and feared.

College caused me authority problems right from the beginning. There were rules against women wearing pants to classes or to the dining room, and rules against wearing curlers in public. There was even a "suggestion" that women shouldn't smoke cigarettes standing up. Soon there was a new regulation concerning hypnosis.

The Dean's summons came right after second semester began. For my audience I wore a madras wrap-around skirt, a Gant button-down shirt, and a cardigan that had leather patches on the elbows. I even wore a panty girdle and hose. She would see that I was a normal, healthy young woman, not a troublemaker.

Dean Pottle looked at least forty years old. Her hair was brown and she was wearing a brown tailored suit. Her skin revealed that she'd once had a mild case of acne. She was smoking a cigarette and seemed quite friendly as she invited me to sit down across from her.

"Ellen," she said comfortingly, "we have had a report that you went to Dr. Hillyer's class in the medical school wearing nothing but a bathing suit and carrying a bottle of champagne on a silver tray."

I tried to think of how best to reply. "I'm not in the medical school, Dean Pottle, so I didn't think the regular rules would apply. Anyway, it was Dr. Hillyer's birthday, and some of his students asked me to deliver the champagne. It seemed harmless enough. I would never have agreed to do it if I'd known the class was at eight-thirty in the morning, I can assure you of that."

When she said nothing, I elaborated. "I wore my trenchcoat over my bathing suit until I got to the door of the classroom, and I put it right back on as soon as I gave him the champagne."

Her eyes were less affable. "The same trenchcoat you've been wearing to your regular classes?"

I nodded.

"Is it true you've been wearing your trenchcoat to classes with nothing under it?"

"It certainly is not true, Dean Pottle. I wear a slip and a bra. I even wear hose."

"Ellen, you do know about the dress code, don't you?"

"I'm within the dress code, Dean Pottle. It just says you can't wear pants, it doesn't say you have to wear skirts. Also, a slip is a kind of skirt, isn't it?"

The Dean was trying to look stern, but I began to suspect she might like me. "Do you think of yourself as an unusual girl, Ellen?"

I nodded miserably. "Listen, Dean Pottle, would you mind if I smoked too? I'm pretty nervous."

"Go ahead. You have a tendency to bend the rules a bit, don't you think?"

I lit a Winston. "I don't know."

"Let's start with the hypnosis."

"There was no rule against hypnosis."

The Dean took a final meditative drag on her own cigarette and crushed it out in a brown glass ashtray.

"Anyway, there's not much to it," I said. "To hypnosis. I saw it on TV one night. I say corny stuff like 'Look only at the tip of my cigarette, your eyelids are getting heavy.' Most people are just dying to go into a trance."

The Dean was staring at the smoke curling slowly from my cigarette.

"Hello?" I said.

With effort she looked up at me. When she didn't speak, I continued. "I tell them, look at the glowing ember of the cigarette. Let your mind relax."

The Dean looked right back at my cigarette. She seemed like a nice person. She probably thought the rules were dumb too.

"Your eyelids will close by themselves."

Her eyelids lowered quietly, like dancers bowing.

Slowly I counted to ten. "That's good. You're feeling very good. Just rest now."

A manila folder with my name on it was lying on her desk. In it were my college application, my board scores, and a handwritten report on the hypnosis incidents. The conclusion said I had difficulty accepting discipline and was on academic probation for poor grades.

I replaced the folder and said in my most soothing voice, "When you wake up, you'll feel great. You won't have any memory of this trance. No memory of it at all. You'll think Ellen Burns is a nice, interesting girl with no problems. Nod your head if you understand me."

The Dean nodded.

I was curious to know what kind of dog she might be, but someone could walk in and I wanted to put this unexpected opportunity to good use. Several acquaintances of mine were going to Harvard for the summer.

"When you wake up, I'm going to ask you about recommending me for summer school, and you're going to think that Harvard's a wonderful idea, in spite of my academic record. You'll say that Harvard is bound to help me with my authority problems. Do you understand?"

She nodded again.

I counted slowly backwards from ten to one, then said, "Wake up now."

The Dean's eyes opened. "I feel great. You're a wonderful girl, Ellen, with no serious problems."

I put out my cigarette in her brown glass ashtray. "Dean Pottle, I wanted to ask you about going to Harvard this summer."

•

Julia A. Boyd (contemporary)

∽℘ ℘∾

FROM *Something Ain't Right*

Beth is always telling me how women are oppressed and over-looked in the world. Funny thing is she never talks about oppression until she can't get what she wants.

•

Wanting equal rights is yesterday's news for me and other Black women, and jumping on the bandwagon behind a white woman hollering to get her equal rights wouldn't help my cause any. Hell, they forget we Black women built that wagon they're riding on, and I'll be damned if I'm going to push the wagon too.

Peg Bracken (1918-   )

∽℘ ℘∾

FROM *The I Hate to Cook Book*

Unnecessary dieting is because everything from television and fashion ads have made it seem wicked to cast a shadow. This wild, emaciated look appeals to some women, though not to many men, who are seldom seen pinning up a *Vogue* illustration in a machine shop.

Anne Bradstreet (c. 1612–1672)

The Prologue

1.

To sing of wars, of captains, and of kings,
Of cities founded, commonwealths begun,
For my mean pen are too superior things:
Or how they all, or each their dates have run,
Let poets and historians set these forth,
My obscure lines shall not so dim their worth.

2.

But when my wondering eyes and envious heart
    Great Bartas' sugared lines do but read o'er,
Fool, I do grudge the Muses did not part
'Twixt him and me, that overfluent store;
A Bartas can do what a Bartas will,
But simple I, according to my skill.

3.

From schoolboy's tongue, no Rhetoric we expect,
Nor yet a sweet consort from broken strings,
Nor perfect beauty, where's a main defect:
My foolish, broken, blemished Muse so sings;
And this to mend, alas, no art is able,
'Cause Nature made it so irreparable.

4.

Nor can I, like that fluent, sweet tongued Greek,
Who lisped at first, in future times speak plain.
By art, he gladly found what he did seek,

A full requital of his striving pain:
Art can do much, but this maxim's most sure:
A weak or wounded brain admits no cure.

5.

I am obnoxious to each carping tongue
Who says my hand a needle better fits,
A poet's pen, all scorn I should thus wrong,
For such despite they cast on female wits:
If what I do prove well, it won't advance,
They'll say it's stolen, or else it was by chance.

6.

But sure the antique Greeks were far more mild,
Else of our sex why feigned they those nine,
And poesy made Calliope's own child,
So 'mongst the rest, they placed the arts divine:
But this weak knot they will full soon untie,
The Greeks did nought but play the fool and lie.

7.

Let Greeks be Greeks, and women what they are,
Men have precedency, and still excel.
It is but vain unjustly to wage war;
Men can do best, and women know it well;
Preeminence in all and each is yours;
Yet grant some small acknowledgement of ours.

8.

And oh, ye high flown quills that soar the skies,
And ever with your prey, still catch your praise,
If e're you deign these lowly lines your eyes,
Give thyme or parsley wreath, I ask no bays;
This mean and unrefinèd ore of mine
Will make your glistering gold but more to shine.

The Author to Her Book

Thou ill-formed offspring of my feeble brain,
Who after birth did'st by my side remain,
Till snatched from thence by friends, less wise than true,
Who thee abroad, exposed to public view,
Made thee in rags, halting to th' press to trudge,
Where errors were not lessened (all may judge).
At thy return my blushing was not small,
My rambling brat (in print) should mother call,
I cast thee by as one unfit for light,
Thy visage was so irksome in my sight;
Yet being mine own, at length affection would
Thy blemishes amend, if so I could:
I washed thy face, but more defects I saw,
And rubbing off a spot, still made a flaw.
I stretched thy joints to make thee even feet,
Yet still thou run'st more hobbling than is meet;
In better dress to trim thee was my mind,
But nought save homespun cloth i' th' house I find.
In this array, 'mongst vulgars mayst thou roam,
In critics' hands, beware thou dost not come;
And take thy way where yet thou art not known;
If for thy father asked, say thou hadst none:
And for thy mother, she alas is poor,
Which caused her thus to send thee out of door.

Clare Bretecher (contemporary)

FROM *Frustration*

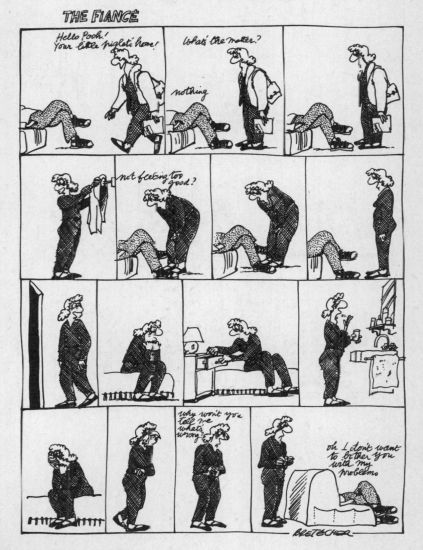

WRITINGS

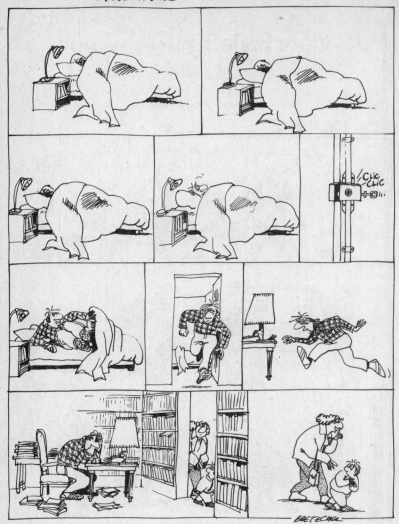

A woman's work

casanova

Anne Brontë (1820-1849)

~e 9e~

FROM *The Tenant of Wildfell Hall*

"I beg your pardon, Mrs. Graham—but you get on too fast. I have not yet said that a boy should be taught to rush into the snares of life,—or even wilfully to seek temptation for the sake of exercising his virtue by overcoming it;—I only say that it is better to arm and strengthen your hero, than to disarm and enfeeble the foe;—and if you were to rear an oak sapling in a hothouse, tending it carefully night and day, and shielding it from every breath of wind, you could not expect it to become a hardy tree, like that which has grown up on the mountain-side, exposed to all the action of the elements, and not even sheltered from the shock of the tempest."

"Granted;—but would you use the same argument with regard to a girl?"

"Certainly not."

"No; you would have her to be tenderly and delicately nurtured, like a hothouse plant—taught to cling to others for direction and support, and guarded, as much as possible, from the very knowledge of evil. But will you be so good as to inform me why you make this distinction? Is it that you think she *has* no virtue?"

"Assuredly not."

"Well, but you affirm that virtue is elicited by temptation;—and you think that a woman cannot be too little exposed to temptation, or too little acquainted with vice, or anything connected therewith—It *must* be, either, that you think she is essentially so vicious, or so feeble-minded, that she *cannot* withstand temptation,—and though she may be pure and innocent as long as she is kept in ignorance and restraint, yet, being destitute of *real* virtue, to teach her how to sin is at once to make her a sinner, and the greater her knowledge, the wider her liberty, the deeper will be her depravity,—whereas, in the nobler sex, there is a natural tendency to goodness, guarded by a superior fortitude, which, the more it is exercised by trials and dangers, is only the further developed—"

"Heaven forbid that I should think so!" I interrupted, at last.

"Well then, it must be that you think they are *both* weak and prone to err, and the slightest error, the merest shadow of pollution, will ruin the one, while the character of the other will be strengthened and embellished—his education properly finished by a little practical acquaintance with forbidden things. Such experience, to him, (to use a trite simile) will be like the storm to the oak, which, though it may scatter the leaves, and snap the smaller branches, serves but to rivet the roots, and to harden and condense the fibres of the tree. You would have us encourage our sons to prove all things by their own experience, while our daughters must not even profit by the experience of others. Now *I* would have both so to benefit by the experience of others, and the precepts of a higher authority, that they should know beforehand to refuse the evil and choose the good, and require no experimental proofs to teach them the evil of transgression. I would not send a poor girl into the world unarmed against her foes, and ignorant of the snares that beset her path; nor would I watch and guard her, till, deprived of self-respect and self-reliance, she lost the power, or the will, to watch and guard herself;—and as for my son—if I thought he would grow up to be what you call a man of the world—one that has *'seen life,'* and glories in his experience, even though he should so far profit by it, as to sober down, at length, into a useful and respected member of society—I would rather that he died to-morrow!—rather a thousand times!" she earnestly repeated, pressing her darling to her side and kissing his forehead with intense affection. He had, already, left his new companion, and been standing for some time beside his mother's knee, looking up into her face, and listening in silent wonder to her incomprehensible discourse.

"Well! you ladies must always have the last word, I suppose," said I, observing her rise and begin to take leave of my mother.

"You may have as many words as you please,—only I can't stay to hear them."

"No; that is the way: you hear just as much of an argument as you please; and the rest may be spoken to the wind."

"If you are anxious to say anything more on the subject," replied she, as she shook hands with Rose, "you must bring your sister to see me some fine day, and I'll listen, as patiently as you could wish, to whatever you please to say. I would rather be lectured by you than the vicar, because I should have less remorse in telling you, at the end of the discourse, that I preserve my own opinion precisely the same as at the beginning—as would be the case, I am persuaded, with regard to either logician."

"Yes, of course," replied I, determined to be as provoking as herself; "for, when a lady does consent to listen to an argument against her own opinions, she is always predetermined to withstand it—to listen only with her bodily ears, keeping the mental organs resolutely closed against the strongest reasoning."

"Good morning, Mr. Markham," said my fair antagonist, with a pitying smile; and deigning no further rejoinder, she slightly bowed, and was about to withdraw; but her son, with childish impertinence, arrested her by exclaiming,—

"Mamma, you have not shaken hands with Mr. Markham!"

She laughingly turned round, and held out her hand. I gave it a spiteful squeeze; for I was annoyed at the continual injustice she had done me from the very dawn of our acquaintance. Without knowing anything about my real disposition and principles, she was evidently prejudiced against me, and seemed bent upon showing me that her opinions respecting me, on every particular, fell far below those I entertained of myself. I was naturally touchy, or it would not have vexed me so much. Perhaps, too, I was a little bit spoiled by my mother and sister, and some other ladies of my acquaintance;—and yet, I was by no means a fop— of that I am fully convinced, whether *you* are or not.

I was too late for tea; but my mother had kindly kept the teapot and muffin warm upon the hobs, and, though she scolded me a little, readily admitted my excuses; and when I complained of the flavour of the over-drawn tea, she poured the remainder into the slop-basin, and bade Rose put some fresh into the pot and reboil the kettle, which offices were performed with great commotion and certain remarkable comments:—

"Well!—if it had been *me* now, I should have had no tea at all— If it had been Fergus, even, he would have had to put up with such as there was, and been told to be thankful, for it was far too good for him; but *you*—we can't do too much for you—It's always so—if there's anything particularly nice at table, mamma winks and nods at me to abstain from it, and if I don't attend to that, she whispers, 'Don't eat so much of that, Rose, Gilbert will like it for his supper'—*I'm* nothing at all—in the parlour, it's 'Come, Rose, put away your things, and let's have the room nice and tidy against they come in; and keep up a good fire; Gilbert likes a cheerful fire.' In the kitchen—'Make that pie a large one, Rose, I dare say the boys'll be hungry;—and don't put so much pepper in, they'll not like it I'm sure'—or, 'Rose, don't put so many spices in the pudding, Gilbert likes it plain,'—or, 'Mind you put plenty of currants in the cake, Fergus likes plenty.' If I say, 'Well, mamma, *I* don't,' I'm told I ought not to think of myself—'You know, Rose, in all household matters, we have only two things to consider, first, what's proper to be done, and secondly, what's most agreeable to the gentlemen of the house—anything will do for the ladies.' "

"And very good doctrine too," said my mother. "Gilbert thinks so, I'm sure."

"Very convenient doctrine, for us at all events," said I; "but if you would really study my pleasure, mother, you must consider your own comfort and convenience a little more than you do—as for Rose, I have no doubt she'll take care of herself; and whenever she does make a sacrifice or perform a remarkable act of devotedness, she'll take good care to let me know the extent of it. But for *you*, I might sink into the grossest condition of self-indulgence and carelessness about the wants of others, from the mere habit of being constantly cared for myself, and having all my wants anticipated or immediately supplied, while left in total ignorance of what is done for me,—if Rose did not enlighten me now and then; and I should receive all your kindness as a matter of course, and never know how much I owe you."

"Ah! and you never *will* know, Gilbert, till you're married. Then, when you've got some trifling, self-conceited girl like Eliza Millward, careless of everything but her own immediate pleasure and advantage, or some misguided, obstinate woman like Mrs. Graham, ignorant of her principal duties, and clever only in what concerns her least to know— then, you'll find the difference."

"It will do me good, mother; I was not sent into the world merely to exercise the good capacities and good feelings of others—was I?— but to exert my own towards them; and when I marry, I shall expect to find more pleasure in making my wife happy and comfortable, than in being made so by her: I would rather give than receive."

"Oh! that's all nonsense, my dear—It's mere boy's talk that! You'll soon tire of petting and humouring your wife, be she ever so charming, and *then* comes the trial."

"Well, then, we must bear one another's burdens."

"Then, you must fall each into your proper place. You'll do your business, and she, if she's worthy of you, will do hers; but it's your business to please yourself, and hers to please you. I'm sure your poor, dear father was as good a husband as ever lived, and after the first six months or so were over, I should as soon have expected him to fly, as to put himself out of his way to pleasure me. He always said I was a good wife, and did my duty; and he always did his—bless him!—he was steady and punctual, seldom found fault without a reason, always did justice at my good dinners, and hardly ever spoiled my cookery by delay—and that's as much as any woman can expect of any man."

Is it so, Halford? Is that the extent of *your* domestic virtues; and does your happy wife exact no more?

Charlotte Brontë (1816–1855)

FROM *Shirley*

Tea was a long time in progress: all the guests gabbled as their hostess had expected they would. Mr. Helstone, being in excellent spirits,—when, indeed, was he ever otherwise in society, attractive female society?—it being only with the one lady of his own family that he maintained a grim taciturnity,—kept up a brilliant flow of easy prattle with his right-hand and left-hand neighbours, and even with his *vis-à-vis*, Miss Mary: though as Mary was the most sensible, the least coquettish of the three, to her the elderly widower was the least attentive. At heart, he could not abide sense in women: he liked to see them as silly, as light-headed, as vain, as open to ridicule as possible; because they were then in reality what he held them to be, and wished them to be,—inferior: toys to play with, to amuse a vacant hour and to be thrown away.

Hannah was his favourite. Harriet, though beautiful, egotistical, and self-satisfied, was not quite weak enough for him: she had some genuine self-respect amidst much false pride, and if she did not talk like an oracle, neither would she babble like one crazy: she would not permit herself to be treated quite as a doll, a child, a plaything; she expected to be bent to like a queen.

Hannah, on the contrary, demanded no respect; only flattery: if her admirers only *told* her that she was an angel, she would let them *treat* her like an idiot. So very credulous and frivolous was she; so very silly did she become when besieged with attention, flattered and admired to the proper degree, that there were moments when Helstone actually felt tempted to commit matrimony a second time, and to try the experiment of taking her for his second helpmeet: but, fortunately, the salutary recollection of the ennuis of his first marriage, the impression still left on him of the weight of the millstone he had once worn round his neck, the fixity of his feelings respecting the insufferable evils of conjugal existence, operated as a check to his tenderness, suppressed the sigh leaving his old iron lungs, and restrained him from whispering to Hannah proposals it would have been high fun and great satisfaction to her to hear.

It is probable she would have married him if he had asked her; her parents would have quite approved the match: to them his fifty-five years, his bend-leather heart, could have presented no obstacles; and, as he was a rector, held an excellent living, occupied a good house, and was supposed even to have private property (though in that the world was mistaken: every penny of the £5000 inherited by him from his father had been devoted to the building and endowing of a new church at his native village in Lancashire—for he could show a lordly munificence when he pleased, and, if the end was to his liking, never hesitated about making a grand sacrifice to attain it),—her parents, I say, would have delivered Hannah over to his loving-kindness and his tender mercies without one scruple; and the second Mrs. Helstone, inversing the natural order of insect existence, would have fluttered through the honeymoon a bright, admired butterfly, and crawled the rest of her days a sordid, trampled worm.

•

"A very dangerous dog that, Miss Keeldar. I wonder you should keep such an animal."

"Do you, Mr. Donne? Perhaps you will wonder more when I tell you I am very fond of him."

"I should say you are not serious in the assertion. Can't fancy a lady fond of that brute—'tis so ugly—a mere carter's dog—pray hang him."

"Hang what I am fond of?"

"And purchase in his stead some sweetly pooty pug or poodle: something appropriate to the fair sex: ladies generally like lap-dogs."

"Perhaps I am an exception."

"Oh! you can't be, you know. All ladies are alike in those matters: that is universally allowed."

•

"How pleasant and calm it is!" said Caroline.

"And how hot it will be in the church!" responded Shirley; "and what a dreary long speech Dr. Boultby will make! and how the curates will hammer over their prepared orations! For my part, I would rather not enter."

"But my uncle will be angry, if he observes our absence."

"I will bear the brunt of his wrath: he will not devour me. I shall be sorry to miss his pungent speech. I know it will be all sense for the Church, and all causticity for Schism: he'll not forget the battle of Royd-lane. I shall be sorry also to deprive you of Mr. Hall's sincere friendly homily, with all its racy Yorkshireisms; but here I must stay. The grey church and greyer tombs look divine with this crimson gleam on them. Nature is now at her evening prayers: she is kneeling before those red hills. I see her prostrate on the great steps of her altar, praying for a fair night for mariners at sea, for travellers in deserts, for lambs on moors, and unfledged birds in woods. Caroline, I see her! and I will tell you what she is like: she is like what Eve was when she and Adam stood alone on the earth."

"And that is not Milton's Eve, Shirley."

"Milton's Eve! Milton's Eve! I repeat. No, by the pure Mother of God, she is not! Cary, we are alone: we may speak what we think. Milton was great; but was he good? His brain was right; how was his heart? He saw heaven: he looked down on hell. He saw Satan, and Sin his daughter, and Death their horrible offspring. Angels serried before him their battalions: the long lines of adamantine shields flashed back on his blind eyeballs the unutterable splendour of heaven. Devils gathered their legions in his sight: their dim, discrowned, and tarnished armies passed rank and file before him. Milton tried to see the first woman; but, Cary, he saw her not."

"You are bold to say so, Shirley."

"Not more bold than faithful. It was his cook that he saw; or it was Mrs. Gill, as I have seen her, making custards, in the heat of summer, in the cool dairy, with rose-trees and nasturtiums about the latticed window, preparing a cold collation for the rectors,—preserves, and 'dulcet creams'—puzzled 'what choice to choose for delicacy best; what order so contrived as not to mix tastes, not well-joined, inelegant; but bring taste after taste, upheld with kindliest change.' "

"All very well too, Shirley."

"I would beg to remind him that the first men of the earth were Titans, and the Eve was their mother: from her sprang Saturn, Hyperion, Oceanus; she bore Prometheus—"

"Pagan that you are! what does that signify?"

"I say, there were giants on the earth in those days: giants that strove to scale heaven. The first woman's breast that heaved with life on this world yielded the daring which could contend with Omnipotence: the strength which could bear a thousand years of bondage,—the vitality which could feed that vulture death through uncounted ages,—the unexhausted life and uncorrupted excellence, sisters to immortality, which, after millenniums of crimes, struggles, and woes, could conceive and bring forth a Messiah. The first woman was heaven-born: vast was the heart whence gushed the well-spring of the blood of nations; and grand the undegenerate head where rested the consort-crown of creation."

"She coveted an apple, and was cheated by a snake: but you have got such a hash of Scripture and mythology into your head that there is no making any sense of you. You have not yet told me what you saw kneeling on those hills."

"I saw—I now see—a woman-Titan: her robe of blue air spreads to the outskirts of the heath, where yonder flock is grazing; a veil white as an avalanche sweeps from her head to her feet, and arabesques of lightning flame on its borders. Under her breast I see her zone, purple like that horizon: through its blush shines the star of evening. Her steady eyes I cannot picture; they are clear—they are deep as lakes—they are lifted and full of worship—they tremble with the softness of love and the lustre of prayer. Her forehead has the expanse of a cloud, and is paler than the early moon, risen long before dark gathers: she reclines her bosom on the ridge of Stilbro' Moor; her mighty hands are joined beneath it. So kneeling, face to face she speaks with God. That Eve is Jehovah's daughter, as Adam was his son."

•

FROM *Villette*

I laughed, as, indeed, it was impossible to do otherwise.

•

I don't know what he said, except that he recommended each to penetrate herself well with a sense of her personal significance. God knows, I thought this advice superfluous for some of us.

•

"My 'beautiful young friend' ought to know that, and to know or feel who is worthy of her," said I. "If her beauty or her brains will not serve her so far, she merits the sharp lesson of experience."

"Are you not a little severe?"

"I am excessively severe—more severe than I choose to show you. You should hear the strictures with which I favour my 'beautiful young friend,' only that you would be unutterably shocked at my want of tender considerateness for her delicate nature."

"She is so lovely, one cannot but be loving towards her. You—

every woman older than herself, must feel for such a simple, innocent, girlish fairy, a sort of motherly or elder-sisterly fondness. Graceful angel! Does not your heart yearn towards her when she pours into your ear her pure, child-like confidences? How you are privileged!" And he sighed.

"I cut short these confidences somewhat abruptly now and then," said I. "But excuse me, Dr. John, may I change the theme for one instant? What a god-like person is that de Hamal! What a nose on his face—perfect! Model one in putty or clay, you could not make a better, or straighter, or neater; and then, such classic lips and chin—and his bearing—sublime."

"De Hamal is an unutterable puppy, besides being a very white-livered hero."

"You, Dr. John, and every man of a less refined mould than he, must feel for him a sort of admiring affection, such as Mars and the coarser deities may be supposed to have borne the young graceful Apollo."

"An unprincipled, gambling, little jackanapes!" said Dr. John curtly, "whom, with one hand, I could lift up by the waistband any day, and lay low in the kennel, if I liked."

"Sweet seraph!" said I. "What a cruel idea? Are you not a little severe, Dr. John?"

•

. . . this picture, I say, seemed to consider itself the queen of the collection. It represented a woman, considerably larger, I thought than life. I calculated that this lady, put into a scale of magnitude suitable for the reception of a commodity of bulk, would infallibly turn from fourteen to sixteen stone. She was, indeed, extremely well fed: very much butcher's meat—to say nothing of bread, vegetables, and liquids—must she have consumed to attain that breadth and height, that wealth of muscle, that affluence of flesh. She lay half-reclined on a couch: why it would be difficult to say; broad daylight blazed round her; she appeared in hearty health, strong enough to do the work of two plain cooks; she could not plead a weak spine; she ought to have been standing, or at least sitting bolt upright. She had no business to lounge away the noon on a sofa. She ought likewise to have worn decent garments; a gown covering her properly, which was not the case: out of abundance of material—seven-and-twenty yards, I should say, of drapery—she managed to make inefficient raiment. Then, for the wretched untidiness surrounding her, there could be no excuse. Pots and pans—perhaps I ought to say vases and goblets—were rolled here and there on the foreground; a perfect rubbish of flowers was mixed amongst them, and an absurd and disorderly mass of curtain upholstery smothered the couch and cumbered the floor. On referring to the catalogue, I found that this notable production bore the name "Cleopatra."

•

And "laids," indeed, they were; being a set of four, denominated in the catalogue "La vie d'une femme." They were painted rather in remarkable style—flat, dead, pale and formal. The first represented a "Jeune Fille," coming out of a church-door, a missal in her hand, her dress very prim, her eyes cast down, her mouth pursed up—the image of a most villainous little precocious she-hypocrite. The second, a "Mariée" with a long white veil, kneeling at a prie-dieu in her chamber, holding her hands plastered together, finger to finger, and showing the whites of her eyes in a most exasperating manner. The third, a "Jeune Mère," hanging disconsolate over a clayey and puffy baby with a face like an unwholesome full moon. The fourth, a "Veuve," being a black woman, holding by the hand a black little girl and the twain studiously surveying an elegant French monument, set up in a corner of some Père la Chaise. All these four "Anges" were grim and gray as burglars, and cold and vapid as ghosts. What women to live with! insincere, ill-humoured, bloodless, brainless nonentities! As bad in their way as the indolent gipsy-giantess; the Cleopatra, in hers.

•

How daintily he held a glass to one of his optics! with what admiration he gazed upon the Cleopatra! and then, how engagingly he tittered and whispered a friend at his elbow! Oh, the man of sense! Oh, the refined gentleman of superior taste and tact! I observed him for about ten minutes, and perceived that he was exceedingly taken with this dusk and portly Venus of the Nile.

•

"Woman of intellect" was his next theme: here he was at home. A "woman of intellect," it appeared, was a sort of *"lusus naturae,"* a luckless accident, a thing for which there was neither place nor use in creation, wanted neither as wife nor worker. Beauty anticipated her in the first office. He believed in his soul that lovely, placid, and passive feminine mediocrity was the only pillow on which manly thought and sense could find rest for its aching temples; and as to work, male mind alone could work to any good practical result—hein?

•

FROM *Jane Eyre*

"Missis was, she dared say, glad enough to get rid of such a tiresome ill-conditioned child, who always looked as if she were watching everybody, and scheming plots underhand." Abbot, I think, gave me credit for being a sort of infantine Guy Fawkes.

•

"No sight so sad as that of a naughty child," he began, "especially a naughty little girl. Do you know where the wicked go after death?"

"They go to hell," was my ready and orthodox answer.

"And what is hell? Can you tell me that?"

"A pit full of fire."

"And should you like to fall into that pit, and to be burning there for ever?"

"No, sir."

"What must you do to avoid it?"

I deliberated a moment: my answer, when it did come was objectionable: "I must keep in good health and not die."

•

"Oh, shocking! I have a little boy, younger than you, who knows six Psalms by heart: and when you ask him which he would rather have, a ginger-bread-nut to eat, or a verse of a Psalm to learn, he says: 'Oh! the verse of a Psalm! angels sings Psalms,' says he; 'I wish to be a little angel here below.' He then gets two nuts in recompense for his infant piety."

•

Women are supposed to be very calm generally: but women feel just as men feel; they need exercise for their faculties, and a field for their efforts as much as their brothers do; they suffer from too rigid a restraint, too absolute a stagnation, precisely as men would suffer; and it is narrow-minded in their mere privileged fellow creatures to say that they ought to confine themselves to making puddings and knitting stockings, to playing on the piano and embroidering bags. It is thoughtless to condemn them, or laugh at them, if they seek to do more or learn more than custom has pronounced necessary for their sex.

•

"What tale do you like best to hear?"

"Oh, I have not much choice! They generally run on the same theme—courtship; and promise to end in the same catastrophe—marriage."

•

"Leaving superiority out of the question, then, you must still agree to receive my orders now and then, without being piqued or hurt by the tone of command. Will you?"

I smiled: I thought to myself Mr. Rochester *is* peculiar—he seems to forget that he pays me thirty pounds per annum for receiving his orders.

•

". . . unheard-of combinations of circumstances demand unheard-of rules."

•

"Do you doubt me, Jane?"
      "Entirely."
      "You have no faith in me?"
      "Not a whit."

•

I laughed at him as he said this. "I am not an angel," I asserted; "and I will not be one till I die: I will be myself. Mr. Rochester, you must neither expect nor exact anything celestial of me—for you will not get it, any more than I shall get it of you: which I do not at all anticipate."

•

"Am I hideous, Jane?"
      "Very, sir; you always were, you know."
      "Humph! The wickedness has not been taken out of you, wherever you have sojourned."

•

I laughed and made my escape, still laughing as I ran upstairs. "A good idea!" I thought with glee. "I see I have the means of fretting him out of his melancholy for some time to come."

•

"I like you more than I can say; but I'll not sink into a bathos of sentiment: and with this needle of repartee I'll keep you from the edge of the gulf, too; and, moreover, maintain by its pungent aid that distance between you and myself most conducive to our real mutual advantage."

Emily Brontë (1818–1848)

❧ ❧

FROM *Wuthering Heights*

While enjoying a month of fine weather at the sea-coast, I was thrown into the company of a most fascinating creature, a real goddess, in my eyes, as long as she took no notice of me. I "never told my love" vocally; still, if looks have language, the merest idiot might have guessed I was over head and ears; she understood me, at last, and looked a return— the sweetest of all imaginable looks—and what did I do? I confess it with shame—shrunk icily into myself, like a snail, at every glance retired colder and farther; till, finally, the poor innocent was led to doubt her own senses, and, overwhelmed with confusion at her supposed mistake, persuaded her mamma to decamp.

By this curious turn of disposition I have gained the reputation of deliberate heartlessness, how undeserved, I alone can appreciate.

•

Not anxious to come in contact with their fangs, I sat still; but, imagining they would scarcely understand tacit insults, I unfortunately indulged in winking and making faces at the trio, and some turn of my physiognomy so irritated madam, that she suddenly broke into a fury and leapt on my knees. I flung her back, and hastened to interpose the table between us.

•

The snow began to drive thickly. I seized the handle to essay another trial; when a young man, without coat, and shouldering a pitchfork, appeared in the yard behind. He hailed me to follow him, and, after marching through a washhouse, and a paved area containing a coal-shed, pump, and pigeon cote, we at length arrived in the huge, warm, cheerful apartment, where I was formerly received.

It glowed delightfully in the radiance of an immense fire, compounded of coal, peat, and wood: and near the table, laid for a plentiful evening meal, I was pleased to observe the "missis," an individual whose existence I had never previously suspected.

I bowed and waited, thinking she would bid me take a seat. She looked at me, leaning back in her chair, and remained motionless and mute.

"Rough weather!" I remarked. "I'm afraid, Mrs. Heathcliff, the door must bear the consequence of your servants' leisure attendance: I had hard work to make them hear me!"

She never opened her mouth. I stared—she stared also. At any rate, she kept her eyes on me, in a cool, regardless manner, exceedingly embarrassing and disagreeable.

"Sit down," said the young man, gruffly. "He'll be in soon."

I obeyed; and hemmed, and called the villain Juno, who deigned, at this second interview, to move the extreme tip of her tail, in token of owning my acquaintance.

"A beautiful animal!" I commenced again. "Do you intend parting with the little ones, madam?"

"They are not mine," said the amiable hostess more repellingly than Heathcliff himself could have replied.

"Ah, your favourites are among these!" I continued, turning to an obscure cushion full of something like cats.

"A strange choice of favourites," she observed scornfully.

Unluckily, it was a heap of dead rabbits—I hemmed once more, and drew closer to the hearth, repeating my comment on the wildness of the evening.

"You should not have come out," she said, rising and reaching from the chimney-piece two of the painted canisters.

Her position before was sheltered from the light: now, I had a distinct view of her whole figure and countenance. She was slender, and apparently scarcely past girlhood: an admirable form, and the most exquisite little face that I have ever had the pleasure of beholding: small features, very fair; flaxen ringlets, or rather golden, hanging loose on her delicate neck; and eyes—had they been agreeable in expression, they would have been irresistible—fortunately for my susceptible heart, the only sentiment they evinced hovered between scorn and a kind of desperation, singularly unnatural to be detected there.

The canisters were almost out of her reach; I made a motion to aid her; she turned upon me as a miser might turn, if any one attempted to assist him in counting his gold.

"I don't want your help," she snapped, "I can get them for myself."

"I beg your pardon," I hastened to reply.

"Were you asked to tea?" she demanded, tying an apron over her neat black frock, and standing with a spoonful of the leaf poised over the pot.

"I shall be glad to have a cup," I answered.

"Were you asked?" she repeated.

"No," I said, half smiling. "You are the proper person to ask me."

She flung the tea back, spoon and all, and resumed her chair in a pet, her forehead corrugated, and her red underlip pushed out, like a child's, ready to cry.

Meanwhile, the young man had slung onto his person a decidedly shabby upper garment, and, erecting himself before the blaze, looked down on me, from the corner of his eyes, for all the world as if there were some mortal feud unavenged between us. I began to doubt whether he were a servant or not; his dress and speech were both rude, entirely devoid of the superiority observable in Mr. and Mrs. Heathcliff; his thick, brown curls were rough and uncultivated, his whiskers encroached bearishly over his cheeks, and his hands were embrowned like those of the common labourer: still his bearing was free, almost haughty; and he showed none of a domestic's assiduity in attending on the lady of the house.

In the absence of clear proofs of his condition, I deemed it best to abstain from noticing his curious conduct, and, five minutes afterwards, the entrance of Healthcliff relieved me, in some measure, from my uncomfortable state.

"You see, sir, I am come according to promise!" I exclaimed, assuming the cheerful "and I fear I shall be weatherbound for half an hour, if you can afford me shelter during that space."

"Half an hour?" he said, shaking the white flakes from his clothes; "I wonder you should select the thick of a snowstorm to ramble about in. Do you know that you run a risk of being lost in the marshes? People familiar with these moors often miss their road on such evenings, and, I can tell you, there is no chance of a change at present."

"Perhaps I can get a guide among your lads, and he might stay at the Grange till morning—could you spare me one?"

"No, I could not."

"Oh, indeed! Well, then, I must trust to my own sagacity."

"Umph!"

"Are you going to mak' th' tea?" demanded he of the shabby coat, shifting his ferocious gaze from me to the young lady.

"Is *he* to have any?" she asked, appealing to Heathcliff.

"Get it ready, will you?" was the answer, uttered so savagely that I started. The tone in which the words were said, revealed a genuine bad nature. I no longer felt inclined to call Heathcliff a capital fellow.

When the preparations were finished, he invited me with—

"Now, sir, bring forward your chair." And we all, including the rustic youth, drew round the table, an austere silence prevailing while we discussed our meal.

I thought, if I had caused the cloud, it was my duty to make an effort to dispel it. They could not every day sit so grim and taciturn, and it was impossible, however ill-tempered they might be, that the universal scowl they wore was their everyday countenance.

"It is strange," I began in the interval of swallowing one cup of tea and receiving another, "it is strange how custom can mould our tastes and ideas; many could not imagine the existence of happiness in a life of such complete exile from the world as you spend, Mr. Heathcliff; yet, I'll venture to say, that, surrounded by your family, and with your amiable lady as the presiding genius over your home and heart—"

"My amiable lady!" he interrupted, with an almost diabolical sneer on his face. "Where is she—my amiable lady?"

"Mrs. Heathcliff, your wife, I mean."

"Well, yes—Oh! you would intimate that her spirit has taken the post of ministering angel, and guards the fortunes of Wuthering Heights, even when her body is gone. Is that it?"

Perceiving myself in a blunder, I attempted to correct it. I might have seen that there was too great a disparity between the ages of the parties to make it likely that they were man and wife. One was about forty; a period of mental vigour at which men seldom cherish the delusion of being married for love, by girls: that dream is reserved for the solace of our declining years. The other did not look seventeen.

Then it flashed upon me—"The clown at my elbow, who is drinking his tea out of a basin, and eating his bread with unwashed hands, may be her husband. Heathcliff, junior, of course. Here is the consequence of being buried alive: she has thrown herself away upon that boor, from sheer ignorance that better individuals existed! A sad pity—I must beware how I cause her to regret her choice."

The last reflection may seem conceited; it was not. My neighbour struck me as bordering on repulsive. I knew, through experience, that I was tolerably attractive.

"Mrs. Heathcliff is my daughter-in-law," said Heathcliff, corroborating my surmise. He turned, as he spoke, a peculiar look in her direction, a look of hatred unless he has a most perverse set of facial muscles that will not, like those of other people, interpret the language of his soul.

"Ah, certainly—I see now; you are the favoured possessor of the beneficent fairy," I remarked, turning to my neighbour.

This was worse than before: the youth grew crimson, and clenched his fist with every appearance of a meditated assault. But he seemed to recollect himself, presently; and smothered the storm in a brutal curse, muttered on my behalf, which, however, I took care not to notice.

"Unhappy in your conjectures, sir!" observed my host; "we neither of us have the privilege of owning your good fairy; her mate is dead. I said she was my daughter-in-law, therefore, she must have married my son."

"And this young man is—"

"Not my son, assuredly!"

Heathcliff smiled again, as if it were rather too bold a jest to attribute the paternity of that bear to him.

"My name is Hareton Earnshaw," growled the other; "and I'd counsel you to respect it."

"I've shown no disrespect," was my reply, laughing internally at the dignity with which he announced himself.

He fixed his eye on me longer than I cared to return the stare, for fear I might be tempted either to box his ears, or render my hilarity audible. I began to feel unmistakably out of place in that pleasant family circle. The dismal spiritual atmosphere overcame, and more than neutralized the glowing physical comforts round me; and I resolved to be cautious how I ventured under those rafters a third time.

The business of eating being concluded, and no one uttering a word of sociable conversation, I approached a window to examine the weather.

A sorrowful sight I saw; dark night coming down prematurely, and sky and hills mingled in one bitter whirl of wind and suffocating snow.

"I don't think it possible for me to get home now, without a guide," I could not help exclaiming. "The roads will be buried already; and if they were bare, I could scarcely distinguish a foot in advance."

"Hareton, drive those dozen sheep into the barn porch. They'll be covered if left in the fold all night; and put a plank before them," and Heathcliff.

"How must I do?" I continued, with rising irritation.

There was no reply to my question; and on looking round, I saw only Joseph bringing in a pail of porridge for the dogs and Mrs. Heathcliff, leaning over the fire, diverting herself with burning a bundle of matches which had fallen from the chimney-piece as she restored the tea-canister to its place.

The former, when he had deposited his burden, took a critical survey of the room; and, in cracked tones, grated out:

"Aw woonder hagh yah can faishion tuh stand thear i' idleness un war, when all on 'em's goan aght! Bud yah're a nowt, and it's noa use talking—yah'll niver mend uh yer ill ways; bud, goa raight tuh t' divil, like yer mother afore ye!"

I imagined, for a moment, that this piece of eloquence was addressed to me; and, sufficiently enraged, stepped towards the aged rascal with an intention of kicking him out of the door.

Mrs. Heathcliff, however, checked me by her answer.

"You scandalous old hypocrite!" she replied. "Are you not afraid of being carried away bodily, whenever you mention the devil's name? I warn you to refrain from provoking me, or I'll ask your abduction as a special favour. Stop, look here, Joseph," she continued, taking a long, dark book from a shelf. "I'll show you how far I've progressed in the Black Art—I shall soon be competent to make a clear house of it. The red cow didn't die by chance; and your rheumatism can hardly be reckoned among providential visitations!"

"Oh, wicked, wicked!" gasped the elder; "may the Lord deliver us from evil!"

"No, reprobate! you are a castaway—be off, or I'll hurt you seriously! I'll have you all modelled in wax and clay; and the first who passes the limits I fix, shall—I'll not say what he shall be done to—but, you'll see! Go, I'm looking at you!"

The little witch put a mock malignity into her beautiful eyes, and Joseph, trembling with sincere horror, hurried out praying and ejaculating "wicked" as he went.

I thought her conduct must be prompted by a species of dreary fun; and, now that we were alone, I endeavoured to interest her in my distress.

"Mrs. Heathcliff," I said, earnestly, "you must excuse me for troubling you—I presume, because, with that face, I'm sure you cannot help being good-hearted. Do point out some landmarks by which I may know my way home—I have no more idea how to get there than you would have how to get to London!"

"Take the road you came," she answered, ensconcing herself in a chair, with a candle, and the long book open before her. "It is brief advice; but as sound as I can give."

"Then, if you hear of me being discovered dead in a bog, or a pit full of snow, your conscience won't whisper that it is partly your fault?"

"How so? I cannot escort you. They wouldn't let me go to the end of the garden-wall."

"*You!* I should be very sorry to ask you to cross the threshold, for my convenience, on such a night," I cried. "I want you to *tell* me my way, not to *show* it, or else to persuade Mr. Heathcliff to give me a guide."

"Who? There is himself, Earnshaw, Zillah, Joseph, and I. Which would you have?"

"Are there no boys at the farm?"

"No, those are all."

"Then, it follows that I am compelled to stay."

"That you may settle with your host. I have nothing to do with it."

"I hope it will be a lesson to you, to make no more rash journeys on these hills," cried Heathcliff's stern voice from the kitchen entrance. "As to staying here, I don't keep accommodations for visitors; you must share a bed with Hareton, or Joseph, if you do."

"I can sleep on a chair in this room," I replied.

"No, no. A stranger is a stranger, be he rich or poor—it will not suit me to permit any one the range of the place while I am off guard!" said the unmannerly wretch.

With this insult, my patience was at an end. I uttered an expression of disgust, and pushed past him into the yard, running against Earnshaw in my haste. It was so dark that I could not see the means of exit, and, as I wandered round, I heard another specimen of their civil behaviour amongst each other.

At first, the young man appeared about to befriend me.

"I'll go with him as far as the park," he said.

"You'll go with him to hell!" exclaimed his master, or whatever relation he bore. "And who is to look after the horses, eh?"

"A man's life is of more consequence than one evening's neglect of the horses; somebody must go," murmured Mrs. Heathcliff, more kindly than I expected.

"Not at your command!" retorted Hareton. "If you set store on him, you'd better be quiet."

"Then I hope his ghost will haunt you; and I hope Mr. Heathcliff will never get another tenant, till the Grange is a ruin!" she answered sharply.

"Hearken, hearken, shoo's cursing on 'em!" muttered Joseph, towards whom I had been steering.

He sat within earshot, milking the cows by the light of a lantern, which I seized unceremoniously, and, calling out that I would send it back on the morrow, rushed to the nearest postern.

"Maister, maister, he's staling t' lantern!" shouted the ancient, pursuing my retreat. "Hey, Gnasher! Hey, dog! Hey, Wolf, holld him, holld him!"

On opening the little door, two hairy monsters flew at my throat, bearing me down and extinguishing the light, while a mingled guffaw, from Heathcliff and Hareton, put the copestone on my rage and humiliation.

Fortunately, the beasts seemed more bent on stretching their paws, and yawning, and flourishing their tails, than devouring me alive; but, they would suffer no resurrection, and I was forced to lie till their malignant masters pleased to deliver me: then hatless, and trembling with wrath, I ordered the miscreants to let me out—on their peril to keep me one minute longer—with several incoherent threats of retaliation that, in their indefinite depth of virulency, smacked of King Lear.

The vehemence of my agitation brought on a copious bleeding at the nose, and still Heathcliff laughed, and still I scolded. I don't know what would have concluded the scene had there not been one person at hand rather more rational than myself, and more benevolent than my entertainer. This was Zillah, the stout housewife; who at length issued forth to inquire into the nature of the uproar. She thought that some of them had been laying violent hands on me and, not daring to attack her master, she turned her vocal artillery against the younger scoundrel.

"Well, Mr. Earnshaw," she cried, "I wonder what you'll have agait next! Are we going to murder folk on our very door-stones? I see this house will never do for me—look at t' poor lad, he's fair choking! Wisht, wisht! you mun'n't go on so—come in, and I'll cure that. There now, hold ye still."

With these words she suddenly splashed a pint of icy water down my neck, and pulled me into the kitchen. Mr. Heathcliff followed, his accidental merriment expiring quickly in his habitual moroseness.

I was sick exceedingly, and dizzy and faint; and thus compelled, perforce, to accept lodgings under his roof. He told Zillah to give me a glass of brandy, and then passed on to the inner room, while she condoled with me on my sorry predicament, and having obeyed his orders, whereby I was somewhat revived, ushered me to bed.

•

"Well, if I cannot keep Heathcliff for my friend—if Edgar will be mean and jealous, I'll try to break their hearts by breaking my own. That will be a prompt way of finishing all, when I am pushed to extremity! But it's a deed to be reserved for a forlorn hope—I'd not take Linton by surprise with it. To this point he has been discreet in dreading to provoke me; you must represent the peril of quitting that policy; and remind him of my passionate temper verging, when kindled, on frenzy. I wish you could dismiss that apathy out of your countenance, and look rather more anxious about me!"

•

"Neither, replied I; "if you mean Mr. Linton. He's tolerably well, I think, though his studies occupy him rather more than they ought; he is continually among his books, since he has no other society."

"Among his books!" she cried, confounded. "And I dying! I on the brink of the grave! My God! does he know how I'm altered?" continued she, staring at her reflection in a mirror hanging against the opposite wall. "Is that Catherine Linton? He imagines me in a pet—in play, perhaps. Cannot you inform him that it is frightful earnest? Nelly, if it be not too late, as soon as I learn how he feels, I'll choose between these two—either to starve at once, that would be no punishment unless he had a heart—or to recover and leave the country."

•

I could not bear the employment. I took my dingy volume by the scroop, and hurled it into the dog-kennel, vowing I hated a good book.
Healthcliff kicked his to the same place.
Then there was a hubbub!
"Maister Hindley!" shouted our chaplain. "Maister, coom hither! Miss Cathy's riven th' back off 'Th' Helmet uh Salvation,' un' Heathcliff's pawsed his fit intuh t' first part uh 'T' Broad Way to Destruction'! It's fair flaysome ut yah, let 'em goa on this gait. Ech! th' owd man ud uh laced 'em properly—bud he's goan!"

•

Her spirits were always at high-water mark, her tongue always going—singing, laughing, and plaguing everybody who would not do the same. A wild, wicked slip she was—but she had the bonniest eye, and sweetest smile, and lightest foot in the parish; and, after all, I believe she meant no harm.

•

That made her cry, at first; and then, being repulsed continually hardened her, and she laughed if I told her to say she was sorry for her faults, and beg to be forgiven.

•

"Why canst thou not always be a good lass, Cathy?"
And she turned her face up to his, and laughed, and answered—"Why cannot you always be a good man, father?"

•

But it was one of their chief amusements to run away to the moors in the morning and remain there all day, and the after punishment grew a mere thing to laugh at.

•

"I wish I were a girl again, half savage and hardy, and free . . . and laughing at injuries, not maddening under them!"

Gwendolyn Brooks (1917-   )

❧ ❧

White Girls Are Peculiar People

White girls are peculiar people.
They cannot keep their hands out of their hair.
Also
they are always shaking it away from their eyes
when it is not in their eyes.
Sometimes when it is braided they forget—
and shake and shake
and smooth what is nothing
away from their shameless eyes.

I laugh.

My hair is short.
It is close to my head.
It is almost a crown of dots.
My head is clean and free.
I do not shake my head to make
my brains like a crazy dust.

•

On Marriage

They ate, drank, and read together. She read *Of Human Bondage*. He read *Sex in the Married Life*. They were silent.

Helen Gurley Brown (1922–)

~ ~

FROM *Sex and the Single Girl*

There is a catch to achieving single bliss. You have to work like a son of a bitch.

•

Even if enlightened parents answer this little girl's questions in a direct, factual way (I know one fortunate little boy whose parents told him the facts of life so satisfactorily, he said in the next breath, "Now tell me how they make peanut butter"), she will still learn to equate sex with dirtiness from her playmates, her playmates' parents, her teachers and other benighted adults.

Rita Mae Brown (1944–)

~ ~

A Note

If you don't like my book, write your own. If you don't think you can write a novel, that ought to tell you something. If you think you can, do. No excuses. If you still don't like my novels, find a book you do like. Life is too short to be miserable. If you like my novels, I commend your good taste.

•

FROM *Rubyfruit Jungle*

Carrie, Carrie, whose politics are to the right of Genghis Khan. Who believes that if the good Lord wanted us to live together he'd have made us all one color. Who believes a woman is only as good as the man she's with. And I love her. Even when I hated her, I loved her. Maybe all kids love their mothers, and she's the only mother I've ever known. Or maybe underneath her crabshell of prejudice and fear there's a human being that's loving. I don't know but either way I love her.

•

. . . I don't feel like having to fight until I'm fifty. But if it does take that long then watch out world because I'm going to be the hottest fifty-year-old this side of the Mississippi.

•

I'd never seen men hold each other. I thought the only thing they were allowed to do was shake hands or fight.

•

They [boyfriends] were a convenience, something you had to wear when you went to school functions, like a bra.

•

FROM *Six of One*

Celeste looked at Fannie, "When it comes to sex, women don't have the sense God gave a goose."

"We make out all right."

"We are the exceptions that prove the rule," Celeste dealt another hand.

"Well, I never was one of those creatures who thought the road to higher truth lay through my vagina."

"Hear, Hear."

"Do you know what always irritated me the most about Sigourny?"

"What?" Celeste asked.

"She's always crowing about being a self-made woman."

"It's big of her to take the blame. Sigourny Romaine is an aesthetic prophylactic."

•

Strange, it's all so strange. I don't feel guilty. I don't feel I've betrayed her. I feel it's the most natural thing in the world to love you. Loving you makes me love her more and loving her makes me love you. Do you think it's possible that love multiplies? We're taught to think it divides. There's only so much to go around, like diamonds. It multiplies.

•

> *"Life is a carnival,*
> *Believe it or not.*
> *Life is a carnival,*
> *Two bets and a shot."*

Elizabeth Barrett Browning (1806-1861)

~❧ ❧~

A Man's Requirements

I

Love me, Sweet, with all thou art,
   Feeling, thinking, seeing;
Love me in the lightest part,
   Love me in full being.

II

Love me with thine open youth
   In its frank surrender;
With the vowing of thy mouth.
   With its silence tender.

III

Love me with thine azure eyes,
   Made for earnest granting;
Taking color from the skies,
   Can Heaven's truth be wanting?

IV

Love me with their lids, that fall
   Snow-like at first meeting;
Love me with thine heart, that all
   Neighbors then see beating.

V

Love me with thine hand stretched out
    Freely—open-minded:
Love me with thy loitering foot,—
    Hearing one behind it.

VI

Love me with thy voice, that turns
    Sudden faint above me;
Love me with thy blush that burns
    When I murmur *Love me!*

VII

Love me with thy thinking soul,
    Break it to love-sighing;
Love me with thy thoughts that roll
    On through living—dying.

VIII

Love me in thy gorgeous airs,
    When the world has crowned thee;
Love me, kneeling at thy prayers,
    With the angels round thee.

IX

Love me pure, as musers do,
    Up the woodlands shady:
Love me gaily, fast and true,
    As a winsome lady.

X

Through all hopes that keep us brave,
    Farther off or nigher,
Love me for the house and grave,
    And for something higher.

XI
Thus, if thou wilt prove me, Dear,
Woman's love no fable,
I will love *thee*—half a year—
As a man is able.

Frances (Fanny) Burney 1752–1840)

~❧ ❧~

FROM *A Letter to Her Sister Esther*

Directions for coughing, sneezing, or moving, before the King and Queen:

In the first place you must not cough. If you find a cough tickling in your throat, you must arrest it from making any sound; if you find yourself choking with the forbearance, you must choke—but not cough. In the second place, you must not sneeze. If you have a vehement cold, you must take no notice of it; if your nose membranes feel a great irritation, you must hold your breath; if a sneeze still insists upon making its way, you must oppress it, by keeping your teeth grinding together; if the violence of the repulse breaks some blood-vessel, you must break the blood vessel—but not sneeze.

Brett Butler (contemporary)

~❧ ❧~

One-liner

In response to Pat Buchanan's speech at the 1992 Republican national convention, where women's reproductive rights were considered the handmaidens of witchcraft, Brett Butler suggested that we could not condemn Buchanan's speech "because, after all, it was much better in the original German."

Liz Carpenter (1920-   )

❧ ❧

One-liner

When Arthur Schlesinger, Jr., stopped Carpenter to make the following comment, "I liked your book, Liz. Who wrote it for you?" she replied brightly, "I'm glad you like it, Arthur. Who read it to you?"

Rosario Castellanos (1925-1974)

❧ ❧

FROM *Learning About Things*

They taught me things all wrong,
the ones who teach things:
my parents, the teacher, the priest.
You have to be a good girl, they told me.

It's enough to be good. Because the good person
gets a piece of candy, a medal, all the love, and heaven, too.

And it's very easy to be good. All you have to do is lower
your eyelids
in order not to see or judge what others do
because it does not pertain to you.

You just don't have to open your mouth not to protest
when someone shoves you because they didn't
mean to hurt you or
they couldn't help it or
because God is testing the mettle of your soul.

But, anyhow, when something bad does happen to you
you must accept it, even be grateful for it

but not return it. And don't ask why.
Because good people
are not curious.

And you have to give. If you own a cape, cut it in two
and give one-half to someone else
—even though that someone else may very well be
a collector of other halves of capes.
That's his business and your right hand must ignore
what your left hand . . . etc., etc.

And you must turn both cheeks. Ah, yes.

They won't always be blows.

It may be a bouquet of flowers that gives you
hay fever. Or the seafood that gives
you an allergy.
Sometimes praise,
which if not false cuts to the quick
and if it is false offends. Forgive,
because that is what good people do.

So I obeyed. For it is known that
obedience is the greatest virtue.

So the years went by
And I was that stumbling block
the absent-minded tripped over or, better yet,
a punching bag
the strong tried out their skill on.

Sometimes at cards I would deal a royal flush
but this cleverness rained indifferently
upon my friends
and my friends' friends,
I mean, my enemies.

So then I sat down to wait for the medal,
the piece of candy, and the smile, in short,
the prize in this world.

But all I saw was scorn for my own weakness,
hate for having been the tool
of others' malice.

Since when did I have the right to want to canonize
myself using others' vices or defects?
Why was I electing myself
the only chosen one?
Why was I that grain of sand in the works
that paralyzes every function?
Paralyzed, the doers were thinking.
And I was the efficient cause of their thoughts.
So for me there was only contempt.

Until I finally understood. So I made myself
into a well-oiled cog with which the machine
now turns perfectly.

A cog. I don't have
any specific name or any attribute
according to which I can classify myself
as any better or any worse or even more or less useful
than any of the other cogs.

If I should have to come up with a justification
for someone (and there isn't anyone—there never was any
witness for what happens)
I would say that I was in my place,
that I spun in the right direction at
the required speed and the required frequency.
That I never tried to get them to replace me
ahead of time or to allow me to continue once
I had been declared useless.

Before I finish I want to make it perfectly clear
that I did none of these things
out of humility. Since when are cogs humble?
Ridiculous! And that certainly
my behavior cannot be attributed to hope.

No, for a long time now heaven is a factor
that doesn't figure in my calculations.

Conformity? Perhaps. Which, in a cog, like me,
is not in any way a merit
but rather, at best, a condition.

M.A.
En la tierra de en medio, in *Poesía no eres tú* (1972)

•

FROM *If Not Poetry, Then What?*

We have to laugh. Because laughter, we already know, is the first evidence of freedom.

•

FROM *Woman and Her Image*

Thus, throughout the centuries, woman has been raised to the altar of the gods and has breathed the incense of the faithful. That is, when she is not locked up in a gymnasium or a harem to share the yoke of slavery with her own kind; when she is not confined to the courtyards of the unclean, when she is not branded with the mark of the prostitute; crushed by the servant's burden; expelled from the religious congregation, the political arena, or the university classroom.

•

The antithesis of Pygmalion, man does not aspire, by means of beauty, to convert a statue into a living being, but rather a living being into a statue.

•

FROM *Cooking Lesson*

The kitchen is shining white. It's a shame to have to get it dirty. One ought to sit down and contemplate it, describe it, close one's eyes, evoke it. . . . My place is here. I've been here from the beginning of time. In the German proverb woman is synonymous with *Küche, Kinder, Kirche.* I wandered astray through classrooms, streets, offices, cafés, wasting my time on skills that now I must forget in order to acquire others. For example, choosing the menu. How could one carry out such an arduous task without the cooperation of society—of all history? On a special shelf, just right for my height, my guardian spirits are lined up, those acclaimed jugglers that reconcile the most irreducible contradictions among the pages of their recipe books: slimness and gluttony, pleasing appearance and economy, speed and succulence. With their infinite combinations: slimness and economy, speed and pleasing appearance, succulence and . . . What can you suggest to me for today's meal, O experienced housewife, inspiration of mothers here and gone, voice of tradition, clamoring secret of the supermarkets? I open a book at random and read: "Don Quijote's Dinner." Very literary but not very satisfying, because Don Quijote was not famous as a gourmet but as a bumbler. Although a more profound analysis of the text reveals etc., etc., etc.

Charlotte Charke (1713–c. 1760)

~❦ ❧~

FROM *A Narrative of the Life of Mrs. Charlotte Charke*

THE AUTHOR TO HERSELF

MADAM,

Tho' Flattery is universally known to be the Spring from which Dedication frequently flow, I hope I shall escape that Odium so justly thrown on poetical Petitioners, notwithstanding my Attempt to illustrate those wonderful Qualifications by which you have so eminently distinguish'd Yourself, and gives you a just Claim to the Title of a Nonpareil of the Age.

That thoughtless Ease (so peculiar to yourself) with which you have run thro' many strange and unaccountable Vicissitudes of Fortune, is an undeniable Proof of the native indolent Sweetness of your Temper. With what Fortitude of Mind have you vanquished Sorrow, with the fond Imagination and promissary Hopes (only from Yourself) of a Succession of Happiness, neither within your Power or View?

Your exquisite Taste in Building must not be omitted: The magnificent airy Castles, for which you daily drew out Plans without Foundation, must, could they have been distinguishable to Sight, long ere this have darken'd all the lower World; nor can you be match'd, in Oddity of Fame, by any but that celebrated Knight-Errant of the Moon, G——E A————R ST——S; whose Memoirs, and yours conjoin'd, would make *great Figures in History,* and might justly claim a Right to be transmitted to Posterity; as you are, without Exception, two of *the greatest Curiosities* that ever were the Incentives to the most *profound Astonishment.*

My Choice of you, Madam, to patronize my Works, is an evidential Proof that I am not disinterested in that Point; as the World will easily be convinc'd, from your natural Partiality to all I have hitherto produc'd, that you will tenderly overlook *their Errors,* and, to the utmost of your Power, endeavour *to magnify their Merits.* If, by your Approbation, the World may be perswaded into a tolerable Opinion of my Labours, I shall, for the Novelty-sake, venture for once to call you, friend; a Name, I own, I never *as yet have known you by.*

I hope, dear Madam, as Manly says in *The Provok'd Husband,* that "Last Reproach has struck You," and that you and I may ripen our Acquaintance into a perfect Knowledge of each other, that may establish a lasting and social Friendship between us.

Your two Friends, Prudence and Reflection, I am inform'd, have lately ventur'd to pay you a Visit; for which I heartily congratulate you, as nothing can possibly be more joyous to the Heart than the Return of absent Friends, after a long and painful Peregrination.

Permit me, Madam, to subscribe myself for the future, what I ought to have been some Years ago,

> *Your real Friend,*
> *And humble Servant,*
> Charlotte Charke.

A NARRATIVE OF THE LIFE OF MRS. CHARLOTTE CHARKE

As the following History is the Product of a Female Pen, I tremble for the terrible Hazard it must run in venturing into the World, as it may very possibly suffer, in many Opinions, without perusing it; I therefore humbly move for its having the common Chance of a Criminal, at least to be properly examin'd, before it so condemn'd . . .

As I have instanc'd, that my Education was not only a genteel, but in Fact a liberal one, and such indeed as might have been sufficient for a Son instead of a Daughter; I must beg Leave to add, that I was never made much acquainted with that necessary Utensil which forms the housewifely Part of a young Lady's Education, call'd a Needle; which I handle with the same clumsey Awkwardness a Monkey does a Kitten, and am equally capable of using the one, as Pug is of nursing the other.

As I have promised to conceal nothing that might raise a Laugh, I shall begin with a small Specimen of my former Madness, when I was but four Years of Age. Having, even then, a passionate Fondness for a Perriwig, I crawl'd out of Bed one Summer's Morning at *Twickenham,* where my Father had Part of a House and Gardens for the Season, and, taking it into my small Pate, that by Dint of a Wig and a Waistcoat, I should be the perfect Representative of my Sire, I crept softly into the Servants-Hall, where I had the Night before espied all Things in Order, to perpetrate the happy Design I had framed for the next Morning's Expedition. Accordingly I paddled down Stairs, taking with me my Shoes, Stockings, and little Dimity Coat; which I artfully contrived to pin up, as well as I could, to supply the Want of a Pair of Breeches. By the Help of a long Broom, I took down a Waistcoat of my Brother's, and an enormous bushy Tie-wig of my Father's, which entirely enclos'd my Head and Body, with the Knots of the Ties thumping my little Heels as I marched along, with flow and solemn Pace. The Covert of Hair in which I was concealed, with the Weight of a monstrous Belt and large Silver-hilted Sword, that I could scarce drag along, was a vast Impediment in my Procession: And, what still added to the other Inconveniences I laboured under, was whelming myself under one of my Father's large Beaver-hats, laden with Lace, as thick and broad as a Brickbat.

Being thus accoutred, I began to consider that 'twould be impossible for me to pass for Mr. *Cibber* in Girl's Shoes, therefore took an Opportunity to flip out of Doors after the Gardener, who went to his Work, and roll'd myself into a dry Ditch, which was as deep as I was high; and, in this Grotesque Pigmy-State, walked up and down the Ditch bowing to all who came by me. But, behold, the Oddity of my Appearance soon assembled a Croud about me; which yielded me no small Joy, as I conceived their Risibility on this Occasion to be Marks of Approbation, and walked myself into a Fever, in the happy Thought of being taken for the 'Squire.

Ilka Chase (1903–1978)

~≫ ⋙~

One-liner

Ilka Chase had been married to Louis Calhern, who divorced her in order to marry Julia Hoyt. Sorting through her possessions shortly after the unhappy episode she found some visiting cards she had had printed for herself with the name Mrs. Louis Calhern. Generously, and bearing in mind her own experience, she sent them on to the new Mrs. Louis Calhern with a short note: "Dear Julia, I hope these reach you in time."

Roz Chast (1954-)

FROM *The Four Elements*

FROM *Parallel Universes*

COLLECTOR'S ITEMS

Barbie Real ~
Teenage doll comes
complete with acne,
weight problem, and
tacky wardrobe.

Phobic Barbie ~
The doll that never
leaves her
packing case.

Conceptual Barbie ~
A small book of essays
by various people on
the idea of Barbie.

FROM *Unscientific Americans*

CINDERELLA ~
WHERE ARE THEY NOW?

Cinderella ~

Divorced Prince,
married Count Von Helsinki.
Lives in Geneva, Switzerland.

Prince ~

After divorce, lost
much of fortune in
Monte Carlo, but made
gains through development
of own line of perfume.

Stepmother ~

After truce with
Cinderella, opened
chain of family restaurants
in Florida.

Two Stepsisters ~

Both live within 5 miles of
each other, with their families,
in trailer parks somewhere
on the outskirts of Los Angeles.

The Fairy Godmother ~

Went back to the land,
1971.

FROM *Proof of Life on Earth*

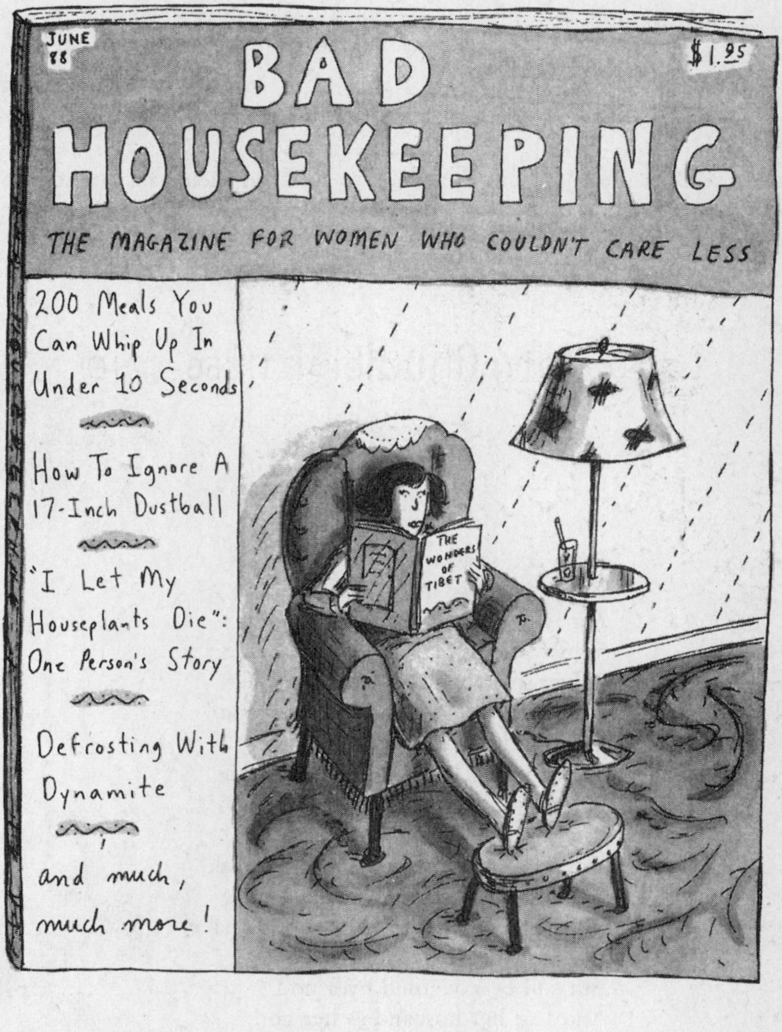

Margaret Cho (contemporary)

One-liner

Men look at me and think I'm going to walk on their backs or something. I tell them, "The only time I'll walk on your back is if there's something on the other side of you that I want."

Lady Mary Chudleigh (1656–1710)

To the Ladies

Wife and servant are the same,
But only differ in the name:
For when that fatal knot is tied,
Which nothing, nothing can divide,
When she the word *Obey* has said,
And man by law supreme has made,
Then all that's kind is laid aside,
And nothing left but state and pride.
Fierce as an eastern prince he grows,
And all his innate rigour shows:
Then but to look, to laugh, or speak,
Will the nuptial contract break.
Like mutes, she signs alone must make,
And never any freedom take,
But still be governed by a nod,
And fear her husband as her god:
Him still must serve, him still obey,
And nothing act, and nothing say,
But what her haughty lord thinks fit,
Who, with the power, has all the wit.

Then shun, oh! shun that wretched state,
And all the fawning flatterers hate.
Value yourselves, and men despise:
You must be proud, if you'll be wise.

Caryl Churchill (1938-   )

FROM *Top Girls*

The first half of my life was all sin and the second / all repentance.

Ina Claire (1895-1985)

One-liner

Ina Claire was a well-known stage actress who successfully made a break into the early "talkies" of Hollywood. For a brief three years she was married to John Gilbert, idol of the silent movies. One day a movie magazine reporter asked her how it felt to be married to a celebrity. "You'd better ask my husband," was Miss Claire's reply.

Ellen Cleghorn (contemporary)

One-liner

When this judge let a rapist go because the woman had been wearing a miniskirt and so was "asking for it" I thought, ladies, what we all should

do is this: next time we see an ugly guy on the street, shoot him. After
all, he knew he was ugly when he left the house. He was asking for it.

Lucille Clifton (1936-   )

~e e~

homage to my hair

when i feel her jump up and dance
i hear the music! my God
i'm talking about my nappy hair!
she is a challenge to your hand
black man,
she is as tasty on your tongue as good greens
black man,
she can touch your mind
with her electric fingers and
the grayer she do get, good God,
the blacker she do be!

•

aunt agnes hatcher tells (about my daddy)

your daddy, he decided to spread the wealth
as they say, and made another daughter.
just before the war she come calling
looking like his natural blood.
your mama surprised us and opened her heart.
none of his other tricks worked that good.

Kate Clinton (contemporary)

~⋖&⋗~

FROM *Making Light: Some Notes
on Feminist Humor*

Consider feminist humor and consider the lichen. Growing low and lowly on enormous rocks, secreting tiny amounts of acid, year after year, eating into the rock. Making places for water to gather, to freeze and crack the rock a bit. Making soil, making way for grasses to grow. Making way for rosehips and sea oats, for aspen and cedar. It is the lichen which begins the splitting apart of the rocks, the changing of the shoreline, the shape of the earth. Feminist humor is serious, and it is about the changing of this world.

•

Masculine humor is deflective. It allows denial of responsibility, the oh-I-was-just-kidding disclaimer. It is escapist, something to gloss over and get through the hard times, without ever having to do any of the hard work of change. Masculine humor is essentially not about change. It is about the maintenance of the status quo. There is nothing new under the sons: they are always dead serious.

•

Humor leads the way; it moves us past those inbred, ingrained resistances. We make light. We see where to go and we are light enough to move there. In a male culture which places all emphasis on the serious, we women sometimes feel we need to outserious the man. Not often enough then, in the midst of excruciating conversations, do I have the good sense to remember that the whole point of our talking is that we are both working to make room for more joy in our lives.

Jane Collier (1710–1755)

~❧ ❧~

FROM *An Essay on the Art of Tormenting*

Suppose your stock of children too large; and that, by your care for their support, you should be abridged of some of your own luxuries and pleasures. To make away with the troublesome and expensive brats, I allow, would be the desirable thing: but the question is, how to effect this without subjecting yourself to that punishment which the law has thought proper to affix to such sort of jokes. Whipping and starving, with some caution, might do the business: but, since a late execution for a fact of that kind may have given a precedent for the magistrates to examine into such affairs, you may, by these means, find your way to the gallows, if you are low enough for such a scrutiny into your conduct: and, if you are too high to have your actions punished, you may possibly be a little ill spoken of amongst your acquaintance. I think, therefore, it is best not to venture, either your neck, or your reputation, by such a proceeding; especially as you may effect the thing, full as well, by following the directions I have given, of holding no restraint over them.

Suffer them to climb, without contradiction, to heights from whence they may break their necks: let them eat every thing they like, and at all times; not refusing them the richest meats, and highest sauces, with as great a variety as possible; because even excess in one dish of plain meat cannot, as I have been told by physicians, do much harm. Suffer them to sit up as late as they please at night, and make hearty meat-suppers; and even in the middle of the night, if they call for it, don't refuse the poor things some victuals. By this means, nobody can say you starve your children: and if they should chance to die of a surfeit, or of an ill habit of body, contracted from such diet, so far will you be from censure, that your name will be recorded for a kind and indulgent parent. If any impertinent person should hint to you, that this manner of feeding your children was the high road to destruction, you may answer, "That the poor people suffer their children to eat and drink what they please, not feeding them upon bread-pudden, milk and water,

and such stuff, as the physicians advise; and (you may say) where do you
see anything more healthful, than the children of the poor?"

Patricia Collinge (1894-?)

~≪ ℀~

Sickroom Visitors

I love visitors, especially the cheery ones. They just don't believe there
is anything the matter with you at all, they think you are just fooling
everyone—you little rascal! They never saw you look better in your life.
My, they would be sick themselves if they could look like that, and if
that is what hospitals do for you they guess they will go into one and
stay there forever. Which is all right with you.

And I love the doleful ones. They get an awful shock when they
see you, but at that they think you are lucky to have pulled through at
all, because look at what happened to Amy. And, oh yes, they know
you feel pretty good now, but wait till you get up. Which they hope
for your sake will be soon, because they don't know what it is, but there
is something awfully depressing about a hospital. Well, you could give
them an idea.

And then the suspicious ones. They watch every move the nurse
makes. They ask you if you *really* like your doctor, and do you *really*
feel that his treatment is helping you? . . . so few doctors *know*, dear.
They have very little faith in doctors since their own doctor died. And
they can't help wondering if it is really necessary for you to be here at
all; somehow they don't quite *trust* hospitals. For themselves they would
rather be right in their own homes. Which makes it unanimous.

And of course there are the ones who have had it themselves. You
can't tell *them*. Not that you get the chance. They had the most terrible
pain right there . . . they couldn't describe it. But they have an awfully
good try. The way they suffered! They used to scream if anyone so much
as came in the room. And the nights . . . the long sleepless nights! They
always say about sickness that the nights are the worst part. Which is
open to argument.

And, oh dear Heaven, there are the hearty ones. You can hear them
coming up in the elevator, and even if they are visiting at the other end

of the corridor, they might as well be right in your room. The hospital rings with their laughter, and you ought to hear the way they josh the nurse. They are bursting with wisecracks, and they just kid the life out of you. Just about.

And what of the timid ones? They speak in whispers and sit on the edge of the chair. They don't dare to look about them, and they jump at the slightest sound. They are sure that somebody is being tortured somewhere, and they *know* that there are dead bodies in the halls. And they have to leave almost as soon as they come, because the mere odor of a hospital makes them sick. Well, there is good in everything.

But I do love visitors. For aren't there the nice ones? They want to hear all about what is the matter with you, and they bring you the most elegant gossip. They are perfectly sure that one cigarette won't hurt you, and a monument could be erected to them with the simple inscription: "They never sat on the bed."

Certainly I love visitors. They come and they go. Which helps.

Julie Connelly (contemporary)

FROM *The CEO's Second Wife*

First wives invariably think their husbands were lured away by hot tomatoes proficient at the kind of sex formerly banned in most states. One look at those desiccated bodies, the knees and elbows sharp enough to puncture a tire, might suggest that sex is the last thing on men's minds.

Lucha Corpi (1945–)

FROM *Delia's Song*

A frowning Virginia Woolf and a dandy Baudelaire greeted Delia, looked at her literary scapulary and she at theirs. Following the rules of the game, they folded their hands together and bowed their heads. In unison they exclaimed, "Benediction, dear Saint Theresa." Delia wanted to lose herself in the game, forget everything that had happened that evening. She reached for a plastic tumbler, poured herself some wine from a half-empty bottle, drank it in one gulp, then raised her right hand and made the sign of the cross in the air. Baudelaire and Woolf laughed and applauded.

Delia elbowed her way through the dining room where Emily Dickinson was dancing cheek-to-cheek with Edgar Allan Poe. Ezra Pound lectured T.S. Eliot on the evils of anti-semitic attitudes, while Hemingway eyed Delmira Agustini, Fitzgerald admired Sor Juana from afar, and José Montoya, Luis Valdez and Pancho Villa applauded Alurista's ritual sundance.

Mephistopheles and Faust approached her, extending their hands to her as an invitation to dance with them. She joined them, but after a few steps she felt dizzy. She had not eaten anything since lunchtime and the wine was making her feel sick. She reached the hall and went up the short flight of stairs to Mattie's bedroom, hoping to find it empty so she could lie down for a while. Instead, she found Mattie pouring warm water into a footbath for George Sand. Mattie was happy to see Delia and signaled her to come in. George was obviously in pain.

"Joyce bumped the table and that heavy bust of Beethoven fell on her foot." Mattie winked at Delia.

"Is there anything I can do?" Delia asked solicitously. She welcomed the idea of nursing George's foot and not going out of the bedroom for a while. She moved toward the bed but stopped suddenly. "Who did you say knocked over the bust?"

"James Joyce—"

Elena Tajena Creef (contemporary)

～❦ ❧～

FROM *Notes from a Fragmented Daughter*

"Clara speaks in tongues at the Ladies Prayer Meetings and has seen angels in the sky through her Kodak Instamatic. She turns to me and shouts in a thick New York accent, 'So what are you studying?' I say,

'English.' She says, 'Gee your English is very good. How long have you been in this country?' I say, 'All of my life.' She shouts, 'Are you Chinese?' I say, 'Japanese.' She says, 'I admire your people very much!' I smile and say, 'Yes and we are very good with our hands, too.' "

Amanda Cross
(Carolyn G. Heilbrun) (1926–   )

FROM *Death in a Tenured Position*

Professors of literature collect books the way a ship collects barnacles, without seeming effort. A literary academic can no more pass a bookstore than an alcoholic can pass a bar.

Ellen Currie (contemporary)

FROM *Available Light*

I like men, God help me. Not that I'm a siren on a rock, I just like them, the way some women like cats and some others hate spiders. I tried to explain all this to Eileen, but she tends to go a bit dim on you in areas. Sex, to Eileen, is basically what you do to avoid an argument.

"You'll bring trouble down on us," my mother used to say. "You're just inviting trouble. Don't start trouble. Don't make trouble. You're far more trouble than you're worth. You'll cause trouble." It was because I talked too much. I talked to divert them. I babbled all the time to distract them. Asked questions, offered observations. I was desperate to stop them fighting. I said wrong things, I filled in all the silences, talked up, talked back. Eileen was different. She went off inside herself.

She was disdainful. I was more horrified. She was more ashamed. "After all," my mother used to say, "he is your father."

Mary Daly (1928-   )

FROM *Gyn/Ecology*

Why has it seemed "appropriate" in this culture that the plot of a popular book and film (*The Exorcist*) centers around a Jesuit who "exorcises" a girl who is "possessed"? Why is there no book or film about a woman who exorcises a Jesuit?

Another example is the term *glamour,* whose first definition as given in Merriam-Webster is "a magic spell." Originally it was believed that witches possessed the power of glamour, and according to the authors of the *Malleus Maleficarum*, witches by their glamour could cause the male "member" to disappear.

Thus, the Latin term *texere,* meaning to weave, is the origin and root both for *textile* and for *text*. It is important for women to note the irony in this split of meanings.

Women's minds have been mutilated and muted to such a state that "Free Spirit" has been branded into them as a brand name for girdles and bras.

Moronized, women believe that male-written texts (bibical, literary, medical, legal, scientific) are "true."

Breaking through the foreground which is the Playboys' Playground means letting out the bunnies, the bitches, the beavers, the squirrels, the chicks, the pussycats, the cows, the nags, the foxy ladies, the old bats and biddies, so that they can at last begin naming themselves.

Amazon expeditions into the male-controlled "fields" are necessary in order to leave the fathers' caves and live in the sun. A crucial problem for us has been to learn how to re-possess righteously while avoiding being caught too long in the caves. In universities, and in all of the professions, the omnipresent poisonous gases gradually stifle women's minds and spirits. Those who carry out the necessary expeditions run the risk of shrinking into the mold of the mystified Athena, the twice-born, who forgets and denies her Mother and Sisters, because she has forgotten her original Self. "Re-born" from Zeus, she becomes Daddy's Girl, the mutant who serves the master's purposes. The token woman, who in reality is enchained, possessed, "knows" that she is free. She is a useful tool of the patriarchs, particularly against her sister Artemis, who knows better, respects her Self, bonds with her Sisters, and refuses to sell her freedom, her original birthright, for a mess of respectability.

A-mazing Amazons must be aware of the male methods of mystification. Elsewhere I have discussed four methods which are essential to the games of the fathers. First, there is *erasure* of women. (The massacre of millions of women as witches is erased in patriarchal scholarship.) Second, there is *reversal*. (Adam gives birth to Eve, Zeus to Athena, in patriarchal myth.) Third, there is *false polarization*. (Male-defined "feminism" is set up against male-defined "sexism" in the patriarchal media.) Fourth, there is *divide and conquer*. (Token women are trained to kill off feminists in patriarchal professions.)

•

Webster's defines *titter* as follows: "to give vent to laughter one is seeking to suppress; laugh lightly or in a subdued manner; laugh in a *nervous, affected, or restrained* manner, especially at a high pitch and with short catches of the voice [emphasis mine]." Self-loathing ladies titter; Hags and Harpies roar. Fembots titter at themselves when Daddy turns the switch. They totter when he pulls the string. They titter especially at the spinning of Spinsters, whom they have been trained to see as dizzy dames. Daddy's little Titterers try to intimidate women struggling for greatness. This is what they are made for and paid for. There is only one taboo for titterers: they must never laugh seriously at Father—only at his jokes.

There is nothing like the sound of women really laughing. The roaring laughter of women is like the roaring of the eternal sea. Hags can cackle and roar at themselves, but more and more, one hears them roaring at the reversal that is patriarchy, that monstrous jock's joke, the Male Mothers Club that gives birth only to putrefaction and deception. One can hear pain and perhaps cynicism in the laughter of Hags who witness the spectacle of Male Mothers (Murderers) dismembering a planet they have already condemned to death. But this laughter is the one true hope, for as long as it is audible there is evidence that someone is seeing through the Dirty Joke. It is in this hope that this Hag-ography is written.

•

For example, the cliché, "She lacks a sense of humor"—applied by men to every threatening woman—is one basic "electrode" embedded just deeply enough into the fearful foreground of women's psyches to be able to conduct female energy against the Self while remaining disguised. The comment is urbane, insidious. It is boring and predictable if seen through, devastating if believed. The problem is that the victim who "sees through" this dirty trick on one level may "believe" the judgment literally on more vulnerable levels. It is perfectly consistent with patriarchal patterns that this device is used especially against the wittiest women, who are dismissed as "sharp-tongued." The Godfather is the Father of Lies and favors the most blatant lies.

•

Overcoming the silencing of women is an extreme act, a sequence of extreme acts. Breaking our silence means living in existential courage. It means dis-covering our deep sources, our spring. It means finding our native resiliency, springing into life, speech, action.

Josephine Daskam (1876-1961)

~ゆ ゆ~

FROM *The Woman Who Caught the Idea*

There was once a Woman whose Fiancé had a Decided Theory regarding the most Desirable Characteristics of the Sexes. This Theory, in a Word, was that a Woman should be Like a Clinging Vine, while a Man should Resemble a Sturdy Oak. For Many Years, therefore, the Woman had Practiced Clinging with Great Success. One day, However, her Fiancé grew Critical of her Method . . .

So they Broke off the Engagement. The Fiancé found a Progressive and Stimulating Woman who Agreed to Criticize him and March Abreast of him. The only Trouble with this was that Not Only did she March Abreast, but it Seemed Probable that she would Get Ahead. Also she had a Work of Her Own, which sometimes Interfered with His. . . .

So he Returned to his Old Love and said, "Let All Be as it was Before."

"I am Afraid that can Not be," she replied, Sadly. "Since I Lost You I have Given Up Clinging, and I have Caught Your Idea. I had to Sympathize with Someone, so I have Taken Up a Work of My Own. Judging from your Tone I think you Would Fail to Comprehend it. The Century is Progressing and Things can Never Be as they Were Before."

This teaches us that It's Well to Be On with the Old Love Before you are Off with the New.

Emily Dickinson (1830–1886)

Witchcraft was hung, in History,
But History and I
Find all the Witchcraft that we need
Around us, every Day—
.

The Riddle we can guess
We speedily despise—
Not anything is stale so long
As Yesterday's surprise—
.

Forever is composed of Nows—
.

The butterfly obtains
But little sympathy,
Though favorably mentioned
In Entomology.
Because he travels freely
And wears a proper coat,
The circumspect are certain
That he is dissolute.
Had he the homely scutcheon of modest Industry,
'Twere fitter certifying for Immortality.
.

I

I fear a man of scanty speech,
I fear a silent man,
Haranguer I can overtake
Or babbler entertain—

But he who waiteth while the rest
Expend their inmost pound,
Of this Man I am wary—
I fear that He is Grand.

II

Publication is the auction
Of the mind of man,
Poverty be justifying
For so foul a thing.

Possibly,—but we would rather
From our garret go
White unto the White Creator,
Than invest our snow.

Thought belongs to Him who gave it—
Then to him who bear
Its corporal illustration.
Sell the Royal air
In the parcel,—be the merchant
Of the Heavenly Grace,
But reduce no human spirit
To disgrace of price!

Annie Dillard (1945-   )

❧ ❧

FROM *An American Childhood*

During a family trip to the Highland Park Zoo, Mother and I were alone for a minute. She approached a young couple holding hands on a bench by the seals, and addressed the young man in dripping tones:

"Where have you been? Still got those baby-blue eyes; always did slay me. And this"—a swift nod at the dumbstruck young woman, who had removed her hand from the man's—"must be the one you were telling me about. She's not so bad, really, as you used to make out. But listen, you know how I miss you, you know where to reach me, same old place. And there's Ann over there—see how she's grown? See the blue eyes?"

And off she sashayed, taking me firmly by the hand, and leading us around briskly past the monkey house and away. She cocked an ear back, and both of us heard the desperate beginning, in a high-pitched wail, "I swear, I never saw her before in my life. . . ."

Phyllis Diller (1917–   )

❧ ❧

FROM *Phyllis Diller's Marriage Manual*

Let me tell you, a discussion that starts, "I'll tell you something you do that irritates me, if you tell me something I do that bothers you," never ends in a hug and a kiss.

•

It might help you to be more satisfied with your mate if you remember that when you made the selection it was not multiple choice. I was sort of tricked into marrying. One night I was out with Fang and a girl said, "You better hang on to him." I thought I had a prize. I didn't know she meant that after one drink he falls down.

•

Fang told me he was a self-made man. It wasn't until later that I discovered that he would have been wise to get some help.

•

If your husband wants to lick the beaters on the mixer, shut them off before you give them to him.

•

FROM *Phyllis Diller's Housekeeping Hints*

I know people who are so clean you can eat off their floors. You can't eat off my table. Fang, my husband, says the only thing domestic about me is that I was born in this country.

•

If somebody—like a husband—tells you to get busy, say, "All right, if you want that bare, clean, sterile look." Often say, "I let my family *live* in our house." Use the words "casual," "comfortable," "informal," a lot. Our house has gone past the "lived in" look. It has more a "no survivors" look.

•

Do not taste food while you're cooking. You may lose your nerve to serve it.

If your cooking is as bad as mine, train your family to eat fast.

Above all, use imagination in your cooking. Imagine it's good.

•

Give a sentimental value to any piece that looks beat-up. Say "We'd get rid of that chair with the springs showing, but I was sitting on it when Ronnie brought home his first report card with a grade above an F." *Never* say, "It's either that or sitting on the floor."

FROM *The Joys of Aging—and how to avoid them*

HOME REMEDIES—"Feed a cold and starve a fever"; "Get plenty of hot water and blankets"; "Wrap a dirty woolen sock around his neck"; "If she has morning sickness, give her Tabasco sauce and slap her with an ear of corn." These are not lines from a Randolph Scott Film Festival, but are actual home remedies and cures for illness. Some make sense, others are pure superstition. My Aunt Becky used to warn me, "Phyllis, if you sleep outside in the back yard, be sure to close the gate or you'll catch a draft." Soon after this my Aunt Becky was placed in a home. Another bit of advice was, "You will avoid respiratory illness if you face the east and sneeze into a shoe." This was from my Uncle Florsheim.

•

The doors are never marked "Men" and "Women." They always have names that take a Berlitz student to decipher. In Mexican restaurants it's

"Caballeros" and "Señoritas." In medieval restaurants, "Lords" and "Wenches." A lamb specialty place had "Rams" and "Ewes." My sister-in-law was stranded for three hours in a fish restaurant trying to figure out whether to go into "Fluke" or "Flounder."

•

If you're going to dress young, you must shop at young stores. After all, you're not going to find cut-off jeans and tube tops at a place called Senile la Mode. Also when shopping large department stores it's psychologically helpful to seek out young "sounding" clothing sections: "Junior World," "The Campus Shop," "Teen Togs." Avoid departments with names like "Ambulatory Fashions," and "One Step Before The Grave Boutique." Above all, avoid any shopping center called the "Menopause Mall."

•

CAN THEY EVER BE TOO YOUNG?

Yes, they can. After all, you don't want to be going through change-of-life the same time your date is going through change-of-voice.

There are some sure-fire ways to tell if your date is too young for you.

- Can he fly for half-fare?
- Are his love letters to you written in Crayola?
- Is his bedroom wallpapered in a clown motif?
- Do his pajamas have feet?
- When you ask him a question, does he raise his hand before answering?

•

When I was a little girl my mother told me, "Phyllis, save it any way you can." Then we started talking about money.

I've always linked sex and finance anyway. I guess it's because my dates have always been Standard and Poor.

•

One-liners

A friend told me the longer you keep Romano cheese, the better it gets.
So, I kept it three years. And this thing turned mean. Now and then
I'd open the refrigerator door and throw it some food. I'd have to walk
it now and then. And then it grew this one leg. And it's got this ugly
fuzz all over it. And the dogs won't run with it.

•

By the time she was eighteen she had sown enough wild oats to make
a grain deal with Russia.

Sarah Dixon (1672–1765)

The Returned Heart

It must be mine! no other heart could prove
Constant so long, yet so ill-used in love.
How bruised and scarified! how deep the wound!
Senseless, of life no symptom to be found!
Can it be this, that left me young and gay?
Just in the gaudy bloom it fled away:
Unhappy rover! what couldst thou pretend?
Where tyrants reign, can innocence defend?
I'll vow thou art so altered, I scarce know
Thou art the thing, which Strephon sighed for so:
Look how it trembles! and fresh drops declare
It is the same, and he the murderer.

    Thus lawless conquerors our town restore,
With the sad marks of their inhuman power;
No art, nor time, such ravage can repair;
No superstructure can these ruins bear.

Margaret Drabble (1939-)

❧ ❧

FROM *The Middle Ground*

. . . Kate realized, more or less overnight, that one of the ways to avoid being a butt or laughingstock yourself is to make people laugh—not as in the pious old cliché "*with* you rather than *at* you"; no they had to laugh at you, but they had to laugh because *you made them,* because you were funny . . . she realised that it was fine to be the centre of attention on one's own terms, and that there was nothing, literally, nothing, that couldn't be turned into a joke. In fact, the more horrible and discreditable the subject matter, the better the joke.

•

FROM *The Garrick Year*

There the picture ended. It would not have done to show the public the crumbs and the chewing.

•

I tried not to side with either of them, I tried to balance myself neatly in the middle, and I thought, as I often used to think, though more rarely these days, of that fable, Aesop's no doubt, in which a boy and his father and a donkey set off on a journey and cannot satisfy any passerby that they are rightly employed. "Oh, the poor child," cries one as the father rides, and "Oh, your poor old father," cries another as the boy rides, and "Oh, the poor donkey," cries a third as they both ride, and "Oh, what fools to walk and to take no advantage of your donkey," cries a fourth as they both dismount, and these are the cries that echo regularly and more or less in sequence in my ears.

•

FROM *The Waterfall*

She was treacherously afraid that he would look a fool, in his goggles and helmet, and she could not bear him to look anything less than perfect, but luckily, when he had them on, he looked all right. She realized that he knew he looked all right in them or he would not have risked putting them on.

•

Had I not expected such events, they would not have occurred: the force of the current admits them, and a shifting of the landscape effects them.

•

If I were drowning I couldn't reach out a hand to save myself, so unwilling am I to set myself up against my fate.

•

Learning was so dangerous: for how could one tell in advance, while still ignorant, whether a thing could ever be unlearned or forgotten, or if, once known and named, it would invalidate by its significance the whole of one's former life, all of those years wiped out, convicted at one blow, retrospectively darkened by one sudden light? It seemed at times too dangerous to find out those most important things, in case, having found them, one should also find that nothing else would do, no other word, no other act. Yet how could one know? Like a nun, she had held on, in wise alarm, to her virginity: through marriage, through children, she had held on to it, motionless, passive, as pure as a nun, because she had always known it would destroy her, such knowledge.

•

Reader, I loved him: as Charlotte Brontë said. Which was Charlotte Brontë's man, the one she created and wept for and longed for, or the poor curate that had her and killed her, her sexual measure, her sexual match?

•

I married Malcolm because I thought he was safe. I thought I was safe with him. I thought that he would be safe with me. In view of the mutual damage that we finally inflicted, this seems a curious basis for choice, but so it was. I thought that our weaknesses and virtues were well matched: and so in a sense they were, alas, on all levels but that most profound one that might have saved us. Malcolm is a guitar player, of the most elevated classical nature; he also sings. He does not descend toward the popular; he is a purist, a musician, and just good enough to be able to afford to be so, even in so competitive a world. Guitarists and garage owners: God knows what defects in me this lunatic selection represents. Where are the proper people, the politicians, the academics, the lawyers, and the company directors? Cast out on the family rubbish heap: gone forever.

•

I blame Campion, I blame the poets, I blame Shakespeare for that farcical moment in *Romeo and Juliet* where he sees her at the dance, from far off, and says, I'll have her, because she is the one that will kill me.

•

I liked having a safe dependable reliable man to go around with and kill time with. I was so much at ease with him; I behaved so well, I was so agreeable and even-tempered that he can't possibly have believed some of the dark and airy hints about my true nature that from time to time I honorably threw about. I misled him, I gave him a false impression of myself, though not of course intentionally: the truth was that when I was with him I felt a different, better, safer person, a person well able to look any shop attendant or bus conductor in the eye. I remember thinking, as the months rolled by into a year, that this calm kind person was surely my real self and that the other person had been a mistake, an adolescent, unhappy mistake, lacking Malcolm, lacking a man. Thus I cast off more than twenty years of experience, thinking I could abandon them and emerge from them as a butterfly emerges from its scrappy dingy inelegant case.

•

I thought then, oddly enough, that I was denying myself tragedy, that I was choosing companionship and safety and dignity, and avoiding thus the bloody black denouement that I had been sure, as a girl, would be mine: the lyric note, I thought I had chosen in Malcolm, not those profound cries that I was later to hear issuing from my own throat in childbirth and abandon. Often, in jumping to avoid our fate, we meet it: as Seneca said. It gets us in the end. What treachery to all that I had been, to think that I could evade it. Needless treachery. We walked to the altar, Malcolm and I, a hopeful couple, waiting for time to unite us, poised delicately together, hand in hand. At the wedding reception Malcolm's father, in a carefully written speech, said that he trusted we would live together in harmony, creating one sweet melody, I the words and he the tune, I the verse and he the musical refrain. It was a lovely image and he worked it out well, hindered only by the fact that it would have been more appropriate to our respective sexes had I been the musical and Malcolm the verbal element. I was moved, I wept.

It is a curious business, marriage. Nobody seems to pay enough attention to its immense significance. Nobody seemed to think that in approaching the altar, garbed in white, I was walking toward unknown disaster of unforeseeable proportions: and so I tried to emulate —I emulated successfully—the world's fine confident unconcern. Such an emulation had paid off so well on so many other alarming occasions (anaesthesia, for instance, or diving off the top diving board, both events which, I was assured, despite a natural reluctant fear, would not harm me) that I was prepared to take the world's calm view of marriage too, distrusting and ignoring the forebodings that even then possessed me: in such a mood, assured that it is a normal event or a commonplace sacrifice, one might well lay one's head upon the block or jump from a high window. Such images are not wholly retrospective.

•

Did I marry because monogamy, cruel though it may be in its initial selection, seemed safer, more honorable, more innocent, than endless choice and endless realignment, in which the victims could merely lose more and more often, and the takers more often, more surely, take all, take each other, take all? Better a bad match and stick to it than to form a part of the endless snatch and grab. Better to be nothing, better to weep by the wall, the twenty-ninth child. Better to lose than to endure the guilt of winning; better to lose than to be a capitalist of the emotions, staring down from one's guilt-constructed office tower at the hurrying throng below.

•

Firstly, and briefly I hope, I don't think I could have slept with James if the house I did it in hadn't been technically mine. I've always worried about women having to commit adultery on their husband's money: It seems hard, to have to betray one's husband twice over, both sexually and financially.

•

There is something so ludicrous about efforts to subdue trivial phobias, unfounded fears: even the most heroic victory on this field has a quality of the pitiable. When we see a woman walk along the street, how do we know she is not some brave agoraphobe, flinching for the brutal sky? Some people are afraid of insects, of water, of green leaves. Of the very air. They fight against unseen impediments to perform the most simple human acts—speaking, hearing, making love. They expose themselves to their own ridicule, in efforts to avoid a stammer or a fit of impotence. And yet we dare to judge each other, we dare to suppose a norm. We continue to live, as though life were a practical possibility, as though we could know something of one another.

•

I would have liked to be one of those women who, fortified by love, could nurse the severed heads of their lovers, but I am afraid of blood and flesh and gaping organs.

•

. . . It was our meeting that was not foreseen: though what lovers had not believed that the whole of time has been watching over their convergence?

•

In the past, in old novels, the price of love was death, a price which virtuous women paid in childbirth, and the wicked, like Nana, with the pox. Nowadays it is paid in thrombosis or neurosis: one can take one's pick.

Lady Dorothea Dubois (1728-1774)

Song

A scholar first my love implored,
And then an empty titled lord;
The pedant talked in lofty strains;
Alas! his lordship wanted brains:
I listened not to one or t' other,
But straight referred them to my mother.

A poet next my love assailed,
A lawyer hoped to have prevailed;
The bard too much approved himself;
The lawyer thirsted after pelf:
I listened not to one or t' other,
But still referred them to my mother.

An officer my heart would storm,
A miser sought me too, in form;
But Mars was over-free and bold;

The miser's heart was in his gold:
I listened not to one or t' other,
Referring still unto my mother.

And after them, some twenty more
Successless were, as those before;
When Damon, lovely Damon came,
Our hearts straight felt a mutual flame:
I vowed I'd have him, and no other,
Without referring to my mother.

Maria Edgeworth (1767-1849)

FROM *Belinda*

"Was not he?—Ho! ho!—He's off then!—Ay, so I prophesied; she's
not the thing for him: he has some strength of mind—some soul—
above vulgar prejudices; so must a woman be to hold him. He was
caught at first by her grace and beauty, and that sort of stuff; but I knew
it could not last—knew she'd dilly dally with Clary, till he would turn
upon his heel and leave her there."

"I fancy that you are entirely mistaken both with respect to Mr.
Hervey and Lady Delacour," Belinda very seriously began to say. But
Mrs. Freke interrupted her, and ran on; "No! no! no! I'm not mistaken;
Clarence has found her out. She's a *very* woman—*that* he could forgive
her, and so could I; but she's a *mere* woman—and that he can't
forgive—no more can I."

There was a kind of drollery about Mrs. Freke, which, with some
people, made the odd things she said pass for wit. Humour she really
possessed; and when she chose it, she could be diverting to those who
like buffoonery in women. She had set her heart upon winning Belinda
over to her party. She began by flattery of her beauty; but as she saw
that this had no effect, she next tried what could be done by insinuating
that she had a high opinion of her understanding, by talking to her as
an esprit fort.

"For my part," said she, "I own I should like a strong devil better
than a weak angel."

"You forget," said Belinda, "that it is not Milton, but Satan, who says,

'Fallen spirit, to be weak is to be miserable.' "

"You read, I see!—I did not know you were a reading girl. So was I once; but I never read now. Books only spoil the originality of genius: very well for those who can't think for themselves—but when one has made up one's opinion, there is no use in reading."

"But to *make* them up," replied Belinda, "may it not be useful?"

"Of no use upon earth to minds of a certain class. You, who can think for yourself, should never read."

"But I read that I may think for myself."

"Only ruin your understanding, trust me. Books are full of trash— nonsense, conversation is worth all the books in the world."

"And is there never any nonsense in conversation?"

"What have you here?" continued Mrs. Freke, who did not choose to attend to this question; exclaiming, as she reviewed each of the books on the table in their turns, in the summary language of presumptuous ignorance, "Smith's Theory of Moral Sentiments—milk and water! Moore's Travels—hasty pudding! La Bruyère—nettle porridge! This is what you were at when I came in, was it not?" said she, taking up a book in which she saw Belinda's mark: "Against Inconsistency in our Expectations. Poor thing! who bored you with this task?"

"Mr. Percival recommended it to me, as one of the best essays in the English language."

"The devil! they seem to have put you in a course of the bitters— a course of the woods might do your business better. Do you ever hunt?—Let me take you out with me some morning—you'd be quite an angel on horseback; or let me drive you out some day in my unicorn."

Belinda declined this invitation, and Mrs. Freke strode away to the window to conceal her mortification, threw up the sash, and called out to her groom, "Walk those horses about, blockhead!"

Mr. Percival and Mr. Vincent at this instant came into the room.

"Hail, fellow! well met!" cried Mrs. Freke, stretching out her hand to Mr. Vincent.

It has been remarked, that an antipathy subsists between creatures, who, without being the same, have yet a strong external resemblance. Mr. Percival saw this instinct rising in Mr. Vincent, and smiled.

"Hail fellow! well met! I say. Shake hands and be friends, man! . . ."

Then turning towards Mr. Percival, she measured him with her eye, as a person whom she longed to attack. She thought, that if Belinda's opinion of the understanding of *these Percivals* could be lowered, she should rise in her esteem: accordingly, she determined to draw Mr. Percival into an argument.

"I've been talking treason, I believe, to Miss Portman," cried she; "for I've been opposing some of your opinions, Mr. Percival."

"If you opposed them all, madam," said Mr. Percival, "I should not think it treason."

"Vastly polite!—But I think all our politeness hypocrisy: what d'ye say to that?"

"You know that best, madam!"

"Then I'll go a step farther; for I'm determined you shall contradict me: I think all virtue is hypocrisy."

"I need not contradict you, madam," said Mr. Percival, "for the terms which you make use of contradict themselves."

"It is my system," pursued Mrs. Freke, "that shame is always the cause of the vices of women."

"It is sometimes the effect," said Mr. Percival; "and, as cause and effect are reciprocal, perhaps you may, in some instances, be right."

"Oh! I hate qualifying arguers—plump assertion or plump denial for me: you sha'n't get off so. I say shame is the cause of all women's vices."

"False shame, I suppose you mean?" said Mr. Percival.

"Mere play upon words! All shame is false shame—we should be a great deal better without it. What say you, Miss Portman?—Silent, hey? Silence that speaks."

"Miss Portman's blushes," said Mr. Vincent, "speak *for* her."

"*Against* her," said Mrs. Freke: "women blush because they understand."

"And you would have them understand without blushing?" said Mr. Percival. "I grant you that nothing can be more different than innocence and ignorance. Female delicacy—"

"This is just the way you men spoil women," cried Mrs. Freke, "by talking to them of the *delicacy of their sex*, and such stuff. This *delicacy* enslaves the pretty delicate dears."

"No; it enslaves us," said Mr. Vincent.

"I hate slavery! Vive la liberté!" cried Mrs. Freke. "I'm a champion for the Rights of Woman."

"I am an advocate for their happiness," said Mr. Percival, "and for their delicacy, as I think it conduces to their happiness."

"I'm an enemy to their delicacy, as I am sure it conduces to their misery."

"You speak from experience?" said Mr. Percival.

"No, from observation. Your most delicate women are always the greatest hypocrites; and, in my opinion, no hypocrite can or ought to be happy."

"But you have not proved the hypocrisy," said Belinda. "Delicacy is not, I hope, an indisputable proof of it? If you mean *false* delicacy—"

"To cut the matter short at once," cried Mrs. Freke, "why, when a woman likes a man, does not she go and tell him so honestly?"

Belinda, surprised by this question from a woman, was too much abashed instantly to answer.

"Because she's a hypocrite. That is and must be the answer."

"No," said Mr. Percival; "because, if she be a woman of sense, she knows that by such a step she would disgust the object of her affection."

"Cunning!—cunning!—cunning!—the arms of the weakest."

"Prudence! prudence!—the arms of the stongest. Taking the best means to secure our own happiness without injuring that of others is the best proof of sense and strength of mind, whether in man or woman. Fortunately for society, the same conduct in ladies which best secures their happiness most increases ours."

Mrs. Freke beat the devil's tattoo for some moments, and then exclaimed, "You may say what you will, but the present system of society is radically wrong:—whatever is, is wrong."

"How would you improve the state of society?" asked Mr. Percival, calmly.

"I'm not tinker-general to the world," said she.

"I'm glad of it," said Mr. Percival; "for I have heard that tinkers often spoil more than they mend."

"But if you want to know," said Mrs. Freke, "what I would do to improve the world, I'll tell you: I'd have both sexes call things by their right names."

"This would doubtless be a great improvement," said Mr. Percival; "but you would not overturn society to attain it, would you? Should we find things much improved by tearing away what has been called the decent drapery of life?"

"Drapery, if you ask me my opinion," cried Mrs. Freke, "drapery, whether wet or dry, is the most confoundedly indecent thing in the world."

"That depends on *public* opinion, I allow," said Mr. Percival. "The Lacedæmonian ladies, who were veiled only by public opinion, were better covered from profane eyes than some English ladies are in wet drapery."

"I know nothing of the Lacedæmonian ladies: I took my leave of them when I was a schoolboy—girl, I should say. But pray, what o'clock is it by you? I've sat till I'm cramped all over," cried Mrs. Freke, getting up and stretching herself so violently that some part of her habiliments gave way. "Honi soit qui mal y pense!" said she, bursting into a horse laugh.

Without sharing in any degree that confusion which Belinda felt for her, she strode out of the room saying, "Miss Portman, you understand these things better than I do; come and set me to rights."

When she was in Belinda's room, she threw herself into an armchair, and laughed immoderately.

"How I have trimmed Percival this morning!" said she.

"I am glad you think so," said Belinda; "for I really was afraid he had been too severe upon you."

"I only wish," continued Mrs. Freke, "I only wish his wife had been by. Why the devil did not she make her appearance? I suppose the prude was afraid of my demolishing and unrigging her."

"There seems to have been more danger of that for you than for any body else," said Belinda, as she assisted to set Mrs. Freke's *rigging,* as she called it, to rights.

"I do of all things delight in hauling good people's opinions out of their musty drawers, and seeing how they look when they're all pulled to pieces before their faces! Pray, are those Lady Anne's drawers or yours?" said Mrs. Freke, pointing to a chest of drawers.

"Mine."

"I'm sorry for it; for if they were hers, to punish her for *shirking* me, by the Lord, I'd have every rag she has in the world out in the middle of the floor in ten minutes! You don't know me—I'm a terrible person when provoked—stop at nothing!"

•

"People who expect sentiment from children of six years old will be disappointed, and will probably teach them affectation. Surely it is much better to let their natural affections have time to expand. If we tear the rosebud open we spoil the flower." Belinda smiled at this parable of the rosebud, which, she said, might be applied to men and women, as well as to children.

"And yet, upon reflection," said Lady Anne, "the heart has nothing in common with a rosebud. Nonsensical allusions pass off very prettily in conversation. I mean, when we converse with partial friends: but we should reason ill, and conduct ourselves worse, if we were to trust implicitly to poetical analogies. Our affections," continued Lady Anne, "arise from circumstances totally independent of our will."

"That is the very thing I meant to say," interrupted Belinda, eagerly.

"They are excited by the agreeable or useful qualities that we discover in things or in persons."

"Undoubtedly,' said Belinda.

"Or by those which our fancies discover," said Lady Anne.

Belinda was silent; but, after a pause, she said, "That it was certainly very dangerous, especially for women, to trust to fancy in bestowing their affections."

•

"It is difficult in society," said Mr. Percival, "especially for women, to do harm to themselves, without doing harm to others. They may begin in frolic, but they must end in malice. They defy the world—the world in return excommunicates them—the female outlaws become desperate, and make it the business and pride of their lives to disturb the peace of their sober neighbours. Women who have lowered themselves in the public opinion cannot rest without attempting to bring others to their own level."

"Mrs. Freke, notwithstanding the blustering merriment that she affects, is obviously unhappy," said Belinda; "and since we cannot do her any good, either by our blame or our pity, we had better think of something else."

•

FROM *Castle Rackrent*

And all the young ladies, who used to be in her room dressing of her, said in Mrs. Jane's hearing that my lady was the happiest bride ever they had seen, and that to be sure a love-match was the only thing for happiness, where the parties could any way afford it.

•

It is curious to observe how customs and ceremonies degenerate. The present Irish cry, or howl, cannot boast of such melody, nor is the funeral procession conducted with much dignity. The crowd of people who assemble at these funerals sometimes amounts to a thousand, often to four or five hundred. They gather as the bearers of the hearse proceed on their way, and when they pass through any village, or when they come near any houses, they begin to cry—Oh! Oh! Oh! Oh! Oh! Agh! Agh! raising their notes from the first *Oh!* to the last *Agh!* in a kind of mournful howl. This gives notice to the inhabitants of the village that *a funeral is passing,* and immediately they flock out to allow it. In the province of Munster it is a common thing for the women to follow a funeral, to join in the universal cry with all their might and main for some time, and then to turn and ask—"Arrah! who is it that's dead?— who is it we're crying for?"

A raking pot of tea.—We should observe, this custom has long since been banished from the higher orders of Irish gentry. The mysteries of a raking pot of tea, like those of the Bona Dea, are supposed to be sacred to females; but now and then it has happened that some of the male species, who were either more audacious, or more highly favoured than the rest of their sex, have been admitted by stealth to these orgies. The time when the festive ceremony begins varies according to circumstances, but it is never earlier than twelve o'clock at night the joys of a raking pot of tea depending on its being made in secret, and at an unseasonable hour. After a ball, when the more discreet part of the company has departed to rest, a few chosen female spirits, who have footed it till they can foot it no longer, and till the sleepy notes expire under the slurring hand of the musician, retire to a bedchamber, call the favourite maid who alone is admitted, bid her *put down the kettle,* lock the door, and amidst as much giggling and scrambling as possible, they get round a tea-table, on which all manner of things are huddled together. Then begin mutual railleries and mutual confidences amongst the young ladies, and the faint scream and the loud laugh is heard, and the romping for letters and pocket-books begins, and gentlemen are called by their sur- names, or by the general name of fellows! pleasant fellows! charming fellows! odious fellows! abominable fellows! and then all prudish deco- rums are forgotten, and then we might be convinced how much the satirical poet was mistaken when he said—

There is no woman where there's no reserve.

The merit of the original idea of a raking pot of tea evidently be- longs to the washerwoman and the laundry-maid. But why should not we have *Low life above stairs* as well as *High life below stairs?*

Sarah Egerton (1670-1723)

❧ ❧

The Emulation

Say, tyrant Custom, why must we obey
The impositions of thy haughty sway?
From the first dawn of life unto the grave,
Poor womankind's in every state a slave,
The nurse, the mistress, parent and the swain,
For love she must, there's none escape that pain.
Then comes the last, the fatal slavery:
The husband with insulting tyranny
Can have ill manners justified by law,
For men all join to keep the wife in awe.
Moses, who first our freedom did rebuke,
Was married when he writ the Pentateuch.
They're wise to keep us slaves, for well they know,
If we were loose, we soon should make them so.
We yield like vanquished kings whom fetters bind,
When chance of war is to usurpers kind;
Submit in form; but they'd our thoughts control,
And lay restraints on the impassive soul.
They fear we should excel their sluggish parts,
Should we attempt the sciences and arts;
Pretend they were designed for them alone,
So keep us fools to raise their own renown.
Thus priests of old, their grandeur to maintain,
Cried vulgar eyes would sacred laws profane;
So kept the mysteries behind a screen:
Their homage and the name were lost had they been seen.
But in this blessèd age such freedom's given,
That every man explains the will of heaven;
And shall we women now sit tamely by,
Make no excursions in philosophy,
Or grace our thoughts in tuneful poetry?
We will our rights in learning's world maintain;

Wit's empire now shall know a female reign.
Come, all ye fair, the great attempt improve,
Divinely imitate the realms above:
There's ten celestial females govern wit,
And but two gods that dare pretend to it.
And shall these finite males reverse their rules?
No, we'll be wits, and then men must be fools.

George Eliot
(Mary Ann Evans) (1819–1880)

❦ ❧

FROM *Daniel Deronda*

Men can do nothing without the make-believe of a beginning.

•

Since she was not winning strikingly, the next best thing was to lose strikingly.

•

But her thoughts never dwelt on marriage as the fulfilment of her ambition; the dramas in which she imagined herself a heroine were not wrought up to that close. To be very much sued or hopelessly sighed for as a bride was indeed an indispensable and agreeable guarantee of womanly power; but to become a wife and wear all the domestic fetters of that condition, was on the whole a vexatious necessity. Her observation of matrimony had inclined her to think it rather a dreary state, in which a woman could not do what she liked, had more children than were desirable, was consequently dull, and became irrevocably immersed in humdrum.

•

"Imagination is often truer than fact," said Gwendolen, decisively, though she could no more have explained these glib words than if they had been Coptic or Etruscan.

•

. . . and if she wanders into a swamp, the pathos lies partly, so to speak, in her having on her satin shoes.

•

Gwendolen rather valued herself on her superior freedom in laughing where others might only see matter for seriousness. Indeed, the laughter became her person so well that her opinion of its gracefulness was often shared by others.

•

The perception that poor Rex wanted to be tender made her curl up and harden like a sea-anemone at the touch of a finger.

•

Some readers of this history will doubtless regard it as incredible that people should construct matrimonial prospects on the mere report that a bachelor of good fortune and possibilities was coming within reach, and will reject the statement as a mere outflow of gall: they will aver that neither they nor their first cousins have minds so unbridled; and that in fact this is not human nature, which would know that such speculations might turn out to be fallacious, and would therefore not entertain them. But, let it be observed, nothing is here narrated of human nature generally: the history in its present stage concerns only a few people in a corner of Wessex—whose reputation, however, was un-impeached, and who, I am in the proud position of being able to state, were all on visiting terms with persons of rank.

•

"Are you converted to-day?" said Gwendolen.

(Pause, during which she imagined various degrees and modes of opinion about herself that might be entertained by Grandcourt.)

•

"Yes, indeed: I never like my life so well as when I am on horseback, having a great gallop. I think of nothing. I only feel myself strong and happy."

(Pause, wherein Gwendolen wondered whether Grandcourt would like what she said, but assured herself that she was not going to disguise her tastes.)

•

"I don't know that. I have great rivals. Did you not observe how well Miss Arrowpoint shot?"

(Pause, wherein Gwendolen was thinking that men had been known to choose some one else than the woman they most admired, and recalled several experiences of that kind in novels.)

•

"We must stay where we grow, or where the gardeners like to transplant us. We are brought up like the flowers, to look as pretty as we can, and be dull without complaining. That is my notion about the plants: they are often bored, and that is the reason why some of them have got poisonous. What do you think?"

•

"Indeed he has all the qualities that would make a husband tolerable— battlement, veranda, stable, etc., no grins and no glass in his eye."

•

FROM *The Mill on the Floss*

MAGGIE TRIES TO RUN AWAY FROM HER SHADOW

Maggie's intentions, as usual, were on a larger scale than Tom had imagined. The resolution that gathered in her mind, after Tom and Lucy had walked away, was not so simple as that of going home. No! she would run away and go to the gypsies, and Tom should never see her any more. That was by no means a new idea to Maggie: she had been so often told she was like a gypsy and "half wild" that when she was miserable it seemed to her the only way of escaping opprobrium and being entirely in harmony with circumstances, would be to live in a little brown tent on the commons: the gypsies, she considered, would gladly receive her and pay her much respect on account of her superior knowledge. She had once mentioned her views on this point to Tom, and suggested that he should stain his face brown and they should run away together; but Tom rejected the scheme with contempt, observing that gypsies were thieves and hardly got anything to eat and had nothing to drive but a donkey. Today, however, Maggie thought her misery had reached a pitch at which gypsydom was her only refuge, and she rose from her seat on the roots of the tree with the sense that this was a great crisis in her life; she would run straight away till she came to Dunlow Common, where there would certainly be gypsies, and cruel Tom, and the rest of her relations who found fault with her, should never see her any more. She thought of her father as she ran along, but she reconciled herself to the idea of parting with him, by determining that she would secretly send him a letter by a small gypsy who would run away without telling where she was, and just let him know that she was well and happy, and always loved him very much.

Maggie soon got out of breath with running, but by the time Tom got to the pond again, she was at the distance of three long fields and was on the edge of the lane leading to the high road. She stopped to pant a little, reflecting that running away was not a pleasant thing until one had got quite to the common where the gypsies were, but her resolution had not abated: she presently passed through the gate into the lane, not knowing where it would lead her, for it was not this way that they came from Dorlcote Mill to Garum Firs, and she felt all the safer for that, because there was no chance of her being overtaken. But she was soon aware, not without trembling, that there were two men coming along the lane in front of her: she had not thought of meeting strangers—she had been too much occupied with the idea of her friends coming after her. The formidable strangers were two shabby-looking men with flushed faces, one of them carrying a bundle on a stick over his shoulder: but to her surprise, while she was dreading their disapprobation as a runaway, the man with the bundle stopped, and in a half whining half coaxing tone asked her if she had a copper to give a poor man. Maggie had a sixpence in her pocket—her uncle Glegg's present —which she immediately drew out and gave this poor man with a polite smile, hoping he would feel very kindly towards her as a generous person. "That's the only money I've got," she said, apologetically. "Thank you, little miss," said the man in a less respectful and grateful tone than Maggie anticipated, and she even observed that he smiled and winked at his companion. She walked on hurriedly, but was aware that the two men were standing still, probably to look after her, and she presently heard them laughing loudly. Suddenly it occurred to her that they might think she was an idiot:—Tom had said that her cropped hair made her look like an idiot, and it was too painful an idea to be readily forgotten. Besides she had no sleeves on—only a cape and a bonnet. It was clear that she was not likely to make a favourable impression on passengers, and she thought she would turn into the fields again: but not on the same side of the lane as before, lest they should still be uncle Pullet's fields. She turned through the first gate that was not locked, and felt a delighted sense of privacy in creeping along by the hedgerows after her recent humiliating encounter. She was used to wandering about the fields by herself, and was less timid there than on the high-road. Sometimes she had to climb over high gates, but that was a small evil; she was getting out of reach very fast, and she should probably soon come within sight of Dunlow Common, or at least of some other common, for she had heard her father say that you couldn't go very far without coming to a common. She hoped so, for she was getting rather tired and hungry, and until she reached the gypsies there was no definite prospect of bread-and-butter. It was still broad daylight, for aunt Pullet, retaining the early habits of the Dodson family, took tea at half-past four by the sun and at five by the kitchen clock; so, though it was nearly an hour since Maggie started, there was no gathering gloom on the fields to remind her that the night would come. Still, it seemed to her that she had been walking a very great distance indeed, and it was really surprising that the common did not come within sight. Hitherto she had been in the rich parish of Garum where there was a great deal of pasture-land, and she had only seen one labourer at a distance: that was fortunate in some respects, as labourers might be too ignorant to understand the propriety of her wanting to go to Dunlow Common; yet it would have been better if she could have met some one who would tell her the way without wanting to know anything about her private business. At last, however, the green fields came to an end and Maggie found herself looking through the bars of a gate into a lane with a wide margin of grass on each side of it. She had never seen such a wide lane before, and without her knowing why, it gave her the impression that the common could not be far off; perhaps, it was because she saw a donkey with a log to his foot feeding on the grassy margin, for she had seen a donkey with that pitiable encumbrance on Dunlow Common when she had been across it in her father's gig. She crept through the bars of the gate and walked on with new spirit, though not without haunting images of Apollyon, and a highwayman with a pistol, and a blinking dwarf in yellow with a mouth from ear to ear, and other miscellaneous dangers. For poor little Maggie had at once the timidity of an active imagination, and the daring that comes from overmastering impulse. She had rushed into the adventure of seeking her unknown kindred, the gypsies, and now she was in this strange lane she hardly dared look on one side of her, lest she should see the diabolical blacksmith in his leathern apron grinning at her with arms akimbo. It was not without a leaping of the heart that she caught sight of a small pair of bare legs sticking up, feet uppermost, by the side of a hillock; they seemed something hideously preternatural—a diabolical kind of fungus; for she was too much agitated at the first glance to see the ragged clothes and the dark shaggy head attached to them. It was a boy asleep, and Maggie trotted along faster and more lightly lest she should wake him: it did not occur to her that he was one of her friends the gypsies, who in all probability would have very genial manners. But the fact was so, for at the next bend in the lane, Maggie actually saw the little semicircular black tent with the blue smoke rising before it which was to be her refuge from all the blighting obloquy that had pursued her in civilised life. She even saw a tall female figure by the column of smoke—doubtless the gypsy-mother, who provided the tea and other groceries: it was astonishing to herself she did not feel more delighted. But it was startling to find the gyspies in a lane, after all, and not on a common: indeed, it was rather disappointing; for a mysterious illimitable common where there were sand-pits to hide in, and one was out of everybody's reach, had always made part of Maggie's picture of gypsy life. She went on, however, and thought with some comfort that gypsies most likely knew nothing about idiots, so there was no danger of their falling into the mistake of setting her down at the first glance as an idiot. It was plain she had attracted attention, for the tall figure, who proved to be a young woman with a baby in her arm, walked slowly to meet her. Maggie looked up in the new face rather tremblingly as it approached, and was reassured by the thought that her aunt Pullet and the rest were right when they called her a gypsy, for this face with the bright dark eyes and the long hair was really something like what she used to see in the glass before she cut her hair off.

"My little lady, where are you going to?" the gypsy said, in a tone of coaxing deference.

It was delightful, and just what Maggie expected: the gypsies saw at once that she was a little lady, and were prepared to treat her accordingly.

"Not any farther," said Maggie, feeling as if she were saying what she had rehearsed in a dream. "I'm come to stay with *you*, please."

"That's pritty; come then—why, what a nice little lady you are, to be sure," said the gypsy, taking her by the hand. Maggie thought her very agreeable, but wished she had not been so dirty.

There was quite a group round the fire when they reached it. An old gypsy-woman was seated on the ground nursing her knees, and occasionally poking a skewer into the round kettle that sent forth an odorous steam: two small shock-headed children were lying prone and resting on their elbows something like small sphinxes: and a placid donkey was bending his head over a tall girl who, lying on her back, was scratching his nose and indulging him with a bite of excellent stolen hay. The slanting sunlight fell kindly upon them, and the scene was really very pretty and comfortable, Maggie thought, only she hoped they would soon set out the tea-cups. Everything would be quite charming when she had taught the gypsies to use a washing-basin and to feel an interest in books. It was a little confusing, though, that the young woman began to speak to the old one in a language which Maggie did not understand, while the tall girl who was feeding the donkey, sat up and stared at her without offering any salutation. At last, the old woman said,

"What, my pretty lady, are you come to stay with us? Sit ye down, and tell us where you come from."

It was just like a story: Maggie liked to be called pretty lady and treated in this way. She sat down and said,

"I'm come from home, because I'm unhappy, and I mean to be a gypsy. I'll live with you, if you like, and I can teach you a great many things."

"Such a clever little lady," said the woman with the baby, sitting down by Maggie, and allowing baby to crawl, "and such a pritty bonnet and frock," she added, taking off Maggie's bonnet and looking at it while she made an observation to the old woman, in the unknown language. The tall girl snatched the bonnet and put it on her own head hindforemost with a grin; but Maggie was determined not to show any weakness on this subject, as if she were susceptible about her bonnet.

"I don't want to wear a bonnet," she said, "I'd rather wear a red handkerchief, like yours" (looking at her friend by her side). "My hair was quite long till yesterday, when I cut it off: but I dare say it will grow again very soon," she added apologetically, thinking it probable the gypsies had a strong prejudice in favour of long hair. And Maggie had forgotten even her hunger at that moment in the desire to conciliate gypsy opinion.

"O what a nice little lady—and rich, I'm sure," said the old woman. "Didn't you live in a beautiful house at home?"

"Yes, my home is pretty, and I'm very fond of the river where we go fishing—but I'm often very unhappy. I should have liked to bring my books with me, but I came away in a hurry, you know. But I can tell you almost everything there is in my books, I've read them so many times—and that will amuse you. And I can tell you something about Geography too—that's about the world we live in—very useful and interesting. Did you ever hear about Columbus?"

Maggie's eyes had begun to sparkle and her cheeks to flush—she was really beginning to instruct the gypsies, and gaining great influence over them. The gypsies themselves were not without amazement at this talk, though their attention was divided by the contents of Maggie's pocket, which the friend at her right hand had by this time emptied, without attracting her notice.

"Is that where you live, my little lady?" said the old woman, at the mention of Columbus.

"O no!" said Maggie, with some pity, "Columbus was a very wonderful man, who found out half the world and they put chains on him and treated him very badly, you know—it's in my Catechism of Geography—but perhaps it's rather too long to tell before tea. . . . *I want my tea so.*"

The last words burst from Maggie, in spite of herself, with a sudden drop from patronising instruction to simple peevishness.

"Why, she's hungry, poor little lady," said the younger woman. "Give her some o' the cold victual. You've been walking a good way, I'll be bound, my dear. Where's your home?"

"It's Dorlcote Mill, a good way off," said Maggie. "My father is Mr. Tulliver, but we mustn't let him know where I am, else he'll fetch me home again. Where does the queen of the gypsies live?"

"What! do you want to go to her, my little lady?" said the younger woman. The tall girl, meanwhile, was constantly staring at Maggie and grinning. Her manners were certainly not agreeable.

"No," said Maggie, "I'm only thinking that if she isn't a very good queen you might be glad when she died, and you could choose another. If I was a queen, I'd be a very good queen, and kind to everybody."

"Here's a bit o' nice victual, then," said the old woman, handing to Maggie a lump of dry bread, which she had taken from a bag of scraps, and a piece of cold bacon.

"Thank you," said Maggie, looking at the food, without taking it, "but will you give me some bread and butter and tea instead? I don't like bacon."

"We've got no tea nor butter," said the old woman with something like a scowl, as if she were getting tired of coaxing.

"O, a little bread and treacle would do," said Maggie.

"We ha'n't got no treacle," said the old woman crossly, whereupon there followed a sharp dialogue between the two women in their un-known tongue, and one of the small sphinxes snatched at the bread-and-bacon and began to eat it. At this moment the tall girl who had gone a few yards off, came back and said something, which produced a strong effect. The old woman seeming to forget Maggie's hunger, poked the skewer into the pot with new vigour, and the younger crept under the tent, and reached out some platters and spoons. Maggie trembled a little, and was afraid the tears would come into her eyes. Meanwhile the tall girl gave a shrill cry and presently came running up to the boy whom Maggie had passed as he was sleeping—a rough urchin about the age of Tom. He stared at Maggie, and there ensued much incomprehensible chattering. She felt very lonely, and was quite sure she should begin to cry before long: the gypsies didn't seem to mind her at all, and she felt quite weak among them. But the springing tears were checked by a new terror, when two men came up, whose approach had been the cause of the sudden excitement. The elder of the two carried a bag, which he flung down, addressing the women in a loud and scolding tone, which they answered by a shower of treble sauciness; while a black cur ran barking up to Maggie and threw her into a tremor that only found a new cause in the curses with which the younger man called the dog off, and gave him a rap with a great stick he held in his hand.

Maggie felt that it was impossible she should ever be queer of these people, or ever communicate to them amusing and useful knowledge.

Both the men now seemed to be inquiring about Maggie, for they looked at her, and the tone of the conversation became of that pacific kind which implies curiosity on one side and the power of satisfying it on the other. At last the younger woman said in her previous deferential coaxing tone,

"This nice little lady's come to live with us: aren't you glad?"

"Ay, very glad," said the younger man, who was looking at Maggie's silver thimble and other small matters that had been taken from her pocket. He returned them all except the thimble to the younger woman, with some observation, and she immediately restored them to Maggie's pocket, while the men seated themselves and began to attack the contents of the kettle—a stew of meat and potatoes—which had been taken off the fire and turned out into a yellow platter.

Maggie began to think that Tom might be right about the gypsies—they must certainly be thieves, unless the man meant to return her thimble by and by. She would willingly have given it him, for she was not at all attached to her thimble; but the idea that she was among thieves prevented her from feeling any comfort in the revival of deference and attention towards her—all thieves except Robin Hood were wicked people. The women saw she was frightened.

"We've got nothing nice for a lady to eat," said the old woman, in her coaxing tone. "And she's so hungry, sweet little lady."

"Here, my dear, try if you can eat a bit o' this," said the younger woman, handing some of the stew on a brown dish with an iron spoon to Maggie, who remembering that the old woman had seemed angry with her for not liking the bread and bacon, dared not refuse the stew, though fear had chased away her appetite. If her father would but come by in the gig and take her up! Or even if Jack the Giantkiller or Mr. Greatheart or St. George who slew the dragon on the half-pennies, would happen to pass that way! But Maggie thought with a sinking heart that these heroes were never seen in the neighborhood of St. Ogg's—nothing very wonderful ever came there.

Maggie Tulliver, you perceive was by no means that well-trained, well-informed young person that a small female of eight or nine necessarily is in these days: she had only been to school a year at St. Ogg's, and had so few books that she sometimes read the dictionary; so that in travelling over her small mind you would have found the most unexpected ignorance as well as unexpected knowledge. She could have informed you that there was such a word as "polygamy" and being also acquainted with "polysyllable," she had deduced the conclusion that "poly" meant "many;" but she had had no idea that gypsies were not well supplied with groceries, and her thoughts generally were the oddest mixture of clear-eyed acumen and blind dreams.

Her ideas about gypsies had undergone a rapid modification in the last five minutes. From having considered them very respectful companions, amenable to instruction, she had begun to think that they meant perhaps to kill her as soon as it was dark, and cut up her body for gradual cooking: the suspicion crossed her that the fierce-eyed old man was in fact the devil who might drop that transparent disguise at any moment, and turn either into the grinning blacksmith or else a fiery-eyed monster with dragon's wings. It was no use trying to eat the stew, and yet the thing she most dreaded was to offend the gypsies by betraying her extremely unfavourable opinion of them, and she wondered with a keenness of interest that no theologian could have exceeded, whether if the devil were really present he would know her thoughts.

"What, you don't like the smell of it, my dear," said the young woman, observing that Maggie did not even take a spoonful of the stew. "Try a bit, come."

"No, thank you," said Maggie, summoning all her force for a desperate effort, and trying to smile in a friendly way. "I haven't time, I think—it seems getting darker. I think I must go home now, and come again another day, and then I can bring you a basket with some jam tarts and things."

Maggie rose from her seat as she threw out this illusory prospect, devoutly hoping that Apollyon was gullible; but her hope sank when the old gypsy-woman said, "Stop a bit, stop a bit, little lady—we'll take you home, all safe, when we've done supper: you shall ride home, like a lady."

Maggie sat down again, with little faith in this promise, though she presently saw the tall girl putting a bridle on the donkey and throwing a couple of bags on his back.

"Now then, little missis," said the younger man, rising, and leading the donkey forward, "tell us where you live—what's the name o' the place?"

"Dorlcote Mill is my home," said Maggie, eagerly. "My father is Mr. Tulliver—he lives there."

"What, a big mill a little way this side o' St. Ogg's?"

"Yes," said Maggie. "Is it far off? I think I should like to walk there, if you please."

"No, no, it'll be getting dark, we must make haste. And the donkey'll carry you as nice as can be—you'll see."

He lifted Maggie as he spoke and set her on the donkey. She felt relieved that it was not the old man who seemed to be going with her, but she had only a trembling hope that she was really going home.

"Here's your pretty bonnet," said the younger woman putting that recently despised but now welcome article of costume on Maggie's head; "and you'll say we've been very good to you, won't you, and what a nice little lady we said you was."

"O, yes, thank you," said Maggie, "I'm very much obliged to you. But I wish you'd go with me too." She thought anything was better than going with one of the dreadful men alone: it would be more cheerful to be murdered by a larger party.

"Ah, you're fondest o' me, aren't you?" said the woman. "But I can't go—you'll go too fast for me."

It now appeared that the man also was to be seated on the donkey holding Maggie before him, and she was as incapable of remonstrating against this arrangement as the donkey himself, though no nightmare had ever seemed to her more horrible. When the woman had patted her on the back and said goodbye, the donkey, at a strong hint from the man's stick, set off at a rapid walk along the lane towards the point Maggie had come from an hour ago, while the tall girl and the rough urchin, also furnished with sticks, obligingly escorted them for the first hundred yards, with much screaming and thwacking.

Not Leonore in that preternatural midnight excursion with her phantom lover, was more terrified than poor Maggie in this entirely natural ride on a short-paced donkey, with a gypsy behind her who considered that he was earning half-a-crown. The red light of the setting sun seemed to have a portentous meaning, with which the alarming bray of the second donkey, with the log on its foot, must surely have some connection. Two low thatched cottages—the only houses they passed in this lane—seemed to add to its dreariness: they had no windows, to speak of, and the doors were closed: it was probable that they were inhabited by witches, and it was a relief to find that the donkey did not stop there.

At last—O sight of joy—this lane, the longest in the world, was coming to an end, was opening on a broad high road, where there was actually a coach passing! And there was a finger-post at the corner: she had surely seen that finger-post before—"To St. Ogg's, 2 miles." The gypsy really meant to take her home, then: he was probably a good man, after all, and might have been rather hurt at the thought that she didn't like coming with him alone. This idea became stronger as she felt more and more certain that she knew the road quite well and she was con-

sidering how she might open a conversation with the injured gypsy, and
not only gratify his feelings but efface the impression of her cowardice,
when, as they reached a cross road, Maggie caught sight of some one
coming on a white-faced horse.

"O stop, stop!" she cried out. "There's my father! O father, father!"
The sudden joy was almost painful, and before her father reached
her, she was sobbing. Great was Mr. Tulliver's wonder, for he had made
a round from Basset, and had not yet been home.

"Why, what's the meaning o' this?" he said, checking his horse,
while Maggie slipped from the donkey and ran to her father's stirrup.

"The little miss lost herself, I reckon," said the gypsy. "She'd come
to our tent, at the far end o' Dunlow Lane, and I was bringing her
where she said her home was. It's a good way to come after being on
the tramp all day."

"O, yes, father, he's been very good to bring me home," said Maggie. "A very kind, good man!"

"Here then, my man," said Mr. Tulliver, taking out five shillings.
"It's the best day's work *you* ever did. I couldn't afford to lose the little
wench. Here, lift her up before me."

"Why, Maggie, how's this, how's this," he said, as they rode along,
while she laid her head against her father and sobbed. "How came you
to be rambling about and lose yourself?"

"O father," sobbed Maggie, "I ran away, because I was so
unhappy—Tom was so angry with me. I couldn't bear it."

"Pooh, pooh," said Mr. Tulliver, soothingly, "you mustn't think
o' running away from father. What 'ud father do without his little
wench?"

"O no—I never will again, father—never."

Mr. Tulliver spoke his mind very strongly when he reached home
that evening, and the effect was seen in the remarkable fact that Maggie
never heard one reproach from her mother or one taunt from Tom
about this foolish business of her running away to the gypsies. Maggie
was rather awestricken by this unusual treatment, and sometimes thought
that her conduct had been too wicked to be alluded to.

•

"I don't think I *am* well, father," said Tom. "I wish you'd ask Mr.
Stelling not to let me do Euclid—it brings on the toothache, I think."

(The toothache was the only malady to which Tom had ever been
subject.)

"Euclid, my lad—why, what's that?" said Mr. Tulliver.

"O I don't know: it's definitions and axioms and triangles and
things. It's a book I've got to learn in—there's no sense in it."

"Go, go!" said Mr. Tulliver, reprovingly, "you mustn't say so. You must learn what your master tells you. He knows what it's right for you to learn."

"*I'll* help you now, Tom," said Maggie, with a little air of patronising consolation. "I'm come to stay ever so long, if Mrs. Stelling asks me. I've brought my box and my pinafores, haven't I, father?"

"*You* help me, you silly little thing!" said Tom, in such high spirits at this announcement, that he quite enjoyed the idea of confounding Maggie by showing her a page of Euclid. "I should like to see you doing one of *my* lessons! Why, I learn Latin too! Girls never learn such things. They're too silly."

"I know what Latin is very well," said Maggie, confidently. "Latin's a language. There are Latin words in the Dictionary. There's bonus, a gift."

"Now, you're just wrong there, Miss Maggie!" said Tom, secretly astonished. "You think you're very wise. But 'bonus' means 'good,' as it happens—bonus, bona, bonum."

"Well, that's no reason why it shouldn't mean 'gift,' " said Maggie, stoutly. "It may mean several things. Almost every word does. There's 'lawn'—it means the grass plot, as well as the stuff pocket-handkerchiefs are made of."

"Well done, little 'un," said Mr. Tulliver, laughing, while Tom felt rather disgusted with Maggie's knowingness, though beyond measure cheerful at the thought that she was going to stay with him. Her conceit would soon be overawed by the actual inspection of his books.

Mrs. Stelling, in her pressing invitation, did not mention a longer time than a week for Maggie's stay, but Mr. Stelling, who took her between his knees and asked her where she stole her dark eyes from, insisted that she must stay a fortnight. Maggie thought Mr. Stelling was a charming man, and Mr. Tulliver was quite proud to leave his little wench where she would have an opportunity of showing her cleverness to appreciating strangers. So it was agreed that she should not be fetched home till the end of the fortnight.

"Now then, come with me into the study, Maggie," said Tom, as their father drove away. "What do you shake and toss your head now for, you silly?" he continued; for though her hair was now under a new dispensation and was brushed smoothly behind her ears, she seemed still in imagination to be tossing it out of her eyes. "It makes you look as if you were crazy."

"But I shall be a *clever* woman," said Maggie, with a toss.

"O, I dare say, and a nasty conceited thing. Everybody'll hate you."

•

She presently made up her mind to skip the rules in the Syntax,—the examples became so absorbing. These mysterious sentences snatched from an unknown context,—like strange horns of beasts and leaves of unknown plants, brought from some far-off region, gave boundless scope to her imagination, and were all the more fascinating because they were in a peculiar tongue of their own, which she could learn to interpret. It was really very interesting—the Latin Grammar that Tom had said no girls could learn: and she was proud because she found it interesting. The most fragmentary examples were her favourites.

"Now, then, Magsie, give us the Grammar!"

"O Tom, it's such a pretty book!" she said, as she jumped out of the large arm-chair to give it him, "it's much prettier than the Dictionary. I could learn Latin very soon. I don't think it's at all hard."

"O I know what you've been doing," said Tom, "you've been reading the English at the end. Any donkey can do that."

Tom seized the book and opened it with a determined and business-like air as much as to say that he had a lesson to learn which no donkeys would find themselves equal to. Maggie, rather piqued, turned to the bookcases to amuse herself with puzzling out the titles.

Maggie obeyed and took the open book.

"Where do you begin, Tom?"

"O, I begin at *'Appellativa arborum,'* because I say all over again what I've been learning this week."

Tom sailed along pretty well for three lines; and Maggie was beginning to forget her office of prompter, in speculating as to what *mas* could mean, which came twice over, when he stuck fast at *Sunt etiam volucrum.*

"Don't tell me, Maggie; *Sunt etiam volucrum . . . Sunt etiam volucrum . . . ut ostrea, cetus . . ."*

"No," said Maggie, opening her mouth and shaking her head.

"Sunt etiam volucrum," said Tom, very slowly, as if the next words might be expected to come sooner, when he gave them this strong hint that they were waited for.

"C, e, u," said Maggie, getting impatient.

"O, I know—hold your tongue," said Tom. *"Ceu passer, hirundo, ferarum . . . ferarum . . ."* Tom took his pencil and made several hard dots with it on his book-cover . . . *"ferarum . . ."*

"O dear, O dear Tom," said Maggie, "what a time you are! *Ut . . ."*

"Ut, ostrea . . ."

"No, no," said Maggie, *"ut, tigris . . ."*

"O yes, now I can do," said Tom, "it was *tigris, vulpes,* I'd forgotten: *ut tigris, vulpes, et piscium.*"

With some further stammering and repetition, Tom got through the next few lines.

"Now then," he said, "the next is what I've just learnt for tomorrow. Give me hold of the book a minute."

After some whispered gabbling, assisted by the beating of his fist on the table, Tom returned the book.

"Mascula nomina in a," he began.

"No, Tom," said Maggie, "that doesn't come next. It's *Nomen non creskens genittivo . . .*"

"Creskens genittivo," exclaimed Tom, with a derisive laugh, for Tom had learned this omitted passage for his yesterday's lesson, and a young gentleman does not require an intimate or extensive acquaintance with Latin before he can feel the pitiable absurdity of a false quantity. *"Creskens genittivo!* What a little silly you are, Maggie!"

"Well, you needn't laugh, Tom, for you didn't remember it at all. I'm sure it's spelt so. How was I to know?"

"Phee-e-e-h! I told you girls couldn't learn Latin. It's *Nomen non crescens genitivo.*"

"Very well, then," said Maggie, pouting. "I can say that as well as you can. And you don't mind your stops. For you ought to stop twice as long at a semicolon as you do at a comma, and you make the longest stops where there ought to be no stop at all."

"O, well, don't chatter. Let me go on."

They were presently fetched to spend the rest of the evening in the drawing-room, and Maggie became so animated with Mr. Stelling, who, she felt sure, admired her cleverness, that Tom was rather amazed and alarmed at her audacity. But she was suddenly subdued by Mr. Stelling's alluding to a little girl of whom he had heard that she once ran away to the gypsies.

"What a very odd little girl that must be!" said Mrs. Stelling, meaning to be playful, but a playfulness that turned on her supposed oddity was not at all to Maggie's taste. She feared Mr. Stelling, after all, did not think much of her, and went to bed in rather low spirits. Mrs. Stelling, she felt, looked at her as if she thought her hair was very ugly because it hung down straight behind.

Nevertheless it was a very happy fortnight to Maggie—this visit to Tom. She was allowed to be in the study while he had his lessons, and in her various readings got very deep into the examples in the Latin Grammar. The astronomer who hated women generally caused her so much puzzling speculation that she one day asked Mr. Stelling if all astronomers hated women, or whether it was only this particular astronomer. But, forestalling his answer, she said,

"I suppose it's all astronomers: because you know, they live up in high towers, and if the women came there, they might talk and hinder them from looking at the stars."

Mr. Stelling liked her prattle immensely, and they were on the best terms. She told Tom she should like to go to school to Mr. Stelling, as he did, and learn just the same things. She knew she could do Euclid, for she had looked into it again, and she saw what A B C meant: they were the names of the lines.

"I'm sure you couldn't do it, now," said Tom. "And I'll just ask Mr. Stelling if you could."

"I don't mind," said the little conceited minx. "I'll ask him myself."

"Mr. Stelling," she said, that same evening, when they were in the drawing-room, "couldn't I do Euclid, and all Tom's lessons, if you were to teach me instead of him?"

"No; you couldn't," said Tom, indignantly. "Girls can't do Euclid: can they, sir?"

"They can pick up a little of everything, I daresay," said Mr. Stelling. "They've a great deal of superficial cleverness: but they couldn't go far into anything. They're quick and shallow."

Tom, delighted with this verdict, telegraphed his triumph by wagging his head at Maggie behind Mr. Stelling's chair. As for Maggie, she had hardly ever been so mortified: she had been so proud to be called "quick" all her little life, and now it appeared that this quickness was the brand of inferiority. It would have been better to be slow, like Tom.

"Ha, ha! Miss Maggie!" said Tom, when they were alone, "you see it's not such a fine thing to be quick. You'll never go far into anything, you know."

And Maggie was so oppressed by this dreadful destiny that she had no spirit for a retort.

But when this small apparatus of shallow quickness was fetched away in the gig by Luke, and the study was once more quite lonely for Tom, he missed her grievously. He had really been brighter and had got through his lessons better since she had been there; and she had asked Mr. Stelling so many questions about the Roman Empire, and whether there really ever was a man who said in Latin, "I would not buy it for a farthing or a rotten nut," or whether that had only been turned into Latin—that Tom had actually come to a dim understanding of the fact that there had once been people upon the earth who were so fortunate as to know Latin without learning it through the medium of the Eton

Grammar. This luminous idea was a great addition to his historical acquirements during this half year which were otherwise confined to an epitomised History of the Jews.

But the dreary half year *did* come to an end. How glad Tom was to see the last yellow leaves fluttering before the cold wind! The dark afternoons and the first December snow seemed to him far livelier than the August sunshine; and that he might make himself the surer about the flight of the days that were carrying him homeward,—he stuck twenty-one sticks deep in a corner of the garden when he was three weeks from the holidays, and pulled one up every day with a great wrench, throwing it to a distance, with a vigour of will which would have carried it to limbo, if it had been in the nature of sticks to travel so far.

But it was worth purchasing, even at the heavy price of the Latin Grammar—the happiness of seeing the bright light in the parlour at home as the gig passed noiselessly over the snow-covered bridge: the happiness of passing from the cold air to the warmth and the kisses and the smiles of that familiar hearth where the pattern of the rug and the greate and the fire-irons were "first ideas" that it was no more possible to criticise than the solidity and extension of matter. There is no sense of ease like the ease we felt in those scenes where we were born, where objects became dear to us before we had known the labour of choice, and where the outer world seemed only an extension of our own personality: we accepted and loved it as we accepted our own sense of existence and our own limbs. Very commonplace, even ugly, that furniture of our early home might look if it were put up to auction: an improved taste in upholstery scorns it; and is not the striving after something better and better in our surroundings, the grand characteristic that distinguishes man from the brute—or, to satisfy a scrupulous accuracy of definition, that distinguishes the British man from the foreign brute? But heaven knows where that striving might lead us, if our affections had not a trick of twining round those old inferior things, if the loves and sanctities of our life had no deep immovable roots in memory. One's delight in an elderberry bush overhanging the confused leafage of a hedgerow bank as a more gladdening sight than the finest cistus or fuchsia spreading itself on the softest undulating turf, is an entirely unjustifiable preference to a landscape-gardener, or to any of those severely regulated minds who are free from the weakness of any attachment that does not rest on a demonstrable superiority of qualities. And there is no better reason for preferring this elderberry bush than that it stirs an early memory—that it is no novelty in my life speaking to me merely through my present sensibilities to form and colour, but the long companion of my existence that wove itself into my joys when joys were vivid.

•

"Take back your *Corinne*," said Maggie, drawing a book from under her shawl. "You were right in telling me she would do me no good. But you were wrong in thinking I should wish to be like her."

"Wouldn't you really like to be a tenth Muse, then, Maggie?" said Philip, looking up in her face as we look at a first parting in the clouds, that promises us a bright heaven once more.

"Not at all," said Maggie, laughing. "The Muses were uncomfortable goddesses, I think—obliged always to carry rolls and musical instruments about with them. If I carried a harp in this climate, you know, I must have a green baize cover for it—and I should be sure to leave it behind me by mistake."

"You agree with me in not liking Corinne, then?"

"I didn't finish the book," said Maggie. "As soon as I came to the blond-haired young lady reading in the park, I shut it up and determined to read no further. I foresaw that that light complexioned girl would win away all the love from Corinne and make her miserable. I'm determined to read no more books where the blond-haired women carry away all the happiness. I should begin to have a prejudice against them —If you could give me some story, now, where the dark woman triumphs, it would restore the balance—I want to avenge Rebecca and Flora Mac-Ivor, and Minna and all the rest of the dark unhappy ones. Since you are my tutor you ought to preserve my mind from prejudices, you are always arguing against prejudices."

"Well, perhaps you will avenge the dark women in your own person;—carry away all the love from your cousin Lucy. She is sure to have some handsome young man of St. Ogg's at her feet now—and you have only to shine upon him—your fair little cousin will be quite quenched in your beams."

"Philip, that is not pretty of you, to apply my nonsense to anything real," said Maggie, looking hurt. "As if I, with my old gowns, and want of all accomplishments, could be a rival of dear little Lucy, who knows and does all sorts of charming things, and is ten times prettier than I am—even if I were odious and base enough to wish to be her rival. Besides, I never go to aunt Deane's when any one is there: it is only because dear Lucy is good and loves me that she comes to see me, and will have me got to see her sometimes."

"Maggie," said Philip, with surprise, "it is not like you to take playfulness literally. You must have been in St. Ogg's this morning, and brought away a slight infection of dulness."

"Well," said Maggie, smiling, "if you meant that for a joke, it was a poor one; but I thought it was a very good reproof. I thought you wanted to remind me that I am vain, and wish every one to admire me most. But it isn't for that, that I'm jealous for the dark women—not because I'm dark myself. It's because I always care the most about the unhappy people: if the blonde girl was forsaken, I should like *her* best. I always take the side of the rejected lover in the stories."

"Then you would never have the heart to reject one yourself—should you, Maggie?" said Philip, flushing a little.

"I don't know," said Maggie, hesitatingly. Then with a bright smile—"I think perhaps I could if he were very conceited. And yet, if he got extremely humiliated afterwards, I should relent."

"I've often wondered, Maggie," Philip said, with some effort, "whether you wouldn't really be more likely to love a man that other women were not likely to love."

"That would depend on what they didn't like him for," said Maggie, laughing. "He might be very disagreeable. He might look at me through an eyeglass stuck in his eye, making a hideous face, as young Torry does. I should think other women are not fond of that; but I never felt any pity for young Torry. I've never any pity for conceited people, because I think they carry their comfort about with them."

.

FROM *Middlemarch*

The really delightful marriage must be that where your husband was a sort of father, and could teach you even Hebrew, if you wished it.

.

A man's mind—what there is of it—has always the advantage of being masculine—as the smallest birch-tree is of a higher kind than the most soaring palm—and even his ignorance is of a sounder quality. Sir James might not have originated this estimate; but a kind Providence furnishes the limpest personality with a little gum or starch in the form of tradition.

.

"O Mrs. Cadwallader, I don't think it can be nice to marry a man with a great soul."

"Well, my dear, take warning. You know the look of one now; when the next comes and wants to marry you, don't you accept him."

.

"He has got no good red blood in his body," said Sir James.

"No. Somebody put a drop under a magnifying-glass, and it was all semicolons and parentheses," said Mrs. Cadwallader.

.

Plain women he regarded as he did the other severe facts of life, to be faced with philosophy and investigated by science.

•

Having once embarked on your marital voyage, it is impossible not to be aware that you make no way and that the sea is not within sight— that in fact, you are exploring an enclosed basin.

•

Solomon's Proverbs, I think, have omitted to say, that as the sore palate findeth grit, so an uneasy consciousness heareth innuendoes.

•

"Mamma," said Rosamond, "when Fred comes down I wish you would not let him have red herrings. I cannot bear the smell of them all over the house at this hour of the morning."

"Oh, my dear, you are so hard on your brothers! It is the only fault I have to find with you. You are the sweetest temper in the world, but are so tetchy with your brothers."

"Not tetchy, mamma; you never hear me speak in an unladylike way."

"Well, but you want to deny them things."

"Brothers are so unpleasant."

"Oh, my dear, you must allow for young men. Be thankful if they have good hearts. A woman must learn to put up with little things. You will be married some day."

"Not to any one who is like Fred."

"Don't decry your own brother, my dear. Few young men have less against them, although he couldn't take his degree—I'm sure I can't understand why, for he seems to me most clever. And you know yourself he was thought equal to the best society at college. So particular as you are, my dear, I wonder you are not glad to have such a gentlemanly young man for a brother. You are always finding fault with Bob because he is not Fred."

"Oh no, mamma, only because he is Bob."

"Well, my dear, you will not find any Middlemarch young man who has not something against him."

"But"—here Rosamond's face broke into a smile which suddenly revealed two dimples. She herself thought unfavourably of these dimples and smiled little in general society. "But I shall not marry any Middlemarch young man."

•

"Are you beginning to dislike slang, then?" said Rosamond, with mild gravity.

"Only the wrong sort. All choice of words is slang. It marks a class."

"There is correct English: that is not slang."

"I beg your pardon: correct English is the slang of prigs who write history and essays. And the strongest slang of all is the slang of poets."

•

"Fred's studies are not very deep," said Rosamond, rising with her mamma, "he is only reading a novel."

•

"I want the ride so much, it is indifferent to me where we go." Rosamond really wished to go to Stone Court, of all other places.

"Oh, I say, Rosy," said Fred, as she was passing out of the room, "if you are going to the piano, let me come and play some airs with you."

"Pray do not ask me this morning."

"Why not this morning?"

"Really, Fred, I wish you would leave off playing the flute. A man looks very silly playing the flute. And you play so out of tune."

"When next any one makes love to you, Miss Rosamond, I will tell him how obliging you are."

"Why should you expect me to oblige you by hearing you play the flute, any more than I should expect you to oblige me by not playing it?"

"And why should you expect me to take you out riding?"

This question led to an adjustment, for Rosamond had set her mind on that particular ride.

So Fred was gratified with nearly an hour's practice of "Ar hyd y nos," "Ye banks and braes," and favourite airs from his "Instructor on the Flute"; a wheezy performance, into which he threw much ambition and an irrespressible hopefulness.

•

FROM *Silly Novels by Lady Novelists*

We may remark, by the way, that we have been relieved from a serious scruple by discovering that silly novels by lady novelists rarely introduce us into any other than very lofty and fashionable society. We had imagined that destitute women turned novelists, as they turned governesses, because they had no other "lady-like" means of getting their bread. On this supposition, vacillating syntax and improbable incident had a certain pathos for us, like the extremely supererogatory pincushions and ill-devised nightcaps that are offered for sale by a blind man. We felt the commodity to be a nuisance, but we were glad to think that the money went to relieve the necessitous, and we pictured to ourselves lonely women struggling for a maintenance, or wives and daughters devoting themselves to the production of "copy" out of pure heroism,—perhaps to pay their husband's debts, or to purchase luxuries for a sick father. Under these impressions we shrank from criticising a lady's novel: her English might be faulty, but, we said to ourselves, her motives are irreproachable; her imagination may be uninventive, but her patience is untiring. Empty writing was excused by an empty stomach, and twaddle was consecrated by tears. But no! This theory of ours, like many other pretty theories, has had to give way before observation. Women's silly novels, we are now convinced, are written under totally different circumstances. The fair writers have evidently never talked to a tradesman except from a carriage window; they have no notion of the working-classes except as "dependents"; they think five hundred a-year a miserable pittance; Belgravia and "baronial halls" are their primary truths, and they have no idea of feeling interest in any man who is not at least a great landed proprietor, if not a prime minister. It is clear that they write in elegant boudoirs, with violet-coloured ink and a ruby pen; that they must be entirely indifferent to publishers' accounts, and inexperienced in every form of poverty except poverty of brains. It is true that we are constantly struck with the want of verisimilitude in their representations of the high society in which they seem to live; but then they betray no closer acquaintance with any other form of life. If their peers and peeresses are improbable, their literary men, tradespeople, and cottagers are impossible; and their intellect seems to have the peculiar impartiality of reproducing both what they *have* seen and heard, and what they have *not* seen and heard, with equal unfaithfulness.

•

Thus, for Evangelical young ladies there are Evangelical love stories, in which the vicissitudes of the tender passion are sanctified by saving views of Regeneration and the Atonement. These novels differ from the oracular ones, as a Low Churchwoman often differs from a High Churchwoman: they are a little less supercilious, and a great deal more ignorant, a little less correct in their syntax, and a great deal more vulgar.

•

"Be not a baker if your head be made of butter," says a homely proverb, which, being interpreted, may mean, let no woman rush into print who is not prepared for the consequences.

•

No sooner does a woman show that she has genius or effective talent, than she receives the tribute of being moderately praised and severely criticised. By a peculiar thermometric adjustment, when a woman's talent is at zero, journalistic approbation is at the boiling pitch; when she attains mediocrity, it is already at no more than summer heat; and if ever she reaches excellence, critical enthusiasm drops to the freezing point.

Mary Ellmann (contemporary)

~❧ ❧~

FROM *Thinking About Women*

With a kind of inverted fidelity, the discussion of women's books by men will arrive punctually at the point of preoccupation, which is the fact of femininity. Books by women are treated as though they themselves were women, and criticism embarks, at its happiest, upon an intellectual measuring of busts and hips. Of course, this preoccupation has its engaging and compensatory sides. Like such minor physical disorders as shingles and mumps, it often seems (whether or not it feels so to the critic) comical as well as distressing.

•

Norman Mailer, for example, is pleased to think that Joseph Heller's *Catch-22* is a man's book to read, a book which merely "puzzles" women. Women cannot comprehend male books, men cannot tolerate female books. The working rule is simple, basic: there must always be two literatures like two public toilets, one for Men and one for Women.

Nora Ephron (1941-)

~❧ ❧~

FROM *Crazy Salad*

I have no desire to be dominated. Honestly I don't. And yet I find myself becoming angry when I'm not. My husband has trouble hailing a cab or flagging a waiter, and suddenly I feel a kind of rage; ball-breaking anger rises to my T-zone. I wish he were better at hailing taxis than I am; on the other hand, I realize that expectation is culturally conditioned, utterly foolish, has nothing to do with anything, is exactly the kind of thinking that ought to be got rid of in our society; on still another hand, having that insight into my reaction does not seem to calm my irritation.

•

FROM the Introduction to
When Harry Met Sally

[Writing a script is] like delivering a great big beautiful plain pizza, the one with only cheese and tomatoes. And then you give it to the director, and the director says, "I love this pizza. I am willing to commit to this pizza. But I really think this pizza should have mushrooms on it." And you say, "Mushrooms! Of course! I meant to put mushrooms on the pizza. Why didn't I think of that? Let's put some on immediately." And then someone else comes along and says, "I love this pizza too, but it really needs green peppers." "Great," you say. "Green peppers. Just the thing." And then someone else says, "Anchovies." There's always a fight over the anchovies. And when you get done, what you have is a pizza with everything. Sometimes, it's wonderful. And sometimes you look at it and you think, I knew we shouldn't have put the green peppers onto it. Why didn't I say so at the time? Why didn't I lie down in traffic to prevent anyone's putting green peppers into the pizza?

•

FROM *Heartburn*

I finished being interviewed by Detective Nolan, and gave him my father's telephone number and my number at home in Washington just in case. It wasn't until I was past the newspaper photographers and on the subway that I wondered whether Detective Nolan was single. He wasn't exactly my type, but look where my type had gotten me. Then I wondered if he was uncircumcised. Then I wondered if I could be happily married to a policeman. Then I wondered why I was so hopelessly bourgeois that I couldn't even have a fantasy about a man without moving on to marriage.

•

The first is that I have always believed that crying is a highly overrated activity: women do entirely too much of it, and the last thing we ought to want is for it to become a universal excess. The second thing I want to say is this: beware of men who cry. It's true that men who cry are sensitive to and in touch with feelings, but the only feelings they tend to be sensitive to and in touch with are their own.

•

It's hard when you don't like someone a friend marries. . . . [I]t means that even a simple flat inquiry like "How's Helen?" is taken amiss, since your friend always thinks that what you hope he's going to say is "Dead." You feel irritated because your darling friend has married beneath himself, and he feels irritated because you don't see the virtues of his beloved. Then, if your friend's marriage fails, he becomes even more irritated at you, because if you had been a real friend, you would have prevented him physically from making the mistake, you would have locked him up in a closet until the urge to get married had passed.

•

Vera said: "Why do you feel you have to turn everything into a story?"
So I told her why:
Because if I tell the story, I control the version.
Because if I tell the story, I can make you laugh, and I would rather have you laugh at me than feel sorry for me.
Because if I tell the story, it doesn't hurt as much.
Because if I tell the story, I can get on with it.

Fanny Fern
(Sara Payson [Willis] Parton) (1811–1872)

~⊰⊱~

Aunt Hetty on Matrimony

"Now girls," said Aunt Hetty, "put down your embroidery and worsted work; do something sensible, and stop building air-castles, and talking of lovers and honey-moons. It makes me sick; it is perfectly antimonial. Love is a farce; matrimony is a humbug; husbands are domestic Napoleons, Neroes, Alexanders,—sighing for other hearts to conquer, after they are sure of yours. The honey-moon is as short-lived as a lucifer-match; after that you may wear your wedding-dress at breakfast, and your night-cap to meeting, and your husband wouldn't know it. You may pick up your own pocket-handkerchief, help yourself to a chair, and split your gown across the back reaching over the table to get a piece of butter, while he is laying in his breakfast as if it was the last meal he should eat in this world. When he gets through he will aid your digestion,—while you are sipping your first cup of coffee,—by inquiring what you'll have for dinner; whether the cold lamb was all ate yesterday; if the charcoal is all out, and what you gave for the last green tea you bought. Then he gets up from the table, lights his cigar with the last evening's paper, that you have not had a chance to read; gives two or three whiffs of smoke,—which are sure to give you a headache for the afternoon,—and, just as his coattail is vanishing through the door, apologizes for not doing "that errand" for you yesterday,—thinks it doubtful if he can to-day,—"so pressed with business." Hear of him at eleven o'clock, taking an ice-cream with some ladies at a confectioner's, while you are at home new-lining his coat-sleeves. Children by the ears all day; can't get out to take the air; feel as crazy as a fly in a drum. Husband comes home at night; nods a "How d'ye do, Fan?"

•

Women and Money

"A wife shouldn't ask her husband for money at meal-times."—EXCHANGE.

By no manners of means; *not at any other time;* because, it is to be hoped, he will be gentlemanly enough to spare her that humiliating necessity. Let him hand her his porte-monnaie every morning, with *carte-blanche* to help herself. The consequence would be, she would lose all desire for the contents, and hand it back, half the time without abstracting a single *sou*.

It's astonishing men have no more dipolomacy about such matters. *I* should like to be a husband! There *are* wives whom I verily believe might be trusted to make way with a ten dollar bill without risk to the connubial donor! I'm not speaking of those doll-baby libels upon womanhood, whose chief ambition is to be walking advertisements for the dressmaker; but a rational, refined, sensible woman, who knows how to look like a lady upon small means; who would both love and respect a man less for requiring an account of every copper; but who, at the same time, would willingly wear a hat or garment that is "out of date," rather than involve a noble, generous-hearted husband in unnecessary expenditures.

I repeat it—"It *isn't every man who has a call to be a husband.*" Half the married men should have their "licenses" taken away, and the same number of judicious bachelors put in their places. I think the attention of the representatives should be called to this. They can't expect to come down to town and peep under all the ladies' bonnets the way they do, and have all the newspapers free gratis, and two dollars a day besides, without "paying their way"!

It's none of *my* business, but I question whether their wives, whom they left at home, stringing dried apples, know how spruce they look in their new hats and coats, or how facetious they grow with their landlady's daughter; or how many of them pass themselves off for bachelors, to verdant spinsters. Nothing truer than that little couplet of *Shakspeare's*—

> "When the cat's away
> The mice will play."

•

A Law More Nice Than Just

NUMBER II

After all, having tried it I affirm that nothing reconciles a woman quicker to her femininity than an experiment in male apparel, although I still maintain that she should not be forbidden by law to adopt it when necessity requires; at least, not till the practice is amended by which a female clerk, who performs her duty equally well with a male clerk, receives less salary, simply because she is a woman.

To have to jump on to the cars when in motion, and scramble yourself on to the platform as best you may without a helping hand; to be nudged roughly in the ribs by the conductor with, "your fare, sir?" to have your pretty little toes trod on, and no healing "beg your pardon," applied to the smart; to have all those nice-looking men who used to make you such crushing bows, and give you such insinuating smiles, pass you without the slightest interest in your coat tails, and perhaps push you against the wall or into the gutter, with a word tabooed by the clergy. In fine, to dispense with all those delicious little politenesses (for men are great bears to each other) to which one has been accustomed, and yet feel no inclination to take advantage of one's corduroys and secure an equivalent by making interest with the "fair sex," stale to you as a thrice-told tale. Isn't *that* a situation?

To be subject to the promptings of that unstifleable feminine desire for adornment, which is right and lovely within proper limits, and yet have no field for your operations. To have to conceal your silken hair, and yet be forbidden a becoming moustache, or whiskers, or beard— (all hail beards, I say!). To choke up your nice throat with a disguising cravat; to hide your bust (I trust no Miss Nancy is blushing) under a baggy vest. To have nobody ask you to ice cream, and yet be forbidden, by your horrible disgust of tobacco, to smoke. To have a gentleman ask you "the time sir?" when you are new to the geography of your watch-pocket. To accede to an invitation to test your "heft," by sitting down in one of those street-weighing chairs, and have one of the male by-standers, taking hold of your foot, remark, "Halloo, sir, you must not rest these upon the ground while you are being weighed"; and go grinning away in your coat-sleeve at your truly feminine faux pas.

And yet—and yet—to be able to step over the ferry-boat chain when you are in a distracted hurry, like any other fellow, without waiting for that tedious unhooking process, and quietly to enjoy your triumph over scores of impatient-waiting crushed petticoats behind you; to taste that nice lager beer "on draught"; to pick up contraband bits of science in a Medical Museum, forbidden to crinoline, and hold conversations with intelligent men, who supposing you to be a man, consequently talk sense to you. That is worth while.

Take it all in all, though, I thank the gods I am a woman. I had rather be loved than make love; though I could beat the makers of it, out and out, if I did not think it my duty to refrain out of regard to their feelings, and the final disappointment of the deluded women! But—oh, dear, I want to do such a quantity of "improper" things, that there is not the slightest real harm in doing. I want to see and know a thousand things which are forbidden to flounces—custom only can tell why—I can't. I want the free use of my ankles, for this summer at least, to take a journey; I want to climb and wade, and tramp about, without giving a thought to my clothes; without carrying about with me a long procession of trunks and boxes, which are the inevitable penalty of femininity as at present appareled. I hate a Bloomer, such as we have seen —words are weak to say how much; I hate myself as much in a man's

dress; and yet I want to run my fingers through my cropped hair some
fine morning without the bore of dressing it; put on some sort of loose
blouse affair—it must be pretty, though—and a pair of Turkish
trousers—*not* Bloomers—and a cap, or hat—and start; nary a trunk—
"nary" a bandbox. Wouldn't that be fine? But propriety scowls and says,
"ain't you ashamed of yourself, Fanny Fern?" *Yes, I am,* Miss Nancy. I
am ashamed of myself, that I haven't the courage to carry out what
would be so eminently convenient, and right, and proper under the
circumstances. I am ashamed of myself that I sit like a fool on the piazza
of some hotel every season, gazing at some distant mountain, which
every pulse and muscle of my body, and every faculty of my soul, are
urging me to climb, that I may "see the kingdoms of the earth and the
glory of them." I *am* ashamed of myself that you, Miss Nancy, with your
uplifted forefinger and your pursed-up mouth, should keep me out of a
dress in which only I can hope to do such things. Can't I make a compromise with you, Miss Nancy? for I'm getting restless, as these lovely
summer days pass on. I'd write you such long accounts of beautiful
things, Miss Nancy—things which God made for female as well as male
eyes to see; and I should come home so strong and healthy, Miss
Nancy—a freckle or two, perhaps—but who cares? O-h-n-o-w, Miss
Nancy, d-o—Pshaw! you cross old termagant! May Lucifer fly away
wid ye.

•

A Reasonable Being

If there's anything I hate, it is "a reasonable being." Says the lazy mother
to her restless child whom she has imprisoned within doors and whose
active mind seeks solutions of passing remarks, "Don't bother, Tommy;
do be *reasonable,* and not tease with your questions." Says the husband
to his sick or overtasked wife, when she cries from mere mental or
physical exhaustion, "How I hate tears; do be a reasonable being." Says
the conservative father to his son, whom he would force into some
profession or employment for which nature has utterly disqualified him,
"Are you wiser than your father? do be a reasonable being." Says the
mother to sweet sixteen, whom she would marry to a sixty-five-year-
old money-bag, "Think what a thing it is to have a fine establishment;
do be a reasonable being."

As near as I can get at it, to be a reasonable being, is to laugh when
your heart aches; it is to give confidence and receive none; it is faithfully

to keep your own promises, and never mind such a trifle as having promises broken to you. It is never to have or to promulgate a dissenting opinion. It is either to be born a fool, or in lack of that to become a hypocrite, trying to become a "reasonable being."

Geraldine Ferraro (1935-   )

On Progress

It was not so long ago that people thought that semiconductors were part-time orchestra leaders and microchips were very, very small snack foods.

Anne Finch (1661-1720)

FROM *The Introduction*

Did I my lines intend for public view,
How many censures, would their faults pursue.
Some would, because such words they do affect,
Cry they're insipid, empty, uncorrect.
And many have attained, dull and untaught,
The name of wit, only by finding fault.
True judges might condemn their want of wit,
And all might say, they're by a woman writ.
Alas! a woman that attempts the pen,
Such an intruder on the rights of men,
Such a presumptuous creature is esteemed,
The fault can by no virtue be redeemed.
They tell us, we mistake our sex and way;
Good breeding, fashion, dancing, dressing, play
Are the accomplishments we should desire;

To write, or read, or think, or to enquire
Would cloud our beauty, and exhaust our time,
And interrupt the conquests of our prime;
Whilst the dull manage of a servile house
Is held by some, our utmost art, and use.

Sure 'twas not ever thus, nor are we told
Fables, of women that excelled of old;
To whom, by the diffusive hand of Heaven
Some share of wit and poetry was given.
On that glad day, on which the Ark returned,
The holy pledge, for which the land had mourned,
The joyful tribes attend it on the way,
The Levites do the sacred charge convey,
Whilst various instruments before it play;
Here, holy virgins in the concert join,
The louder notes to soften and refine,
And with alternate verse, complete the hymn divine.
Lo! the young poet, after God's own heart,
By Him inspired and taught the Muses' art,
Returned from conquest, a bright chorus meets,
That sing his slain ten thousand in the streets.
In such loud numbers they his acts declare,
Proclaim the wonders of his early war,
That Saul upon the vast applause does frown,
And feels its mighty thunder shake the crown.
What, can the threatened judgment now prolong?
Half of the kingdom is already gone;
The fairest half, whose influence guides the rest,
Have David's empire o'er their hearts confessed.

A woman here leads fainting Israel on,
She fights, she wins, she triumphs with a song,
Devout, majestic, for the subject fit,
And far above her arms exalts her wit,
Then, to the peaceful, shady palm withdraws,
And rules the rescued nation with her laws.
How are we fallen, fallen by mistaken rules?
And Education's more than Nature's fools,
Debarred from all improvements of the mind
And to be dull, expected and designed;
And if someone would soar above the rest,
With warmer fancy and ambition pressed,

So strong, th' opposing faction still appears,
The hopes to thrive can never outweigh the fears;
Be cautioned then, my Muse, and still retired;
Nor be despised, aiming to be admired;
Conscious of wants, still with contracted wing,
To some few friends, and to thy sorrows sing;
For groves of laurel thou wert never meant;
Be dark enough thy shades, and be thou there content.

Mary (1865-1963) and Jane (1866-1946) Findlater

~❦ ❦~

FROM *Crossriggs*

"Surely you read novels sometimes! I couldn't live without reading novels," she began.

"No—very seldom," said the Admiral. . . . "all that nonsense about *love*, so-called. Why, the books now are a disgrace! In my young days . . . there was none of this sort of thing. If a man was going to run away with his friend's wife, he *did* it, and said no more about it, like Lord Nelson. But now in some of these books a man will shilly-shally and talk about feelings and so on through two whole volumes, and many pages of pestilent trash about 'love.' . . .

"I don't defend such an action, but it *was action*, Miss Hope, not that everlasting talk, talk, talk, that the world is full of now."

•

It is one of the curious effects of a too passionate imaginative nature that its forebodings outrun time. So that often when the dreaded circumstance really arrives, it seems as nothing compared to the hours of imaginative misery that went before, as a line that has been already burnt will stop a prairie fire.

•

"Alex," Matilda cried, half angrily, half pityingly, "what do you want, what do you expect from life?"

"All or nothing. All is what I want, and nothing is what I expect."

Fannie Flagg (contemporary)

~≈ ℈~

FROM *Fried Green Tomatoes at the Whistle Stop Cafe*

So in the long run, it didn't matter at all if you had been good or not. The girls in high school who had "gone all the way" had not wound up living in back alleys in shame and disgrace, like she thought they would; they wound up happily or unhappily married, just like the rest of them.

•

About ten years ago, when Ed had started seeing a woman he worked with down at the insurance company, she had attended a group called The Complete Woman, to try and save her marriage. She wasn't sure she loved Ed all that much, but she loved him just enough to not want to lose him. Besides, what would she do? She had lived with him as long as she had lived with her parents. The organization believed that women could find complete happiness if they, in turn, would dedicate their entire lives to just making their man happy.

Their leader had informed them that all the rich and successful career women out there who appeared to be so happy were, in reality, terribly lonely and miserable and secretly envied them their happy Christian homes.

It was a stretch to imagine that Barbara Walters might want to give it all up for Ed Couch, but Evelyn tried her hardest. Of course, even though she was not religious, it was a comfort to know that the Bible backed her up in being a doormat. Hadn't the apostle St. Paul said for women not to usurp power over the men, but to be in silence?

•

Evelyn had even made up a secret code name for herself . . . a name feared around the world: TOWANDA THE AVENGER!

And while Evelyn went about her business with a smile, Towanda was busy poking child molesters with electric cattle prods until their hair stood on end. She placed tiny bombs inside *Playboy* and *Penthouse* magazines that would expode when they were opened. She gave dope dealers overdoses and left them in the streets to die; forced that doctor, who had told her mother she had cancer, to walk down the street naked while the entire medical profession, including dentists and oral hygienists, jeered and threw rocks. A merciful avenger, she always waited until he finished his walk and then beat his brains out with a sledgehammer.

Towanda was able to do anything she wanted. She went back in time and punched out the apostle Paul for writing that women should remain silent. Towanda went to Rome and kicked the pope off the throne and put a nun there, with the priests cooking and cleaning for her, for a change.

Towanda appeared on *Meet the Press*, and with a calm voice, a cool eye, and a wry smile, debated everyone who disagreed with her until they became so defeated by her brilliance that they burst into tears and ran off the show. She went to Hollywood and ordered all the leading men to act opposite women of their own age, not twenty-year-old girls with perfect bodies. She allowed rats to chew all slumlords to death, and sent food and birth control methods, for men as well as women, to the poor people of the world.

And because of her vision and insight, she became known the world over as Towanda the Magnanimous, Righter of Wrongs and Queen without Compare.

Towanda ordained that: an equal number of men and women would be in the government and sit in on peace talks; she and her staff of crack chemical scientists would find a cure for cancer and invent a pill that would let you eat all you want and not gain weight; people would be forced to get a license to have children and must be found fit, financially and emotionally—*no more starving or battered children*. Jerry Falwell would be responsible for the raising of all illegitimate children who had no homes; no kittens or puppies would be put to sleep, and they would be given a state of their own, maybe New Mexico or Wyoming; teachers and nurses would receive the same salary as professional football players.

She would stop the construction of all condos, especially ones with red tile roofs; and Van Johnson would be given a show of his own . . . he was one of Towanda's favorites.

Graffiti offenders were to be dipped in a vat of indelible ink. No more children of famous parents could write books. And she'd personally see to it that all the sweet men and daddies, who had worked so hard, would each receive a trip to Hawaii and an outboard motor to go with it.

Towanda went to Madison Avenue and took control of all the fashion magazines; all models weighing under 135 were fired, and wrinkles suddenly became sexually desirable. Low-fat cottage cheese was banned from the land forever. Ditto, carrot sticks.

Why, just yesterday, Towanda had marched into the Pentagon, taken all the bombs and missiles away, and had given them toys to play with instead, while her sisters in Russia were doing the same thing. Then she went on the six o'clock nightly news and gave the entire military budget to all the people in the United States over sixty-five. Towanda would be so busy all day that Evelyn was exhausted by bedtime.

Diane Ford (contemporary)

One-liner

"I had to hold down three jobs to put him through school. Then when I turned twenty-six and thought that I should go back to college, he divorced me. For a nineteen-year-old bimbette with straw for brains who walks seven feet behind him so that when he stops to read a road map she wipes his butt . . . But I'm not bitter."

Margaret Fuller (1810–1850)

One-liners

"But early I perceived that men never, in any extreme of despair, wished to be women. On the contrary, they were ever ready to taunt one another, at any sign of weakness, with,

'Art thou not like the women, who,'—

The passage ends various ways, according to the occasion and rhetoric of the speaker. When they admired any woman, they were inclined to speak of her as 'above her sex.' "

Man has gone but little way; now he is waiting to see whether Woman can keep step with him; but, instead of calling out, like a good brother, "You can do it, if you only think so," or impersonally, "Any one can do what he tries to do"; he often discourages with school-boy brag: "Girls can't do that; girls can't play ball." But let any one defy their taunts, break through and be brave and secure, they rend the air with shouts. . . .

Zsa Zsa Gabor (1918?-   )

~≈ ✽≈~

One-liners

A girl must marry for love, and keep on marrying until she finds it.

•

I'm a wonderful housekeeper. Every time I get a divorce, I keep the house.

Elizabeth Gaskell (1810-1865)

~≈ ✽≈~

FROM *Cranford*

My next visit to Cranford was in the summer. There had been neither births, deaths, nor marriages since I was there last. Everybody lived in the same house, and wore pretty nearly the same well-preserved, old-fashioned clothes. The greatest event was, that Miss Jenkyns had purchased a new carpet for the drawing-room. Oh, the busy work Miss Matty and I had in chasing the sunbeams, as they fell in an afternoon right down on this carpet through the blindless window! We spread newspapers over the places and sat down to our book or our work; and, lo! in a quarter of an hour the sun had moved, and was blazing away on a fresh spot; and down again we went on our knees to alter the position of the newspapers. We were very busy, too, one whole morning, before Miss Jenkyns gave her party, in following her directions, and in cutting out and stitching together pieces of newspaper so as to form little paths to every chair set for the expected visitors, lest their shoes might dirty or defile the purity of the carpet.

•

"Well, Miss Matty! men will be men. Every mother's son of them wishes to be considered Samson and Solomon rolled into one—too strong ever to be beaten or discomfited—too wise ever to be outwitted. If you will notice, they have always foreseen events, though they never tell one for one's warning before the events happen; my father was a man, and I know the sex pretty well."

•

"Listen to reason—"

"I'll not listen to reason," she said—now in full possession of her voice, which had been rather choked with sobbing. "Reason always means what some one else has got to say."

Stella Gibbons (1902–1989)

~✤ ✤~

FROM *Cold Comfort Farm*

Flora, observing the faces of the Brethren as they crowded into the dog-kennel, thought that Amos had probably underestimated the strength of their nerves. Seldom had she seen so healthy and solid-looking an audience.

As an audience, it compared most favourably with audiences she had studied in London; and particularly with an audience seen once—but only once—at a Sunday afternoon meeting of the Cinema Society to which she had, somewhat unwillingly, accompanied a friend who was interested in the progress of the cinema as an art.

That audience had run to beards and magenta shirts and original ways of arranging its neckwear; and not content with the ravages produced in its over-excitable nervous system by the remorseless workings of its critical intelligence, it had sat through a film of Japanese life called "Yĕs," made by a Norwegian film company in 1915 with Japanese actors, which lasted an hour and three-quarters and contained twelve close-ups of water-lilies lying perfectly still on a scummy pond and four suicides, all done extremely slowly.

All round her (Flora pensively recalled) people were muttering how lovely were its rhythmic patterns and what an exciting quality it had and how abstract was its formal decorative shaping.

But here was one little man sitting next to her, who had not said a word; he had just nursed his hat and eaten sweets out of a paper bag. Something (she supposed) must have linked their auras together, for at the seventh close-up of a large Japanese face dripping with tears, the little man held out to her the bag of sweets, muttering:

"Peppermint creams. Must have something."

And Flora had taken one thankfully, for she was extremely hungry.

When the lights went up, as at last they did, Flora had observed with pleasure that the little man was properly and conventionally dressed; and, for his part, his gaze had dwelt upon her neat hair and well-cut coat with incredulous joy, as of one who should say: "Dr. Livingstone, I presume?"

He then, under the curious eyes of Flora's highbrow friend, said that his name was Earl P. Neck, of Beverly Hills, Hollywood; and he gave them his "cyard" very ceremoniously and asked if they would go and have tea with him? He seemed the nicest little creature, so Flora disregarded the raised eyebrows of her friend (who, like all loose-living persons, was extremely conventional) and said that they would like to very much, so off they went.

At tea, Mr. Neck and Flora had exchanged views on various films of a frivolous nature which they had seen and enjoyed (for of "Yes" they could not yet trust themselves to speak), and Mr. Neck had told them that he was a guest-producer at the new British studios at Wendover, and would Flora and her friend come and visit the studios some time? It must be soon, said Mr. Neck, because he was returning to Hollywood with the annual batch of England's best actors and actresses in the autumn.

Somehow she had never found time to visit Wendover, though she had dined twice with Mr. Neck since their first meeting, and they liked each other very much. He had told Flora all about his slim, expensive mistress, Lily, who made boring scenes and took up the time and energy which he would much sooner have spent with his wife, but he had to have Lily, because in Beverly Hills, if you did not have a mistress, people thought you were rather queer, and if, on the other hand, you spent all your time with your wife, and were quite firm about it, and said that you liked your wife, and, anyway, why the hell shouldn't you, the papers came out with repulsive articles headed "Hollywood Czar's Domestic Bliss," and you had to supply them with pictures of your wife pouring your morning chocolate and watering the ferns.

So there was no way out of it, Mr. Neck said.

Anyway, his wife quite understood, and they played a game called "Dodging Lily," which gave them yet another interest in common.

Now Mr. Neck was in America, but he would be flying over to England, so his last letter told Flora, in the late spring.

Flora thought that when he came she would invite him to spend a day with her in Sussex. There was somebody about whom she wished to talk to him.

She was reminded of Mr. Neck, as she stood pensively watching the Brethren going into the chapel, by the spectacle of the Majestic Cinema immediately opposite. It was showing a stupendous drama of sophisticated passion called "Other Wives' Sins." Probably Seth was inside, enjoying himself.

The dog-kennel was nearly full.

Somebody was playing a shocking tune on the poor little wheezy organ near the door. Except for this organ, Flora observed, peering over Amos's shoulder, the chapel looked like an ordinary lecture hall, with a little round platform at the end farthest from the door, on which stood a chair.

"Is that where you preach, Cousin Amos?"

"Aye."

"Does Judith or either of the boys ever come down to hear you preach?" She was making conversation because she was conscious of a growing feeling of dismay at what lay before her, and did not wish to give way to it.

Amos frowned.

"Nay. They struts like Ahab in their pride and their eyes drip fatness, nor do they see the pit digged beneath their feet by the Lord. Aye, 'tes a terrible wicked family I'm cursed wi', and the hand o' the Lord it lies heavy on Cold Comfort, pressin' the bitter wine out o' our souls."

"Then why don't you sell it and buy another farm on a really *nice* piece of land, if you feel like that about it?"

"Nay . . . there have always been Starkadders at Cold Comfort," he answered, heavily. " 'Tes old Mrs. Starkadder—Ada Doom as she was, before she married Fig Starkadder. She's sot against us leavin' the farm. She'd never see us go. 'Tes a curse on us. And Reuben sits awaitin' for me to go, so as he can have the farm. But un shall niver have un. Nay, I'll leave it to Adam first."

Before Flora could convey to him her lively sense of dismay at the prospect indicated in this threat, he moved forward saying, " 'Tes nearly full. We mun go in," and in they went.

Flora took a seat at the end of a row near the exit; she thought it would be as well to sit near the door in case the double effect of Amos's preaching and no ventilation became more than she could bear.

Amos went to a seat almost directly in front of the little platform, and sat down after directing two slow and brooding glances, laden with promise of terrifying eloquence to come, upon the Brethren sitting in the same row.

The dog-kennel was now packed to bursting, and the organ had begun to play something like a tune. Flora found a hymn-book being pressed into her hand by a female on her left.

"It's number two hundred, 'Whatever shall we do, O Lord,' " said the female, in a loud conversational voice.

Flora had supposed from impressions gathered during her wide reading, that it was customary to speak only in whispers in a building devoted to the act of worship. But she was ready to learn otherwise, so she took the book with a pleasant smile and said, "Thank you so much."

The hymn went like this:

> *Whatever shall we do, O Lord,*
> *When Gabriel blows o'er sea and river,*
> *Fen and desert, mount and ford?*
> *The earth may burn, but we will quiver.*

Flora approved of this hymn, because its words indicated a firmness of purpose, a clear path in the face of a disagreeable possibility, which struck an answering note in her own character. She sang industriously in her pleasing soprano. The singing was conducted by a surly, excessively dirty old man with long, grey hair who stood on the platform and waved what Flora, after the first incredulous shock, decided was a kitchen poker.

"Who is that?" she asked her friend.

" 'Tes Brother Ambleforth. He leads the quiverin' when we begins to quiver."

"And why does he conduct the music with a poker?"

"To put us in mind of hell fire," was the simple answer, and Flora had not the heart to say that as far as she was concerned, at any rate, this purpose was not achieved.

After the hymn, which was sung sitting down, everybody crossed their legs and arranged themselves more comfortably, while Amos rose from his seat with terrifying deliberation, mounted the little platform, and sat down.

For some three minutes he slowly surveyed the Brethren, his face wearing an expression of the most profound loathing and contempt, mingled with a divine sorrow and pity. He did it quite well. Flora had never seen anything to touch it except the face of Sir Henry Wood when pausing to contemplate some late-comers into the stalls at the Queen's Hall just as his baton was raised to conduct the first bar of the "Eroica." Her heart warmed to Amos. The man was an artist. At last he spoke. His voice jarred the silence like a broken bell.

"Ye miserable, crawling worms, are ye here again, then? Have ye come like Nimshi, son of Rehoboam, secretly out of yer doomed houses to hear what's comin' to ye? Have ye come, old and young, sick and well, matrons and virgins (if there is any virgins among ye, which is not likely, the world bein' in the wicked state it is), old men and young lads, to hear me tellin' o' the great crimson lickin' flames o' hell fire?"

A long and effective pause, and a further imitation of Sir Henry. The only sound (and it, with the accompanying smell, was quite enough) was the wickering hissing of the gas flares which lit the hall and cast sharp shadows from their noses across the faces of the Brethren.

Amos went on:

"Aye, ye've come." He laughed shortly and contemptuously. "Dozens of ye. Hundreds of ye. Like rats to a granary. Like field-mice when there's harvest home. And what good will it do ye?"

Second pause, and more Sir Henry stuff.

"Nowt. Not the flicker of a whisper of a bit o' good."

He paused and drew a long breath, then suddenly leaped from his seat and thundered at the top of his voice:

"Ye're all damned!"

An expression of lively interest and satisfaction passed over the faces of the Brethren, and there was a general rearranging of arms and legs, as though they wanted to sit as comfortably as possible while listening to the bad news.

"Damned," he repeated, his voice sinking to a thrilling and effective whisper. "Oh, do ye ever stop to think what that word *means* when ye use it every day, so lightly, o' yer wicked lives? No. Ye doan't. Ye never stop to think what anything means, do ye? Well, I'll tell ye. It means endless horrifyin' torment, with yer poor sinful bodies stetched out on hot gridirons in the nethermost fiery pit of hell, and demons mockin' ye while they waves cooling jellies in front of ye, and binds ye down

tighter on yer dreadful bed. Aye, an' the air'll be full of the stench of
burnt flesh and the screams of your nearest and dearest . . ."

He took a gulp of water, which Flora thought he more than deserved. She was beginning to feel that she could do with a glass of water
herself.

Amos's voice now took on a deceptively mild and conversational
note. His protruding eyes ranged slowly over his audience.

"Ye know, doan't ye, what it feels like when ye burn yer hand in
takin' a cake out of the oven or wi' a match when ye're lightin' one of
they godless cigarettes? Aye. It stings wi' a fearful pain, doan't it? And
ye run away to clap a bit o' butter on it to take the pain away. Ah, but'
(an impressive pause) *'there'll be no butter in hell!* Yer whoal body will be
burnin' and stingin' wi' that unbearable pain, and yer blackened tongues
will be stickin' out of yer mouth, and yer cracked lips will try to scream
out for a drop of water, but no sound woan't come because yer throat
is drier nor the sandy desert and yer eyes will be beatin' like great red-
hot balls against yer shrivelled eyelids . . ."

It was at this point that Flora rose quietly and with an apology to
the woman sitting next to her, passed rapidly across the narrow aisle to
the door. She opened it, and went out. The details of Amos's description, the close atmosphere and the smell of the gas made the inside of
the chapel quite near enough to hell, without listening to Amos's conducted tour of the place thrown in. She felt that she could pass the
evening more profitably elsewhere.

But where? The fresh air smelled deliciously sweet. She regained
her composure while she stood in the porch putting on her gloves. She
wondered if she should drop in to see "Other Wives' Sins," but thought
not; she had heard enough about sin for one evening.

What, then, should she do? She could not return to the farm except
with Amos in the buggy, for it was seven miles from Beershorn, and
the last bus to Howling left at half past six during the winter months. It
was now nearly eight o'clock and she was hungry. She looked crossly
up and down the street; most of the shops were shut, but one a few
doors from the cinema was open.

It was called Pam's Parlour. It was a tea-shop, and Flora thought it
looked pretty grim; there were cakes in its windows all mixed up with
depressing little boxes made of white wood and raffia bags and linen
bags embroidered with hollyhocks. But where there were cakes there
might also be coffee. She crossed the road and went in.

No sooner did she stand inside than she realized that she had gone
out of hell fire into an evening of boredom. For someone was seated at

one of the tables whom she recognized. She seemed to remember meeting him at a party given by a Mrs. Polswett in London. And he could only be Mr. Mybug. That was who he looked like, and that, of course, was who he was. There was no one else in the shop. He had a clear field, and she could not escape.

•

"I think it's *degrading* of you, Flora," cried Mrs. Smiling at breakfast. "Do you truly mean that you don't ever want to work at *anything*?"

Her friend replied after some thought:

"Well, when I am fifty-three or so I would like to write a novel as good as *Persuasion*, but with a modern setting, of course. For the next thirty years or so I shall be collecting material for it. If anyone asks me what I work at, I shall say, 'Collecting material.' No one can object to that. Besides, so I shall be."

Mrs. Smiling drank some coffee in silent disapproval.

"If you ask me," continued Flora, "I think I have much in common with Miss Austen. She liked everything to be tidy and pleasant and comfortable about her, and so do I. You see, Mary"—and here Flora began to grow earnest and to wave one finger about—"unless everything is tidy and pleasant and comfortable all about one, people cannot even begin to enjoy life. I cannot *endure messes*."

"Oh, neither can I," cried Mrs. Smiling, with fervour. "If there is one thing I do detest it is a mess. And I do think *you* are going to be messy, if you go and live with a lot of obscure relations."

"Well, my mind is made up, so there is no purpose in arguing," said Flora. "After all, if I find I cannot abide Scotland or South Kensington or Sussex, I can always come back to London and gracefully give in, and learn to work, as you suggest. But I am not anxious to do that, because I am sure it would be more amusing to go and stay with some of these dire relatives. Besides, there is sure to be a lot of material I can collect for my novel; and perhaps one or two of the relations will have messes or miseries in their domestic circle which I can clear up."

"You have the most revolting Florence Nightingale complex," said Mrs. Smiling.

"It is not that at all, and well you know it. On the whole I dislike my fellow-beings; I find them so difficult to understand. But I have a tidy mind, and untidy lives irritate me. Also, they are uncivilized."

"I think if I find that I have any third cousins living at Cold Comfort Farm (young ones, you know, children of Cousin Judith) who are named Seth, or Reuben, I shall decide not to go."

"Why?"

"Oh, because highly sexed young men living on farms are always called Seth or Reuben, and it would be such a nuisance. And my cousin's name, remember, is Judith. That in itself is most ominous. Her husband is almost certain to be called Amos; and if he *is*, it will be a typical farm, and you know what *they* are like."

•

The waitress went away, and Mr. Mybug could once more concentrate upon Flora. He leaned his elbows on the table, sank his chin in his hands, and looked steadily at her. As Flora merely went on eating her orange, he was forced to open the game with, "Well?" (A gambit which Flora, with a sinking heart, recognized as one used by intellectuals who had decided to fall in love with you.)

"You are writing a book, aren't you?" she said, rather hastily. "I remember that Mrs. Polswett told me you were. Isn't it a life of Branwell Brontë?" (She thought it would be best to utilize the information artlessly conveyed to her by Mrs. Murther at the Condemn'd Man, and conceal the fact that she met Mrs. Polswett, a protégée of Mrs. Smiling's, only once, and thought her a most trying female.)

"Yes, it's goin' to be dam' good," said Mr. Mybug. "It's a psychological study, of course, and I've got a lot of new matter, including three letters he wrote to an old aunt in Ireland, Mrs. Prunty, during the period when he was working on *Wuthering Heights*."

He glanced sharply at Flora to see if she would react by a laugh or a stare of blank amazement, but the gentle, interested expression upon her face did not change, so he had to explain.

"You see, it's obvious that it's his book and not Emily's. No woman could have written that. It's male stuff . . . I've worked out a theory about his drunkenness, too—you see, he wasn't really a drunkard. He was a tremendous genius, a sort of second Chatterton—and his sisters hated him because of his genius."

"I thought most of the contemporary records agree that his sisters were quite devoted to him," said Flora, who was only too pleased to keep the conversation impersonal.

"I know . . . I know. But that was only their cunning. You see, they were devoured by jealousy of their brilliant brother, but they were afraid that if they showed it he would go away to London for good, taking his manuscripts with him. And they didn't want him to do that because it would have spoiled their little game."

"Which little game was that?" asked Flora, trying with some difficulty to imagine Charlotte, Emily, and Anne engaged in a little game.

"Passing his manuscripts off as their own, of course. They wanted to have him under their noses so that they could steal his work and sell it to buy more drink."

"Who for—Branwell?"

"No—for themselves They were all drunkards, but Anne was the worst of the lot. Branwell, who adored her, used to pretend to get drunk at the Black Bull in order to get gin for Anne. The landlord wouldn't let him have it if Branwell hadn't built up—with what devotion, only God knows—that false reputation as a brilliant, reckless, idle drunkard. The landlord was proud to have young Mr. Brontë in his tavern; it attracted custom to the place, and Branwell could get gin for Anne on tick—as much as Anne wanted. Secretly, he worked twelve hours a day writing *Shirley* and *Villette*—and, of course, *Wuthering Heights*. I've proved all this by evidence from the three letters to old Mrs. Prunty."

"But do the letters," inquired Flora, who was fascinated by this recital, "actually say that he is writing *Wuthering Heights*?"

"Of course not," retorted Mr. Mybug. "Look at the question as a psychologist would. Here is a man working fifteen hours a day on a stupendous masterpiece which absorbs almost all his energy. He will scarcely spare the time to eat or sleep. He's like a dynamo driving itself on its own demoniac vitality. Every scrap of his being is concentrated on finishing *Wuthering Heights*. With what little energy he has left he writes to an old aunt in Ireland. Now, I ask you, would you expect him to mention that he was working on *Wuthering Heights*?"

"Yes," said Flora.

Mr. Mybug shook his head violently.

"No—no—no! Of course he wouldn't. He'd want to get away from it for a little while, away from this all-obsessing work that was devouring his vitality. Of course he wouldn't mention it—not even to his aunt."

"Why not even to her? Was he so fond of her?"

"She was the passion of his life," said Mr. Mybug, simply, with a luminous gravity in his voice. "Think—he'd never seen her. She was not like the rest of the drab angular women by whom he was surrounded. She symbolized mystery . . . woman . . . the eternal unsolvable and unfindable X. It was a perversion, of course, his passion for her, and that made it all the stronger. All we have left of this fragile, wonderfully delicate relationship between the old woman and the young man are these three short letters. Nothing more."

"Didn't she ever answer them?"

"If she did, her letters are lost. But his letters to her are enough to go on. They are little masterpieces of repressed passion. They're full of tender little questions . . . he asks her how is her rheumatism . . . has her cat, Toby, 'recovered from the fever' . . . what is the weather like at Derrydownderry . . . at Haworth it is not so good . . . how is Cousin Martha (and what a picture we get of Cousin Martha in those simple words, a raw Irish chit, high-cheekboned, with limp black hair and clear blood in her lips!) . . . It didn't matter to Branwell that in London the Duke was jockeying Palmerston in the stormy Corn Reforms of the 'forties.' Aunt Prunty's health and welfare came first in interest."

Mr. Mybug paused and refreshed himself with a spoonful of orange juice. Flora sat pondering on what she had just heard. Judging by her personal experience among her friends, it was not the habit of men of genius to refresh themselves from their labours by writing to old aunts; this task, indeed, usually fell to the sisters and wives of men of genius, and it struck Flora as far more likely that Charlotte, Anne, or Emily would have had to cope with any old aunts who were clamouring to be written to. However, perhaps Charlotte, Anne, or Emily had all decided one morning that it really *was* Branwell's turn to write to Aunt Prunty, and had sat on his head in turn while he wrote the three letters, which were afterwards posted at prudently spaced intervals.

She glanced at her watch.

It was half past eight. She wondered what time the Brethren came out of the dog-kennel. There was no sign of their release so far; the kennel was thundering to their singing, and at intervals there were pauses, during which Flora presumed that they were quivering. She swallowed a tiny yawn. She was sleepy.

"What are you going to call it?"

She knew that intellectuals always made a great fuss about the titles of their books. The titles of biographies were especially important. Had not *Victorian Vista*, the scathing life of Thomas Carlyle, dropped stone cold last year from the presses because everybody thought it was a boring book of reminiscences, while *Odour of Sanctity*, a rather dull history of Drainage Reform from 1840 to 1873, had sold like hot cakes because everybody thought it was an attack on Victorian morality.

"I'm hesitating between *Scapegoat; A Study of Branwell Brontë*, and *Pard-spirit; A Study of Branwell Brontë*—you know . . . A pard-like spirit, beautiful and swift."

Flora did indeed know. The quotation was from Shelley's "Adonais." One of the disadvantages of almost universal education was the fact that all kinds of persons acquired a familiarity with one's favourite writers. It gave one a curious feeling; it was like seeing a drunken stranger wrapped in one's dressing-gown.

"Which do you like best?" asked Mr. Mybug.

"Pard-spirit," said Flora, unhesitatingly, not because she did, but because it would only lead to a long and boring argument if she hesitated.

"Really . . . that's interesting. So do I. It's wilder somehow, isn't it? I mean, I think it does give one something of the feeling of a wild thing bound down and chained, eh? And Branwell's colouring carries out the analogy—that wild reddish-leopard colouring. I refer to him as the Pard throughout the book. And then, of course, there's an under-current of symbolism . . ."

He thinks of everything, reflected Flora.

"A leopard can't change his spots, and neither could Branwell, in the end. He might take the blame for his sisters' drunkenness and let them, out of some perverted sense of sacrifice, claim his books. But in the end his genius has flamed out, blackest spot on richest gold. There isn't an intelligent person in Europe to-day who really believes Emily wrote the *Heights.*"

Flora finished her last biscuit, which she had been saving, and looked hopefully across at the dog-kennel. It seemed to her that the hymn now being sung had a sound like the tune of those hymns which are played just before people come out of church.

In the interval of outlining his work, Mr. Mybug had been looking at her very steadily, with his chin lowered, and she was not surprised when he said, abruptly:

"Do you cah about walking?"

Flora was now in a dreadful fix, and earnestly wished that the dog-kennel would open and Amos, like a fiery angel, come to rescue her. For if she said that she adored walking, Mr. Mybug would drag her for miles in the rain while he talked about sex, and if she said that she liked it only in moderation, he would make her sit on wet stiles, while he tried to kiss her. If, again, she parried his question and said that she loathed walking, he would either suspect that she suspected that he wanted to kiss her, or else he would make her sit in some dire tea-room while he talked more about sex and asked her what she felt about it.

There really seemed no way out of it, except by getting up and rushing out of the shop.

But Mr. Mybug spared her this decision by continuing in the same low voice:

"I thought we might do some walks together, if you'd cah to? I'd better warn you—I'm—pretty susceptible."

And he gave a curt laugh, still looking at her.

"Then perhaps we had better postpone our walks until the weather is finer," said she, pleasantly. "It would be too bad if your book were held up by your catching a cold, and if you really have a weak chest you cannot be too careful."

Mr. Mybug looked as though he would have given much to have brushed this aside with a brutal laugh. He had planned that his next sentence should be, in an even lower voice:

"You see, I believe in utter frankness about these things—Flora."

But somehow he did not say it. He was not used to talking to young women who looked as clean as Flora looked. It rather put him off his stroke. He said instead, in a toneless voice: "Yes . . . oh, yes, of course," and gave her a quick glance.

Flora was pensively drawing on her gauntlets and keeping her glance upon the stream of Brethren now issuing from the dog-kennel. She feared to miss Amos.

Mr. Mybug rose abruptly, and stood looking at her with his hands thrust into his pockets.

"Are you with anybody?" he asked.

"My cousin is preaching at the Church of the Quivering Brethren opposite. He is driving me home."

Mr. Mybug murmured his, "dear, how amusing." He then said:

"Oh . . . I thought we might have walked it."

"It is seven miles, and I am afraid my shoes are not stout enough," countered Flora firmly.

Mr. Mybug gave an ironical smile and muttered something about "Check to the King," but Flora had seen Amos coming out of the kennel and knew that rescue had come, so she did not mind who was checked.

She said, pleasantly, "I must go, I am afraid; there is my cousin looking for me. Good-bye, and thank you so much for telling me about your book. It's been so interesting. Perhaps we shall meet again some-time . . ."

Mr. Mybug leapt on this remark, which slipped out unintentionally from Flora's social armoury, before she could prevent it, and said eagerly that it would be great fun if they could meet again. "I'll give you my card." And he brought out a large, dirty, nasty one, which Flora with some reluctance put into her bag.

"I warn you," added Mr. Mybug, "I'm a queer moody brute. No-body likes me. I'm like a child that's been rapped over the knuckles till it's afraid to shake hands—but there's something there if you cah to dig for it."

Flora did not cah to dig, but she thanked him for his card with a smile, and hurried across the road to join Amos, who stood towering in the middle of it.

As she came up to him he drew back, pointed at her, and uttered the single word:

"Fornicator!"

"No—dash it, Cousin Amos, that wasn't a stranger; it was a person I'd met before at a party in London," protested Flora, her indignation a little roused by the unjustness of the accusation, especially when she thought of her real feelings for Mr. Mybug.

" 'Tes all one—aye, and worse too, comin' from London, the devil's city," said Amos, grimly.

However, his protest had apparently been a matter more of form than of feeling. He said nothing more about it, and they drove home in silence, save for a single remark from him to the effect that the Brethren had been mightily stirred by his preaching and that Flora had missed a good deal by not staying for the quivering.

To which Flora replied that she was sure she had, but that his eloquence had been altogether too much for her weak and sinful spirit. She added firmly that he really ought to see about going round on that Ford van; and he sighed heavily, and said that no doubt she was a devil sent to tempt him.

•

Urk gave a wild laugh. His hand fell on her shoulder, and he drew her to him and pressed a savage kiss full on her open mouth. Aunt Ada Doom, choking with rage, struck at them with the *Milk Producers' Weekly Bulletin and Cowkeepers' Guide*, but the blow missed. She fell back, gasping, exhausted.

"Come, my beauty—my handful of dirt. I mun carry thee up to Ticklepenny's and show 'ee to the water-voles." Urk's face was working with passion.

"What! At this time o' night?" cried Mrs. Beetle, scandalized.

Urk put one arm round Meriam's waist and heaved away, but could not budge her from the floor. He cursed aloud, and, kneeling down, placed his arms about her middle, and heaved again. She did not stir. Next he wrapped his arms about her shoulders, and below her knees. She declined upon him, and he, staggering beneath her, sank to the floor. Mrs. Beetle made a sound resembling "t-t-t-t."

Mark Dolour was heard to mutter that th' Fireman's Lift was as good a hold as any he knew.

Now Urk made Meriam stand in the middle of the floor, and with a low, passionful cry, ran to her.

"Come, my beauty."

The sheer animal weight of the man bore her up into his clutching arms. Mark Dolour (who dearly loved a bit of sport) held open the door, and Urk and his burden rushed out into the dark and the earthy scents of the young spring night.

A silence fell.

The door remained open, idly swinging in a slow, cold wind which had risen.

As though frozen, the group within the kitchen waited for the distant crash which should tell them that Urk had fallen down.

Pretty soon it came; and Mark Dolour shut the door.

•

This was his idea of romance, Flora could see. She knew from experience that intellectuals thought the proper—nay, the only—way to fall in love with somebody was to do it the very instant you saw them. You met somebody, and thought they were "A charming person. So gay and simple." Then you walked home from a party with them (preferably across Hampstead Heath, about three in the morning) discussing whether you should sleep together or not. Sometimes you asked them to go to Italy with you. Sometimes they asked you to go to Italy (preferably to Portofino) with them. You held hands, and laughed, and kissed them and called them your "true love." You loved them for eight months, and then you met somebody else and began being gay and simple all over again, with small-hours' walk across Hampstead, Portofino invitation, and all.

It was very simple, gay, and natural, somehow.

Charlotte Perkins Gilman (1869–1935)

❧ ❧

Queer People

The people people work with best
   Are often very queer,
The people people own by birth
   Quite shock your first idea;
The people people choose for friends

Your common sense appall,
But the people people marry
Are the queerest ones of all.

•

FROM *The Yellow Wallpaper*

It is very seldom that mere ordinary people like John and myself secure ancestral halls for the summer.

A colonial mansion, a hereditary estate, I would say a haunted house, and reach the height of romantic felicity—but that would be asking too much of fate!

Still I will proudly declare that there is something queer about it.

Else, why should it be let so cheaply? And why have stood so long untenanted?

John laughs at me, of course, but one expects that in marriage.

John is practical in the extreme. He has no patience with faith, an intense horror of superstition, and he scoffs openly at any talk of things not to be felt and seen and put down in figures.

John is a physician, and *perhaps*—(I would not say it to a living soul, of course, but this is dead paper and a great relief to my mind)—*perhaps* that is one reason I do not get well faster.

You see he does not believe I am sick!

And what can one do?

If a physician of high standing, and one's own husband, assures friends and relatives that there is really nothing the matter with one but temporary nervous depression—a slight hysterical tendency—what is one to do?

My brother is also a physician, and also of high standing, and he says the same thing.

So I take phosphates or phosphites—whichever it is, and tonics, and journeys, and air, and exercise, and am absolutely forbidden to "work" until I am well again.

Personally, I disagree with their ideas.

Personally, I believe that congenial work, with excitement and change, would do me good.

But what is one to do?

I did write for a while in spite of them; but it *does* exhaust me a good deal—having to be so sly about it, or else meet with heavy opposition.

I sometimes fancy that in my condition if I had less opposition and more society and stimulus—but John says the very worst thing I can do is to think about my condition, and I confess it always makes me feel bad.

So I will let it alone and talk about the house.

The most beautiful place! It is quite alone, standing well back from the road, quite three miles from the village. It makes me think of English places that you read about, for there are hedges and walls and gates that lock, and lots of separate little houses for the gardeners and people.

There is a *delicious* garden! I never saw such a garden—large and shady, full of box-bordered paths, and lined with long grape-covered arbors with seats under them.

There were greenhouses, too, but they are all broken now.

There was some legal trouble, I believe, something about the heirs and coheirs; anyhow, the place has been empty for years.

That spoils my ghostliness, I am afraid, but I don't care—there is something strange about the house—I can feel it.

I even said so to John one moonlight evening, but he said what I felt was a *draught*, and shut the window.

I get unreasonably angry with John sometimes. I'm sure I never used to be so sensitive. I think it is due to this nervous condition.

But John says if I feel so, I shall neglect proper self-control; so I take pains to control myself—before him, at least, and that makes me very tired.

I don't like our room a bit. I wanted one downstairs that opened on the piazza and had roses all over the window, and such pretty old-fashioned chintz hangings! but John would not hear of it.

He said there was only one window and not room for two beds, and no near room for him if he took another.

He is very careful and loving, and hardly lets me stir without special direction.

I have a schedule prescription for each hour in the day; he takes all care from me, and so I feel basely ungrateful not to value it more.

He said we came here solely on my account, that I was to have perfect rest and all the air I could get. "Your exercise depends on your strength, my dear," said he, " and your food somewhat on your appetite; but air you can absorb all the time." So we took the nursery at the top of the house.

It is a big, airy room, the whole floor nearly, with windows that look all ways, and air and sunshine galore. It was nursery first and then playroom and gymnasium, I should judge; for the windows are barred for little children, and there are rings and things in the walls.

The paint and paper look as if a boys' school had used it. It is stripped off—the paper—in great patches all around the head of my bed, about as far as I can reach, and in a great place on the other side of the room low down. I never saw a worse paper in my life.

One of those sprawling flamboyant patterns committing every artistic sin.

It is dull enough to confuse the eye in following, pronounced enough to constantly irritate and provoke study, and when you follow the lame uncertain curves for a little distance they suddenly commit suicide—plunge off at outrageous angles, destroy themselves in unheard of contradictions.

The color is repellent, almost revolting; a smouldering unclean yellow, strangely faded by the slow-turning sunlight.

It is a dull yet lurid orange in some places, a sickly sulphur tint in others.

No wonder the children hated it! I should hate it myself if I had to live in this room long.

There comes John, and I must put this away,—he hates to have me write a word.

•

Similar Cases

There was once a little animal,
    No bigger than a fox,
And on five toes he scampered
    Over Tertiary rocks.
They called him Eohippus,
    And they called him very small,
And they thought him of no value—
    When they thought of him at all;
For the lumpish old Dinoceras
    And Coryphodon so slow
Were the heavy aristocracy
    In days of long ago.

Said the little Eohippus,
    "I am going to be a horse!
And on my middle finger-nails
    To run my earthly course!

I'm going to have a flowing tail!
    I'm going to have a mane!
I'm going to stand fourteen hands high
    On the psychozoic plain!"
The Coryphodon was horrified,
    The Dinoceras was shocked;
And they chased young Eohippus,
    But he skipped away and mocked.

"We are going to turn life upside down
    About a thing called gold!
We are going to want the earth, and take
    As much as we can hold!
We are going to wear great piles of stuff
    Outside our proper skins!
We are going to have Diseases!
    And Accomplishments!! And sins!!!"

Then they all rose up in fury
    Against their boastful friend,
For prehistoric patience
    Cometh quickly to an end.
Said one, "This is chimerical!
    Utopian! Absurd!"
Said another, "What a stupid life!
    Too dull, upon my word!"

Cried all, "Before such things can come,
    You idiotic child,
You must alter Human Nature!"
    And they all sat back and smiled.
Thought they, "An answer to that last
    It will be hard to find!"
It was a clinching argument
    To the Neolithic Mind!

•

FROM *Herland*

"Well—there are some rather high forms of insect life in which it occurs. Parthenogenesis, we call it—that means virgin birth."
    She could not follow him.

"*Birth*, we know, of course; but what is *virgin*?"

Terry looked uncomfortable, but Jeff met the question quite calmly. "Among mating animals, the term *virgin* is applied to the female who has not mated," he answered.

"Oh, I see. And does it apply to the male also? Or is there a different term for him?"

He passed this over rather hurriedly, saying that the same term would apply, but was seldom used.

"No?" she said. "But one cannot mate without the other surely. Is not each then—virgin—before mating?"

Nikki Giovanni (1943-)

Rituals

i always wanted to be a bridesmaid
honest to god
i could just see me floating
down that holy aisle leading
some dear friend to heaven
in pink and purple organza with lots and lots
of crinoline pushing the violets out from my dress
hem
or maybe in a more sophisticated endeavor
one of those lovely sky blue slinky numbers
fitting tight around my abounding twenty-eights
holding a single red rose white gloves open in the back
always forever made of nylon and my feet nestled gently
in *chandlers* number 699 which was also the price plus
one dollar to match it pretty near the dress color

wedding rituals have always intrigued me
and i'd swear to friends i wouldn't say goddamn not even
once no matter what neither would i give a power
sign but would even comb my hair severely
back and put that blue shit under my eyes
i swear i wanted to be in a wedding

Straight Talk

i'm giving up
on language
my next book will be blank
pages of various textures and hues
i have touched in
certain spots and patterns
and depending upon the mood the reader can come
with me or take me somewhere else

     i smell blood a'cookin

"but why" i asked when she said "i'm afraid
to see men cry"
"because i depend" she replied "on their strength"
"but are they any less strong for crying
nylon stockings wear better if they're washed first"

     mommy said it's only pot
     luck but you can have some

science teaches us matter
is neither created nor destroyed
and as illogical as it is there is nothing
worthwhile but people
and lord knows how irrational we are

     i'll just have a scrambled egg
     if it's all right

the question turns on a spelling problem
i mean i hate
to squash a roach and thought about giving up
meat between the shadow
and the act falls the essence   encore!
the preceding paragraph was brought to you by the letter E
in the name of hue*manity*

an acorn to an ant
is the same as a white man to a Black JOB
enjoyed waiting on

the lord tell me
why can't i

and i'm glad i'm smart cause i know
smart isn't enough and i'm glad
i'm young cause "youth and truth are making love" i'm glad
i'm Black not only
because it's beautiful but because it's me
and i can be dumb and old and petty and ugly
and jealous but i still need love

   your lunch today was brought to you
   by the polytech branch of your local
   spear o agnew association
   HEY! this is straight talk!

have a good day

                    •

Housecleaning

   i always liked housecleaning
   even as a child
   i dug straightening
   the cabinets
   putting new paper on
   the shelves
   washing the refrigerator
   inside out
   and unfortunately this habit has
   carried over and i find
   i must remove you
   from my life

                    •

Nikki Rosa

childhood remembrances are always a drag
if you're Black
you always remember things like living in Woodlawn

with no inside toilet
and if you become famous or something
they never talk about how happy you were to have your mother
all to yourself and
how good the water felt when you got your bath from one of those
big tubs that folk in chicago barbecue in
and somehow when you talk about home
it never gets across how much you
understood their feelings
as the whole family attended meetings about Hollydale
and even though you remember
your biographers never understand
your father's pain as he sells his stock
and another dream goes
and though you're poor it isn't poverty that
concerns you
and though they fought a lot
it isn't your father's drinking that makes any difference
but only that everybody is together and you
and your sister have happy birthdays and very good christ-
masses and I really hope no white person ever had cause to
write about me because they never understand Black love
is Black wealth and they'll probably talk about my hard
childhood and never understand that all the while I was
quite happy

Whoopi Goldberg (1950-)

One-liners

It's bull that people throw paint on fur coats. Come near me with a can,
and I'll take out your trachea.

•

[I]t's great being a grandmother—you can send *those* kids home.

Ellen Goodman (1941–   )

❧ ❧

FROM *Making Sense*

I, too, am leery of chemicals and squeamish about factory farming. Yet I have the sense that the advent of friendly farming will get out of hand. We are entering an era when the very best people will only eat food that's been well-bred, hand-raised, indeed, scratched behind the ears. Purveyors to the finest will be required to prove that they were kind and caring to all the little piggies who went to market.

It does not take much of an imagination to see where this is leading. "This flank steak comes from Bessie, who was hand-raised by the Johnsons after a difficult labor. Bessie spent her first year of life frolicking around the crystal-clear pond behind the Johnsons' Vermont house where she became a favorite of Pearl Johnson, who always slipped her the finest of grains."

Will the restaurants that now wheel raw platters of meat and fish for our choosing bring along testimonials about how well each item was brought up? Will our leather shoes require a certificate proving that the animals were all volunteers?

I know where you think this is heading: toward vegetarianism. But sliced tomatoes are said to scream, and even zucchini may need a certificate attesting to a happy summer in the sun before they were killed with kindness.

The truth is that I don't want to get any closer to my food. It is bad enough to have to know the cholesterol content of eggs, the country of origin of grapes, the chemical content of apples. I do not want to feel responsible for the workplace conditions and psychological profile of my dinner.

Pass me two more eggs. Crack them. Cook them. Eat them. Just don't tell their mama.

•

The twenty-fifth reunion reports are full of our "mistakes." The very mistakes younger graduates want to avoid. Our lives are littered with mid-course corrections. A full half of us divorced. Many of the women have had career paths that look like games of Chutes and Ladders. We have changed directions and priorities again and again. But our "mistakes" became crucial parts, sometimes the best parts, of the lives we have made.

As a writer, I believe that a blank slate is very much overrated. It's terrifying. It's easier to get some words down, to just get rolling, than to wait for the perfect ones to come to mind. You can always rewrite.

•

Husbands and wives now come to court pleading "no fault." It is a reform that takes into account absolutely everything except the human desire for revenge and absolution. How many couples leave secretly longing for a verdict that declares their ex to be: Cad! Heel! Louse! By order of the court.

•

Last year, the big phrase was post-feminist. Any young woman who had not personally signed up for Radical Feminist Cell 16 was called a member of the post-feminist generation. The label managed to wear-date the women's movement so that it seemed unfashionable. Feminism itself was described as something the country had outgrown, like a singed training bra.

Serena Gray (contemporary)

~≈ ❦ ≈~

FROM *Beached on the Shores of Love*

Suddenly, having a man, like having a miniskirt, has become important again. Where ten or twenty years ago the books written for women were all about asserting ourselves and understanding the ways in which men had historically manipulated and taken advantage of us, about being independent and enjoying our freedom and our rights as human beings, about finding ourselves and not turning into Barbie Dolls, now they are all about finding HIM—and having found him, understanding him, keeping him happy, and keeping him, come hell or high water. Where ten or twenty years ago women were dressing in sensible clothes and practical shoes (having broken that last high heel over his head when he suggested that her opinion on *ciné vérité* wasn't worth having), repair manual gripped under the arm and a sureness in the step, decking any man who dared to hold a door open or pull back a chair, now those same women have stilettos, tortured hair-dos and tight skirts that make running from muggers difficult, and sing "I Enjoy Being A Girl."

•

Men and children are equally sensitive to minor illnesses and injuries (the mild headache, the banged hand, the stomachache from mixing chocolate and chips or bourbon and wine), liable to take to the sofa in need of cold compresses and cups of tea and someone to offer assurances that death is not imminent and that there's chocolate custard for dessert for anyone who survives. Men and children do not like doing yukky things like cleaning out the swing bin or changing the cat litter or mopping up sick or fishing out things that fell in the toilet. Men and children do not like waiting around while you chat to a friend you just bumped into or try on just one more swimming costume. They hate it when you talk on the telephone at a time when you are supposed to be playing with them. They think that if you're sitting down it means you're waiting for someone to give you something to do. Both men and children are given to tantrums, though in the case of the latter you usually both say you're sorry in the end, and in the case of the former only you say you're sorry.

•

You live with Stan for six years. And for six years he drives you crazy. Even though he has lived in the flat as long as you have, he can never remember where the coffee or the tin opener are kept, and even though he is a nuclear physicist of some distinction he has yet to work out the complexities of the washing machine. If you go away for a weekend, it is guaranteed that when you return you will discover that Stan has run out of toilet paper, milk and cat food while you were gone and that it has not occurred to him that he is permitted to replace them (so the cats are eating tinned tuna, last week's colour supplement is in the bog, and the fridge contains one empty milk carton). Despite all this, Stan is a fussbudget. If you leave something on the table (other than the coffee or the tin opener) he will put it away. If you put the newspaper to one side because there was something you wanted to read in it he will throw it out. If you put out the cheese dip to reach room temperature before the guests arrive, Stan will put it back in the fridge so that you have to serve it with knives instead of celery sticks. Stan is also a workaholic hypochondriac, torn between spending all his spare time doing the "just a few things" he brought home from the office and taking his temperature and pulse. In many ways, living with Stan is like being alone—

but with none of the benefits (you can't eat toast in bed because it makes him break out in a rash; you can't play your Talking Heads albums because it disturbs his concentration; you can't stay out too late on your own because it causes him anxiety). A typical evening with Stan consists of you rushing home to fix a meal that he doesn't eat because he works late and isn't hungry by the time he slumps through the door, or because someone left a copy of *Your Health Today* on the train and he now realizes that he's allergic to wheat. Then Stan will lock himself away to work, unless you have something you wanted to do, in which case he is overcome with the need to spend some time with you. And Stan is very competitive. He is a bad Scrabble loser, the sort of man who quibbles over the rules and re-checks the scores. If you say that "Lola" came out in 1969 and he says that it came out in 1970, he will leave no stone unturned and no record shop uncalled in proving you are wrong (and on every occasion for the next few months that someone introduces music into the conversation, Stan will immediately say, "My God, speaking of that, did I tell you what she came out with the other day? She . . . she thought 'Lola' came out in 1969 . . ."). Because he gets restless on weekends, when he is locked out of his lab on Sunday, holidays with Stan are few, brief, and far between—and normally spent with him felled by food poisoning, sunstroke, or a sensitivity to foreign water, even if it comes in bottles, and you staying close by in case he needs something (so that, though you and Stan have been to some of the world's great beauty spots, in your memory they all meld into one medium-sized hotel room with a view of the car park or the swimming pool).

•

A cautionary tale. Several years ago, for no good reason that any of us could see, my friend Jenny fell in love with a man in her office. A married man with four young children. According to Jenny, this man was not only brilliant (a quality she admired) but had a simmering sensuality cleverly camouflaged by the fact that he looked like a hobbit. They began by playing footsie at board meetings. Then they went for chaste, professional lunches in the executive dining room where she chose the wine and he asked her opinions on world affairs. They started going to bars out of town frequented by long-distance lorry drivers and held hands across the table while, on the jukebox Robert Gordon sang "It's Only Make Believe." They made out in the car, just like teenagers. "He makes me feel so young," she said. "She makes me feel like a kid again," he said. Finally, after a number of false starts (one date was cancelled because of his guilt, one date was cancelled because of her guilt, one date was cancelled because his daughter had a severe nosebleed), she invited him over for dinner. She bought two hand-blown champagne glasses and two bottles of Bollinger to mark the occasion. She paid a small fortune for a dress that barely weighed in at half an ounce. He passed out. Soon, of course, they were both madly, passionately, and hopelessly in love. He said that she was the only woman who had ever made him feel really alive. He said it was as though she'd broken a spell. He could never go back to the tedious, life-sapping existence he had had before. He couldn't continue living a lie. He told his wife. His wife felt as though a spell had been broken, as well. She reminded him of their fifteen years together, their children, their plans. She made him go to family counselling with her. Any time she called the office and a woman answered she burst into tears. Jenny was hurt that he seemed to be making more effort to save a marriage he claimed had been dead for fourteen years than to begin a new one. Jenny was hurt because his children wouldn't speak to her. She was upset because although he was always just about to leave his wife something happened to delay him (the youngest had chicken-pox, his wife threatened to kill herself, it was one of the children's birthdays, it was Christmas, it was Easter, it was his birthday, he couldn't find a flat, his wife had given all his clothes away to the Salvation Army). Finally, heartsick, underweight, and having given most of her friends compassion fatigue with her endless unhappiness, Jenny decided to go to Australia for a year or two. While she was away, her lover left his wife and children and moved in with a twenty-year-old designer named Aire. He is now on his third marriage. Jenny has yet to start her first.

•

One of the few interesting things about office affairs is that no matter how discreet and clever you think you are, everyone else in the office, if not the entire building, will know what's going on approximately four hours before you do. They will know when you meet. They will know at every step what stage the relationship is at. "They went away for the weekend," Sandra will tell Inez as they remove the covers from their computers on Monday morning. "Where to?" asks Inez. "His brother's place at the seaside." "How do you know?" asks Inez. "I heard him on the phone on Friday and when he came in this morning there was seaweed stuck to his shoe." "Wow," says Inez. "They're sure moving fast. I wonder what it was like . . ." Sandra rolls her eyes. "Oohwee," says Sandra. "You should see him. He looks like Don Johnson on a roll. I bet he hasn't slept or shaved since Friday morning. 'Oh, Mr. Smothers,' I said to him. 'You look like you've been working too hard again.' " "And what did he say?" asks Inez. "He said, 'I know, Sandra, but some-

body's got to do it.' " Inez and Sandra both start laughing rather uncontrollably here. "And what about Ms. Wishbone?" asks Inez once
she's recovered. "I haven't seen her yet this morning." Sandra can barely
answer, she's laughing so hard. "Oh her," chokes Sandra, "she called in
sick." Inez nearly falls off her chair.

They will not only know every time you and your lover have an
orgasm, they will know every time you have a fight. "Stay away from
the two of them today," Inez will warn Sandra. "Why?" asks Sandra,
glancing up from her terminal. "What's up?" "Not him," says Inez.
"They had a real knock-down-drag-out because he went out drinking
with the boys last night and forgot he had a date with her."

They will know long before you do when the relationship is coming to an end. "Did you see that?" Sandra asks Inez one Friday night as
the hands of the clock are skipping towards five-thirty. "Am I blind?"
Inez wants to know. "I haven't seen him move so fast since he set fire
to his waste basket that time." Just then you come by, looking as though
you have one or two little things you have to finish up before you go
home for the weekend, and looking as though it only occurred to you
a few minutes ago that if Mr. Smothers hasn't gone home yet he might
be able to answer one or two of your questions. "He's gone," says
Sandra as you come to an abrupt halt at the entrance to Mr. Smothers'
office, noticing, not for the first time, just how much its neatness, its
white walls and chrome fixtures reminds you of his bathroom at home.
"Gone home?" you say, as though it is impossible to understand how a
man who has not "gone home" on a Friday evening for the past six
months but has lingered in the office until everyone else had left so that
you and he could do some heavy breathing against the filing cabinets
could possibly have changed his habits. "Yes," says Inez, exchanging
with Sandra a look that is not without its sisterly compassion. "Gone
home."

•

The only thing to remember when your best friend says, "Come over
to supper on Thursday, I've got someone I'm just dying for you to
meet," is not to get your hopes up. Remember the time she threw a
summer solstice party so you could meet this great guy who turned out
to be a manic depressive who took you back to his place to show you
all the holes he'd punched in the walls? Remember how many broken
hearts you've had to see her through? Go thinking not, I'm about to
meet a man who looks like Robert de Niro and can play "Girls from
Texas" on the guitar, but, I'm about to get a free meal and with any
luck she'll make that chocolate pie I like so much. Keep in mind that

God does work in some pretty mysterious ways, and so, as Chuck Berry once noted, you never can tell. You might get really lucky.

Germaine Greer (1939-   )

~~❧ ❧~~

FROM *The Female Eunuch*

The occupational hazard of being a Playboy Bunny is the aching facial muscles brought on by the obligatory smiles.

So what is the beef? Maybe I couldn't make it. Maybe I don't have a pretty smile, good teeth, nice tits, long legs, a cheeky arse, a sexy voice. Maybe I don't know how to handle men and increase my market value, so that the rewards due to the feminine will accrue to me. Then again, maybe I'm sick of the masquerade. I'm sick of pretending eternal youth. I'm sick of belying my own intelligence, my own will, my own sex. I'm sick of peering at the world through false eyelashes, so everything I see is mixed with a shadow of bought hairs; I'm sick of weighting my head with a dead mane, unable to move my neck freely, terrified of rain, of wind, of dancing too vigorously in case I sweat into my lacquered curls. I'm sick of the Powder Room. I'm sick of pretending that some fatuous male's self-important pronouncements are the objects of my undivided attention, I'm sick of going to films and plays when someone else wants to, and sick of having no opinions of my own about either. I'm sick of being a transvestite. I refuse to be a female impersonator. I am a woman, not a castrate.

•

Freud is the father of psychoanalysis. It had no mother. He is not its only begetter, and subsequent structures of theory have challenged as well as reinforced his system. Probably the best way to treat it is as a sort of metaphysic but usually it is revered as a science. Freud himself lamented his inability to understand women, and became progressively humbler in his pronouncements about them. The best approach to Freud's assumptions about women is probably the one adopted by Dr. Ian Suttie, that of psychoanalyzing Freud himself. The cornerstone of the Freudian theory of womanhood is the masculine conviction that a women is a castrated man. It is assumed that she considers herself to be thus deprived and that much of her motivation stems either from the attempt to pretend that this is not so, typical of the immature female who indulges in clitoral sexuality, or from the attempt to compensate herself for this lack by having children. Basically the argument is a tautology which cannot proceed beyond its own terms, so that it is neither demonstrable nor refutable. Ernest Jones, himself a devout Freudian, began to suspect that something was wrong with the basic hypothesis because he took the trouble to observe the sexuality of female children. . . .

•

Women have always been well represented in journalism, partly because of the existence of the pulp female market, but the names of the good ones like Katherine Whitehorn really stick. In the States the difficulty seems to be breaking through the writer (male)–researcher (female) setup, but in England things seem easier for the right girl, like Sally Beaumann who was offered the editorship of *Queen* when hardly out of her teens.

It seems that woman has more likelihood of success the higher she pitches her sights, and the more uncommon she is in her chosen environment. The highest value is placed by this society upon creativity, either in designing goods for large-scale consumption, or writing advertising copy or novels, or inventing forms of organization geared to current demand. British trade depends upon the export of ideas and expertise and men have no monopoly of either. Neither is incompatible with femininity, for even Mary Quant has had her pubic hair shaved into a heartshape by her adoring husband, if that is what you fancy. One of my favorite stories of female success is that of Mrs. Pamela Porter, who owns her own car transporter and drives 1,500 miles a week with three spaniels in the cab for company. The onus is on women, who must not only equal men in the race for employment, but outstrip them. Such an incentive must ultimately be an advantage.

•

In love, as *in* pain, *in* shock, *in* trouble.

Thus love is a state, presumably a temporary state, an aberration from the norm.

The outward symptoms of this state are sleeplessness, distraction, loss of appetite, alternations of euphoria and depression, as well as starry eyes (as in fever), and agitation.

The principal explanation of the distraction, which leads to the mislaying of possessions, confusion, forgetfulness and irresponsibility, is the overriding obsession with the love object, which may only have been seen from a distance on one occasion. The love object occupies the thoughts of the person diagnosed "in love" all the time despite the probability that very little is actually known about it. To it are ascribed all qualities considered by the obsessed as good, regardless of whether the object in question possesses those qualities in any degree. Expectations are set up which no human being could fulfill. Thus the object chosen plays a special role in relation to the ego of the obsessed, who decided that he or she is the *right* or the *only* person for him. In the case of a male this notion may sanction a degree of directly aggressive behavior either in pursuing the object or driving off competition. In the case of a female, no aggressive behavior can be undertaken and the result is more likely to be brooding, inexplicable bad temper, a dependence upon the telephone and gossip with other women about the love object, or even acts of apparent rejection and scorn to bring herself to the object's attention.

Nicole Gregory and Judith Stone

(contemporary)

~&~ &~

FROM *Heeling Your Inner Dog*

ARE YOU A SICK PUP?

A Questionnaire

Since a quarter past the dawn of time, humankind has been attempting to reduce the psyche to its component parts. Perhaps that's why there's so little mental health today.

In the late nineteenth century Sigmund Freud divided the mind into the ego (the rational self), the superego (the conscience), and the id (primal, uncontrollable urges such as sex, looking into a Kleenex after you blow your nose, putting your tongue in the hole left by a missing tooth, or saying "Peep!" after your father says "One more peep out of you and you'll be sorry").

Freud's disciple, the Swiss psychologist Carl Jung, added to the master's schema the notion of a collective unconscious, a part of the psyche that retains and transmits the common psychological inheritance of mankind. He also coined the terms *extrovert, introvert,* and *nutbag.*

Later, the founder of Transactional Analysis, Eric Berne, preferred yet another mental breakdown: child, adult, and parent. Dr. Jean-Claude Pep, the noted psychiatrist and automotive-parts magnate, followed nearly the same model but called the components Manny, Moe, and Jack.

(Curiously, Pep's Austrian rival, Dr. Fritz Dreistoogen, echoed the work of his nemesis by segmenting the psyche into three parts designated Larry, Moe, and Curly. For a detailed study of the importance of both Pep's and Dreistoogen's Moe mode in psychological rebirth and recovery, see our book *Moe Better Blues: A Poke in the Eye from the Wise Guy Within*.)

Inner Dog theory is a synthesis of all that came before it, and then some. The sooner you complete the following questionnaire, the sooner Inner Dog theory can work for you.

1. I am the adult child of former children.
   YES _____   NO _____

2. I tend to confuse pity with love, and Upton Sinclair with Sinclair Lewis.
   YES _____   NO _____

3. I was always teacher's pet.
   YES _____   NO _____

4. Squirrels interest me strangely.
   YES _____   NO _____

5. When I saw *Cats*, I felt the urge to rush the stage.
   YES _____   NO _____

6. My two favorite colors are Old Rose and Old Yeller.
   YES _____   NO _____

7. I'm easy—I'll roll over for anyone.
   YES _____   NO _____

8. One crack of thunder and I'm under the bed.
   YES _____   NO _____

9. I like to drive with my head out the window.
   YES _____   NO _____

10. I'm most loyal to someone who feeds me, tells me I'm good, and clips my toenails.
    YES _____   NO _____

11. I'm a people pleaser.

    YES _____   NO _____

12. I'm a people eater.

    YES _____   NO _____

13. I drool over my friends' good fortune.

    YES _____   NO _____

14. I drool over my friends.

    YES _____   NO _____

15. I have trouble making decisions; I respond well to commands.

    YES _____   NO _____

16. Which statement best matches what you feel:

    _____ Why shouldn't I tip over garbage cans? If I didn't, someone else would.
    _____ If I don't do tricks, no one will like me.
    _____ Why bother to carry a tennis ball in my mouth? No one's going to throw it for me anyway.
    _____ I have to beg for whatever scraps I can get.

SCORING: If you answered yes to any question above, your Inner Dog is wounded, and you need professional help. If you answered no to any question above, you are in deep denial and need professional help.

In either case, this book—a distillation of what we* teach at our famous Inner Dog Workshops—will help you get in touch with and transform your Inner Dog. Keep a copy by your bedside and another in the bathroom, near the Victoria's Secret catalog; carry a copy with you. Dip into it daily. If you're short on time, simply skim the aphorisms that we think of as soulchow and brain kibble for the Inner Dog—tender, meaty nuggets of wisdom served up in a rich gravy of experience.

Communicate anger in healthy ways. Baring your teeth and barking are fine in a workshop setting, but they may be counterproductive at

---

* We, George and Harriet, refer to ourselves throughout the book as both "we" and "us"—a tribute to our newfound commitment to togetherness—and as "George," "Harriet," "he," and "she," as an acknowledgment of our separate uniqueness.

home—for example, when your lover tells you he or she forgot to make your coffee in the morning.

Try saying this: "What's true for me today is that I have angry feelings concerning what I heard you say when you said what you said. It reminds me of what my mother said when she said what she said, and that hurts me and so that's where I'm at with this, and it's not all right with me for today." This should help to avoid a lot of communication problems.

Sarah Moore Grimké (1792–1873)

~❦ ❧~

FROM *The Pastoral Letter of the General Association of Congregational Ministers of Massachusetts*

I am persuaded that when the minds of men and women become emancipated from the thraldom of superstition and "traditions of men," the sentiments contained in the Pastoral Letter will be recurred to with as much astonishment as the opinions of Cotton Mather and other distinguished men of his day, on the subject of witchcraft; nor will it be deemed less wonderful, that a body of divines should gravely assemble and endeavor to prove that woman has no right to "open her mouth for the dumb," than it now is that judges should have sat on the trials of witches, and solemnly condemned nineteen persons and one dog to death for witchcraft.

•

"Her influence is the source of mighty power." This has ever been the flattering language of man since he laid aside the whip as a means to keep woman in subjection.

•

I do long to see the time when it will no longer be necessary for women to expend so many precious hours in furnishing "a well spread table," but that their husbands will forego some of their accustomed indulgences in this way, and encourage their wives to devote some portion of their time to mental cultivation, even at the expense of having to dine sometimes on baked potatoes, or bread and butter.

Cathy Guisewite (contemporary)

Cathy

Modine Gunch (contemporary)

~ჯ 9&~

FROM *Never Heave Your Bosom in a
Front-Hook Bra*

But I'll tell you, when I was fifteen, we didn't worry none about getting P.G., or catching one of them transmission diseases you get from sex. We knew we wouldn't live long enough. If we committed a mortal sin, like kissing a boy for longer than thirty seconds or wearing immodest shoes that showed the cleavage of our toes, a bus would hit us on our way to church to go to confession and that would be it. If God was in a bad mood, we could get struck down for even *thinking* about doing something like that. Sister Gargantua warned us we'd go straight into the flames of hell for all eternity—on a technicality.

And if you wasn't allowed to think about s-e-x, then you couldn't ask any questions. I got my sex education from the underwear and hernia section of the Sears catalog.

But some things don't change. Every few months, the nuns give a little speech about inviting a nice young man to the school dance. Which was asking the impossible. At a all-girls school, you don't get too much chance to meet any kind of young man. After a while, the guy who sweeps up the place after hours starts to look good. At least he got hair on his legs.

I remember my senior year. I am so desperate for a date to the Senior Prom, I decide to make a sacrificial offering. (Catholics do this sometimes. Other people mostly try a lucky rabbit's foot or just plain pray.) I walk around with a rock in my shoe for a entire week. And it works. Hanna Bunkart, a girl who could find a eligible man if she was stranded at a eunuchs' convention, fixes me up with a date. She says he looks like he'd be great at basketball. I think tall, so I buy real high heels— modest ones, of course, that don't show no cleavage. Our dance dresses have to pass inspection too. No strapless, no spaghetti straps. If the nice young man goes totally out of control, the nuns want us dressed in something that will hold up under assault.

Margaret Halsey (1910-   )

FROM *With Malice Toward Some*

Today, when one of my blanks said OCCUPATION, I wrote down *none*, though I suspected this would not do. A severe but courteous official confirmed this impression. So I crossed it out and wrote *parasite*, which, not to be too delicate about it, is what I am. This made the official relax a little and he himself put *housewife* in what space there was left. "Be a prince," I said. "Make it *typhoid carrier*." But he only smiled and blotted out *parasite* so that it would not show.

•

I am a big girl now and too old to believe in Shakespeare.

•

We left the suitcases and went out to eat, as—if the smell in the corridors was any indication—it was Human Sacrifice Night at the hotel. Three-quarters of an hour of walking failed to disclose a restaurant which was still open. Just as I was saying tragically that we would have to go back to the room and eat toothpaste, Henry noticed a place of decidedly humble aspect which seemed in two minds about closing up. We hurried in, and an absent-minded waitress gave us a pot of tea, supplemented after fifteen minutes by a piece of steak which had evidently been put to bed for the night and resented being disturbed.

•

Today is Sunday, and the English Sunday has started right in to live up to what I had read about it Everything is closed up, the streets are empty, and the citizens have all gone down into their cellars and pulled pillowcases over their heads. I keep having an impulse to go up to one of those sealed front doors, tap on it and say politely, "May I suggest a raven?"

•

Humility is not my forte, and whenever I dwell for any length of time on my own shortcomings, they gradually begin to seem mild, harmless, rather engaging little things, not at all like the staring defects in other people's characters.

•

The poor man has all the machinery of an intellectual (the books, the attitudes and the vocabulary), but not juice enough to run it, which makes him bad-tempered.

•

American men look at women when (they think) the women are not aware of it; Englishmen do not look at them at all; but Frenchmen look at them with such thoroughness and intensity that you half expect them to approach and ask dubiously, "Is it washable?"

Eliza Haywood (c. 1693-1756)

FROM *The Female Spectator*

How glorious a Privilege has Man beyond all other sublunary Beings! who, tho' indigent, unpitied, forsaken by the World, and even chain'd in a Dungeon, can by the Aid of Divine Contemplation, enjoy all the Charms of Pomp, Respect, and Liberty!—Transport himself in Idea to whatever Place he wishes, and grasp in Theory imagin'd Empires!

Unaccountable is it, therefore, that so many People find an Irksomeness in being alone, tho' for never so small a Space of Time!— Guilt indeed creates Perturbations, which may well make Retirement horrible, and drive the self-tormented Wretch into any Company to avoid the Agonies of Remorse; but I speak not of those who are *afraid* to reflect, but of those who seem to me not to have the *Power* to do it.

There are several of my Acquaintance of both Sexes, who lead Lives perfectly inoffensive, and when in Company appear to have a Fund of Vivacity capable of enlivening all the Conversation they come into; yet if you happen to meet them after half an Hour's Solitude, are for some Minutes the most heavy lumpish Creatures upon Earth:—Ask them if they are indispos'd? they will drawl out—*No, they are well enough*—If any Misfortune has befallen them? still they answer—*No*, in the same stupid Tone as before, and look like Things inanimate till something is said or done to reinspire them.—One would imagine they were but half awoke from a deep Sleep, and indeed their Minds, during this Lethargy, may be said to have been in a more inactive State than even of Sleep, for they have not so much as dream'd; but I think they may justly enough be compar'd to Clock-work, which has Power to do nothing of itself till wound up by another.

Whatever Opinion the World may have of the Wit of Persons of this Cast, I cannot help thinking there is a Vacuum in the Mind:—that they have no Ideas of their own, and only through Custom and a genteel Education are enabled to talk agreeably on those of other People. A real fine Genius can never want Matter to entertain itself, and tho' on the Top of a Mountain without Society, and without Books, or any *exterior* Means of Employment, will always find that *within* which will keep it from being idle—*Memory* and *Recollection* will bring the Transactions of *past* Times to View:—*Observation* and *Discernment* point out the *present* with their Causes; and *Fancy*, temper'd with *Judgment*, anticipate the *future*,—This Power of Contemplation and Reflection it is that chiefly distinguishes the *Human* from the *Brute* Creation, and proves that we have Souls which are in reality Sparks of that Divine, Omniscient, Omnipresent Being whence we all boast to be deriv'd.

The Pleasures which an agreeable Society bestows are indeed the most elegant we can taste; but even that Company we like best would grow insipid and tiresome were we to be for ever in it; and to a Person who knows how to think justly, it would certainly be as great a Mortification never to be alone, as to be always so.

Conversation, in effect, but furnishes Matter for Contemplation;—it exhilarates the Mind, and fits it for Reflection afterward:—Every new thing we hear in Company raises in us new Ideas in the Closet or on the Pillow; and as there are few People but one may gather something from, either to divert or improve, a good Understanding will, like the industrious Bee, suck out the various Sweets, and digest them in Retirement. But those who are perpetually hurrying from one Company to another, and never suffer themselves to be alone but when weary Nature summonses them to Repose, will be little amended, tho' the Maxims of a *Seneca* were to be deliver'd to them in all the enchanting Eloquence of a *Tully*.

But not to be more improved is not the worst Mischief that attends an immoderate Aversion to Solitude—People of this Humour, rather than be alone, fly into all Company indiscriminately, and sometimes fall into such as they have Reason to repent their whole Lives of having ever seen: for tho' they may not possibly reap any Advantage from the *Good*, their Reputations must certainly, and perhaps their Morals and Fortunes too, will suffer very much from the *Bad*; and where we do not give ourselves Leisure to chuse, it is rarely we happen on the former, as they being infinitely the smaller Number, and also less easy of Access to those whose Characters they are unacquainted with. . . .

But suppose we make some Allowances to a few of the very Young and Gay, especially the Beautiful and High-born, who, by a mistaken Fondness in their Parents, from the Moment they were capable of understanding what was said to them, heard nothing but Flattery, and are made to believe they came into the World for no other Purpose than to be adored and indulged, what can we say for those who had a different Education, and are of riper Years?—How little Excuse is there for a gadding Matron, or for a Woman who ought to have the Care of a House and Family at Heart!—How odd a Figure does the Mother of five or six Children make at one of these nocturnal Rambles; and how ridiculous is it for a Person in any Trade or Avocation, to be, or affect to be, above the Thought of all Economy, and make one in every Party of Pleasure that presents itself?—Yet such as these are no Prodigies.— All kinds of Regulation and Management require some small Reflection and Recess from Company, and these are two Things so terrible to some People, that they will rather suffer every thing to be ruined than endure the Fatigue of Thought. . . .

There are People so uncharitable, as to believe some latent Crime hangs heavy on the Minds of all those who take so much Pains to avoid being alone; but I am far from being of that Number:—It is my Opinion that neither this old Rattle I have mentioned, nor many others who act in the same manner, ever did a real Hurt to any one.—Those who are incapable of *Thinking*, are certainly incapable of any *premeditated* Mischief; and, as I have already said, seem to me a Set of Insensibles, who never act of themselves, but are acted upon by others.

Before one passes so cruel a Censure, one should therefore examine, I mean not the Lives and Characters, for they may deceive us, but at what Point of Time this Aversion to Solitude commenced—If from Childhood, and so continued even to the extremest old Age, it can proceed only from a Weakness in the Mind, and is deserving our Compassion; but if from taking that Satisfaction in Contemplation and Retirement, which every reasonable Soul finds in it, one sees a Person has turned to the reverse,—starts even while in Company at the bare mention of quitting it, and flies Solitude as a House on Fire, one may very well suspect some secret Crime has wrought so great a Transition, and that any Conversation, tho' the most insipid and worthless, seems preferable to that which the guilty Breast can furnish to itself.

I am well aware that there is another Motive besides either a Want of Power to think, or a Consciousness of having done what renders Thought a Pain, that induces many People to avoid being alone as much as possible; and that is, when the Mind is oppress'd with any very severe Affliction.—To be able to reflect on our Misfortunes, goes a great way towards bearing them with that Fortitude which is becoming the Dignity of human Nature; but all have not Courage to do it, and those who have not would sink beneath the Weight of Grief, were they to indulge the Memory of what occasion'd it.

This I am sensible is the Case of many who pass for Persons of very good Understanding, and the Excuse is allowed by the Generality of the World as a reasonable one; but yet I must beg their Pardon when I say, that whatsoever Share of fine Sense they may shew in other Things, they betray a very great Deficiency in this:—The Relaxation which Noise and Hurry may afford is but short-liv'd, and are so far from removing that Burthen which the Spirit labours under, that they afterward make it felt with double Weight.

Some are so madly stupid as to attempt to lose the Thoughts of one Evil by running into others of perhaps worse Consequence,—I mean that of Drinking, and some other Excesses equally pernicious both to Fortune and Constitution; but how false a Relief this gives I need only appeal to those who have made the Trial.

Would such People be prevail'd upon to make a little Reflection before it is too late, they would certainly have Recourse to more solid Consolations:—Would not the Works of some of our celebrated Poets divert a melancholy Hour much more than all the Rhodomontades of a vague idle Conversation!—Would not the Precepts of Philosophy, of which so many excellent Treaties have been wrote, give them more true Courage than all the Bottle can inspire!—And above all, would not the Duties of an entire Submission and Resignation to the Almighty Disposer of all Things, so often and so strenuously recommended, be infinitely more efficacious to quiet all Perturbations of the Mind than any vain Amusements of what kind soever!

It is not that I would perswade any one to a continual poreing over Books, too much Reading, tho' of the best Authors, is apt to dull the Spirits, and destroy that Attention which alone can render this Employment profitable.—A few good Maxims, well digested by Reflection, dwell upon the Memory, and are not only a Remedy for present Ills, but also a kind of Antidote against any future ones that Fate may have in Store.

But it may be said that this Advice can only be complied with by Persons of Condition; and as for the meaner Part, it cannot be imagined that they have either Time or Capacities to enable them to square themselves by such Rules:—This indeed must be allowed; but then it must also be allowed, that they can the least afford to waste what Time they have in such fruitless Attempts as they generally make use of for forgetting their Cares; and as to their Capacities, we are to suppose that every one understands the Trade or Business to which he has been bred, and in my Opinion, nothing is more plain than that an industrious Application to that would be his best Relief for any Vexation he is involved in, as well as the surest Means of avoiding falling into others.

Upon the whole, it denotes a Meanness of Soul, not to be forgiven even in the lowest Rank of People, much less in those of a more refined Education, when to shun the Remembrance of perhaps a trifling Affliction, they rush into Irregularities, each of which their Reason might inform them would be productive of greater Ills than any they yet had to lament; and is so far from affording any Relief, that it serves only to give new Additions to their former Disquiets, according to the Poet, justly describing this Fever of the Mind.

> *Restless they toss, and turn about their feavorish Will,*
> *When all their Ease must come by lying still.*

But what can be more amazing, than that Persons, who have no one thing on Earth to incommode them, should not be able to take any Pleasure in contemplating on the Tranquillity of their Situation!—Yet so it is: There are those in the World, and in the great World too, who being possessed of every thing they can wish, and frequently much more than either they deserve or could ever expect, seem altogether insensible of the Benefits they receive from Heaven, or any Obligations they may have to Man.—This, methinks, is an Indolence of Nature which can never be too much guarded against, because whoever is guilty of it becomes ungrateful and unjust without knowing he is so, and incurs the Censure of all who are acquainted with him for Omissions which himself is wholly ignorant of, and if he were not so, would perhaps be very far from meriting. . . .

But after all that has, or can be said, the World is more inclinable to excuse this Defect than any other I know of:—A person who loves to be always in Company, and accept of any sort rather than be alone, is accounted a good-natur'd harmless Creature; and tho' it is impossible they can be magnified for any extraordinary Virtues or Qualifications, what they lose in *Respect* is for the most Part made up with *Love*.—They have rarely any Enemies, and the Reason is plain, they are generally merry, never contradict whatever is said or done, nor refuse any thing that is asked of them:—People of a middling Understanding like their Conversation;—the most Weak are in no Awe of them; and the Wisest will sometimes suffer themselves to be diverted by them.—In fine, every body is easy with them, and how easy they are to themselves in all Events there are unnumerable Instances.

Cynthia Heimel (1947-   )

FROM *If You Can't Live Without Me, Why Aren't You Dead Yet?*

"Well, did he have the boy disease?"

"You know," said Felicity (brunette, stunning), "when everything's just great and you're having a wonderful time and then he suddenly becomes very weird and disappears. It's epidemic nowadays. I believe it was first isolated by Natalia Schiffrin, who noticed that if her friends were looking starry-eyed and walking on air one week, they were bound to be hollow-eyed, pale, and listless the next. Apparently boys are being disappointing in droves these days."

•

"But you don't know Will Wenham's famous theory?" she asked me.

"It's perfectly simple," said Louisa. "All women are either girls, women, or men. And all men are either men, boys, or hairdressers.

"Sigourney Weaver is a man. Jane Fonda is a man. Diane Keaton is a girl," said Louisa. "Jessica Lange is a woman. Mel Gibson is a boy, Clint Eastwood is a man. Cary Grant was a hairdresser."

"No, it's perfectly okay. There's nothing wrong with being a hairdresser, and it has nothing to do with sexual orientation," said Felicity. "Very good people are hairdressers. Louisa's father is a hairdresser, and he's a great man."

•

Most men are boys. Men who are men are probably the best, but almost impossible to find."

•

"We even know that girls tend to have women for daughters."

•

Get a job, your husband hates you. Get a good job, your husband leaves you. Get a stupendous job, your husband leaves you for a teenager.

•

[*His Girl Friday*] concerns an ace reporter, Hildy, who wants a "normal" life, so she's quitting her job and marrying Ralph Bellamy. But somehow, just as she is leaving, she is embroiled in *one last story*. She can't help herself, the story, involving murder, is too good to resist. At a crucial moment, just when she must get on the train with her fiancé or forfeit all, Hildy sees the sheriff, who has essential information. She goes after him. He runs away. She runs after him and, with a giant leap, she grabs him around the legs and tackles him.

Now, this is a great comedic moment, the audience piss themselves laughing. Not me, I burst into tears every time.

Do you see? She can't help herself, she has to do a good job! Even deeper than her need for normalcy, for marriage, is this wellspring of commitment to the work she loves.

•

FROM *But Enough About You*

FEAR OF DATING

The realization hit me heavily, like a .44 Magnum smashing into my skull. My heart started beating with a quick dread, and my blood froze in my veins. My stomach did backflips; I had to race to the bathroom to avoid a major incident. The ordeal I was about to face is one of the most grisly, macabre, and chilling experiences known to woman.

Dating. I will have to start dating again.

Please God no, don't make me do it! I'll be good from now on, I promise! I'll stop feeding the dog hashish! I'll wear that mauve acrylic sweater my grandmother knitted me! I'll never again have ten pizzas with extra cheese delivered to the Kiwi! I'll be kind, thoughtful, sober, industrious—anything. But please God, not the ultimate torture of dating!

I mean, I can't even stand the thought of the shower beforehand, and the shower used to be my favorite ritual, giving my hair three sudsings for good measure, thoughtfully shaving my legs way past my knees, keeping my face under the hot stream of water until every old crust of mascara was dissolved.

That's why I stayed with him so long, probably. I couldn't stand going through it all again. Sure, he might be a trifle wild and intractable, I kept telling myself, but at least I know I'll get laid tonight, and to-morrow night. At least he'll be used to the fact that I try on seven outfits so that I'll look okay when I run to the corner for a quart of milk. At least someone will go to the movies with me and not try to hold my hand.

Hand-holding—the worst thing about dating. The fellow, or maybe even I, will decide that holding hands is a sweet simple way to start. Hah! It's the most nerve-racking experience of life! Once I start holding hands, I'm afraid to stop. If I pull my hand away, will he think I'm being cold, or moody? Should I squeeze his hand and kind of wiggle my fingers around suggestively? Or is that too forward? What if we're holding hands in the movies and I have to scratch my nose? If I let his hand go, and then scratch the offending nose, and then don't grab his hand again immediately, will he think I'm rejecting him? Will he be relieved? What if my hand is clammy? A clammy hand is more offensive than bad breath or right-wing politics! A clammy hand means you are a lousy lay! Everybody knows that.

And what, dear spiteful God, will I wear? I'll need new dresses, new jewelry, new sweaters, trousers, underwear. And shoes! Shoes tell everything; shoes have to be perfect! Men like high heels, right? I can't walk in high heels. Well, I can try. For a really important date, I can just see myself spending $250 on a pair of drop-dead suede heels, maybe with some fanciful stitching and sweet bows to tie around my ankles. This time it will be different, I'll tell myself; this time I will be able to walk. But after an hour the ball of my foot will cramp up, I know it, and I'll hobble. "Is anything wrong?" he'll ask me solicitously. "You're limping." And I won't know where to look. I won't be able to say, "These fucking shoes are crippling me and if I don't take them off this minute I'll be maimed for life," because then he'll know I just bought them, that I bought them to go out on a date with him. And that will make him feel weird and pressured knowing that this date was a big deal for me and he'll realize that maybe I'm not as popular and sophisticated as he thought I was if I had to buy a special pair of shoes that I can't even walk in for chrissakes just for a date with *him*. So I have to explain the limping in such a way that it won't have to do with the shoes. An old war wound? Fell down the stairs earlier?

What if my hair refuses to behave? What if it's all recalcitrant and cranky and goes all limp and flat on one side and then sort of bends at a right angle over one ear? I mean, sometimes I apply precisely the right amount of mousse and hang upside down when I blow-dry it and yet something still goes drastically wrong and I end up looking like Margaret Thatcher. Sometimes the suspense of what I will look like is so terrible that I have to take a Valium.

I have been known to apply four shades of lipstick, one on top of the other, in a pathetic attempt to achieve a certain I'm-not-actually-wearing-lipstick-I-just-naturally-have-pink-moist-luscious-lips effect. I have been known to put green eye pencil below my lower lashes, look in the mirror, realize that I look like a gangrenous raccoon, quickly remove it, look in the mirror, realize that I'd rather look like a gangrenous raccoon than an anemic buffalo, and reapply the stuff. I have been known to start trying on outfits in an entirely tidy room and somehow when I am finished every single item of clothing I own is off the rack and on the floor and then when the phone rings there is no way on earth I can find it. I can't even find my *bed*. God, I hate dating.

And when he rings my doorbell and my stockings are still around my ankles because my garter belt is missing but with mad, deep, quick thought I finally remember it's in my black satin purse (don't ask) and I get it on and get the stockings up and answer the door smiling casually, what precisely do I say?

What will I talk about on a date?

Not one thing that's on my mind will be a suitable topic of conversation. "Do you think we'll sleep together tonight?" "Are you one of those guys who can't make a commitment? Or can only make a commitment to a woman with really smooth, finely muscled thighs?" "Is my deodorant working?" "What kind of relationship did you have with your mother?" "How do you think we're getting along so far?" "Do you like me?" "How much do you like me?" "Are you sure you really like me?" "Have you happened to contract any exotic social diseases?" "Ever been plagued by impotence?" "You're not going out with me because you feel sorry for me, are you?"

No, we'll talk about movies. What we've seen recently. What if he tells me that he finally got around to seeing *Cocoon* and it turned out to be one of the greatest experiences of his life? Will I pretend to agree? I bet I will. I bet something slimy inside myself will cause me to nod my head encouragingly and say, "Yes, wasn't it lovely? I especially liked the sex scene in the pool." And then I'll hate myself because I've turned our date into a tissue of lies. I'll become distracted thinking about what a hypocrite I really am and my eyes will glaze over and I'll nod absently when he tries to draw me out and then he'll get all paranoid, thinking I hate him because he liked *Cocoon*. He'll be right.

But what if it turns out that his favorite movie is *The Man Who Came to Dinner*, with *Slapshot* a close second? Then I could fall in love. Then I'll really be terrified.

●

WHEN IN DOUBT, ACT LIKE MYRNA LOY

Just for a gag, take this quiz:

1

There you are, being pulled along the floor of an incredibly posh drinking establishment by a small, strongly effusive fox terrier. The dozens of wrapped Christmas presents that were once in your arms are now scattered in every direction. You finally come to rest, and happen to glance up. Your husband, dressed impeccably and holding a martini, is looking down at you, astonished. At this point, do you

A Burst into tears and demand to be taken home?
B Grasp your husband around his ankles, pleading forgiveness and promising never to do it again?
C Simulate an epileptic fit?
D Pick yourself up, brush yourself off, and say, "Oh, so it's you! He's dragged me to every gin mill on the block."

One more, for luck:

2

Your husband is about to go off on a dangerous adventure. To make sure he doesn't leave you behind, you get into the taxi before him. Your husband tells the cabbie to take you to Grant's tomb and the taxi speeds away with only you inside. When your husband enquires later how you liked Grant's tomb, you say,

A You are a filthy pig and I want a divorce immediately.
B I'll never get over what you've done to me.
C Please may I have a sedative?
D It was lovely. I'm having a copy made for you.

If I know you, you smart cookie, you answered D to both the above questions. As well as you should. It's exactly what Myrna Loy would have done. Did.

If you've ever seen The Thin Man, with Myrna Loy as Nora Charles, you recognize these scenes. But these are more than simply great moments in cinematic history; they are behavioral lessons on which one can base one's life. Forget est, forget years of grueling psychotherapy, forget taking off your clothes in the presence of other consenting adults and "sharing" your most excruciating childhood memories.

I sure have. Whenever I'm too crazy, too paranoiac, or too mentally feeble to deal with a situation, I pretend I'm Myrna Loy. It works.

Consider: the Myrna Loy who appeared as Nora in *The Thin Man* movies was a real pip. She was beautiful, she was witty, she was self-possessed, she was adventuresome, she wore great hats. (*Note:* If you're a man, it might be more profitable to pretend you're William Powell as Nicky, another perfect role model.)

When Nora discovered that Nicky had had six martinis to her paltry one, she told the barman to "bring me five more martinis, Bill, line 'em up right here." When Nicky took her to her first jazz club, she was bemused for a moment, but before he knew it she was saying to some creep, "Oh, get lost, you off-beat rinky-dink, you're nowhere!" When Nicky happened to ask her if she possessed a nice evening gown, she didn't blink or twiddle her fingers or pick her nose but said straightaway, "Yes, I've got a lulu. Why?"

This is all good stuff.

Movie stars have traditionally been used as role models; that's what they're there for. But so many of us pick silly ones to ape. Who can forget 1976, when every third woman in the world decided she was *exactly* like Diane Keaton in *Annie Hall*? Everywhere one went that year, one ran into hordes of females in baggy trousers and their boyfriend's ties, stuttering and saying "lah-di-dah, lah-di-dah." Most depressing. And who will ever get over that ghastly moment in history when otherwise sensible women decided to act just like Liza Minnelli in *Cabaret* and painted their fingernails green while discussing "divine decadence"? Soon after, one could not leave one's home without colliding with hordes of women wearing artfully and expensively ripped sweatshirts and the sultry, vapid look of some person called, I believe, Jennifer Beales.

Modern movie stars will get you nowhere, role model–wise. I can't think of one who has wit, moral integrity, and terrific outfits. One must stick with the old girls, who knew what was what.

Instead of Myrna Loy, you may if you wish emulate Lauren Bacall in *To Have and Have Not*, the one where she asks, "You know how to whistle, don't you?" Or Katharine Hepburn in *The Philadelphia Story*. Or Bette Davis in *All About Eve*.

But I personally stick with Myrna. She's got the lightest touch. Who else could play poker with the boys in the baggage car and never remove her hat? Who else, when Nicky was ogling a stacked heiress, could say, "The earrings are higher up" and leave it at that?

I'm not kidding; I really do this. Not, mind you, as a matter of course, since I often have a perfectly fine personality of my own, and one must, whenever possible, to one's own self be true.

But there are times when I am completely boggled—I know for a fact that the minute I open my mouth, I'm going to turn into my mother, my grandmother, or my Aunt Selma. Which is unfortunate, since my family were all very big on a particularly noxious brand of sullen martyrdom.

Witness last summer. There I was, minding my own business, when the Kiwi suddenly turned horrible. He became furiously impatient with me because I was afraid to climb a (small) mountain in the dark and left me alone on some wet rocks while he went exploring. Even took my cigarette lighter.

When the thoughtless cad reappeared, my first impulse was to sniffle a lot. The first words that sprung to my mind went something like this:

"After all I've done for you, look how you treat me! [Sob.] You obviously don't care about me at all, oh no you don't, I can tell. [Stifled moans!] Oh, how could you? What have I done to deserve this?"

Awful. The worst thing about the what-have-I-done-to-deserve-this gag is that people will tell you. Had I said something along the lines of the above, Mr. Adorable would have felt perfectly justified in starting a huge row in which he touched upon all my inadequacies, fears, and lousy nutritional habits.

Luckily, some still voice of sanity cautioned me that this was the wrong tack, even though it was the one I was brought up with. And luckily, like a lightning bolt, Myrna Loy flashed through my sniveling brain. What would Myrna do in such a situation? Would one ever catch *her* being so wimpily wretched?

I held my piece during the car ride home, letting Loyness filter through my being. When we got inside the house, I calmly filled the kettle and put it on the stove. Then I turned around.

"Darling," I said, "you are an inconsiderate brat. I absolutely refuse to be left alone and terrified on any more dark mountainsides. Next time the climbing lust overtakes you, warn me first so that I can take in a nice, warm movie instead of sitting around like a fool on wet rocks, you abysmal warthog."

"But, but—" he said.

"Don't *but* me, you twit," I continued silkily. "I simply won't have it, and that's that."

All right, the words may have been a bit clumsy, since I had to write my own material on the spot. But things never got ugly. By morning he apologized prettily, I accepted him happily, and we were in perfect accord as I slipped into my satin dressing gown to go down to breakfast.

Myrna would have been proud.

•

MAKING FRIENDS WITH ANXIETY

Anxiety attack!

I'm on the subway and it's stopped I don't know why and I'm late already the car is packed and sharing the strap I'm hanging from is a little pale man with no eyelashes at all and he's—yes, *I'm not imagining it!*—he's rubbing his crotch against my thigh but I can't move away because I'm a sardine in here and I'm so late, will probably lose this job, is that a hand going into my bag? *I can't breathe.* Will the train move again? Never.

Anxiety attack!

It's ten-thirty at night I sent my son to the corner for milk at nine-thirty he's not back yet what's he doing, where is he, is he still alive? Although this is New York City I'll call the cops anyway. They won't come. They will come; they'll *laugh* at me getting hysterical. I'm waiting I'm waiting any second now he'll come through the door, "Mom!" and I'll break his jaw. *Where is he?* Decided to take a little stroll? Got into a car with a *child-molesting murderer?*

Anxiety attack!

Nothing is wrong. Everything's fine it's just that I wish I had a Valium because *my head hurts my heart's pounding I can't breathe.* I'm pacing. I'm frightened. My head is swimming with strange images. I'm running to the bathroom. I can't read, can't sleep, can't think. I'm going to die I can tell this is a death premonition. *Nothing's wrong! Really.*

Okay, I'm fine now.

If you've never had an anxiety attack, I don't want to know you. I'm sure you're very nice, very pleasant, but I can't relate. I once had a two-year anxiety attack (1973–75). Now I privately think of myself as a connoisseur of anxiety attacks, having successfully cataloged at least thirty-seven different variations of the species, each with its own piquant bouquet of emotions.

Here are some:

The Blancmange: Hardly an anxiety attack at all, this is the normal state of consciousness for those of us in big cities. Unexpected sounds make the heart jump into the throat; a moving shadow glimpsed from the corner of the eye precedes a monster adrenaline rush. A huge crowd of business suits congesting the steps of a favorite and heretofore undiscovered eatery causes nausea and despondence.

The Petite Weirdness: There you are, minding your own business, when, suddenly and out of nowhere, everything is *too much*. The man in front of you at the movie theater eating something wrapped in cellophane and telling his date what a fabulous *auteur* Sylvester Stallone is must be immediately assassinated. Your shopping bag disintegrates in the rain on Fourteenth Street and you must check into a mental hospital.

The Sudden Abyss: These are the little pockets of dread that punctuate our days and riddle our nights. We're sitting happily at lunch and someone says something like, "How's your book coming?" and we immediately need CPR. We're standing at the bar in the Mike Todd room and someone whispers, "Don't look now, but isn't that your ex-boyfriend over there?" and we consume three double tequilas before we know it.

The Full-Throttle Blow-out: The activity of the brain speeds up to 45 rpms while the rest of the body stays at 33⅓. This causes an insistent inner hum and a whirling sensation, which in turn produces a terrible and strange heart-throbbing and a desire for instant unconsciousness. Occasionally the mind actually floats away from the body—the last thing you remember is being in a shop trying on a mauve sweater and how suddenly you're on a bus hurtling toward Cincinnati.

"Anger," your shrink will probably tell you while you quiver and shake with the heebie-jeebies, "massive homicidal rage you felt against your parents as a child but which you considered inappropriate and dangerous since it would never do to do in mom and dad, so you took this blinding fury and turned it in upon yourself, where it has caused dreadful attacks which to this day cripple and inconvenience you."

"Pooh pooh," I say to shrinks, anxiety isn't that at all. Here's what anxiety *really* is:

Anxiety is your friend. Anxiety is telling you in the nicest possible way that you are being threatened and it really would be better for all concerned if you stopped lollygagging and did something, anything, instead of sitting around behaving helpless. Anxiety wants you to *do it now*.

Son missing? Go out and find him. Man rubbing against you against your will? Scream piercingly. Groceries all over the street? Pick them up. Ex-boyfriend sighted? Pour a drink over his head. Book not done? Get your agent to call your editor to say you've broken both arms.

"That's all very well," I hear you say, "but what about when I really *can't* do anything? What if my hands are tied? Like if it's my boss torturing me but I need the job or I'll starve. Or if it's Jerry Falwell?"

The solution is simple: Become a writer. Work hard and long until some publication somewhere gives you a column. Elbow your way into as much prominence as possible, and then write about people. By simply changing a name slightly, you can reduce to mincemeat any person, place, or thing that has incurred your displeasure. Remember: revenge is the best revenge.

Nicole Hollander (contemporary)

FROM *The Whole Enchilada*

Marietta Holley (1836-1926)

❧ ❧

FROM *The Widder Doodle's Courtship*

I WISH I WAS A WIDDER.

by Betsey Bobbet

Oh, "Gimlet," back again I float
   With broken wings, a weary bard;
I cannot write as once I wrote,
   I have to work so very hard.
So hard my lot, so tossed about,
My muse is fairly tuckered out.

My musie aforesaid, once hath flown,
   But now her back is broke, and breast;
And yet she fain would crumble down
   On "Gimlet" pages she would rest;
And sing plain words as there she's sot
Haply they'll rhyme, and haply not.

I spake plain words in former days,
   No guile I showed, clear was my plan;
My gole it matrimony was.
   My earthly aim it was a man.
I gained my man, I won my gole,
Alas, I feel not as I fole.

Yes, ringing through my maiden thought
   This clear voice rose, "Oh come up higher"
To speak plain truth with cander fraught,
   To married be, was my desire.
Now sweeter still this lot doth seem
To be a widder is my theme.

For toil hath claimed me for her own,
   In wedlock I have found no ease;
I've cleaned and washed for neighbors round;
   And took my pay in beans and pease;
In boiling sap no rest I took
Or husking corn in barn and stook.

Or picking wool from house to house,
   White-washing, painting, papering,
In stretching carpets, boiling souse,
   E'en picking hops it hath a sting
For spiders there assembled be,
Mosqueetoes, bugs, and etcetree.

I have to work, oh! very hard;
   Old Toil, I know your breadth, and length.
I'm tired to death; and in one word
   I have to work beyond my strength,
And mortal men are very tough
To get along with—nasty, rough.

Yes, tribulation's doomed to her
   Who weds a man, without no doubt
In peace a man is singuler
   His ways, they are past finding out,
And oh! the wrath of mortal males
To paint their ire, earth's language fails.

And thirteen children in our home
   Their buttons rend, their clothes they burst.
Much bread and such do they consume;
   Of children they do seem the worst;
And Simon and I do disagree,
He's prone to sin continualee.

·

On Marriage

"Good land!" says I, "is marryin' the only theme that anybody can lay
holt of?" says I, "it seems to me it would be the best way to lay holt
of duty now, and then, if a bo come, lay holt of him. If they ketch a
bo with such a hook as they are a-fishin' with now, what kind of a bo

will it be? Nobody but a fool would lay holt of a hook baited with dime novels and pups. Learn your girls to be industrious, and to respect themselves. They can't now, Delila Ann, I know they can't. No woman can feel honorable and reverential toward themselves, when they are foldin' their useless hands over their empty souls, waitin' for some man, no matter who, to marry 'em and support 'em. When in the agony of suspense and fear, they have narrowed down to this one theme, all their hopes and prayers, Good Lord; *anybody!*"

"But when a woman lays holt of life in a noble, earnest way, when she is dutiful, and cheerful, and industrious, God-fearin', and self-respectin', though the world sinks, there is a rock under her feet that won't let her down far enough to hurt her any. If love comes to her to brighten her pathway, so much the better. She will be ready to receive them royally, and keep him when she gets him. Some folks don't know how to use love worth a cent. But no matter whether she be single or double, I am not afraid of her future."

Josiah Allen, . . . Anybody would think to hear you talk that a woman couldn't do but just one of the two things any way—marry or vote, and had got to take her choice of the two at the pint of the bayonet.

On Competition

Tirzah Ann burst right out a-crying, and says she:

"Mother, one week's more rest would have tuckered me completely out; I should have died off."

I wiped my own spectacles, I was so affected, and says I, in choked up axents:

"You know I told you just how it would be; I told you you wus happy enough to home, and you hadn't better go off in search of rest or of pleasure."

And says she, breakin' right down agin, "One week more of such pleasure and recreation, would have been my death blow."

Says I, "I believe it, I believe you; you couldn't have stood another mite of rest and recreation, without it's killin' of you—anybody can see that by lookin' at your mean." But says I, knowin' it wus my duty to be calm, "It is all over now, Tirzah Ann; you hain't got to go through it agin; you must try to overcome your feelin's. Tell your ma all about it. Mebby it will do you good, in the words of the him, 'Speak, and let the worst be known, Speakin' may relieve you.' "

And I see, indeed, that she needed relief. Wall, she up and told me the hull on it. And I found out that Mrs. Skidmore wus to the bottom of it all—she, and Tirzah Ann's ambition. I could see that them two wus to blame for the hull on it.

Mrs. Skidmore is the wife of the other lawyer in Janesville; they moved there in the spring. She wus awful big feelin', and wus determined from the first to lead the fashion—tried to be awful genteel and put on sights of airs.

And Tirzah Ann bein' ambitius, and knowin' that she looked a good deal better than Mrs. Skidmore did, and knew as much agin, and knowin' that Whitfield wus a better lawyer than her husband wus, and twice as well off, wusn't goin' to stand none of her airs. Mrs. Skidmore seemed to sort o' look down on Tirzah Ann, for she never felt as I did on that subject.

Now, if anybody wants to feel above me, I look on it in this light, I filosofize on it in this way: it probably does them some good, and it don't do me a mite of hurt, so I let 'em feel. I have always made a practice of it—it don't disturb me the width of a horse-hair. Because somebody feels as if they wus better than I am, that don't make 'em so; if it did, I should probably get up more interest on the subject. . . .

"Such folks have to put on more airs than them that have got sunthin' to feel big over." Says I, "It is reeson and filosify that if anybody has got a uncommon intellect, or beauty, or wealth, they don't, as a general thing, put on the airs that them do that hain't got nothin'; they don't *have* to; they have got sunthin' to hold 'em up—they can stand without airs. But when anybody hain't got no intellect, nor riches, nor nothin'—when they hain't got nothin' only jest air to hold 'em up, it stands to reeson that they have got to have a good deal of it."

I had studied it all out, so it wus as plain to me as anything. But Tirzah Ann couldn't see it in that light, and would get as mad as a hen at Mrs. Skidmore ever sense they came to Jonesville, and was bound she shouldn't go by her and out-do her. And so when Mrs. Skidmore gin it out in Janesville that she and her husband wus a goin' away for the summer, for rest and pleasure, Tirzah Ann said to herself that she and her husband would go for rest and pleasure, if they both died in the attempt. Wall, three days before they started, Tirzah Ann found that Mrs. Skidmore had got one dress more than she had, and a polenay, so she went to the store and got the material and ingredients, and sot up day and night a-makin' of 'em up; it most killed her a-hurryin' so.

Wall, they started the same day, and went to the same place the Skidmores did—a fashionable summer resort—and put up to the same tavern, to rest and recreate. But Mrs. Skidmore bein' a healthy, raw-boned woman, could stand as much agin rest as Tirzah Ann could. Why, Tirzah Ann says the rest wus enough to wear out a leather wemen, and how she stood it for two weeks wus more than she could tell. You see she wusn't used to hard work. I had always favored her and gone ahead with the work myself, and Whitfield had been as careful of her, and as good as a woman to help her, and the rest came tough on it; it wus dretful hard on her to be put through so.

You see she had to dress up two or three times a day, and keep the babe dressed up slick. And she had to promenade down to the waterin'-place, and drink jist such a time, and it went against her stomach, and almost upset her every time. And she had to go a-ridin', and out on the water in boats and yots, and that made her sick, too, and had to play erokey, and be up till midnight to parties. You see she had to do all this, ruther than let Mrs. Skidmore get in ahead on her, and do more than she did, and be more genteel than she wus, and rest more.

And then the town bein' full, and runnin' over, they wus cooped up in a little mite of a room up three flights of stairs; that in itself, wus enough to wear Tirzah Ann out; she never could climb stairs worth a cent. And their room wus very small, and the air close, nearly tight, and hot as an oven; they wus used to great, cool, airy rooms to hum; and the babe couldn't stand the hotness and the tightness, and she began to enjoy poor health, and cried most all the time, and that wore on Tirzah Ann; and to hum, the babe could play round in the yard all day a'most, but here she hung right on to her ma.

And then the rooms on one side of 'em wus occupied by a young man a-learnin' to play on the flute; he had been disappointed in love, and he would try to make up tunes as he went along sort o' tragedy style, and dirge-like, the most unearthly and woe-begone sounds, they say, that they ever heard or heard on. They say it wus enough to make anybody's blood run cold in their veins to hear 'em; he kept his room most of the time, and played day and night. He had ruther be alone day times and play, than go into company, and nights he couldn't sleep, so he would set up and play. They wus sorry for him, they said they wus; they knew his mind must be in a awful state, and his sufferin's intense, or he couldn't harrow up anybody's feelin's so. But that didn't make it more the easier for them.

Tirzah Ann and Whitfield both says that tongue can't never tell the sufferin's they underwent from that flute, and their feelin's for that young man; they expected every day to hear he had made way with himself, his agony seemed so great, and he would groan and rithe so fearful, when he was playin'.

And the room on the other side of 'em wus occupied by a young woman who owned a melodien; she went into company a good deal, and her spells of playin' and singin' would come on after she had got home from parties. She had a good many bo's, and wus happy disposi-tioned naturally; and they said some nights, it would seem as if there wouldn't be no end to her playin' and singin' love songs, and performin' quiet pieces, polkys, and waltzes, and such. Tirzah Ann and Whitfield are both good-hearted as they can be, and they said they didn't want to throw no shade over young hearts; they had been young themselves not much more than two years ago; they knew by experience what it wus to be sentimental, and they felt to sympathize with the gladness and highlarity of a young heart, and they didn't want to do nothin' to break it up. But still it came tough on 'em—dretful. I s'pose the sufferin's couldn't be told that they suffered from them two musicianers. And the babe not bein' used to such rackets, nights, would get skairt, and almost go into hysterick fits. And two or three nights, Tirzah Ann had 'em, too—the hystericks. I don't know what kept Whitfield up; he says no money would tempt him to go through it agin; I s'pose she almost tore him to pieces; but she wasn't to blame, she didn't know what she was a-doin'.

It hain't no use to blame Tirzah Ann now, after it is all over with; but she sees it plain enough now, and she's a-sufferin' from the effects of it, her tryin' to keep up with Mrs. Skidmore, and do all she done. And there is where her morals get all run down, and Whitfield's, too.

Judy Holliday (1922–1965)

~≈€ ℥~

On Falsies

Judy Holliday was being chased around the room by an aroused casting director, she finally stopped running and removed the "falsies" she had tucked into her bra. "Here," she told him, handing him two spheres of foam rubber, "I believe it's these you're after."

Marie Jenney Howe (c. 1871–1934)

~e 9~

An Anti-Suffrage Monologue

Please do not think of me as old-fashioned. I pride myself on being a modern up-to-date woman. I believe in all kinds of broad-mindedness, only I do not believe in woman suffrage because to do that would be to deny my sex.

Woman suffrage is the reform against nature. Look at these ladies sitting on the platform. Observe their physical inability, their mental disability, their spiritual instability and general debility! Could they walk up to the ballot box, mark a ballot, and drop it in? Obviously not. Let us grant for the sake of argument that they could mark a ballot. But could they drop it in? Ah, no. All nature is against it. The laws of man cry out against it. The voice of God cries out against it—and so do I.

Enfranchisement is what makes man man. Disfranchisement is what makes woman woman. If women were enfranchised every man would be just like every woman and every woman would be just like every man. There would be no difference between them. And don't you think this would rob life of just a little of its poetry and romance?

Man must remain man. Woman must remain woman. If man goes over and tries to be like woman, if woman goes over and tries to be like man, it will become so very confusing and so difficult to explain to our children. Let us take a practical example. If a woman puts on a man's coat and trousers takes a man's cane and hat and cigar, and goes out on the street, what will happen to her? She will be arrested and thrown into jail. Then why not stay at home?

I know you begin to see how strongly I *feel* on this subject, but I have some reasons as well. These reasons are based on logic Of course I am not logical. I am a creature of impulse, instinct, and intuition—and I glory in it. But I know that these reasons are based on logic because I have culled them from the men whom it is my privilege to know.

My first argument against suffrage is that the women would not use it if they had it. You couldn't drive them to the polls. My second argument is, if the women were enfranchised they would neglect their homes, desert their families, and spend all their time at the polls. You may tell me that the polls are only open once a year. But I know women. They are creatures of habit. If you let them go to the polls once a year, they will hang round the polls all the rest of the time.

I have arranged these arguments in couplets. They go together in such a way that if you don't like one you can take the other. This is my second anti-suffrage couplet. If the women were enfranchised they would vote exactly as their husbands do and only double the existing vote. Do you like that argument? If not, take this one. If the women were enfranchised they would vote against their own husbands, thus creating dissension, family quarrels, and divorce.

My third anti-suffrage couplet is—women are angels. Many men call me an angel and I have a strong instinct which tells me it is true; that is why I am anti, because "I want to be an angel and with the angels stand." And if you don't like that argument take this one. Women are depraved. They would introduce into politics a vicious element which would ruin our national life.

Fourth anti-suffrage couplet: women cannot understand politics. Therefore there would be no use in giving women political power, because they would not know what to do with it. On the other hand, if the women were enfranchised, they would mount rapidly into power, take all the offices from all the men, and soon we would have women governors of all our states and dozens of women acting as President of the United States.

Fifth anti-suffrage couplet: women cannot band together. They are incapable of organization. No two women can even be friends. Women are cats. On the other hand, if women were enfranchised, we would have all the women banded together on one side and all the men banded together on the other side, and there would follow a sex war which might end in bloody revolution.

Just one more of my little couplets: the ballot is greatly over-estimated. It has never done anything for anybody. Lots of men tell me this. And the corresponding argument is—the ballot is what makes man man. It is what gives him all his dignity and all of his superiority to women. Therefore if we allow women to share this privilege, how could a woman look up to her own husband? Why, there would be nothing to look up to.

I have talked to many woman suffragists and I find them very unreasonable. I say to them: "Here I am, convince me." I ask for proof. Then they proceed to tell me of Australia and Colorado and other places where women have passed excellent laws to improve the condition of working women and children. But I say, "What of it?" These are facts. I don't care about facts. I ask for proof.

Then they quote the eight million women of the United States who are now supporting themselves, and the twenty-five thousand married women in the City of New York who are self-supporting. But I say again, what of it? These are statistics. I don't believe in statistics. Facts and statistics are things which no truly womanly woman would ever use.

I wish to prove anti-suffrage in a womanly way—that is, by personal example. This is my method of persuasion. Once I saw a woman driving a horse, and the horse ran away with her. Isn't that just like a woman? Once I read in the newspapers about a woman whose house caught on fire, and she threw the children out of the window and carried the pillows downstairs. Does that show political acumen, or does it not? Besides, look at the hats that women wear! And have you ever known a successful woman governor of a state? Or have you ever known a really truly successful woman president of the United States? Well, if they could they would, wouldn't they? Then, if they haven't, doesn't that show they couldn't? As for the militant suffragettes, they are all hyenas in petticoats. Now do you want to be a hyena and wear petticoats?

Now, I think I have proved anti-suffrage; and I have done it in a womanly way—that is, without stooping to the use of a single fact or argument or a single statistic.

I am the prophet of a new idea. No one has ever thought of it or heard of it before. I well remember when this great idea first came to me. It waked me in the middle of the night with a shock that gave me a headache. This is it: woman's place is in the home. Is it not beautiful as it is new, new as it is true? Take this idea away with you. You will find it very helpful in your daily lives. You may not grasp it just at first, but you will gradually grow into understanding of it.

I know the suffragists reply that all our activities have been taken out of the home. The baking, the washing, the weaving, the spinning are all long since taken out of the home. But I say, all the more reason that something should stay in the home. Let it be woman. Besides, think of the great modern invention, the telephone. That has been put into the home. Let woman stay at home and answer the telephone.

We antis have so much imagination! Sometimes it seems to us that we can hear the little babies in the slums crying to us. We can see the children in factories and mines reaching out their little hands to us, and the working women in the sweated industries, the underpaid, underfed women, reaching out their arms to us—all, all crying as with one voice,

"Save us, save us, from Woman Suffrage." Well may they make this appeal to us, for who knows what woman suffrage might not do for such as these. It might even alter the conditions under which they live.

We antis do not believe that any conditions should be altered. We want everything to remain just as it is. All is for the best. Whatever is, is right. If misery is in the world, God has put it there; let it remain. If this misery presses harder on some women than others, it is because they need discipline. Now, I have always been comfortable and well cared for. But then I never needed discipline. Of course I am only a weak, ignorant woman. But there is one thing I do understand from the ground up, and that is the divine intention toward woman. I *know* that the divine intention toward woman is, let her remain at home.

The great trouble with the suffragists is this; they interfere too much. They are always interfering. Let me take a practical example.

There is in the City of New York a Nurses' Settlement, where sixty trained nurses go forth to care for sick babies and give them pure milk. Last summer only two or three babies died in this slum district around the Nurses' Settlement, whereas formerly hundreds of babies have died there every summer. Now what are these women doing? Interfering, interfering with the death rate! And what is their motive in so doing? They seek notoriety. They want to be noticed. They are trying to show off. And if sixty women who merely believe in suffrage behave in this way, what may we expect when all women are enfranchised?

What ought these women to do with their lives? Each one ought to be devoting herself to the comfort of some man. You may say, they are not married. But I answer, let them try a little harder and they might find some kind of a man to devote themselves to. What does the Bible say on this subject? It says, "Seek and ye shall find." Besides, when I look around me at the men, I feel that God never meant us women to be too particular.

Let me speak one word to my sister women who are here to-day. Women, we don't need to vote in order to get our own way. Don't misunderstand me. Of course I want you to get your own way. That's what we're here for. But do it indirectly. If you want a thing, tease. If that doesn't work, nag. If that doesn't do, cry—crying always brings them around. Get what you want. Pound pillows. Make a scene. Make home a hell on earth, but do it in a womanly way. That is so much more dignified and refined than walking up to a ballot box and dropping in a piece of paper. Can't you see that?

Let us consider for a moment the effect of woman's enfranchisement on man. I think some one ought to consider the men. What makes husbands faithful and loving? The ballot, and the monopoly of that privilege. If women vote, what will become of men? They will all slink off drunk and disorderly. We antis understand men. If women were enfranchised, men would revert to their natural instincts such as regicide, matricide, patricide and race-suicide. Do you believe in race-suicide or do you not? Then, isn't it our duty to refrain from a thing that would lure men to destruction?

It comes down to this. Someone must wash the dishes. Now, would you expect man, man made in the image of God, to roll up his sleeves and wash the dishes? Why, it would be blasphemy. I know that I am but a rib and so I wash the dishes. Or I hire another rib to do it for me, which amounts to the same thing.

Let us consider the argument from the standpoint of religion. The Bible says, "Let the women keep silent in the churches." Paul says, "Let them keep their hats on for fear of the angels." My minister says, "Wives, obey your husbands." And my husband says that woman suffrage would rob the rose of its fragrance and the peach of its bloom. I think that is so sweet.

Besides did George Washington ever say, "Votes for women"? No. Did the Emperor Kaiser Wilhelm ever say, "Votes for women"? No. Did Elijah, Elisha, Micah, Hezekiah, Obadiah, and Jeremiah ever say, "Votes for women"? No. Then that settles it.

I don't want to be misunderstood in my reference to woman's inability to vote. Of course she could get herself to the polls and lift a piece of paper. I don't doubt that. What I refer to is the pressure on the brain, the effect of this mental strain on woman's delicate nervous organization and on her highly wrought sensitive nature. Have you ever pictured to yourself Election Day with women voting? Can you imagine how women, having undergone this terrible ordeal, with their delicate systems all upset, will come out of the voting booths and be led away by policemen, and put into ambulances, while they are fainting and weeping, half laughing, half crying, and having fits upon the public highway? Don't you think that if a woman is going to have a fit, it is far better for her to have it in the privacy of her own home?

And how shall I picture to you the terrors of the day after election? Divorce and death will rage unchecked, crime and contagious disease will stalk unbridled through the land. Oh, friends, on this subject I feel—I feel, so strongly that I can—not think!

Josephine Humphreys (contemporary)

~❧ ❧~

FROM *Dreams of Sleep*

She doesn't see other women much, especially since her husband took
up with one.

•

In real estate it is part of the business to know of impending divorce and
disease, the harbingers of real estate transactions.

•

Her own dolls were either babies or storybook characters like Cinderella
and Snow White who though past childhood were somehow not yet
into the world, girls who kept themselves apart from the world without
really knowing what for. Now girls know what for. They menstruate
when they are ten, and their dolls are sluts.

•

He let Claire redecorate [the office] last year, when she first started acting
sad.

•

A doctor's wife. That is what the girl would be expecting. And it is
living up to baby-sitters' expectations that keeps households civilized.

•

We were always modern parents, me and Carol. Enlightened, I think
you would call us. We did Lamaze, we did Leboyer. Then we did
divorce.

•

Children might tend the plots of their parents, weed them and keep the
stones clean, but sooner or later the living forget the dead, and the dead's
stones, too. In a golf-course cemetery you pay the company for perpetual
care. They mow you for eternity.

Zora Neale Hurston (1909-1960)

FROM *Their Eyes Were Watching God*

There was no doubt that the town respected him and even admired him in a way. But any man who walks in the way of power and property is bound to meet hate. So when speakers stood up when the occasion demanded and said "Our beloved Mayor," it was one of those statements that everybody says but nobody actually believes like "God is everywhere." It was just a handle to wind up the tongue with.

•

Joe returned to the store full of pleasure and good humor but he didn't want Janie to notice it because he saw that she was sullen and he resented that. She had no right to be, the way he thought things out. She wasn't even appreciative of his efforts and she had plenty cause to be. Here he was just pouring honor all over her; building a high chair for her to sit in and overlook the world and she here pouting over it! Not that he wanted anybody else, but just too many women would be glad to be in her place. He ought to box her jaws! But he didn't feel like fighting today, so he made an attack upon her position backhand.

"Ah had tuh laugh at de people out dere in de woods dis mornin', Janie. You can't help but laugh at de capers they cuts. But all the same, Ah wish mah people would git mo' business in 'em and not spend so much time on foolishness."

"Everybody can't be lak you, Jody. Somebody is bound tuh want tuh laugh and play."

"Who don't love tuh laugh and play?"

"You make out like you don't, anyhow."

"I god, Ah don't make out no such uh lie! But it's uh time fuh all things. But it's awful tuh see so many people don't want nothin' but uh full belly and uh place tuh lay down and sleep afterwards. It makes me sad sometimes and then agin it makes me mad. They say things sometimes that tickles me nearly tuh death, but Ah won't laugh jus' tuh discourage 'em." Janie took the easy way away from a fuss. She didn't change her mind but she agreed with her mouth. Her heart said, "Even so, but you don't have to cry about it."

But sometimes Sam Watson and Lige Moss forced a belly laugh out of Joe himself with their eternal arguments. It never ended because there was no end to reach. It was a contest in hyperbole and carried on for no other reason.

Maybe Sam would be sitting on the porch when Lige walked up. If nobody was there to speak of, nothing happened. But if the town was there like on Saturday night, Lige would come up with a very grave air. Couldn't even pass the time of day, for being so busy thinking. Then when he was asked what was the matter in order to start him off, he'd say, "Dis question done 'bout drove me crazy. And Sam, he know so much into things, Ah wants some information on de subject."

Walter Thomas was due to speak up and egg the matter on. "Yeah, Sam always got more information than he know what to do wid. He's bound to tell yuh whatever it is you wants tuh know."

•

Jody must have noticed it too. Maybe, he had seen it long before Janie did, and had been fearing for her to see. Because he began to talk about her age all the time, as if he didn't want her to stay young while he grew old. It was always "You oughta throw somethin' over yo' shoulders befo' you go outside. You ain't no young pullet no mo'. You'se uh ole hen now." One day he called her off the croquet grounds. "Dat's somethin' for de young folks, Janie, you out dere jumpin' round and won't be able tuh git out de bed tuhmorrer." If he thought to deceive her, he was wrong. For the first time she could see a man's head naked of its skull. Saw the cunning thoughts race in and out through the caves and promontories of his mind long before they darted out of the tunnel of his mouth. She saw he was hurting inside so she let it pass without talking. She just measured out a little time for him and set it aside to wait.

It got to be terrible in the store. The more his back ached and his muscle dissolved into fat and the fat melted off his bones, the more fractious he became with Janie. Especially in the store. The more people in there the more ridicule he poured over her body to point attention away from his own. So one day Steve Mixon wanted some chewing tobacco and Janie cut it wrong. She hated that tobacco knife anyway. It worked very stiff. She fumbled with the thing and cut way away from the mark. Mixon didn't mind. He held it up for a joke to tease Janie a little.

"Looka heah, Brother Mayor, whut yo' wife done took and done." It was cut comical, so everybody laughed at it. "Uh woman and uh knife—no kind of uh knife, don't b'long tuhgether." There was some more good-natured laughter at the expense of women.

Jody didn't laugh. He hurried across from the post office side and took the plug of tobacco away from Mixon and cut it again. Cut it exactly on the mark and glared at Janie.

"I god amighty! A woman stay round uh store till she get old as Methusalem and still can't cut a little thing like a plug of tobacco! Don't stand dere rollin' yo' pop eyes at me wid yo' rump hangin' nearly to yo' knees!"

A big laugh started off in the store but people got to thinking and stopped. It was funny if you looked at it right quick, but it got pitiful if you thought about it awhile. It was like somebody snatched off part of a woman's clothes while she wasn't looking and the streets were crowded. Then too, Janie took the middle of the floor to talk right into Jody's face, and that was something that hadn't been done before.

"Stop mixin' up mah doings wid mah looks, Jody. When you git through tellin' me how tuh cut uh plug uh tobacco, then you kin tell me whether mah behind is on straight or not."

"Wha—whut's dat you say, Janie? You must be out yo' head."

"Naw, Ah ain't outa mah head neither."

"You must be. Talkin' any such language as dat."

"You de one started talkin' under people's clothes. Not me."

"Whut's de matter wid you, nohow? You ain't no young girl to be gettin' all insulted 'bout yo' looks. You ain't no young courtin' gal. You'se uh ole woman, nearly forty."

"Yeah, Ah'm nearly forty and you'se already fifty. How come you can't talk about dat sometimes instead of always pointin' at me?"

"T'ain't no use in gettin' all mad, Janie, 'cause Ah mention you ain't no young gal no mo'. Nobody in heah ain't lookin' for no wife outa yuh. Old as you is."

"Naw, Ah ain't no young gal no mo' but den Ah ain't no old woman neither. Ah reckon Ah looks mah age too. But Ah'm uh woman every inch of me, and Ah know it. Dat's uh whole lot more'n *you* kin say. You big-bellies round here and put out a lot of brag, but 'tain't nothin' to it but yo' big voice. Humph! Talkin' 'bout *me* lookin' old! When you pull down yo' britches, you look lak de change uh life."

"Great God from Zion!" Sam Watson gasped. "Y'all really playin' de dozens tuhnight."

"Wha—whut's dat you said?" Joe challenged, hoping his ears had fooled him.

"You heard her, you ain't blind," Walter taunted.

"Ah ruther be shot with tacks than tuh hear dat 'bout mahself," Lige Moss commiserated.

Then Joe Starks realized all the meanings and his vanity bled like a flood. Janie had robbed him of his illusion of irresistible maleness that all men cherish, which was terrible. The thing that Saul's daughter had done to David. But Janie had done worse, she had cast down his empty armor before men and they had laughed, would keep on laughing. When he paraded his possessions hereafter, they would not consider the two together. They'd look with envy at the things and pity the man that owned them. When he sat in judgment it would be the same. Good-for-nothing's like Dave and Lum and Jim wouldn't change place with him. For what can excuse a man in the eyes of other men for lack of strength?

•

Ed laughed and said, "Git off de muck! You ain't nothin'. Dat's all! Hot boilin' water won't help yuh none." Ed kept on laughing because he had been so scared before. "Sop, Bootyny, all y'all dat lemme win yo' money: Ah'm sending it straight off to Sears and Roebuck and buy me some clothes, and when Ah turn out Christmas day, it would take a doctor to tell me how near Ah is dressed tuh death."

•

"Sometimes God gits familiar wid us womenfolks too and talks His inside business. He told me how surprised He was 'bout y'all turning out so smart after Him makin' yuh different; and how surprised y'all is goin' tuh be if you ever find out you don't know half as much 'bout us as you think you do. It's so easy to make yo'self out God Almighty when you ain't got nothin' tuh strain against but women and chickens."

•

One day they were working near where the beans ended and the sugar cane began. Janie had marched off a little from Tea Cake's side with another woman for a chat. When she glanced around Tea Cake was gone. Nunkie too. She knew because she looked.

"Where's Tea Cake?" she asked Sop-de-Bottom.

He waved his hand towards the cane field and hurried away. Janie never thought at all. She just acted on feelings. She rushed into the cane and about the fifth row down she found Tea Cake and Nunkie struggling. She was on them before either knew.

"Whut's de matter heah?" Janie asked in a cold rage. They sprang apart.

"Nothin'," Tea Cake told her, standing shamefaced.

"Well, whut you doin' in heah? How come you ain't out dere wid de rest?"

"She grabbed mah workin' tickets outa mah shirt pocket and Ah run tuh git 'em back," Tea Cake explained, showing the tickets, considerably mauled about in the struggle.

Janie made a move to seize Nunkie but the girl fled. So she took out behind her over the humped-up cane rows. But Nunkie did not mean to be caught. So Janie went on home. The sight of the fields and the other happy people was too much for her that day. She walked slowly and thoughtfully to the quarters. It wasn't long before Tea Cake found her there and tried to talk. She cut him short with a blow and they fought from one room to the other, Janie trying to beat him, and Tea Cake kept holding her wrists and wherever he could to keep her from going too far.

"Ah b'lieve you been messin' round her!" she panted furiously.

"No sich uh thing!" Tea Cake retorted.

"Ah b'lieve yuh did."

"Don't keer how big uh lie get told, somebody kin b'lieve it!"

They fought on. "You done hurt mah heart, now you come wid uh lie tuh bruise mah ears! Turn go mah hands!" Janie seethed. But Tea Cake never let go. They wrestled on until they were doped with their own fumes and emanations; till their clothes had been torn away; till he hurled her to the floor and held her there melting her resistance with the heat of his body, doing things with their bodies to express the inexpressible; kissed her until she arched her body to meet him and they fell asleep in sweet exhaustion.

The next morning Janie asked like a woman, "You still love ole Nunkie?"

"Naw, never did, and you know it too. Ah didn't want her."

"Yeah, you did." She didn't say this because she believed it. She wanted to hear his denial. She had to crow over the fallen Nunkie.

"Whut would Ah do wid dat lil chunk of a woman wid you around? She ain't good for nothin' exceptin' tuh set up in uh corner by de kitchen stove and break wood over her head. You'se something tuh make uh man forget tuh git old and forget tuh die."

•

FROM *Drenched in Light*

Now there are certain things that Grandma Potts felt no one of this female persuasion should do—one was to sit with the knees separated, "settin' brazen" she called it; another was whistling, another playing with boys. Finally, a lady must never cross her legs.

Ann E. Imbrie (contemporary)

~≈≈ ≈≈~

FROM *Spoken in Darkness*

Learning about sex was a little bit like learning grammar. Every teacher you had assumed some other teacher taught you the year before, or the year before that, as if none of them wanted to talk about it, as if grammar was a bunch of dirty words. A massive silence surrounded dangling participles and infinitive clauses, and you learned to fear making mistakes you didn't know how to avoid.

Elizabeth Inchbald (1753–1821)

~≈≈ ≈≈~

FROM *A Simple Story*

"What, love a rake, a man of professed gallantry? impossible.—To me, a common rake is as odious, as a common prostitute is to a man of the nicest feelings.—Where can be the pride of inspiring a passion, fifty others can equally inspire? or the transport of bestowing favours, where the appetite is already cloyed by fruition of the self-same enjoyments?"

"Strange," cried Miss Woodley, "that you, who possess so many follies incident to your sex, should, in the disposal of your heart, have sentiments so contrary to women in general."

"My dear Miss Woodley," returned she, "put in competition the languid love of a debauchee, with the vivid affection of a sober man, and judge which has the dominion? Oh! in my calendar of love, a solemn lord chief justice, or a devout archbishop ranks before a licentious king."

Miss Woodley smiled at an opinion which she knew half her sex would laugh at; but by the air of sincerity with which it was delivered, she was convinced, her late behaviour to Lord Frederick was but the mere effect of chance.

Lord Elmwood's carriage drove to his door just at the time hers did; Mr. Sandford was with him, and they were both come from passing the evening at Mr. Fenton's.

"So, my lord," said Miss Woodley, as soon as they met in the apartment, "you did not come to us."

"No," answered his lordship, "I was sorry; but I hope you did not expect me."

"Not expect you, my lord?" cried Miss Milner, "did not you say you would come?"

"If I had, I certainly should have come," returned he, "but I only said so conditionally."

"That I am witness to," cried Sandford, "for I was present at the time, and his lordship said it should depend upon Miss Fenton."

"And she, with her gloomy disposition," said Miss Milner, "chose to sit at home."

"Gloomy disposition?" repeated Sandford, "She is a young lady with a great share of sprightliness—and I think I never saw her in better spirits than she was this evening, my lord?"

Lord Elmwood did not speak.

"Bless me, Mr. Sandford," cried Miss Milner, "I meant no reflection upon Miss Fenton's disposition; I only meant to censure her taste for staying at home."

"I think," replied Sandford, "a much greater censure should be passed upon those, who prefer rambling abroad."

"But I hope, ladies, my not coming," said his lordship, "was no cause of inconvenience to you; you had still a gentleman with you, or I should certainly have come."

"Oh! yes, two gentlemen," answered the young son of Lady Evans, a lad from school, whom Miss Milner had taken along with her, and to whom his lordship had alluded.

"What two?" asked Lord Elmwood.

Neither Miss Milner or Miss Woodley answered.

"You know, madam," said young Evans, "that handsome gentleman who handed you into your carriage, and you called my lord."

"Oh! he means Lord Frederick Lawnly," said Miss Milner carelessly, but a blush of shame spread over her face.

"And did he hand you into your coach?" asked his lordship, earnestly.

"By mere accident, my lord," Miss Woodley replied, "for the crowd was so great—"

"I think, my lord," said Sandford, "it was very lucky you were *not* there."

"Had Lord Elmwood been with us, we should not have had occasion for the assistance of any other," said Miss Milner.

"Lord Elmwood has been with you, madam," returned Sandford, "very frequently, and yet—"

"Mr. Sandford," said his lordship, interrupting him, "it is near bedtime, your conversation keeps the ladies from retiring."

"Your lordship's does not," said Miss Milner, "for you say nothing."

"Because, madam, I am afraid to offend."

"But does not your lordship also hope to please? and without risking the one, it is impossible to arrive at the other."

"I think, at present, the risk of one would be too hazardous, and so I wish you a good night." And he went out of the room somewhat abruptly.

"Lord Elmwood," said Miss Milner, "is very grave—he does not look like a man who has been passing his evening with the woman he loves."

"Perhaps he is melancholy at parting from her," said Miss Woodley.

"More likely offended," said Sandford, "at the manner in which that lady has spoken of her."

"Who, I?" cried Miss Milner, "I protest I said nothing but—"

"Nothing, madam? did not you say she was gloomy?"

"But, what I thought—I was going to add, Mr. Sandford."

"When you think unjustly, you should not express your thoughts."

"Then, perhaps, I should never speak."

"And it were better you did not, if what you say, is to give pain.—Do you know, madam, that my lord is going to be married to Miss Fenton?"

"Yes," answered Miss Milner.

"Do you know that he loves her?"

"No," answered Miss Milner.

"How, madam! do you suppose he does not?"

"I suppose he does, yet I don't know it."

"Then supposing he does, how can you have the imprudence to find fault with her before him?"

"I did not—to call her gloomy, was, I knew, to praise her both to him and to you, who admire such tempers."

"Whatever her temper is, *every one* admires it; and so far from its being what you have described, she has a great deal of vivacity; vivacity which proceeds from the heart."

"No, if it proceeded, I should admire it too; but it rests there, and no one is the better for it."

"Come, Miss Milner," said Miss Woodley, "it is time to retire; you and Mr. Sandford must finish your dispute in the morning."

"Dispute, madam!" said Sandford, "I never disputed with any one beneath a doctor of divinity in my life.—I was only cautioning your friend not to make light of virtues, which it would do her honour to possess.—Miss Fenton is a most amiable young woman, and worthy just such a husband as my Lord Elmwood will make her."

"I am sure," said Miss Woodley, "Miss Milner thinks so—she has a high opinion of Miss Fenton—she was at present only jesting."

"But, madam, jests are very pernicious things, when delivered with a malignant sneer.—I have known a jest destroy a lady's reputation—I have known a jest give one person a distaste for another—I have known a jest break off a marriage."

"But I suppose there is no apprehension of that, in the present case?" said Miss Woodley—wishing he might answer in the affirmative.

"Not that I can foresee," replied he.—"No, Heaven forbid; for I look upon them to be formed for each other—their dispositions, their pursuits, their inclinations the same.—Their passions for each other just the same—pure—white as snow."

"And I dare say, not warmer," replied Miss Milner.

He looked provoked beyond measure.

"Dear Miss Milner," cried Miss Woodley, "how can you talk thus? I believe in my heart you are only envious my lord did not offer himself to you."

"To her!" said Sandford, affecting an air of the utmost surprise, "to her? Do you think his lordship received a dispensation from his vows to become the husband of a coquette—a—" he was going on.

"Nay, Mr. Sandford," cried Miss Milner, "I believe my greatest crime in your eyes, is being a heretic."

"By no means, madam—it is the only circumstance that can apologize for your faults; and had you not that excuse, there would be none for you."

"Then, at present, there is an excuse—I thank you, Mr. Sandford; this is the kindest thing you ever said to me. But I am vext to see you are sorry, you have said it."

"Angry at your being a heretic?" he resumed, "Indeed I should be much more concerned to see you a disgrace to our religion."

Miss Milner had not been in a good humour during the whole evening—she had been provoked to the full extent of her patience several times; but this harsh sentence hurried her beyond all bounds, and she arose from her seat in the most violent agitation, and exclaimed, "What have I done to be treated thus?"

Though Mr. Sandford was not a man easily intimidated, he was on this occasion evidently alarmed; and stared about him with so strong an expression of surprise, that it partook in some degree of fear.—Miss Woodley clasped her friend in her arms, and cried with the tenderest affection and pity, "My dear Miss Milner, be composed."

Miss Milner sat down, and was so for a minute; but her dead silence was nearly as alarming to Sandford as her rage had been; and he did not perfectly recover himself till he saw a flood of tears pouring down her face; he then heaved a sigh of content that it had so ended, but in his heart resolved never to forget the ridiculous affright into which he had been put.—He stole out of the room without uttering a syllable—But as he never retired to rest before he had repeated a long form of evening prayers, so when he came to that part which supplicates "Grace for the wicked," he named Miss Milner's name, with the most fervent devotion.

Molly Ivins (1944–   )

FROM *Molly Ivins Can't Say That, Can She?*

[To] be a feminist country music fan is an exercise in cultural masochism. There you are trying to uphold the personhood of the female sex, while listening to "She Got the Gold Mine, I Got the Shaft" or "Don't the Girls All Get Prettier at Closing Time." Women in country music are either saints or sluts, but they're mostly sluts. She's either a "good-hearted woman" or a "honky-tonk angel." There are more hard-hearted women in country music ("I Gave Her a Ring, She Gave Me the Finger"), despicable bimbos ("Ruuuby, Don't Take Your Love to Town"), and heartless gold diggers ("Satin Sheets to Lie On, Satin Pillow to Cry On") than the scholars can count. Even the great women country singers aren't much help. The immortal Patsy Cline was mostly lovesick for some worthless heel ("I Fall to Pieces") and Tammy Wy-

nette's greatest contribution was to advise us "Stand by Your Man."
(Tammy has stood by several of them.)

•

They kept telling us we had to get in touch with our bodies. Mine isn't
all that communicative but I heard from it on Tuesday morning when
I genially proposed, "Body, how'd you like to go to the nine o'clock
class in vigorous toning with resistance?"

Clear as a bell my body said, "Listen, bitch, do it and you die."

Great, I'm finally in touch with my body and it turns out to have
the personality of a Mafioso. They tell you to listen to your body, so I
went to the hot tub instead.

•

It's illegal to be gay in Texas again, thanks to the Fifth Circuit. They
reinstated our sodomy statute, so people can legally screw pigs in public
but not each other in private.

•

Speaking of Baton Rouge, when David Duke, the newest member of
the Louisiana Legislature, was the chief cheese and sheet-washer for the
Knights of the Ku Klux Klan, he took the Dale Carnegie course in how
to win friends and influence people. Honest. At the time, the case of
the Klansman who took the Carnegie course (where they teach you to
say heartily, "Gosh, isn't this a good party?" and "My, aren't we having
a lot of fun?") seemed to be just another reason not to write fiction.

•

If we were to go for honesty instead of public relations, we'd wind up
with something like TOO MUCH IS NOT ENOUGH or TEXAS—
LAND OF WRETCHED EXCESS. Or, perhaps, HOME OF THE
FDIC.

If honesty were a national license plate policy, we'd see

- RHODE ISLAND—LAND OF OBSCURITY

- OKLAHOMA—THE RECRUITING VIOLATIONS STATE

- MAINE—HOME OF GEORGE BUSH

- MINNESOTA—TOO DAMN COLD

- WISCONSIN—EAT CHEESE OR DIE

- CALIFORNIA—FREEWAY CONGESTION WITH OCCASIONAL
  GUNFIRE

- NEW JERSEY—ARMPIT OF THE NATION

- NORTH DAKOTA—INCREDIBLY BORING

- NEBRASKA—MORE INTERESTING THAN NORTH DAKOTA

- NEW YORK—WE'RE NOT ARROGANT, WE'RE JUST BETTER THAN YOU

•

Many cultures have popular song forms that reflect the people's concerns. In Latin cultures the *corridos*, written by immortal poets such as García Lorca, give voice to the yearnings of the voiceless. In our culture, "Take This Job and Shove It" serves much the same function.

If you want to take the pulse of the people in the country, listen to country-western music.

•

[A] surprising number of men are alarmed by the thought of a witty woman. They think of women's wit as sarcastic, cutting, "ball-busting": it was one of the unstated themes of the campaign and one reason why Ann Richards didn't say a single funny thing during the whole show. Margaret Atwood, the Canadian novelist, once asked a group of women at a university why they felt threatened by men. The women said they were afraid of being beaten, raped, or killed by men. She then asked a group of men why they felt threatened by women. They said they were afraid women would laugh at them.

•

FROM *Nothin' but Good Times Ahead*

Although a lifelong fashion dropout, I have absorbed enough by reading *Harper's Bazaar* while waiting at the dentist's to have grasped that the purpose of fashion is to make A Statement. (My own modest Statement, discerned by true cognoscenti, is, "Woman Who Wears Clothes So She Won't Be Naked.")

•

Fellow citizens, as we stagger toward the millennium, I can only hope that this modest oeuvre—as we often say in Amarillo—will remind you that we need to stop and laugh along the way. We live in a Great Nation, but those who attempt to struggle through it unarmed with a sense of humor are apt to wind up in my Aunt Eula's Fort Worth Home for the

Terminally Literal-Minded, gibbering like some demented neoconservative about the Decline of Civilization.

•

On the occasion of the bicentennial of the Constitution, the ACLU was fixin' to lay some heavy lifetime freedom-fighter awards on various citizens, and one of 'em was Joe Rauh, the lawyer who defended so many folks during the McCarthy era and the civil rights movement (note that the rightness of those stands is always easier to see in retrospect). Rauh was sick in the hospital at the time and asked a friend of his to go down and collect the award for him. His friend went to see him in the hospital and said, "Joe, what you want me to tell these folks?"

So there was Rauh lyin' there sick as a dog, thinkin' back on all those bad, ugly, angry times—the destroyed careers, the wrecked lives —and he said, "Tell 'em how much fun it was. Tell 'em how much fun it was."

So keep fightin' for freedom and justice, beloveds, but don't you forget to have fun doin' it. Lord, let your laughter ring forth. Be outrageous, ridicule the fraidy-cats, rejoice in all the oddities that freedom can produce. And when you get through kickin' ass and celebratin' the sheer joy of a good fight, be sure to tell those who come after how much fun it was.

Elaine Jackson (contemporary)

~❧ ❧~

FROM *Paper Dolls*

LIZZIE: I told him I was fifty-five years old and he nearly fell out of his seat.

M-E: No wonder! He was in shock. You're sixty-nine!

LIZZIE: That's it! That's *it!* I'm not saying another word to you! I'm not going to talk to you anymore, Margaret. . . . *If* I happen to speak to you again, it's because you're the only somebody in here that I know.

•

M-E: Only made *one* picture where they let my legs show . . . can't remember her name. I played . . . a native girl . . . what was her name? . . . Goodness knows, I'd almost forgotten that. (*Calling in to* LIZZIE.) Darn it, Lizzie! I'd almost forgotten that movie. "Bugga Wanna, Bugga Wanna, Bugga Wanna Wanna Na."

    Those were my lines. Those were the lines I had to say when they brought me back to my tribe. "Bugga Wanna, Bugga Wanna, Bugga Wanna Wanna Na."

LIZZIE: It's too bad you remembered them, Margaret. It sorta makes you want to throw up.

                                        •

M-E: They took all the natural things of life and made a mess out of them! Do you realize that we spent our entire lives traumatizing over things that had been carefully worked out? Someone decided everything was too simple . . . the Grand Design just wasn't complex enough . . . so they threw a monkey wrench into the whole goddamn works. Life! Growing up! Growing old! . . . Beauty! . . . *but,* finally, Death! . . . Now that's unnatural!

LIZZIE: The only unnatural thing I've done recently is to come here with you.

M-E: Oh, poo poo! When I was thirteen years old, my mother went around telling everyone I was nine. When I was sixteen, she told people I was twelve! I've lived my whole life never experiencing my true age. I wore ribbons in my hair until I was thirty-five years old! Mother said, "When you're young, people allow you to make mistakes. They forgive you."

Shirley Jackson (1919–1965)

                         ❧ ❧

FROM *Life Among the Savages*

She is one of those impressive women who usually head committees on supervising movies, taking the entire sixth grade on a tour of one of our local factories, or outlawing slingshots, and I daresay she would be the first person everyone would think of if there should arise an occasion for the mothers to lift the school building and carry it bodily to another location.

•

I am wholeheartedly afraid of fuses and motorcycles and floor plugs and lightning rods and electric drills and large animals and most particularly of furnaces. Laboriously, over the span of years of married life, my husband has taught me to use such hazardous appliances as a toaster and an electric coffee pot, but no one is ever going to get me to go down cellar and fool around with a furnace.

•

"Name?" the desk clerk said to me politely, her pencil poised.
"Name." I said vaguely. I remembered, and told her.
"Age?" she asked. "Sex? Occupation?"
"Writer," I said.
"Housewife," she said.
"Writer," I said.
"I'll just put down housewife," she said.

•

FROM *Raising Demons*

I was not bitter about being a faculty wife, very much, although it did occur to me once or twice that young men who were apt to go on and become college teachers someday ought to be required to show some clearly distinguishable characteristic, or perhaps even wear some large kind of identifying badge, for the protection of innocent young girls who might in that case go on to be the contented wives of furniture repairmen or disc jockeys or even car salesmen. The way it is now, almost any girl is apt to find herself hardening slowly into a faculty wife when all she actually thought she was doing was just getting married.

•

FROM *Come Along with Me*

I've just buried my husband," I said.
"I've just buried mine," she said.
"Isn't it a relief?" I said.
"What?" she said.

"It was a very sad occasion," I said.
"You're right," she said. "It's a relief."

Bonnie Januszewski-Ytuarte (1957-)

~❦ ❦~

One-liners

The phrase "working mother" is redundant.

•

Dress casually? I don't own casual clothes. Either I show up in shorts or in my wedding gown.

•

I woke up one morning and thought, "Here I am with two kids at home, doing all kinds of stuff I never thought I'd do. For example, who made me into the Queen of Jello Molds?"

Jenny Jones (contemporary)

~❦ ❦~

On Men

If you want to seduce a woman, invite her over and cook for her. Afterwards, she'll sit on a couch and say, "I want to show you how much I appreciate that wonderful dinner . . . I love macaroni and cheese . . . I just never had to slice it before . . . oh, maybe a metal knife and fork would be better . . . it's just so romantic eating over the sink. More? Oh, don't open a can just for me."

•

You guys who went to Catholic school need to loosen up. This one guy said to me, "Am I the first one?" I said, "Yeah. Today."

Erica Jong (1942-   )

~∘ e ✺ ∘~

FROM *Fear of Flying*

We drove to the hotel and said goodbye. How hypocritical to go upstairs with a man you don't want to fuck, leave the one you do sitting there alone, and then, in a state of great excitement, fuck the one you don't want to fuck while pretending he's the one you do. That's called fidelity. That's called monogamy. That's called civilization and its discontents.

•

I was a little appalled at my own promiscuity, that I could go from one man to another and feel so glowing and intoxicated. I knew I would have to pay for it later with the guilt and misery which I alone know how to give myself in such good measure. But right now I was happy. I felt properly appreciated for the first time. Do two men perhaps add up to one whole person?

•

Bennett's careful, compulsive, and boring steadfastness was my own panic about change, my fear of being alone, my need for security. Adrian's antic manners and ass-grabbing was the part of me that wanted exuberance above all. I had never been able to make peace between the two halves of myself. All I had managed to do was suppress one half (for a while) at the expense of the other. I had never been happy with the bourgeois virtues of marriage, stability, and work above pleasure. I was too curious and adventurous not to chafe under those restrictions. But I also suffered from night terrors and attacks of panic at being alone. So I always wound up living with somebody or being married.

Besides I really believed in pursuing a longstanding and deep relationship with one person. I could easily see the sterility of hopping from bed to bed and having shallow affairs with lots of shallow people. I had had the unutterably dismal experience of waking up in bed with a man I couldn't bear to talk to—and that was certainly no liberation either. But still, there just didn't seem to be any way to get the best of both exuberance and stability into your life. The fact that greater minds than mine had pondered these issues and come up with no very clear answers didn't comfort me much either. It only made me feel that my concerns were banal and commonplace. If I were really an exceptional person, I thought, I wouldn't spend hours worrying my head about marriage and adultery. I would just go out and snatch life with both hands and feel no remorse or guilt for anything. My guilt only showed how thoroughly bourgeois and contemptible I was. All my worrying this sad old bone only showed my ordinariness.

•

The ultimate sexist put-down: the prick which lies down on the job. The ultimate weapon in the war between the sexes: the limp prick. The banner of the enemy's encampment: the prick at half-mast. The symbol of the apocalypse: the atomic warhead prick which self-destructs. *That* was the basic inequity which could never be righted: not that the male had a wonderful added attraction called a penis, but that the female had a wonderful all-weather cunt. Neither storm nor sleet nor dark of night could faze it. It was always there, always ready. Quite terrifying, when you think about it. No wonder men hated women. No wonder they invented the myth of female inadequacy.

•

Why should a bad marriage have been so much more compelling than no marriage? Why had I clung to my misery so? Why did I believe it was all I had?

As I read the notebook, I began to be drawn into it as into a novel. I almost began to forget that I had written it. And then a curious revelation started to dawn. I stopped blaming myself; it was that simple. Perhaps my finally running away was not due to malice on my part, nor to any disloyalty I need apologize for. Perhaps it was a kind of loyalty to myself. A drastic but necessary way of changing my life.

You did not have to apologize for wanting to own your own soul. Your soul belonged to you—for better or for worse. When all was said and done, it was all you had.

Marriage was tricky because in some ways it was always a *folie à deux*. At times you scarcely knew where your own lunacies left off and those of your spouse began. You tended to blame yourself too much, or not enough, or for the wrong things. And you tended to confuse dependency with love.

I went on reading and with each page I grew more philosophical. I knew I did not want to return to the marriage described in that notebook. If Bennett and I got back together again, it would have to be under very different circumstances. And if we did not, I knew I would survive.

No electric light bulb went on in my head with that recognition.

Nor did I leap into the air and shout *Eureka!* I sat very quietly looking at the pages I had written. I knew I did not want to be trapped in my own book.

It was also heartening to see how much I had changed in the past four years. I was able to send my work out now. I was not afraid to drive. I was able to spend long hours alone writing. I taught, gave lectures, traveled. Terrified of flying as I was, I didn't allow that fear to control me. Perhaps someday I'd lose it altogether. If some things could change, so could other things. What right had I to predict the future and predict it so nihilistically? As I got older I would probably change in hundreds of ways I couldn't foresee. All I had to do was wait it out.

It was easy enough to kill yourself in a fit of despair. It was easy enough to play the martyr. It was harder to do nothing. To endure your life. To wait.

I slept. I think I actually fell asleep with my face pressed to my spiral notebook. I remember waking up in the blue hours of early morning and feeling a spiral welt on the side of my cheek. Then I pushed away the notebook and went back to sleep.

And my dreams were extravagant. Full of elevators, platforms in space, enormously steep and slippery staircases, ziggurat temples I had to climb, mountains, towers, ruins. . . . I had some vague sense that I was *assigning* myself dreams as a sort of cure. I remember once or twice waking and then falling back to sleep thinking: "Now I will have the dream which makes my decision for me." But what was the decision I sought? Every choice seemed so unsatisfactory in one way or another. Every choice excluded some other choice. It was as if I were asking my dreams to tell me who I was and what I ought to do. I would wake with my heart pounding and then sink back to sleep again. Maybe I was hoping I'd wake up somebody else.

Fragments of those dreams are still with me. In one of them, I had to walk a narrow plank between two skyscrapers in order to save someone's life. Whose? Mine? Bennett's? Chloe's? The dream did not say. But it was clear that if I failed, my own life would be over. In another, I reached inside myself to take out my diaphragm, and there, floating over my cervix, was a large contact lens. Womb with a view. The cervix was really an eye. And a nearsighted eye at that.

Then I remember the dream in which I was back in college preparing to receive my degree from Millicent McIntosh. I walked up a long flight of steps which looked more like the steps of a Mexican temple than the steps of Low Library. I teetered on very high heels and worried about tripping over my gown.

As I approached the lectern and Mrs. McIntosh held out a scroll to me, I realized that I was not merely graduating but was to receive some special honor.

"I must tell you that the faculty does not approve of this," Mrs. McIntosh said. And I knew then that the fellowship conferred on me the right to have three husbands simultaneously. They sat in the audience wearing black caps and gowns: Bennett, Adrian, and some other man whose face was not clear. They were all waiting to applaud when I got my diploma.

"Only your high academic achievement makes it impossible for us to withhold this honor," Mrs. McIntosh said, "but the faculty hopes you will decline of your own volition."

"But why?" I protested. "Why *can't* I have all three?"

After that I began a long rationalizing speech about marriage and my sexual needs and how I was a poet not a secretary. I stood at the lectern and ranted at the audience. Mrs. McIntosh looked soberly disapproving. Then I was picking my way down the steep steps, half crouching and terrified of falling. I looked into the sea of faces and suddenly realized that I had forgotten to take my scroll. In a panic I knew that I had forfeited everything: graduation, my fellowship grant, my harem of three husbands.

The final dream I remember is strangest of all. I was walking up the library steps again to reclaim my diploma. This time it was not Mrs. McIntosh at the lectern, but Colette. Only she was a black woman with frizzy reddish hair glinting around her head like a halo.

"There is only one way to graduate," she said, "and it has nothing to do with the number of husbands."

"What do I have to do?" I asked desperately, feeling I'd do anything.

She handed me a book with my name on the cover. "That was only a very shaky beginning," she said, "but at least you *made* a beginning."

I took this to mean I still had years to go.

"Wait," she said, undoing her blouse. Suddenly I understood that making love to her in public was the real graduation, and at that moment it seemed like the most natural thing in the world. Very aroused, I moved toward her. Then the dream faded.

Judith Katz (contemporary)

~&~

FROM *Running Fiercely Toward a High Thin Sound*

Sarah reached up and pinched my cheek. "So you're the maid of honor. Let me set you ladies up in dressing room three."

It took me a minute to remember they were talking about me, that I was the honor maiden. Nonetheless, when Sarah led us to a far corner of the bridal boutique, I followed. Sarah jingled a huge ring of keys and unlocked a white door. "You go in and make yourselves comfortable. Mimi will be in to fit you in a minute."

"It's lovely, isn't it?" my mother gestured broadly at the small private room. Mirrors covered three walls, a white shag rug was on the floor. The furniture was early Barbie doll—two plump white hassocks and a satin couch.

"I hope you have a decent bra on," my mother said as I unbuttoned my shirt. I suddenly couldn't remember if I had on any bra at all, but before I could pull my shirt back on the door swung open and there stood Mimi, who must have been Sarah's depressed twin. She had a tape measure around her neck, a long pink dress slung over one arm, and a pair of white linen pumps clutched between her thick fingers. Sighing deeply, Mimi hung the dress on a chrome hook and set the shoes down at my feet. Then she kneeled in front of me and with the help of a shoe horn slipped my foot into one of the pumps.

"Like a glove," Mimi said as she got me into the other shoe.

"I don't think I can walk." I stood and wobbled from one end of the dressing room to the other.

"A little practice, you'll be fine," my mother said.

"Besides, you'll kick them off as soon as the dancing starts."

I was surprised to hear my sister Electa's voice. She hadn't said a word since we got into the department store.

"She won't kick them off," my mother argued.

"I probably will," I answered, disturbed at the whine in my voice, "but still, I have to walk down the aisle—"

"Don't worry, Janie, we've got a nice strong best man for you to
lean on when it comes to that." Electa winked conspiratorially.

Best man? I never even considered I'd have to wobble on some
strange guy's arm on top of every other thing. "But I still have to stand
up at the altar teetering—"

"For God's sake," burst my mother, "the heel is only a half inch
—less than that. You can practice standing. It won't kill you—"

"I could break my neck," I said softly.

"Yes, think of the headlines," Electa said, "FEMINIST SISTER
DIES IN TRAGIC HIGH HEEL ACCIDENT: 'I DIDN'T THINK
IT COULD HAPPEN HERE' SAYS SHOCKED BRIDE."

"Alright Electa, cut the comedy," my mother said. "Mimi, the
shoes fit. Let's try the dress."

"*Oi*, the dress."

"It's not gonna kill you to wear a dress and heels and look like a
mentsh for five hours."

"It totally contradicts my political world view."

"Stop talking nonsense. Mimi! The dress."

The dress was worse than I'd imagined. The sleeves were sheer, the
bodice and hem frilly. I cringed at the thought of wearing it in public.
"Electa, this is a real girly outfit."

"I know, Jane. I'm sorry, but it's the best of what they're offering
this year."

"What's wrong with it?" my mother wanted to know. "A dress is
for girls to wear. What were you expecting? Lace overalls?"

"It's just so—"

"Feminine?" my mother sneered. "Look, we haven't got all day.
Try it on."

I slipped out of the rest of my clothes. To my relief, I had remembered to wear a bra and if it wasn't clean, my mother didn't notice. I
climbed into the dress, which pinched at the waist as my mother zipped it.

"It's too small, Ma."

She pulled up at the zipper, and my sister Electa empathetically held
her breath. Mimi the seamstress evilly fingered the pins in the cushion
on her wrist.

"It really doesn't fit," I said weakly.

"It fits. With a different bra—you know, it wouldn't hurt to lose
a few pounds before the wedding anyway . . . *oi* . . . there." My mother
triumphantly slipped the zipper all the way shut. I saw myself in the
three dressing room mirrors. I recognized the face, but I couldn't place
the body anywhere. "Ma, if I turn purple because I can't breathe it's
gonna spoil the effect."

"You only have to wear it once. It's fine."

"I'm gonna faint."

"Alright, we can let it out, can't we, Mimi? Jane, take it off."

Mimi unzipped, and I dutifully stepped out of the dress.

My mother snatched the dress out of Mimi's hands and carefully examined the seams. "There's plenty here to play with."

"Ma," Electa looked our mother in the eye, "let Jane try the next size."

"It will fit like a tent."

"Please, can we try the next size?" Electa asked the seamstress directly, by-passing my mother, taking matters into her own bride-to-be hands.

Mimi returned in a few minutes bearing another gown exactly like the first but bigger. I numbly climbed into it. It zipped like a charm but hung oddly in strange places.

"What did I tell you," my mother said triumphantly, "a tent."

Electa again went over my mother's head. "Mimi, what's easier? To take in or to let out?"

"In my professional opinion, it would be easier to find a style that fit the young lady to begin with."

A tear formed in the corner of my eye. Electa sat back in her chair with her head in her hands. "This is impossible. I can't find one dress that looks good on five different women!"

"Try the smaller size again."

"Ma, I can't fit in the smaller size."

"*Can't* means *won't*."

I stood looking at myself in the larger dress. I pressed my eyes in to hold back a fit of crying. Electa touched my shoulder. "Really, Jane, it's not so bad."

"The smaller one is better," my mother said flatly. "Jane, try the smaller one just one last time."

I stood paralyzed in the middle of the dressing room.

"Really," said my mother, "I just want to prove a point. Please step into this."

She held the dress open like an envelope. I looked at Electa who looked at Mimi who silently washed her hands of the entire matter. Then Mimi unzipped the bigger gown and held it while I carefully stepped out.

The other women held their breath as I wedged myself into the first dress. My mother once again tugged at the zipper.

"It's gonna rip."

My mother squeezed the flesh of my back in under the zipper

and yanked. "I could use a little cooperation. Pull your tummy in."

"It's in as far as it will go."

"Mommy," Electa pulled herself up to her full height, which in the space of the dressing room was rather impressive. "I'm not going to watch you torture Jane one more minute. Jane, you put on the large dress. Mimi, you pin it."

My mother threw up her hands and sat in a corner where she sulked until the pinning was complete. Normally I would have been nervous that she was going to lapse into her depression again, but right now I had troubles of my own.

"It's not my fault I can't fit into a size-eleven dress."

"No comment," my mother muttered.

She was still alive, and I was an adolescent again. The fluorescent light made my skin green, my teeth yellow, my face puffy and full of tear streaks. I wobbled in my white linen pumps while Mimi took pin after pin from her pin cushion wrist watch, poked, adjusted, and sighed.

At last, the seamstress got up off her knees. She dusted her hands and opened them to my reflection in the mirror. "You look like a million," she said.

Even through the straight pins, I could see that the dress looked better, although it was nothing I would ever choose for myself.

I picked my way out of the dress. My mother said, "Don't scratch yourself. If you get blood on that dress it's ruined."

I put my own clothes on but still could not recognize myself in the bridal boutique mirrors.

"You look exhausted," said my mother. "C'mon. I'm gonna buy you girls some lunch."

Pamela Katz (contemporary)

~❦ ❦~

The Long Ride

Completely unthreatened for a change, not caring what I said, or how it made me look, or seem, I asked my old friend Mark a question.

"Do you ever take buses?"

He smiled whimsically. He thought about how to answer most

humorously. He thought more about how the answer reflected on him, than on how the question revealed my character. Or the lack of it. He looked up grandly:

"I am at such a station in life that I no longer take buses."

Vindicated, I laughed. He laughed.

A light feeling filled me up. Drinking, eating, happy. Why?

I lived, at that time, with a man who wanted to take the bus home to the midwest. 24 hours. With me. Casually, at first, I complained. I didn't want to take the bus. Let's fly. I'll pay. Little did I know the onslaught of recriminations this would bring. For this minor opinion, I was condemned. Bourgeois. Not adventurous. I was not, in short, many things that I thought I was. And I was everything I didn't want to be. Or he didn't want me to be. In one sentence.

A minor issue in a relationship. To be rejected out of hand by people who would say: "Why didn't she fly, and let him take the bus?" "Couldn't she stand up for her own opinion?" Or a hundred other sentences which can all be summed up by the phrase: "What's the big deal?"

But does anyone reading this really doubt its significance? Doesn't everyone have a similar story? Don't all larger differences finally explode over the most trivial?

More importantly, though, is that almost no one recognizes such issues as trivial at the time, nor see what it is that they actually represent.

I only knew, then, that I felt helpless. I felt trapped by my comment. Forced to take the bus or accept everything that he said about me. Everything. I didn't consider why he would want to think them.

It's always the same simple equation. I liked him, or loved him, or thought I did. And I wanted him to love me, no doubt about that. If taking the bus would work, I would do it.

My moment with Mark was an undreamed-for freedom. I felt that I was right. Nobody likes to take the bus. I was right.

When we "landed" in his midwestern town, his father made many jokes: "Grueling trip, huh?" But his father was a hypocrite. He was glad we took the bus. And glad that I was unhappy about it. It proved something to him. At the time I was innocent of the game his family played. The game of tests. The possibility of failing a test given by someone who said they loved you.

The test went on. We packed a lunch for the bus. But we couldn't eat it right away. I snuck a candy bar in the Holland Tunnel. Weakness. I got car sick trying to read. Demerit. I fell asleep and woke up with a stiff neck. Complainer.

But I took the bus, I would later scream in my defense! To be expected, he would shrug. It's the fight that wasn't right. That I would even suggest not taking it. It hadn't mattered that I gave in. My objection damned me. I could have flown and received the same status. My unfortunate protest. One sentence. 24 hours on the bus couldn't redeem me. (I wished I'd known that.)

When I think now of how large this issue loomed, I could kick myself. Sometimes I do kick myself. How could I not have known then? It was so obvious. He didn't care about me. He enjoyed my discomfort. He thought it a moral act to disagree with me. It was so clear.

Now I am happily married. The absurdity of my arguments with this other man multiply in my mind. They become my own personal sickness. I cannot explain what it was I was thinking or feeling. It was blind love, it was something else. If he had waved a flag saying "I hate you" would I have seen it? Probably. So why?

And then I talk to my friends.

One who can't play a tape her friend made her of 100 great dance tunes. Her husband is one year younger than her and likes contemporary rock music. The tape is from the 50's and 60's and he tells her that she reveals her age, and her lack of interest in modern music, by playing it. What she reveals by actually LIKING it he can hardly utter.

One who can't buy extravagant items even though she is the only one in the house earning money.

One who can't wear make-up because it's phoney.

One who can't buy a couch because furniture is stupid.

One who couldn't pay off their credit cards (with money she earns) because her husband bought a Corvette.

One who has to live in her boyfriend's parents' house, with his parents (who hate her) because he wants to write a book about his home town.

So what is the point? Is this essay simply a list of complaints about women who don't know how to help themselves?

No. The point is to know for yourself when the trivial issue in your relationship is significant. We always find ourselves saying "No, I don't agree with him, but what am I going to do, break up over his choice in silverware?"

What am I going to do, break up with him because he needs one more year to decide! (And we've been going out for five years, think of what I'll lose.)

Break up with him because he was unfaithful just this once?

Break up with the man I love? Oh no, I'll need a good reason for that.

Good reasons are not universal, or universally recognized. But there are some questions which help us down the garden path. For example:

DOES HE LOVE ME?
DOES HE APPRECIATE ME?
DOES HE CARE ABOUT ME?
DOES HE WANT TO MAKE IT WORK, OR IS IT ALWAYS ME WHO TRIES TO SOLVE OUR PROBLEMS?
DOES HE MAKE ME FEEL INADEQUATE? HOW OFTEN? IN WHAT WAYS?
WHY DOES HE MAKE ME FEEL INADEQUATE? DOES HE ENJOY IT? DOES HE NEED IT?

Sound like obvious questions? Think about your relationship If you are happy, think about a relationship you regret. Is anything ever obvious when you are in that torture chamber of self-doubt, known as relationship hell?

Pray to the Saint of the Obvious for vision. Even if you are not religious.

Florynce Kennedy (1916-)

~℩ ℀~

One-liners

When a male heckler called out "Are you a lesbian?" she immediately replied, "Are you my alternative?"

•

There's a lady in the dentist's chair who is pretty nervous about what's going on. The dentist works on her for about three minutes and all of a sudden he realizes that she has managed to obtain a very tight grip on his testicles, and she's squeezing just short of agony. So he stops and says, "What is this?" and she says, "We are not going to hurt each other, are we, doctor?"

•

I'm just a loud-mouthed middle-aged colored lady . . . and a lot of people think I'm crazy. Maybe you do too, but I never stop to wonder why I'm not like other people. The mystery to me is why more people aren't like me.

•

When women began wearing pants there was a tremendous backlash. I can remember—I was still practicing law at that time—going to court in pants and the judge's remarking that I wasn't properly dressed, that the next time I came to court I should be dressed like a lawyer. He's sitting there in a long black dress gathered at the yoke, and I said, "Judge, if you won't talk about what I'm wearing, I won't talk about what you're wearing."

Jean Kerr (1923-   )

FROM *Go Josephine, in Your Flying Machine*

By the time the plane is ready to depart I have been fortified with tranquilizers, dramamine, and intoxicating beverages. Nevertheless I creep up the entrance ramp a craven creature, escorted usually by the copilot, who recognizes a case of nerves when he sees one. "I suppose you've checked all the engines," I say, laughing wildly—giving a performance like James Cagney being led to the chair in one of those old Warner Brothers movies. The only reason I don't change my mind and make a break for it right down the ramp is because they have by this time absconded with my luggage, which is now, I presume, locked away in the hold.

I never bring reading material aboard a plane because I am convinced that if I'm not right there, alert every minute, keeping my eye on things, heaven knows what might happen to us. When it comes to selecting a seat I am torn between my wish to sit well back in the tail (surely the safest place to be when we crash) and the feeling that it is my civic duty to take a place next to the window where I can keep a constant watch over the engines. You have no idea how heedless and selfish some passengers are—reading magazines and munching sandwiches the while that I, alone, am keeping that plane aloft by tugging upward on the arms of my chair and concentrating intensely, sometimes for hours. And when it becomes absolutely clear that something is amiss, who has to ask that simple, straightforward question that will clarify things? I do. Honestly, I don't think these people care whether they live or die.

On a recent daylight flight to Washington, D.C., I was quick to notice that in spite of the fact that the weather was brilliantly clear our plane kept losing altitude. By which I mean it was dropping and dropping and dropping. "Stewardess," I said, raising my voice to a whisper, "is something the matter?" She flashed me a wide, Cinemascope smile and said, "I'll ask the Captain, if you wish." By this time my stomach was in such a precarious condition that I didn't trust myself to vocalize, so I merely made a little gesture meaning "that would be very nice." She disappeared into the cockpit, where, evidently, the intercom between pilot and passengers had been left open. Presently we were all able to hear the stewardess reporting, "The passengers want to know if something is the matter." The next thing we heard was a short oath and a hoarse male voice saying, "The hell with the passengers, I'm up to my ears in trouble."

Well, talk about a conversation stopper. Even the jaunty junior executives who, a moment before, had been exchanging noisy jokes about an extremely co-operative girl named Mildred retreated into silence behind their copies of *The Wall Street Journal*, which could be seen to flap and rustle in their trembling hands. Mercifully, there were no more bulletins from the cabin and we landed uneventfully, none the worse for wear. Well, I can't speak for the other passengers, of course. But after five days' bed rest I felt fine.

I know perfectly well that people who talk about "their flights" are on a par, conversationally, with people who talk about their operations. Consequently at social gatherings I always try to find a subject that is genuinely interesting, like, for instance, my dishwasher. (The man was here *three* times and still the water pours out all over the kitchen floor.) However I barely get started when someone interrupts me to say, "Listen, do you want to hear a really hair-raising story?" And I know we are off on another saga of the perils of this age of flight. A songwriter recently told me that his plane from the Coast was barely aloft when he overheard the following exchange between dear old lady across the aisle from him and the stewardess:

DEAR OLD LADY: I hate to mention this, stewardess, but I think one
                 of the engines is on fire.

STEWARDESS:	No, indeed, madam, those little sparks you see are part of the normal functioning. May I ask, is this your first flight?
DEAR OLD LADY:	That's right. My children gave me this trip as a present for my eighty-sixth birthday.
STEWARDESS:	I thought so. Many of our first-time passengers are a little nervous, but there is nothing to worry about. Not one member of the crew has had less than two thousand hours in the air.
DEAR OLD LADY:	Thank you, my dear. I felt I was being a little silly. But before you go would you mind taking a look out my window here?
STEWARDESS:	Why, certainly. If it will make you feel a little better I'll be glad to—*oh my God!*

The engine, needless to say, was on fire, but I won't wear you out with all the details—except to say that all landed safely, including the old lady, who was heard remarking to her son-in-law, "You won't believe this, Henry, but *I* had to tell them the plane was on fire."

•

This always reminds me of a story about a friend of mine. One Easter she had to prepare dinner for fifteen people, counting children and relatives. For reasons of economy she decided to make a ham loaf instead of the traditional baked ham. Obviously it was going to be four times the trouble, since the recipe for the ham loaf was extremely elaborate: there were a dozen different ingredients and the whole thing had to be made in advance and allowed to "set" overnight in pineapple juice. But she went gamely ahead, convinced that she was going to produce something tastier than baked ham, if not indeed a gourmet's dish. As she took the square pink loaf out of the oven, a sinister thought crossed her mind. She cut off a little slice and tasted it, her worst suspicions confirmed. In tears she flew out of the kitchen to find her husband. "Oh, Frank," she said, "do you know what I've *got*? I've got Spam!"

•

FROM *Penny Candy*

I couldn't appear at a chic dinner party in a dress that buttoned down the front. I knew I had to take steps.

I went to Lord & Taylor and bravely marched into "Better

Dresses." Then I stood in a corner for a while and studied the salesladies. What I did *not* want was an elegant saleslady. I knew, from past experience, that in the presence of a really elegant saleslady with a really elegant European accent I tend to drop my purse and my gloves and to develop coughing spells.

I finally selected one who seemed a little shy and nervous. I went over to her and took hold of her elbow. "Don't *argue* with me," I said, "I want to buy a dress. I want to buy a fancy dress. And I want to buy it this afternoon." She didn't seem startled by my outburst. She just sighed a little sigh that seemed to say "Boy, I get all the nuts!" Then she went to work and found me a pretty dress. It was made of yellow silk pongee with metallic gold thread woven through the fabric. And so I went to the party calm in my conviction that for once I was wearing something that did not look as though it had been run up by loving hands at home.

My husband and I were the first to arrive because we had made the youthful error of arriving at precisely the time for which we had been invited. The editor and his wife greeted us in the foyer and were most gracious. I felt, however, that the wife's smile was a little bit strained. I understood everything when we walked into the living room. Three walls of the room were covered from floor to ceiling with draperies. And the draperies were made of exactly the same material as my new dress. What depressed me most was my feeling that I *wouldn't* die of embarrassment.

I tried to appraise the over-all situation. It wasn't so terrible. It just looked as though they'd had enough material left over to make a dress. But then why, in heaven's name, would I be wearing it? Actually, it didn't matter so much to me that when I was standing in front of a drapery I seemed to be a disembodied head. It mattered more to the other guests, who were hard put to analyze what they assumed must be an optical illusion. Conversations with me had a way of sputtering out. In fact, one man left my side in the middle of a sentence muttering, "I don't know *what* they put in this drink." Finally, I had to devote all of my energies to keeping near the one undraped—or safe—wall, where the heat from the open fireplace promptly took the curl out of my hair. Needless to say, we were not invited back.

Another reason I have so many dreary dresses is that I *know* I am a difficult size, which means that whenever a saleslady produces a dress that actually fits me I feel a sporting obligation to buy it. (I consider a dress fits me when it reaches to my knees and can be zipped up by only one person.) I seem unable to make plain statements like "I can't wear beige because I *am* beige." I may venture a feeble question, "Don't you think it's a little on the beige side?", but if I do the saleslady instantly counters with "Madam must imagine it dressed up with spanking white accessories." So naturally I buy the dress. I'm certainly not going to confess to that girl that I don't own one single spanking white accessory.

•

We live in Larchmont, a small community about twenty miles from New York. Most of our friends live in New York City, and they invite us to dinner calm in the assumption that we will find our way to the great metropolis in less than forty minutes. To a reasonable person it would appear that the distance between New York and Larchmont is approximately the same as the distance between Larchmont and New York. However, when I invite people out here I am left with the feeling that I am inviting them to Ice Station Zebra and that I should offer to provide Sherpa guides for those last tortuous miles through the mountain passes. You understand that Larchmont is on Long Island Sound and flat as can be. The only place a guide will be required is to get them through our garage where, for reasons I couldn't explain under oath, our six children have stored nineteen battered bicycles.

•

I DON'T WANT TO SEE THE UNCUT VERSION OF *ANYTHING*

Reflections of a Part-Time Playwright

I do not like to hear the most explicit four-letter words spoken from the stage because I number among my acquaintance persons of such candor and quick temper that, for me, the thrill is gone.

I have noticed that in plays where the characters on stage laugh a great deal, the people out front laugh very little. This is notoriously true of productions of Shakespeare's comedies. "Well, sirrah," says one buffoon, "he did go heigh-ho upon a bird-bolt." This gem is followed by such guffaws and general merriment as would leave Olsen and Johnson wondering how they failed.

It may have been bearable the first time it was done, but it is no longer bearable to see a comedy in which the ingenue yap yap yaps the whole first act long about the burdens of her virginity.

Also—speaking of the same kind of play—the heroine always does look as cute as all get out when, for reasons of the plot, she has to wear the hero's bathrobe. On the other hand (and this is happening more and more), when the hero is required to wear her brunch coat, he looks just plain terrible.

I have noticed that an entertainment that opens or closes with the setting up or dismantling of a circus tent always gets good notices. I don't know what to make of this.

I have seen plays performed on steps in front of a cyclorama that I enjoyed—but not many.

I am wary of plays in which God or the devil appear as characters. We will waive any discussion of theology and I don't mean to be irreverent when I say that, for all practical purposes in the theater, God is a lousy part. (A play I really loved, *The Tenth Man*, had to do with a girl who was being exorcised of the devil, but it may be relevant to note that we never saw the devil.)

I don't want to see productions that run four and one-half hours. (I don't want to see the "uncut version" of *anything*.) In a recent production of *King Lear*, the first act ran for two and one-half hours. By that time I considered that I had given up smoking, and I spent the entire intermission wondering if I should begin again. And I was once more made aware—during that interminable first act—that the most serious materials eventually seem comic if they are allowed to go on too long. For instance, during the protracted scene in which Lear (now mad) is talking to poor, blinded Gloucester, all I could think was: first they put his eyes out, now they're going to talk his ears off.

•

When *The Little Foxes* was revived recently, there were those who said it was too well constructed. To me, that's like saying a Pan Am pilot is too conscientious. What I like about Lillian Hellman's play is that you couldn't play the second act first. I know all about improvisation and the free-form that mirrors the chaos of our time, but I do like to feel that the playwright has done *some* work before I got there.

•

For Men

What is the proper answer when the little woman asks the following questions:

How is the roast beef?
    (a) Roast beef? I thought it was potroast.
    (b) Honey, do we have any ketchup?
    (c) Great.

My best friend from college is coming for a couple of days. Is that all right?

    (a) Okay, but don't expect me to steer her through the Guggenheim again.

    (b) Do you mean Grace who twitters like a parakeet and leaves squashed Kleenex all over the house because of her sinus condition?

    (c) Of all your friends, Honey, I think Grace is the one most like you.

Can you tell I've lost weight?

    (a) Not really. I'd say you'd have to lose another ten pounds before it begins to show.

    (b) If you say so.

    (c) Wow.

I suppose you wish I was as good as cook as Emily?

    (a) Or even half as good.

    (b) I'm sure you could cook as well as Emily if you were willing to put the same amount of time into it.

    (c) Oh, I'd get pretty sick of all that rich food day after day. And they say Bill's getting a liver condition.

Do you love me as much as the day we were married?

    (a) Yeah, yeah, yeah, I love you as much as the day we were married.

    (b) Oh, God, not again.

    (c) If you have to ask that question. Honey, it must be my fault. I mustn't be showing all the love I really feel.

Will you lower that damn ballgame?

    (a) If I lower that ballgame, all I'll hear is you screaming at the kids.

    (b) When *you're* listening to Ol' Dave and Ol' Chet, I can hear it as I step off the New Haven.

    (c) Oh, is it bothering you? Why don't I go up to the bedroom and watch it on the portable? You'll be coming up, won't you?

Would you say that I have been a help to you in your work?

    (a) Honey, don't make dumb jokes.

    (b) Undoubtedly, undoubtedly. If I didn't have you and the kids I'd be a beachcomber today. And very happy.

    (c) Honey! Could I ever have got to teach third grade without you right here beside me?

You never talk to me.

    (a) I don't talk to you because the only topics in the world that interest you are Billy's rotten report card, your rotten dishwasher, and that rotten milkman who keeps tracking up your linoleum.

    (b) Of course I talk to you. What am I doing now, pantomime?

    (c) And here I was, sitting here and thinking how beautiful you are and how lucky I am and how peaceful it was.

For Women

What is the proper answer when hubby makes the following observations:

What happens to all my clean handkerchiefs?

    (a) I eat them.

    (b) You don't have clean handkerchiefs because you don't put them in the wash. You leave them all scrunched up in your slacks which are on the floor of the closet.

    (c) Here's a clean one of mine. We'll fold it so the lace doesn't show.

Hey, Abe's new wife is attractive as hell, don't you think?

    (a) Everybody's new wife is attractive. Your problem is that you're stuck with your old one.

    (b) Yes, but I think she might do something about that little mustache.

    (c) I think *all* Abe's new wives are attractive.

When you write a check, will you for God's sake, please, please, write down the amount somewhere, anywhere?

    (a) Why do you carry on like a madman? Nothing ever ever happens, the checks never bounce.

    (b) Okay, you're Paul Getty, *you* make out the checks.

    (c) Yes.

Ye gods, does that kid have to eat that way?

    (a) No, I coach him to eat that way because I know it drives you absolutely crazy.

    (b) That kid just also happens to be your kid, and anytime you want to give him your famous lecture on table manners, I'll be rooting for you all the way.

    (c) Darling, I *want* to reprimand him but he's so exactly like you I just melt.

Oh, Lord, you're crying again. What is it this time?

    (a) I spent three hours stuffing the veal and you never even said it was good. I had my hair done and you didn't notice. It rained all day and the kids were like maniacs. And after I sewed all the buttons back on Brucie's sweater he lost it in the park. And you never, never, never offer to do anything to help me.

(b) Because I want to marry Aristotle Onassis and live on the island of Scorpia and have a hundred servants and my own airline.

(c) Oh, because I'm silly and I don't count my blessings. Come on, give me a little squeeze and take out the garbage and I'll be through here in no time.

There. Of course I don't mean to suggest that this test is either foolproof or definitive. I mean only to be the first pebble in the avalanche that must surely come. But perhaps I should add just one final cautionary note. Those persons who found themselves anticipating the correct answer *in each instance* are probably so perfect that they would drive any other human being bonkers. I suggest that they remain single.

•

FROM *Please Don't Eat the Daisies*

The thing that worries me is that I am so different from other writers. Connecticut is just another state to me. And nature—well, nature is just nature. When I see a tree whose leafy mouth is pressed against the earth's sweet flowing breast, I think, "Well, *that's* a nice-looking oak," but it doesn't change my way of life.

•

We were in Anatole's open car. Overhead the sky was blue as a bruise.

The gleaming white road slipping under our wheels seemed like a ribbon of cotton candy. As I realized we were nearing the château, my heart turned over once, quickly and neatly, like a pancake on a griddle.

Anatole's voice seemed to come from a great distance.

"Bored, darling?"

I turned to him.

"Of course—and you?"

His answering smile told me that he was.

And now we were running up the long flight of steps to the château hand in hand like two happy children, stopping only when Anatole had to recover his wind.

At the doorway he paused and gathered me into his arms. His voice, when he spoke, was like a melody played sweetly and in tune.

"My darling," he said, "I hope I have made it perfectly clear that so far as I am concerned you are just another pickup."

"Of course," I whispered. How adult he was, and how indescribably dear.

So the golden days passed. Mostly we were silent, but occasionally we sat in the twilight and spoke wistfully of Dorette and Banal and what suckers they were.

And who could describe those nights? Never in my relationship with Banal had I felt anything like this. Ah, how rewarding it is to share the bed of a really mature man. For one thing, there was the clatter and the excitement four times a night as he leaped to the floor and stamped on his feet in an effort to get the circulation going. My little pet name for him, now, was Thumper.

•

Where do people get all these diets, anyway? Obviously from the magazines; it's impossible to get a diet from a newspaper. For one thing, in a newspaper you can never catch the diet when it *starts*. It's always the fourth day of Ada May's Wonder Diet and, after a brief description of a simple slimming exercise that could be performed by anybody who has had five years' training with the ballet, Ada May gives you the menu for the day. One glass of skim, eight prunes, and three lamb kidneys. This settles the matter for most people, who figure—quite reasonably —that if this is the *fourth* day, heaven deliver them from the first.

However, any stoics in the group who want to know just how far Ada May's sense of whimsey will take her can have the complete diet by sending twenty-five cents in stamps to the newspaper. But there you are. Who has twenty-five cents in stamps? You're not running a branch of the post office. And if you're going to go out and get the stamps you might as well buy a twenty-five-cent magazine which will give you not only the same diet (now referred to as *Our* Wonder Diet) but will, in addition, show you a quick and easy way to turn your husband's old socks into gay pot holders.

•

What actually holds a husband through thick and thick is a girl who is fun to be with. And any girl who has had nothing to eat since nine o'clock this morning but three hard-boiled eggs will be about as jolly and companionable as an income-tax inspector.

So I say, ladies, find out why women everywhere are switching from old-fashioned diets to the *modern* way: no exercise, no dangerous drugs, no weight loss. (And what do they mean, "ugly fat"? It's *you*, isn't it?)

Laura Kightlinger (contemporary)

❧ ❧

FROM *Return the Favor*

In college I wrote comedy sketches for my roommate and soon after joined a comedy troupe on campus and that's where I started. My mother's single most encouraging comment after seeing my first MTV 'spot' some two years ago was, "well, you're a lot funnier than the guy who wears the glove on his head." She was, of course, referring to Howie Mandell; she was of course, dead-on in her assessment but I could feel the undercurrent of her disbelief in my talent . . . she really said more than she knew as far as quality vs. quantity and what sells, etc. . . .

My favorite example of "How It Isn't" is the time when my grandma had it all figured out for me, and she said, "Wouldn't more people know about you if you were on the Johnny Carson show?", to which I replied, "yes." And then she said, "you should just ask him (Johnny) if you could do your routine some night on his show." I said, "you know, you're right!" TV shows like "David Letterman" or "The Tonight Show" are usually a three or four (sometimes eight or nine) audition-process. A comic must be highly recommended before a talent coordinator or show producer will come out to see the comic perform in a club. The average overnight success takes six to ten years.

Florence King (1936–   )

❧ ❧

Fiftysomething

Lear's is the magazine "For The Woman Who Wasn't Born Yesterday."

Shakespearean buffs who think it is named for the Lear who said, "Let it stamp wrinkles in her brow of youth, with cadent tears fret channels in her cheeks," must think again. *Lear's* is the brainchild of sixtyish Frances Lear, the former Mrs. Norman Lear, who decided to build the confidence of older women by giving them their own magazine and naming it after the man who paid her $112 million for divorcing him.

Considering the way they edited my copy, they ought to call themselves *The Battle-Ax*. As far as I could tell, they do nothing for older women unless you want to count the ten years they took off my life.

Writing for women's magazines is a matter of skirting their various taboos. Pedophobia at *Family Circle* and Lesbianism at *Cosmopolitan* make sense, but the great taboo at *Lear's*, according to one of their many former editors, is the word *menopause*.

A shame, because I would have loved to write an article on it for them.

My thoughts on the menopause do not go over well with the kind of middle-aged women who say, "You're only as old as you feel," and then give a pert toss of the head. These are the women who buy the most surgical collars. They are also the women who buy the most plastic surgery; I have a professional acquaintance whose recent eyelid job has left her with a permanent expression of such poleaxed astonishment that she looks at all times as if she had just read one of my books.

About the most these women will say on the forbidden subject is a wistful murmur of "I miss my periods." If you reply, as I did, "That's like missing the Spanish Inquisition," your name will be entered in the *Index of Insensitivity* under Twatist. Between the upbeat seventies' psychobabble about "passages" and feminism's attempt to reduce menopause to a sheaf of mendacious stereotypes invented by the patriarchy, many women come so close to claiming that there is no such thing as menopause that they come very close to sounding like Mrs. Eddy.

I grew up hearing a very different sort of wishful thinking. My grandmother's disquisition on the menopause always began with a doleful sigh. "Ahhh! That time of life. . . . It's got to come to all of us someday."

In the South of my childhood, no woman could weather the "Change" completely unscathed; it was femininity's Appomattox and you had to milk it for every possible drop of theater.

A definite menopause class system existed. The Brahmins, of course, were the women who went hopelessly, gothically, permanently insane. In the next caste down were women with such severe female trouble that their "parts" fell out like gifts from a piñata, known as "she felt a *whoosh*! and then it just went *plop!*" The last of the Big Three patricians, officially disapproved of but providing a perfect plum of gossip, was the woman who developed another form of looseness known as "she *likes* men."

The pelvic bourgeoisie were the women who did "something peculiar," a catch-all phrase that might refer to a woman who became a spit-and-polish housekeeper after years of sloth; or one who took to shoplifting inane items like pen wipers; or one who suddenly began wearing white anklets (Granny: "whoopee socks") with black patent leather high heels.

The working class had the "sleeping Change," an extreme form of fatigue manifested by a neighbor of Granny's, who never did see the end of *The Sheik* despite ten trips to the theater. The phlegmatic quality of the sleeping Change made it déclassé because menopausal women are supposed to be "nervous." It always provoked the disappointed assessment. "She slept right through it," accompanied by a ski-slope gesture going off into infinity where, the speaker left no doubt, the calm one deserved to be banished.

The untouchables were the women who had no trouble whatsoever, known contemptuously as "She sailed right through it."

I started looking forward to the menopause at the age of twelve due to what male gynecologists call "discomfort"—wracking, knotting, waves of cramps and vomiting that lasted the whole of the first day and left me wrung out for most of the second. In high school I missed the annual French contest because of cramps. In college, as soon as the exam schedule was posted, I checked the dates in abject fear that one or more of mine would fall on Der Tag. Gradually my whole concept of time changed until I thought of a month as having twenty-five days of humanness and five others when I might just as well have been an animal in a steel trap. When I heard other women say, "My periods are what make me a woman," I always thought, "My periods are what keep me from being myself."

None of the doctors I consulted could find anything wrong with me. I thought I might have what Granny & Company called a "tilted womb" but my pelvis was normal in every way. Finally, at the age of thirty, I decided to try to get a partial hysterectomy. I picked that particular cut-off age because I had heard that a woman of thirty who had three children could have her tubes tied at her own request on the assumption that her whelping days were over (this was 1966). Since I did not intend to have any children at all, I figured that some version of the same rule would apply to me. (I was working for the *Raleigh News and Observer* and writing "30" at the end of copy, so it made a certain sense.)

One day while editing canned features I came across one about a contraceptive operation in which the lining of the uterus—the endometrium—is removed via the vagina. Without the porous lining, said the article, menstrual blood had no place to collect; the woman would stop menstruating, and her eggs, if fertilized, would simply slide down the slippery slope and be passed off unnoticed.

It sounded perfect. No surgery. Merely a matter of what Granny, in the fruitiness of her idiom, would have called: "They just reach right up and pull it right out—*whisk!*"

Feminists are right and wrong about male gynecologists. Yes, they are supercilious bastards; no, they are not swept by irresistible forces of sadism and greed at the thought of performing unnecessary operations on female organs—if they were, I would have gotten what I wanted.

The first one listened to my story, his mouth twitching in amusement, then patted my hand and said, "You'll change your mind when you hold your first baby in your arms."

The second one threw me out of his office.

"We have ways of curing monthly discomfort with medication! If you had a sore toe, would you want to get it cut off?"

"Sure, if it was sore enough," I said. "You can live with nine toes unless you're a ballet dancer, and I'm not."

"I hope you don't have children," he said, his voice shaking. "I'd hate to see what they'd turn out to be like."

A few weeks later while editing the social notes, I saw his daughter's name in a ballet recital list. Doubtless he was as sick of dying swans as I was of twat artists. I gave up the idea of having my endometrium ripped untimely from my womb and went on menstruating.

I began missing periods at forty-six and had my last one four years ago at fifty. Since then, I have been living proof of Simone de Beauvoir's assessment of menopause in *The Second Sex*:

> In many, a new endocrine balance becomes established. Woman is now delivered from the servitude imposed by her female nature, but she is not to be likened to a eunuch, for her vitality is unimpaired. And what is more, she is no longer the prey of overwhelming forces; she is herself, she and her body are one. It is sometimes said that women of a certain age constitute "a third sex"; and, in truth, while they are not males, they are no longer females. Often, indeed, this release from female physiology is expressed in a health, a balance, a vigor that they lacked before.

This is the calamity known as "losing your femininity" that women's magazines are so eager to help us stave off.

The prospect of being feminine always makes me think of James M. Cain's reply when asked to write for *The New Yorker:* "On the whole, I'd rather be dead."

In my youth I did a fairly credible imitation of femininity. I never could manage the big things, such as playing dumb or being undemanding in bed, but I did remember to soften my voice, shorten my stride, and be sweetly helpless about electricity. I played my part so well that eventually I came to believe it. It was easy to convince myself that I was feminine because I thought masculine women had to be athletic and good at sports, which I was not. It took the menopause to teach me that another, more agreeable kind of tomboyhood awaited me.

There are four stages of woman, best defined by looking at a commonplace task: taking the car to the shop. When you are a sweet young thing, the mechanics don't want you to hang around the shop for fear you will get dirty. When you are a sexy broad, they don't want you to hang around the shop for fear you will create such a tempting distraction that they will get hurt. And when you are a little old lady, they don't want you to hang around the shop for fear you will get in the way.

But there is another stage, the one between siren and dear old thing. Stage Three: sexually over the hill but still alert and able to move fast —*when the mechanics don't worry about you!* It lasts about fifteen years, from fifty to Social Security, but they are the best fifteen years of a woman's life; the debriefing years, the detoxification years, when she can shed her skin and become, for a brief shining moment, a female good ole boy.

It is de rigueur for post-menopausal women to say, "I didn't get older, I got better," and describe how intense their orgasms are now that they no longer have to worry about getting pregnant.

There may be some women who suddenly discover that they "*like* men," but usually it's because they saved it up too long and must make up for lost time (Granny: "A candle always flares up before it goes out").

In the majority of cases, however, I suspect that the older-but-better brigade are fibbing in the cause of the American economy, which encourages them to do it. If the advertising-dependent women's magazines can make them believe that they never stop feeling horny, they will buy more clothes, cosmetics, vacations, plastic surgery, eighty-dollar haircuts, and Kellogg's Product 19 to feel like nineteen again even though it's as dry as a bone—and I don't mean the cereal.

The sacrilegious truth is, my sex drive diminished sharply when I started skipping periods, and vanished entirely as soon as they stopped for good. Now the only thing I miss about sex is the cigarette afterwards. Next to the first one in the morning, it's the best one of all. It tasted so good that even if I had been frigid I would have pretended otherwise just to be able to smoke it.

There is much to be said for post-menopausal celibacy. Sex is rough on loners because you have to have somebody else around, but now I don't. No more diets to stay slim and desirable: I've had sex and I've had food, and I'd rather eat. Although Mother Nature rather than will-power crafted my celibacy, the result has been the same. My powers of concentration are now as awesome as those of the most successful artistic or priestly practitioner of sublimation; sexual need no longer distracts me from my work.

There is a wholeness to celibacy. For a woman, a sexual relationship is an invasion of privacy, an absorption of individuality, a fragmentation of the personality that poses an everpresent threat to the character. The Roman historian Tacitus wrote: "When a woman has lost her chastity she will shrink from no crime." He did not mean that non-virgins routinely become murderers and bank robbers, but that a woman in a sexual relationship makes emotional choices rather than ethical ones—what Tammy Wynette was recommending when she sang "Stand By Your Man." I never wanted to stand by anybody except myself, and now I can.

Let's not forget the menopausal blessings of thrift. My heating bill has gone down by more than half over the last few years. So much, in fact, that a compassionate soul from the utility company called me last winter to see if I was in dire economic straits.

"If you've had financial difficulties . . ."

"I haven't had financial difficulties, I've had the Change. My hot flashes keep me warm now. I've turned into my own furnace."

"Oh. . . ."

I love those gulpy *oh's*. They are part and parcel of another menopausal benefit I call the "boldness syndrome."

When I was menstruating, I used to avoid controversy because I was afraid that when the situation came to a head, I wouldn't "feel well." Always, in the back of my mind, lay the knowledge that if I shot off my mouth on, say, the fourteenth of the month, that by the thirtieth, when everybody was good and mad, I would have cramps and be unable to follow through. Now, I no longer worry.

A woman must wait for her ovaries to die before she can get her rightful personality back. Post-menstrual is the same as pre-menstrual; I am once again what I was before the age of twelve: a female human being who knows that a month has thirty days, not twenty-five, and who can spend every one of them free of the shackles of that defect of body and mind known as femininity.

•

The Silver Scream

As one born in 1936, I am a member of America's most movie-influenced generation, raised on the great films of Hollywood's golden age.

Children of the thirties and forties went to the movies every time the picture changed, which was two or three times a week. In that era of non-working mothers and live-in grandmothers, I would get home from school to find Mama and Granny ready and waiting for our after-noon treat at the Tivoli, our neighborhood theater at 14th and Park Road.

We never paid any attention to the schedule. The idea was to go to the movies right after school let out so we would be home in time for dinner. If we happened to arrive when the picture was starting, fine; if not, that was fine too. More often than not, we got in at the middle just in time to see Miriam Hopkins burst into tears, or Bette Davis shoot somebody, without having the faintest idea why. We watched from the middle to the end, then saw the "selected short subjects," then the "pre-views of coming attractions," and finally, when the next continuous showing started, we saw the beginning.

Seeing movies backwards was not merely our family eccentricity, but a national practice. The catch phrase, "This is where I came in," originated at this time, though with three mindsets to deal with, we never could agree on when that was. Granny, a Victorian, remembered deathbed scenes: Mama, an unregenerate tomboy, noticed fights and cars; and I was in the animal-loving stage when children want to grow up to be veterinarians.

"We got here when she fell off the horse."

"No, we didn't *see* her fall off, we just heard the doctor say she was paralyzed for life while we were buying popcorn."

"George Raft was beating somebody up when we sat down."

"Oh, look, there's Charles Coburn with his head in his hands! *That's* where we came in."

If it wasn't too late, remaining to see a favorite scene over again was also common practice, with the child as arbiter: "I wanna see her fall off the horse again."

The movie theaters of the era were rightly called "palaces." The lush dreams of romance and adventure in faraway places began when we bought our tickets from a cashier seated in an ornate box modeled on a Turkish caliph's sedan chair.

Inside, the theater was an opulent cave with thick carpeting and a sweeping marble staircase leading to the balcony. The walls of the auditorium were covered in plush brocade; I remember pushing my small fist against it and marveling that it yielded like a pillow. The brocade was shot with gilded thread in whose whorls I saw other pictorial dramas of my own imagining—a pirate, a lady in a big hat, a prancing horse—just as I did when I lay in bed at home and looked up at the paintbrush marks on the ceiling. But these images were more ingratiating because they emerged from luxuriant silk instead of plain white plaster.

When the movie ended and the soft amber lights came up, the magic remained. No one moved for a moment; staying seated quietly in the cool penumbra was a gentle transition the audience could not resist. Finally, with what seemed like a collective sigh, people rose and walked slowly up the aisle, stumbling a little from the combined effects of the spongy carpet and the lingering daze of enchantment.

The spell was not broken until we left the theater and emerged onto the street. My first attack of depression came on a sizzling afternoon in September. What struck me was the contrast—the unbearably sudden contrast between dark and light; between air-conditioned chill and heat-baked sidewalks; between the storybook vistas of the movie just seen and the stark reality of tawdry, noisy 14th Street.

A lump formed in my throat. I wanted to cry but I didn't dare. I knew from experience what would happen. My combative mother would have jumped to her favorite conclusion and demanded, "Did somebody at school pick on you? Why didn't you beat the shit out of them?" While Mama was getting all worked up, Granny, who wanted me to be a delicate Southern lady, would have chimed in with, "The child isn't well." It was easier to keep my troubles to myself, so I did.

The depression receded once we got home and back into our usual routine, but the memory of it remained with me. I kept thinking about the contrast, which I called "the different." Not the different light, or the different temperature, just *The Different*, as in a Stephen King title.

Over the next several weeks, it happened each time we left the theater. Although I managed not to cry on the street, ultimately I did something worse: I broke down in the crowded ladies' lounge of the Tivoli.

Many years later when I went to Versailles, all I could think of was that ladies' lounge. They were furnished the same way; Louis Quinze chairs, tables, and settees, ornate gilded mirrors, curlicued gilded frames containing pictures of Fragonard courtiers chasing nymphs through sylvan glades.

But the lounge contained something that Versailles did not: ashtrays. Tall, tubular, stainless steel receptacles like umbrella stands, filled with sand and stuck with lipstick-smeared butts. There was one beside each Louis Quinze settee. The contrast between the modern, gleaming steel containers and the kind of furniture I had so often seen in costume movies was too much. Past and present, reality and fantasy, movie and life, were side by side, next to each other, *touching*.

I started crying.

"What's the matter?" asked Granny.

"Jesus Christ on roller skates!" Mama, of course.

"Oh, the poor little thing," some woman quavered.

"Did the movie scare you, honey?" asked another.

"It's those cartoons," said a third. "They're supposed to be funny but everybody gets run over by steamrollers."

"Did somebody at school pick on you?"

"The poor little thing, she reminds me of Margaret O'Brien in that movie—oh, what was the name of that? You remember, when she cried and cried and cried?"

"What's the matter?" Granny asked again.

"I don't know!" I sobbed. "It's the different!"

"What's different?"

"The ashtrays! They make me sad! I can't stand them!"

"Jesus Christ on roller skates! Who do you think you are, Greta Garbo?"

Despite the stark reality I was pumping into the atmosphere, even my down-to-earth mother drew on the movies for her shouted analogy. The woman across the lounge was still more captive to fantasy; she had forgotten all about me and was back in the Margaret O'Brien movie.

"It was about the war and she was an orphan in London and Robert Young wanted to adopt her but something happened that he couldn't and then she just started crying and crying and crying. She wore a little peaked cap like a gremlin and wouldn't let go of her telescope, and I think somebody died. Was it Loretta Young? Anyhow, she just kept crying and crying and crying like her poor little heart would break. Oh, *what* was the name of that?"

"The child isn't well," Granny decreed.

On that note we left. By the time we got home, she had remembered a distant cousin "who was never well," and spent the rest of the evening sighing. "It runs in the family." I had to spend the rest of the evening convincing Mama that nobody had picked on me.

Maybe it was knowing that I had played into their hands that helped me pull myself together. Maybe my public crying jag had drained me of pity and terror. Maybe children are emotionally resilient. Or maybe it was simply because I loathed Margaret O'Brien. For whatever reason, The Different never returned after that.

Everyone quickly forgot about it. Mama shrugged it off with her all-purpose explanation—"You're deep, just like your father"—and Granny shortly got interested in something else that ran in the family. For my part, ever eager to dissociate myself from the genus children and fiercely proud of puffs like *mature for her age* and *beyond her years* that my teachers wrote on my report cards. I decided that The Different was the last vestige of childhood, the emotional counterpart of my last skinned knee.

I was wrong. It came back again and again throughout my life, albeit in subtler ways. Nor did I suffer alone. The Different is America's eternal, universal emotion; it stays with us for life and attacks everybody except the Amish because the only way to avoid it is never to go to the movies.

My childhood version of The Different was like Emily Dickinson's "certain slant of light," a simple revulsion against abrupt contrast. Being a city child who wanted to live in a country house like the ones in *Wuthering Heights* and *Kings Row*, the grinding streetcars and sunbaked sidewalks were sudden, unbearable reminders of where I did live. Later, as an adult, I came to like cities, but by then I was susceptible to another kind of post-movie depression.

There is more sexism in a year's worth of movies than actually exists in a woman's entire lifetime. The movies of the fifties and early sixties were constant reminders that every inclination I had was wrong. Close-ups of babies had to be greeted with "Awwwww," not the "Uggghhh" I was thinking. The contemptuous hoots that greeted the sexually erring woman and the casting-office spinster in hornrim glasses filled me with angry confusion. In a contrary way I wanted to be both women, and somehow I sensed that I would be both.

Countless scripts called for the female star to deliver some version of the ringing line, "I just want to be a *woman!*" When Eleanor Parker as opera star Marjorie Lawrence gave up her career to marry Glenn Ford, silencing his protests with, "I've *had* all that! I just want to be Mrs. Thomas King!" the audience burst into applause that sent me into a cringing sulk.

By the time the show was over I felt like a stainless steel ashtray next to a Louis Quinze settee: instead of suffering from The Different, I had become it.

The post-movie mood is more often than not a bad one. How many arguments have you had or heard on leaving the theater? The young woman suddenly snaps at her date after spending two hours with Charlton Heston or Robert Redford. The husband still under the spell of the French Foreign Legion suddenly yells at the wife and kids who are keeping him from a life of adventure. The child emerging from *My Friend Flicka* gets slapped because he keeps whining "Why can't we go live on a ranch?" The wife who has just seen *Gaslight* goes wild when her husband says he can't find the car keys, and the two middle-aged women who have just seen *Mildred Pierce* together can't wait to get home and give their daughters hell.

Mama and I had an awful fight the night we went to see *To Catch a Thief.* I was then about the same age as the Grace Kelly character. I smelled trouble during the show when Jessie Royce Landis, who played Kelly's rip-snortin' mother, said: "My daughter's ashamed of me." My own rip-snortin' mother grunted and leaned as far away from me as she could get, so what happened later in the parking lot came as no surprise.

"I guess you're ashamed of me, huh? Because I don't speak French, huh? Shit on French!" she bellowed, banging her fist on the hood. "Shit on you! I'm as good as you are, you little snot, so take your French and shove it!" Some people a few cars over burst into applause.

It was what screenwriters aim for: Mama had "identified" with a character. I had not: I didn't like Grace Kelly but I did identify with one of her lines: "The only difference between Mother and me is a little grammar." I found it very touching because it was a perfect description of Mama and me, but when I tried to tell her this, she refused to believe it. A movie had come between us, and I wondered how many others had. What did she feel when she saw *Stella Dallas*? Did that hurt her too?

I like to imagine how pleasant and confident life would be if movies had never been invented. An insignificant mishap like a crumbled wine cork would not make a man feel like an unsophisticated clod because he never would have seen Cary Grant extract one with a single adroit twist. With no one to imitate, everyone would have his own bona fide personality, and it would be a stronger one for being real. We would not be burdened with our current "crisis in self-esteem" because untold millions of people would not have spent the last seven decades walking off into the night brooding, "If only I could look like that . . . dance like that . . . swim like that." And we would be free of the kind of sheer idiocy that makes people set their hearts on owning a car whose doors close with a whooshy *snick!* because it's the "rich car door sound" they heard in movies.

Whenever I speculate on what women would be like had movies never been invented, I need look no further than Granny. Thirty-six in 1915 when *Birth of a Nation* and Theda Bara's *A Fool There Was* inaugurated the movie era, her personality was formed long before Hollywood encouraged women to exchange identity for identification.

By the time I knew her, she got to the movies at least twice a week, but the movies never got to her. Her favorite scenes involved sickbeds and terminal illness, but her reaction was that of a technical adviser rather than a hypnotized spectator in the throes of romantic masochism. Old enough and rural enough to have witnessed real home deaths from a variety of grim causes, she was unimpressed when Jennifer Jones swallowed arsenic in *Madame Bovary*.

"You never look that pretty when you're full of arsenic," she whispered to me. "I'll never forget the time Willie Codrick swallowed the rat poison. He was spewing like a fountain—from *both* ends."

Obsessive love moved her not. "The worse you treat a man, the better he treats you," she whispered during *Letter From an Unknown Woman.* "The *man* should be the one who's in love," she advised throughout *Back Street.* Equally lost on her were hankering dissatisfaction and hopeless yearning. Her resolute contentment was never more in evidence than when we went to see Bette Davis in *Beyond the Forest*.

There was Davis as nostril-flaring Rosa Moline, married to good, dull Joseph Cotten, stuck in a small town and a shabby house ("What a dump!") that she hates. Consumed by the desire to run away to Chicago, her eyes stretch open every time she hears the train whistle. Bosom heaving in frustration, she gazes in the direction of Chicago and then paces, paces, paces like a caged animal while the background music plays "Chicago, Chicago."

Finding herself pregnant, she throws herself down a hill to get rid of the baby who is keeping her from fleeing to Chicago. Dying of blood poisoning from the botched miscarriage, she drags herself out of bed and crawls on her hands and knees through the town to the railroad station while the background music plays a labored version of "Chicago, Chicago." As she collapses on the platform and claws the air, the Chicago train pulls in and momentarily hides her from view. When it pulls out again, we see her lying dead as the background music plays "Chicago, Chicago" in funeral-march time.

The women seated around us were clutching their throats and moaning "Oh, no, no!" Mama was sitting forward in her seat and I, too young to appreciate Rosa's problems but knowing real tragedy when I saw it, was drooling soggy popcorn from a corner of my open mouth.

"Why would anybody want to go to Chicago?" Granny asked irritably. "It's full of Yankees."

Maxine Hong Kingston (1940-   )

~❦ ❦~

FROM *The Woman Warrior*

Marriage promises to turn strangers into friendly relatives—a nation of siblings.

•

I went away to college—Berkeley in the sixties—and I studied, and I marched to change the world, but I did not turn into a boy. I would have liked to bring myself back as a boy for my parents to welcome with chickens and pigs. That was for my brother, who returned alive from Vietnam.

If I went to Vietnam, I would not come back; females desert families. It was said, "There is an outward tendency in females," which meant that I was getting straight A's for the good of my future husband's family, not my own. I did not plan ever to have a husband. I would show my mother and father and the nosey emigrant villagers that girls have no outward tendency. I stopped getting straight A's.

And all the time I was having to turn myself American-feminine, or no dates.

There is a Chinese word for the female *I*—which is "slave." Break the women with their own tongues!

I refused to cook. When I had to wash dishes, I would crack one or two. "Bad girl," my mother yelled, and sometimes that made me gloat rather than cry. Isn't a bad girl almost a boy?

"What do you want to be when you grow up, little girl?"

"A lumberjack in Oregon."

Even now, unless I'm happy, I burn the food when I cook. I do not feed people. I let the dirty dishes rot. I eat at other people's tables but won't invite them to mine, where the dishes are rotting.

If I could not-eat, perhaps I could make myself a warrior like the swordswoman who drives me.

•

Her daughter pointed toward Brave Orchid. And at last Moon Orchid looked at her—two old women with faces like mirrors.

Their hands reached out as if to touch the other's face, then returned to their own, the fingers checking the grooves in the forehead and along the sides of the mouth. Moon Orchid, who never understood the gravity of things, started smiling and laughing, pointing at Brave Orchid. Finally Moon Orchid gathered up her stuff, strings hanging and papers loose, and met her sister at the door, where they shook hands, oblivious to blocking the way.

"You're an old woman," said Brave Orchid.

"Aiaa. *You're* an old woman."

"But you are really old. Surely, you can't say that about me. I'm not old the way you're old."

"But *you* really are old. You're one year older than I am."

"Your hair is white and your face all wrinkled."

"You're so skinny."

"You're so fat."

"Fat women are more beautiful than skinny women."

The children pulled them out of the doorway. One of Brave Orchid's children brought the car from the parking lot, and the other heaved the luggage into the trunk. They put the two old ladies and the niece in the back seat. All the way home—across the Bay Bridge, over the Diablo hills, across the San Joaquin River to the valley, the valley moon so white at dusk—all the way home, the two sisters exclaimed every time they turned to look at each other, "Aiaa! How old!"

•

"You must make it plain to your husband right at the start what you expect of him. That is what a wife is for—to scold her husband into becoming a good man."

•

When my sisters and I ate at their house, there we would be—six girls eating. The old man opened his eyes wide at us and turned in a circle, surrounded. His neck tendons stretched out. "Maggots!" he shouted. "Maggots! Where are my grandsons? I want grandsons! Give me grandsons! Maggots!" He pointed at each one of us, "Maggot! Maggot! Maggot! Maggot! Maggot! Maggot!" Then he dived into his food, eating fast and getting seconds. "Eat, maggots," he said. "Look at the maggots chew."

"He does that at every meal," the girls told us in English.

"Yeah," we said. "Our old man hates us too. What assholes."

Sarah Kemble Knight (1666-1727)

～✌ ✌～

FROM *The Private Journal of a Journey
from Boston to New York in the Year
1704, Kept by Madam Knight*

Tuesday, October the third, about eight in the morning, I with the post proceeded forward without observing any thing remarkable; And about two, afternoon, arrived at the post's second stage, where the western post met him and exchanged letters. Here, having called for something to eat, the woman brought in a twisted thing like a cable, but something whiter, and laying it on the board, tugged for life to bring it into a capacity to spread; which having with great pains accomplished, she served in a dish of pork and cabbage, I suppose the remains of dinner. The sauce was of a deep purple, which I thought was boiled in her dye kettle; the bread was Indian, and everything on the table service agreeable to these. I, being hungry, got a little down; but my stomach was soon cloyed, and what cabbage I swallowed served me for a cud the whole day after.

Having here discharged the ordinary for self and guide (as I understood was the custom), about three, afternoon, went on with my third guide, who rode very hard; and having crossed Providence Ferry, we come to a river which they generally ride through. But I dare not venture; so the post got a lad and canoe to carry me to t'other side, and he rid through and led my horse. The canoe was very small and shallow, so that when we were in she seemed ready to take in water, which greatly terrified me and caused me to be very circumspect, sitting with my hands fast on each side, my eyes steady, not daring so much as to lodge my tongue a hair's breadth more on one side of my mouth than t'other, nor so much as think on Lot's wife, for a wry thought would have overset our wherry.

I went to bed, which, though pretty hard, was yet neat and handsome. But I could get no sleep, because of the clamor of some of the town topers in the next room, who were entered into a strong debate concerning the signification of the name of their country: viz., *Narragansett.* One said it was named so by the Indians because they grew a brier there of a prodigious height and bigness, the like hardly ever known, called by the Indians Narragansett; and quotes an Indian of so barbarous a name for his author, that I could not write it. His antagonist replied no—it was from a spring it had its name, which he well knew where it was, which was extreme cold in summer and as hot as could be imagined in the winter, which was much resorted to by the natives, and by them called Narragansett (hot and cold), and that was the original of their place's name—with a thousand impertinences not worth notice, which he uttered with such a roaring voice and thundering blows with the fist of wickedness on the table, that it pierced my very head. I heartily fretted, and wished them tongue-tied; but with as little success as a friend of mine once, who was (as she said) kept a whole night awake on a journey by a country lieutenant and a sergeant, ensign and a deacon, contriving how to bring a triangle into a square. They kept calling for t'other gill, which while they were swallowing, was some intermission, but presently, like oil to fire, increased the flame. I set my candle on a chest by the bedside, and sitting up, fell to my old way of composing my resentments, in the following manner:

> *I ask thy aid, O potent rum!*
> *To charm these wrangling topers dumb.*
> *Thou hast their giddy brains possessed—*
> *The man confounded with the beast—*
> *And I, poor I, can get no rest.*
> *Intoxicate them with thy fumes:*
> *O still their tongues till morning comes!*

And I know not but my wishes took effect; for the dispute soon ended with t'other dram; and so good night!

Nella Larsen (1891–1964)

FROM *Helga Crane*

Her mind trailed off to the highly important matter of clothes. What should she wear? White? No, everybody would, because it was hot. Green? She shook her head, Anne would be sure to. The blue thing. Reluctantly she decided against it; she loved it, but she had worn it too often. There was that cobwebby black net touched with orange, which she had bought last spring in a bit of extravagance and never worn, because on getting it home both she and Anne had considered it too *décolleté*, and too *outré*. Anne's words: "There's not enough of it, and what there is gives you the air of something about to fly," came back to her, and she smiled as she decided that she would certainly wear the black net. For her it would be a symbol. She was about to fly.

Mary Leapor (1722–1746)

Upon her Play being returned to her, stained with Claret

Welcome, dear wanderer, once more!
　　Thrice welcome to thy native cell!
Within this peaceful humble door
　　Let thou and I contented dwell!

But say, O whither hast thou ranged?
　　Why dost thou blush a crimson hue?
Thy fair complexion's greatly changed:
　　Why, I can scarce believe 'tis you.

Then tell, my son, O tell me, where
　　Didst thou contract this sottish dye?

You kept ill company, I fear,
    When distant from your parent's eye.

Was it for this, O graceless child!
    Was it for this you learned to spell?
Thy face and credit both are spoiled:
    Go drown thyself in yonder well.

I wonder how thy time was spent:
    No news, alas, hast thou to bring?
Hast thou not climbed the Monument?
    Nor seen the lions, nor the King?

But now I'll keep you here secure:
    No more you view the smoky sky;
The Court was never made, I'm sure,
    For idiots like thee and I.

Fran Lebowitz (1951?-   )

FROM *Metropolitan Life*

PLANTS: THE ROOTS OF ALL EVIL

The Unabridged Second Edition of Webster's Dictionary—a volume of no small repute—gives the following as the second definition of the word *plant:* "any living thing that cannot move voluntarily, has no sense organs and generally makes its own food. . . ." I have chosen the second definition in favor of the first because it better serves my purpose. which is to prove once and for all that, except in extreme rare instances, a plant is really not the sort of thing that one ought to have around the house. That this might be accomplished in an orderly manner, I have elected to consider each aspect of the above definition individually. Let us begin at the beginning:

Any Living Thing

In furnishing one's place of residence one seeks to acquire those things which will provide the utmost in beauty, comfort, and usefulness. In the beauty department one is invariably drawn to such fixtures as Cocteau drawings, Ming vases, and Aubusson rugs. Comfort is, of course, assured by the ability to possess these objects. Usefulness is something best left to those trained in such matters.

It should, then, be apparent that at no time does Any Living Thing enter the picture except in the past tense. In other words, it is perfectly acceptable to surround oneself with objects composed of that which while alive may have been Any Living Thing but in death has achieved dignity by becoming a nice white linen sheet.

That Cannot Move Voluntarily

Here one is confronted with the problem that arises when Any Living Thing takes the form of an extra person. An extra person is quite simply a person other than oneself. Living things of this nature undoubtedly have their place in both town and country, as they usually prove to be the most adept at typing, kissing, and conversing in an amusing fashion. It must be pointed out, however, that moving voluntarily is the very key to their success in performing these functions; the necessity of having to actually operate them would quite eliminate their appeal.

I have previously stated my contention that plants are acceptable in extremely rare instances. This type of extremely rare instance occurs when one is presented with a leaf-ridden token of affection by an extra person who has provided valuable service. Refusal of a plant thus offered will almost certainly result in the termination of this bond. Therefore, while the decision as to who exactly should be allowed to burden one with such a memento is, of course, a matter of personal conscience, one is wise to remember that talk is cheap, a kiss is just a kiss, but manuscripts do not type themselves.

Has No Sense Organs

It is necessary to remember that, although No Sense Organs does most assuredly guarantee no meaningful glances, no snorting derisively, and no little tastes, it also, alas, guarantees no listening spellbound.

And Generally Makes Its Own Food

There is, I believe, something just the tiniest bit smug in that statement. And Generally Makes Its Own Food, does it? Well, bully for It. I do not generally make my own food, nor do I apologize for it in the least. New York City is fairly bristling with restaurants of every description and I cannot help but assume that they are there for a reason. Furthermore, it is hard to cherish the notion of a cuisine based on photosynthesis. Thus, since I have yet to detect the aroma of Fettuccine Alfredo emanating from a Boston fern, I do not consider And Generally Makes Its Own Food to be a trait of any consequence whatsoever. When you run across one that Generally Makes Its Own Money, give me a call.

•

FOOD FOR THOUGHT AND VICE VERSA

Summer has an unfortunate effect upon hostesses who have been unduly influenced by the photography of Irving Penn and take the season as a cue to serve dinners of astonishingly meager proportions. These they call light, a quality which while most assuredly welcome in comedies, cotton shirts, and hearts, is not an appropriate touch at dinner.

It is not surprising that a number of such hostesses seem to be associated with the world of high fashion, for it follows that a person whose idea of a hard day's work is posing for Deborah Turbeville might also be of the opinion that parsley is an adequate meat course.

Thin, almost transparent slices of lemon do indeed go a long way in dressing up a meal but they should not be counted as a separate vegetable.

•

Cold soup is a very tricky thing and it is the rare hostess who can carry it off. More often than not the dinner guest is left with the impression that had he only come a little earlier he could have gotten it while it was still hot.

•

A salad is not a meal. It is a style.

•

Japanese food is very pretty and undoubtedly a suitable cuisine in Japan, which is largely populated by people of below average size. Hostesses hell-bent on serving such food to occidentals would be well advised to supplement it with something more substantial and to keep in mind that almost everybody likes french fries.

•

Vegetables are interesting but lack a sense of purpose when unaccompanied by a good cut of meat.

•

Water chestnuts are supposed to go in a thing, not to be the thing itself.

•

White grapes are very attractive but when it comes to dessert people generally like cake with icing.

•

Candied violets are the Necco Wafers of the overbred.

There are a number of restaurants in New York that cater primarily to the confirmed bachelor. These establishments share many characteristics with the summer hostess and then some.

One such local eatery is a remodeled diner that looks like what Busby Berkeley would have done if only he hadn't had the money. It is open twenty-four hours a day—one supposes as a convenience to the hungry truck driver who will belly up to the takeout counter and bellow, "Two cucumber soups—good and cold; one endive salad—red wine vinaigrette; and one order of fresh asparagus—hold the hollandaise."

•

Saffron should be used sparingly if at all. No matter how enamored one might be of this seasoning, there are few who would agree that it is equal to salt in the versatility department.

•

A native-born American who has spent the entire day in what he knows to be New York City and has not once stepped aboard a ship or plane is almost invariably chagrined and disoriented by a menu that uses the French counterpart for the perfectly adequate English word *grapefruit*.

•

Watercress is pleasant enough in a salad or sandwich, but when placed alongside a hamburger it is merely an annoyance.

•

While it is undeniably true that people love a surprise, it is equally true that they are seldom pleased to suddenly and without warning happen upon a series of prunes in what they took to be a normal loin of pork.

•

People have been cooking and eating for thousands of years, so if you are the very first to have thought of adding fresh lime juice to scalloped potatoes try to understand that there must be a reason for this.

•

Technological innovation has done great damage not only to reading habits but also to eating habits. Food is now available in such unpleasant forms that one frequently finds smoking between courses to be an aid to the digestion.

•

A loaf of bread that is more comfortable than a sofa cannot help but be unpalatable.

•

The servant problem being what it is, one would think it apparent that a society that provides a Helper for tuna but compels a writer to pack her own suitcases desperately needs to reorder its priorities.

•

Chocolate is an excellent flavor for ice cream but both unreasonable and disconcerting in chewing gum.

•

Breakfast cereals that come in the same colors as polyester leisure suits make oversleeping a virtue.

•

When one asks for cream one should receive either cream or the information that the establishment in question favors instead a combination of vegetable oil and cancer-causing initials.

•

Cheese that is required by law to append the word *food* to its title does not go well with red wine or fruit.

•

Thoroughly distasteful as synthetic foods might be, one cannot help but accord them a certain value when confronted with the health food buff. One is also ever mindful of the fact that the aficionado of whole foods is a frequent champion of excessive political causes.

•

Brown rice is ponderous, overly chewy, and possessed of unpleasant religious overtones.

•

Civilized adults do not take apple juice with dinner.

•

Inhabitants of underdeveloped nations and victims of natural disasters are the only people who have ever been happy to see soybeans.

•

Bread that must be sliced with an ax is bread that is too nourishing.

•

Large, naked, raw carrots are acceptable as food only to those who live in hutches eagerly awaiting Easter.

•

Food is such a common occurrence in our daily lives that few have taken the time to consider it in the broader sense and thus cannot truly appreciate its impact on society.

•

Food is welcome at both meal and snack time. It goes well with most any beverage and by and large makes the best sandwich.

•

Food gives real meaning to dining room furniture.

•

Food goes a long way in rounding out a CARE package.

•

Food offers the perfect excuse to use the good dishes.

•

Food is an important part of a balanced diet.

•

Food plays a crucial role in international politics. If there was no such thing as food, state dinners would be replaced by state bridge games and, instead of fasting, political activists would probably just whine.

•

A foodless world would have the disastrous effect of robbing one's initiative. Ambition has no place in a society that refuses its members the opportunity to become top banana.

•

Without food, one of man's most perplexing yet engaging problems would be rendered meaningless when one realized that the chicken and the egg both didn't come first.

•

If food did not exist it would be well-nigh impossible to get certain types off the phone, as one would be unable to say, "Look, I've got to run but let's have dinner sometime soon."

•

Food was a very big factor in Christianity. What would the miracle of the loaves and fishes have been without it? And the Last Supper—how effective would that have been?

•

If there was no such thing as food, Oyster Bay would be called just Bay, and for the title of *The Cherry Orchard* Chekhov would have chosen *A Group of Empty Trees, Regularly Spaced*.

•

WRITING: A LIFE SENTENCE

Contrary to what many of you might imagine, a career in letters is not without its drawbacks—chief among them the unpleasant fact that one is frequently called upon to actually sit down and write. This demand is peculiar to the profession and, as such, galling, for it is a constant reminder to the writer that he is not now, nor will he ever really be, like other men. For the requirements of the trade are so unattractive, so not fair, and so foreign to regular people that the writer is to the real world what Esperanto is to the language world—funny, maybe, but not *that* funny. This being the case, I feel the time has come for all concerned to accept the writer's differences as inherent and acknowledge once and for all that in the land of the blind the one-eyed man is a writer and he's not too thrilled about it.

Thus I offer the following with the hope that it will bring about much-needed compassion. Points 1 through 5 are for parents—the later explication for masochists. Or vice versa.

How to Tell If Your Child Is a Writer

Your child is a writer if one or more of the following statements are applicable. Truthfulness is advised—no amount of fudging will alter the grim reality.

1. Prenatal
    A. You have morning sickness at night because the fetus finds it too distracting to work during the day.
    B. You develop a craving for answering services and typists.
    C. When your obstetrician applies his stethoscope to your abdomen he hears excuses.
2. Birth
    A. The baby is at least three weeks late because he had a lot of trouble with the ending.
    B. You are in labor for twenty-seven hours because the baby left everything until the last minute and spent an inordinate amount of time trying to grow his toes in a more interesting order.
    C. When the doctor spanks the baby the baby is not at all surprised.
    D. It is definitely a single birth because the baby has dismissed being twins as too obvious.
3. Infancy
    A. The baby refuses both breast and bottle, preferring instead Perrier with a twist in preparation for giving up drinking.

B. The baby sleeps through the night almost immediately. Also through the day.

C. The baby's first words, uttered at the age of four days, are "Next week."

D. The baby uses teething as an excuse not to learn to gurgle.

E. The baby sucks his forefinger out of a firm conviction that the thumb's been done to death.

4. Toddlerhood

A. He rejects teddy bears as derivative.

B. He arranges his alphabet blocks so as to spell out derisive puns on the names of others.

C. When he is lonely he does not ask his mother for a baby brother or sister but rather for a protégé.

D. When he reaches the age of three he considers himself a trilogy.

E. His mother is afraid to remove his crayoned handiwork from the living room walls lest she be accused of excessive editing.

F. When he is read his bedtime story he makes sarcastic remarks about style.

5. Childhood

A. At age seven he begins to think about changing his name. Also his sex.

B. He balks at going to summer camp because he is aware that there may be children there who have never heard of him.

C. He tells his teachers that he didn't do his homework because he was blocked.

D. He refuses to learn how to write a Friendly Letter because he knows he never will.

E. With an eye to a possible movie deal, he insists upon changing the title of his composition "What I Did on My Summer Vacation" to the far snappier "Vacation."

F. He is thoroughly hypochondriac and is convinced that his chicken pox is really leprosy.

G. On Halloween he goes out trick-or-treating dressed as Harold Acton.

By the time this unfortunate child has reached puberty there is no longer any hope that he will outgrow being a writer and become something more appealing—like a kidnap victim. The concern, then, as he enters the difficult period of adolescence, is that he receive the proper education in a sympathetic environment. For this reason it is strongly recommended that the teen writer attend a school geared to his dilemma—Writing High. At Writing High the student will be among his own kind—the ungrateful. He will be offered a broad range of subjects relevant to his needs: Beginning Badly, Avoiding Los Angeles One and Two, Remedial Wakefulness, Magazine Editors: Why?, and Advanced Deftness of Phrase—all taught by jealous teachers who would really rather be students. Extracurricular activities (such as the Jacket Flap Club, where students have fun while learning the rudiments of acquiring colorful temporary jobs such as lumberjack, numbers runner, shepherd, and pornographer) are in plentiful supply. The figure of speech team, the Metaphors, are mighty effective. They can mix it up with the best of them, and Janet Flanner, their lovable mascot, is a great campus favorite.

Although the yearbook—*The Contempt*—is rarely finished in time for graduation, it is nevertheless a treasured memento of the years spent at Writing High. The cafeteria is presided over by an overweight woman of great ambition and serves mediocre Italian food at ridiculously inflated prices. School spirit is encouraged by holding in the auditorium a weekly gathering known as Asimile. Tutoring is available for the slow student, or "ghost," as he is referred to at Writing High. Upon graduation or expulsion (and expulsion is favored by the more commercial students, who prize it for its terrific possibilities as a talk-show anecdote) the writer is as ready as he'll ever be to make his mark upon the world.

It is unnecessary to detail the next, or actual career, stage, for all writers end up the same—either dead or in Homes for the Aged Writer. The prospect of being put in such an establishment is viewed by all writers with gread dread and not without reason. Recent scandals have revealed the shockingly widespread sadistic practice of slipping the aged writer unfavorable reviews, and more than one such victim has been found dead from lack of sufficient praise.

Not a very pretty picture, I'm afraid, and not a very accurate one either. But don't be encouraged by *that*—two wrongs don't make you write.

•

THE WORD *LADY:* MOST OFTEN USED TO DESCRIBE SOMEONE YOU
WOULDN'T WANT TO TALK TO FOR EVEN FIVE MINUTES
For years and years people who had them referred to their girl friends as their girl friends. With the advent of that unattractive style known as

hip, many people stole the term *old lady* from perfectly innocent black jazz musicians and began using it in regard to their own girl friends. Then came women's lib and quite a number of people apparently felt that the word *old* was sexist. These people began to call their girl friends their "ladies."

Lest you get the impression that I am totally opposed to the word *lady* I rush to assure you that I think it is a perfectly nice word when used correctly. The word *lady* is used correctly only as follows:

A. To refer to certain female members of the English aristocracy.

B. In reference to girls who stand behind lingerie counters in department stores, but only when preceded by the word *sales*.

C. To alert a member of the gentle sex to the fact that she is no longer playing with a full deck. As in, "Lady, what are you—nuts or something?"

D. To differentiate between girls who put out and girls who don't. Girls who put out are tramps. Girls who don't are ladies. This is, however, a rather archaic usage of the word. Should one of you boys happen upon a girl who doesn't put out, do not jump to the conclusion that you have found a lady. What you have probably found is a lesbian.

•

A FEW WORDS ON A FEW WORDS

Democracy is an interesting, even laudable, notion and there is no question but that when compared to Communism, which is too dull, or Fascism, which is too exciting, it emerges as the most palatable form of government. This is not to say that it is without its drawbacks—chief among them being its regrettable tendency to encourage people in the belief that all men are created equal. And although the vast majority need only take a quick look around the room to see that this is hardly the case, a great many remain utterly convinced. -

The major problem resulting from this conviction is that it causes such people to take personally the inalienable right of freedom of speech. This in itself would be at least tolerable were this group not given to such a broad interpretation of the word *freedom* or such a slender interpretation of the word *speech*.

It would further ameliorate the situation were these equality buffs to recall that one of the distinguishing characteristics of democracy is the division between the public sector and the private sector. The founding fathers may have had any number of things in mind when they made this admirable distinction, but surely their primary consideration was to protect the articulate against the possibility of overhearing the annoying conversation of others.

Since the Bill of Rights in its present form leaves far too much to the imagination, it is obviously necessary for some sane, responsible citizen to step forward and explain in detail just exactly what is meant by freedom of speech. Being as civic-minded as the next girl, I willingly accept this challenge. Lest you assume that I possess unreasonable and dangerous dictatorial impulses, I assure you that my desire to curtail undue freedom of speech extends only to such public arenas as restaurants, airports, streets, hotel lobbies, parks, and department stores. Verbal exchanges between consenting adults in private are of as little interest to me as they probably are to them. I wish only to defend the impressionable young and the fastidious old against the ravages of unseemly word usage. To this end I have prepared a list of words which should be used in public only as specified.

1. *art*—This word may be publicly used in only two instances:
   A. As a nickname—in which case the suffix *ie* may be added to form the word *Artie*.
   B. By a native of the East End of London to describe a vital organ, as in the sentence, "Blimy, I feel poorly—must be my bleedin' 'art."
2. *love*—The word *love* may be used in public only to refer to inanimate or totally inaccessible objects.
   A. "I love linguini with clam sauce" is always acceptable.
   B. "I love Truman Capote" is acceptable only if one is not personally acquainted with him. If one is personally acquainted with Mr. Capote it is rather unlikely at this time that one would be moved to express such a sentiment.
3. *relationship*—The civilized conversationalist uses this word in public only to describe a seafaring vessel carrying members of his family.
4. *diaphragm*—Public decency demands that this word be used

only to refer to the midriff area of the body and then only by doctors—never by singers.

5. *Ms.*—The wise avoid this word entirely but:
   A. It may be used on paper by harried members of the publishing world who find it necessary to abbreviate the word manuscript.
   B. Or by native residents of the south and southwestern portions of the United States as follows: "I sho do ms. that purty little gal."

6. *honest*—This word is suitable for public use only to indicate extreme distaste, as in the sentence "Dorothy has become absolutely unbearable—I think she must be on est."

7. *internalize*—To be used (if at all) only to describe that process by which a formerly harmless medical student becomes a menace to the sick and helpless.

8. *fair*—This word is to be used only in reference to a carnival-type event and not as an expression of justice—for not only is such usage unpleasant but also, I assure you, quite useless.

9. *assert*—One would do well to remember that as far as public utterance is concerned, *assert* refers only to that which is two mints in one.

Carol Leifer (contemporary)

~⊱ ⊰~

On Marriage

I got divorced recently. It was a mixed marriage. I'm human, he was Klingon.

•

I'm thirty-six years old and I have no children. At least, none that I know of . . .

Charlotte Lennox (1729-1804)

~⋇ ⋇~

FROM *The Female Quixote*

From her earliest youth she had discovered a fondness for reading, which extremely delighted the marquis; he permitted her therefore the use of his library, in which, unfortunately for her, were great stores of romances, and what was still more unfortunate, not in the original French, but very bad translations.

•

Her ideas, from the manner of her life, and the objects around her, had taken a romantic turn; and supposing romances were real pictures of life, from them she drew all her notions and expectations. By them she was taught to believe, that love was the ruling principle of the world; that every other passion was subordinate to this; and that it caused all the happiness and miseries of life. Her glass, which she often consulted, always shewed her a form so extremely lovely, that, not finding herself engaged in such adventures as were common to the heroines in the romances she read, she often complained of the insensibility of mankind, upon whom her charms seemed to have so little influence.

•

. . . Lovers think every thing possible which they fear.

•

Some of the wiser sort took her for a foreigner: others, of still more sagacity, supposed her a Scotch lady, covered with her plaid; and a third sort, infinitely wiser than either, concluded she was a Spanish nun, that had escaped from a convent, and had not yet quitted her veil.—Arabella, ignorant of the diversity of opinions to which her appearance gave rise, was taken up in discoursing with Mr. Glanville upon the medicinal virtue of the springs, the economy of the baths, the nature of the diversions, and such other topics as the objects around them furnished her with.—In the mean time, Miss Glanville was got amidst a crowd of her acquaintance, who had hardly paid the civilities of a first meeting, before they eagerly inquired who that lady she brought with her was.—Miss Glanville informed them, that she was her cousin, and daughter to the deceased Marquis of ————; adding, with a sneer, that she had been brought up in the country, knew nothing of the world and had some very peculiar notions. As you may see, said she, by that odd kind of covering she wears.

•

Mr. Selvin, so was the other gentleman called, was of a much graver cast; he affected to be thought deep-read in history, and never failed to take all opportunities of displaying his knowledge of antiquity, which was indeed but very superficial: but having some few ancedotes by heart, which he would take occasion to introduce as often as he could, he passed among many persons for one who, by application and study, had acquired an universal knowledge of ancient history.—Speaking of any particular circumstance, he would fix the time, by computing the year with the number of the Olympiads. It happened, he would say, in the 141st Olympiad.

•

When actions are a censure upon themselves, the reciter will always be considered as a satirist.

•

FROM *Henrietta*

She could not help fancying herself the future heroine of some affecting tale, whose life would be varied with surprizing vicissitudes of fortune. . . . But these reflections were succeeded by others more reasonable and which indeed afforded her a more solid satisfaction. . . .

Baird Leonard (c. 1890-?)

FROM *The Columnist*

The Class-A Wife.
          She has no living relatives,
          And all her girlhood friends are brilliant and beautiful women. . . .

She does not quote poetry, diet, or read anything aloud except by request. . . .

She has no curiosity concerning her husband's recent whereabouts so long as he does not come home accompanied by policemen or interns. . . .

She knows a good joke when she hears it, even for the fifteenth or sixteenth time. . . .

Her earrings stay put, whatever their weight, and an open handbag never falls from her lap. . . .

She does not insist on starting for a train an hour before the gate opens.

In telling an anecdote, she does not confuse or omit its point,

And her chequebook is as neat and accurate as that of a certified accountant.

She takes no notice of her husband's dancing partners, keeps no record of his libations, and gladly allows him to attend to his own business or profession. . . .

The Class-A Husband.

When something good is coming over the radio, he is perfectly willing to let well enough alone. . . .

He is not skeptical when she thinks she hears a burglar, and he rises quickly and cheerfully to adjust a flapping window shade or subdue an insurgent radiator.

He sleeps with his mouth closed.

His private secretary is a man.

. . . When the waiter brings the bill, he does not pore over it as though he were committing it to memory. . . .

He is lucky when he gambles, and splits all his winnings with his wife.

He doesn't reminisce with old college classmates about former pranks of inebriety, or the time they dressed Nathan Hale's statue in the Dean's pajamas. . . .

When he says he can be reached at his club, he is speaking the truth.

He enjoys walking the dog, is handy around the house, scrambles perfect eggs at odd hours. . . .

Doris Lessing (1919–   )

How I Finally Lost My Heart

It would be easy to say that I picked up a knife, slit open my side, took my heart out, and threw it away; but unfortunately it wasn't as easy as that. Not that I, like everyone else, had not often wanted to do it. No, it happened differently, and not as I expected.

It was just after I had had a lunch and a tea with two different men. My lunch partner I had lived with for (more or less) four and seven-twelfths years. When he left me for new pastures I spent two years, or was it three, half-dead, and my heart was a stone, impossible to carry about, considering all the other things weighing on one. Then I slowly, and with difficulty, got free, because my heart cherished a thousand adhesions to my first love—though from another point of view he could be legitimately described as either my second *real* love (my father being the first) or my third (my brother intervening).

As the folk song has it:

> *I have loved but three men in my life,*
> *My father, my brother, and the man that*
> *took my life.*

But if one were going to look at the thing from outside, without insight, he could be seen as (perhaps, I forget) the thirteenth, but to do that means disregarding the inner emotional truth. For we all know that those affairs or entanglements one has between *serious* loves, though they may number dozens and stretch over years, *don't really count.*

This way of looking at things creates a number of unhappy people, for it is well known that what doesn't really count for me might very well count for you. But there is no way of getting over this difficulty, for a *serious* love is the most important business in life, or nearly so. At any rate, most of us are engaged in looking for it. Even when we are in fact being very serious indeed with one person we still have an eighth of an eye cocked in case some stranger unexpectedly encountered might turn out to be even more serious. We are all entirely in agreement that we are in the right to taste, test, sip and sample a thousand people on our way to the *real* one. It is not too much to say that in our circles tasting and sampling is probably the second most important activity, the first being earning money. Or to put it another way, if you are serious about this thing, you go on laying everybody that offers until something clicks and you're all set to go.

I have digressed from an earlier point: that I regarded this man I had lunch with (we call him A) as my first love; and still do, despite the Freudians, who insist on seeing my father as A and possibly my brother as B, making my (real) first love C. And despite, also, those who might ask: What about your two husbands and all those affairs?

What about them? I did not *really* love them, the way I loved A.

I had lunch with him. Then, quite by chance, I had tea with B. When I say B, here, I mean my *second* serious love, not my brother, or the little boys I was in love with between the ages of five and fifteen, if we are going to take fifteen (arbitrarily) as the point of no return . . . which last phrase is in itself a pretty brave defiance of the secular arbiters.

In between A and B (my count) there were a good many affairs, or samples, but they didn't score. B and I *clicked*, we went off like a bomb, though not quite as simply as A and I had clicked, because my heart was bruised, sullen, and suspicious because of A's throwing me over. Also there were all those ligaments and adhesions binding me to A still to be loosened, one by one. However, for a time B and I got on like a house on fire, and then we came to grief. My heart was again a ton weight in my side.

> *If this were a stone in my side, a stone,*
> *I could pluck it out and be free. . . .*

Having lunch with A, then tea with B, two men who between them had consumed a decade of my precious years (I am not counting the test or trial affairs in between) and, it is fair to say, had balanced all the delight (plenty and intense) with misery (oh Lord, Lord)—moving from one to the other, in the course of an afternoon, conversing amiably about this and that, with meanwhile my heart giving no more than slight reminiscent tugs, the fish of memory at the end of a long slack line . . .

To sum up, it was salutary.

Particularly as that evening I was expecting to meet C, or someone who might very well turn out to be C; though I don't want to give too much emphasis to C, the truth is I can hardly remember what he looked

like, but one can't be expected to remember the unimportant ones one
has sipped or tasted in between. But after all, he might have turned out
to be C, we might have *clicked,* and I was in that state of mind (in which
we all so often are) of thinking: He might turn out to be the one. (I use
a woman's magazine phrase deliberately here, instead of saying, as I
might: *Perhaps it will be serious.*)

So there I was (I want to get the details and atmosphere right)
standing at a window looking into a street (Great Portland Street, as a
matter of fact) and thinking that while I would not dream of regretting
my affairs, or experiences, with A and B (it is better to have loved and
lost than never to have loved at all), my anticipation of the heart because
of spending an evening with a possible C had a certain unreality, because
there was no doubt that both A and B had caused me unbelievable pain.
Why, therefore, was I looking forward to C? I should rather be running
away as fast as I could.

It suddenly occurred to me that I was looking at the whole phenomenon quite inaccurately. My (or perhaps I am permitted to say our?)
way of looking at it is that one must search for an A, or a B, or a C or
a D with a certain combination of desirable or sympathetic qualities so
that one may click, or spontaneously combust: or to put it differently,
one needs a person who, like a saucer of water, allows one to float off
on him/her, like a transfer. But this wasn't so at all. Actually one carries
with one a sort of burning spear stuck in one's side, that one waits for
someone else to pull out; it is something painful, like a sore or a wound,
that one cannot wait to share with someone else.

I saw myself quite plainly in a moment of truth: I was standing at
a window (on the third floor) with A and B (to mention only the
mountain peaks of my emotional experience) behind me, a rather attractive woman, if I may say so, with a mellowness that I would be the
first to admit is the sad harbinger of age, but is attractive by definition,
because it is a testament to the amount of sampling and sipping (I nearly
wrote "simpling" and "sapping") I have done in my time. . . . There I
stood, brushed, dressed, red-lipped, kohl-eyed, all waiting for an evening
with a possible C. And at another window overlooking (I think I am
right in saying) Margaret Street, stood C, brushed, washed, shaved, smiling: an attractive man (I think), and *he* was thinking: Perhaps she will
turn out to be D (or A or 3 or ? or %, or whatever symbol he used).
We stood, separated by space, certainly, in identical conditions of pleasant uncertainty and anticipation, and we both held our hearts in our
hands, all pink and palpitating and ready for pleasure and pain, and we
were about to throw these hearts in each other's face like snowballs, or

cricket balls (How's that?) or, more accurately, like great bleeding wounds: "Take my wound." Because the last thing one ever thinks at such moments is that he (or she) will say: Take *my* wound, please remove the spear from *my* side. No, not at all; one simply expects to get rid of one's own.

I decided I must go to the telephone and say, C!—You know that joke about the joke-makers who don't trouble to tell each other jokes, but simply say Joke 1 or Joke 2, and everyone roars with laughter, or snickers, or giggles appropriately. . . . Actually one could reverse the game by guessing whether it was Joke C(b) or Joke A(d) according to what sort of laughter a person made to match the silent thought. . . . Well, C (I imagined myself saying), the analogy is for our instruction: Let's take the whole thing as read or said. Let's not lick each other's sores; let's keep our hearts to ourselves. Because just consider it, C, how utterly absurd—here we stand at our respective windows with our palpitating hearts in our hands. . . .

At this moment, dear reader, I was forced simply to put down the telephone with an apology. For I felt the fingers of my left hand push outwards around something rather large, light, and slippery—hard to describe this sensation, really. My hand is not large, and my heart was in a state of inflation after having had lunch with A, tea with B, and then looking forward to C. . . . Anyway, my fingers were stretching out rather desperately to encompass an unknown, largish, lightish object, and I said: Excuse me a minute, to C, looked down, and there was my heart, in my hand.

I had to end the conversation there.

For one thing, to find that one has achieved something so often longed for, so easily, is upsetting. It's not as if I had been trying. To get something one wants simply by accident—no, there's no pleasure in it, no feeling of achievement. So to find myself heart-whole, or, more accurately, heart-less, or at any rate, rid of the damned thing, and at such an awkward moment, in the middle of an imaginary telephone call with a man who might possibly turn out to be C—well, it was irritating rather than not.

For another thing, a heart, raw and bleeding and fresh from one's side is not the prettiest sight. I'm not going into that at all. I was appalled, and indeed embarrassed that *that* was what had been loving and beating away all those years, because if I'd had any idea at all—well, enough of that.

My problem was how to get rid of it.

Simple, you'll say, drop it into the waste bucket.

Well, let me tell you, that's what I tried to do. I took a good look

at this object, nearly died with embarrassment, and walked over to the
rubbish-can, where I tried to let it roll off my fingers. It wouldn't. It
was stuck. There was my heart, a large red pulsing bleeding repulsive
object, stuck to my fingers. What was I going to do? I sat down, lit a
cigarette (with one hand, holding the matchbox between my knees),
held my hand with the heart stuck on it over the side of the chair so
that it could drip into a bucket, and considered.

> *If this were a stone in my hand, a stone,*
> *I could throw it over a tree. . . .*

When I had finished the cigarette, I carefully unwrapped some tin
foil of the kind used to wrap food in when cooking, and I fitted a sort
of cover around my heart. This was absolutely and urgently necessary.
First, it was smarting badly. After all, it had spent some forty years protected by flesh and ribs, and the air was too much for it. Secondly, I
couldn't have any Tom, Dick and Harry walking in and looking at it.
Thirdly, I could not look at it for long myself, it filled me with shame.
The tin foil was effective, and indeed rather striking. It is quite pliable
and now it seemed as if there were a stylised heart balanced on my palm,
like a globe, in glittering, silvery substance. I almost felt I needed a
sceptre in the other hand to balance it. . . . But the thing was, there is
no other word for it, in bad taste. I then wrapped a scarf around hand
and tin-foiled heart, and felt safer. Now it was a question of pretending
to have hurt my hand until I could think of a way of getting rid of my
heart altogether, short of amputating my hand.

Meanwhile I telephoned (really, not in imagination) C, who now
would never be C. I could feel my heart, which was stuck so close to
my fingers that I could feel every beat or tremor, give a gulp of resigned
grief at the idea of this beautiful experience now never to be. I told him
some idiotic lie about having 'flu. Well, he was all stiff and indignant,
but concealing it urbanely, as I would have done, making a joke but
allowing a tiny barb of sarcasm to rankle in the last well-chosen phrase.
Then I sat down again to think out my whole situation.

There I sat.

What was I going to do?

There I sat.

I am going to have to skip about four days here, vital enough in
all conscience, because I simply cannot go heartbeat by heartbeat through
my memories. A pity, since I suppose this is what this story is about;
but in brief: I drew the curtains, I took the telephone off the hook, I

turned on the lights, I took the scarf off the glittering shape, then the tin foil; then I examined the heart. There were two-fifths of a century's experience to work through, and before I had even got through the first night, I was in a state hard to describe. . . .

> *Or if I could pull the nerves from my skin*
> *A quick red net to drag through a sea for fish. . . .*

By the end of the fourth day I was worn out. By no act of will, or intention, or desire, could I move that heart by a fraction—on the contrary, it was not only stuck to my fingers, like a sucked boiled sweet, but was actually growing to the flesh of my fingers and my palm.

I wrapped it up again in tin foil and scarf, and turned out the lights and pulled up the blinds and opened the curtains. It was about ten in the morning, an ordinary London day, neither hot nor cold nor clear nor clouded nor wet nor fine. And while the street is interesting, it is not exactly beautiful, so I wasn't looking at it so much as waiting for something to catch my attention while thinking of something else.

Suddenly I heard a tap-tap-tapping that got louder, sharp and clear, and I knew before I saw her that this was the sound of high heels on a pavement though it might just as well have been a hammer against stone. She walked fast opposite my window and her heels hit the pavement so hard that all the noises of the street seemed absorbed into that single tap-tap-clang-clang. As she reached the corner at Great Portland Street two London pigeons swooped diagonally from the sky very fast, as if they were bullets aimed to kill her; and then as they saw her they swooped up and off at an angle. Meanwhile she had turned the corner. All this has taken time to write down, but the thing happening took a couple of seconds: the woman's body hitting the pavement bang-bang through her heels then sharply turning the corner in a right angle; and the pigeons making another acute angle across hers and intersecting it in a fast swoop of displaced air. Nothing to all that, of course, nothing—she had gone off down the street, her heels tip-tapping, and the pigeons landed on my windowsill and began cooing. All gone, all vanished, the marvellous exact co-ordination of sound and movement, but it had happened, it had made me happy and exhilarated, I had no problems in this world, and I realised that the heart stuck to my fingers was quite loose. I couldn't get it off altogether, though I was tugging at it under the scarf and the tin foil, but almost.

I understood that sitting and analysing each movement or pulse or beat of my heart through forty years was a mistake. I was on the wrong track altogether: this was the way to attach my red, bitter, delighted heart to my flesh for ever and ever. . . .

> *Ha! So you think I'm done! You think. . . .*
> *Watch, I'll roll my heart in a mesh of rage*
> *And bounce it like a handball off*
> *Walls, faces, railings, umbrellas and pigeons' backs. . . .*

No, all that was no good at all; it just made things worse. What I must do is to take myself by surprise, as it were, the way I was taken by surprise over the woman and the pigeons and the sharp sounds of heels and silk wings.

I put on my coat, held my lumpy scarfed arm across my chest, so that if anyone said: What have you done with your hand? I could say: I've banged my finger in the door. Then I walked down into the street.

It wasn't easy to go among so many people, when I was worried that they were thinking: What has that woman done to her hand? because that made it hard to forget myself. And all the time it tingled and throbbed against my fingers, reminding me.

Now I was out, I didn't know what to do. Should I go and have lunch with someone? Or wander in the park? Or buy myself a dress? I decided to go to the Round Pond, and walk around it by myself. I was tired after four days and nights without sleep. I went down into the underground at Oxford Circus. Midday. Crowds of people. I felt self-conscious, but of course need not have worried. I swear you could walk naked down the street in London and no one would even turn round.

So I went down the escalator and looked at the faces coming up past me on the other side, as I always do; and wondered, as I always do, how strange it is that those people and I should meet by chance in such a way, and how odd that we would never see each other again, or, if we did, we wouldn't know it. And I went on the crowded platform and looked at the faces as I always do, and got into the train, which was very full, and found a seat. It wasn't as bad as at rush hour, but all the seats were filled. I leaned back and closed my eyes, deciding to sleep a little, being so tired. I was just beginning to doze off when I heard a woman's voice muttering, or rather, declaiming:

> "A gold cigarette case, well, that's a nice thing, isn't it, I must say, a gold case, yes. . . ."

There was something about this voice which made me open my eyes: on the other side of the compartment, about eight persons away, sat a youngish woman, wearing a cheap green cloth coat, gloveless hands, flat brown shoes, and lisle stockings. She must be rather poor—a woman dressed like this is a rare sight, these days. But it was her posture that struck me. She was sitting half-twisted in her seat, so that her head was turned over her left shoulder, and she was looking straight at the stomach of an elderly man next to her. But it was clear she was not seeing it: her young staring eyes were sightless, she was looking inwards.

She was so clearly alone, in the crowded compartment, that it was not as embarrassing as it might have been. I looked around, and people were smiling, or exchanging glances, or winking, or ignoring her, according to their natures, but she was oblivious of us all.

She suddenly aroused herself, turned so that she sat straight in her seat, and directed her voice and her gaze to the opposite seat:

"Well so that's what you think, you think that, you think that do you, well, you think I'm just going to wait at home for you, but you gave her a gold case and . . ."

And with a clockwork movement of her whole thin person, she turned her narrow pale-haired head sideways over her left shoulder, and resumed her stiff empty stare at the man's stomach. He was grinning uncomfortably. I leaned forward to look along the line of people in the row of seats I sat in, and the man opposite her, a young man, had exactly the same look of discomfort which he was determined to keep amused. So we all looked at her, the young, thin, pale woman in her private drama of misery, who was so completely unconscious of us that she spoke and thought out loud. And again, without particular warning or reason, in between stops, so it wasn't that she was disturbed from her dream by the train stopping at Bond Street, and then jumping forward again, she twisted her body frontways, and addressed the seat opposite her (the young man had got off, and a smart grey-curled matron had got in):

"Well I know about it now, don't I, and if you come in all smiling and pleased well then I know, don't I, you don't have to tell me, I know, and I've said to her, I've said, I know he gave you a gold cigarette case. . . ."

At which point, with the same clockwork impulse, she stopped, or was checked, or simply ran out, and turned herself half-around to stare at the stomach—the same stomach, for the middleaged man was still there. But we stopped at Marble Arch and he got out, giving the compartment, rather than the people in it, a tolerant half-smile which said: I am sure I can trust you to realise that this unfortunate woman is stark staring mad. . . .

His seat remained empty. No people got in at Marble Arch, and the two people standing waiting for seats did not want to sit by her to receive her stare.

We all sat, looking gently in front of us, pretending to ourselves and to each other that we didn't know the poor woman was mad and that in fact we ought to be doing something about it. I even wondered what I should say: Madam, you're mad—shall I escort you to your home? Or: Poor thing, don't go on like that, it doesn't do any good, you know—just leave him, that'll bring him to his senses. . . .

And behold, after the interval that was regulated by her inner mechanism had elapsed, she turned back and said to the smart matron who received this statement of accusation with perfect self-command:

"Yes, I know! Oh yes! And what about my shoes, what about them, a golden cigarette case is what she got, the filthy bitch, a golden case. . . ."

Stop. Twist. Stare. At the empty seat by her.

Extraordinary. Because it was a frozen misery, how shall I put it? A passionless passion—we were seeing unhappiness embodied; we were looking at the essence of some private tragedy—rather, Tragedy. There was no emotion in it. She was like an actress doing Accusation, or Betrayed Love, or Infidelity, when she has only just learned her lines and is not bothering to do more than get them right.

And whether she sat in her half-twisted position, her unblinking eyes staring at the greenish, furry, ugly covering of the train seat, or sat straight, directing her accusation to the smart woman opposite, there was a frightening immobility about her—yes, that was why she frightened us. For it was clear that she might very well (if the inner machine ran down) stay silent, forever, in either twisted or straight position, or at any point between them—yes, we could all imagine her, frozen perpetually in some arbitrary pose. It was as if we watched the shell of some woman going through certain predetermined motions.

For *she* was simply not there. *What* was there, who she was, it was impossible to tell, though it was easy to imagine her thin, gentle little face breaking into a smile in total forgetfulness of what she was enacting now. She did not know she was in a train between Marble Arch and Queensway, nor that she was publicly accusing her husband or lover, nor that we were looking at her.

And we, looking at her, felt an embarrassment and shame that was not on her account at all. . . .

Suddenly I felt, under the scarf and the tin foil, a lightening of my fingers, as my heart rolled loose.

I hastily took it off my palm, in case it decided to adhere there again, and I removed the scarf, leaving balanced on my knees a perfect stylised heart, like a silver heart on a Valentine card, though of course it was three-dimensional. This heart was not so much harmless, no that isn't the word, as artistic, but in very bad taste, as I said. I could see that the people in the train, now looking at me and the heart, and not at the poor madwoman, were pleased with it.

I got up, took the four or so paces to where she was, and laid the tin-foiled heart down on the seat so that it received her stare.

For a moment she did not react, then with a groan or a mutter of relieved and entirely theatrical grief, she leaned forward, picked up the glittering heart, and clutched it in her arms, hugging it and rocking it back and forth, even laying her cheek against it, while staring over its top at her husband as if to say: Look what I've got, I don't care about you and your cigarette case, I've got a silver heart.

I got up, since we were at Notting Hill Gate, and, followed by the pleased congratulatory nods and smiles of the people left behind, I went out onto the platform, up the escalators, into the street, and along to the park.

No heart. No heart at all. What bliss. What freedom . . .

Hear that sound? That's laughter, yes.
That's me laughing, yes, that's me.

Esther Lewis (fl. 1747–1789)

A Mirror for Detractors. Addressed to a Friend

This wit was with experience bought
(And that's the best of wit, 'tis thought),
That when a woman dares indite,
And seek in print the public sight,
All tongues are presently in motion
About her person, mind, and portion;
And every blemish, every fault,
Unseen before, to light is brought.
Nay, generously they take the trouble
Those blemishes and faults to double.

Whene'er you chance her name to hear,
With a contemptuous, smiling sneer,
A prude exclaims, "O, she's a wit!"
And I've observed that epithet
Means self-conceit, ill-nature, pride,
And fifty hateful things beside.

The men are mighty apt to say,
"This silly girl has lost her way;
No doubt she thinks we must admire
And such a rhyming wit desire;
But here her folly does appear,
We never choose a learned fair,
Nor like to see a woman try
With our superior parts to vie.
She ought to mind domestic cares,
The sex were made for such affairs.
She'd better take in hand the needle,
And not pretend to rhyme and riddle.
Shall women thus usurp the pen?
That weapon nature made for men.

Presumptuous thing! how did she dare
This implement from us to tear?

"In short, if women are allowed
(Women by nature vain and proud)
Thus boldly on the press to seize,
And say in print what'er they please,
They'll soon their lawful lords despise,
And think themselves as Sybils wise."

Thus far the men their wit display;
Let's hear now what the women say.

Now we'll suppose a tattling set
Of females o'er tea-table met,
While from its time-consuming streams
Arise a hundred idle themes,
Of fans, of flounces, flies, and faces,
Of lap-dogs, lovers, lawns and laces.
At length this well-known foe to fame
In luckless hour brings forth my name;
Then all exclaim with great good-nature,
"O Lord! that witty, rhyming creature!"
Alternate then their parts sustain:
"Pray, don't you think she's mighty vain?,"
Says one; "No doubt," another cries;
"Vain, Lord, of what?," a third replies;
"What though suppose the thing can rhyme,
And on the changing numbers chime,
No merit lies in that, 'tis plain,
And others, if they were as vain,
I make no doubt could write as well,
Would they but try, perhaps excel."

Then thus Philantha, in whose breast
Good-nature is a constant guest:
"I own I've heard before, with pain,
Some people call her proud and vain;
I know her well, yet ne'er could see
This mighty pride and vanity."

"You, Madam, are, I find, her friend;
But I can never apprehend
She ever yet a poem penned.

They're all another's works, no doubt,
With which she makes this mighty rout."

"That's very like, but, Miss, suppose
She does the tedious stuff compose,
Yet for my part, though some may praise,
And stick the creature out with bays,
I can see nothing in the scrawls,
That for such vast encomiums calls.
'Tis true, in length if merit lies,
From all she'll bear away the prize.

"This for her poems may be said,
They're mighty good to lull the head;
For nothing there piquant you'll find,
To raise a laugh, or rouse the mind.
No doctor's opiate can exceed 'em,
Whene'er I want a nap I read 'em."

Philantha then—" 'Tis so well known
That all those poems are her own,
I wonder anyone can doubt it,
Or have a single thought about it,
And oft I've heard the lines commended;
Then all allow they're well intended."

"That may perhaps be true enough;
But who's the better for her stuff?
I see no difference in the times,
The world's not mended by her rhymes.
She to the men, I apprehend,
Intends herself to recommend
By scribbling verses, but she'll find
They don't so much regard the mind;
For though they're civil to her face,
'Tis all a farce, and mere grimace;
Her back once turned, I've heard 'em swear
They hated wisdom in the fair.

"Then she's so nice and so refined
About the morals, and the mind,
That really, Madam, I'm afraid
This rhyming wit will die a maid;

And if she weds, it is high time,
I think she's almost past her prime.
Why, with the men, as I've been told,
She'll paper-conversation hold."

"Madam, that's fact, I long have known it,
Without a blush I've heard her own it."

"Good Lord! some women are so bold,
I vow I blush to hear it told;
I hate censoriousness, but when
Girls freely correspond with men,
I can't forbear to speak my mind,
Although to scandal ne'er inclined.
Well, I protest I never yet
To any man a letter writ;
It may be innocent, 'tis true,
But 'tis a thing I ne'er could do."

"Well," cried Philantha, "I protest
I almost think you are in jest,
For really, Miss, I cannot see
In this the breach of modesty;
With men we chat away our time,
And none regard it as a crime;
And where's the difference, if we write:
'Tis but our words in black and white.
I think we may, without offence,
Converse by pen with men of sense."

"Well, let us say no more about her,
But entertain ourselves without her;
No harm I meant, nor none I wish;
Miss, won't you drink another dish?"
"Not one drop more, I thank you, Madam."
"Here, take away the tea-things, Adam.
And bring the cards, and since we're met,
Pray let us make at whist a set."

Thus tea and scandal, cards and fashion,
Destroy the time of half the nation.

But, Sir, methinks 'tis very hard
From pen and ink to be debarred:

Are simple women only fit
To dress, to darn, to flower, or knit,
To mind the distaff, or the spit?

   Why are the needle and the pen
Thought incompatible by men?
May we not sometimes use the quill,
And yet be careful housewives still?
Why is it thought in us a crime
To utter common sense in rhyme?
Why must each rhymer be a wit?
Why marked with that loathed epithet?
For envy, hatred, scorn, or fear
To wit, you know, is often near.
Good-natured wit, polite, refined,
Which seeks to please, not pain the mind,
How rare to find! for O, how few
Have true and generous wit like you!
Your mind in different mould was cast,
To raise a character, not blast;
Pleased to encourage what I write,
And smile upon my humble flight.

Judy Little (contemporary)

꡴ℰ ℰ꡴

FROM *Comedy and the Woman Writer*

In fact, a major theme of women's humor is precisely the differences
between women's and men's lives and values.

Anita Loos (1893-1981)

~e e~

FROM *Kiss Hollywood Goodby*

I recall an occasion on the set where the camera was to cease grinding abruptly at a moment when Jean [Harlow] started to remove her jacket. But for some reason the boy in charge of the clap-board failed to give the signal to cut, so Jean "innocently" continued to take off her jacket, under which she was nude to the waist. Nudity was rarely seen in those days, and Jean's had the startling quality of an alabaster statue. Visitors on the set scarcely believed their eyes. The lighting crew almost fell out of the flies in shock. Wide-eyed in her "apology," Jean addressed the director. "I'm sorry, but nobody gave the order to cut."

Every MGM movie was taken out to one of the Los Angeles suburbs for a preview, Irving being the first producer to make use of audiences for constructive criticism. At each preview, postcards were distributed with a request for the audience to mail in suggestions. Irving paid small attention to professional critics, putting them down as impersonal theorists; but he read those postcards with the greatest respect, and, guided by them, he would re-edit the movie. In some cases no retakes at all were required but there were times when those amateur critics demanded as much as a third of the film to be reshot; a procedure which Irving never hesitated to follow. In those days MGM released a new picture every week: fifty-two movies a year, and every one a success— all due to the fact that Irving took the trouble to find out what pleased audiences and then gave it to them.

The initial preview of *Red-Headed Woman* took place in Glendale on that momentous date in June of 1932. Irving and I hid out in that suburban audience with our ears nervously tuned for its reaction. And during the first ten minutes we were deeply disturbed, for the audience was as confused as Jack Conway had been. It didn't know whether to laugh at our sex pirate or not, and, as every producer of comedy knows, a half-laugh is worse than none at all. Only after the movie was well along did the audience catch on and begin to enjoy the jokes.

There was no need to wait for postcards on that movie. Irving called me to his office the first thing next morning. "Look," said he, "I'd like you to contrive a prologue which will tip the audience off that the movie's a comedy." I proceeded to concoct a scene which showed Jean describing to her girl friend the all-abiding depth of her love for her married boss; as proof of which Jean revealed a photo of her loved one on a flashy dime-store garter.

Our second preview was in Pasadena and the movie started off with the garter scene. That did it! Laughs began at once and never ceased to mount to the end of the film.

When *Red-Headed Woman* was released, it instantly catapulted Jean Harlow into stardom. The picture enjoyed all sorts of fringe successes. It won the award of *Vanity Fair* magazine as the best film of the year; and the London office of MGM reported that the royal family kept a copy at Buckingham Palace for entertaining guests after dinner. Among its many distinctions, *Red-Headed Woman* made film history because it brought on more stringent censorship and caused massive difficulties to the industry for years to come. It outraged ladies' clubs throughout the land, but not because of any episode which might be termed salacious. It was because our heroine, the bad girl of whom all good husbands dream, ended her career as many such scalawags do, rich, happy, and respected, without ever having paid for her sins.

•

FROM *Gentlemen Prefer Blondes*

MARCH 20TH:

Mr. Eisman gets in tomorrow to be here in time for my birthday. So I thought it would really be delightful to have at least one good time before Mr. Eisman got in, so last evening I had some literary gentlemen in to spend the evening because Mr. Eisman always likes me to have literary people in and out of the apartment. I mean he is quite anxious for a girl to improve her mind and his greatest interest in me is because I always seem to want to improve my mind and not waste any time. And Mr. Eisman likes me to have what the French people call a "salo" which means that people all get together in the evening and improve their minds. So I invited all of the brainy gentlemen I could think up. So I thought up a gentleman who is the proffessor of all of the economics up at Columbia College, and the editor who is the famous editor of the New York Transcript and another gentleman who is a famous playright who writes very, very famous plays that are all about Life. I mean anybody would recognize his name but it always seems to slip my memory because all of we real friends of his only call him Sam. So Sam asked if he could bring a gentleman who writes novels from England, so I said yes, so he brought him. And then we all got together and I called up Gloria and Dorothy and the gentleman brought their own liquor. So of course the place was a wreck this morning and Lulu and I worked like proverbial dogs to get it cleaned up, but Heaven knows how long it will take to get the chandelier fixed.

MARCH 22ND:

Well my birthday has come and gone but it was really quite depressing. I mean it seems to me a gentleman who has a friendly interest in educating a girl like Gus Eisman, would want her to have the biggest square cut diamond in New York. I mean I must say I was quite disappointed when he came to the apartment with a little thing you could hardly see. So I told him I thought it was quite cute, but I had quite a headache and I had better stay in a dark room all day and I told him I would see him the next day, perhaps. Because even Lulu thought it was quite small and she said, if she was I, she really would do something definite and she said she always believed in the old addage, "Leave them while you're looking good." But he came in at dinner time with really a very very beautiful bracelet of square cut diamonds so I was quite cheered up. So then we had dinner at the Colony and we went to a show and supper at the Trocadero as usual whenever he is in town. But I will give him credit that he realized how small it was. I mean he kept talking about how bad business was and the button profession was full of bolshevicks who make nothing but trouble. Because Mr. Eisman feels that the country is really on the verge of the bolshevicks and I become quite worried. I mean if the bolshevicks do get in, there is only one gentleman who could handle them and that is Mr. D. W. Griffith. Because I will never forget when Mr. Griffith was directing Intolerance. I mean it was my last cinema just before Mr. Eisman made me give up my career and I was playing one of the girls that fainted at the battle when all of the gentlemen fell off the tower. And when I saw how Mr. Griffith handled all of those mobs in Intolerance I realized that he could do anything, and I really think that the government of America ought to tell Mr. Griffith to get all ready if the bolshevicks start to do it.

Well I forgot to mention that the English gentleman who writes novels seems to have taken quite an interest in me, as soon as he found

out that I was literary. I mean he has called up every day and I went to
tea twice with him. So he has sent me a whole complete set of books
for my birthday by a gentleman called Mr. Conrad. They all seem to be
about ocean travel although I have not had time to more than glance
through them. I have always liked novels about ocean travel ever since
I posed for Mr. Christie for the front cover of a novel about ocean travel
by McGrath because I always say that a girl never really looks as well as
she does on board a steamship, or even a yacht.

So the English gentleman's name is Mr. Gerald Lamson as those
who have read his novels would know. And he also sent me some of
his own novels and they all seem to be about middle age English gentlemen who live in the country over in London and seem to ride bicycles, which seems quite different from America, except at Palm Beach.
So I told Mr. Lamson how I write down all of my thoughts and he said
he knew I had something to me from the first minute he saw me and
when we become better acquainted I am going to let him read my diary.
I mean I even told Mr. Eisman about him and he is quite pleased.
Because of course Mr. Lamson is quite famous and it seems Mr. Eisman
has read all of his novels going to and fro on the trains and Mr. Eisman
is always anxious to meet famous people and take them to the Ritz to
dinner on Saturday night. But of course I did not tell Mr. Eisman that
I am really getting quite a little crush on Mr. Lamson, which I really
believe I am, but Mr. Eisman thinks my interest in him is more literary.

•

So Dorothy and I came to the Ritz and it is delightfully full of Americans. I mean you would really think it was New York because I always
think that the most delightful thing about traveling is to always be running into Americans and to always feel at home.

•

I mean I always seem to think that when a girl really enjoys being with
a gentleman, it puts her to quite a disadvantage and no real good can
come of it.

And when a girl walks around and reads all of the signs with all of
the famous historical names it really makes you hold your breath. Because when Dorothy and I went on a walk, we only walked a few blocks
but in only a few blocks we read all of the famous historical names, like
Coty and Cartier and I knew we were seeing something educational at
last and our whole trip was not a failure. I mean I really try to make
Dorothy get educated and have reverance. So the Place Vandome, if
you turn your back on a monument they have in the middle and look
up, you can see none other than Coty's sign. So I said to Dorothy, does

it not really give you a thrill to realize that that is the historical spot where Mr. Coty makes all the perfume? So then Dorothy said that she supposed Mr. Coty came to Paris and he smelled Paris and he realized that something had to be done. So Dorothy will really never have any reverance.

•

MAY 27TH:

Well finaly I broke down and Mr. Spoffard said that he thought a little girl like I, who was trying to reform the whole world was trying to do to much, especially beginning on a girl like Dorothy. So he said there was a famous doctor in Vienna called Dr. Froyd who could stop all of my worrying because he does not give a girl medicine but he talks you out of it by psychoanalysis. So yesterday he took me to Dr. Froyd. So Dr. Froyd and I had quite a long talk in the english landguage. So it seems that everybody seems to have a thing called inhibitions, which is when you want to do a thing and you do not do it. So then you dream about it instead. So Dr. Froyd asked me, what I seemed to dream about. So I told him that I never really dream about anything. I mean I use my brains so much in the day that at night they do not seem to do anything else but rest. So Dr. Froyd was very very surprized at a girl who did not dream about anything. So then he asked me all about my life. I mean he is very very sympathetic, and he seems to know how to draw a girl out quite a lot. I mean I told him things that I really would not even put in my diary. So then he seemed very very intreeged at a girl who always seemed to do everything she wanted to do. So he asked me if I really never wanted to do a thing that I did not do. For instance did I ever want to do a thing that was really vialent, for instance, did I ever want to shoot someone for instance. So then I said I had, but the bullet only went in Mr. Jennings lung and came right out again. So then Dr. Froyd looked at me and looked at me and he said he did not really think it was possible. So then he called in his assistance and he pointed at me and talked to his assistance quite a lot in the Viennese landguage. So then his assistance looked at me and looked at me and it really seems as if I was quite a famous case. So then Dr. Froyd said that all I needed was to cultivate a few inhibitions and get some sleep.

•

FROM *But Gentlemen Marry Brunettes*

. . . I gave Henry a supscription to the Book of the Month Club that tells you the book you have to read every month to make your individuality stand out. And it really is remarkable, because it makes over 50,000 people read the same book every month.

•

Dorothy said that if I wanted to meet High Brows, she was going to a literary party that was being held by George Jean Nathan at a place in Jersey that is noted for serving the kind of beer that is made without ether. And Mr. H. L. Mencken, Theadore Dreiser, Sherwood Anderson, Sinclare Lewis, Joseph Hergesheimer and Ernest Boyd would be there. So I said to Dorothy "If they are so literary, why do they go to a place like New Jersey, which is chiefly noted for being inartistic?" And the only reason that Dorothy could think up, was on account of the *Beer*. But I finally decided to go, because some of them do write quite well-read novels.

•

"[W]hen a genius falls in love with a lady genius," Tony says, "there is h—— to pay," because he cannot go off and have an affair and keep his mouth shut like a waiter, but he has to talk it over with his wife, and then they have to look it up in Psychoanalisis, and then they have to talk it all over with all of the other geniuses, and they really never get to any conclusion on the subjeck.

•

[T]his girl was a beautiful tall immitation Russian Countess of the vampire type. And she had black hair and black eyes and quite a desperate kind of an anti-Bolshivic expression, with a leaning towards long anteek ear rings. And Dorothy says you had to give her credit, because she had almost solved the problem of how to look well groomed without the use of water.

•

Dorothy is the cool type of temprament who quite frequently think that two is a crowd.

•

Charlie Breene's Mother had always been quite anxious for him to be married, and settle down, and drink in his own home instead of in night clubs, where everybody saw him disgrace the old family name.

•

So Dorothy says the first word she learned from the French was the word "Sal," which always goes before the mention of foreign names.

For instants, "Sal Americaines," "Sal Anglaises," "Sal Allemangs," "Sal Autruches," "Sal Italyens," etc.

"Moms" Mabley (1894–1975)

Stand-up routines

One day she was sitting on the porch and I said, "Granny, how old does a woman get before she don't want no more boyfriends?" (She was around 106 then.) She said, "I don't know, Honey. You have to ask somebody older than me." She said, "A woman is a woman as long as she lives; there's a certain time in a man's life when he has to go to a place called over the hill."

•

Now his sporting days are over, and his tail light is out,
And what used to be his sex appeal now is just his water spout.
So that's the story, alas and alack,
When he's squeezed out the toothpaste, he just can't squeeze it back.

So if we want to make whoopie, don't wait until—
We get—over the hill, over the hill.

•

My daddy liked him so I had to marry that old man. My daddy should have married him; he the one liked him (*laughter*). The nearest thing to death you ever seen in your life. His shadow weighed more than he did. He got out of breath threading a needle. And UGLY! He was so ugly he hurt my feelings. . . . He was so ugly he had to tip up on a glass to get a drink of water. . . . I thought he never would die. . . . I shouldn't talk like that about him though. He's dead. They say you shouldn't say nothing about the dead unless you can say something good. He's dead, GOOD!

Betty MacDonald (1908–1958)

~❧ ❧~

FROM *Onions in the Stew*

In fact, if I were to be absolutely truthful, and I wouldn't dare because we are so happily married, I would say that Don is a charter member, perhaps the founder, of that old Scottish brotherhood sworn always to bring bad news home even if it means mounting a rabid camel and riding naked over the Himalayas in winter.

•

FROM *The Egg and I*

I entered all of the soap contests in the vain hope that I would win $5000 and never have to use theirs or any other washing powder ever again as long as I lived. I failed to understand why farmers' wives were always talking about the sense of accomplishment they derived from doing a large washing. I would have had a lot more feeling of accomplishment lying in bed while someone else did the washing.

Patricia Mainard (contemporary)

~❧ ❧~

On the Politics of Housework

"I don't mind sharing the work, but you'll have to show me how to do it."

Meaning: I ask a lot of questions and you'll have to show me everything every time I do it because I don't remember so good. Also, don't try to sit down and read while I'm doing my jobs because I'm going to annoy the hell out of you until it's easier to do them yourself.

Mary Manley (1663-1724)

~⊱ ⊰~

FROM *Corinna*

The next house furnishes with a scene no less an object of satire: you will see there a young lady, who has long suffered under the barbarous persecution of her mother; she would persuade her she was a lunatic, and used her accordingly, till at length she has in reality made her not very far from one. As a proof of it, she is gone to live with her again; notwithstanding all her ill usage. We find the lady born with an elevated genius in a family of considerable circumstances, her father a chevalier. Corinna had a genteel, agreeable person, with an abundance of roving wit, superficial sparklings, without much conduct or any judgment. Her mother, a severe parsimonious lady, allowed her no advantages from education at home, or conversations abroad, so that Corinna bred herself, and took a bent not easily to be straightened. She had so much of my lady in her temper, as to be covetous; to which she has owed her misfortunes. The original of her mother's aversion for her, had its rise from an intercepted letter that Corinna wrote to a confidant; where complaining of the little diversions she met with at home, she summed up the family in these two lines.

> *A hen-pecked father, an imperious mother,*
> *A deaf sister, and a lame brother.*

From which she desired her to make a judgment of the agreeableness of her entertainment, and whether such company could have any part in her fondness. My lady was resolved to make good the character her daughter gave her, and used her with such tyranny and ill-nature, that Corinna could not support it. The chevalier her father was concerned at it; but according to what his daughter had said, durst not complain. The young lady made him a request, that she could not very easily expect to have had granted. My dear Papa, says the caressing Corinna, I know you do; as if you loved my mother, never contradicting her anything; but I am sure you love your girl, because you are uneasy at her contradicting me in every thing: you know, my dear Papa, that I'm an excellent housewife, my lady herself can't say against it; all she will allow me to be her daughter in, is, because I have a great deal of her preserving temper. I have no inclination to marry, rather an aversion that way; you have said my fortune shall be forty thousand crowns, this you would not scruple to pay down upon the nail, to any old curmudgeonly deformed abject monster, that shall hit my mother's foible. For if she says it must be done, there's no remedy; we must both consent, tho' my eternal quiet is sacrificed to her caprice. Such a one I'm informed she is in treaty with; old Adorno, you know him, my dear Papa; but what are his large possessions to me? I shall ever hate him; can your girl be happy with such unequal merit? When my lady has brought things to a conclusion, if you refuse your consent, it will make a perpetual quarrel; if you grant, then Corinna's mortified and undone. Therefore, my dear Papa, trust your poor girl for once; give me the possession of those crowns, I'll take a little house, two maidservants, a woman, one footman, and a coachman, and you shall see how distinguishingly I shall live. Resolving never to marry, you will have my house to be easy in, when my mother makes you otherwise at home. If you can be so obliging, you will render me eternally happy, and if I prophesy right, you'll have no occasion to repent of it. I will at least answer on my part, unless some unfortunate whirl of fate thrust between me and happiness, to poison that quiet I promise to my self; but however, this I may almost venture to be a sybil in, my disappointment shall never arise from love; and what young woman was ever yet known entirely miserable without it?

To be short, she gained her point, the chevalier made her absolute mistress of forty thousand crowns, and of her own conduct, settled her in a very pretty house, for which he paid the highest price, I mean his own life. My lady grew so outrageous to see her daughter entirely out of her dominion, that she never ceased a moment from teasing her husband; who so well knew her temper, and the ascendancy she had over him, by his love of ease, and refusing to exert himself, that he had put it out of his power to recall Corinna's fortune, as he certainly must have done, if possible. My lady would, however, take out her revenge upon his quiet, and so successfully pursued her point, that he fell a martyr to her tongue. A landmark for husbands, how they suffer the growth of authority in that tyrannical unruly member!

The gentleman who owned the house Corinna lived in, was a cadet of justice, with no large estate, but that was then the worst part of him, for his person was agreeable enough, his temper soft and amorous, exact in his dress, not wholly free from foppery in his manner; he could not see his fair tenant without a tenderness for her. She had many pretenders, and some admirers; but Don Alonzo, so was he called, proved to be the man. She had some relish of his conversation, had read a great deal, and much of love, but was never touched with anything that interfered with interest; she liked with her eyes, but her heart had still a true regard to the world, more than merit. However, finding her self mistress of an easy fortune, resolved against the marriage chain, and entirely at her own dispose, she waived too scrupulous an inquiry into what she owed her virtue, and determined not to deny her satisfaction for a circumstance. She had an idea of the joys of love from others; all who have ever felt it, speak with rapture of its delights. Those who can write but indifferently on other subjects, if once they have been truly agitated by it, write well of that. Her curiosity taught her to prove whether there was in it that pang of pleasure, as she had been made to believe; but the affair was a little nice, Don Alonzo had an honorable opinion of her virtue, and visited her accordingly. 'Twas true she was a virgin, but weary of being such, and yet she did not know how to exchange her condition, without making her self that slave a wife, as she called it. However, a lady, or her lover, must be very dull indeed, in the freedom of conversation, if one cannot give, and the other explain, their desires without speaking. Don Alonzo was perhaps as long again in guessing at her design, as another less prepossessed would have been; because he desired to marry her, and was very unwilling to believe but indifferently of a lady he had such an intention towards: he pressed hard upon the point, but she was deaf as storms on that side; but when he would urge the excess of his passion, the height of his respective flames, the ardor of his pains, his impatiency for happiness; she would smile him a gracious look of approbation, suffered him to kneel at her feet, to grasp her knees, to meet the softness of her eyes, with greater of his own; would lean her face to his, where (all coward, as love had made him) the kindling youth could not be so lost to native hope and instinct, as not to attempt the hanging cherry of her lip, that seemed to stoop for pressure. But oh! which was greater, his astonishment or delight? when he found that an action which he feared had merited death, was feelingly received, and repayed with blushing usury; his heart throbbed as if 'twould leave his breast; he felt inestimable pleasures, between his fears and his desires. Her sparkling eyes cast a day of hope around him, to animate his doubting love. The virgin-guard of awful modesty was willingly thrown by, she left the dazzled youth no time to pause or recollect, but answering all his eager sighs, his kisses and desires, she leaned upon a bed was near her, whither the amorous youth in heat of ecstasy pursued her. Then was his time (he thought) to gain the warmed, the yielding maid's consent; he pressed for happiness, he pressed to marry her—to lengthen out his part of bliss, and make it durable as great—Corinna paused—and yawned upon the importunity.—Have you ever seen water thrown upon aspiring flames, that rise to cover all they meet with ruin? such, and so damped, seemed the burnings of the defeated maid. At length obliged to answer his repeated proposition, emboldened as he grew by that degree of favor she had lately shown him;—Why, ay, Alonzo— answered she—'tis true—marriage is indeed for life,—but who can tell what sort of a life?—Do you think we can't love without marrying? at least it seems rational to us that have our understanding about us, to try those nearer intimacies, which are said, either to ravish or disgust! to make us fonder or more indifferent. Whatever false notion the world or you may have of virtue, I must confess I should be very loathe to bind my self to a man for ever, before I was sure I should like him for a night; I don't take you to be so dull, that I need explain my self any further. I have hinted to you my inclinations, I think it is now your business to convince me of the extent of yours.

Don Alonzo, who had an early taint in his composition of self-conceit, did not fear that possession could abate of her inclination towards his fine person; he rather believed it would heighten it, a received maxim, that women become fonder of whomsoever they admit to those intimacies. He did not doubt his charms, nor his good fortune, by a mistaken notion, concluding it would give him a right over the dishonored fair, and that then she would be glad to marry him with the soonest, at least if she should happen to be pregnant.

But he had to deal with a lady infinitely more politic; she had gratified her curiosity, and became dotingly fond of his conversation, perpetually teasing and sending after him when he was never so little a time absent from her; but still she would not, she was too wise, or too covetous, to marry him. A neighboring lady, whom he had introduced to her intimacy, pressed her hard on Don Alonzo's part, to make his happiness lawful, representing a thousand things to engage; among the rest, his vast respect, nay, adoration for her person. Corinna said, she was indeed obliged to him; but, Madam, she pursued, what should I marry him for, to make him the master of my self and fortune, only for a name? I love his company, whilst he is thus obliging, insinuating, careful of displeasing, tender, complaisant, amorous and ardent; but these qualities, so conspicuous and valuable in a lover, will be lost, or vanish in the husband: neglectful, sullen, perhaps morose; all his attributes will be inverted; he will then expect to be pleased, 'twill be my turn to

oblige and obey, at least I must endeavor it, and perhaps without suc-
ceeding, I shall find him positive, arbitrary, cold, as if he never had had
any fire, or that I had lost the art of kindling it; tho' I must confess to
you, the defect of my own constitution, I should not stick with him for
that trifle, because whatever lovers may talk of joys, I find there's nothing
in't. If I were to judge of all ladies by my self, I should think it lay
chiefly in the head; therefore must be mad to give up my possessions
for nothing, to lose all that is endearing in Don Alonzo's conversation,
and not be able to find my account any other way: no, no, madam, I'm
wiser than that comes to. I am mistress of my own liberty and fortune,
I shall put on none of his fetters, since all I shall be entitled to by 'em
is, clearing his mortgaged estate, and paying his other debts.

Mean time, her mother (thro' some extravagant sparklings in the
daughter's unheeded conversation, with her intimates, who ridiculed a
wit they did not understand) failed not to represent her in all companies
as lunatic; she thought if she could but succeed, her forty thousand
crowns would fall to her share: the truly covetous have never enough!
The charge of keeping her under those circumstances would be insignificant; at length she proceeded so far, as to have her seized in her own
house, by doctors and nurses, and put under the operation. Don Alonzo
rescued her, they had a trial at law, where Corinna's woman deposed,
that for a length of time together, she had given her a powder every
morning in her chocolate, that my lady had furnished her with, pernicious to health, and capable, by slow degrees, of ruining the strongest
constitution. Don Alonzo pleaded merit from the service he had done
her, and urged her to marry him, which perhaps she might have been
brought to, since the name and quality of a husband, was all that was
left to screen her from her mother's malicious designing pretenses, if an
unlucky story had not reached her ear. It seems, during the time of her
persecution, Don Alonzo had the reputation of courting a lady only for
his pleasure, who made no scruple to receive his visits and his presents;
but yet at the long run refused him her favors: he was out of patience
with the jilting fair one, and as the scandalous chronicle recites, having
one day found a lone opportunity, he very robustly gave her two or
three sound blows that stunned her and threw her on the ground; where,
as 'tis reported, he took the opportunity of accomplishing his desire. The
cadet so used to do justice to others, would not refuse it to himself; for,
as he said, his presents had bought the lady; the favors she had to bestow
were his, and he would take 'em where-ever he had an opportunity.

This ruined him with Corinna, who tho' she had found nothing
in't, was not very willing another should. Her mother got her again, and

kept her a prisoner at a house in the country, whence to free her self, she did the thing in the world she had least inclination for, and that was to marry the son of the family she was in, a pert young man, without the ballast of understanding. He might have made himself and Corinna happy; but with weak heads, good fortune has fumes that very often turns the brain. They were forced to submit to another trial at law, to acquit her from being a lunatic; one (no undiverting) circumstance, inclined the judge to give sentence in her favor. A gentleman of the long robe, named Vagellius, was eminently against her.

> ————One reputed long,
> *For strength of lungs and pliancy of tongue:*
> *Which way he pleases, he can mold a cause,*
> *The worst has merits, and the best has flaws.*
> *Five pieces makes a criminal to day,*
> *And ten to morrow takes the stain away:*
> *Whatever he affirms is undenied, &c.*

To be short, nothing can be added to the satirist's excellent description of him, but a word or two of his person: where we find a studied elegance of dress, and stiffness of behavior, that distinguishes him as much as his tongue. This spruce, affected, not unhandsome lawyer, had made the overture of his fair person to Corinna. You have heard that only necessity could determine her resolutions (against her inclinations) to marry at all, and therefore when she was not under that necessity, she refused Vagellius, who as little in his revenge, as he was great in rhetoric, engaged himself of her mother's side, and said all that could be said, to convince the judge she was a lunatic. Corinna begged his lordship to hear her but one word upon that head, related the circumstances of Vagellius's courtship, and then appealed to his lordship's judgment, if they could rationally condemn her for a lunatic, who had been so wise as to refuse to marry him, with his little share of real estate, and his large portion of children, for he had six. This determined the court of her side; she was discharged, and left to her own and her husband's management, who in a little time behaved himself unworthily to her, kept two women for his pleasure, in her very eye, and rioted out the income of her fortune in such blamable diversions, till he had quite wearied her out, and forced her to take up with her mother's house, to revenge herself upon her husband. He quickly, upon her desertion, fell into a want of money, and failing to carry her off, when he came to my lady's to demand her, he fell into a lunacy; the first effects of it was fatal to

his friend, whom he had brought to assist him; for, without any prov-
ocation, as they were walking, he let him go a little before, and then
discharging a pistol behind, shot him into the body, of which he died.
He also let fly another at the first person that he saw in the road. He
was seized, and brought to justice; but his madness saved his life. He is
now under cure, and Corinna buried and forgotten in her mother's
persecutions; a lady, who bating some circumstances, deserved better
fortune, all her misery and wrongs being derived from her that should,
by nature and duty, have done her utmost to shelter her from being
wronged by others.

Katherine Mansfield (1888-1923)

~ԑ ঙ~

The Singing Lesson

With despair—cold, sharp despair—buried deep in her heart like a
wicked knife, Miss Meadows, in cap and gown and carrying a little
baton, trod the cold corridors that led to the music hall. Girls of all ages,
rosy from the air, and bubbling over with that gleeful excitement that
comes from running to school on a fine autumn morning, hurried,
skipped, fluttered by; from the hollow classrooms came a quick drum-
ming of voices; a bell rang; a voice like a bird cried, "Muriel." And
then there came from the staircase a tremendous knock-knock-knock-
ing. Some one had dropped her dumbbells.

The Science Mistress stopped Miss Meadows.

"Good mor-ning," she cried, in her sweet, affected drawl. "Isn't it
cold? It might be win-ter."

Miss Meadows, hugging the knife, stared in hatred at the Science
Mistress. Everything about her was sweet, pale, like honey. You would
not have been surprised to see a bee caught in the tangles of that yellow
hair.

"It is rather sharp," said Miss Meadows, grimly.

The other smiled her sugary smile.

"You look fro-zen," said she. Her blue eyes opened wide; there
came a mocking light in them. (Had she noticed anything?)

"Oh, not quite as bad as that," said Miss Meadows, and she gave the Science Mistress, in exchange for her smile, a quick grimace and passed on. . . .

Forms Four, Five, and Six were assembled in the music hall. The noise was deafening. On the platform, by the piano, stood Mary Beazley, Miss Meadows' favourite, who played accompaniments. She was turning the music stool. When she saw Miss Meadows she gave a loud, warning "Sh-sh! girls!" and Miss Meadows, her hands thrust in her sleeves, the baton under her arm, strode down the centre aisle, mounted the steps, turned sharply, seized the brass music stand, planted it in front of her, and gave two sharp raps with her baton for silence.

"Silence, please! Immediately!" and, looking at nobody, her glance swept over that sea of coloured flannel blouses, with bobbing pink faces and hands, quivering butterfly hair-bows, and music-books outspread. She knew perfectly well what they were thinking. "Meady is in a wax." Well, let them think it! Her eyelids quivered; she tossed her head, defying them. What could the thoughts of those creatures matter to some one who stood there bleeding to death, pierced to the heart, to the heart, by such a letter—

. . . "I feel more and more strongly that our marriage would be a mistake. Not that I do not love you. I love you as much as it is possible for me to love any woman, but, truth to tell, I have come to the conclusion that I am not a marrying man, and the idea of settling down fills me with nothing but—" and the word "disgust" was scratched out lightly and "regret" written over the top.

Basil! Miss Meadows stalked over to the piano. And Mary Beazley, who was waiting for this moment, bent forward; her curls fell over her cheeks while she breathed, "Good morning, Miss Meadows," and she motioned towards rather than handed to her mistress a beautiful yellow chrysanthemum. This little ritual of the flower had been gone through for ages and ages, quite a term and a half. It was as much part of the lesson as opening the piano. But this morning, instead of taking it up, instead of tucking it into her belt while she leant over Mary and said, "Thank you, Mary. How very nice! Turn to page thirty-two," what was Mary's horror when Miss Meadows totally ignored the chrysanthemum, made no reply to her greeting, but said in a voice of ice, "Page fourteen, please, and mark the accents well."

Staggering moment! Mary blushed until the tears stood in her eyes, but Miss Meadows was gone back to the music stand; her voice rang through the music hall.

"Page fourteen. We will begin with page fourteen. 'A Lament.' Now, girls, you ought to know it by this time. We shall take it all together; not in parts, all together. And without expression. Sing it, though, quite simply, beating time with the left hand."

She raised the baton; she tapped the music stand twice. Down came Mary on the opening chord; down came all those left hands, beating the air, and in chimed those young, mournful voices:

> *Fast! Ah, too Fast Fade the Ro-o-ses of Pleasure;*
> *Soon Autumn yields unto Wi-i-nter Drear.*
> *Fleetly! Ah, Fleetly Mu-u-sic's Gay Measure*
> *Passes away from the Listening Ear.*

Good Heavens, what could be more tragic than that lament! Every note was a sigh, a sob, a groan of awful mournfulness. Miss Meadows lifted her arms in the wide gown and began conducting with both hands. " . . . I feel more and more strongly that our marriage would be a mistake. . . ." she beat. And the voices cried: *Fleetly! Ah, Fleetly.* What could have possessed him to write such a letter! What could have led up to it! It came out of nothing. His last letter had been all about a fumed-oak bookcase he had bought for "our" books, and a "natty little hall stand" he had seen, "a very neat affair with a carved owl on a bracket, holding three hat-brushes in its claws." How she had smiled at that! So like a man to think one needed three hat-brushes! *From the Listening Ear,* sang the voices.

"Once again," said Miss Meadows. "But this time in parts. Still without expression." *Fast! Ah, too Fast.* With the gloom of the contraltos added, one could scarcely help shuddering. *Fade the Roses of Pleasure.* Last time he had come to see her, Basil had worn a rose in his buttonhole. How handsome he had looked in that bright blue suit, with that dark red rose! And he knew it, too. He couldn't help knowing it. First he stroked his hair, then his moustache; his teeth gleamed when he smiled.

"The headmaster's wife keeps on asking me to dinner. It's a perfect nuisance. I never get an evening to myself in that place."

"But can't you refuse?"

"Oh, well, it doesn't do for a man in my position to be unpopular."

Music's Gay Measure, wailed the voices. The willow trees, outside the high, narrow windows, waved in the wind. They had lost half their leaves. The tiny ones that clung wriggled like fishes caught on a line. " . . . I am not a marrying man. . . ." The voices were silent; the piano waited.

"Quite good," said Miss Meadows, but still in such a strange, stony tone that the younger girls began to feel positively frightened. "But now that we know it, we shall take it with expression. As much expression as you can put into it. Think of the words, girls. Use your imaginations. *Fast! Ah, too Fast,*" cried Miss Meadows. "That ought to break out—a loud, strong *forte*—a lament. And then in the second line, *Winter Drear,* make that *Drear* sound as if a cold wind were blowing through it. *Dreear!*" said she so awfully that Mary Beazley, on the music stool, wriggled her spine. "The third line should be one crescendo. *Fleetly! Ah, Fleetly Music's Gay Measure.* Breaking on the first word of the last line, *Passes.* And then on the word, *Away,* you must begin to die . . . to fade . . . until *The Listening Ear* is nothing more than a faint whisper. . . . You can slow down as much as you like almost on the last line. Now, please."

Again the two light taps; she lifted her arms again. *Fast! Ah, too Fast.* " . . . and the idea of settling down fills me with nothing but disgust—" Disgust was what he had written. That was as good as to say their engagement was definitely broken off. Broken off! Their engagement! People had been surprised enough that she had got engaged. The Science Mistress would not believe it at first. But nobody had been as surprised as she. She was thirty. Basil was twenty-five. It had been a miracle, simply a miracle, to hear him say, as they walked home from church that very dark night, "You know, somehow or other, I've got fond of you." And he had taken hold of the end of her ostrich feather boa. *Passes away from the Listening Ear.*

"Repeat! Repeat!" said Miss Meadows. "More expression, girls! Once more!"

Fast! Ah, too Fast. The older girls were crimson; some of the younger ones began to cry. Big spots of rain blew against the windows, and one could hear the willows whispering, " . . . not that I do not love you. . . ."

"But, my darling, if you love me," thought Miss Meadows, "I don't mind how much it is. Love me as little as you like." But she knew he didn't love her. Not to have cared enough to scratch out the word "disgust," so that she couldn't read it! *Soon Autumn yields unto Winter Drear.* She would have to leave the school, too. She could never face the Science Mistress or the girls after it got known. She would have to disappear somewhere. *Passes away.* The voices began to die, to fade, to whisper . . . to vanish. . . .

Suddenly the door opened. A little girl in blue walked fussily up the aisle, hanging her head, biting her lips, and twisting the silver bangle on her red little wrist. She came up the steps and stood before Miss Meadows.

"Well, Monica, what is it?"

"Oh, if you please, Miss Meadows," said the little girl, gasping, "Miss Wyatt wants to see you in the mistress's room."

"Very well," said Miss Meadows. And she called to the girls, "I shall put you on your honour to talk quietly while I am away." But they were too subdued to do anything else. Most of them were blowing their noses.

The corridors were silent and cold; they echoed to Miss Meadows' steps. The head mistress sat at her desk. For a moment she did not look up. She was as usual disentangling her eye-glasses, which had got caught in her lace tie. "Sit down, Miss Meadows," she said very kindly. And then she picked up a pink envelope from the blotting-pad. "I sent for you just now because this telegram has come for you."

"A telegram for me, Miss Wyatt?"

Basil! He had committed suicide, decided Miss Meadows. Her hand flew out, but Miss Wyatt held the telegram back a moment. "I hope it's not bad news," she said, so more than kindly. And Miss Meadows tore it open.

"Pay no attention to letter, must have been mad, bought hat-stand to-day—Basil," she read. She couldn't take her eyes off the telegram.

"I do hope it's nothing very serious," said Miss Wyatt, leaning forward.

"Oh, no, thank you, Miss Wyatt," blushed Miss Meadows. "It's nothing bad at all. It's"—and she gave an apologetic little laugh—"it's from my *fiancé* saying that . . . saying that—" There was a pause. "I *see*," said Miss Wyatt. And another pause. Then—"You've fifteen minutes more of your class, Miss Meadows, haven't you?"

"Yes, Miss Wyatt." She got up. She half ran towards the door.

"Oh, just one minute, Miss Meadows," said Miss Wyatt. "I must say I don't approve of my teachers having telegrams sent to them in school hours, unless in case of very bad news, such as death," explained Miss Wyatt, "or a very serious accident, or something to that effect. Good news, Miss Meadows, will always keep, you know."

On the wings of hope, of love, of joy, Miss Meadows sped back to the music hall, up the aisle, up the steps, over to the piano.

"Page thirty-two, Mary," she said, "page thirty-two," and, picking up the yellow chrysanthemum, she held it to her lips to hide her smile. Then she turned to the girls, rapped with her baton: "Page thirty-two, girls. Page thirty-two."

> *We come here To-day with Flowers o'erladen,*
> *With Baskets of Fruit and Ribbons to boot,*
> *To-oo Congratulate. . . .*

"Stop! Stop!" cried Miss Meadows. "This is awful. This is dreadful." And she beamed at her girls. "What's the matter with you all? Think, girls, think of what you're singing. Use your imaginations. *With Flowers o'erladen. Baskets of Fruit and Ribbons to boot.* And *Congratulate.*" Miss Meadows broke off. "Don't look so doleful, girls. It ought to sound warm, joyful, eager. *Congratulate.* Once more. Quickly. All together. Now then!"

And this time Miss Meadows' voice sounded over all the other voices—full, deep, glowing with expression.

Merrill Markoe (contemporary)

~⅊ ⅋~

FROM *What the Dogs Have Taught Me*

Put on alert by my foolproof "dumb-movie sensory system"—a highly developed sixth sense that reminds me to stay away from movies with titles containing numbers or accompanied by the words *produced by Simpson and Bruckheimer*—I had been purposely avoiding *Pretty Woman.* But *Pretty Woman* was the thing that wouldn't die. I kept seeing ads that called it "the feel-good hit of the season." And then it was rereleased so everyone would have a chance to see it *again.* And then came a barrage of new ads proclaiming that at long last the movie was available on videocassette.

Finally, I started to hear that ten-year-old girls were watching it over and over, and this was when I began to get concerned, because my own ten-year-old-girl fantasy fixations were the early starting point for a whole lot of trouble later on. So I gave in and saw the darn thing, and my short review is this: It really sucks and it pissed me off.

To recap briefly, the amazingly appealing Julia Roberts plays the most improbable hooker in the history of unlikely TV and movie hookers. She might as well have been portraying the Bean Goddess from Neptune, so unhookerlike is her character. (In fact, what we have here is the first true Disney hooker! The story could almost have been serialized on the old *Mickey Mouse Club* with Annette in the starring role!)

Anyway, here's the hooker dressed like Rocker Barbie, leading a life just a tad less brutal, alienating or problematic than that of any cosmetics counter saleswoman when she encounters repressed, handsome, egomaniac john Richard Gere. This man has just been dumped by his girlfriend because, she says, she is "sick of being at his beck and call." So he decides to hire this (wink, wink) *hooker* to be his temporary social companion. And as it turns out, not only does she not have any kind of a "beck and call" problem, something about this situation causes her to blossom, flower and *thrive!* Even though he never offers her anything in the way of emotional interaction, that doesn't affect her *incredible joie de vivre!* Because she's just so darned full of this drug-free, childlike wonderment at life! Wow! A hotel lobby! Yikes! Room service! A hat! A dress! A *really big* bathtub! Oh, my God! Pinch me! I'm dreaming!

Because this is a movie, she pretty soon falls in love with this guy. And now, when he offers to *pay* her to stay, she is hurt and packs up to leave. "It's just not good enough anymore," she says to him. "I want *the whole fairy tale!!*" (And I'm thinking to myself, *Excuse me, but where was I when they rewrote the fairy tale to start, "Once upon a time, in a land far, far away, there was this hooker . . ."?*)

Anyway, these are the easy, lighthearted reasons to hate the movie. That it is evil and loathsome to glorify hooking and sociopathic men is kind of obvious. But the ending was the final straw. Moved to the kind of white-knight behavior that I have never seen exhibited, even in the name of love, by a human male of any race, creed or religion anywhere except in a movie, the Richard Gere character shows up at the last minute to *rescue* Julia Roberts and bring us to the super-disgusting last line. As he lifts her into his arms, she says, "And now I'll rescue you right back."

That was when the uncontrollable barfing started for me. Because I knew that the guys who made this movie were all patting themselves on the back, thinking that the line added some kind of Nineties contemporary woman's egalitarian spin to the proceedings. I really got revved up, thinking about the insanity of that mainstay of Hollywood romantic plot devices: *rescuing*.

(You: "Gee, Merrill is certainly very grumpy today. I wonder if she's getting enough potassium and magnesium.")

It's certainly a time-honored tradition to have women be the *rescued* party. (Cinderella and Sleeping Beauty spring to mind.) But the fantasies that had the tightest hold on me involved the woman as the *rescuer*. In my preteen years I went repeatedly to see *West Side Story* because I had the hots for all the (wink, wink) teenage gang members. They were the first versions of a fantasy prototype that I have always found a real winner—I speak of the wounded, brooding, tough-guy loner with the mysterious tragic past, running, ever running, from unjust circumstances, his sad eyes the only clue to the horrible lack of love that has driven him to unfortunate acts of rage, rebellion and self-destruction. Now he is hurt, and dangerous to everyone except that one woman whose love might make a difference. It is she he can come to in the middle of the night as he hides from the "authorities" who have wronged him. Together they will walk through the turbulent weather, joint observers of life's cruelties, until he kisses her with such ferocity that she has no choice but to devote her very being to trying to save him.

Various versions of this scenario accompanied me through my girlhood in the form of James Dean, Clint Eastwood or even the young Bob Dylan; then, more recently, Sean Penn, Gary Oldman or Johnny Depp. (Girlhood nothing; I was mesmerized *last weekend* by the several male cast members who have been doing this dance on *Twin Peaks.*) And that got me to thinking, *Who are these guys playing? Who are these wounded, brooding guys in real life?* Finally, I realized that wounded, brooding loners in real life are the emotionally crippled, paranoid, narcissistic guys with drug and alcohol and commitment problems who drove the woman of the Eighties into a frenzy, writing, reading and buying that endless series of bestselling books with the long, annoying titles. I refer, of course, to the *Men Who Hate Women and the Women Who Love Them*, etc., genre.

Just about all these books are devoted to the premise that rescuing is not only futile, it is *impossible* (because someone can rescue himself, but no one can rescue another person). These books contain chapter after chapter of advice on how to rebuild your decimated life and your shattered self-esteem—just two of the cute little by-products of your full-out rescuing attempt. In fact, in the past decade we have become a nation of Twelve-Step Programs (AA, ACOA, CODA, etc.), each set up to instruct participants in how to regain their sanity and stop rescuing.

(You again: "Gee, Merrill really *is* grumpy today. I'll bet she isn't getting enough vitamin B complex. Someone should check.")

If the characters in *Pretty Woman* had lived real people's lives, here is how the story would have continued after the movie. Longing to feel more legitimate, the Julia Roberts character would succeed in getting the Richard Gere character to marry her. And, feeling more legitimized, she would begin to build a sense of identity, power and self-worth, all of which would become threatening to the Richard Gere character even though she would be imagining that it made her more appealing. After all, the only reason she never moved in this direction before was her unfortunate social circumstances. Of course, she also loses interest in being at his beck and call, which is maybe when she notices that he has begun to withdraw emotionally. But who can blame him? He feels hurt and betrayed. This is not the woman he married. And so he secretly starts searching for another naive, joie-de-vivre-driven, beck-and-call girl to serve his needs. In other words, if I am not mistaken, *Pretty Woman* turns into the story of Donald and Ivana Trump and Marla Maples!

Well! Now that I have proven how pernicious this whole rescuing business can be (in fact, it's even at the core of that most pathetic of female situations—waiting for the unhappily trapped married man), then what, oh what, you are probably wondering, are we to put in its place? How do we rebuild our romantic fantasies? Well, I think there is a solution. And, as they say on the sitcoms, "It's kinda crazy but it just might work."

Here it is: Entertain the notion that the rescuing isn't what we crave. After all, there's a lot of *work*. Couldn't it be the theatrical behavior? All of those appealing facial expressions and great moves are being totally wasted on the wrong bunch of guys. And so I call for a national retraining program in which pleasant, good-natured accountants and management trainees can learn to pout and brood and wear leather jackets. One class could be devoted to the dramatic uses of staring into nature—the pounding surf, the driving rain, the howling wind. Learn which seasonal precipitate is right for you.

In other words, if we could just get the good, well-intentioned but dowdy guys to take all this over, it would be a whole lot easier and more doable than trying to get women like me to stop falling in love with the screwed-up, weaselly guys who use that behavior to such good effect.

Well, it's just an idea. I'm off now to see about some kind of meditation plan and maybe consult with a dietician.

Penny Marshall (contemporary)

On Acting

I remember once being in an acting class and watching a girl do a scene. She was crying through the scene and I thought it had some of the funniest words I'd ever heard in my life, but this girl had tears running down her face: And then I actually read the words and I said, "This is a *funny* monologue." I don't know—maybe she was doing an exercise on how to cry. So I waited a respectable amount of time so people would forget she did the scene crying and I came in and got laughs. So anything can be played either way. It's the way you envision it.

Judith Martin (1938-   )

~≈ ≈~

FROM *Miss Manners' Guide to Excruciatingly Correct Behavior*

SAYING NO: SILENCE AS A SOCIAL SKILL

Quick: What are the correct answers to the following questions?

1. "It was so nice of you to ask us for the weekend. We can't, but you know who would love to? Rhino's first wife is getting married this summer, so she can't take the kids, and frankly Rhino and I have got to be alone now—I don't count Kristen; she's only two—if we're going to salvage anything. Anyway, his kids are big now, you'd be surprised, and they're dying to come down and spend some time there. They won't be any trouble because they'll bring their own sleeping bags and I told them they have to get summer jobs, and when they do, I'm sure they'll want to get their own place. They're great kids; you'll love them; and they think this is so great of you. OK?"

2. "My twins are in your son's class and we're asking all the mothers to help out. It's about the school dance. They need a strobe light and a new amplifier, and the school simply will not supply them, and we thought of asking the kids to pitch in but some of them are, you know, uh, well, scholarship students and it might not be fair to ask them, if you know what I mean. Anyway, we decided to have a raffle, and each mother just has to sell twenty tickets so it's not much work for anyone. You could sell them around your neighborhood in no time, or some people who can't be bothered are just buying them all themselves. OK?"

3. "Are you and Buckley free for dinner three weeks from Wednesday? Marvelous—we have some darling friends you'll just love. When they heard you were a tax lawyer, they were thrilled, because they have

some kind of terrible tax situation they'd love to ask you about, and of course everyone is dying to meet Buckley. We're counting on his putting in a good word for us on this secret project we'll tell you all about at dinner. Is seven thirty all right?"

Notice that Miss Manners has asked for *correct* answers. She can hear all those answers that sprang to your minds, through inspiration, assertiveness training, or self-defense, and they are not *correct* answers. What is more, they are not answers that many people would say to friends or acquaintances. It's all very well to talk about the need for saying "No"; but the real need in the lives of civilized people is to say, "No, thank you."

Because of this lack, people who refuse to be rude—and bless them for that—find themselves answering either, "Well, we'd love to, but we think Noah might be getting appendicitis then and there's been an electrical fire in our family room and I find my time is so limited now that I have to keep reporting to my probation officer"; or, what is worse, they answer, "Yes."

The correct answers are simple. All they require, to be both gracious and effective, is that one close one's mouth after saying them and not continue talking. The correct answer to any of the initial questions is "Oh, I'm so terribly sorry, I just can't." Got that? In most cases, that is enough. However, if anyone asks why not, the correct answer is "Because I'm afraid it's just impossible."

The sentences are not difficult to pronounce, but many people find the silence following them impossible to accomplish. They fill it by running off at the mouth with increasingly complicated and farfetched excuses until the only hope of wiping out all their dreadful lies is to turn themselves in and do what was asked of them. They would do well to practice shutting up. It is a social grace few can afford to be without. In the meantime, Miss Manners has an exercise for intermediate students. They may say, "I have to check with my husband (wife, broker, boss, dog's baby-sitter, house plants)" and then call back later and try again to give the correct answer.

·

THE SILENT TYPE

Dear Miss Manners:

My boyfriend is very shy, and we never seem to have anything to talk about. On the phone—he calls me every night before bedtime— the silences are awful. Can you suggest something I could say to him?

Gentle Reader:
"Do you have any nice friends?"

•

NOMENCLATURE

Dear Miss Manners:
What can you do after accidentally calling your present lover by your former lover's name?
Gentle Reader:
Seek a future lover. Such a mistake is easy to do and impossible to undo. Why do you think the term "darling" was invented?

•

WHEN THE LADY PAYS

Dear Miss Manners:
As a businessman, how do I allow a businesswoman to pay for my lunch?
Gentle Reader:
With credit card or cash, as she prefers.

•

HAIR

Dear Miss Manners:
I cannot understand why the hair stylists of this world won't do anything about this long sloppy hair on girls and letting it go on forever. We always have to see them brushing their hair away from their faces and having to eat with them in diners, etc., it's a sickening sight.
Gentle Reader:
It will take Miss Manners a moment to collect herself before answering you. She is shocked and upset and even has a tear or two to brush away from *her* face before she can trust herself to think. You see, Miss Manners has very long hair herself. She doesn't wear it down at her age, but she always thought it proper for young girls to do so, and never worried that hair stylists or other free-lance critics, such as yourself, were policing the streets, looking for visual offenders. If you must, please try to remember: It's the girls who bob their hair who are fast.

•

ANNOUNCING DIVORCE

Dear Miss Manners:

What is the correct way of announcing that I am divorced? Do I send out cards (and if so, how are they properly worded)? Can I give a party? Hire a billboard? Shout it from the housetops? I don't want to do anything in poor taste, but I am delighted with my new freedom and want to let people know about it.

Gentle Reader:

This will come as a shock, but society's laws about which events one may rejoice over and which one may not do not necessarily correspond to the true feelings of the participant. For example, if your nasty, crotchety, quarrelsome, critical old great-uncle dies and leaves you a fortune, you must try to look solemn, if not actually grieved. If your fourteen-year-old daughter is having a baby, you are supposed to act delighted. You may call this hypocrisy. As a matter of fact, Miss Manners calls it hypocrisy, too. The difference is probably that you don't consider hypocrisy one of the social graces, and she does. In any case, one does not brag about a divorce, however much personal satisfaction it may bring one. There is no formal announcement. Anything along the lines of hiring an airplane to write it in the sky is considered to be in poor taste.

Naturally, you want everyone to know. Miss Manners appreciates that. If you can write notes announcing a change of name or address and explain in them that it is a result of your recent divorce, that is a solution. You may even give a party, provided that the excuse is not the divorce itself, but a result of it, such as a party to show off your newly redecorated house, even if the redecoration is only the fact that you have put your clothes in both bedroom closets after emptying one of them of someone else's clothes.

Failing this pretext, you must be alert for opportunities of working the news into conversation. This is not difficult. If someone says, "Tell me, how have you been?" You may answer, "Well, I think everything is settled down now, since the divorce." Miss Manners urges you, for the sake of propriety, to keep a straight face.

•

A GAY INTRODUCTION

Dear Miss Manners:

What am I supposed to say when I am introduced to a homosexual "couple"?

Gentle Reader:
"How do you do?" "How do you do?"

Harriet Martineau (1802-1876)

❧ ❧

On Marriage

Any one must see at a glance that if men and women marry those whom they do not love, they must love those whom they do not marry.

Bobbie Ann Mason (1942-   )

❧ ❧

FROM *Love Life*

In bed, he watches his wife reading. Nancy zooms through a new novel from the library almost every evening. The covers of the books picture sexy women sprawling in the clutches of virile, dark-haired men. The women wear long, lowcut dresses, with their breasts bulging out the tops. Nancy calls the books "Bodice Busters," and for a long time Dean thought that was a brand name. Nancy is wittier than he gives her credit for.

•

"My brother couldn't get in the Army because he had high arches, so he became a Holy Roller preacher instead. He used to cuss like the devil, but now he's preaching up a storm." Jane looks Mrs. Bush straight in the eyes. She's not old but looks old. If she died, maybe Jane could get her job.

"My cousin was a Holy Roller," says Mrs. Bush. "He got sanctified and then got hit by a truck the next day."

Phyllis McGinley (1905-1978)

~≈ ✤~

Why, Some of My Best Friends
Are Women!

I learned in my credulous youth
    That women are shallow as fountains.
Women make lies out of truth
    And out of a molehill their mountains.
Women are giddy and vain,
    Cold-hearted or tiresomely tender;
Yet, nevertheless, I maintain
    I dote on the feminine gender.

For the female of the species may be deadlier than the male
But she can make herself a cup of coffee without reducing
The entire kitchen to a shambles.

Perverse though their taste in cravats
    Is deemed by their lords and their betters,
They know the importance of hats
    And they write you the news in their letters.
Their minds may be lighter than foam,
    Or altered in haste and in hurry,
But they seldom bring company home
    When you're warming up yesterday's curry.

And when lovely woman stoops to folly,
She does not invariably come in at four A.M.
Singing Sweet Adeline.

Oh, women are frail and they weep.
    They are recklessly given to scions.
But, wakened unduly from sleep,
    They are milder than tigers or lions.

Women hang clothes on their pegs
    Nor groan at the toil and the trouble.

Women have rather nice legs
    And chins that are guiltless of stubble.
Women are restless, uneasy to handle,
But when they are burning both ends of the scandal,
They do not insist with a vow that is votive,
How high are their minds and how noble the motive.

As shopping companions they're heroes and saints;
They meet you in tearooms nor murmur complaints;
They listen, entranced, to a list of your vapors;
At breakfast they sometimes emerge from the papers;
A Brave Little Widow's not apt to sob-story 'em,
And they keep a cool head in a grocery emporium.
Yes, I rise to defend
    The quite possible She.
For the feminine gend-
    Er is O.K. by me.

Besides everybody admits it's a Man's World.
And just look what they've done to it!

Terry McMillan (1951-)

FROM *Waiting to Exhale*

I think life is one long introductory course in tolerance, but in order for a woman to get her PhD., she's gotta pass Men 101.

•

My mother told me a long time ago that a woman should never tell a man the whole truth. She said some things you keep to yourself, because they'll use it against you later. She said a woman should never tell a man how many times she's been in love, how many men she's slept with, and under no circumstances should you give him any details about your past relationships. Well, I forgot.

•

I see fields of cotton and think it's ironic that it's Mexicans now who pick it. I laugh when I pass the sign by the prison that says DO NOT STOP FOR HITCHHIKERS.

As much as I want to get married, I realize that just because I want to settle down doesn't mean I have to settle.

Beverly Mickins (contemporary)

On Sex

"Please, I'll only put it in for a minute." She replies with "What does he think I am, a microwave?"

Edna St. Vincent Millay (1892–1950)

First Fig

My candle burns at both ends;
   It will not last the night;
But ah, my foes, and oh, my friends—
   It gives a lovely light!

Second Fig

Safe upon the solid rock the ugly houses stand:
Come and see my shining palace built upon the sand!

Sometimes when I am wearied suddenly
Of all the things that are the outward you,
And my gaze wanders ere your tale is through

To webs of my own weaving, or I see
Abstractedly your hands about your knee
And wonder why I love you as I do,
Then I recall, "Yet *Sorrow* thus he drew";
Then I consider, "*Pride* thus painted he."
Oh, friend, forget not, when you fain would note
In me a beauty that was never mine,
How first you knew me in a book I wrote,
How first you loved me for a written line:
So are we bound till broken is the throat
Of Song, and Art no more leads out the Nine.

•

Oh, oh, you will be sorry for that word!
Give back my book and take my kiss instead.
Was it my enemy or my friend I heard,
"What a big book for such a little head!"
Come, I will show you now my newest hat,
And you may watch me purse my mouth and prink!
Oh, I shall love you still, and all of that.
I never again shall tell you what I think.
I shall be sweet and crafty, soft and sly;
You will not catch me reading any more:
I shall be called a wife to pattern by;
And some day when you knock and push the door,
Some sane day, not too bright and not too stormy,
I shall be gone, and you may whistle for me.

•

Sonnet XI

Not in a silver casket cool with pearls
Or rich with red corundum or with blue,
Locked, and the key withheld, as other girls
Have given their loves, I give my love to you;
Not in a lovers'-knot, not in a ring
Worked in such fashion, and the legend plain—
Semper fidelis, where a secret spring
Kennels a drop of mischief for the brain:
Love in the open hand, no thing but that,
Ungemmed, unhidden, wishing not to hurt,

As one should bring you cowslips in a hat
Swung from the hand, or apples in her skirt,
I bring you, calling out as children do:
"Look what I have!—And these are all for you."

·

Sonnet XII

Olympian gods, mark now my bedside lamp
Blown out; and be advised too late that he
Whom you call sire is stolen into the camp
Of warring Earth, and lies abed with me.
Call out your golden hordes, the harm is done:
Enraptured in his great embrace I lie;
Shake heaven with spears, but I shall bear a son
Branded with godhead, heel and brow and thigh.
Whom think not to bedazzle or confound
With meteoric splendours or display
Of blackened moons or suns or the big sound
Of sudden thunder on a silent day;
Pain and compassion shall he know, being mine,—
Confusion never, that is half divine.

·

Sonnet XIX

My most distinguished guest and learnèd friend,
The pallid hare that runs before the day
Having brought your earnest counsels to an end
Now have I somewhat of my own to say:
That it is folly to be sunk in love,
And madness plain to make the matter known,
These are no mysteries you are verger of;
Everyman's wisdoms these are, and my own.
If I have flung my heart unto a hound
I have done ill, it is a certain thing;
Yet breathe I freer, walk I the more sound
On my sick bones for this brave reasoning?
Soon must I say, " 'Tis prowling Death I hear!"
Yet come no better off, for my quick ear.

·

Sonnet XX

Think not, nor for a moment let your mind,
Wearied with thinking, doze upon the thought
That the work's done and the long day behind,
And beauty, since 'tis paid for, can be bought.
If in the moonlight from the silent bough
Suddenly with precision speak your name
The nightingale, be not assured that now
His wing is limed and his wild virtue tame.
Beauty beyond all feathers that have flown
Is free; you shall not hood her to your wrist,
Nor sting her eyes, nor have her for your own
In any fashion; beauty billed and kissed
Is not your turtle; treat her like a dove—
She loves you not; she never heard of love.

Sonnet XXIX

Heart, have no pity on this house of bone:
Shake it with dancing, break it down with joy.
No man holds mortgage on it; it is your own;
To give, to sell at auction, to destroy.
When you are blind to moonlight on the bed,
When you are deaf to gravel on the pane,
Shall quavering caution from this house instead
Cluck forth at summer mischief in the lane?
All that delightful youth forbears to spend
Molestful age inherits, and the ground
Will have us; therefore, while we're young, my friend—
The Latin's vulgar, but the advice is sound.
Youth, have no pity; leave no farthing here
For age to invest in compromise and fear.

Sonnet XXX

Love is not all: it is not meat nor drink
Nor slumber nor a roof against the rain;
Nor yet a floating spar to men that sink
And rise and sink and rise and sink again;
Love can not fill the thickened lung with breath,
Nor clean the blood, nor set the fractured bone;
Yet many a man is making friends with death
Even as I speak, for lack of love alone.
It well may be that in a difficult hour,
Pinned down by pain and moaning for release,
Or nagged by want past resolution's power,
I might be driven to sell your love for peace,
Or trade the memory of this night for food.
It well may be. I do not think I would.

Alice Duer Miller (1874-1942)

Why We Don't Want Men to Vote

1. Because man's place is in the army.
2. Because no really manly man wants to settle any question otherwise than by fighting about it.
3. Because if men should adopt peaceable methods women will no longer look up to them.
4. Because men will lose their charm if they step out of their natural sphere and interest themselves in other matters than feats of arms, uniforms and drums.
5. Because men are too emotional to vote. Their conduct at baseball games and political conventions shows this, while their innate tendency to appeal to force renders them unfit for government.

Carol Mitchell (contemporary)

On Quickies

A guy and a girl are in the front seat of a car adjusting themselves after a quickie. The guy looks a little uncomfortable and says to the girl, "If I'd known you were a virgin I would have taken more time." The girl looks back at him and says, "If I'd known you weren't in such a hurry, I'd have taken off my panty hose."

Lady Mary Wortley Montagu (1689–1762)

FROM *Verses Addressed to the Imitator of the First Satire of the Second Book of Horace*

[A REPLY TO ALEXANDER POPE]
When God created thee, one would believe
He said the same as to the snake of Eve:
"To human race antipathy declare,
'Twixt them and thee be everlasting war."
But oh! the sequel of the sentence dread,
And whilst you bruise their heel, beware your head.
    Nor think thy weakness shall be thy defence,
The female scold's protection in offence.
Sure 'tis as fair to beat who cannot fight,
As 'tis to libel those who cannot write.
And if thou draw'st thy pen to aid the law,
Others a cudgel, or a rod, may draw.
    If none with vengeance yet thy crimes pursue,
Or give thy manifold affronts their due;
If limbs unbroken, skin without a stain,

Unwhipped, unblanketed, unkicked, unslain,
That wretched little carcase you retain,
The reason is, not that the world wants eyes,
But thou'rt so mean, they see, and they despise:
When fretful porcupine, with rancorous will,
From mounted back shoots forth a harmless quill,
Cool the spectators stand; and all the while
Upon the angry little monster smile.
Thus 'tis with thee:—whilst impotently safe,
You strike unwounding, we unhurt can laugh.
"Who but must laugh, this bully when he sees,
A puny insect shivering at a breeze?"
One over-matched by every blast of wind,
Insulting and provoking all mankind.

   Is this the thing to keep mankind in awe,
"To make those tremble who escape the law?"
Is this the ridicule to live so long,
"The deathless satire and immortal song?"

               •

The Reasons that Induced Dr. S[wift] to Write a Poem Called "The Lady's Dressing-Room"

The Doctor, in a clean starched band
His golden snuff-box in his hand,
With care his diamond ring displays,
And artful shows its various rays;
While grave he stalks down —— Street,
His dearest Betty —— to meet.

   Long had he waited for this hour,
Nor gained admittance to the bower;
Had joked, and punned, and swore, and writ,
Tried all his gallantry and wit;
Had told her oft what part he bore
In Oxford's schemes in days of yore;
But bawdy, politics, nor satyr
Could move this dull hard-hearted creature.

   Jenny, her maid, could taste a rhyme,
And grieved to see him lose his time,

Had kindly whispered in his ear,
"For twice two pounds you enter here;
My lady vows without that sum,
It is in vain you write or come."
    The destined offering now he brought,
And in a paradise of thought,
With a low bow approached the dame,
Who smiling heard him preach his flame.
His gold she took (such proofs as these
Convince most unbelieving she's)
And in her trunk rose up to lock it
(Too wise to trust it in her pocket),
And then, returned with blushing grace,
Expects the Doctor's warm embrace.

    But now this is the proper place
Where morals stare me in the face;
And for the sake of fine expression,
I'm forced to make a small digression.

    Alas! for wretched humankind,
With learning mad, with wisdom blind!
The ox thinks he's for saddle fit
(As long ago friend Horace writ);
And men their talents still mistaking,
The stutterer fancies his is speaking.

    With admiration oft we see
Hard features heightened by toupee;
The beau affects the politician,
Wit is the citizen's ambition;
Poor P[ope] philosophy displays on,
With so much rhyme and little reason;
And though he argues ne'er so long
That *all is right*, his head is wrong.
None strive to know their proper merit,
But strain for wisdom, beauty, spirit,
And lose the praise that is their due,
While they've th' impossible in view.

    [So have I seen the injudicious heir,
To add one window, the whole house impair.]

    Instinct the hound does better teach,
Who never undertook to preach;
The frighted hare from dogs does run,

But not attempts to bear a gun—
Here many noble thoughts occur,
But I prolixity abhor;
And will pursue th' instructive tale,
To show the wise in some things fail.
  The reverend lover with surprise,
Peeps in her bubbies and her eyes,
And kisses both—and tries—and tries.
The evening in this hellish play,
Besides his guineas thrown away,
Provoked the priest to that degree,
He swore, "*The fault is not in me.*
Your damned close-stool so near my nose,
Your dirty smock, and stinking toes
Would make a Hercules as tame
As any beau that you can name."
  The nymph grown furious, roared, "By God,
The blame lies all in sixty-odd";
And scornful, pointing to the door,
Cried, "*Fumbler, see my face no more.*"
"With all my heart I'll go away,
But nothing done, I'll nothing pay;
Give back the money"—"How," cried she,
"Would you palm such a cheat on me?
I locked it in the trunk stands there,
And break it open if you dare;
For poor four pounds to roar and bellow,
Why sure you want some new prunella?
What if your verses have not sold,
Must therefore I return your gold?
Perhaps you have no better luck in
The knack of rhyming than of ———.
I won't give back one single crown,
To wash your band, or turn your gown."
  "I'll be revenged, you saucy quean,"
(Replies the disappointed Dean)
"I'll so describe your *dressing room*,
The very *Irish* shall not come."
She answered short, "I'm glad you'll write,
You'll furnish paper when I shite."

Marianne Moore (1887-1972)

I May, I Might, I Must

If you will tell me why the fen
appears impassable, I then
will tell you why I think that I
can get across it if I try.

•

Values in Use

I attended school and I liked the place—
grass and little locust-leaf shadows like lace.

Writing was discussed. They said, "We create
values in the process of living, daren't await

their historic progress." Be abstract
and you'll wish you'd been specific; it's a fact.

What was I studying? Values in use,
"judged on their own ground." Am I still abstruse?

Walking along, a student said offhand,
" 'Relevant' and 'plausible' were words I understand."

A pleasing statement, anonymous friend.
Certainly the means must not defeat the end.

Toni Morrison (1931–   )

~❧ ❧~

FROM *Beloved*
(On visiting a carnival)

The barker called them and their children names ("Pickaninnies free!") but the food on his vest and the hole in his pants rendered it fairly harmless. In any case it was a small price to pay for the fun they might not ever have again. Two pennies and an insult were well spent if it meant seeing the spectacle of whitefolks making a spectacle of themselves. So, although the carnival was a lot less than mediocre (which is why it agreed to a Colored Thursday), it gave the four hundred black people in its audience thrill upon thrill upon thrill.

One-Ton Lady spit at them, but her bulk shortened her aim and they got a big kick out of the helpless meanness in her little eyes. Arabian Nights Dancer cut her performance to three minutes instead of the usual fifteen she normally did—earning the gratitude of the children, who could hardly wait for Abu Snake Charmer, who followed her.

Denver bought horehound, licorice, peppermint and lemonade at a table manned by a little whitegirl in ladies' high-topped shoes. Soothed by sugar, surrounded by a crowd of people who did not find her the main attraction, who, in fact, said, "Hey, Denver," every now and then, pleased her enough to consider the possibility that Paul D wasn't all that bad. In fact there was something about him—when the three of them stood together watching Midget dance—that made the stares of other Negroes kind, gentle, something Denver did not remember seeing in their faces. Several even nodded and smiled at her mother, no one, apparently, able to withstand sharing the pleasure Paul D was having. He slapped his knees when Giant danced with Midget; when Two-Headed Man talked to himself. He bought everything Denver asked for and much she did not. He teased Sethe into tents she was reluctant to enter. Stuck pieces of candy she didn't want between her lips. When Wild African Savage shook his bars and said wa wa, Paul D told everybody he knew him back in Roanoke.

Paul D made a few acquaintances; spoke to them about what work he might find. Sethe returned the smiles she got. Denver was swaying with delight. And on the way home, although leading them now, the shadows of three people still held hands.

Judith Sargent Murray (1751-1820)

On the Equality of the Sexes

Is it upon mature consideration we adopt the idea that nature is thus partial in her distributions? Is it indeed a fact that she hath yielded to one-half of the human species so unquestionable a mental superiority? I know that to both sexes elevated understandings, and the reverse, are common. But, suffer me to ask in what the minds of females are so notoriously deficient or unequal. May not the intellectual powers be ranged under these four heads—imagination, reason, memory and judgment? The province of imagination hath long since been surrendered up to us, and we have been crowned undoubted sovereigns of the regions of fancy. Invention is perhaps the most arduous effort of the mind; this branch of imagination hath been particularly ceded to us, and we have been time out of mind invested with that creative faculty. Observe the variety of fashions (here I bar the contemptuous smile) which distinguish and adorn the female world; how continually are they changing, insomuch that they almost render the wise man's assertion problematical, and we are ready to say, *there is something new under the sun.* Now what a playfulness, what an exuberance of fancy, what strength of inventive imagination, doth this continual variation discover? Again, it hath been observed that if the turpitude of the conduct of our sex hath been ever so enormous, so extremely ready are we, that the very first thought presents us with an apology so plausible as to produce our actions even in an amiable light. Another instance of our creative powers is our talent for slander; how ingenious are we at inventive scandal! what a formidable story can we in a moment fabricate merely from the force of a prolific imagination! how many reputations, in the fertile brain of a female, have been utterly despoiled! how industrious are we at improving a hint! suspicion how easily do we convert into conviction, and conviction, embellished by the power of eloquence, stalks abroad to the surprise and confusion of unsuspecting innocence. Perhaps it will be asked if I furnish these facts as instances of excellency in our sex. Certainly not; but as proofs of a creative faculty, of a lively imagination. Assuredly great activity of mind is thereby discovered, and was this activity properly directed, what beneficial effects would follow. Is the needle and kitchen sufficient to employ the operations of a soul thus organized? I should conceive not. Nay, it is a truth that those very departments leave the intelligent principle vacant, and at liberty for speculation. Are we deficient in reason? we can only reason from what we know, and if an opportunity of acquiring knowledge hath been denied us, the inferiority of our sex cannot fairly be deduced from thence. Memory, I believe, will be allowed us in common, since every one's experience must testify that a loquacious old woman is as frequently met with as a communicative old man; their subjects are alike drawn from the fund of other times, and the transactions of their youth or of maturer life entertain, or perhaps fatigue you, in the evening of their lives. "But our judgment is not so strong—we do not distinguish so well."—Yet it may be questioned, from what doth this superiority, in this determining faculty of the soul, proceed? May we not trace its source in the difference of education, and continued advantages? Will it be said that the judgment of a male of two years old is more sage than that of a female's of the same age? I believe the reverse is generally observed to be true. But from that period what partiality! how is the one exalted, and the other depressed, by the contrary modes of education which are adopted! the one is taught to aspire, and the other is early confined and limited. As their years increase, the sister must be wholly domesticated, while the brother is led by the hand through all the flowery paths of science. Grant that their minds are by nature equal, yet who shall wonder at the *apparent* superiority, if indeed custom becomes *second nature*; nay, if it taketh place of nature, and that it doth the experience of each day will evince. At length arrived at womanhood, the uncultivated fair one feels a void, which the employments allotted her are by no means capable of filling. What can she do? to books she may not apply; or if she doth, *to those only of the novel kind*, lest she merit the appellation of a *learned lady*; and what ideas have been affixed to this term, the observation of many can testify. Fashion, scandal, and sometimes what is still more reprehensible, are then called in to her relief; and who can say to what lengths the liberties she takes may proceed. Meantime she herself is most unhappy; she feels the want of a cultivated mind. Is she single, she in vain seeks to fill up time from sexual employments or amusements. Is she united to a person whose soul nature made equal to her own, education hath set him so far above her that in those entertainments which are productive of such rational felicity, she is not qualified to accompany him. She experiences a mortifying consciousness of inferiority, which embitters every enjoyment. Doth the person to whom her adverse fate hath consigned her possess a mind incapable of improvement, she is equally wretched, in being so closely connected with an individual whom she cannot but despise. Now, was she permitted the same instructors as her brother (with an eye however to their particular departments), for the employment of a rational mind an ample field would be opened. In astronomy she might catch a glimpse of the immensity of the Deity, and thence she would form amazing conceptions of the august and supreme Intelligence. In geography she would admire Jehovah in the midst of his benevolence: thus adapting this globe to the various wants and amusements of its inhabitants. In natural philosophy she would adore the infinite majesty of heaven, clothed in condescension; and as she traversed the reptile world, she would hail the goodness of a creating God. A mind thus filled would have little room for the trifles with which our sex are, with too much justice, accused of amusing themselves; and they would thus be rendered fit companions for those, who should one day wear them as their crown. Fashions, in their variety, would then give place to conjectures which might perhaps conduce to the improvement of the literary world; and there would be no leisure for slander or detraction. Reputation would not then be blasted, but serious speculations would occupy the lively imaginations of the sex. Unnecessary visits would be precluded, and that custom would only be indulged by way of relaxation, or to answer the demands of consanguinity and friendship. Females would become discreet, their judgments would be invigorated, and their partners for life being circumspectly chosen, an unhappy Hymen would then be as rare as is now the reverse.

Will it be urged that those acquirements would supersede our domestic duties? I answer that every requisite in female economy is easily attained; and, with truth I can add, that when once attained, they require no further *mental attention*. Nay, while we are pursuing the needle or the superintendency of the family, I repeat that our minds are at full liberty for reflection; that imagination may exert itself in full vigor; and that if a just foundation is early laid, our ideas will then be worthy of rational beings. If we were industrious, we might easily find time to arrange them upon paper, or should avocations press too hard for such an indulgence, the hours allotted for conversation would at least become more refined and rational. Should it still be vociferated, "Your domestic employments are sufficient"—I would calmly ask, is it reasonable that a candidate for immortality, for the joys of heaven, an intelligent being, who is to spend an eternity in contemplating the works of Deity, should at present be so degraded as to be allowed no other ideas than those which are suggested by the mechanism of a pudding or the sewing of the seams of a garment? Pity that all such censurers of female improvement do not go one step further and deny their future existence; to be consistent they surely ought.

Yes, ye lordly, ye haughty sex, our souls are by nature *equal* to yours; the same breath of God animates, enlivens, and invigorates us; and that we are not fallen lower than yourselves, let those witness who have greatly towered above the various discouragements by which they have been so heavily oppressed; and though I am unacquainted with the list of celebrated characters on either side, yet from the observations I have made in the contracted circle in which I have moved, I dare confidently believe, that from the commencement of time to the present day, there hath been as many females, as males, who, by the *mere force of natural powers*, have merited the crown of applause; who, *thus unassisted*, have seized the wreath of fame. I know there are who assert, that as the animal powers of the one sex are superior, of course their mental faculties also must be stronger; thus attributing strength of mind to the transient organization of this earth-born tenement. But if this reasoning is just, man must be content to yield the palm to many of the brute creation, since by not a few of his brethren of the field, he is far surpassed in bodily strength. Moreover, was this argument admitted, it would prove too much, for ocular demonstration evinceth, that there are many robust masculine ladies, and effeminate gentlemen. Yet I fancy that Mr. Pope, though clogged with an enervated body, and distinguished by a diminutive stature, could nevertheless lay claim to greatness of soul; and perhaps there are many other instances which might be adduced to combat so unphilosophical an opinion. Do we not often see, that when the clay-built tabernacle is well nigh dissolved, when it is just ready to mingle with the parent soil, the immortal inhabitant aspires to, and even attaineth heights the most sublime, and which were before wholly unexplored. Besides, were we to grant that animal strength proved anything, taking into consideration the accustomed impartiality of nature, we should be induced to imagine that she had invested the female mind with superior strength as an equivalent for the bodily powers of man. But waving this however palpable advantage, for *equality only*, we wish to contend.

I am aware that there are many passages in the sacred oracles which seem to give the advantage to the other sex; but I consider all these as

wholly metaphorical. Thus David was a man after God's own heart, yet
see him enervated by his licentious passions! behold him following Uriah
to the death, and shew me wherein could consist the immaculate Being's
complacency. Listen to the curses which Job bestoweth upon the day of
his nativity, and tell me where is his perfection, where his patience—
literally it existed not. David and Job were types of him who was to
come; and the superiority of man, as exhibited in scripture, being also
emblematical, all arguments deduce from thence, of course fall to the
ground. The exquisite delicacy of the female mind proclaimeth the ex-
actness of its texture, while its nice sense of honor announceth its innate,
its native grandeur. And indeed, in one respect, the preeminence seems
to be tacitly allowed us, for after an education which limits and confines,
and employments and recreations which naturally tend to enervate the
body and debilitate the mind; after we have from early youth been
adorned with ribbons and other gewgaws, dressed out like the ancient
victims previous to a sacrifice, being taught by the care of our parents
in collecting the most showy materials that the ornamenting our exterior
ought to be the principal object of our attention; after, I say, fifteen years
thus spent, we are introduced into the world, amid the united adulation
of every beholder. Praise is sweet to the soul; we are immediately intoxicated by large draughts of flattery, which, being plentifully admin-
istered, is to the pride of our hearts the most acceptable incense. It is
expected that with the other sex we should commence immediate war,
and that we should triumph over the machinations of the most artful.
We must be constantly upon our guard; prudence and discretion must
be our characteristics; and we must rise superior to, and obtain a complete victory over those who have been long adding to the native
strength of their minds by an unremitted study of men and books, and
who have, moreover, conceived from the loose characters which they
have seen portrayed in the extensive variety of their reading, a most
contemptible opinion of the sex. Thus unequal, we are, notwithstanding,
forced to the combat, and the infamy which is consequent upon the
smallest deviation in our conduct, proclaims the high idea which was
formed of our native strength; and thus, indirectly at least, is the preference acknowledged to be our due. And if we are allowed an equality
of acquirement, let serious studies equally employ our minds, and we
will bid our souls arise to equal strength. We will meet upon even
ground, the despot man; we will rush with alacrity to the combat, and,
crowned by success, we shall then answer the exalted expectations which
are formed. Though sensibility, soft compassion, and gentle commiser-
ation are inmates in the female bosom, yet against every deep-laid art,

altogether fearless of the event, we will set them in array; for assuredly the wreath of victory will encircle the spotless brow. If we meet an equal, a sensible friend, we will reward him with the hand of amity, and through life we will be assiduous to promote his happiness; but from every deep-laid scheme for our ruin, retiring into ourselves, amid the flowerly paths of science, we will indulge in all the refined and senti-mental pleasures of contemplation. And should it still be urged that the studies thus insisted upon would interfere with our more peculiar de-partment, I must further reply that *early hours*, and close application, will do wonders; and to her who is from the first dawn of reason taught to fill up time rationally, both the requisites will be easy. I grant that niggard fortune is too generally unfriendly to the mind, and that much of that valuable treasure, time, is necessarily expended upon the wants of the body; but it should be remembered, that in embarrassed circumstances our companions have as little leisure for literary improvement as is af-forded to us; for most certainly their provident care is at least as requisite as our exertions. Nay, we have even more leisure for sedentary pleasures, as our avocations are more retired, much less laborious, and, as hath been observed, by no means require that avidity of attention which is proper to the employments of the other sex. In high life, or, in other words, where the parties are in possession of affluence, the objection respecting time is wholly obviated, and of course falls to the ground; and it may also be repeated that many of those hours which are at present swallowed up in fashion and scandal might be redeemed, were we ha-bituated to useful reflections. But in one respect, O ye arbiters of our fate! we confess that the superiority is undubitably yours; you are by nature formed for our protectors; we pretend not to vie with you in bodily strength; upon this point we will never contend for victory. Shield us then, we beseech you, from external evils, and in return we will transact *your* domestic affairs. Yes, *your*, for are you not equally interested in those matters with ourselves? Is not the elegancy of neatness as agreeable to your sight as to ours, is not the well favored viand equally delightful to your taste; and doth not your sense of hearing suffer as much from the discordant sounds prevalent in an ill regulated family, produced by the voices of children and many *et ceteras?*

Gloria Naylor (1950-)

FROM *Mama Day*

I'd met quite a few guys in restaurants with my box of toothpicks: it was a foolproof way to start up a conversation once I'd checked out what they'd ordered and how they ate it. The way a man chews can tell you loads about the kind of lover he'd turn out to be. Don't laugh—meat is meat.

Itabari Njeri (contemporary)

What's in a Name?

Sophisticated white people, upon hearing my name, approach me as would a cultural anthropologist finding a piece of exotica right in his own living room. This happens a lot, still, at cocktail parties.

"Oh, what an unusual and beautiful name. Where are you from?"

"Brooklyn," I say. I can see the disappointment in their eyes. Just another home-grown Negro.

Sheryl Noethe (contemporary)

Illusion

The pink
neon made a

halfcircle
on your face
while you slept.
From outside
the flashing
light gave you
a question mark
of a look.
From out the
window pink neon
flashed your face
into a circus of
possible expressions.
Living above the
Waffle Shop has
made you a figure
of mystery.

Edna O'Brien (1932–)

FROM *Girls in Their Married Bliss*

. . . people liking you or not liking you is an accident and is to do with them and not you. That goes for love too, only more so.

•

The vote, I thought, means nothing to women, we should be armed.

•

All this thing about women and new freedom. There isn't a man alive wouldn't kill any woman the minute she draws attention to his defects.

Flannery O'Connor (1925-1964)

~❦ ❦~

FROM *The Habit of Being*

My nine copies have to go to a set of relatives who are waiting anxiously to condemn the book until they get a free copy.

•

I certainly am glad you like the stories because now I feel it's not bad that I like them so much. The truth is I like them better than anybody and I read them over and over and laugh and laugh, then get embarrassed when I remember I was the one wrote them.

•

As for the success, my tongue was not in my cheek. Success means being heard and don't stand there and tell me you are indifferent to being heard. Everything about you screams to be heard. You may write for the joy of it, but the act of writing is not complete in itself. It has its end in its audience.

•

FROM *A Temple of the Holy Ghost*

She could never be a saint, but she thought she could be a martyr if they killed her quick.

She could stand to be shot but not to be burned in oil. She didn't know if she could stand to be torn to pieces by lions or not. She began to prepare her martyrdom, seeing herself in a pair of tights in a great arena, lit by the early Christians hanging in cages of fire, making a gold dusty light that fell on her and the lions. The first lion charged forward and fell at her feet, converted. A whole series of lions did the same. The lions liked her so much she even slept with them and finally the Romans were obliged to burn her but to their astonishment she would not burn down and finding she was so hard to kill, they finally cut off her head very quickly with a sword and she went immediately to heaven. She rehearsed this several times, returning each time at the entrance of Paradise to the lions.

•

FROM *Good Country People*

"I didn't intraduce myself," he said. "I'm Manley Pointer from out in the country around Willohobie, not even from a place, just from near a place."

"You wait a minute," she said. "I have to see about my dinner." She went out to the kitchen and found Joy standing near the door where she had been listening.

"Get rid of the salt of the earth," she said, "and let's eat."

Jane O'Reilly (contemporary)

On Feminism

It's so hard to be a feminist if you are a woman.

Dorothy Osborne (1627–1694)

FROM *The Letters of Dorothy Osborne to William Temple*

What an age do we live in where 'tis a miracle if in ten couples that are married two of them live so as not to publish it to the world that they cannot agree . . . A kinswoman of ours . . . had a husband who was not always himself, and when he was otherwise his humour was to rise in the night, and with two bedstaves tabor upon the table an hour together. She took care every night to lay a great cushion upon the table for him to strike on that nobody might hear him and so discover his madness. But 'tis a sad thing that all one's happiness is only that the world does not know you are miserable. For my part I think it were very convenient that all such as intend to marry should live together in the same house some years of probation, and if in all that time they never disagreed they should then be permitted to marry if they pleased. But how few would do it then! I do not remember that I ever saw or heard of any couple that were bred up so together (as many you know are, that are designed for one another from children) but they always disliked one another extremely, and parted if it were left in their choice. If people proceeded with this caution the world would end sooner than is expected, I believe. . . .

•

Just now I have news brought me of the death of an old, rich knight that has promised me these seven years to marry me whensoever his wife died, and now he's dead before her, and has left her such a widow it makes me mad to think on't; £1200 a year jointure and £20,000 in money and personal estate; and all this I might have had if Mr. Death had been pleased to have taken her instead of him: well who can help these things? But since I cannot have him, would you had her! What say you, shall I speak a good word for you? She will marry for certain, and though perhaps my brother may expect I should serve him in it, yet if you give me commission I'll say I was engaged beforehand for a friend and leave him to shift for himself. You would be my neighbour if you had her and I should see you often.

Grace Paley (1922-   )

⊰⊱ ⊰⊱

An Interest in Life

My husband gave me a broom one Christmas. This wasn't right. No one can tell me it was meant kindly.

"I don't want you not to have anything for Christmas while I'm away in the Army," he said. "Virginia, please look at it. It comes with this fancy dustpan. It hangs off a stick. Look at it, will you? Are you blind or cross-eyed?"

"Thanks, chum," I said. I had always wanted a dustpan hooked up that way. It was a good one. My husband doesn't shop in bargain basements or January sales.

Still and all, in spite of the quality, it was a mean present to give a woman you planned on never seeing again, a person you had children with and got onto all the time, drunk or sober, even when everybody had to get up early in the morning.

I asked him if he could wait and join the Army in a half hour, as I had to get the groceries. I don't like to leave kids alone in a three-room apartment full of gas and electricity. Fire may break out from a nasty remark. Or the oldest decides to get even with the youngest.

"Just this once," he said. "But you better figure out how to get along without me."

"You're a handicapped person mentally," I said. "You should've been institutionalized years ago." I slammed the door. I didn't want to see him pack his underwear and ironed shirts.

I never got further than the front stoop, though, because there was Mrs. Raftery, wringing her hands, tears in her eyes as though she had a monopoly on all the good news.

"Mrs. Raftery!" I said, putting my arm around her. "Don't cry." She leaned on me because I am such a horsy build. "Don't cry, Mrs. Raftery, please!" I said.

"That's like you, Virginia. Always looking at the ugly side of things. 'Take in the wash. It's rainin'!' that's you. You're the first one knows it when the dumb-waiter breaks."

"Oh, come on now, that's not so. It just isn't so," I said. "I'm the exact opposite."

"Did you see Mrs. Cullen yet?" she asked, paying no attention.

"Where?"

"Virginia!" she said, shocked. "She's passed away. The whole house knows it. They've got her in white like a bride and you never saw a beautiful creature like that. She must be eighty. Her husband's proud."

"She was never more than an acquaintance; she didn't have any children," I said.

"Well, I don't care about that. Now, Virginia, you do what I say now, you go downstairs and you say like this—listen to me—say, 'I hear, Mr. Cullen, your wife's passed away. I'm sorry.' Then ask him how he is. Then you ought to go around the corner and see her. She's in Witson & Wayde. Then you ought to go over to the church when they carry her over."

"It's not my church," I said.

"That's no reason, Virginia. You go up like this," she said, parting from me to do a prancy dance. "Up the big front steps, into the church you go. It's beautiful in there. You can't help kneeling only for a minute. Then round to the right. Then up the other stairway. Then you come to a great oak door that's arched above you, then," she said, seizing a deep, deep breath, for all the good it would do her, "and then turn the knob slo-owly and open the door and see for yourself: Our Blessed Mother is in charge. Beautiful. Beautiful. Beautiful."

I sighed in and I groaned out, so as to melt a certain pain around my heart. A steel ring like arthritis, at my age.

"You are a groaner," Mrs. Raftery said, gawking into my mouth.

"I am not," I said. I got a whiff of her, a terrible cheap wine lush.

My husband threw a penny at the door from the inside to take my notice from Mrs. Raftery. He rattled the glass door to make sure I looked at him. He had a fat duffel bag on each shoulder. Where did he acquire so much worldly possession? What was in them? My grandma's goose feathers from across the ocean? Or all the diaper-service diapers? To this day the truth is shrouded in mystery.

"What the hell are you doing, Virginia?" he said, dumping them at my feet. "Standing out here on your hind legs telling everybody your business? The Army gives you a certain time, for God's sakes, they're not kidding." Then he said, "I beg your pardon," to Mrs. Raftery. He took hold of me with his two arms as though in love and pressed his body hard against mine so that I could feel him for the last time and suffer my loss. Then he kissed me in a mean way to nearly split my lip. Then he winked and said, "That's all for now," and skipped off into the future, duffel bags full of rags.

He left me in an embarrassing situation, nearly fainting, in front of that old widow, who can't even remember the half of it. "He's a crock," said Mrs. Raftery. "Is he leaving for good or just temporarily, Virginia?"

"Oh, he's probably deserting me," I said, and sat down on the stoop, pulling my big knees up to my chin.

"If that's the case, tell the Welfare right away," she said. "He's a bum, leaving you just before Christmas. Tell the cops," she said. "They'll provide the toys for the little kids gladly. And don't forget to let the grocer in on it. He won't be so hard on you expecting payment."

She saw that sadness was stretched world-wide across my face. Mrs. Raftery isn't the worst person. She said, "Look around for comfort, dear." With a nervous finger she pointed to the truckers eating lunch on their haunches across the street, leaning on the loading platforms. She waves her hand to include in all the men marching up and down in

search of a decent luncheonette. She didn't leave out the six longshore-
men loafing under the fish-market marquee. "If their lungs and stomachs
ain't crushed by overwork, they disappear somewhere in the world.
Don't be disappointed, Virginia. I don't know a man living'd last you a
lifetime."

Ten days later Girard asked, "Where's Daddy?"

"Ask me no questions, I'll tell you no lies." I didn't want the children to know the facts. Present or past, a child should have a father.

"Where *is* Daddy?" Girard asked the week after that.

"He joined the Army," I said.

"He made my bunk bed," said Phillip.

"The truth shall make ye free," I said.

Then I sat down with pencil and pad to get in control of my
resources. The facts, when I added and subtracted them, were that my
husband had left me with fourteen dollars, and the rent unpaid, in an
emergency state. He'd claimed he was sorry to do this, but my opinion
is, out of sight, out of mind. "The city won't let you starve," he'd said.
"After all, you're half the population. You're keeping up the good work.
Without you the race would die out. Who'd pay the taxes? Who'd keep
the streets clean? There wouldn't be no Army. A man like me wouldn't
have no place to go."

I sent Girard right down to Mrs. Raftery with a request about the
whereabouts of Welfare. She responded RSVP with an extra comment
in left-handed script: "Poor Girard . . . he's never the boy my John
was!"

Who asked her?

I called on Welfare right after the new year. In no time I discovered
that they're rigged up to deal with liars, and if you're truthful it's disappointing to them. They may even refuse to handle your case if you're
too truthful.

They asked sensible questions at first. They asked where my husband had enlisted. I didn't know. They put some letter writers and agents
after him. "He's not in the United States Army," they said. "Try the
Brazilian Army," I suggested.

They have no sense of kidding around. They're not the least bit
lighthearted and they tried. "Oh no," they said. "That was incorrect.
He is not in the Brazilian Army."

"No?" I said. "How strange! He must be in the Mexican Navy."

By law, they had to hound his brothers. They wrote to his brother
who has a first-class card in the Teamsters and owns an apartment house
in California. They asked his two brothers in Jersey to help me. They

have large families. Rightfully they laughed. Then they wrote to Thomas, the oldest, the smart one (the one they all worked so hard for years to keep him in college until his brains could pay off). He was the one who sent ten dollars immediately, saying, "What a bastard! I'll send something time to time, Ginny, but whatever you do, don't tell the authorities." Of course I never did. Soon they began to guess they were better people than me, that I was in trouble because I deserved it, and then they liked me better.

But they never fixed my refrigerator. Every time I called I said patiently, "The milk is sour . . ." I said, "Corn beef went bad." Sitting in that beer-stinking phone booth in Felan's for the sixth time (sixty cents) with the baby on my lap and Barbie tapping at the glass door with an American flag, I cried into the secretary's hardhearted ear, "I bought real butter for the holiday, and it's rancid . . ." They said, "You'll have to get a better bid on the repair job."

While I waited indoors for a man to bid, Girard took to swinging back and forth on top of the bathroom door, just to soothe himself, giving me the laugh, dreamy, nibbling calcimine off the ceiling. On first sight Mrs. Raftery said, "Whack the monkey, he'd be better off on arsenic."

But Girard is my son and I'm the judge. It means a terrible thing for the future, though I don't know what to call it.

It was from constantly thinking of my foreknowledge on this and other subjects, it was from observing when I put my lipstick on daily, how my face was just curling up to die, that John Raftery came from Jersey to rescue me.

On Thursdays, anyway, John Raftery took the tubes in to visit his mother. The whole house knew it. She was cheerful even before breakfast. She sang out loud in a girlish brogue that only came to tongue for grand occasions. Hanging out the wash, she blushed to recall what a remarkable boy her John had been. "Ask the sisters around the corner," she said to the open kitchen windows. "They'll never forget John."

That particular night after supper Mrs. Raftery said to her son, "John, how come you don't say hello to your old friend Virginia? She's had hard luck and she's gloomy."

"Is that so, Mother?" he said, and immediately climbed two flights to knock at my door.

"Oh, John," I said at the sight of him, hat in hand in a white shirt and blue-striped tie, spick-and-span, a Sunday-school man. "Hello!"

"Welcome, John!" I said. "Sit down. Come right in. How are you? You look awfully good. You do. Tell me, how've you been all this time, John?"

"How've I been?" he asked thoughtfully. To answer within reason, he described his life with Margaret, marriage, work, and children up to the present day.

I had nothing good to report. Now that he had put the subject around before my very eyes, every burnt-up day of my life smoked in shame, and I couldn't even get a clear view of the good half hours.

"Of course," he said, "you do have lovely children. Noticeable-looking, Virginia. Good looks is always something to be thankful for."

"Thankful?" I said. "I don't have to thank anything but my own foolishness for four children when I'm twenty-six years old, deserted, and poverty-struck, regardless of looks. A man can't help it, but I could have behaved better."

"Don't be so cruel on yourself, Ginny," he said. "Children come from God."

"You're still great on holy subjects, aren't you? You know damn well where children come from."

He did know. His face reddened further. John Raftery has had that color coming out on him boy and man from keeping his rages so inward.

Still he made more sense in his converation after that, and I poured fresh tea to tell him how my husband used to like me because I was a passionate person. That was until he took a look around and saw how in the long run this life only meant more of the same thing. He tried to turn away from me once he came to this understanding, and make me hate him. His face changed. He gave up his brand of cigarettes, which we had in common. He threw out the two pairs of socks I knitted by hand. "If there's anything I hate in this world, it's navy blue," he said. Oh, I could have dyed them. I would have done anything for him, if he were only not too sorry to ask me.

"You were a nice kid in those days," said John, referring to certain Saturday nights. "A wild, nice kid."

"Aaah," I said, disgusted. Whatever I was then, was on the way to where I am now. "I was fresh. If I had a kid like me, I'd slap her cross-eyed."

The very next Thursday John gave me a beautiful radio with a record player. "Enjoy yourself," he said. That really made Welfare speechless. We didn't own any records, but the investigator saw my burden was lightened and he scribbled a dozen pages about it in his notebook.

On the third Thursday he brought a walking doll (twenty-four inches) for Linda and Barbie with a card inscribed, "A baby doll for a couple of dolls." He had also had a couple of drinks at his mother's, and this made him want to dance. "La-la-la," he sang, a ramrod swaying in my kitchen chair. "La-la-la, let yourself go . . ."

"You gotta give a little," he sang, "live a little . . ." He said, "Virginia, may I have this dance?"

"Sssh, we finally got them asleep. Please, turn the radio down. Quiet. Deathly silence, John Raftery."

"Let me do your dishes, Virginia."

"Don't be silly, you're a guest in my house," I said. "I still regard you as a guest."

"I want to do something for you, Virginia."

"Tell me I'm the most gorgeous thing," I said, dipping my arm to the funny bone in dish soup.

He didn't answer. "I'm having a lot of trouble at work," was all he said. Then I heard him push the chair back. He came up behind me, put his arms around my waistline, and kissed my cheek. He whirled me around and took my hands. He said, "An old friend is better than rubies." He looked me in the eye. He held my attention by trying to be honest. And he kissed me a short sweet kiss on my mouth.

"Please sit down, Virginia," he said. He kneeled before me and put his head in my lap. I was stirred by so much activity. Then he looked up at me and, as though proposing marriage for life, he offered—because he was drunk—to place his immortal soul in peril to comfort me.

First I said, "Thank you." Then I said, "No."

I was sorry for him, but he's devout, a leader of the Fathers' Club at his church, active in all the lay groups for charities, orphans, etc. I knew that if he stayed late to love with me, he would not do it lightly but would in the end pay terrible penance and ruin his long life. The responsibility would be on me.

So I said no.

And Barbie is such a light sleeper. All she has to do, I thought, is wake up and wander in and see her mother and her new friend John with his pants around his knees, wrestling on the kitchen table. A vision like that could affect a kid for life.

I said no.

Everyone in this building is so goddamn nosy. That evening I had to say no.

But John came to visit, anyway, on the fourth Thursday. This time he brought the discarded dresses of Margaret's daughters, organdy party dresses and glazed cotton for every day. He gently admired Barbara and Linda, his blue eyes rolling to back up a couple of dozen oohs and ahs.

Even Phillip, who thinks God gave him just a certain number of hellos and he better save them for the final judgment, Phillip leaned on John and said, "Why don't you bring your boy to play with me? I don't have nobody who to play with." (Phillip's a liar. There must be at least seventy-one children in this house, pale pink to medium brown, English-talking and gibbering in Spanish, rough-and-tough boys, the Lone Ranger's bloody pals, or the exact picture of Supermouse. If a boy wanted a friend, he could pick the very one out of his neighbors.

Also, Girard is a cold fish. He was in a lonesome despair. Sometimes he looked in the mirror and said, "How come I have such an ugly face? My nose is funny. Mostly people don't like me." He was a liar too. Girard has a face like his father's. His eyes are the color of those little blue plums in August. He looks like an advertisement in a magazine. He could be a child model and make a lot of money. He is my first child, and if he thinks he is ugly, I think I am ugly.)

John said, "I can't stand to see a boy mope like that. . . . What do the sisters say in school?"

"He doesn't pay attention is all they say. You can't get much out of them."

"My middle boy was like that," said John. "Couldn't take an interest. Aaah, I wish I didn't have all that headache on the job. I'd grab Girard by the collar and make him take notice of the world. I wish I could ask him out to Jersey to play in all that space."

"Why not?" I said.

"Why, Virginia, I'm surprised you don't know why not. You know I can't take your children out to meet my children."

I felt a lot of strong arthritis in my ribs.

"My mother's the funny one, Virginia." He felt he had to continue with the subject matter. "I don't know. I guess she likes the idea of bugging Margaret. She says, 'You goin' up, John?' 'Yes, Mother,' I say. 'Behave yourself, John,' she says. 'That husband might come home and hack-saw you into hell. You're a Catholic man, John,' she says. But I figured it out. She likes to know I'm in the building. I swear, Virginia, she wishes me the best of luck."

"I do too, John," I said. We drank a last glass of beer to make sure of a peaceful sleep. "Good night, Virginia," he said, looping his muffler neatly under his chin. "Don't worry. I'll be thinking of what to do about Girard."

I got into the big bed that I share with the girls in the little room. For once I had no trouble falling asleep. I only had to worry about Linda and Barbara and Phillip. It was a great relief to me that John had taken over the thinking about Girard.

John was sincere. That's true. He paid a lot of attention to Girard, smoking out all his sneaky sorrows. He registered him into a wild pack of cub scouts that went up to the Bronx once a week to let off steam. He gave him a Junior Erector Set. And sometimes when his family wasn't listening he prayed at great length for him.

One Sunday, Sister Veronica said in her sweet voice from another life, "He's not worse. He might even be a little better. How are *you*, Virginia?" putting her hand on mine. Everybody around here acts like they know everything.

"Just fine," I said.

"We ought to start on Phillip," John said, "if it's true Girard's improving."

"You should've been a social worker, John."

"A lot of people have noticed that about me," said John.

"Your mother was always acting so crazy about you, how come she didn't knock herself out a little to see you in college? Like we did for Thomas?"

"Now, Virginia, be fair. She's a poor old woman. My father was a weak earner. She had to have my wages, and I'll tell you, Virginia, I'm not sorry. Look at Thomas. He's still in school. Drop him in this jungle and he'd be devoured. He hasn't had a touch of real life. And here I am with a good chunk of a family, a home of my own, a name in the building trades. One thing I have to tell you, the poor old woman is sorry. I said one day (oh, in passing—years ago) that I might marry you. She stuck a knife in herself. It's a fact. Not more than an eighth of an inch. You never saw such a gory Sunday. One thing—you would have been a better daughter-in-law to her than Margaret."

"Marry me?" I said.

"Well, yes. . . . Aaah—I always liked you, then . . . Why do you think I'd sit in the shade of this kitchen every Thursday night? For God's sakes, the only warm thing around here is this teacup. Yes, sir, I did want to marry you, Virginia."

"No kidding, John? Really?" It was nice to know. Better late than never, to learn you were desired in youth.

I didn't tell John, but the truth is, I would never have married him. Once I met my husband with his winking looks, he was my only interest. Wild as I had been with John and others, I turned all my wildness over to him and then there was no question in my mind.

Still, face facts, if my husband didn't budge on in life, it was my fault. On me, as they say, be it. I greeted the morn with a song. I had a hello for everyone but the landlord. Ask the people on the block, come or go—even the Spanish ones, with their sad dark faces—they have to smile when they see me.

But for his own comfort, he should have done better lifewise and moneywise. I was happy, but I am now in possession of knowledge that this is wrong. Happiness isn't so bad for a woman. She gets fatter, she gets older, she could lie down, nuzzling a regiment of men and little kids, she could just die of pleasure. But men are different, they have to own money, or they have to be famous, or everybody on the block has to look up to them from the cellar stairs.

A woman counts her children and acts snotty, like she invented life, but men *must* do well in the world. I know that men are not fooled by being happy.

"A funny guy," said John, guessing where my thoughts had gone. "What stopped him up? He was nobody's fool. He had a funny thing about him, Virginia, if you don't mind my saying so. He wasn't much distance up, but he was all set and ready to be looking down on us all."

"He was very smart, John. You don't realize that. His hobby was crossword puzzles, and I said to him real often, as did others around here, that he ought to go out on the '$64 Question.' Why not? But he laughed. You know what he said? He said, 'That proves how dumb you are if you think I'm smart.' "

"A funny guy," said John. "Get it all off your chest," he said. "Talk it out, Virginia; it's the only way to kill the pain."

By and large, I was happy to oblige. Still I could not carry through about certain cruel remarks. It was like trying to move back into the dry mouth of a nightmare to remember that the last day I was happy was the middle of a week in March, when I told my husband I was going to have Linda. Barbara was five months old to the hour. The boys were three and four. I had to tell him. It was the last day with anything happy about it.

Later on he said, "Oh, you make me so sick, you're so goddamn big and fat, you look like a goddamn brownstone, the way you're squared off in front."

"Well, where are you going tonight?" I asked.

"How should I know?" he said. "Your big ass takes up the whole goddamn bed," he said. "There's no room for me." He bought a sleeping bag and slept on the floor.

I couldn't believe it. I would start every morning fresh. I couldn't believe that he would turn against me so, while I was still young and even his friends still liked me.

But he did, he turned absolutely against me and became no friend of mine. "All you ever think about is making babies. This place stinks like the men's room in the BMT. It's a fucking *pissoir*." He was strong on truth all through the year. "That kid eats more than the five of us put together," he said. "Stop stuffing your face, you fat dumbbell," he said to Phillip.

Then he worked on the neighbors. "Get that nosy old bag out of here," he said. "If she comes on once more with 'my son in the building trades' I'll squash her for the cat."

Then he turned on Spielvogel, the checker, his oldest friend, who only visited on holidays and never spoke to me (shy, the way some bachelors are). "That sonofabitch, don't hand me that friendship crap, all he's after is your ass. That's what I need—a little shitmaker of his using up the air in this flat."

And then there was no one else to dispose of. We were left alone fair and square, facing each other.

"Now, Virginia," he said, "I come to the end of my rope. I see a black wall ahead of me. What the hell am I supposed to do? I only got one life. Should I lie down and die? I don't know what to do any more. I'll give it to you straight, Virginia, if I stick around, you can't help it, you'll hate me . . ."

"I hate you right now," I said. "So do whatever you like."

"This place drives me nuts," he mumbled. "I don't know what to do around here. I want to get you a present. Something."

"I told you, do whatever you like. Buy me a rattrap for rats."

That's when he went down to the House Appliance Store, and he brought back a new broom and a classy dustpan.

"A new broom sweeps clean," he said. "I got to get out of here," he said. "I'm going nuts." Then he began to stuff the duffel bags, and I went to the grocery store but was stopped by Mrs. Raftery, who had to tell me what she considered so beautiful—death—then he kissed and went to join some army somewhere.

I didn't tell John any of this, because I think it makes a woman look too bad to tell on how another man has treated her. He begins to see her through the other man's eyes, a sitting duck, a skinful of flaws. After all, I had come to depend on John. All my husband's friends were strangers now, though I had always said to them, "Feel welcome."

And the family men in the building looked too cunning, as though they had all personally deserted me. If they met me on the stairs, they carried the heaviest groceries up and helped bring Linda's stroller down, but they never asked me a question worth answering at all.

Besides that, Girard and Phillip taught the girls the days of the week: Monday, Tuesday, Wednesday, Johnday, Friday. They waited for him once a week, under the hallway lamp, half asleep like bugs in the sun, sitting in their little chairs with their names on in gold, a birth present from my mother-in-law. At fifteen after eight he punctually came, to read a story, pass out some kisses, and tuck them into bed.

But one night, after a long Johnday of them squealing my eardrum split, after a rainy afternoon with brother constantly raising up his hand against brother, with the girls near ready to go to court over the proper ownership of Melinda Lee, the twenty-four-inch walking doll, the door-bell rang three times. Not any of those times did John's face greet me.

I was too ashamed to call down to Mrs. Raftery, and she was too mean to knock on my door and explain.

He didn't come the following Thursday either. Girard said sadly, "He must've run away, John."

I had to give him up after two weeks' absence and no word. I didn't know how to tell the children: something about right and wrong, goodness and meanness, men and women. I had it all at my finger tips, ready to hand over. But I didn't think I ought to take mistakes and truth away from them. Who knows? They might make a truer friend in this world somewhere than I have ever made. So I just put them in bed and sat in the kitchen and cried.

In the middle of my third beer, searching in my mind for the next step, I found the decision to go on "Strike It Rich." I scrounged some paper and pencil from the toy box and I listed all my troubles, which must be done in order to qualify. The list when complete could have brought tears to the eye of God if He had a minute. At the sight of it my bitterness began to improve. All that is really necessary for survival of the fittest, it seems, is an interest in life, good, bad, or peculiar.

As always happens in these cases where you have begun to help yourself with plans, news comes from an opposite direction. The door-bell rang, two short and two long—meaning John.

My first thought was to wake the children and make them happy. "No! No " he said. "Please don't put yourself to that trouble. Virginia, I'm dog-tired," he said. "Dog-tired. My job is a damn headache. It's too much. It's all day and it scuttles my mind at night, and in the end who does the credit go to?

"Virginia," he said, "I don't know if I can come any more. I've been wanting to tell you. I just don't know. What's it all about? Could you answer me if I asked you? I can't figure this whole thing out at all."

I started the tea steeping because his fingers when I touched them were cold. I didn't speak. I tried looking at it from his man point of view, and I thought he had to take a bus, the tubes, and a subway to see me; and then the subway, the tubes, and a bus to go back home at 1 A.M. It wouldn't be any trouble at all for him to part with us forever. I thought about my life, and I gave strongest consideration to my chil-dren. If given the choice, I decided to choose not to live without him.

"What's that?" he asked, pointing to my careful list of troubles. "Writing a letter?"

"Oh no," I said, "it's for 'Strike It Rich.' I hope to go on the program."

"Virginia, for goodness' sakes," he said, giving it a glance, "you don't have a ghost. They'd laugh you out of the studio. Those people really suffer."

"Are you sure, John?" I asked.

"No question in my mind at all," said John. "Have you ever seen that program? I mean, in addition to all of this—the little disturbances of man"—he waved a scornful hand at my list—"they *suffer*. They live in the forefront of tornadoes, their lives are washed off by floods— catastrophes of God. Oh, Virginia."

"Are you sure, John?"

"For goodness' sake . . ."

Sadly I put my list away. Still, if things got worse, I could always make use of it.

Once that was settled, I acted on an earlier decision. I pushed his cup of scalding tea aside. I wedged myself onto his lap between his hard belt buckle and the table. I put my arms around his neck and said, "How come you're so cold, John?" He has a kind face and he knew how to look astonished. He said, "Why, Virginia, I'm getting warmer." We laughed.

John became a lover to me that night.

Mrs. Raftery is sometimes silly and sick from her private source of cheap wine. She expects John often. "Honor your mother, what's the matter with you, John?" she complains. "Honor. Honor."

"Virginia dear," she says. "You never would've taken John away to Jersey like Margaret. I wish he'd've married you."

"You didn't like me much in those days."

"That's a lie," she says. I know she's a hypocrite, but no more than the rest of the world.

What is remarkable to me is that it doesn't seem to conscience John as I thought it might. It is still hard to believe that a man who sends out the Ten Commandments every year for a Christmas card can be so easy buttoning and unbuttoning.

Of course we must be very careful not to wake the children or disturb the neighbors who will enjoy another person's excitement just so far, and then the pleasure enrages them. We must be very careful for ourselves too, for when my husband comes back, realizing the babies are in school and everything easier, he won't forgive me if I've started it all up again—noisy signs of life that are so much trouble to a man.

We haven't seen him in two and a half years. Although people have suggested it, I do not want the police or Intelligence or a private eye or anyone to go after him to bring him back. I know that if he expected to stay away forever he would have written and said so. As it is, I just don't know what evening, any time, he may appear. Sometimes, stumbling over a blockbuster of a dream at midnight, I wake up to vision his soft arrival.

He comes in the door with his old key. He gives me a strict look and says, "Well, you look older, Virginia." "So do you," I say, although he hasn't changed a bit.

He settles in the kitchen because the children are asleep all over the rest of the house. I unknot his tie and offer him a cold sandwich. He raps my backside, paying attention to the bounce. I walk around him as though he were a Maypole, kissing as I go.

"I didn't like the Army much," he says. "Next time I think I might go join the Merchant Marine."

"What army?" I say.

"It's pretty much the same everywhere," he says.

"I wouldn't be a bit surprised," I say.

"I lost my cuff link, goddamnit," he says, and drops to the floor to look for it. I go down too on my knees, but I know he never had a cuff link in his life. Still I would do a lot for him.

"Got you off your feet that time," he says, laughing. "Oh yes, I did." And before I can even make myself half comfortable on that polka-dotted linoleum, he got onto me right where we were, and the truth is, we were so happy, we forgot the precautions.

Gail Parent (contemporary)

~e 9~

FROM *Sheila Levine Is Dead and Living in New York*

At four I was madly in love with Alan Hirsch, who was madly in love with Cynthia Fishman. He played doctor with me but swore he would marry her when he grew up. At age four I was already the other woman.

•

The average sex act uses up about a hundred and fifty calories. Really, that is a fact. And you don't eat while you fuck. Therefore, the more you fuck, the less you eat. It's the best diet I've ever been on.

•

Some call New York a jungle. It's not. It's a big jockstrap. It supports the men.

Dorothy Parker (1893-1967)

A Telephone Call

Please, God, let him telephone me now. Dear God, let him call me now. I won't ask anything else of You, truly I won't. It isn't very much to ask. It would be so little to You, God, such a little, little thing. Only let him telephone now. Please, God. Please, please, please.

If I didn't think about it, maybe the telephone might ring. Sometimes it does that. If I could think of something else. If I could think of something else. Maybe if I counted five hundred by fives, it might ring by that time. I'll count slowly. I won't cheat. And if it rings when I get to three hundred, I won't stop; I won't answer it until I get to five hundred. Five, ten, fifteen, twenty, twenty-five, thirty, thirty-five, forty, forty-five, fifty. . . . Oh, please ring. Please.

This is the last time I'll look at the clock. I will not look at it again. It's ten minutes past seven. He said he would telephone at five o'clock. "I'll call you at five, darling." I think that's where he said "darling." I'm almost sure he said it there. I know he called me "darling" twice, and the other time was when he said good-by. "Good-by, darling." He was busy, and he can't say much in the office, but he called me "darling" twice. He couldn't have minded my calling him up. I know you shouldn't keep telephoning them—I know they don't like that. When you do that, they know you are thinking about them and wanting them, and that makes them hate you. But I hadn't talked to him in three days—not in three days. And all I did was ask him how he was; it was just the way anybody might have called him up. He couldn't have minded that. He couldn't have thought I was bothering him. "No, of course you're not," he said. And he said he'd telephone me. He didn't have to say that. I didn't ask him to, truly I didn't. I'm sure I didn't. I don't think he would say he'd telephone me, and then just never do it. Please don't let him do that, God. Please don't.

"I'll call you at five, darling." "Good-by, darling." He was busy, and he was in a hurry, and there were people around him, but he called me "darling" twice. That's mine, that's mine. I have that, even if I never see him again. Oh, but that's so little. That isn't enough. Nothing's enough, if I never see him again. Please let me see him again, God. Please, I want him so much. I want him so much. I'll be good, God. I will try to be better, I will, if You will let me see him again. If You let him telephone me. Oh, let him telephone me now.

Ah, don't let my prayer seem too little to You, God. You sit up there, so white and old, with all the angels about You and the stars slipping by. And I come to You with a prayer about a telephone call. Ah, don't laugh, God. You see, You don't know how it feels. You're so safe, there on Your throne, with the blue swirling under You. Nothing can touch You; no one can twist Your heart in his hands. This is suffering, God, this is bad, bad suffering. Won't You help me? For Your Son's sake, help me. You said You would do whatever was asked of You in His name. Oh, God, in the name of Thine only beloved Son, Jesus Christ, our Lord, let him telephone me now.

I must stop this. I mustn't be this way. Look. Suppose a young man says he'll call a girl up, and then something happens, and he doesn't. That isn't so terrible, is it? Why, it's going on all over the world, right this minute. Oh, what do I care what's going on all over the world? Why can't that telephone ring? Why can't it, why can't it? Couldn't you ring? Ah, please, couldn't you? You damned, ugly, shiny thing. It would hurt you to ring, wouldn't it? Oh, that would hurt you. Damn you, I'll pull your filthy roots out of the wall, I'll smash your smug black face in little bits. Damn you to hell.

No, no, no. I must stop. I must think about something else. This is what I'll do. I'll put the clock in the other room. Then I can't look at it. If I do have to look at it, then I'll have to walk into the bedroom, and that will be something to do. Maybe, before I look at it again, he will call me. I'll be so sweet to him, if he calls me. If he says he can't see me tonight, I'll say, "Why, that's all right, dear. Why, of course it's all right." I'll be the way I was when I first met him. Then maybe he'll like me again. I was always sweet, at first. Oh, it's so easy to be sweet to people before you love them.

I think he must still like me a little. He couldn't have called me "darling" twice today, if he didn't still like me a little. It isn't all gone, if he still likes me a little; even if it's only a little, little bit. You see, God, if You would just let him telephone me, I wouldn't have to ask You anything more. I would be sweet to him, I would be gay, I would be just the way I used to be, and then he would love me again. And then I would never have to ask You for anything more. Don't You see, God? So won't You please let him telephone me? Won't You please, please, please?

Are You punishing me, God, because I've been bad? Are You angry with me because I did that? Oh, but, God, there are so many bad people—You could not be hard only to me. And it wasn't very bad; it couldn't have been bad. We didn't hurt anybody, God. Things are only bad when they hurt people. We didn't hurt one single soul; You know that. You know it wasn't bad, don't You, God? So won't You let him telephone me now?

If he doesn't telephone me, I'll know God is angry with me. I'll count five hundred by fives, and if he hasn't called me then, I will know God isn't going to help me, ever again. That will be the sign. Five, ten, fifteen, twenty, twenty-five, thirty, thirty-five, forty, forty-five, fifty, fifty-five. . . . It was bad. I knew it was bad. All right, God, send me to hell. You think You're frightening me with Your hell, don't You? You think Your hell is worse than mine.

I mustn't. I mustn't do this. Suppose he's a little late calling me up—that's nothing to get hysterical about. Maybe he isn't going to call—maybe he's coming straight up here without telephoning. He'll be cross if he sees I have been crying. They don't like you to cry. He doesn't cry. I wish to God I could make him cry. I wish I could make him cry and tread the floor and feel his heart heavy and big and festering in him. I wish I could hurt him like hell.

He doesn't wish that about me. I don't think he even knows how he makes me feel. I wish he could know, without my telling him. They don't like you to tell them they've made you cry. They don't like you to tell them you're unhappy because of them. If you do, they think you're possessive and exacting. And then they hate you. They hate you whenever you say anything you really think. You always have to keep playing little games. Oh, I thought we didn't have to; I thought this was so big I could say whatever I meant. I guess you can't, ever. I guess there isn't ever anything big enough for that. Oh, if he would just telephone, I wouldn't tell him I had been sad about him. They hate sad people. I would be so sweet and so gay, he couldn't help but like me. If he would only telephone. If he would only telephone.

Maybe that's what he is doing. Maybe he is coming on here without calling me up. Maybe he's on his way now. Something might have happened to him. No, nothing could ever happen to him. I can't picture anything happening to him. I never picture him run over. I never see him lying still and long and dead. I wish he were dead. That's a terrible wish. That's a lovely wish. If he were dead he would be mine. If he were dead, I would never think of now and the last few weeks. I would remember only the lovely times. It would be all beautiful. I wish he were dead. I wish he were dead, dead, dead.

This is silly. It's silly to go wishing people were dead just because they don't call you up the very minute they said they would. Maybe the clock's fast; I don't know whether it's right. Maybe he's hardly late at all. Anything could have made him a little late. Maybe he had to stay at his office. Maybe he went home, to call me up from there, and somebody came in. He doesn't like to telephone me in front of people. Maybe he's worried, just a little, little bit, about keeping me waiting. He might even hope that I would call him up. I could do that. I could telephone him.

I mustn't. I mustn't, I mustn't. Oh, God, please don't let me telephone him. Please keep me from doing that. I know, God, just as well as You do, that if he were worried about me, he'd telephone no matter where he was or how many people there were around him. Please make me know that, God. I don't ask You to make it easy for me—You can't do that, for all that You could make a world. Only let me know it, God. Don't let me go on hoping. Don't let me say comforting things to myself. Please don't let me hope, dear God. Please don't.

I won't telephone him. I'll never telephone him again as long as I live. He'll rot in hell, before I'll call him up. You don't have to give me strength, God; I have it myself. If he wanted me, he could get me. He knows where I am. He knows I'm waiting here. He's so sure of me, so sure. I wonder why they hate you, as soon as they are sure of you. I should think it would be so sweet to be sure.

It would be so easy to telephone him. Then I'd know. Maybe it wouldn't be a foolish thing to do. Maybe he wouldn't mind. Maybe he'd like it. Maybe he has been trying to get me. Sometimes people try and try to get you on the telephone, and they say the number doesn't answer. I'm not just saying that to help myself; that really happens. You know that really happens, God. Oh, God, keep me away from that telephone. Keep me away. Let me still have just a little bit of pride. I think I'm going to need it, God. I think it will be all I'll have.

Oh, what does pride matter, when I can't stand it if I don't talk to him? Pride like that is such a silly, shabby little thing. The real pride, the big pride, is in having no pride. I'm not saying that just because I want to call him. I am not. That's true, I know that's true. I will be big. I will be beyond little prides.

Please, God, keep me from telephoning him. Please, God.

I don't see what pride has to do with it. This is such a little thing, for me to be bringing in pride, for me to be making such a fuss about. I may have misunderstood him. Maybe he said for me to call him up, at five. "Call me at five, darling." He could have said that, perfectly well. It's so possible that I didn't hear him right. "Call me at five, darling." I'm almost sure that's what he said. God, don't let me talk this way to myself. Make me know, please make me know.

I'll think about something else. I'll just sit quietly. If I could sit still. If I could sit still. Maybe I could read. Oh, all the books are about people who love each other, truly and sweetly. What do they want to write about that for? Don't they know it isn't true? Don't they know it's a lie, it's a God damned lie? What do they have to tell about that for, when they know how it hurts? Damn them, damn them, damn them.

I won't. I'll be quiet. This is nothing to get excited about. Look. Suppose he were someone I didn't know very well. Suppose he were another girl. Then I'd just telephone and say, "Well, for goodness' sake, what happened to you?" That's what I'd do, and I'd never even think about it. Why can't I be casual and natural, just because I love him? I can be. Honestly, I can be. I'll call him up, and be so easy and pleasant. You see if I won't, God. Oh, don't let me call him. Don't, don't, don't.

God, aren't You really going to let him call me? Are You sure, God? Couldn't You please relent? Couldn't You? I don't even ask You to let him telephone me this minute, God; only let him do it in a little while. I'll count five hundred by fives. I'll do it so slowly and so fairly. If he hasn't telephoned then, I'll call him. I will. Oh, please, dear God, dear kind God, my blessed Father in Heaven, let him call before then. Please, God. Please.

Five, ten, fifteen, twenty, twenty-five, thirty, thirty-five . . .

•

FROM *Dusk Before Fireworks*

"I watched you just sit there and deliberately talk yourself into it, starting right out of nothing. Now what's the idea of that? Oh, good Lord, what's the matter with women, anyway?"

"Please don't call me 'women,' " she said.

"I'm sorry darling," he said. "I didn't mean to use bad words." He smiled at her. She felt her heart go liquid, but she did her best to be harder won.

•

FROM *The Grandmother of the*
Aunt of the Gardener

I have here before me a small green book called *The Ideal System for Acquiring a Practical Knowledge of French* by Mlle. V. D. Gaudel (who, in case you're going over and you don't know anyone in Paris, lives at 346 Rue Saint-Honoré). Well, everything might have been all right if Mlle. Gaudel—now why do I picture her as fond of dancing and light wines, with a way of flipping up her skirts at the back, to the cry of "Oh-la-la"?—had not subtitled her work *Just the French One Wants to Know*. Somehow, those words antagonized me, by their very blandness, so that I forgot the thirst for knowledge and searched the tome only for concrete examples of just the French one will never need. Oh-la-la, yourself, Mademoiselle, and go on and get the hell back into *La Vie Parisienne*!

Now you know perfectly well that at my time of life it would be just a dissipation of energy for me to learn the French equivalent of "Either now, or this afternoon at five." It is, at best, a matter of dark doubt that I shall ever be in any position in which it will be necessary for me to cry: "Although the captain is far from here, I always think of him." It is possible, of course, but it's a nasty wrench to the arm of coincidence that I shall find occasion for the showing-off of the phrase "Her marriage took place (*eut lieu*) on the 2nd of April, 1905"; or that it will be given me to slide gently into a conversation with "I admire the large black eyes of this orphan." Better rest I silent forever than that I pronounce: "In this case, it is just that you should not like riding and swimming"; or that I inquire: "Are you pleased that they will bring the cricket set?"; or that I swing into autobiography with the confession: "I do not like to play blindman's buff"; or that I so seriously compromise myself as to suggest: "I propose that you breakfast with me and afterwards look for our friends."

The future is veiled, perhaps mercifully, and so I cannot say that never, while I live, shall I have occasion to announce in French: "It was to punish your foster-brother"; but I know which way I would bet. It may be that some day I shall be in such straits that I shall have to remark: "The friend of my uncle who took the quill feather bought a round black rice-straw hat trimmed with two long ostrich feathers and a jet buckle." Possibly circumstances will so weave themselves that it will be just the moment for me to put in: "Mr. Fouchet would have received some eel." It might occur that I must thunder: "Obey, or I will not show you the beautiful gold chain." But I will be damned if it is ever

going to be of any good to me to have at hand Mlle. Gaudel's masterpiece:
"I am afraid he will not arrive in time to accompany me on the harp."

Oh, "Just the French One Wants to Know" *mon oeil*, Mademoiselle.
And you know what you can do, far better than I could tell you.

•

FROM *The Lady's Reward*

Be you wise and never sad,
You will get your lovely lad.
Never serious be, nor true,
And your wish will come to you—
And if that makes you happy, kid,
You'll be the first it ever did.

•

FROM *Mrs. Post Enlarges on Etiquette*

Emily Post's *Etiquette* is out again, this time in a new and an enlarged
edition, and so the question of what to do with my evenings has been
all fixed up for me. There will be an empty chair at the deal table at
Tony's, when the youngsters gather to discuss life, sex, literature, the
drama, what is a gentleman, and whether or not to go on to Helen
Morgan's Club when the place closes; for I shall be at home among my
book. I am going in for a course of study at the knee of Mrs. Post.
Maybe, some time in the misty future, I shall be Asked Out, and I shall
be ready. You won't catch me being intentionally haughty to subordi-
nates or refusing to be a pallbearer for any reason except serious ill health.
I shall live down the old days, and with the help of Mrs. Post and God
(always mention a lady's name first) there will come a time when you
will be perfectly safe in inviting me to your house, which should never
be called a residence except in printing or engraving.

It will not be a grueling study, for the sprightliness of Mrs. Post's
style makes the textbook as fascinating as it is instructive. Her characters,
introduced for the sake of example, are called by no such unimaginative
titles as Mrs. A., or Miss Z., or Mr. X.; they are Mrs. Worldly, Mr.
Bachelor, the Gildings, Mrs. Oldname, Mrs. Neighbor, Mrs. Stranger,
Mrs. Kindhart, and Mr. and Mrs. Nono Better. This gives the work all
the force and the application of a morality play.

•

FROM *Home Is the Sailor*

The Swiss are a neat and an industrious people, none of whom is under seventy-five years of age. They make cheeses, milk chocolate, and watches, all of which, when you come right down to it, are pretty fairly unnecessary. It is all true about yodelling and cowbells. It is, however, not true about St. Bernard dogs rescuing those lost in the snow. Once there was something in the story; but, what with the altitude and the long evenings and one thing and another, the present dogs are of such inclinations that it is no longer reasonable to send them out to work, since they took to eating the travelers. Barry, the famous dog hero, credited with the saving of seven lives, is now on view, stuffed; stuffed, possibly, with the travelers he did not bring home. Skiing is extremely difficult, and none of my affair. The most frequent accident, among ski-jumpers, is the tearing off of an ear. The edelweiss is a peculiarly un-pleasant-looking flower. During the early summer, the natives fling themselves into the sport of watching one cow fight another cow; the winning lady is hung with blossoms and escorted, by her fans, from café to café, all night long. There is a higher consumption of alcohol, per capita, in Switzerland than in any other country in Europe (although there may be some slight change in those figures, now that your cor-respondent has returned to Tony's). The country itself is extravagantly beautiful, and practically crawling with lakes and mountains. And, while we are on that subject, how are you fixed for mountains, anyway? Be-cause, after a year in the Alps, I should be glad to give them to you for your birthday and throw in a mandolin.

Cathie Pelletier (contemporary)

FROM *The Funeral Makers*

"If God had meant for me to be religious, he would have alphabetized the books of the Bible. It was just too hard for me to find what I was looking for, especially if I was looking for it through a few glasses of scotch."

—Gert McKinnon, Atheist and Spinster, 1935

•

September arrived and Marge McKinnon became seriously ill. And while the land and the animals had been in a hurry, Marge was not. She held on to her illness as though it were a brooch, a family heirloom, and in a way it was. She was the only person in Mattagash, Maine, suffering from beriberi. It was the town's only attraction and a well-deserved one considering that Marge contracted beriberi because her father, the missionary Reverend Ralph C. McKinnon, died in China of kala-azar.

Someone in Mattagash looked it up in a medical book and discovered that kala-azar is sometimes called dum dum's fever. Many of the townspeople wondered who had had the foresight to call it dum dum's fever without ever having met the Reverend Ralph.

•

"What's so funny?" asked Pearl.

"Remember the time you wanted to . . ." But Marvin Sr. lost control again. He pressed a hand into his stomach to ease the pain of laughing. Tears filled his eyes.

"Well, for heaven's sakes, tell us," said Pearl. "The time I wanted to do what?" Marvin Sr. still couldn't speak. Junior had slowly inched his way over until his head was lying on his father's shoulder. He was snoring now, mouth wide open.

"Are you laughing at Junior?" asked Pearl, who had begun to laugh along without knowing why. Finally, Marvin Sr. said, "The time you wanted to turn the back room of the funeral home into a beauty shop and call the whole thing *The Ivy Funeral Home and Beauty Salon.*" Marvin Sr. doubled up with laughter.

"It wasn't that bad of an idea. Women can't always get an appointment right away when someone in the family dies. It would have come in real handy." Pearl was indignant, especially when she saw a trace of a smile on Thelma's face.

•

. . . she saw the sign in the camper window. There was no mistaking it, and her heart pounded in recognition of what it clearly meant: FIRE. Pearl's scream caught Thelma, who was trying to imagine an entire row of women sobbing beneath hair dryers in the back room of the funeral home, totally off guard. The Packard swerved into the gravel at the side of the road as Thelma fought to keep it in control. A pickup truck coming at them in the opposite direction left the road to avoid Thelma's recovery of the car, which sent it wildly into the territory of southbound traffic. The brakes screeched. Pearl looked back, expecting to see flames engulfing the camper at any minute then spreading to the gas tank of the Packard. The entire Ivy family would be wiped out in one fell swoop. "The Lord is my shepherd, I shall not want," she began. Marvin Sr. opened his door, thinking Thelma would soon bring the car to a halt.

"The kids are burning!" screamed Pearl.

Thelma *had* slowed the Packard down and had it almost under control until she heard Pearl say that the babies she had brought into the world, the children she had born to this family of death were on fire. Thelma put her face in her hands and screamed uncontrollably, leaving the car to steer itself. The Packard took an alarming plunge for the ditch, threatening to tip the camper, which was swaying dangerously by this time. The door Marvin Sr. had opened, in order that he might rescue his grandchildren from a fiery inferno, rocked on its hinges, then closed on his leg, like the huge jaws of a dinosaur.

Pearl had wanted to slap Thelma from the first moment they met, so she let her have one evenly across the side of her head. Then she grabbed the wheel herself, steering the Packard with her left hand, a task Pearl would never have attempted with two hands. She did not drive. But she was a religious woman and, not about to play with fate, she began to pray. "Yea, though I walk through the valley . . ." Unable to open the heavy door, Thelma had rolled down her window and was attempting to climb out. Pearl reached over with her right hand and caught one of Thelma's winglike arms and held on. In the backseat Marvin Sr. was still trying to extricate the portion of leg that his door had closed on.

"This is worse than the war!" he shouted in pain. Then, "Step on the brake, Pearly!"

Pearl struggled to get her left foot past Thelma's and onto the brake. She managed, but not knowing the complexities of the automobile, she pushed the clutch instead. The big green Packard, with Pearl steering by means of her left hand, snaked down the highway. Thelma's crying was out of control when Marvin Jr. woke up with the full effects of the scotch upon him. By this time Pearl had figured out which pedal was the brake and slammed her left foot down on it. The brakes screamed, and the weaving Packard, complete with a camper of innocent children, slowed down.

"A fire in the camper!" Marvin Sr. shouted to his confused son. Marvin Jr. grabbed the tumbler of scotch and melted ice that was still between his legs. He had heard his father in pain, his wife crying uncontrollably, his mother finishing up a hurried rendition of the 23rd Psalm. In an instant Marvin Ivy Jr. knew that he had before him the means to become the hero of his family. He leapt from the Packard with the tumbler of watered-down sctoch, shouting "Daddy's coming!" Behind him went the sack of egg-and-tuna sandwiches Thelma had packed for the occasion. Wondering why the earth was moving, Junior bounced along the road. The tumbler followed, leaving a wet, dark trail in the gravel.

"My God, we've lost Junior!" shouted Marvin Sr., who had just managed in his newfound drunkenness to retrieve his leg from the clutches of the door. Pearl, who was on her second recital of the same psalm, looked back in horror, sure her husband meant that the flames had reached the backseat and engulfed her only child. She forgot completely about steering the Packard and let go of both the wheel and Thelma. "He maketh me to lie down in green pastures . . ." Pearl shouted as the bewildered Packard left the road and careened through a field of hay and clover. It came to rest rather abruptly against a huge rockpile, only because it did not have the speed to climb it.

Halfway out her window, Thelma looked up expecting to see her maker, but saw instead a state trooper looking suspiciously down at her, then at the half-killed bottle in the backseat.

Pearl glanced back to see if the camper had been blown to smithereens, leaving behind only bits and pieces of her poor little grandchildren: A ribbon particle. A teddy bear's ear. A shard of tweed skirt. But it was still there. In the window Regina Beth's small hand was holding up the sign: FOOD. Cynthia Jane was standing near the trooper at her mother's window, tugging at her panties.

"Regina Beth can't spell at all, Mama. She held up FIRE instead of FOOD. Are we going to have a picnic right here?"

"Cynthia Jane," said Thelma, trying to recapture some dignity. "Please don't tug at your panties in front of strangers."

"We're hungry, Mama. Can we make a fireplace out of them big rocks and roast hot dogs?"

Pearl was examining the bruise on Marvin Sr.'s leg. "This is some way to go to a funeral," she said to the trooper. "We're lucky it isn't our own."

"Regina Beth is holding her breath again," said Cynthia Jane.

"Good for her," said Pearl.

Marvin Jr. lost both knees of his gray Sunday slacks, including most of the skin beneath. Limping through the field to catch up with his family was a painful endeavor. Each time weight was applied to his left foot, he winced. The ankle, he was sure, must be broken or sprained. There was a great deal of pain in his elbow, which was badly scraped. He stuck his head inside the camper door, expecting to find the charred remnants of his tiny children. Instead he found only Regina Beth, who was sitting on the floor holding her breath and the SORRY! game. Junior scooped the child up into his arms and hobbled painfully around to the Packard. They were all there, including a state trooper who was questioning a tearful Thelma. All except for Marvin Randall Ivy III. When Cynthia Jane saw her father, she ran to him, stepping on his painful left foot.

"Get off!" shouted Junior, putting down Regina Beth, who had begun to breathe again when she saw the policeman.

"Daddy," Cynthia Jane pleaded. "Can we camp out right here? Can we? Please?"

"Where's your brother?" Marvin Jr. asked his oldest child.

"He got off at the last gas station to pee and Mama left him," said Cynthia Jane, still chafed.

"Why in God's name didn't you stop us?" asked Pearl.

"We didn't have a sign that said STOP," said Cynthia Jane, now tugging on her father's sore arm.

"I'll give you a sign," Pearl said, holding up a fist.

Ann Petry (1908-   )

❧ ❧

FROM *Mamie*

When she went on these starvation diets, she seemed impelled to torture herself by handling food, by cooking food that smelled to high heaven. She would sit at the table with a cup of black coffee and a package of cigarettes in front of her, sit there and sip the coffee; and smoke one cigarette after another, and watch them eat, watch forkfuls of the great round crusted roast of beef, and the browned potatoes and the beautiful fresh vegetables and the rich buttery dessert go into their mouths; her eyes followed the course of their forks and spoons from the plate to mouth, mouth to plate, her eyes eating the food with them, her lower lip thrust out, mouth a little open. . . .

Then Mamie would catch him staring and turn her belligerent baleful hungry eyes toward him, and he would look away, eating faster and faster, eating more than his stomach could possibly hold, afraid to stop eating. . . .

Once she'd held out for a whole month, a month during which

she watched them eat cream puffs, chocolate éclairs, strawberry short-
cakes piled up with whipped cream, all the rich sweet fattening food she
loved most, while she drank black coffee, and wolfed down some kind
of dry hard tasteless crackers.

Fiona Pitt-Kethley (1954-   )

Men

I sing of Men—crude, thoughtless, kinky men.

The ones who recommend you to a mate
and bring him round—fat, ugly, hopeful too.
('But why object? He only wants to watch—
well, for the first ten minutes, anyway . . .')

Those who are grieved you're not a lesbian—
they'd bargained on two girls to fill their bed.

The guilty types who ask to be abused—
I'll swear alright, but in my own good time—
or leave, muttering, 'Sorry about last night.'

Each who, unwisely seeks comparisons,
needs constant humouring like a lunatic,
wants A-plus marked in teacher's big black book.

Last, those who in the throes of passion drop
your clothes, then, stop to hang their trousers up.

There's nothing *badly* wrong with blokes like these—
they wouldn't use you as a punching-bag
or ask to have their faces shat upon—
a Civil Service taste I heard from some
Madame's good friend. All that they need to make
them perfect men is some *good* woman's love.
I'm glad that I am not that sort.

Penis-Envy

Freud, you were right! I must expose my id
And show the penis-envy that lies hid.
It's not that I admire the look as such,
It seems a strange adornment for a crutch,
Like sets of giblets from a butcher's shop,
Two kidneys with a chicken-neck on top,
Floating serene in baths like lug-worm bait,
Or, jokily bobbing with the jogger's gait.
Fig-leaves, I'm sure, are prettier far than cocks,
And only suffer greenfly not the pox.
As tools, pricks really aren't reliable,
One minute hard, the next too pliable.
If I had bought a hammer or a chisel
As changeable, I'd think it was a swizzle.

It's not that I'm against them in their place,
But simply that I cannot see a case
For cocks to be a sort of union card
In life's closed shop. I think it very hard
That humans with these fickle bits and bobs
Are given a fairer lot and better jobs.
If only I'd had one of them, it seems
I could have had success, fulfilled my dreams.
A female eunuch though, all I'll attain
Is Pyrrhic victory and trifling gain.

Sylvia Plath (1932–1963)

The Applicant

First, are you our sort of a person?
Do you wear
A glass eye, false teeth or a crutch,

A brace or a hook,
Rubber breasts or a rubber crotch,

Stitches to show something's missing? No, no? Then
How can we give you a thing?
Stop crying.
Open your hand.
Empty? Empty. Here is a hand.

To fill it and willing
To bring teacups and roll away headaches
And do whatever you tell it.
Will you marry it?
It is guaranteed

To thumb shut your eyes at the end
And dissolve of sorrow.
We make new stock from the salt.
I notice you are stark naked.
How about this suit——

Black and stiff, but not a bad fit.
Will you marry it?
It is waterproof, shatterproof, proof
Against fire and bombs through the roof.
Believe me, they'll bury you in it.

Now your head, excuse me, is empty.
I have the ticket for that.
Come here, sweetie, out of the closet.
Well, what do you think of *that*?
Naked as paper to start

But in twenty-five years she'll be silver,
In fifty, gold.
A living doll, everywhere you look.
It can sew, it can cook,
It can talk, talk, talk.

It works, there is nothing wrong with it.
You have a hole, it's a poultice.
You have an eye, it's an image.

My boy, it's your last resort.
Will you marry it, marry it, marry it.

•

FROM *The Bell Jar*

It's not that we hadn't enough to eat at home, it's just that my grandmother always cooked economy joints and economy meat loafs and had
the habit of saying, the minute you lifted the first forkful to your mouth,
"I hope you enjoy that, it cost forty-one cents a pound," which always
made me feel I was somehow eating pennies instead of Sunday roast.

•

I had read one of Mrs. Guinea's books in the town library—the college
library didn't stock them for some reason—and it was crammed from
beginning to end with long, suspenseful questions: "Would Evelyn dis-
cern that Gladys knew Roger in her past? wondered Hector feverishly"
and "How could Donald marry her when he learned of the child Elsie,
hidden away with Mrs. Rollmop on the secluded country farm? Griselda
demanded of her bleak, moonlit pillow." These books earned Philomena
Guinea, who later told me she had been very stupid at college, millions
and millions of dollars.

Mrs. Guinea answered my letter and invited me to lunch at her
home. That was where I saw my first fingerbowl.

The water had a few cherry blossoms floating in it, and I thought
it must be come clear sort of Japanese after-dinner soup and ate every
bit of it, including the crisp little blossoms. Mrs. Guinea never said anything, and it was only much later, when I told a debutante I knew at
college about the dinner, that I learned what I had done.

•

Suddenly, after I finished a poem, he said, "Esther, have you ever seen
a man?"

The way he said it I knew he didn't mean a regular man or a man
in general, I knew he meant a man naked.

"No," I said. "Only statues."

"Well, don't you think you would like to see me?"

I didn't know what to say. My mother and my grandmother had
started hinting around to me a lot lately about what a fine, clean boy
Buddy Willard was, coming from such a fine, clean family, and how
everybody at church thought he was a model person, so kind to his

parents and to older people, as well as so athletic and so handsome and so intelligent.

All I'd heard about, really, was how fine and clean Buddy was and how he was the kind of a person a girl should stay fine and clean for. So I didn't really see the harm in anything Buddy would think up to do.

"Well, all right, I guess so," I said.

I stared at Buddy while he unzipped his chino pants and took them off and laid them on a chair and then took off his underpants that were made of something like nylon fishnet.

"They're cool," he explained, "and my mother says they wash easily."

Then he just stood there in front of me and I kept staring at him. The only thing I could think of was turkey neck and turkey gizzards and I felt very depressed.

Buddy seemed hurt I didn't say anything. "I think you ought to get used to me like this," he said. "Now let me see you."

But undressing in front of Buddy suddenly appealed to me about as much as having my Posture Picture taken at college, where you have to stand naked in front of a camera, knowing all the time that a picture of you stark naked, both full view and side view, is going into the college gym files to be marked A B C or D depending on how straight you are.

"Oh, some other time," I said.

Letty Cottin Pogrebin (1939–   )

❧ ❧

FROM *A Question of Appearances*

The ability to keep one's hands free implies not only status and economic privilege but real physical freedom. It is much easier for the unencumbered to use their hands, defend themselves, be mobile, run, or stand tall and retain their dignity whether uniformed or not. Historically and cross-culturally, women have been weighted down by babies in their arms and baskets on their heads while men, carrying only their weapons, move freely in the world. In modern society as in ancient cultures, noticing who schleps and carries tells us a lot about who is usually left holding the bag.

Mimi Pond (contemporary)

⤳ ❧ ⤳

FROM *Shoes Never Lie*

FEMALE BONDING: TEAM SHOPPING

Who says sisterhood isn't poweful? Take your best friend shopping for shoes with you. Urge each other on to more and more and more stores in what can become a marathon competitive consumer event.

Make sure that your friend shares your tastes and has your best interests in mind. She'll steer you away from the insanity of spike-heeled leopard-skin boots unless she's convinced they're truly *you*. When you're in your darkest hour of decision-making, she won't say, "I don't know why on earth you'd ever want shoes like *that*. Come look at these nice brown oxfords over here."

On the dark side of team shopping, make sure that everything between you and your friend is sunny and bright. Those harboring subconscious hostilities *could* lead you far astray into the embarrassing world of salmon Beatle boots, marabou mules, or plastic jeweled Roman sandals.

Once I forced my dearest friend, almost at knifepoint, to buy a pair of Ralph Lauren boots on sale. I wanted them in the worst way, but all they had left was *her* size. This is called Vicarious Shoe Thrills. Sure, I got a few kicks, but I felt just awful about it later. It was too late for her. All sales were final.

•

WHAT BECOMES OF THE BROKEN-HEARTED? THEY BUY SHOES

Did he tell you he wanted his freedom? Did he say you needed yours? Was there Someone Else? Did he leave without saying good-bye . . . or were you forced to throw him out because you had too much self-respect not to? Whatever the reason, all that remains now is an aching in your heart.

Don't make that fatal mistake. Don't pick up that phone and beg him to come back. Show some self-respect. There's an on-ramp to the road of recovery and it's called New Shoes.

Call up your best friend and tell her this: "My man is gone but my feet are still here. There's an empty place in my heart and a draft on my toes. I need love, but right now I'll settle for shoes. Let's hit the stores." If she's a real friend, a shoe-buddy, she'll take a hint and guide you through this therapy for the Heartbroken.

RULE #1: Don't be afraid to spend money. You deserve a treat after what you went through for that louse.

RULE #2: Don't be afraid to buy more than one pair. Buy as many as it takes to forget.

RULE #3: Make sure you're not going to run into him while you're out shopping. That would spoil all the fun.

RULE #4: Don't tell the shoe salesman that you're Shopping to Forget. He may figure you for a chump and take advantage of your delicate emotional state. Act like the fabulous woman you know you really are. If he tries to sell them to you in vermilion when what you want is cerise, tell him where he and his kind can get off.

In no time at all you'll feel like a new woman. New men, better men, will notice that "new shoe glow" and flock to your side. You'll have to beat them away with long-handled shoehorns. Shoes conquer all.

Paula Poundstone (contemporary)

~❧ ❧~

FROM *Why Is Everybody Always Pickin'
on Bill?*

[On criticism of a TV show in development] Why would even a critic criticize something that doesn't exist? It's like seeing a sonogram and saying the baby's ugly.

•

It took twelve long years for the Republicans to drive up the deficit, and now Bob Dole can stand on the Senate floor with pointer and chart and claim that the Republicans can reduce the deficit better than Clinton can, without raising taxes. Apparently they had this plan all along, but only recently got hold of a pointer and a chart.

•

One of the first people we hired was a young receptionist. She answers the phone like she's doing time.

•

FROM *L.A. Laugh Tracks*

The editor guy of this magazine asked me the other day if Hollywood has morals. Gee, I certainly don't think so. He seems like such a bright man; why would he ask a question like that? Hollywood uses the TV laugh track, the very soul of dishonesty. In the years before I understood that they couldn't possibly have performed before a live audience, I thought the Flintstones were funny to adults. I assumed the jokes were just over my head and that, when I matured, the elephant who said, "It's a living," while his trunk was used as the spray nozzle for washing dishes would be a knee-slapper.

Barbara Pym (1913-1980)

~≈ ℈~

FROM *Excellent Women*

I did part-time work at an organisation which helped impoverished gentlewomen, a cause very near to my own heart, as I felt that I was just the kind of person who might one day become one.

•

"It's not the animals so much as the birds," said Mrs. Bone fiercely. "You will hardly believe this, Miss—er—but I was sitting in the window this afternoon and as it was a fine day I had it open at the bottom, when I felt something drop into my lap. And do you know what it was?" She turned and peered at me intently.

I said that I had no idea.

"Unpleasantness," she said, almost triumphantly so that I was reminded of William Caldicote. Then lowering her voice she explained, "From a bird, you see. It had *done* something when I was actually sitting in my own drawing-room."

"How annoying," I said, feeling mesmerised and unable even to laugh. . . .

"I eat as many birds as possible," said Mrs. Bone when we were sitting down to roast chicken. "I have them sent from Harrods or Fortnum's, and sometimes I go and look at them in the cold meats department. They do them up very prettily with aspic jelly and decorations. At least we can eat our enemies."

•

FROM *A Few Green Leaves*

Beatrix . . . found herself thinking that Emma could have made herself look more attractive. She was getting a little too old for the modish drabness and wispyness so fashionable today. Surely a dress of a prettier color and some attempt at a hair style, either curled or neatly cut and set, might have made the evening even more successful? It wasn't as if Emma had ever produced anything that could justify such high-minded dowdiness—here Beatrix considered various contemporary women of distinction—no novel or volume of poetry or collection of paintings, only a few unreadable anthropological papers. Was she not capable of better things?

Gilda Radner (1946–1989)

On Playing the Fool

I just realized: I have such a fear of looking like the fool that I will *play* the fool. It's like the emperor's new clothes. It's like walking outside all naked and not knowing it. If I'm naked, I want to know it. When I was a little girl, my family lived in Florida during the winter. A little boy named Mark, who lived on our street, came by our house one day and yelled from his bike, "Gilda, I saw you outside yesterday in your underwear!" I said, "You did not. . . ." And he kept going, "I saw Gilda in her underwear!" So I went back into the house and I thought, "Oh, God. Did I go outside in my underwear by accident? Did I go insane for a minute and go out the door? Maybe I just walked *by* the door. . . ." And I thought, the *horror* if he saw me in my underwear. He convinced me that maybe I *did* do that. And I thought right then —'cause I felt sick in my stomach if he did see me—if I was gonna go outside in my underwear, when I got out there I was gonna yell, "HEY EVERYBODY! I'M OUTSIDE IN MY UNDERWEAR!" so I wouldn't have that sick feeling inside.

Libby Reid (contemporary)

FROM *You Don't Have to Pet to Be Popular*

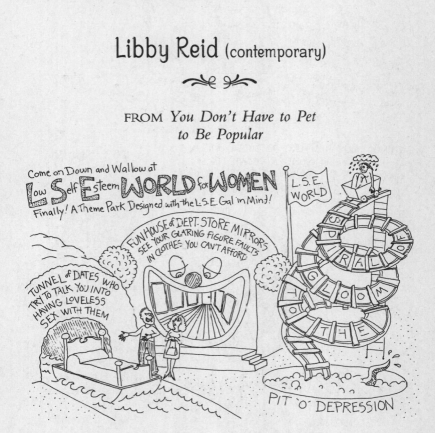

He's a snappy dresser, has curly hair and doesn't smell bad—Real Prime Mate Material! ....I think it would be best if we moved in to a new, bigger apartment instead of his or mine. ....I prefer a simple wedding, but it's o.k. by me if he wants a gala reception. ....Good thing he makes Big $ because we'll need it to hire the nanny for our darling identical twin babies whose birth coincides with the completion of our beautiful country home. ....It's too soon to think about retirement plans.

I wonder what she looks like naked.

THINGS YOU MIGHT LIKE TO DWELL ON AT 4:00 A.M. WHILE WONDERING WHATEVER HAPPENED TO THE GUY WHO NEVER CALLED BACK WHO YOU COULD HAVE SWORN WAS YOUR BOYFRIEND:

I never should have let him see me naked under fluorescent lights

Is there such a thing as Viral Amnesia?

The T.V. commercials were right! It's my breath.

I scared him away because I—
Ⓐ Loved too much
Ⓑ Loved too little
Ⓒ Loved too medium

He's beaten up and bleeding in a ditch somewhere. .....I hope.

Perhaps he's in a time warp where 6 weeks seem like 6 minutes

Agnes Repplier (1855–1950)

~∾ ∾~

FROM *Counter-Currents*

I pick up a very serious and very well-written book on the Brontë sisters, and am told that if I would "touch the very heart of the mystery that was Charlotte Brontë" (I had never been aware that there was anything mysterious about this famous lady), I will find it—save the mark!—in her passionate love for children.

"We are face to face here, not with a want, but with an abyss, depth beyond depth of tenderness, and longing, and frustration; with a passion that found no clear voice in her works because it was one with the elemental nature in her, undefined, unuttered, unutterable!"

It was certainly unuttered. It was not even hinted at in Miss Brontë's novels, nor in her voluminous correspondence. Her attitude toward children—so far as it found expression—was the arid but pardonable attitude of one who had been their reluctant caretaker and teacher. If, as we are now told, "there were moments when it was pain for Charlotte to see the children born of and possessed by other women," there were certainly hours—so much she makes clear to us—in which the business of looking after them wearied her beyond her powers of endurance. It is true that Miss Brontë said a few, a very few friendly words about these little people.. She did not, like Swift, propose that babies should be cooked and eaten. But this temperate regard, this restricted benevolence, gives us no excuse for wallowing in sentiment at her expense.

Joan Rivers (1939?–)

~∾ ∾~

One-liners

A friend of mine confused her valium with her birth control pills—she had fourteen kids but didn't give a shit.

•

The Royal Family? A bunch of Dogs! Go out on the street, call their names: "Queenie, Duke, and Prince." See what shows up!

•

I was dating a transvestite. My mother said, "Marry him. You'll double your wardrobe!"

•

I read the National Enquirer. Don't you read the Enquirer? . . . Who said no? . . . What do you read when you go to the bathroom? I open up the Enquirer—I automatically go mmgh! . . . . It's replacing bran muffins!

Roseanne (1952-   )

≈≈

Stand-up routine

This bugs me the worst. That's when the husband thinks that the wife knows where everything is, huh? Like they think the uterus is a tracking device. He comes in: "Hey, Roseanne! Roseanne! Do we have any Cheetos left?" Like he can't go over and lift up that sofa cushion himself.

•

People say to me, "You're not very feminine." Well, they can *suck my dick*.

Helen Rowland (1875-1950)

≈≈

FROM *Book of Flirts*

Marvellous, oh, my Daughter, is the way of a man with women; for every man hath a *method* and each his favorite *stunt*. And the stunt that he hath found to work successfully with one damsel shall be practised upon each in turn, even unto the finest details thereof.

Behold, one man shall come unto thee saying:

"How foolish are the sentimentalists! But, as for *me*, my motives are altruistic and disinterested; and a woman's *friendship* is what I most desire." Yet, I charge thee, seek among his women "friends" and thou shalt not find an *homely* damsel in all their number.

For this is the *platonic* stunt. . . .

Yet observe how still another seeketh to be more subtle.

Mark how he sitteth afar off and talketh of love in the *abstract*; how he calleth three times a week, yet remaineth always *impersonal*; how he praiseth the shape of thine hand and admireth thy rings, yet toucheth not so much as the *tips* of thy fingers.

"Lo," he thinketh in his heart, "I shall keep her guessing. Yea, I shall wrack her soul with thoughts of how I may be brought to subjection. And when she can no longer contain her curiosity, then will she seek to *lure* me, and I shall gather her in mine arms."

And this is the *elusive* stunt.

. . . Each of these is but as a chainstitch unto a rose pattern, beside him that playeth the *frankly devoted*.

For all women are unto him as one woman—and that one *putty*.

•

FROM *Reflections of a Bachelor Girl*

Flinging yourself at a man's head is like flinging a bone at a cat; it doesn't fascinate him, it frightens him.

•

Never worry for fear you have broken a man's heart; at the worst it is only sprained and a week's rest will put it in perfect working condition again.

•

About the only sign of personal individuality that the average woman is allowed to retain after she marries is her toothbrush.

•

There are moments when the meanest of women may feel a sisterly sympathy for her husband's first wife.

•

A girl who has a brother has a great advantage over one who hasn't; she gets a working knowledge of men without having to go through the matrimonial inquisition in order to acquire it.

•

FROM *It Must Be Thrilling to Be a Man*

It must be thrilling to be a man!

It must be wonderful always to get the best food, the best service and all the waiter's attention. . . .

It must be wonderful to feel that your morals are not your own responsibility, and that it is up to some woman to "guide you to heaven." . . .

It must be thrilling to know that you will always be "as young as you feel," and that you will be fascinating just as long as you have a few strands of hair left to plaster across your forehead.

It must be comforting to face forty without the slightest fear that you will be out of the "vamping" class—and to believe at fifty that a girl of nineteen loves you for yourself alone!

It must be consoling to know that, no matter how poor or plain or passé you may be, you can always find some woman willing to dine with you, flirt with you—and even to marry you! . . .

It must be delightful to be able to carry all your belongings in your pockets, instead of having to struggle with a hand-bag, a vanity case, a change-purse, and half a dozen other pieces of "junk." . . .

It must be wonderful to know that, when you die, if you have managed to keep out of jail and the newspaper, everybody will speak of you as a "good man."

It must be wonderful to have someone believe everything you tell her!

It must be *wonderful* to be a man!

•

One-liners

When you see what some girls marry, you realize how they must hate to work for a living.

•

A bachelor never quite gets over the idea that he is a thing of beauty and a boy forever.

•

From the day on which she weighs 140, the chief excitement of a woman's life consists in spotting women who are fatter than she is

Jill Ruckelshaus (1937?-)

On Following

It occurred to me when I was thirteen and wearing white gloves and Mary Janes and going to dancing school, that no one should have to dance backward all their lives.

Rita Rudner (contemporary)

FROM *Naked Beneath My Clothes*

WHAT IS IT WITH MEN AND THEIR CARS?

What is it with men and their cars? I know I've just repeated myself, but it's a question that bears repeating. What is it with men and their cars?

I've never known a man who wasn't deeply attached on a very emotional level to his beloved vehicle. Whether it was a piece of junk or a masterpiece made no difference. They rode in their metal boxes and were in control of their lives. I think I know why so many men are afraid to make a commitment to women. It's because we can't be steered.

My first boyfriend, who shall remain nameless and probably jobless, had an antique car. It was a 1957 Jaguar. Now, 1991 Jaguars are not all that reliable. This car kept falling apart in the garage. Charles Manson had a better chance of getting out than this car did. My boyfriend had bought this car and rebuilt it himself with the care and precision of a surgeon who had very little idea of what he was doing.

I actually went into his apartment one day to find him sitting at his dining room table trying to fix the brakes. I stared at this greasy picture and decided maybe we shouldn't live together or for that matter drive together.

When I suggested he take the car to the shop or, God forbid, buy a car that worked, he looked at me like I'd just suggested he sleep with his sister. This was his "baby." Someday it would work. He would restore a 1957 Jaguar, and he would drive around the neighborhood for everyone to see. I wished him well. I didn't have that kind of time.

For the sake of my marriage, I'll skip over other boyfriends and their cars and go straight to my husband and his. My husband just bought his "dream car." I won't reveal the manufacturer, but in the early 1940s the makers of this car weren't very nice to Jewish people. My husband says I shouldn't let World War II influence my feelings toward his car. He's always wanted this type of car, and now he has it. He has the car and something more. He has a rattle. This is the most beautiful car you've ever seen, and it comes with its own invisible mariachi band.

No one can find the rattle. The salesman who sold us this car can't hear it. He went deaf about the same time the check cleared. Also the alarm on this car is very temperamental. Often it goes off while we are driving. Concerned citizens write down our license plate number and report my husband and me for stealing our own car.

We hand-wash this car. It can't go through a car wash. It's too delicate. The advertisement on television has a building falling on this vehicle and it coming through intact, but it can't be washed with brushes. It needs a natural sponge and special car shampoo. I think we should put it through a car wash. I think it might fix the rattle.

For all the care my husband takes of his car, he does exhibit some very strange in-car behavior. Basically, my husband has two beliefs in life. He believes in God, and he believes that when the gas gauge is on empty, he still has a quarter of a tank. He thinks the "E" stands for "Eeeggghh, there's still some left." Once we were driving along and we were so low on gas, I didn't know what to do, but I wanted to do something . . . so I turned off the radio.

I don't know why men think their cars don't need gas. I think it's because they love their cars and want to believe their cars love them back. If, in some way, their vehicle will run without the benefit of fuel for a few miles, they will know for sure that theirs is a love that is returned. But a car won't do this for them. To quote a phrase I just made up, "No gasee, no runee."

I'll never understand men and their cars, but I have a little confession to make. There is something comforting about my husband loving cars. When we walk down the street I don't really worry about him looking at other women. More often than not when his head turns he is ogling a Ferrari. If he's going to lust after something, I'd rather it be something that lives in a garage.

•

INHUMAN NATURE

I try to be the best person I can be, but I'm constantly letting myself down. Human nature is largely something that has to be overcome. Lots of the little things in life that give me pleasure are usually connected with someone else's misfortune. Not big misfortunes, not even misfortunes, more inconveniences; little victories in my life that keep me going. Before you start to hate me, let me give you a few examples and see if they sound familiar.

1. You're standing on line for a very popular movie. You're worried about whether or not you will get in. You wait ten minutes. You turn around. You are no longer at the end of the line. There are now at least thirty people behind you who have less chance of getting in than you do, and if they do, you will almost certainly get a better seat. What is your reaction? Do you say to the people behind you, "Hey, you can all get in front of me, I can see this movie tomorrow night." No, you gloat—admit it, you gloat . . . or am I the only one?

2. I'm staying in a hotel, and while walking down the corridor I always peek in other people's hotel rooms to see if they are nicer than mine. If their room is nicer, I rationalize to myself, "It's just a room, I'm going to be sleeping in it most of the time." However, if my room is nicer, I think, "Ha ha, I got a better room, ha, ha, ha, ha, ha, ha, ha, ha." I revert to a three-year-old and say "ha" far too many times.

3. We all know that life isn't fair; but restaurant service should be. When I sit down at a restaurant and the people who sit down fifteen minutes after me get served first, I'm furious, unless I'm the later person who has gotten served. I don't wait and say, "I'm not eating until the people who got here before me are taken care of." I eat. I eat, and it's especially delicious.

4. There are few things that have given me more joy than

Geraldo Rivera being hit in the nose by a chair. It still gives me the giggles when I think about the bandage. I don't like Geraldo Rivera, but I would never wish him harm. I just think it's the chair that makes the image special. A fist would have been too common and a blender too disturbing, but a chair and a nose coming together when the nose belonged to Geraldo Rivera, that was a delight.

5. This is something that must not go farther than this book. Sometimes, when I'm in an elevator and I see someone running toward it, I . . . I . . . I pretend I can't find the Open Door button. There, I said it. It has nothing to do with the character of the person who wants to come in. I don't even particularly want to be alone. I just don't want to press the button.

6. When I'm driving down the street and see someone else fixing a flat tire, I sit a little taller. I know someday that will be me out there, but it hasn't happened yet, so I'm still able to chuckle.

7. In traffic there is only one rule that is a constant. The lane of traffic that you are in is the lane of traffic that isn't moving. If I were in the lane of traffic that was moving, I'm sure I would be happy about it, but this personally has never happened to me.

8. I'm in the movie theater, a woman with an enormous head sits down directly in front of the person sitting next to me. I am amused, but only for a few seconds before she changes her mind and sits directly in front of me.

9. One of my very best friends who has never been able to gain weight (poor thing) recently gained ten pounds and had to go on a diet. Glee. I call her and laugh and hang up. (She does deserve it; all those years of complaining to me about the horrors of having to drink a chocolate shake every day.)

10. My husband found a gray hair on his head. He was upset. I had it framed.

There are more things about myself that I'm ashamed of, but I'm going to stop here, just in case it's not really human nature . . . and I'm the only one.

•

DRIVING EACH OTHER CRAZY

If my husband and I are going to get into an argument, it usually happens in the car. A car is a very small place where you can scrutinize each other's every movement. I think we need a bigger car. I think we need a two-bedroom car, or at least one with a cement wall down the middle.

I have been driving for five years now. I learned how when I moved from New York to L.A. In New York you don't have to know how to drive, you just have to know how to jump out of the way of taxis, which are for some reason speeding along the sidewalks. Taxi drivers in New York are seldom aware of what country they are in. In London, if you want to be a taxi driver, you have to study for years and take an extensive test called "the knowledge" before you are granted a license. In New York, if you want to be a taxi driver, you have to have a foot.

Whenever my husband and I are in my car and I am driving, he is convinced that I am out to kill us both. He has no confidence in my ability to stop. Every time we come up to a red light I see him gripping the side of the car as if he were hanging on to the outside of a speeding train.

"Christ, brake, stop . . . stop, there's a red light!" he bellows.

"I know there's a red light, that's why I'm slowing down. That's what I do right before I stop. I use it as a kind of preparation. I tried speeding up as a preparation for a while, but it made stopping more difficult," I say, trying not to speed up for spite.

"You have such a heavy foot!"

"I don't have a heavy foot. I have lots of other things that are heavy, but my foot is just right."

I don't get it. When I leave in the car on my own he never thinks it's the last time he's going to see me. If he thinks I drive as badly as he obviously thinks I drive, then why does he let me drive at all? If I need to get somewhere, why doesn't he just put me in a sack and call a cab?

My husband is convinced that he is a much safer driver than I am. He has two moving violations, I have none. When he came over from England, we had a huge fight because I told him you had to stop at stop signs, whether someone is coming the other way or not, and he didn't believe me. Evidently they don't have to stop in England. He didn't have time to explain that to the officer. He refused to go to traffic school, where you can get your ticket erased and you can actually learn the rules of another country, so the next officer had to tell him about double yellow lines. Did you know that you can make a U-turn at will in England? One day we were driving along a busy street and all of a sudden he made the most beautiful U-turn right in front of a police car. The policeman flashed his lights and my husband waved; he thought the officer was complimenting him on completing such a pretty turn in such heavy traffic. Instead he was introduced to ticket number two.

And yet I've never once thought that my husband was going to kill me in the car. I had confidence in his ability to drive long before he knew any of the rules. That's why, when we go on trips, he drives and I am left with the unhappy experience of trying to read the map. Because I learned how to drive so late in life, I do not have a very developed sense of map. Very often I will sit in the car and stare at it silently for hours, just hoping that something will magically begin to make sense to me. My husband says we would have a better chance of getting to our destination if he just taped the map on the windshield and drove by feel.

In our travels we have gone into many countries unnecessarily . . . and without our passports . . . and without the correct currency. My indisputable talent is my ability, no matter where we are, to find cows. It doesn't matter if we are going sight-seeing in Germany or to the theater in Pasadena, you give me the map and I will lead you to cows. If only cows could talk and tell us how to get back on the 101.

I am now going to solve our problem; since I'm a safe driver, and he's good at reading maps, why don't we reverse responsibilities? We tried that once, and he was so concentrated on reading the map, he forgot to panic at every red light, my heavy foot remembered to brake, and it just didn't feel right. We missed the screaming . . . and the cows. So for now, we'll keep our roles . . . and look for a two-bedroom car.

•

One-liners

If you never want to see a man again, say, "I love you, I want to marry you. I want to have children . . ."—they leave skid marks.

•

My boyfriend and I broke up. He wanted to get married . . . and I didn't want him to.

Muriel Rukeyser (1913-1980)

Myth

Long afterward, Oedipus, old and blinded, walked the roads.   He
smelled a familiar smell.   It was the Sphinx.   Oedipus said, "I
want to ask one question. Why didn't I recognize my mother?"
"You gave the wrong answer," said the Sphinx.   "But that was what
made everything possible," said Oedipus.   "No," she said. "When
I asked, What walks on four legs in the morning, two at noon, and three
in the evening, you answered, Man.   You didn't say anything about
woman."   "When you say Man," said Oedipus, "you include
women too. Everyone knows that."   She said, "That's what you
think."

Joanna Russ (1937-   )

Somebody's Trying to Kill
Me and I Think It's My Husband:
The Modern Gothic

Here are the elements [of the Modern Gothic]:
    To a large, lonely, usually brooding *House* (always named) comes a
Heroine who is young, orphaned, unloved, and lonely. She is shy and
inexperienced. She is attractive, sometimes even beautiful, but she does
not know it. Sometimes she has spent ten years nursing a dying mother;
sometimes she has (or has had) a wicked stepmother, a bad aunt, a demanding and selfish mother (usually deceased by the time the story
opens) or an ineffectual, absent, or (usually) long-dead father, whom she
loves. The House is set in exotic, vivid and/or isolated *Country*. The
Heroine, whose reaction to people and places tends toward emotional
extremes, either loves or hates the House, usually both.

After a short prologue, this latter-day Jane Eyre forms a personal or professional connection with an older man, a dark, magnetic, powerful, brooding, sardonic *Super-Male*, who treats her brusquely, derogates her, scolds her, and otherwise shows anger or contempt for her. The Heroine is vehemently attracted to him and usually just as vehemently repelled or frightened—she is not sure of her feelings for him, his feelings for her, and whether he (1) loves her, (2) hates her, (3) is using her, or (4) is trying to kill her.

Mary Russo (contemporary)

~€ ৯~

FROM *Female Grotesques: Carnival and Theory*

Making a spectacle out of oneself seemed a specifically feminine danger. The danger was of exposure. Men, I learned somewhat later in life, "exposed themselves," but that operation was quite deliberate and circumscribed. For a woman, making a spectacle out of herself had more to do with inadvertency and loss of boundaries: the possessors of large, aging, and dimpled thighs displayed at the public beach, of overly rouged cheeks, of a voice shrill with laughter, or out of a sliding bra strap—a loose, dingy bra strap especially—were at once caught out by fate and blameworthy . . . anyone, any *woman*, could make a spectacle out of herself if she was not careful.

Dorothy L. Sayers (1893–1957)

~€ ৯~

Are Women Human?

It is the mark of all movements, however well-intentioned, that their pioneers tend, by much lashing of themselves into excitement, to lose sight of the obvious. In reaction against the age-old slogan, "woman is the weaker vessel," or the still more offensive, "woman is a divine creature," we have, I think, allowed ourselves to drift into asserting that "a woman is as good as a man," without always pausing to think what exactly we mean by that. What, I feel, we ought to mean is something so obvious that it is apt to escape attention altogether, viz.: not that every women is, in virtue of her sex, as strong, clever, artistic, level-headed, industrious and so forth as any man that can be mentioned; but, that a woman is just as much an ordinary human being as a man, with the same individual preferences, and with just as much right to the tastes and preferences of an individual. What is repugnant to every human being is to be reckoned always as a member of a class and not as an individual person. A certain amount of classification is, of course, nec-essary for practical purposes: there is no harm in saying that women, as a class, have smaller bones than men, wear lighter clothing, have more hair on their heads and less on their faces, go more pertinaciously to church or the cinema, or have more patience with small and noisy ba-bies. In the same way, we may say that stout people of both sexes are commonly better-tempered than thin ones, or that university dons of both sexes are more pedantic in their speech than agricultural labourers, or that Communists of both sexes are more ferocious than Fascists—or the other way round. What is unreasonable and irritating is to assume that *all* one's tastes and preferences have to be conditioned by the class to which one belongs. That has been the very common error into which men have frequently fallen about women—and it is the error into which feminist women are, perhaps, a little inclined to fall into about themselves.

Take, for example, the very usual reproach that women nowadays always want to "copy what men do." In that reproach there is a great deal of truth and a great deal of sheer, unmitigated and indeed quite wicked nonsense. There are a number of jobs and pleasures which men have in times past cornered for themselves. At one time, for instance, men had a monopoly of classical education. When the pioneers of uni-versity training for women demanded that women should be admitted to the universities, the cry went up at once: "Why should women want to know about Aristotle?" The answer is NOT that *all* women would be the better for knowing about Aristotle—still less, as Lord Tennyson seemed to think, that they would be more companionable wives for their husbands if they did know about Aristotle—but simply: "What women want as a class is irrelevant. *I* want to know about Aristotle. It is true that most women care nothing about him, and a great many male undergraduates turn pale and faint at the thought of him—but I, eccen-tric individual that I am, do want to know about Aristotle, and I submit that there is nothing in my shape or bodily functions which need prevent my knowing about him." . . .

So that when we hear that women have once more laid hands upon something which was previously a man's sole privilege, I think we have to ask ourselves: is this trousers or is it braces? Is it something useful, convenient and suitable to a human being as such? Or is it merely something unnecessary to us, ugly, and adopted merely for the sake of collaring the other fellow's property? These jobs and professions, now. It is ridiculous to take on a man's job just in order to be able to say that "a woman has done it—yah!" The only decent reason for tackling any job is that it is *your* job and *you* want to do it.

At this point, somebody is likely to say: "Yes, that is all very well. But it *is* the woman who is always trying to ape the man. She *is* the inferior being. You don't as a rule find the men trying to take the women's jobs away from them. They don't force their way into the household and turn women out of their rightful occupations."

Of course they do not. They have done it already.

Let us accept the idea that women should stick to their own jobs—the jobs they did so well in the good old days before they started talking about votes and women's rights. Let us return to the Middle Ages and ask what we should get then in return for certain political and educational privileges which we should have to abandon.

It is a formidable list of jobs: the whole of the spinning industry, the whole of the dyeing industry, the whole of the weaving industry. The whole catering industry and—which would not please Lady Astor, perhaps—the whole of the nation's brewing and distilling. All the preserving, pickling and bottling industry, all the bacon-curing. And (since in those days a man was often absent from home for months together on war or business) a very large share in the management of landed estates. Here are the women's jobs—and what has become of them? They are all being handled by men. It is all very well to say that woman's place is the home—but modern civilization has taken all these pleasant and profitable activities out of the home, where the women looked after them, and handed them over to big industry, to be directed and organized by men at the head of large factories. Even the dairy-maid in her simple bonnet has gone, to be replaced by a male mechanic in charge of a mechanical milking plant.

Now, it is very likely that men in big industries do these jobs better than the women did them at home. The fact remains that the home contains much less of interesting activity than it used to contain. What is more, the home has so shrunk to the size of a small flat that—even if we restrict woman's job to the bearing and rearing of families—there is no room for her to do even that. It is useless to urge the modern woman to have twelve children, like her grandmother. Where is she to put them when she has got them? And what modern man wants to be bothered with them? It is perfectly idiotic to take away woman's traditional occupations and then complain because she looks for new ones. Every woman is a human being—one cannot repeat that too often—and a human being *must* have occupation, if he or she is not to become a nuisance to the world.

I am not complaining that the brewing and baking were taken over by the men. If they can brew and bake as well as women or better, then by all means let them do it. But they cannot have it both ways. If they are going to adopt the very sound principle that the job should be done by the person who does it best, then that rule must be applied universally. If the women make better office-workers then men, they must have the office work. If any individual woman is able to make a first-class lawyer, doctor, architect or engineer, then she must be allowed to try her hand at it. Once lay down the rule that the job comes first and you throw that job open to every individual, man or woman, fat or thin, tall or short, ugly or beautiful, who is able to do that job better than the rest of the world.

Now, it is frequently asserted that, with women, the job does not come first. What (people cry) are women doing with this liberty of theirs? What woman really prefers a job to a home and family? Very few, I admit. It is unfortunate that they should so often have to make the choice. A man does not, as a rule, have to choose. He gets both. In fact, if he wants the home and family, he usually has to take the job as well, if he can get it. Nevertheless, there have been women, such as Queen Elizabeth and Florence Nightingale, who had the choice, and chose the job and made a success of it. And there have been and are many men who have sacrificed their careers for women—sometimes, like Antony or Parnell, very disastrously. When it comes to a *choice*, then every man or woman has to choose as an individual human being, and, like a human being, take the consequences.

As human beings! I am always entertained—and also irritated—by the newsmongers who inform us, with a bright air of discovery, that they have questioned a number of female workers and been told by one and all that they are "sick of the office and would love to get out of it." In the name of God, what human being is *not*, from time to time, heartily sick of the office and would *not* love to get out of it? The time of female office-workers is daily wasted in sympathizing with disgruntled male colleagues who yearn to get out of the office. No human being likes work—not day in and day out. Work is notoriously a curse—and if women *liked* everlasting work they would not be human beings at all. *Being* human beings, they like work just as much and just as little as anybody else. They dislike perpetual washing and cooking just as much as perpetual typing and standing behind shop counters. Some of them prefer typing to scrubbing—but that does not mean that they are not, as human beings, entitled to damn and blast the typewriter when they feel that way. The number of men who daily damn and blast typewriters is incalculable; but that does not mean that they would be happier doing a little plain sewing. Nor would the women.

I have admitted that there are very few women who would put their job before every earthly consideration. I will go further and assert that there are very few men who would do it either. In fact, there is perhaps only one human being in a thousand who is passionately interested in his job for the job's sake. The difference is that if that one person in a thousand is a man, we say, simply, that he is passionately keen on his job; if she is a woman, we say she is a freak. It is extraordinarily entertaining to watch the historians of the past, for instance, entangling themselves in what they were pleased to call the "problem" of Queen Elizabeth. They invented the most complicated and astonishing reasons both for her success as a sovereign and for her tortuous matrimonial policy. She was the tool of Burleigh, she was the tool of Leicester, she was the fool of Essex; she was diseased, she was deformed, she was a man in disguise. She was a mystery, and must have some extraordinary solution. Only recently has it occurred to a few enlightened people that the solution might be quite simple after all. She might be one of the rare people who were born into the right job and put that job first. Whereupon a whole series of riddles cleared themselves up by magic. She was in love with Leicester—why didn't she marry him? Well, for the very same reason that numberless kings have not married their lovers—because it would have thrown a spanner into the wheels of the State machine. Why was she so bloodthirsty and unfeminine as to sign the death-warrant of Mary Queen of Scots? For much the same reason that induced King George V to say that if the House of Lords did not pass the Parliament Bill he would create enough new peers to force it through—because she was, in the measure of her time, a constitutional sovereign, and knew that there was a point beyond which a sovereign could not defy Parliament. Being a rare human being with her eye to the job, she did what was necessary; being an ordinary human being, she hesitated a good deal before embarking on unsavory measures—but as to feminine mystery, there is no such thing about it, and nobody, had she been a man, would have thought either her statesmanship or her humanity in any way mysterious. Remarkable they were—but she was a very remarkable person. Among her most remarkable achievements was that of showing that sovereignty was one of the jobs for which the right kind of woman was particularly well fitted.

Which bring us back to this question of what jobs, if any, are women's jobs. Few people would go so far as to say that all women are well fitted for all men's jobs. When people do say this, it is particularly exasperating. It is stupid to insist that there are as many female musicians and mathematicians as male—the facts are otherwise, and the most we can ask is that if a Dame Ethel Smyth or a Mary Somerville turns up, she shall be allowed to do her work without having aspersions cast either on her sex or her ability. What we ask is to be human individuals, however peculiar and unexpected. It is no good saying: "You are a little girl and therefore you ought to like dolls"; if the answer is, "But I don't," there is no more to be said. Few women happen to be natural born mechanics; but if there is one, it is useless to try and argue her into being something different. What we must *not* do is to argue that the occasional appearance of a female mechanical genius proves that all women would be mechanical geniuses if they were educated. They would not.

Where, I think, a great deal of confusion has arisen is in a failure to distinguish between special *knowledge* and special *ability*. There are certain questions on which what is called "the woman's point of view" is valuable, because they involve special *knowledge*. Women should be consulted about such things as housing and domestic architecture because, under present circumstances, they have still to wrestle a good deal with houses and kitchen sinks and can bring special knowledge to the problem. Similarly, some of them (though not all) know more about children than the majority of men, and their opinion, *as women*, is of value. In the same way, the opinion of colliers is of value about coalmining, and the opinion of doctors is valuable about disease. But there are other questions—as for example, about literature or finance—on which the "woman's point of view" has no value at all. In fact, it does not exist. No special knowledge is involved, and a woman's opinion on literature or finance is valuable only as the judgment of an individual. I am occasionally desired by congenital imbeciles and the editors of magazines to say something about the writing of detective fiction "from the woman's point of view." To such demands, one can only say, "Go away and don't be silly. You might as well ask what is the female angle on an equilateral triangle." . . .

A man once asked me—it is true that it was at the end of a very good dinner, and the compliment conveyed may have been due to that circumstance—how I managed in my books to write such natural conversation between men when they were by themselves. Was I, by any chance, a member of a large, mixed family with a lot of male friends? I replied that, on the contrary, I was an only child and had practically never seen or spoken to any men of my own age till I was about twenty-five. "Well," said the man, "I shouldn't have expected a woman [meaning me] to have been able to make it so convincing." I replied that I had coped with this difficult problem by making my men talk, as far as possible, like ordinary human beings. This aspect of the matter seemed to surprise the other speaker; he said no more, but took it away to chew it over. One of these days it may quite likely occur to him that women, as well as men, when left to themselves, talk very much like human beings also.

Indeed, it is my experience that both men and women are fundamentally human, and that there is very little mystery about either sex, except the exasperating mysteriousness of human beings in general. And though for certain purposes it may still be necessary, as it undoubtedly was in the immediate past, for women to band themselves together, as women, to secure recognition of their requirements as a sex, I am sure that the time has now come to insist more strongly on each woman's —and indeed each man's—requirements as an individual person. It used to be said that women had no *esprit de corps*; we have proved that we have—do not let us run into the opposite error of insisting that there is an aggressively feminist "point of view" about everything. To oppose one class perpetually to another—young against old, manual labor against brain-worker, rich against poor, woman against man—is to split the foundations of the State; and if the cleavage runs too deep, there remains no remedy but force and dictatorship. If you wish to preserve a free democracy, you must base it—not on classes and categories, for this will land you in the totalitarian State, where no one may act or think except as the member of a category. You must base it upon the individual Tom, Dick and Harry, on the individual Jack and Jill—in fact, upon you and me.

Florence Guy Seabury (1881-1951)

～❦ ❦～

FROM *The Delicatessen Husband*

. . . Since the beginning, the whole feminine world has been in a conspiracy to shield and protect men. Only in fables of chivalry is woman the sheltered sex. Visit any American home and you will find grandmothers, mothers, wives, sisters, aunts, daughters and female servants consecrated to one great purpose—guarding the male members of the family from the vicissitudes of everyday life.

. . . The life of the business world, like that of the home, is built upon the theory of masculine protection. In every well regulated office, a cordon of women employees vie with each other to keep the outside world from permeating the inner sanctum. A young girl answers the telephone and prevents access of any but the acceptable; a woman secretary is always on duty as buffer and custodian of the sacred presence; feminine stenographers, bookkeepers and file clerks carry on the drab routine, while "he" sits majestically in an inner chamber.

Naturally, this easy and secure life of man and his years of sheltered living, have made him more or less helpless. In many ways he could put a Victorian female to shame. . . .

. . . Man is secretly conscious of a biological inferiority, since he cannot bear children. Therefore, he must be continually propped up by those who do bear them, in order to feel a sure-enough place in the universe.

Women probably sensed this fact before psychologists brought it to the daylight, which accounts for their protection of him. . . . It's almost impossible to find any record of their real opinion about men.

Anne Sexton (1928-1974)

Riding the Elevator into the Sky

As the fireman said:
Don't book a room over the fifth floor
in any hotel in New York.
They have ladders that will reach further
but no one will climb them.
As the New York *Times* said:
The elevator always seeks out
the floor of the fire
and automatically opens
and won't shut.
These are the warnings
that you must forget
if you're climbing out of yourself.
If you're going to smash into the sky.

Many times I've gone past
the fifth floor,
cranking toward,
but only once
have I gone all the way up.
Sixtieth floor:
small plants and swans bending
into their grave.
Floor two hundred:
mountains with the patience of a cat,
silence wearing its sneakers.

Floor five hundred:
messages and letters centuries old,
birds to drink,
a kitchen of clouds.
Floor six thousand:

                    the stars,
                    skeletons on fire,
                    their arms singing.
                    And a key,
                    a very large key,
                    that opens something—
                    some useful door—
                    somewhere—
                    up there.

Ntozake Shange (1948-   )

~≪ ≫~

FROM *For Colored Girls Who Have
Considered Suicide, When the Rainbow
Is Enuf*

without any assistance or guidance from you
i have loved you assiduously for 8 months 2 wks & a day
i have been stood up four times

i want you to know
this waz an experiment
to see how selfish i cd be
if i wd really carry on to snare a possible lover
if i waz capable of debasin my self for the love of another
if i cd stand not being wanted
when i wanted to be wanted
& i cannot
so
with no further assistance & no guidance from you
i am endin this affair
this note is attached to a plant
i've been waterin since the day i met you
you may water it
yr damn self

Joane Sharpe (17th century)

~❧ ❧~

A Defence of Women, Against the Author of the Arraignment of Women

An idle companion was raging of late
Who in fury 'gainst women expresseth his hate:
He writeth a book, an *Arraignment* he calleth,
In which against women he currishly bawleth.
He deserveth no answer but in ballad or rhyme,
Upon idle fantastics who would cast away time:
Any answer may serve an impudent liar,
Any mangy scabbed horse doth fit a scold Squire:
In the ruff of his fury, for so himself saith,
The blasphemous companion he shamefully playeth.
The woman for an helper, God did make he doth say,
But to help to consume and spend all away.
Thus, at God's creation to flout and to jest,
Who but an atheist would so play the beast?
The scriptures do prove that when Adam did fall,
And to death and damnation was thereby a thrall.
Then woman was an helper, for by her blessed seed,
From Hell and damnation all mankind was freed.
He saith, women are froward, which the rib doth declare,
For like as the rib, so they crooked are:
The rib was her subject for body we find,
But from God came her soul, and dispose of her mind.
Let no man think much if women compare,
That in their creation they much better are:
More blessings therein to woman do fall,
Than unto mankind have been given at all.
Women were the last work, and therefore the best,
For what was the end, excelleth the rest.
For woman's more honour, it was so assigned,
She was made of the rib of metal refined:

The country doth also the woman more grace,
For paradise is far the more excellent place.
Yet women are mischevous, this author doth say,
But Scriptures to that directly say nay:
God said, 'twixt the woman and serpent for ever,
Strong hatred he would put, to be qualified never.
The woman being hateful to the serpent's condition,
How excellent is she in her disposition?
The serpent with men in their works may agree,
But the serpent with women that never may be.
If you ask how it happens some women prove naught,
By men turned to serpents they are over-wrought.
What the serpent began, men follow that still,
They tempt what they may to make women do ill.
They will tempt, and provoke, and follow us long:
They deceive us with oaths, and a faltering tongue.
To make a poor maiden or woman a whore,
They care not how much they spend of their store.
But where is there a man that will anything give
That woman or maid may with honesty live?
If they yield to lewd counsel they nothing shall want,
But for to be honest, then all things are scant.
It proves a bad nature in men doth remain.
To make women lewd their purses they strain.
For a woman that's honest they care not a whit,
They'll say she is honest because she lacks wit.
They'll call women whores, but their stakes they might save,
There can be no whore, but there must be a knave.
They say that our dressings, and that our attire
Are causes to move them to lustful fire.
Of all things which are we evermore find,
Such thoughts do arise as are like to the mind.
Men's thoughts being wicked they wrack on us thus,
That scandal is taken, not given by us.
If their sight to be so weak, and their frailty be such,
Why do they then gaze at our beauty so much?
Pluck away those ill roots whence sin doth arise,
Amend wicked thoughts, or pluck out the eyes.
The humours of men, see how froward they be;
We know not to please them in any degree:
For if we go plain we are sluts they do say,
They doubt of our honesty if we go gay;

If we be honest and merry, for giglots they take us,
If modest and sober, than proud they make us:
Be we housewifty *[sic]* quick, then a shrew he doth keep,
If patient and mild, then he scorneth a sheep.
What can we devise to do or to say,
But men do wrest all things the contrary way.
'Tis not so uncertain to follow the wind,
As to seek to please men of so numerous mind.
Their humours are giddy, and never long lasting,
We know not to please them, neither full nor yet fasting.
Either we do too little, or they do too much:
They strain our poor wits, their humours are such.
They say, women are proud, wherein made they trial?
They moved some lewd suit, and had the denial:
To be crossed in such suits, men cannot abide,
And thereupon we are entitled with pride.
They say we are cursed and froward by kind,
Our mildness is changed, where raging we find,
A good Jack says the proverb, doth make a good Jill,
A curst froward husband doth change woman's will.
They use us (they say) as necessary evils,
We have it from them, for they are our devils.
When they are in their rages and numerous fits,
They put us poor women half out of our wits.
Of all naughty women name one if you can,
If she proved bad, it came by a man.
Fair Helen forsook her husband of Greece,
A man called Paris, betrayed that peace.
Medea did rage, and did shamefully murder,
A Jason was cause, which her mischief did further.
A Cressid was false, and changed her love,
Diomedes her heart by constraint did remove.
In all like examples the world may see,
Where women prove bad, there men are not free.
But in those offences they have the most share,
Women would be good, if serpents would spare.
Let women and maids whatsoever they be,
Come follow my counsel, be warned by me.
Trust no men's suits, their love proveth lust,
Both hearts, tongues, and pens, do all prove unjust.
How fair they will speak and write in their love,
But put them to trial how false do they prove?

They love hot at first, when the love is a stranger,
But they will not be tied to rack and to manger.
What call you that when men are a wooing,
And seek nothing else but shame and undoing.
As women in their faults I do not commend,
So wish I all men their lewd suits they would end.
Let women alone, and seek not their shame,
You shall have no cause then women to blame.
'Tis like that this author against such doth bawl,
Who by his temptations have gotten a fall.
For he who of women so wickedly deemeth,
Hath made them dishonest, is probably seemeth.
He hath been a traveller, it may be well so,
By his tales and reports as much we do know.
He promiseth more poison against women to trust,
He doth it for physic, or else he would bust.
Thus I bid him farewell till next we do meet,
And then as cause moveth, so shall we greet.

May Sinclair (1863-1946)

~%€ ℈✠~

FROM *Mr. Waddington of Wyck*

He was propped up by his pillows. On his shoulders, over one of those striped pyjama suits that Barbara had once ordered from the Stores, he wore, like a shawl, a woolly, fawn-coloured motor-scarf of Fanny's. His arms were laid before him on the counterpane in a gesture of complete surrender to his illness. Fanny was always tucking them away under the blankets, but if anybody came in he would have them so. He was sitting up, waiting in an adorable patience for something to be done for him. His face had the calm, happy look of expectation utterly appeased and resigned. It was that look that frightened Barbara; it made her think that Mr. Waddington was going to die. Supposing his congestion turned to pneumonia? There was so much of him to be ill, and those big men always did die when they got pneumonia.

Mr. Waddington could hear Barbara's quiet voice saying something to Fanny; he could see her unhappy, anxious face. He enjoyed Barbara's anxiety. He enjoyed the cause of it, his illness. So long as he was actually alive he even enjoyed the thought that, if his congestion turned to pneumonia, he might actually die. There was a dignity, a prestige about being dead that appealed to him. Even his high temperature and his headache and his shooting pains and his difficulty in breathing could not altogether spoil his pleasure in the delicious concern of everybody about him, and in his exquisite certainty that, at any minute, a moan would bring Fanny to his side. He was the one person in the house that counted. He had always known it, but he had never felt it with the same intensity as now. The mind of every person in the house was concentrated on him now as it had not been concentrated before. He was holding them all in a tension of worry and anxiety. He would apologize very sweetly for the trouble he was giving everybody, declaring that it made him very uncomfortable; but even Fanny could see that he was gratified.

And as he got worse—before he became too ill to think about it at all—he had a muzzy yet pleasurable sense that everybody in Wyck-on-the-Hill and in the county for miles round was thinking of him. He knew that Corbett and Lady Corbett and Markham and Thurston and the Hawtreys, and the Rector and the Rector's wife and Colonel Grainger had called repeatedly to inquire for him. He was particularly gratified by Grainger's calling. He knew that Hitchin had stopped Horry in the street to ask after him, and he was particularly gratified by that. Old Susan-Nanna had come up from Medlicott to see him. And Ralph Bevan called every day. That gratified him, too.

The only person who was not allowed to know anything about his illness was his mother, for Mr. Waddington was certain it would kill her. Every evening at medicine time he would ask the same questions: "My mother doesn't know yet?" And: "Anybody called to-day?" And Fanny would give him the messages, and he would receive them with a gentle, solemn sweetness. You wouldn't have believed, Barbara said to herself, that complacency could take so heartrending a form.

And under it all, a deeper bliss in bliss, was the thought that Barbara was thinking about him, worrying about him, and being, probably, ten times more unhappy about him than Fanny. After working so long by his side, her separation from him would be intolerable to Barbara; intolerable, very likely, the thought that it was Fanny's turn, now, to be by his side. Every day she brought him a bunch of snowdrops, and every day, as the door closed on her little anxious face, he was sorry for Barbara shut out from his room. Poor little Barbara. Sometimes, when he was feeling well enough, he would call to her: "Come in, Barbara." And she would come in and look at him and put her flowers into his hand and say she hoped he was better. And he would answer: "Not much better, Barbara. I'm very ill."

He even allowed Ralph to come and look at him. He would hold his hand in a clasp that he made as limp as possible, on purpose, and would say in a voice artificially weakened: "I'm very ill, Ralph."

Dr. Ransome said he wasn't; but Mr. Waddington knew better. It was true that from time to time he rallied sufficiently to comb his own hair before Barbara was let in with her snowdrops, and that he could give orders to Partridge in a loud, firm tone; but he was too ill to do more than whisper huskily to Barbara and Fanny.

•

FROM *The Three Sisters*

He was aware that Mary Cartaret was sweet and good. But he had found that sweet and good women were not invariably intelligent. As for honesty, if they were always honest they would not always be sweet and good.

•

So long as she knew that Rowcliffe cared for her and always had cared, it did not seem to matter to her so much that he had married Mary. She actually considered that, of the two, Mary was the one to be pitied; it was so infinitely worse to be married to a man who didn't care for you than not to be married to a man who did.

•

She had become a furious reader. She liked hard stuff that her brain could bite on. It fell on a book and gutted it, throwing away the trash. She read all the modern poets and novelists she cared about, English and foreign. They left her stimulated but unsatisfied. There were not enough good ones to keep her going.

Betty Smith (1896–1972)

꧁ ❦ ꧂

FROM *A Tree Grows in Brooklyn*

Sissy wasn't working that day. Knowing that the children would be left alone locked in the rooms, she decided to keep them company.

She knocked at the door calling out that she was Aunt Sissy. Francie opened the door on the chain to make sure before she let her in. The children swarmed over Sissy smothering her with hugs. They loved her. To them, she was a beautiful lady who always smelled sweet, wore beautiful clothes and brought them amazing presents.

Today she brought a sweet-smelling cedar cigar box, several sheets of tissue paper, some red and some white, and a jar of paste. They sat around the kitchen table and went to work decorating the box. Sissy outlined circles on the paper with a quarter and Francie cut them out. Sissy showed her how to make them into little paper cups by molding the circles around the end of a pencil. When they had a lot of cups made, Sissy drew a heart on the box cover. The bottom of each red cup was given a dab of paste and the cup was pasted on the penciled heart. The heart was filled in with red cups. The rest of the lid was filled in with white. When the top was finished it looked like a bed of closely-packed white carnations with a heart of red ones. The sides were filled in with white cups and the inside lined with red tissue. You never could tell it had been a cigar box, it was that beautiful. The box took up most of the afternoon.

Sissy had a chop suey date at five and she got ready to leave. Francie clung to her and begged her not to go. Sissy hated to leave, yet she didn't want to miss her date. She searched in her purse for something to amuse them in her absence. They stood at her knee helping her look. Francie spied a cigarette box and pulled it out. On the cover was a picture of a man lying on a couch, knees crossed, one foot dangling in the air and smoking a cigarette which made a big smoke ring over his head. In the ring was a picture of a girl with her hair in her eyes and her bust popping out of her dress. The name on the box was *American Dreams*. It was out of the stock at Sissy's factory.

The children clamored for the box. Sissy reluctantly let them have it after explaining that the box contained cigarettes and was only to hold and to look at and not under any circumstances to be opened. They must not touch the seals, she said.

After she left, the children amused themselves for a time by staring at the picture. They shook the box. A dull swishing mysterious sound resulted.

"They is snakes in there and not zingarettes," decided Neeley.

"No," corrected Francie. "Worms are in there. Live ones."

They argued, Francie saying the box was too small for snakes and Neeley insisting that they rolled-up snakes like herring in a glass jar. Curiosity grew to such a pitch that Sissy's instructions were forgotten.

The seals were so lightly pasted, it was a simple matter to pull them off. Francie opened the box. There was a sheet of soft dulled tin foil over the contents. Francie lifted the foil carefully. Neeley prepared to crawl under the table if the snakes became active. But there were neither snakes, worms nor cigarettes in the box and its contents were very uninteresting. After trying to devise some simple games, Francie and Neeley lost interest, clumsily tied the contents of the box to a string, trailed the string out of the window and finally secured the string by shutting the window on it. They then took turns jumping on the denuded box and became so absorbed in breaking it into bits that they forgot all about the string hanging out of the window.

Consequently, there was a great surprise waiting for Johnny when he sauntered home to get a fresh dicky and collar for his evening's job. He took one look and his face burned with shame. He told Katie when she came home.

Katie questioned Francie closely and found out everything. Sissy was condemned. That night after the children had been put to bed and Johnny was away working, Katie sat in her dark kitchen with blushes coming and going. Johnny went about his work with a dull feeling that the world had come to an end.

Evy came over later in the evening and she and Katie discussed Sissy.

"That's the end, Katie," said Evy, "the very end. What Sissy does is her own business until her own business makes a thing like this happen. I've got a growing girl, so have you, we mustn't let Sissy come into our homes again. She's bad and there's no getting around it."

"She's good in many ways," temporized Katie.

"You say that after what she did to you today?"

"Well . . . I guess you're right. Only don't tell Mother. She doesn't know how Sissy lives and Sissy is her eye-apple."

When Johnny came home, Katie told him that Sissy was never to come to their house again. Johnny sighed and said he guessed that was the only thing to do. Johnny and Katie talked away the night, and in the morning they had their plans all made for moving when the end of the month came. . . .

In the summer of that same year, Johnny got the notion that his children were growing up ignorant of the great ocean that washed the shores of Brooklyn. Johnny felt that they ought to go out to sea in a ship. So he decided to take them for a rowboat ride at Canarsie and do a little deep sea fishing on the side. He had never gone fishing and he'd never been in a rowboat. But that's the idea he got.

Weirdly tied up with this idea, and by a reasoning process known only to Johnny, was the idea of taking Little Tilly along on the trip. Little Tilly was the four-year-old child of neighbors whom he had never met. In fact, he had never seen Little Tilly but he got this idea that he had to make something up to her on account of her brother Gussie. It all tied up with the notion of going to Canarsie.

Gussie, a boy of six, was a murky legend in the neighborhood. A tough little hellion, with an over-developed underlip, he had been born like other babies and nursed at his mother's great breasts. But there, all resemblance to any child, living or dead, ceased. His mother tried to wean him when he was nine months old but Gussie wouldn't stand for it. Denied the breast, he refused a bottle, food or water. He lay in his crib and whimpered. His mother, fearful that he would starve, resumed nursing him. He sucked contentedly, refusing all other food, and lived off his mother's milk until he was nearly two years old. The milk stopped then because his mother was with child again. Gussie sulked and bided his time for nine long months. He refused cow's milk in any form or container and took to drinking black coffee.

Little Tilly was born and the mother flowed with milk again. Gussie went into hysterics the first time he saw the baby nursing. He lay on the floor, screaming and banging his head. He wouldn't eat for four days and he refused to go to the toilet. He got haggard and his mother got frightened. She thought it wouldn't do any harm to give him the breast just once. That was her big mistake. He was like a dope fiend getting the stuff after a long period of deprivation. He wouldn't let go.

He took all of his mother's milk from that time on and Little Tilly, a sickly baby, had to go on the bottle.

Gussie was three years old at this time and big for his age. Like other boys, he wore knee pants and heavy shoes with brass toe tips. As soon as he saw his mother unbutton her dress, he ran to her. He stood up while nursing, an elbow on his mother's knee, his feet crossed jauntily and his eyes roving around the room. Standing to nurse was not such a remarkable feat as his mother's breasts were mountainous and practically rested in her lap when released. Gussie was indeed a fearful sight nursing that way and he looked not unlike a man with his foot on a bar rail, smoking a fat pale cigar.

The neighbors found out about Gussie and discussed his pathological state in hushed whispers. Gussie's father got so that he wouldn't sleep with his wife; he said that she bred monsters. The poor woman figured and figured on a way to wean Gussie. he *was* too big to nurse, she decided. He was going for four. She was afraid his second teeth wouldn't come in straight.

One day she took a can of stove blackening and the brush and closed herself in the bedroom where she copiously blackened her left breast with the stove polish. With a lipstick she drew a wide ugly mouth with frightening teeth in the vicinity of the nipple. She buttoned her dress and went into the kitchen and sat in her nursing rocker near the window. When Gussie saw her, he threw the dice, with which he had been playing, under the washtubs and trotted over for feeding. He crossed his feet, planted his elbow on her knee and waited.

"Gussie want tiddy?" asked his mother wheedlingly.

"Yup!"

"All right. Gussie's gonna get nice tiddy."

Suddenly she ripped open her dress and thrust the horribly made-up breast into his face. Gussie was paralyzed with fright for a moment, then he ran away screaming and hid under the bed where he stayed for twenty-four hours. He came out at last, trembling. He went back to drinking black coffee and shuddered every time his eyes went to his mother's bosom. Gussie was weaned.

The mother reported her success all over the neighborhood. It started a new fashion in weaning called, "Giving the baby the Gussie."

Johnny heard the story and contemptuously dismissed Gussie from his mind. He was concerned about Little Tilly. He thought she had been cheated out of something very important and might grow up thwarted. He got a notion that a boat ride off the Canarsie shore might wipe out some of the wrong her unnatural brother had done her. He sent Francie around to ask could Little Tilly go with them. The harassed mother consented happily.

The next Sunday, Johnny and the three children set out for Canarsie. Francie was eleven years old, Neeley ten and Little Tilly well past three. Johnny wore his tuxedo and derby and a fresh collar and dicky. Francie and Neeley wore their everyday clothes. Little Tilly's mother, in honor of the day, had dressed her up in a cheap but fancy lace dress trimmed with dark pink ribbon.

On the trolley ride out, they sat in the front seat and Johnny made friends with the motorman and they talked politics. They got off at the last stop which was Canarsie and found their way to a little wharf on which was a tiny shack; a couple of water-logged rowboats bobbed up and down on the frayed ropes which held them to the wharf. A sign over the shack read:

"Fishing tackle and boats for rent."

Underneath was a bigger sign which said:
FRESH FISH TO TAKE HOME FOR SALE HERE.

Johnny negotiated with the man and, as was his way, made a friend of him. The man invited him into the shack for an eye opener saying that he himself only used the stuff for a night cap.

While Johnny was inside getting his eyes opened, Neeley and Francie pondered how a night cap could also be an eye opener. Little Tilly stood there in her lace dress and said nothing.

Johnny came out with a fishing pole and a rusty tin can filled with worms in mud. The friendly man untied the rope from the least sorry of the rowboats, put the rope in Johnny's hand, wished him luck and went back to his shack.

Johnny put the fishing stuff into the bottom of the boat and helped the children in. Then he crouched on the wharf, the bit of rope in his hand and gave instructions about boats.

"There is always a wrong and a right way to get on a boat," said Johnny, who had never been on any boat except an excursion boat once. "The right way is to give the boat a shove and then jump in it before it drifts out to sea. Like this."

He straightened up, pushed the boat from him, leaped . . . and fell into the water. The petrified children stared at him. A second before, papa had been standing on the dock above them. Now he was below them in the water. The water came to his neck and his small waxed mustache and derby hat were in the clear. His derby was still straight on his forehead. Johnny, as surprised as the children, stared at them a moment before he said:

"Don't any of you damned kids dare to laugh!"

He climbed into the boat almost upsetting it. They didn't dare laugh aloud but Francie laughed so hard inside that her ribs hurt. Neeley was afraid to look at his sister. He knew that if their eyes met, he'd burst out laughing. Little Tilly said nothing. Johnny's collar and dicky were a sodden paperish mess. He stripped them off and threw them overboard. He rowed out to sea waveringly, but with silent dignity. When he came to what he thought was a likely spot, he announced that he was going to "drop anchor." The children were disappointed when they discovered that the romantic phrase simply meant that you threw a lump of iron attached to a rope overboard.

Horrified, they watched papa squeamishly impale a muddy worm on the hook. The fishing started. It consisted in baiting the hook, casting it dramatically, waiting awhile, pulling it up minus worm and fish and starting the whole thing over again.

The sun grew bright and hot. Johnny's tuxedo dried to a stiff wrinkled greenish outfit. The children started to get a whopping case of sunburn. After what seemed hours, papa announced to their intense relief and happiness that it was time to eat. He wound up the tackle, put it away, pulled up the anchor and made for the wharf. The boat seemed to go in a circle which made the wharf get further away. Finally they made shore a few hundred yards further down. Johnny tied up the boat, told the children to wait in it and went ashore. He said he was going to treat them to a nice lunch.

He came back after a while walking sideways, carrying hot dogs, huckleberry pie and strawberry pop. They sat in the rocking boat tied to the rotting wharf, looked down into the slimy green water that smelled of decaying fish, and ate. Johnny had had a few drinks ashore which made him sorry that he had hollered at the kids. He told them they could laugh at his falling into the water if they wanted to. But somehow, they couldn't bring up a laugh. The time was past for that. Papa was very cheerful, Francie thought.

"This is the life," he said. "Away from the maddening crowd. Ah, there's nothing like going down to the sea in a ship. We're getting away from it all," he ended up cryptically.

After their amazing lunch, Johnny rowed them out to sea again. Perspiration poured down from under his derby and the wax in the points of his mustache melted causing the neat adornment to change into disorganized hair on his upper lip. He felt fine. He sang lustily as he rowed:

Sailing, sailing, over the bounding main.

He rowed and rowed and kept going around in a circle and never did get out to sea. Eventually his hands got so blistered that he didn't feel like rowing any more. Dramatically he announced that he was going to pull for the shore. He pulled and pulled and finally made it by rowing in smaller and smaller circles and making the circles come near the wharf. He never noticed that the three children were pea green in the spots where they were not beet red from the sunburn. If he had only known it, the hot dogs, huckleberry pie, strawberry pop and worms squirming on the hook weren't doing them much good.

At the wharf, he leaped to the dock and the children followed his example. All made it excepting Tilly who fell into the water. Johnny threw himself flat on the dock, reached in and fished her out. Little Tilly stood there, her lace dress wet and ruined, but she said nothing. Although it was a broiling hot day, Johnny peeled off his tuxedo jacket, knelt down and wrapped it around the child. The arms dragged in the sand. Then Johnny took her up in his arms and strode up and down the dock patting her back soothingly and singing her a lullaby. Little Tilly didn't understand a thing of all that happened that day. She didn't understand why she had been put into a boat, why she had fallen into the water or why the man was making such a fuss over her. She said nothing.

When Johnny felt that she was comforted, he set her down and went into the shack where he had either an eye opener or a night cap. He bought three flounders from the man for a quarter. He came out with the wet fish wrapped in a newspaper. He told his children that he had promised to bring home some fresh-caught fish to mama.

"The principal thing," said papa, "is that I am bringing home fish that were caught at Canarsie. It makes no difference who caught them. The point is that we went fishing and we're bringing home fish."

His children knew that he wanted mama to think he caught the fish. Papa didn't ask them to lie. He just asked them not to be too fussy about the truth. The children understood.

They boarded one of those trolley cars that had two long benches facing each other. They made a queer row. First there was Johnny in green wrinkled salt stiff pants, an undershirt full of big holes, a derby hat and a disorderly mustache. Next came Little Tilly swallowed up in his coat with salt water dripping from under it and forming a brackish pool on the floor. Francie and Neeley came next. Their faces were brick red and they sat very rigid trying not to be sick.

People got on the car, sat across from them and stared curiously. Johnny sat upright, the fish in his lap, trying not to think of the holes in his exposed undershirt. He looked over the heads of the passengers pretending to study an Ex-Lax advertisement.

More people got on, the car got crowded but no one would sit next to them. Finally one of the fish worked its way out of the sodden newspaper and fell on the floor where it lay slimily in the dust. It was too much for Little Tilly. She looked into the fish's glazed eye, said nothing but vomited silently and thoroughly all over Johnny's tuxedo jacket. Francie and Neeley, as if waiting for that cue, also threw up. Johnny sat there with two exposed fish in his lap, one at his feet and kept staring at the ad. He didn't know what else to do.

When the grisly trip was ended, Johnny took Tilly home feeling that his was the responsibility of explaining. The mother never gave him a chance to explain. She screamed when she saw her dripping be-fouled child. She snatched the coat off, threw it into Johnny's face and called

him a Jack-the-Ripper. Johnny tried and tried to explain but she
wouldn't listen. Little Tilly said nothing. Finally Johnny got a word in
edgewise.

"Lady, I think your little girl has lost her speech."

Whereupon the mother went into hysterics. "You did it, you did
it," she screamed at Johnny.

"Can't you make her say something?"

The mother grabbed the child and shook her and shook her.
"Speak!" She screamed. "Say something." Finally Little Tilly opened
her mouth, smiled happily and said.

"T'anks."

Katie gave Johnny a tongue lashing and said that he wasn't fit to have
children. The children in question were alternating between the chills
and hot flashes of a bad case of sunburn. Katie nearly cried when she
saw the ruin of Johnny's only suit. It would cost a dollar to get it cleaned,
steamed and pressed and she knew it would never be the same again.
As for the fish, they were found to be in an advanced state of decay and
had to be thrown into the garbage can.

The children went to bed. Between chills and fever and bouts of
nausea, they buried their heads under the covers and laughed silently
and bed-shakingly at the remembrance of papa standing in the water.

Johnny sat at the kitchen window until far into the night trying to figure
out why everything had been so wrong. He had sung many a song about
ships and going down to the sea in them with a heave ho and a heave
to. He wondered why it hadn't turned out the way it said in songs. The
children should have returned exhilarated and with a deep and abiding
love for the sea and he should have returned with a fine mess of fish.
Why, oh why hadn't it turned out the way it did in a song? Why did
there have to be his blistered hands and his spoiled suit and sunburn and
rotting fish and nausea? Why didn't Little Tilly's mother understand the
intention and overlook the result? He couldn't figure it out—he couldn't
figure it out.

The songs of the sea had betrayed him.

Stevie Smith (1902–1971)

~∞ ∞~

FROM *Novel on Yellow Paper*

I think soon we shall be saying: Really, some of the people who go to church are just as good as those who stay away. But actually I am not a Christian actively. I mean I am actively not a Christian. I have a lot against Christianity though I cannot at the moment remember what it is.

·

But if you do know whether you are a foot-off-the-ground person or a foot-on-the-ground person, then I say, Come on. Come on with me, and find out.

And for my part I will try to punctuate this book to make it easy for you to read, and to break it up, with spaces for a pause, as the publisher has asked me to do. But this I find very extremely difficult.

For this book is the talking voice that runs on, and the thoughts come, the way I said, and the people come too, and come and go, to illustrate the thoughts, to point the moral, to adorn the tale.

Oh talking voice that is so sweet, how hold you alive in captivity, how point you with commas, semi-colons, dashes, pauses and paragraphs?

Foot-on-the-ground person will have his grave grave doubts, and if he is also a smug-pug he will not keep his doubts to himself; he will say: It is not, and it cannot come to good. And I shall say, Yes it is and shall. And he will say: So you think you can do this, so you do, do you?

Yes I do, I do.

That is my final word to smug-pug. You all now have been warned.

·

Harriet is also having troubles with her young man that sweet boy that is so very serious, and very teaching. Harriet is much more intelligent I think because she is not always being so serious. But this boy friend who is called Stephen, he is very serious indeed, and has never grown up out of being an undergraduate. He wishes to save the world. He has a very great deal to say about Major Douglas and Social Credit.

And Harriet is a darling and listens to him and comforts him for the sins of the whole world, which he must have upon his shoulders. But which were never meant for his shoulders at all. And he is suffering from this development-arrested-at-the-university. But Harriet is very adult, and is suffering from no arrestment in development. But has a quick bright flashing and illuminating mind. And sometimes when we are laughing together, and thinking that together it is easier and we have so very much more fun together than ever we do with our exacerbating, sulky messiah-maniacal, or cross-patchy young men, suddenly the talk will touch lightly on some subject and then up it flares, and out. And sweeping up and out, it is an exultation and an agony, but so sweet it should not be missed.

•

Beside the Seaside
A Holiday with Children

It was a particularly fine day. The calm blue sea at unusually high flood washed the highest ridge of the fine shingle beach. It was a particular moment of high summer.

"In England," said Helen, "the hot August day is sufficiently remarkable to make an occasion."

"One could roll off into it," said Margaret dreamily, looking at the bulging sea.

The beach shelved steeply and the deep water lay in to shore; the water was also clear, you could see the toes of the paddlers, perched like fishing birds upon the upper shingle, knee-deep in the sea.

The two girls were in bathing dress, but Margaret's husband Henry sat in his sports shirt and flannel trousers in a deck-chair with his hat on.

"Yes, one could," said Helen, "but you won't, Margaret, you know you always stand up and take fifteen minutes to get right in."

Helen now turned over and lay flat on her back looking from under her hands at the seaside people at their seaside pleasures.

"It is rather like the moral poem I wrote," she said. "Do you mind if I say it to you?" She looked anxiously at Henry.

"Not at all," said Margaret.

"Oh well . . ." Henry sighed.

"Children . . ." said Helen firmly . . .

> *Children who paddle where the ocean bed shelves steeply*
> *Must take great care they do not,*
> *Paddle too deeply.*

Margaret, who was happy, took the poem with a smile, but Henry, who was never really happy, began to speak about the political situation.

"It is certain that the Russians have the atom bomb," he said, "otherwise they would not be pushing us so far over the Berlin business. Professor D.," he went on (naming a once well-known Russian scientist), "used to work with us at the Cavendish Laboratory in Rutherford's day, he went back to Russia several times, and then one day he went and did not come back. He was a most able man, no doubt he is still working, they say nothing about him. . . ."

"Oh, please drop it," said Helen; but she was not speaking to Henry, she was speaking to Hughie. Henry and Margaret Levison had two children: Hughie who was ten and Anna who was eight. Hughie was now coming along the beach from the next breakwater with a large shrimping net in his hands, and in the shrimping net was a jelly fish so large that it brimmed over the net, and all its strings hung down through the holes of the net and waved about as Hughie ran.

"Oh do drop it, Hughie," said Helen again, "or better still put it up at the top of the beach under the sea-wall in the full sun, where it may fry to death and quite burn out. Oh what a wicked face it has."

"I think it looks rather beautiful," said the gentle girl Margaret.

Well, perhaps it did, after all, look rather beautiful. It looks like a fried egg, thought Helen. The frills waved prettily around a large yellow centre, this was the yoke of the egg; it was the underneath side that seemed to have a face. Hughie had disobediently turned it upside down out of the net just beside his father's deck-chair, so now the wicked face was hidden.

"They reproduce themselves by sexual congress," said Henry grudgingly.

Margaret and Helen lay baking in the sun, laughing silently to themselves. Henry was so brilliantly irascible and gloomy, truly he was a care-ridden person, but so simple and open, and of such a violent honesty and of such a violent love of what was beautiful and truthful, one could not help but love him.

Helen began to whisper in Margaret's ear (the two friends were both writers and had a great appreciation for each other's writing, which was quite different): "That poem I showed you the other day, with the

drawing of the man riding the old tired horse, and the old woman close
behind him, is rather like Henry."

"What poem was that?" said kind Margaret, who knew how Helen
liked to say her poems aloud.

> *Behind the Knight sits hooded Care,*
> *And as he rides she speaks him fair,*
> *She lays her hand in his sable muff,*
> *Ride he never so fast he'll not cast her off.*

Margaret sighed, and turned her head away from Helen. "That poem
has rather a gothic feeling," she said; "it is sad too."

At this moment Major Pole-Curtis came galloping by with his little
boy David.

"Hallo, hallo, hallo," he cried in his deep musical voice, "not been
in yet, and a lovely day like this? Slackers," he said, "the water is quite
warm, isn't it, David?"

"So long all," said David, who looked rather blue. "Helen," he
cried, as his father tore off with him, "H-e-l-e-n!"

The baby-wail of "Helen" came back to them on the wind of their
flight, and Hughie, who was squatting rather restlessly beside his mother,
began to jeer.

"Helen!" he mimicked. He got up and began to prance round
Helen, shouting in his shrill penetrating voice, "David loves Helen, David loves Helen."

The major and his family were at the same hotel as Helen and her
friends, and had the next table to theirs in the dining-room. David told
everybody in the hotel that he was going to marry Helen.

"Will you be quiet, Hughie," said Henry. "Ah, the Major," he
said, as if he had just woken up to the fact that they had been running
past. There they were, now in the distance, still running.

"He was awfully cross because David and Colin were late for lunch
yesterday," said Hughie. "Do you know he gave Colin a terrific
thrashing."

"What!" said simple Henry, as impressed and horrified as his son
had meant him to be. He turned to his wife, "I suppose that is the
correct way to bring children up; you and I, Margaret, are of course
quite wrong. I expect he is unfaithful to her frequently, and then he
comes home and confesses 'all' and says, 'Muriel' (or whatever her name
is), 'Muriel, I have behaved like a cad.' "

Henry looked pleased with himself for this flight of fancy, and especially pleased because it was so well received by the girls, with such a lot of laughter.

"I think I shall bathe now," said Margaret.

She stepped into the sea and stood with the sea washing gently round her knees looking out to the horizon of the sea where the heat mists played tricks with the passing ships. The great liner that was passing down channel from Tilbury seemed to be swimming in the high air, because the dark band of mist that hung below her made a false sea-border.

Margaret always took a long time to get into the water, when she was at last right in she would begin to swim strongly up and down parallel with the beach in a leisurely way that was full of pleasure.

"Oh," she said, "I wish there was no such thing as politics and problems, how wicked people are, how beyond hope unhappy, man is the most wretched of all the animals."

"I do not think so," said Helen, who had rushed quickly into the water and was now swimming alongside her friend, "I think men are splendid hopeful creatures, but they have not come very far yet."

How beautiful the water was, warm and milky; the sun burning through the water struck hot upon their shoulders washed by the sea. Helen turned on her back to rise and fall with the swelling sea (there was quite a swell on in spite of the calmness).

"It does not look as if they would come much further," said Margaret.

"Because of the atom bomb, you mean?"

"And a good riddance to them."

"*Them?*" said Helen. ". . . we are also the children of our times and must live and die with them. But oh what nonsense. Have you not, Margaret, seen babies trying to destroy themselves, they feel that they will burst for all that is in them: men and women are like that."

"And perhaps they will burst," said Margaret.

"If they do," said Helen, "they will still have been the high summit of creation, both great and vile beyond dreams."

"Well, I don't think so," said Margaret.

"Well, I do."

"We have been having a rather deep philosophical argument," said Margaret, as the two wet girls flopped down beside Henry, who never bathed.

"I think I shall take my shirt off for a few minutes," said Henry.

He peeled it off over his head and replaced his large straw hat. "How you girls can stand so much hot sun, I do not know," he said.

"And now look at Margaret putting all that cream on her face." Henry sighed. "It is no good nowadays, there used to be a natural vegetable oil in the face creams, but now what is it? nothing but petroleum oil, no good at all, in fact, harmful."

Helen, who was slopping about in the water again at Henry's feet, her elbows on the shingle ridge to keep her steady and her body afloat in the deep water where the shingle dipped, looked up into Henry's anxious face. In his intelligence, she thought, is all his care.

The child Hughie who had run off, now came back, pushing his sister Anna in front of him. "I think Anna has poliomylitis," he said. "She has a stiff neck." (Hughie was going to be a doctor when he grew up.)

"I think my breasts are beginning to grow," said Anna.

"Breasts," jeered Hughie, "at eight years old, breasts, ha ha ha!"

He turned to Henry. "Daddy, can I have sixpence, please, for another boat ride?"

"Nothing but boat rides, ice creams, pony rides. Well," said Henry, giving him sixpence, "I suppose that is what you think I am here for."

"I'll come with you," said Helen, "so will Anna."

They all ran off to the *Lady Grace* which, with Mr. Crask in charge, was just about to start on a trip.

"Off with you," cried Mr. Crask, chivvying the children away from the stern seat where he kept his motor. He tapped them in a friendly way upon the behind. "Oh, beg pardon," he said, when he had tapped Anna, "it's a lady."

Anna went and sat beside her brother. She was a happy, silent child, easily silenced by her clever brother, a fair, silent child, a clever child, far cleverer than Hughie, but she was his loving slave. She had a strong neat comfortable body and wore only a pair of pants. Helen loved Anna; she thought she was like a seal.

Just as they were starting off, Major Pole-Curtis came running up. "Just in time," he said, and popped David on board. "Good-bye, children," he roared as the boat shot off, "don't be late for lunch."

Hughie began to entertain Mr. Crask with his famous imitation of a train coming into King's Cross main-line station. His bright red hair flamed in the sunshine, his thin straight body moved delicately with the movement of the boat. He stood upright on the seat and let out a wild whistle.

"What's that, Mr. Crask?"

"I dunno, me boy, a whistle, eh?"

"It's a goods train going into a tunnel on an incline," said Hughie.

He gave three short barks and a groan. "That's the trucks closing up as the engine slows down. Chug, chug, chug, it's all right now, they're gathering speed again and coming on to the flat."

Helen smiled at Hughie and then sighed. Hughie made himself rather unpopular sometimes, he was devoured by restless energy, he must do his train noises (or whatever it was), and he must have an audience.

"That Levison boy . . ." the Major had said one day with quite a critical eye . . . he had stopped talking when Helen had come up, but there was no doubt he would like to have smacked Hughie. *Levison*, oh of course, Helen sighed again, of course the Major would feel like that . . . he had just come back from Palestine.

She looked down at the Major's little boy David who was lying alongside with a devoted air. David had pale yellow hair and great charm; he was five years old. Helen stroked his hair and, slipping her hand under his chin, turned his face up to hers. The sun-speckled face, she thought, the smiling eyes, the assured and certain eyes, the easy authority of certain charm, there is the quality of sunlight about you, of ancient sunlight in privileged circumstances.

"Daddy is going to take us to church tomorrow," said David. "You come too, Helen. Helen, do!"

Hughie paused in his train noises and glanced furiously across at them. What a nuisance David was, couldn't Helen *see?*

"We are going to that old church at Lyme," went on David in a confiding tone. "Oh, Helen, do come, do . . . *where that nice vicar is.*"

"Oh, I don't know, I don't know," she said, stroking again the daffodil hair, "I don't know, David . . ."

David moved closer. "Come on, Helen, come on, do . . . *it's the best glass in the south of England.*"

Helen laughed, she knew there would be no room for her in the major's car, with mamma who liked vicars, and papa who liked church glass . . . "I haven't got a hat."

"Never mind," said David, "I never wear mine in church."

In the evening the hotel children, marshalled by Hughie, played cricket in the field at the back of the hotel. This was a fine wide closely-mown piece of grass stretching for a distance under the hills where the old town stood. There was also the military canal and the beautiful gardens before you came to the main road. It was now seven o'clock and the sun dropping to the soft hills threw a golden light upon the cricket field and long shadows.

The grown-ups sat on the pavilion steps and watched the game.

Anna, who only played with boys, was batting; she made thirteen runs.
There were a lot of other people in the field, doing different things.
An old mild person stood himself in front of the children's wicket with
his back turned to them; he was watching the tennis players on the other
side of the wire netting.

"Would you mind moving, please," said David firmly; he was
wicket-keeper.

Some runners came charging by. Never mind, they were soon gone.

Suddenly Henry said that he would play too.

"Oh yes," said Margaret, "do play, Henry."

Helen squeezed her friend's arm affectionately as Henry took his
place. "How happy you look," she said and began to laugh softly. What
an irritating girl.

"Oh, why is it," said poor Margaret, "why is it that there is something so sad and tense about fathers when they play with their children;
it really tears at one when they take part in the sports. Why is it?"

"Yes," said Helen, "it is never very touching when the mothers
run in the three-legged race at schools; no, it is different."

She squeezed Margaret's arm again, "It will be all right, you'll see."

Margaret said, "Henry is more locked up in being a Jew than it
seems possible."

Oh dear, thought Helen. "Well," she said, "you are Jewish too,
aren't you, and you do not feel locked up in it."

"No," said Margaret. "But, Helen, you cannot know quite what it
is like; it is a feeling of profound uncertainty, especially if you have
children. There is a strong growing anti-Jewish feeling in England, and
when they get a little older, will they also be in a concentration camp
here in England?"

"One sometimes thinks that is what they want," said Helen flip-
pantly, getting rather cross, "they behave so extremely. Well, that is
rather an extreme remark of yours, is it not, about the concentration
camps, eh, *here*? If there is an anti-Jewish feeling in England at the moment it is because of Palestine." Helen paused and went on again more
seriously, "I do not hold with the theory that the Jewish people is an
appeasing, accommodating people, knowing, as some say, on which side
their bread is buttered, and prepared to make accommodations with
conscience for their own advantage. No, I think that they are an obstinate and unreasonable people, short-sighted about their true interests,
fanatical. They have not the virtues of a slave, you see, but also they
have not the virtues of a wise person."

"Do not speak like this to Henry, please, Helen," said Margaret.
"Oh, please, do not."

"Of course I will not," said Helen, and was about to pursue the subject when a closer glance at Margaret's gentle face showed that to do so would be untimely and indeed fruitless.

Darling Margaret, she thought with a pang, darling darling Margaret.

Margaret liked to live in a vegetable reverie; in this world of her vegetable reverie the delicate life of the plants, and the stones, too, for that matter, and the great trees and the blades of sharp grass and the leaves that were white when they turned upon the breeze, had a delicate obstinate life of their own. Margaret thought that people were the devils of creation. She thought that they were for ever at war for ever trying to oppress the delicate life of the plants and to destroy them; but this of course fortunately they could not do.

After the cricket match Henry went back to town, travelling late by moonlight in the car of a friend. He had to attend a conference early the next day. Margaret and the children and her friend Helen were now alone.

They spent the long days bathing and sunning themselves, and in the evenings they left the children and climbed to the downs at the back of the town and lay to watch the moon come up far out to sea; the turf was soft and the nights were warm.

Helen's old school-friend Phoebe lived in the little seaside town, and now that they were alone Phoebe often came to visit them, bringing her car.

Phoebe was a quiet girl, enjoying a private income and no cares.

They took the children for a picnic on the banks of the military canal far into the country where it turned inland from the coast three miles over the flats. From the banks of the canal that were covered with long grass and shaded by trees that were planted at the time the canal was built to keep Napoleon out, you could see the Martello towers that marked the line of the coast, and in the distance the pale sea that was as pale as the sky, baked clean of colour.

Helen wandered off on her own and explored the marshes which, cut by little sluggish streams, lay over towards the sea. The little quiet streams were like dykes, the water did not seem to move in them, the tall reeds stood up and every now and then a cow, mistaking the reedy margin for firm land, floundered in the soft mud. Swishing her tail the cow stood puzzled; the flies made a black patch over one eye which gave her a dissipated look.

Helen took off her shoes and walked barefoot over the soft marsh grass, and barefoot over the bare patches where the mud lay caked in squares. She sat down on the bank of the stream and looked up from below at the tall reeds and the thick bushes on the river-side. The cow-parsley towered above her head as she sat close down by the water's edge. How hot and solitary it was here on the marsh by the river, and what a hot muddy watery cowparsley smell it had.

Helen fell into her favourite Brobdingnagian dream . . . if she were so high (say three inches) and the rest of the world unchanged, how very exciting and daring would be this afternoon excursion; each puddle a solitary lake, each tussock a grass mountain, the cowparsley mighty jungle trees, the grass, where it rose high by the river, to be cut through with a sharp knife for a pathway. Helen's enjoyment of scenery was as great as her friend Margaret's, but very different. She was rather childish about it and liked to imagine herself on some bold quest, travelling, with gun and compass and perhaps a fishing rod, exploring, enduring—for some reason, of course. But what reason? Ah, that she had never been able to determine. Never mind, it was the movement, and the sun and the grass and the lakes and the forests that made it exciting, and so agreeable. Sometimes there would come the steep face of a great inland cliff, and up the baked surface of its caked mud slopes the intrepid adventurer would slowly climb, hand over hand, step by step, half crawling, half climbing, the sun hot on her back. Until at last, and only just in time (for really it was hard work), she would come to the top and, pulling herself over by a fistful of tough grass most happily to hand, fling herself down on the grassy plateau, saying, "Well, that's over, and not bad, if I may say so."

Full of these agreeable fancies, soaked in sunshine and spattered with smelly mud, Helen now made her way back to where her friends were setting the tea-things on the river bank.

Hughie was grumbling and tossing. "I hate this place," he said, as Helen came up to them. "I wish I was in London again; I would rather be in the Edgware Road. Do you hear, mother?—the Edgware Road."

Helen sighed. She thought there must be something in Margaret's gentleness that drove her son mad. Hughie must wish to see her round on him, to make her angry, to make her cry?

"Do we have to have Hughie with us?" she said coldly.

One day Phoebe came again to fetch them in her car.

"Would you like to come to Dungeness?" she said. She wanted to go there herself, it would make a nice afternoon trip, and they could get some tea at the Ship Inn on the way.

"Would you like to come, Hughie?" she said.

"Yes," said Hughie. "No, I don't know. If it is fine I should like to bathe again."

He ran off to spend some time jumping from the high stone wall on to the beach.

Anna lay in the shade of her mother's deck chair.

"My little seal," said Helen, holding the painting water for her so that she could colour her drawings. She had a temperature and could not bathe or walk or ride.

"Shall we go to Dungeness?" said Phoebe lazily.

"I don't know. Shall we, yes, let's go quickly to Dungeness, now," said Helen, jumping up. "Let's take Anna because she can't ride or swim. Let's go quickly before anyone notices." (She meant Hughie.)

Helen and Phoebe gave Margaret no time to think about it; the three girls and the child Anna ran laughing through the hotel and climbed into Phoebe's car—there was an exciting air of conspiracy.

"To Dungeness, to Dungeness," sang Anna as the car leaped along.

There will be hell to pay, thought Helen glancing quickly at Margaret and away again.

"It is an escape," she said, "an escape from the men." (From Hughie, she thought, from the restless son, the troubled father.) "Hurrah. A car full of women is always an escaping party," she said. The women laugh, their cheeks flush with excitement. They are off again, laughing they say, as they say of giggling schoolgirls, "They're off again, that's set them off!" The boiled mutton is forgotten, the care of the children, the breadwinner's behest, the thought for others; it is an escape.

Phoebe drove with enthusiasm, well and quickly. Now the long line of bungalows gave way to black buildings of military significance, and now on their left, half out of the sea, stood up the great black wheel that had carried Pluto's cables, they were coming now to the home of Pluto and to the great lighthouse of Dungeness. Black barbed-wire curled over the landscape and ramshackle fishing huts straggled to the water's edge, with sparse dry grass growing up from the shingle gardens. The lighthouse establishments and the lighthouse itself were prinked and spry, untouched by the litter of war, bearing their neat fresh colours in stripes of grey, black, ochre and white.

They parked the car and made off through the barbed-wire entanglements to the brink of the sea at the very point of the land where it dropped to fathoms deep so that great ships drew safely close. They sat with their feet dipping in the sea, watching the porpoises at play and the seagulls dipping for fish. Where the North Sea met the Atlantic the waves drove up against each other, but in the lee of the land a great calm left the surface smooth to the winds' track.

Margaret began to be unhappy. She felt that she had been persuaded—over-persuaded—by these bold friends. Already the temperament of Hughie that was the temperament of his father Henry, stretched an accusing finger. They would certainly be late for dinner.

How beautiful the air was, how hot and singing and full of salt and dry. The sea was quite navy blue where the two seas met; out to sea lay a band of white mist: it was a heat haze. "All through the war," the lighthouse man had said, "the lighthouse kept its light burning. Yes, they tried to bomb us once or twice, but then they gave it up, we were too useful to them, too."

Yes, it was Pluto they were after, though they didn't know what it was, but just to be on the safe side; they'd hear rumours—oh no, they'd never got anything, except them bungalows.

"Margaret, dear," said Helen, "do cheer up. It won't do Hughie any harm; in fact, it will do him good."

(Oh no, they did not understand.)

"The wife is the keeper of the peace," laughed Helen, "but take a long view, Margaret, the long peace is not always the peace of the moment. Hughie must learn."

They were fifteen minutes late. Hughie met them with a speechless fury.

"I will explain, darling," said Margaret. Hughie, who was quite pale with passion, would not speak to them, but began an affected conversation with the major's eldest child at the next table. ("Hallo, Helen," said David the lover, "Hallo.")

Margaret and the two children slept in one room. After dinner Helen went up with them, and now Hughie began to speak.

"You are low, disgusting women," he said in a low, fast voice getting louder. "You are liars. I curse the day I was born."

Hughie was beginning to enjoy himself now, he was beating himself into a great passion and Margaret was getting frightened. He went on in a mad voice: "It is always Anna who must come first," he said, "always Anna, naturally Anna. Mother," he shrieked, "you have deliberately humiliated me to give me an inferiority complex to cripple me in my whole life; later I shall go mad, I feel that I am going mad now, and how will you like that, mother? The people will point to you in the street and they will say, 'There is the woman who drove her son mad.'" He began to scream, "Mad, mad, mad! When I am in an asylum you will be sorry."

Helen picked up a rolled bundle of *Life* that had come from America. "Shut up," she said, and hit him sharply across the shin with the rolled magazine, "shut up, you fool; whose car was it, anyway?"

"Anna is the second-born," went on Hughie, "she has displaced me in my mother's affection, as soon as she was born this is what she did."

"You are practically word-perfect," said Helen, with a fearful sneering expression. She hit him again. "Stop putting on an act, shut up."

At this moment the door opened and in walked Henry with his suitcase in his hand.

"Babies," he said, "babies, what hope have they? They are wheeled in prams along the sea-front like lords; often there is a coloured canopy between them and the sun. You can see them from the window, look." He crossed the room and stepped out on to the balcony looking down at the sea walk. "Look, it might be Lord Curzon. No wonder they are megalomaniacs. I've had a most difficult day," he said, "the people at the Clinic, really, it hardly seems worth while going on, really no idea . . . hum, hum, hum . . ." (He began to sing under his breath.)

Suddenly everybody was talking at once.

Daddy, Hughie, Helen, Children, Mother, Anna. . . .

The words tumbled out all together at the same moment. Henry, washing his hands at the washbasin, did not seem to notice, he was still lost in thought for the babies he had seen in their prams along the promenade on his way from the station. "Megalomaniacs," he muttered.

"Well, good-bye," said Helen, choking back the laughter that was now rising in hysterical gusts. "I am staying the night with Phoebe you know. I'll see you all at breakfast. I'll be back for breakfast."

She ran along the beach picking up some mussels as she ran. The moon was coming up in the twilight sky over to the horizon; but on the west there were long red and pink and green streaks where the sun had just settled below the hills: these were a dark soft olive green. She and Phoebe, Helen thought, could cook those mussels and have them for a late supper. One could always eat two suppers these lovely hungry seaside days. Oh, what a pleasant holiday this was, how much she had enjoyed today for instance; hitting Hughie had also been quite agreeable. How much she enjoyed the company, the conversation, her darling friend Margaret, the stormy Hughie, the sleek child Anna, and that excursion to Dungeness, and now dear Henry's unexpected return.

She sat down for a few minutes before turning inland across the fields to Phoebe's house. She sat on the beach by the tall posts of the breakwater where the sea was lapping up quickly to high tide again. The shingle was still warm on the surface with the day's sunshine, but underneath as she dug her fingers deeper it was cold and wet. She leant her head back against the post and closed her eyes and took a deep sniff of the sea-weedy salt smell, that had also some tar in it. Presently there would be the mussels for an extra supper with dear Phoebe, but not just yet, just for a time she could stay here. Helen shifted a bit from the post and lay flat back upon the beach, looking up at the sky. There was the sun and the moon (well, almost the sun) and the stars and the grey sky growing darker, and there was this fascinating smell, and on the other side of the breakwater the sea was already getting deep. If only the beach were really as empty as the moon, and she could stay here and lie out all night, and nobody pass by and no person pass again ever. But that no doubt was what it would be like when one was dead (this was always what Helen thought death was like), and then of course the poor soul would weep for its loneliness and try to comfort itself with the memory of past company. Was not that what Hadrian had been thinking so cold and solitary of the sheeted dead—*quæ nunc abibis in loca?* Best, then, to make best use of the company that was now at hand. Helen got up and walked slowly up the beach and across the fields towards Phoebe's house, pausing only for quite a short time to lean over the bridge that crossed the dark river, and only then because there was a fish swimming that came suddenly into the track of the moonlight, rising to snap at a mosquito that lay out late on the water.

•

FROM *Simply Living*

You must have some money if you are going to live simply. It need not be much, but you must have some. Because living simply means saying No to a great many things. How can you say No to travelling up and down to work and being competitive if you do not have money? If you have a little money and are a poet, there is no greater pleasure than living simply. It is also grand. In my present circumstances I am grand. I can say No when I want to and Yes when I want to. It is important to say Yes sometimes or you will turn into an Oblomov. He stayed in bed all day and was robbed by his servants. There was little enjoyment there.

Le Plaisir aristocratique de déplaire also lies open to those who live simply. But again you must be careful, or you will cut your nose off to spite your face, and so defeat the purpose of simplicity, which is enjoyment.

> *My heart was full of softening showers,*
> *I used to swing like this for hours,*
> *I did not care for war or death,*
> *I was glad to draw my breath.*

I wrote this poem, accompanied by a drawing of a little creature swinging on his stomach on a swing, to show the enjoyment that lurks in
simplicity. "Lurks" is the word, I think. You do not seek enjoyment, it
swims up to you. The writer John Cowper Powys, in his sneering,
fleering humility, and from the depths of that sardonic laughter which
echoes through his books and takes in the whole universe of rocks, pools,
animals and human beings, knew all there is to know about the pleasures
of simplicity. And its grandeurs too. For as I have hinted, there is a great
lordliness in simplicity, very aggravating to bustlers, whether they bustle
by choice or necessity. However, they will probably write off the simple
ones, as they wrote off poor Croft:

> *Aloft,*
> *In the loft,*
> *Sits Croft;*
> *He is soft.*

I enjoy myself now living simply. I look after somebody who used to
look after me. I like this. I find it more enjoyable than being looked
after. And simpler. I used to have very complicated feelings about not
being able to cook, supposing I ever had to, and not being able to keep
house, and wondering if it might not be better being dead than not
being capable. Now I cook and do not worry. I like food, I like stripping
vegetables of their skins, I like to have a slim young parsnip under my
knife. I like to spend a lot of time in the kitchen. Looking out into the
garden where the rat has his home, and the giant hemlock is now ten
feet high. (I sat next to a man at dinner the other day who during the
war specialised in slow-working poisons for use by the resistance movements. He said: You want to distil the roots.) Looking at the date—
1887—on my mincing machine . . . at the name "The White Rose"
on my rusty iron stove. We should thank our lucky stars for these masters
of incongruity who give names . . . A Dutch blue decorated lavatory
pan in a friend's house called "The Shark." A cruiser called Harebell. A
cat, mother of 200 kittens, called "Girlie."

But—*Looking.* That is the major part of the simple life. Yesterday
the cupboard door in my Aunt's bedroom stuck. When I wrenched it
open, her father's sword fell on my head. I peeled off the perishing black
American cloth it was wrapped in and looked at the beautiful sword. Its
hilt was dressed in pale blue, white and gold. I looked at the blade with
its beautiful chasings. *Looking at colours.* The roof-colours opposite are
like the North Sea, in rain they are sapphire.

Looking at animals. The aged dog from the Dog and Duck, wobbling in fat, takes itself for walks. I met it once a mile away from home. When it crosses the road, it looks right and left like a Christian. The man in the round house collects front doors. They stand in his front garden— pink, blue, green. There is a ginger cat near us, born blind. This cat walks like an emperor, head in the air. But he is wild and if touched will fly for your throat.

Regular habits sweeten simplicity. In the middle of every morning I leave the kitchen and have a glass of sherry with Aunt. I can only say that *this is glorious.* There is a great deal of gloriousness in simplicity. There is, for instance, the gloriousness of things you only do seldom. We have not got television. But once, on a friend's set I saw "The Trojan Women." What laughter and argument came to me from the strong impact of this rare treat. Why make Helen out a baggage? She was royal, half-divine, and under the compulsion of a goddess. Why present the play as an argument against war, yet leave in Euripides's ironic line (which he puts in the mouth of his captive women, princesses and slaves, being led into captivity), the line: "If we had not suffered these things we should not be remembered." What an earth-shaking joke this is. Yet, if my life was not simple, if I looked at television all the time, I might have missed it. There are moments of despair that come sometimes, when night sets in and a white fog presses against the windows. Then our house changes its shape, rears up and becomes a place of despair. Then fear and rage run simply—and the thought of Death as a friend. This is the simplest of all thoughts, that Death must come when we call, although he is a god. It is a good thing at these moments to have a ninety-two-year-old creature sitting upstairs in her dignity and lofty intelligence, to be needed and know that she is needed. I do not think happiness in simplicity can be found in solitude, though many must seek it there, because they have no other choice . . . like this poor man I wrote a poem about and will end with:

> Rise from your bed of languor
> Rise from your bed of dismay
> Your friends will not come tomorrow
> As they did not come today
>
> You must rely on yourself, they said,
> You must rely on yourself,
> Oh but I find this pill so bitter said the poor man
> As he took it from the shelf

Crying, O sweet Death come to me
Come to me for company,
Sweet Death it is only you I can
Constrain for company.

Is it to avoid this *final* simplicity, that people run about so much?

FROM *Too Tired for Words*

Being everlastingly "too tired for words" might seem a serious handicap
to a writer. I cannot complain myself that it has turned out quite like
that, though of course the Muse complains endlessly; (or, feeling guilty.
one complains on her behalf:

My Muse sits forlorn
She wishes she had not been born
She sits in the cold
No word she says is ever told.

The fact is one works one's fingers to the bone for the peevish beast).
Well, one is tired and the devil take it. One forces oneself, one gets a
bit feverish (and much more tired) and eventually, out of the strain and
exasperation, the words come headlong. A bit oddly too sometimes.
Why, the scene shifts wonderfully in the light of the words that are, by
reason of the tiredness, just a bit off-beam. So I have written "affable
circumstances" for affluent circumstances, and "nagative" for negative,
and are not these richer thoughts? And yesterday, writing about the great
Freud, instead of Austrian Jew which I meant, I wrote "Autumn Jew."
And that too is an eerie shift. One may get a poem out of these shifts.
Like this one, with its tired reading of Lobster for Lodestar.

"DUTY WAS HIS LODESTAR"
A SONG.
Duty was my Lobster, my Lobster was she,
And when I walked with my Lobster

I was happy.
But one day my Lobster and I fell out,
And we did nothing but
Rave and shout.

Rejoice, rejoice, Hallelujah, drink the flowing champagne,
For my darling Lobster and I
Are friends again.

Rejoice, rejoice, drink the flowing champagne-cup,
My Lobster and I have made it up.

But sometimes the shifts of tiredness are too eerie by half. Riding home
one night on a late bus, I saw the reflected world in the dark windows
of the top deck and thought I was lost for ever in the swirling streets of
that reflected world, with its panic corners and the distances that end
too soon; lost and never to come home again.

One gets strained, feels guilty, sad, and bad. And so falls into despair.
It is then that the great thought of Death comes to puff one up for
comfort. For however feeble one may seem, however much "of poor
tone" as they say at school, and negligible, Death lies at one's command,
and this is a very invigorating thought and a very proud thought too. I
remember once when I was feeling too tired to write an original poem
I fell to translating Dido's Farewell to Aeneas, putting something into
the last two lines that is not quite in Virgil, to express this proud thought
of commanding the great god Thanatos (you remember she is stabbing
herself). So the lines go like this:

"*Come Death, you know you must come when you're called*
Although you're a god. And this way, and this way, I call you."

Yes, that thought of Death at command is a great relief to the tired.
Indeed, if one is tired all the time I do not see how one can accept the
Christian religion that is so exhausting and neat, and tied up neatly for
all eternity with rewards and punishment and plodding on (that too
much bears the mark of our humanity with its intolerable urge to boss,
confine and intimidate.) And no, it will not, Christianity absolutely will
not allow us this delicious idea of command over Death, preferring to
team up on this point with Old Mother Nature, that bloody-minded
Stakhanovite with her brassy slogan "Production at all costs." But one
wants that idea of Death, you know, as something large and unknowable,
something that allows a person to stretch himself out. Especially one

wants it if one is tired. Or perhaps what one wants is simply a release from sensation, from all consciousness for ever (the Catullus idea of *nox est perpetua una dormienda*.)

I often try to pull myself together, having been well brought up in the stiff-upper-lip school of thought and not knowing either whether other people find Death as merry as I do. But it's a tightrope business, this pulling oneself together, and can give rise to misunderstandings which may prove fatal, as in this poem I wrote about a poor fellow who got drowned. His friends thought he was waving to them but really he was asking for help.

NOT WAVING BUT DROWNING

Nobody heard him, the dead man,
But still he lay moaning:
I was much further out than you thought
And not waving but drowning.

Poor chap, he always loved larking
And now he's dead
It must have been too cold for him his heart gave way,
They said.

Oh, no no no, it was too cold always
(Still the dead one lay moaning)
I was much too far out all my life
And not waving but drowning.

•

FROM *Cats in Colour*

Most of the pussycats in this beautiful picture book are little deb creatures, sweet little catsy-watsies of family, offspring of prizewinners and prizewinners themselves, "daughters" (and sons) "of the game"; the game in this case not being Shakespeare's Ulysses' game, as you will find it in *Troilus and Cressida*, when that cunning Greek general, in high-ranking Army company, refuses to kiss Cressida, because she is too easy by half, too much everyman's armful.

No, here "the game," though not to my mind entirely removed from a hidden tartiness, is the game that human beings have been playing with the animal world since the first dog owned a human master and the first cat settled down upon a human hearth. It is we who have made these little catsy-watsies so sweet, have dressed them up and set them up, in their cultivated coats and many markings, and thrown our own human love upon them and with it our own egocentricity and ambition. I should have liked some little common cats alongside our beauties, some ash-cats going sorrowful about the palings of a poor London street, and not only for contrast with the beauties but for the truth of it as to the whole at nature. Or is the cat-nature disguised as much by misery as it is by grandeur? And what in heaven's name is the cat-nature? Does it shine in the pretty eyes of our cat gathering in this sumptuous book, or is that a humanisation too? Really to look in an animal's eyes is to be aware of stupidity, so bland and shining these eyes are, so cold. It is mind that lights the human eyes, but what mind have animals? We do not know, and as we do not like not to know, we make up stories about them, give our own feelings and thoughts to our poor pets, and then turn in disgust, if they catch, as they do sometimes, something of our own fevers and unquietness. Tamed animals can grow neurotic, as the Colonel in a poem I wrote knew but too well (he was in India, hunting tiger):

> *Wild creatures' eyes, the colonel said,*
> *Are innocent and fathomless*
> *And when I look at them I see*
> *That they are not aware of me*
> *And oh I find and oh I bless*
> *A comfort in this emptiness*
> *They only see me when they want*
> *To pounce upon me at the hunt;*
> *But in the tame variety*
> *There couches an anxiety*
> *As if they yearned, yet knew not what*
> *They yearned for, nor they yearned for not.*
> *And so my dog would look at me*
> *And it was pitiful to see*
> *Such love and such dependency.*
> *The human heart is not at ease*
> *With animals that look like these.*

But I think all animal life, tamed or wild, the cat life, the dog life and the tiger life alike, are hidden from us and protected by darkness, they are too dark for us to read. . . .

Why should such an animal provoke our love? It was the indifference of course, the beastly, truly beastly—that is as appertaining to beasts—indifference of poor dear Tizdal I so relished. There is something about the limitless inability of a beast to meet us on human ground, that cannot but pique, and by pique attract; at least if we are in the mood for it, perhaps, at the moment, too thronged by too-ready human responses, sick of the nerves and whining of our own human situation *vis-à-vis* our fellow mortals. At such a moment the Cat-Fact lifts the human mind and relieves its pressures. As little girls love their dolls, so we love our pets. And use them quite often (I am afraid this is all too common, especially if we suffer from feelings of loneliness) as a stick to beat our human companions, who fail us in some way, are not affectionate enough, do not "understand" us. How nice then to turn to the indifferent cat who can be made to mean so many things—and think them —being as it were a blank page on which to scrawl the hieroglyphics of our own grievance, bad temper and unhappiness, and scrawl also, of course, the desired sweet responses to these uncomfortable feelings.

I had an unlikeable elderly female cousin once and she had a very unlikeable cat, who was in himself I expect no better and no worse than any other animal. Fluff was this cat's name, and "Fluff understands me" was my cousin's constant cry. Looking back from kindlier later years, I can only hope that my cantankerous old cousin's gullibility—for certainly Fluff cared nothing and understood nothing—went on being a comfort to her.

I like to see cats in movement. A galloping cat is a fine sight. See it cross the road in a streak, cursed by the drivers of motor cars and buses, dodging the butcher's bicycle, coming safe to the kerb and bellying under its home gate. See the cat at love, rolling with its sweetheart, up and over, with shriek and moan. But if a person comes by, they break away, sit separate upon a fence washing their faces—and might never have met at all. Better still to see this going on at night, as, if the moon is up and the roofs handy, you sometimes may. And what a wild cry they make, this moan and shriek on an ascending scale, how very wild the cat is then—very different, besotted cat-lovers may say, from "our own dear Queen Cat's home life." But there's not a prim beauty in this handsome book who is not capable of it and happy at it—provided of course our cats are whole cats and not "fixed." Alas, as D. H. Lawrence, in his ratty way, was always saying, so much of our modern life is "fixed" and our animals are most "fixed" of all. That is only one part of the sweetness and cruelty—and necessity too—of taking wild beasts and making pets of them.

Well, you may say, their lives without it were brutish and short.
And has not dear Nip our own dear cat, just completed his seventeenth
year in quiet peacefulness and jolly feeding, and enjoyed every moment
of his life (well, has he?) though a doctored tom and firmly "fixed" from
kithood? Lawrence was a bit of a sentimentalist too, though in the opposite way from such doting cat fanciers as my late old cousin. But a bit
of a sentimentalist in his idea of the satisfactions of animal life; I doubt
for instance if the tomcat is ever satisfied; in the hands of Nature, sex is
a tyrant's weapon.

I like to watch cats when they do not know they are being watched.
Especially I like to watch them hunting . . . flies, perhaps, on the window
pane—cat at fishpond, cat slinking with bird in mouth, cruel cat, cat
stretching on tree bark to sharpen claws, then along the branch he goes
to the fledglings' nest. Cat turning at bay, street-cornered by dogs.
Scared cat.

Cats, by the way, for all their appearance of indifference and self-
sufficiency are nervous creatures, all tamed animals are nervous, we have
given them reason to be, not only by cruelty but by our love too, that
presses upon them. They have not been able to be entirely indifferent
to this and untouched by it.

Best of all, is the cat hunting. Then indeed it might be a tiger, and
the grass it parts in passing, not our green English, or sooty town grass,
but something high in the jungle, and sharp and yellow. But cats have
come a long way from tigers, this tiger-strain is also something that can
be romanticised. In Edinburgh's beautiful zoo, last summer with some
children, I stopped outside the tiger's glass-bound cage. He was pacing
narrowly, turning with a fine swing in a narrow turn. Very close to me
he was, the glass-confinement needing no guard-rails. I looked in his
cold eyes reading cruelty there and great coldness. Cruelty? . . . is not
this also a romanticism? To be cruel one must be self-conscious. Animals
cannot be cruel, but he was I think hungry. To try it out, to see whether
I—this splendid human "I"—could impinge in any way upon this creature in his anteprandial single-mindedness, I made a quick hissing panting
sound, and loud, so that he must hear it—hahr, hahr, hahr, that sort of
sound, but loud. At once the great creature paused in his pacing and
stood for a moment with his cold eyes close to mine through the pro-
tecting glass (and glad I was to have it there). Then suddenly, with my
"hahrs" increasing in violence, this animal grows suddenly mad with
anger. Ah then we see what a tiger—a pussycat too?—driven to it, can
do with his animal nature and his passion. Up reared my tiger on his
hind legs, teeth bared to the high gums, great mouth wide open on the
gorge of his terrible throat. There, most beautifully balanced on his hind

legs he stood, and danced a little too on these hind paws of his. His forepaws he waved in the air, and from each paw the poor captive claws scratched bare air and would rather have scratched me. This great moment made the afternoon for me, and for the children too and for my old friend, their mama (and for the tiger I daresay) and cosily at tea afterwards in Fullers we could still in mind's eye see our animal, stretched and dancing for anger.

Though pussycat has come so far down the line from his tiger ancestry, from jungle to hearthrug, or to those London graveyards where the grass grows "as thin as hair in leprosy" as Browning put it, and where I have often seen tib and tom at work, there does still remain a relationship, something as between a Big Cat and a little one, that you will not find between cat big or little and a dog.

I will now tell you about a hunting cat I once observed. As I put this hunting cat scene in a novel I once wrote, I will if I may lift it straight from that novel as then it was fresh to me and if I told it over again it would not be. It was a hot day in summer, and I was swimming at the seaside with a cousin, not my elderly old lady cousin this time, but a boy cousin and a dear one, his name was Caz. So this is how it goes:

"We were now swimming above a sandbank some half mile or so out from the shore. Presently the sandbank broke surface and we climbed out and stood up on it. All around us was nothing but the sea and the sand and the hot still air. Look, I said, what is this coming? (It was a piece of wreckage that was turning round in the current by the sandbank and coming towards us.) Why, I said, it is a cat. And there sure enough, standing spitting upon the wooden spar was a young cat. We must get it in, said Caz, and stretched out to get it. But I saw that the cat was not spitting for the thought of its plight—so far from land, so likely to be drowned—but for a large sea-beetle that was marooned upon the spar with the cat, and that the cat was stalking and spitting at. First it backed from the beetle with its body arched and its tail stiff, then, lowering its belly to the spar, it crawled slowly towards the beetle, placing its paws carefully and with the claws well out. Why look, said Caz, its jaws are chattering. The chatter of the teeth of the hunting cat could now be heard as the spar came swinging in to the sandbank. Caz made a grab for the spar, but the young cat, its eyes dark with anger, pounced upon his hand and tore it right across. Caz let go with a start and the piece of wreckage swung off at right angles and was already far away upon the current. We could not have taken it with us, I said, that cat is fighting mad, he does not wish to be rescued, with his baleful eye and his angry teeth chattering at the hunt, he does not wish for security."

How curious the observance of cats has been when great artists have been observing them, to paint and sculpture them, or work them in tapestry. The great early artists seem no happier with cats than they are with babies. Yet there is the cat for all to see, and the baby too. And do not say they extract the essence of cat or baby, because that they do not do. Did Raphael extract the essence of infants, in those stiff nativity little monsters, dropsical, wizened and already four years old though born but an hour ago? He did not, nor did Leonardo on his rocks, nor Dürer, nor anyone I can think of.

Who first among artists gave the essence and outline of infancy? . . . of cathood and doghood? Look at the Grecian cats and the Egyptian cats. To do so comfortably and without the need of visiting museums and libraries of ancient manuscripts, you should take a look at Christobel Aberconway's splendid compilation—*A Dictionary of Cat Lovers XV Century B.C. to XX Century A.D.*

It is not only the cats of antiquity that seem so peculiar (3,000 years may allow some difference in form) but . . . scaled to the size of a thin mouse, as we observe an Egyptian puss, couched beneath his master's chair? The Grecian cats, though better scaled, seem dull and the cats of our Christian era not much better. There is a horrible cat drawing in Topsell's *The Historie of Four-Footed Beastes*, dated 1607; there he sits, this cat, with a buboe on his hip, frozen and elaborate. In every line of this drawing, except for the cold sad eyes, the artist wrongs cathood. Quick sketchers do better, by luck perhaps. We all know Lear's drawings of his fat cat Foss. There is true cathood here, though much, too, of course, of Mr. Lear, so "pleasant to know." Quick sketchers too can catch the cat in movement, and, though much addicted to, and fitted for, reclining, the cat moves—gallops, leaps, climbs and plays—with such elegance, one must have it so. Yet only this morning, I saw a cat quite motionless that looked so fine I could not have disturbed it. Hindways on, on top of a gray stone wall, its great haunches spred out beyond the wall's narrow ledge, this animal was a ball of animate ginger fur; no shape but a ball's, no head, no tail that was visible, had this old cat, but he caught all there was of winter sunshine and held it.

Why I particularly like Edward Lear's drawings of cat Foss, is one peculiar character they have that the cats of ancient Greece and Egypt, and our own Christian cats as shown by master painters, do not have. I mean that impression he gives of true cat-intransigeance, of the cat in its long drawn-out "love-affair" with the human race—loved, mocked, cross and resisting. Why should we not mock our cats a little? We know we cannot understand them, as still less can they understand us, nor can we do much to them on the mental plane, except to make them nervous. Then let us not try to, but mock them a little and let them be a little cross. This is good-natured and sensible, it is much better than trying to invade their world, as some cat lovers do, with the likelihood of ending up, like that poor old female cousin of mine, in a no-man's (and no animal's) land of grievance and pretence. But to be frankly fanciful, to invent stories about cats, to give them human clothing and human feelings, to put words in their mouths, and accompanying the tales we tell of them with bright pictures, there is no harm in this—so long as we do not pretend they are not fancies—no harm and much pleasure.

Yes, these animal fables and fairy stories are full of pleasure. My own favourite of all the cat fairy stories is the one called "The White Cat." I forget exactly how it goes, but there was I think the usual youngest of three royal brothers, and this young prince, adventuring in search of treasure beyond gold, finds himself in a great underground candelabra-ed palace. So lofty are these chambers, and so distant their painted walls, the soft lights cannot light them but leave many shadows. The servants in this palace were invisible except for their hands and the Queen of it all was a great white cat, very fine, and finely dressed and bejewelled, and all the lords and ladies who attended her were cats also and wore their rich silks and velvets in fine style, with swords for the gentlemen-cats and high Spanish boots. I remember the great silence of this story, and the strangeness of the hands, the human hands moving in the high air, bringing service to the lordly cats and rich food on golden plates.

This was my favourite story when I was a child. But now I think Grandville stands first with me for cat-fancies, certainly for cat fancies in pictures, he is so mad. This eerie and savage artist, as savage and eerie as Fuseli, is at his best with pussycats. But they are not the pussycats of our present book, indeed they are not. I am thinking of one of Grandville's drawings which Lady Aberconway uses in her *Dictionary of Cat Lovers*, so you may see it there. Well, in this picture a young girl-cat stands in front of some very peculiar cowled chimney-pots (one of them has a human face, all might have). This girl-cat is too gaily dressed, in cheap frills and cheap satin. On one side of her stands a nightgown-clad angel cat with wings. But she does not have an angel face, rather sly she looks, this angel, with a grin and a double chin a madam might have. Yes, there is the debased bridal theme about this cat-picture, as well as the angel theme. I think it is truly depraved. On the other side of the girl cat, and pulling her by one arm, as Madam pulls the other, stands the devil-cat, her dark angel, and I fear it is to him she looks. The devil-cat's eyes stare, his body looks hard beneath his hard fur, but it is a very tough muscular body, you can see how strong he is. And unfurled for flight against the belching chimney cowls of the dark chimneys are his great bats' wings, leathery and clawed.

Well, you do not often get the English drawing cats like this, they will leave this sort of drawing to Monsieur Grandville. Even our mad English, like the strange cat-mad artist Louis Wain, who while he was residing at the Maudsley Hospital for his madness, drew all the nursing staff and the doctors and psychiatrists in cat forms but true likenesses, are mild and sweet in their fancies, though of rich comicality. Mild and sweet, with occasionally a sly nip, just to show puss he must not get too big for his boots, that is the English cat-comical mood, and it can be a true feeling and not sentimental, though sentimentality is the danger. Cats in art, cats on comic postcards, cats in stories. Could any of our pretty pussies in this nice book of ours play their part, given a chance, in our favourite cat stories? Yes, certainly they could. They look demure and prim, fixed in a studio portrait mood, but true cats they are and any fanciful dramatic human being, with a gift for it, could use any one of them, as his own pet cat may often have been used, for any extravagance you like. Pick your Puss-in-Boots from these pages of photographs, your Dick Whittington cat, your Queen White Cat from my favourite fairy story.

And there are the other stories, too, the "true" stories of cat heroes . . . and cat villains. The only cat villains I can think of are the cats in the witch trials, and this by reason of the devil's choice that he so often appeared to the witches as "a greate blacke catte," or gave a cat to a witch to be her familiar, "the devil brought her a cat and said she must feed him with a drop of her blood and call the said cat Mamillian." But witchcraft is too grim a story for here and its rites too cruel for our pampered pets. Yet I remembered the witch legends of history, as when the Scottish witches were accused of attempting the death of the King and Queen on their sea-passage home to Scotland. The witches swam a cat off the coast of North Berwick, having first christened it "Margaret," they cast it into the sea to drown and thus—they said—raise a storm-wind to sink the King's ship. For this they were convicted and burnt, for the Scots law was crueller than ours and sent witches to the stake, while we only hanged them. But in both countries the poor cat that belonged to the witch, if he was "apprehended," might also suffer death by burning or hanging.

People in those days did not recognise, to respect, the two worlds —of the Human Creature and the Animal. There was a cock that turned into a hen—and was tried by Canon Law and burnt for it. We have come a little forward from those days, I think, for nowadays any lack of respect we show for the Animal World, such as to attempt an invasion of it in pursuit of understanding, is something we do out of love, that mistaken too-fond love that makes nervous wrecks of our pets. A witch-cat poem I wrote is called "My Cats." You can tell they are witch's cats by their names, and by the second line of the first verse, that is a punning spell-line to bring death.

> *I like to toss him up and down*
> *A heavy cat weighs half a Crown*
> *With a hey do diddle my cat Brown.*
>
> *I like to pinch him on the sly*
> *When nobody is passing by*
> *With a hey do diddle my cat Fry.*
>
> *I like to ruffle up his pride*
> *And watch him skip and turn aside*
> *With a hey do diddle my cat Hyde.*
>
> *Hey Brown and Fry and Hyde my cats*
> *That sit on tombstones for your mats.*

There are witches' cats too in another poem I wrote, (and after this I will let the witch cats go, but they haunt my memory, these poor animals, these simple beasts, to have been so taken and used, their animal nature so wronged, and all for mischief of our human minds that will never let well alone). So here comes the last of the witches' cats, and here they do not do very much but to step in and set the ghostly scene: (The poem is called "Great Unaffected Vampires and the Moon"):

> *It was a graveyard scene. The crescent moon*
> *Performed a devil's purpose for she shewed*
> *The earth a-heap where smooth it should have lain;*
> *And in and out the tombs great witches' cats*
> *Played tig-a-tag and sang harmoniously.*
> *Beneath the deathly slopes the palings stood*
> *Catching the moonlight on their painted sides,*
> *Beyond, the waters of a mightly lake*
> *Stretching five furlongs at its fullest length*
> *Lay as a looking-glass, framed in a growth*
> *Of leafless willows; all its middle part*
> *Was open to the sky, and there I saw*
> *Embosomed in the lake together lie*
> *Great unaffected vampires and the moon.*
> *A Christian crescent never would have lent*

Unchristian monsters such close company
And so I say she was no heavenly light
But devil's in that business manifest
And as the vampires seemed quite unaware
I thought she'd lost her soul for nothing lying there.

This poem, for all that the cats play so small a part in it, brings to mind
another favourite aspect of cat-fancying—I mean, the cat in ghost stories.
A writer who used them much in this way, and always with the deepest
respect and affection—perhaps too much respect, for are they quite as
"grand" as he paints them?—was Algernon Blackwood. There is one
story of his one cannot forget, not only because it is in all the anthologies, but for its quality. It is called "Ancient Sorceries." Do you remember . . . ? But of course, now I come to think of it, this, too, is a
witch story. Poor pussycats, how linked they are with the black arts, so
plump and peaceful by day, so feared by night, crossing the moon on
their perilous broomsticks. In this story of Blackwood's there is a young
man of French descent who is traveling in France on holiday. Suddenly
the train he is on pulls up at a little station and he feels he must get
down at this station. The inn he goes to is sleepy and comfortable, the
proprietress is also sleepy and comfortable, a large fat lady who moves
silently on little fat feet. Everybody in this inn treads silently, and all the
people in the town are like this too, sleepy, heavy and treading softly.
After a few days the young man begins to wonder; and at night, waking
to look out over the ancient roof-tops, he wonders still more. For there
is a sense of soft movement in the air, of doors opening softly, of soft
thuds as soft bodies drop to the ground from wall or window; and he
sees the shadows moving too. It was the shadow of a human being that
dropped from the wall, but the shadow moved on the ground as a cat
runs, and now it was not a human being but a cat. So in the end of
course the young man is invited by the cat-girl, who is the plump inn
owner's daughter and serves by day in the inn, to join "the dance" that
is the witch's sabbath. For this old French town is a mediaeval witchtown
and bears the past alive within it. Being highminded, as most ghost-
writers are, Blackwood makes the young man refuse the invitation and
so come safe off with his soul, which had been for a moment much
imperilled.

    In other stories Blackwood keeps his cats on the side of the angels,
the good angels that is. They serve then to give warning of evil ghosts
coming up on the night hour in some house of evil history. Blackwood
thought, as many people think to this day, that cats have an especial

awareness of ghosts and ghostliness, even more so than dogs, who are allowed all the same I believe, by people who are informed in such matters, some disturbance of their hackles when ghosts walk.

I have come a long way from the pages of cat photographs you will soon be turning to, or perhaps have already turned to, as introductions are written to be skipped. But if you look at these pretty cats and think I have wronged them, or look at them and think they do not tell the whole cat-story and wish some other sort of cat was there, remember —the cat for all its prettiness or ugliness, high bred under human discipline or got by chance, is a blank page for you to write what you like on. Remember too that what you write throws no light on puss but only on yourself, and so be happy and leave him to his darkness. As I was content to do, I hope, in the poem I called "My Cat Major":

> Major is a fine cat
> What is he at?
> He hunts birds in the hydrangea
> And in the tree
> Major was ever a ranger
> He ranges where no one can see.
>
> Sometimes he goes up to the attic
> With a hooped back
> His paws hit the iron rungs
> Of the ladder in a quick kick
> How can this be done?
> It is a knack.
>
> Oh Major is a fine cat
> He walks cleverly
> And what is he at, my fine cat?
> No one can see.

I will finish with the Story of a Good Cat. This was the cat who came to the cruel cold prison in which Richard III had cast Sir Henry Wyatt when young. Because of his Lancastrian sympathies Henry had already been imprisoned several times, and even put to the torture. The cat saved his life by drawing pigeons into the cell which the gaoler agreed to cook and dress for the poor prisoner, though for fear of his own life he dared not by other means increase his diet. There is a picture of Sir Henry as an old man sitting in a portrait with the prison cell for background and the cat, a peculiar sad-looking little cat, drawing a pigeon through the prison bars. Underneath is written, but so faintly it is difficult to read, "This Knight with hunger, cold and care neere starved, pyncht, pynde away, The sillie Beast did feede, heat, cheere with dyett, warmth and playe."

It is an amiable part of human nature, that we should love our animals; it is even better to love them to the point of folly, than not to love them at all.

•

Marriage I Think

Marriage I think
For women
Is the best of opiates.
It kills the thoughts
That think about the thoughts,
It is the best of opiates.
So said Maria.
But too long in solitude she'd dwelt,
And too long her thoughts had felt
Their strength. So when the man drew near,
Out popped her thoughts and covered him with fear.
Poor Maria!
Better that she had kept her thoughts on a chain,
For now she's alone again and all in pain;
She sighs for the man that went and the thoughts that stay
To trouble her dreams by night and her dreams by day.

•

No Matter Who Rides

No matter who rides in my Ford
Nothing happens at all untoward
Because I simply will not
Have it. Have what?
Oh I don't know—well, THAT! In a Ford!

•

Lulu

I do not care for Nature,
She does not care for me;
You can be alone with a person,
You can't be alone with a tree.

•

Carrie Snow (contemporary)

～ℰ ℋ～

One-liner

Going to a male gynecologist is like going to a mechanic who doesn't own his own car.

Muriel Spark (1918–   )

～ℰ ℋ～

FROM *The Playhouse Called Remarkable*

"And if ever you produce a decent poem or a story, it won't be on account of anything you've got in this world but of something remarkable which you haven't got."

•

FROM *The Driver's Seat*

"This stuff is poison, full of toxics and chemicals. It's far too Yin. You know what Yin is?" he says.

She says, "Well, sort of" . . . "but it's only a snack, isn't it?"

"You understand what Yin is?"

"Well, it's a kind of slang, isn't it. You say a thing's a bit too yin . . . "; plainly she is groping.

"Yin," says Bill, "is the opposite of Yang."

•

. . . "but I never trust the airlines from those countries where the pilots believe in the after-life. You are safer when they don't."

•

FROM *The Girls of Slender Means*

Once you admit that you can change the object of a strongly felt affection, you undermine the whole structure of love and marriage, the whole philosophy of Shakespeare's sonnet.

•

Jane . . . wrote poetry of a strictly non-rational order, in which occurred, in about the proportion of cherries in a cherry-cake, certain words that she described as "of a smouldering nature," such as loins and lovers, the root, the rose, the seawrack and the shroud.

•

. . . she did not think, except in terms of these phrase-ripples of hers: "Filthy lunch." "Thee most gorgeous wedding." "He actually raped her, she was amazed." "Ghastly film." "I'm desperately well, thanks, how are you?"

•

. . . it never really occurred to her that literary men, if they like women at all, do not want literary women but girls.

•

If I had stayed at home, there might have been a fire in the house, or I might have been run over, or murdered, or have committed a mortal sin. There is no absolute method of judging whether one course of action is less dangerous than another.

•

FROM *Robinson*

"You're a nice piece of homework," he said.

I think I could have saved the soup. Really, I do not know, maybe I deliberately let go of the tray.

•

"No man is an island."

"Some are," I said. "Their only ground of meeting is concealed under the sea. If words mean anything, and islands exist, then some people are islands."

•

. . . although my tastes did no longer exactly incline to the scholarly type of man, such as I had married, my taste in books was largely a perpetuation of his.

•

FROM *The Hothouse by the East River*

If it were only true that all's well that ends well, if only it were true.

•

New York, home of the vivisectors of the mind, and of the mentally vivisected still to be reassembled, of those who live intact, habitually wondering about their states of sanity, and home of those whose minds have been dead, bearing the scars of resurrection.

•

"You should never take guidance from one man only. From many men, many women, yes, by watching them and hearing, and finally consulting with yourself."

•

. . . it is infinitely easier for a man to leave a beautiful woman, to walk out and leave her, and be free, than to leave a woman of intelligence beyond his calculation and her own grasp.

Elizabeth Cady Stanton (1815-1902)

FROM *A Letter to Susan B. Anthony, 1853*

How strange it is that man will apply all the improvements in the arts and sciences to everything about him, animate or inanimate, but himself.

•

So long as the mass of men spend most of their time on the fence, not knowing which way to jump, they are surely in no condition to tell us where we had better stand.

Linda Stasi (contemporary)

~୧ ୨~

FROM *A Field Guide to Impossible Men*

IMPOSSIBLE MAN #7

MAMA–SON

Beware the man who loves his mother's macaroni and cheese more than he loves sex. Or you. Or anything. This is the classic sign of a Mama's fave. It's not that he doesn't love women. After all, his mother is one. It's just that he learned early on that loving one (a woman, *any* woman) more than, or even as much as, his mother, could and probably *would* kill her (his mother, that is).

Now although this relationship (his with *her* versus his with '*you*) leads you to imagine (especially if this is your first one) that he and his mother trade clothes and set each other's hair, it's simply not so. That's not to say that they haven't spent many a misty Saturday antiquing and hitting the swap meets for vintage wicker and God-knows-what-else together. But he's really never worn her clothes. Except for laughs.

I can hear you, even now, saying to yourself, "Ho, ho, ha, ha, not me. I would be able to spot a loser like that from a mile away!" Hmmm. Yes? Maybe. But probably not. Mama's favorite son doesn't necessarily go around garbed in sheep's clothing, you know. In fact, he's probably spent a good deal of time garbed in wolf's clothing . . . or what he considers wolf's clothing. Unfortunately he still uses the term "wolf" to mean a "swinger," so his clothing is usually an embarrassingly bad attempt at hipness, worldliness, or style.

Alas, he lacks hipness, worldliness, and style, thanks to the woman who gave him life. If you doubt my word, test him. Chances are good that: 1) He's been to at least one Wayne Newton or Barry Manilow show in Las Vegas or Atlantic City; 2) he's not ashamed to admit that the farthest he's been from his home town (of his own free will besides the company trip to Las Vegas or Atlantic City) was to Club Med, where he nearly lost his mind at the sight of so much flesh; and 3) he still owns (and has been seen wearing) a Huckapoo shirt and/or gold chain. The other possibilities get downright frightening, and there's no sense getting ugly early on.

HOW YOU MEET

It's not hard to meet Mr. Mom. He does, after all, hold down a job, and he does go to singles' things. Usually he holds a job in some kind of civil service organization, where he may be a supervisor of something ambiguous like systems-testing production or a special-procedures evaluation unit. No one, except Mr. Mom and Mom herself, knows exactly what it is that he does. But chances are good that he's been told that he does it real well. Chances are even better that no one except he and Mom are even sure that he goes to work every day. In fact, if you asked one of his fellow workers whether he was at work yesterday, they'd have to think a couple minutes before answering.

At any rate, you might meet him at the company Christmas party (he doesn't bring his mother), or the company picnic (where he may be forced to drink too much beer because he feels guilty that he didn't bring his mother *and* didn't even visit her before he left, even though it was a Sunday). If it is the Christmas party, you somehow end up dancing one dance with him, which he does well, if a bit stiffly. If it's the company picnic, you notice that he pitches the curve ball in the softball game your way once too often. He blushes when you call him on it after the game. He blushes when you flirt with him, even though he's already feeling very little pain.

Sweet, you think. Nice, you think. A decent guy for a change, you think. So, okay, he *is* a bit of a nerd, and he does get himself done up at times like a mad cross between Sonny Bono and Mr. Rogers, you can always teach him to dress. You think. What you are not aware of at the time is that he gives a whole new dimension to the phrase, "You're ugly, and your mother dresses you funny."

WHAT HE DOES ON YOUR FIRST DATE

- Talk about his mother.

- Talk about his mother's neighbors. (They don't appreciate the effort she makes to keep the neighborhood decent!)

- Talk about how his brother(s) and/or sister(s) moved out of town and didn't offer to move back when his father died and/or retired, and life became tough on Mom.

- Take you to the movies and to a diner for hamburgers afterward.

- Drive you home and walk you to your door not expecting to come in unless you live at home with your parents, and then he would love to come in and have coffee with your mother.

WHAT HE DOES ON YOUR SECOND DATE
- Try to get lucky.

WHAT HE DOES ON YOUR THIRD DATE
- Take you to his cousin's wedding.

WHAT HE DOES ON YOUR FOURTH DATE
- Cancel. His mother called him at work to say she's had a fainting spell.

WHAT HE DOES ON YOUR FIFTH DATE
- Get stood up, if you're smart. No sense in trying to compete with you-know-who. The most you can hope for if you continue is that he'll marry you just when she gets around to needing a full-time nurse!

Remember, in the mama's boy category it's better if he has a live wife than a mother who's still breathing. Worried that he's married? Who cares? The only prerequisite should be dead parents.

Okay, so you think, "I've gone too far." Ha! You will be saying the same thing every Sunday of your life when Mom is making her famous chicken and rice just for you (him).

Here's how it goes: She invites you early in your relationship to her house for dinner. She fusses over you and smooths the fabric of your dress as she smiles warmly. What a sweet thing, she says about you. What a dear woman, you say about her. Then you make the mistake of going to the bathroom, and she stabs you in the back. Women of your religion sleep with various farm animals, she's heard. Women of your nationality drink. She knows that for a fact. And dirty? Wow! Did he ever remember visiting Joey's mother's house growing up? Not that she let him go there but once . . . but even once was enough. Laundry piled up for a week at least, and the woman didn't know what an iron was, for God's sake! If he's willing to take on that kind of life . . . well, he can be her guest, but she hopes she doesn't live long enough to see it. Somehow, he's different when you come back into the room.

Now, don't get me wrong: Mama-Son is a nice, if not especially exciting guy. And his mother seems sweet, if a bit whiny. He's usually the last- or first-born son, and he honestly feels in his heart of hearts that his mother couldn't manage without him. He believes that he does everything for her, even if he doesn't.

If you feel you must have him to call your own, then you must be everything his mother has warned him about. Be a crazed nymphomanical stripping vampire who insists on taking him to nude beaches where you feed him cold chicken while he's lying on his back. Send him erotic chocolates at work without a card, teach him to smoke pot in your living room, buy him an oversized rag sweater from L. L. Bean, and take him trout fishing and then take him white-water rafting on the Colorado River. (He pays, of course.) When he calls you from his mother's house, be completely tasteless and tell him that you're hungry and have no one to eat. When he asks you, tell him you're crazy about his mother but don't go with him when he visits, no matter how much you hate her.

Then find a new boyfriend to occupy your time when he's with Mom. Even he will crumble under this onslaught, even she will capitulate. He will hire someone to cut her grass (when he knows he should be doing it), to be with you . . . and to make sure you are not being a stripping vampire who is white-water rafting with someone else.

MAMA'S FAVORITE SON, MOON, AND STARS AS MATE

Somehow through the miracle of high-speed sleight of hand, you do get wonder-son to marry you. What kind of husband and father will he make? Not as good at either as he is at being a son, that's for sure. His mother's illnesses will always come before his wife's or his kids'. His mother will continue to fuss over him when he comes in the door, and to give you an air kiss. She will like the children because they are his, but she will never love them because they are also yours. You will find yourself bundling up children with colds and sore throats for Sunday visits to Nana's. You will get sick and tired of her constant, "Really, it's nothing, just a little heart attack/cancer/stroke . . . don't ruin your plans just to come over and get me an ambulance/doctor/off the floor and back into my iron lung."

She'll invite you to her garage sale where everything you've ever given her is on sale. You'll ask for the unused wok back, and she'll say, "Sure. That'll be $10.50."

But my dear, my dear, what will you have won if you win? A lifetime subscription to *Prevention*, and the constant chore of finding new and different exotic undies to lure him back home? Is that really what you want . . . no matter how crazy not being able to have him all to yourself can make any normally secure woman? And besides, what if you finally *do* turn him normal? Then you just know he'll resent *you* for it when she kicks the bucket. That's when he'll decide that he needs to find someone more understanding. Someone more like his mother.

BEST OF BREED

Mama-son

Aren't You Being a Little Extreme
in Terms of Your Mother? Award:
NORMAN BATES

Weren't You Being a Little Extreme
in Terms of Your Mother
and Her Clothing? Award:
LIBERACE

Aren't You Being a Little Extreme
in Terms of Your Mother Who
Needed a Mobile Home So She Could
Follow You Around When You Got
Drafted? Award:
ELVIS PRESLEY

IMPOSSIBLE MAN #8

DAN, DAN, THE MARRIED MAN

What can you say about Dan besides the fact that he's married? Well, you can say that he fools around. He says he doesn't (except in this particular case, with you, if you happen to be the girlfriend on the side), but he does. Well, he does, unless of course you're married to him and then he probably doesn't fool around. With you. What he does do with or *to* you (if you're his wife), is make occasional love . . . which is different from fooling around—occasionally or habitually.

If Dan isn't *your* husband, then you've probably met him at or through your job, and he may or may not admit his connubial arrangement to you right off the bat. One type lies and pretends to be divorced while the other type feels compelled to tell you within the first five minutes of meeting you that: 1) he's married; 2) he never cheats on his wife; and 3) he and his wife don't sleep together. At this point you can say, "Excuse me, but who asked?" and then you can tell him that you've recently discovered that only 50 percent of all married people sleep together. It seems that all the wives sleep with their husbands, but none of the husbands sleep with their wives. If that doesn't shut him up, you're probably in trouble.

WHAT HE WAS LIKE THEN . . . WHAT HE'S LIKE NOW

Unlike his 1950s counterpart, the modern Dan is a hip, unsleazy guy. (So it seems.) If, however, he is over the age of fifty, he will wear suits that have been tailored too much and he may even have a hairdo like a middle-aged suburban housewife and/or God forbid, Fred the Furrier.

But since he considers himself a modern guy, you won't catch him saying horrible things about his wife in order to get you into the sack. For example, the old-fashioned Dan would have told you how he only stayed with her for the children, but that she was frigid, uncaring, unconcerned about his work, and that he grew over the years but she hadn't. He had to say those things about her to get you. But somewhere along the way (probably around 1973), we all got liberated, which not only gave women the right to work harder but allowed men to work less. Now he doesn't even have to make up clever lies to get you into bed. Also (in spite of all that extra work), we started believing the popular notion (begun no doubt by married men) that there were so many more of us than there were of them that we'd better take what we could get and learn to make soufflé for breakfast.

This was like a bonus from heaven for Dan. Now he could fool around and only have to make up stories *for* his wife and not *about* her. Therefore, he won't tell you he's about to: 1) leave her; 2) marry you.

WHAT YOU'RE LIKE NOW . . . WHAT YOU WERE LIKE THEN

Everyone knows that fooling around with married men is deadly, particularly on your birthday, his birthday, Christmas, Thanksgiving, Guy Fawkes day, Memorial Day, or any other holiday. The only time you can be assured of seeing him is during Tuesday afternoon trysts, when he says he's with clients, or Thursday night liaisons, when he tells his wife that he's playing racquet ball. (We'll get to that later.)

Even though everyone knows that he's deadly, millions of women foolishly think that they will be able to handle it and that they are different and therefore immune. Unfortunately these same women are the very ones to start doodling their *first* names with his *last* name as soon as he boards the 11:15 back to Larchmont. Now, call me extreme, but that doesn't sound immune to me. In reality, the only difference between the woman who is stuck with Dan now and the woman who was stuck with this kind of guy in your mother's day was that she got better presents.

TRYSTING THE NIGHT AWAY

You will meet Dan and somehow end up having a drink with him. If you haven't met him at work, you might also meet him at a singles bar, where he will pretend to be single. If you suspect that he entered with false ID, ask him for his phone number when he asks you for yours, and say that you'll be out of town, but you can call him the next night or so. If he gives you his work number and *not* his home number, he's married or living with someone. It's that simple.

The best way to spot him is that he has a commuter rail pass stuck in his wallet when he pays for the drinks. He also is probably carrying in his briefcase a duplicate of the shirt he left home wearing this morning. After all, it wouldn't do to go home with lipstick on his collar, now would it? If his wife notices the shirt in his briefcase, he tells her that he still takes his favorite shirts to his favorite Chinese laundry in the city. Somehow, even though he would die before he ever would go to the dry cleaners in the burbs, she buys this story of his inexplicable loyalty to a Chinese laundry.

WHAT HE KNOWS THAT YOU DON'T KNOW IF YOU ARE HIS GIRLFRIEND

1. He will never use the Cashmere Bouquet soap in the motel bathroom when he showers. Motels are the only places in the world that have the stuff, and an alert wife can smell it at 100 paces . . . or less.
2. His thoughtful perfume presents to you happen to match his thoughtful observance of his wife's favorite fragrance.

She thinks she's smelling herself on him when he comes home.

3. If all else fails, and he *has* used the Cashmere Bouquet and you have *refused* to use the perfume, he will stop in a bar on his way home, order a Scotch and pour a good part of it on himself. He might even ask someone to blow smoke on him. That's because "getting drunk with the boys" is less life threatening than fooling around with some dame on the at-home scoreboard.

4. Yes, he probably will have a command performance with his wife when he gets home, just so that she doesn't accuse him of fooling around. God knows (she thinks), he'd be too exhausted to make love to two women in one night.

WHAT HE KNOWS THAT YOU DON'T KNOW IF YOU ARE HIS WIFE

1. The switchboard of the hotel he's staying at on business really does accept incoming calls.

2. The reason your joint American Express bill goes directly to his office now really doesn't have anything to do with his expense account. It's because they send receipts with the bill, and these stubs have caused more men to pay more alimony and child support than all the private detectives on earth.

3. He will leave on a business trip one night early, and spend that night with "her." "Her" will be very grateful, which is why you will probably never get rid of the creep. She's grateful and you're not.

4. If she pressures him into taking her away for a weekend, he will concoct some insane story about going to a sales conference or on a hunting/fishing trip where he can't be reached. If you find evidence that he didn't go, he will have proof that he did.

5. It's not true that the reason he comes home from racquet ball with still-pressed, unsweaty clothes in his gym bag is because they have a laundress on staff at the court.

6. Yes, he *can* make love to two different women on one single night. If even *he* thinks the effort will kill him, he will come in the door holding his stomach and claiming it must be something he ate.

WHAT TO DO IF YOU ARE HIS WIFE

1. Get a good lawyer before he does.
2. Tell him that you are interested in investing, and you want a parking lot of your own.
3. Switch your perfume if you want to be sure.
4. Take up with his best friend since college the second you have a separation agreement.
5. Charge at least two thousand dollars on your joint American Express card (the one with the receipts that go directly to his office) for lingerie and never wear one stitch for him. Leave it around, however.
6. After he moves in with "her," drop the kids, the turtle, the dog with oozing sores, and the kids' laundry off at his new love nest before you go away on vacation by yourself.

THE REALITY OF THE RELATIONSHIP IF YOU'RE THE GIRLFRIEND

Somehow against all your better instincts, you find that you *are* involved with him. Even though you swore that you were just in it for the sex, and until something better came along it would be fun. Besides, you thought, having a secret lover would make you more confident and sexier, and that's when other men would flock around like flies. For some insane reason, this equation only works when you are involved with an available man. When you are involved with an available man, all you meet are wonderful other available men. When you are involved with a married man, all you meet are other women who are involved with married men. And, let's face it, everyone else is busy Christmas Day (except you).

Now, of course there are advantages to this involvement. For one thing, it's easier than taking a chance with an available man and then getting rejected. Let me explain: When you are involved with a Dan, you can easily convince yourself that it's not that he doesn't *want* to be with you on Christmas, it's just that he *can't* be with you on Christmas. If an available man suddenly takes a powder on Christmas and heads for the Bahamas without you, then it's pretty clear that drinking hot mulled wine with you on Christmas Eve isn't his first choice. If Dan ends up with wife and kiddies in the Bahamas on Christmas, however, he says it was against his will. He will be tortured while skin diving, snorkeling, drinking out of coconuts, and motor scootering around without you. He would, he says with his eyes, much rather be drinking hot mulled wine with you. He's lying. And so are his eyes.

DEALING THE CARDS AND WINNING THE GAME

First, admit to yourself that he's probably not going to leave his hearth and home for you and even if he does, chances are good that he won't discover what freedom is like until after you've nursed him through his divorce.

There are two approaches that can make your life less miserable. The first is to date every other man in the world, and only see him when it's convenient for you. Drive him looney with your schedule and don't reserve Thursday nights for him because that's the night he can get away the easiest. Send yourself flowers, and buy yourself cocktail dresses and leave them on hangers over your bedroom door. *If* he gets angry and accuses you of cheating on him, laugh in his face. Don't—I repeat—*don't ever let him get you somehow into a monogamous relationship. This relationship is not monagamous. He's got a wife.*

ONLY WOMEN WITH NO SELF-ESTEEM WHATSOEVER TAKE UP WITH MARRIED MEN WHO ARE ALSO POOR

The other alternative is to refine your bad taste in men to men who can afford to cheat. Only rich men should have the audacity to cheat on their wives. All others should be beaten about the head and neck. Now, provided that you really like the guy in the first place (we're not talking about Mayflower Madam sleaze here), tell him you are interested in the bond market, and learning about investing. Let him invest his money for you, and when he wants to buy you fur coats tell him to buy you a parking lot instead. You mustn't be ashamed to accept presents . . . after all, if he were your boyfriend and he didn't have a wife, you two would certainly be exchanging presents. Then when he finally admits that he can never leave his wife for you or anyone, you can cry all the way to the parking lot to pick up your weekly receipts. It only makes sense.

WHAT'S IT ALL ABOUT, RALPHIE?

It's all about getting him before he gets you. He is a playboy who hides behind domesticity. He wants his cake and to eat you too. Well, that's not the way you should let it be. You certainly deserve better than that, don't you? First of all, he's not nice for cheating on his wife. That's a really low-life betrayal of someone who is also supposed to be the closest person in the world to him. And secondly, if he cheats once, he cheats twice and so on and so forth. There really is only one thing to do. Leave him and marry someone else. If you think you don't deserve a man to call your own, you won't get one. If you think you deserve a man who belongs to someone else, chances are good that's what you'll get.

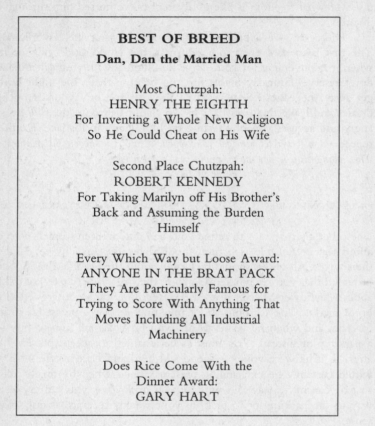

BEST OF BREED

Dan, Dan the Married Man

Most Chutzpah:
HENRY THE EIGHTH
For Inventing a Whole New Religion
So He Could Cheat on His Wife

Second Place Chutzpah:
ROBERT KENNEDY
For Taking Marilyn off His Brother's
Back and Assuming the Burden
Himself

Every Which Way but Loose Award:
ANYONE IN THE BRAT PACK
They Are Particularly Famous for
Trying to Score With Anything That
Moves Including All Industrial
Machinery

Does Rice Come With the
Dinner Award:
GARY HART

IMPOSSIBLE MAN #10
AWESOMELY UNCOMMITTED MAN

Awesome resembles many of the other impossibles in some uncontrollable ways. In fact, he can be the best and the worst of the lot. When you let him enter your life, you allow in a true erotic nightmare. Erotic because he can be very sexy and loving, and a nightmare because he never gets beyond the "going out" stage even if you've been going out for seventeen years. He can't help it, poor guy; he has a fear of engraved

invitations. It runs in his family . . . his father sent one out once and
got stuck with his mother. For life. His mother sent one out once and
got stuck with a life sentence. Yeah, *they're* happy all right.

So early on he decided that a lifetime of bickering just so you could
get laid on a regular basis by someone who got on your nerves and who
probably hated sex (or why would she go to bed wearing goop on her
face?) didn't make a whole lot of sense.

So now, you've got this prize and you completely believe that if
you can just hang in there *long* enough you'll win him over and he'll
be calling you up to discuss engraved invitations sooner or probably later.
And you are wrong. Longevity breeds contempt with this one.

WHERE HE BREEDS, WHAT HE NEEDS

Awesome knows no boundaries. He's been spotted all over the world,
and is not indigenous to any climate. At all. He may not be hip, but he
is in point of fact clean. He loves starched shirts, nice ties, and slacks
with good creases. He is more yuppie than Jerry Rubin, if possible, and
is probably as intellectually deep as ol' Jer, which means that if you
scratch the surface you'll come up empty.

His insatiable passions are music and movies and the right equipment to play them on. He had the first VCR ever made and nearly went
into cardiac arrest the first time he heard a compact disc. Therefore, you
can find him at Radio Shack or Crazy Eddie's on any given night, in
deep conversation with the salesmen who honestly care about finding
him the perfect connecting wire widget. Or he may simply be browsing
the amplifiers or buying obscure records that you've never heard of and,
with any luck, never *will* hear of.

The local video store has a shrine in his name.

So does his favorite car dealer. That's his second favorite passion.
He buys cars the way normal people buy groceries. He loves cars and
always thinks he can find an even better car than the one he has. His
car has a stereo system that sounds like a recording studio. Riding in his
car is like being in other people's living rooms. Only cleaner.

THE MAN WITH A PLAN

His most distinguishing characteristic, however, is his unrivaled ability
to make confirmed plans with his friends for all vacations, summers, and
holidays years in advance, while being unable to make future plans with
you that extend beyond the next fifteen minutes. If you say you'd like

to plan to spend Memorial Day weekend together, he'll say something clever like "whatever." It makes no sense, but then, neither does he.

SPOTTING AN AWESOMELY UNCOMMITTED MAN

Awesome is likely to be spotted in any place that caters to singles and exceptionally clean people. So you might find him (when he's not at Crazy Eddie's) in a gourmet food shop, Chinese laundry, nouvelle cuisine restaurant, any Hampton except Lionel, Club Med, the cleaning aisle of the supermarket, in the best seat of an obscure classical or sixties rock concert, at the local exotic car dealership.

He wears jeans on the weekends and always has a great pair of sneakers on his feet. He is obsessed by his hair and always has a decent haircut that's never quite right. If he's losing his hair, it is to him the equivalent of having cancer. You are sure to find Monoxidil somewhere in his home, or in his bag if you are away together. He spends a great deal of time gently patting the top of his head in a bizarre manner. It's his way of testing to see if any more hair has come loose in the last three minutes.

He wears glasses and has tried contacts, and he is on a first-name basis with his eye doctor called Larry who's one of his Hampton housemates.

YOUR FIRST DATE

He'll pick you up and take you somewhere nice. He's wearing an all-cotton starched shirt with French cuffs. He smells vaguely of Aramis or some other annoying shaving lotion. He'll drink either single malt Scotch or vodka, and will definitely order the pasta whatever it is. He'll be especially thrilled if they have gnocchi on the menu. Don't even be tempted to ask what gnocchi is.

YOUR FIRST CONVERSATION

HE SAYS:	I'd like to be married, have kids, the whole nine yards. I'm getting too old to be a bachelor . . . I'm ready to get married.
HE MEANS:	*If* I found someone who looked like Christie Brinkley, took her clothes off as quickly as Debra Winger in a movie, raised children with the skill of Mrs. Cleaver, had the pa-

	tience of Mother Teresa, and could earn a hundred grand or more in a nice part-time job, I'd marry her in a minute.
YOU SAY:	Oh, really?
YOU SHOULD HAVE SAID:	If there's anything I don't want to be it's married. Why do I only meet men who want to get married?
HE SAYS:	Huh?
HE MEANS:	This is a new one for me!
YOU SAY:	Is the food good here?

Completely ignoring his lies about wanting to get married makes him totally insane. Every woman he's ever been out with hears the wedding march upon the utterance of these magic words and is sure that he means her, he thinks. (Therefore, if you disregard all his nonsense it will make him—if not mad for you—at least anxious enough to keep calling. Lucky you.)

If the wedding talk hasn't budged you, he will switch tactics to show you that he's a man with *plans*. Plans are his life. He already has plans to take a house in the Hamptons with the same group of survivors that he's housed with for the last five summers. He plans to summer with them this year and next, and by the third summer, he will have accrued enough sick time and vacation time to take a month and a half off, at which he will take a house in Spain with four of his housemates from the Hamptons. He's found out that you can get a cleaning lady in Spain for four dollars a day, including laundry! This may in fact be the most telling part of his whole litany. Because, like it or not, cleaning women mean a great deal to him. Cleanliness and order mean a great deal to him. He is anal to the point of turning it into a religious experience.

His present cleaning lady is the most important woman in his life. She's competent, she's amusing, she's organized, she starches his sheets. He's happy when she's there. She makes no demands and all he has to do is give her a bonus at Christmas. He doesn't even have to make a pretense of going into Gucci's.

He would like, in theory at least, to be married. But in reality he sees no need for it, although he does like to have a steady girlfriend he can see (sleep with) a predictable number of days a week and probably on Saturday night. He would like to have relationships with women that could stay on that basis forever. Why spoil the fun? he thinks. And besides, if you're married, you have to get a station wagon.

Here's the kicker: He may have even been married before. What did she have that you don't have? Him, when he was young enough *not* to know that he didn't want to be married.

WHAT HE LIKES TO DO WITH YOU

• Make love and then roll over so fast you'd think he had ball bearings on his back.

• Go shopping for stereo equipment for his apartment.

• Go to the movies and out for dinner on the weekends.

• Keep your relationship in that gray limbo-land for as long as he's comfortable with it, which could be forever or maybe next week.

• Go for rides with his kids and take them places.

WHAT HE LIKES TO DO WITHOUT YOU

• Attend family functions (his).

• See old girlfriends for dinner and lunch.

• Have dinner with his parents and siblings and *their* spouses or dates.

• Go to his best friend's wedding in another state.

• Escort other women to black tie functions as though you were his mistress and he was secretly keeping you, when as far as you know all you've ever gotten out of him is a Trivial Pursuit game to keep at your house.

• *Make plans.* While you aren't looking, he books a mountain-climbing course for every Sunday for three months, signs on for his share of the summer house, books his Club Med trip.

• Keep all of the above from you until each one is a fait ac-compli. When you get crazy and scream about being excluded, he'll say, "I thought you wouldn't enjoy it." Or, "I need some space to do my own things once in a while. I don't understand why you don't find things of your own to do. I'm not your social director." Then you'll have a huge fight, and somehow or other *you* end up apologizing.

MORE FUN WITH ANAL AND ORAL ROBERTS

He will probably never tell you he loves you, although there *is* one Awesome species in particular that says it right away and says it constantly for a few months before he tapers off. Don't get excited by all that love talk. He very rarely makes the leap over into commitment.

If he's the more readily available type, you will go out with him for months, see each other on many weekends, and never hear anything like "I love you." He will actually have the nerve after seeing you for a year to scream out his *fondness* for you in the clinches. Maddening *and* embarrassing is what it is.

He slips out of commitment talk like a greased swimmer out of a pool. The more you push the worse it gets. If you push too much he'll leave, which would be okay, if you honestly could see him for what he is, which you simply will not be able to do until he's ancient history.

You attempt to take him for dinner at happily married friends' homes. He brings the wine and doesn't get the setup. At all. Instead of seeing blessed domesticity, he says they look like they live in student digs. See what marriage does to people? Instead of envying them their lovely children, he gets you alone and says that he hates out-of-control children who use the floor to lie around on, and how much longer does he have to endure this, anyway?

HOW HE DIFFERS FROM ALL THE REST

Unlike most of the others, he is definitely *there*. If he says he'll call you on Monday, he'll call you on Monday. He doesn't disappear and not call again. He simply never allows the relationship to go beyond a certain point. You'll never know whether you're going to see him on the weekends. He seems to go away on weekends a lot. But where? And with whom? Through osmosis, you get the feeling that to ask would be unpleasant, embarrassing, and/or infuriating. He may or may not lie about his whereabouts, and besides he sees you a lot. He says.

WHAT YOU WILL NEVER KNOW ABOUT HIM. EVER.

- Whether or not he's seeing other women while he's seeing you. You think he's not, but who knows? .

- If his parents hate you and that's why you've only met them once.

- If the rumors are true that one of his ex-girlfriends is really in the looney bin because of him.

- If there really was some woman in his past that made every other pale by comparison.

- If he really did want to marry her and she broke his heart.

- How much money he earns, has, or spends.

WHAT YOU WILL ALWAYS KNOW ABOUT HIM

- He has nieces and nephews that he spends a lot of time with.

- He has siblings that he spends a lot of time with.

- His brother or his brother-in-law is his best friend.

- He has dinner with ex-girlfriends a lot.

- He's very close to his family.

- They want to marry him off.

- It's the only concession he won't make.

AVOIDING "FAT-GIRL-WITHOUT-A-DATE-
FOR-THE-PROM" BEHAVIOR

Fat-Girl-Without-a-Date-for-the-Prom behavior truly gets on my nerves. This is the kind of behavior that makes you take the most desperate actions and do the most life-humiliating things.

In this type of mind-set, you immediately become hundreds of pounds overweight the minute the man you crave doesn't call. You absolutely know that he'll never call, and that you'll never, in fact, have another date with *any*one ever again. You begin to cower and pout and whine and generally behave in ways that make everyone hate you. In other words, like the fat girls in your graduating class who didn't have dates for the you know what.

Once you get into Fat-Girl-Without-a-Date-for-the-Prom syndrome, you will do things like send the man of your dreams (who hasn't called you back) nauseating "sensitivity" or cutesy greeting cards. You will find yourself calling your best friend at 3:00 A.M. to ask her to make wrong-number calls to his house. You will make shameless hang-up calls. You will act like everytime you enter McDonald's they have to up the "billions-sold" sign. In short, you act like you need a size 22½ prom gown, even though you'll go to the prom alone and it's your father who'll be buying you the wrist corsage.

This is a natural-response trigger mechanism that happens whenever the guy you've had a great time with doesn't call back. Depending on your self-image, it can happen anywhere from one day to one week later. It is genetically programmed to occur to every woman except Pia Zadora, and it's something that happened even before telephones were invented. In those days women would sit by a wall where a telephone, if it had been invented, would have been. They would stare at the wall and say, "Why doesn't he call?" At this point someone would point out to her that he was unable to call because telephones weren't invented yet, and she'd have to go sit by the mailbox and humiliate herself in front of the mailman. And even though we no longer have to show our grief and longing to the mailman, we *have* invented new and exciting ways to act like "Fat Girl."

Here, then, are several surefire ways to avoid making an ass of yourself or at least of not appearing as though you needed a half-size prom gown . . . pronto!

EMERGENCY FIRST AID: HOW TO NOT SEND CUTE CARDS WHEN HE
HASN'T CALLED AND OTHER DESPERATE MEASURES

Let's face it, pretending that you don't care in spite of a spate of magazine articles that tell you to simply move on to the next one when this one doesn't call you back, is next to impossible. Most women have found solace in the Hallmark store. There amidst "Happy Birthday to My Favorite Aunt" and the condolence cards sit the sensitive cards . . . and worse, the cute cards. The sensitive cards say things like "Seeing You Was Close to My Thoughts" and other completely inane and insane phrases. They make no sense unless you are desperate, and then they seem to be the only things besides Country and Western songs that *do* make any sense.

Worse even than these maudlin pieces of cardboard with out-of-focus pictures of women wearing chiffon dresses and large hats in fields, are the cute cards. These completely insidious little numbers come complete with Peanuts characters (who've never been funny in the first place), Ziggy, and other cartoon characters, and are *designed* to appeal only to the extremely lonely, the desperate, and the extraordinarily obese.

Be honest here, would you actually send one of these cards to anyone else? No! You'd be ashamed to even sign your name. A lifetime of good taste and sensible judgment simply flies out the window in a crazed attempt to get the attention of the fool who hasn't called back.

It won't work. In fact, one male friend of mine says that it's a formula. When he doesn't call a woman back, he can almost calculate to the day just when the cute card will arrive in the mail. Up until he told me that, I honestly believed that I was the only woman who had found a friend at Hallmark. He also told me if I ever felt the urge to send another one, I should sublimate that urge in exercise, meditation, or suicide.

He admits to having received dozens of cards from women that range from the maudlin (baskets of pathetic kittens) to the downright sickening (Ziggy holding a "miss you" sign). He even discovered that if he wanted to get some woman to pay more attention to him, he'd simply not call her back and wait for the cute card to arrive.

Unfortunately, he also admits that as soon as this same woman stooped to the greeting card stage, he'd dislike her. It's a no-win situation and a blight on the face of this country. It's the hidden disease no one talks about.

WHAT TO DO WHEN THE HALLMARK URGE HITS

- Buy the sappiest card you can find and send it to someone you hate. At least you can get *him* to stop calling.

- Start a riot in the card store by laughing out loud at the religious cards.

- Hold up a Jesus card and ask the person next to you if it's a picture of Jesus or George Harrison.

- If you can't resist the urge to get *something* in the mail to him by the next post, send him a Spanish-language card and sign it Carlos. If, however, he *is* Spanish, send him a Ziggy card and sign it Carlos. He will go crazy and worry about his sexuality.

- Send him a condolence card for his birthday and sign it Carlos.

- Make a sign and put it over your bed that says: THE ONLY CARD WORTH ANYTHING IS PLASTIC.

- Throw yourself on the mercy of the clerk and beg her not to sell you anything.

- Form your own chapter of C.A.R.D. (Cards Are *Really* Desperate), and ask other women to share their humiliating card experiences. When the urge hits, you can call your C.A.R.D. "partner," and she'll talk you out of further humiliating yourself by sending it.

- Call your mother and blame it all on her.

●

HOW TO NOT MAKE HANG-UP CALLS WHEN YOU KNOW HE'LL KNOW THAT IT'S YOU ACTING DESPERATE

There is one more activity as humiliating as sending cute cards, and that's the hang-up call. Now, have you ever gotten a hang-up call and *not* known who it was?

It's bad enough that he will be sure that any *legit* hang-up call (when someone really *has* reached a wrong number and hangs up without speaking) is you, without you furthering the spread of the disease. Personally, I don't think there is such a thing as a legit hang-up call, but in all fairness I had to include it.

The subcategory of hang-up calls is the "I'll get my friend to call up and ask for someone else" call. Or in layman's terms, the fake wrong-number call. Now, excuse me, but what are you supposed to find out with these insane calls? Personally, I have never asked a friend to make one of these, but I sure have made them at 3:00 A.M. *for* crazed friends. The only reason I've never asked a friend to make one is because I was sure that the guy would know that I had coerced someone to make a wrong-number call. I am, obviously, extremely paranoid. Besides, all that I could find out from a call like that would be that:

A. He wasn't home, which would make me depressed.
B. He *was* home, which would make me depressed. (Because he wasn't, as I suspected, lying in some hospital, desperate to call me, but alas, paralyzed and unable to pick up the phone. This, incidentally, is the only legit reason for him not to call; all other reasons mean that he's not interested.)
C. He had a woman there (if one answered). From that I

would conclude that they were engaged, which would
make me depressed.
D. If a man answered his phone I would be sure that he was
gay, which would make me depressed.
E. If his mother answered, I would have to kill myself, and
reaffirm "D."

WHAT TO DO INSTEAD OF MAKING HANG-UP CALLS AND WAITING BY
THE PHONE LIKE A FAT-GIRL-WITHOUT-A-DATE-FOR-THE-PROM

• Take a walk . . . cross-country. It's healthy and you may
meet Mr. Right at the Grand Canyon or when you go to
get your shoes resoled in Philadelphia.

• Make hang-up calls to his parents' house at 3:00 A.M.

• Get out a Ouija board and call up dead relatives for advice.

• Go to a past-life therapist to find out if Mr. Wonderful was
St. Anthony in a previous life and that's why he gets to be
so cavalier in this one.

• Go to a past-life therapist to find out if you were Charles
Manson, Goebbels, or Hitler in a previous life and that's why
you have to be tormented in this one.

• Call your mother and blame it all on her.

• Call the phone company and blame it all on them.

• Go out and buy the *National Enquirer* or *The Weekly World
News* and count the number of alien babies born in England
last week. If you're lucky, they will have a story about someone who spontaneously exploded as well. Stories like these
will always cheer you up. After all, you could be stuck with
a glowing, bossy, alien baby right now, or even one of those
children in Brazil who get old-age disease at three. It's
enough to make you count your blessings! A subscription to
one of these can keep you happy for the rest of your life.
After all, what's a little misery when other people are spontaneously exploding?

Abby Stein (contemporary)

On Sleazy Men

I have this thing where I'm attracted to incredibly sleazy men. [I'd love
to go to bed with one of them] if I can shoot him in the head afterwards.
Because if he tells anyone I slept with him, I'll have to move off earth.

Gertrude Stein (1874-1946)

FROM *Gertrude Stein's America*

The thing that struck me most all over the United States was the physical
beauty of the country, and the great beauty of the cities. In Chicago,
when I was teaching there, I hired myself a "Drive Yourself" car—I
adore the phrase—and drove myself into Chicago every way possible. I
don't know a place in the world more beautiful, and I lost my heart to
Texas. Then, Toledo was very beautiful, and the way that the city towers
rise out of the dead level Northwestern plains was marvelous, and New
England under the snow and now in the spring was so lovely.

•

They told us that the modern high buildings had been invented in Chicago and not in New York. That is interesting. It is interesting that it
should have been done where there was plenty of land to build on and
not in New York where it is narrow and so must be high of necessity.
Choice is always more pleasing than anything necessary.

•

We talked about and that has always been a puzzle to me why American
men think that success is everything when they know that eighty percent
of them are not going to succeed more than to just keep going and why
if they are not why they do not keep on being interested in the things

that interested them when they were college men and why American men different from English men do not get more interesting as they get older. We talked about that a lot at Wesleyan.

•

I was much taken with what one American soldier said when he was in England. He said we did not get along at all with the English until they finally did get it into their heads that we were not cousins, but foreigners, once they really got that, there was no more trouble.

The trouble of course is or was that by the time America became itself everybody or very nearly everybody could read and write and so the language which would naturally have changed as Latin languages changed to suit each country, French, Italian and Spanish, Saxon countries England and Germany, Slav countries etcetera, America as everybody knew how to read and write the language instead of changing as it did in countries where nobody knew how to read and write while the language was being formed, the American language instead of changing remained English, long after the Americans in their nature their habits their feelings their pleasures and their pains had nothing to do with England.

So the only way the Americans could change their language was by choosing words which they liked better than other words, by putting words next to each other in a different way than the English way, by shoving the language around until at last now the job is done, we use the same words as the English do but the words say an entirely different thing.

•

FROM *The Autobiography of Alice B. Toklas*

I went to dinner. The dinner was cooked by Hélène. . . .

Hélène had her opinions, she did not for instance like Matisse. She said a frenchman should not stay unexpectedly to a meal particularly if he asked the servant beforehand what there was for dinner. She said foreigners had a perfect right to do these things but not a frenchman and Matisse had once done it. So when Miss Stein said to her, Monsieur Matisse is staying for dinner this evening, she would say, in that case I will not make an omelette but fry the eggs. It takes the same number of eggs and the same amount of butter but it shows less respect, and he will understand.

Gloria Steinem (1934-   )

~ع ۶~

FROM *If Men Could Menstruate*

So what would happen if suddenly, magically, men could menstruate and women could not?

Clearly, menstruation would become an enviable, boast-worthy, masculine event:

Men would brag about how long and how much.

Young boys would talk about it as the envied beginning of manhood. Gifts, religious ceremonies, family dinners, and stag parties would mark the day.

To prevent monthly work loss among the powerful, Congress would fund a National Institute of Dysmenorrhea. Doctors would research little about heart attacks, from which men were hormonally protected, but everything about cramps.

Sanitary supplies would be federally funded and free. Of course, some men would still pay for the prestige of such commercial brands as Paul Newman Tampons, Muhammad Ali's Rope-a-Dope Pads, John Wayne Maxi Pads, and Joe Namath Jock Shields—"For These Light Bachelor Days."

Statistical surveys would show that men did better in sports and won more Olympic medals during their periods.

Generals, right-wing politicians, and religious fundamentalists would cite menstruation ("*men*-struation") as proof that only men could serve God and country in combat ("You have to give blood to take blood"), occupy high political office ("Can women be properly fierce without a monthly cycle governed by the planet Mars?"), be priests, ministers, God Himself ("He gave this blood for our sins"), or rabbis ("Without a monthly purge of impurities, women are unclean").

Male liberals or radicals, however, would insist that women are equal, just different; and that any woman could join their ranks if only she were willing to recognize the primacy of menstrual rights ("Everything else is a single issue") or self-inflict a major wound every month ("You *must* give blood for the revolution").

Street guys would invent slang ("He's a three-pad man") and "give

fives" on the corner with some exchange like, "Man, you lookin' *good!*"
"Yeah, man, I'm on the rag!"

TV shows would treat the subject openly. (*Happy Days*: Richie and
Potsie try to convince Fonzie that he is still "The Fonz," though he has
missed two periods in a row. *Hill Street Blues*: The whole precinct hits
the same cycle.) So would newspapers. (SUMMER SHARK SCARE
THREATENS MENSTRUATING MEN. JUDGE CITES MONTHLIES IN PAR-
DONING RAPIST.)

Men would convince women that sex was *more* pleasurable at "that
time of the month." Lesbians would be said to fear blood and therefore
life itself, though all they needed was a good menstruating man.

Medical schools would limit women's entry ("they might faint at
the sight of blood").

Of course, intellectuals would offer the most moral and logical arguments. Without that biological gift for meauring the cycles of the
moon and planets, how could a woman master any discipline that demanded a sense of time, space, mathematics—or the ability to measure
anything at all? In philosophy and religion, how could women compensate for being disconnected from the rhythm of the universe? Or for
their lack of symbolic death and resurrection every month?

Menopause would be celebrated as a positive event, the symbol that
men had accumulated enough years of cyclical wisdom to need no more.

Liberal males in every field would try to be kind. The fact that
"these people" have no gift for measuring life, the liberals would explain,
should be punishment enough.

Eliza "Mother" Stewart (1816-1908)

❦ ❦

On Sweet Women

But you must know the class of sweet women—who are always so
happy to declare "they have all the rights they want"; "they are perfectly
willing to let their husbands vote for them"—are and always have been
numerous, though it is an occasion for thankfulness that they are becoming less so.

Deanne Stillman (contemporary)

~~ ♆ ~~

FROM *Girls in Suits at Lunch*

Instead of prenuptial agreements, you could urge paranoid clients to have
sex contracts. The groom relinquishes all claim to his wife's body if
cunnilingus is not performed on the wedding night.

Catharine R. Stimpson (1936–   )

~~ ♆ ~~

The F-Word

Feminism, like other movements for social justice, is demanding. Erasing
the images of Betty Crocker or Aunt Jemima and generating new models
is much harder than whipping up a waffle. Even feminists fear feminism.
We underestimated how difficult it would be to wipe out the psychological residue of the feminine mystique. Many of us still carry within
ourselves a conflict about what gender and change mean. We say, "I am
a feminist," but we often whisper, with irritation, guilt, and ennui, "I
wish I did not have to be."

   If all women's lives continue to change as they have been changing,
many people will be able to say "feminist" as casually as they now say
"wife" or "kid" or "snack."

Pam Stone (contemporary)

~❦ ❧~

On Female Problems

I'm not much of a Southern belle. Southern women tend to be real demure. They don't like to talk about anything graphic. I had a girlfriend who told me she was in the hospital for female problems. I said, "Get real! What does that mean?" She says, "You know, *female* problems." I said, "What? You can't parallel park? You can't get credit?"

Harriet Beecher Stowe (1811–1896)

~❦ ❧~

FROM *Love versus Law*

When a young lady states that she is not going to believe a thing, good judges of human nature generally give up the case; but Miss Silence, to whom the language of opposition and argument was entirely new, could scarcely give her ears credit for veracity in the case; she therefore repeated over exactly what she said before, only in a much louder tone of voice, and with much more vehement forms of asseveration—a mode of reasoning which, if not strictly logical, has at least the sanction of very respectable authorities among the enlightened and learned.

Linda Sunshine (contemporary)

~え ッネ

FROM *Women Who Date Too Much (And Those Who Should Be So Lucky)*

THE WEDDING MARCH OF CIVILIZATION: DATING FROM ADAM AND EVE TO MADONNA AND SEAN

Mankind's first official attempt at dating took place in the Garden of Eden, and, like most dates, it was based on a profound misunderstanding.

Adam was eating breakfast one morning when he spied a young woman staring at him from behind a rubber tree. Upon closer inspection, Adam thought he detected a certain hungry look in this strange creature's eyes, so he kindly offered her a piece of his fruit. "Wanna date?" Adam asked.

Eve, the original single woman, heard opportunity knocking loud and clear. "You bet," she said. "Let's do lunch." And she rushed off to wash her hair.

Historians note that the phenomenon of dating might've been radically altered if Adam had been eating a grapefruit that fateful morning.

But he wasn't, and, as we know, Adam and Eve continued to "date"—on and off—for the remainder of their lives, which wasn't all that difficult considering Eve had virtually no competition in Eden and millions of years would pass before the discovery of cellulite.

Throughout the Ages we now call Stone, Ice, Bronze, and Iron, dating consisted mainly of informal gatherings for the purpose of hunting and foraging (sort of like Woodstock in a fur coat). Romance during this time was minimal, since primitive man had yet to create Snoopy greeting cards. In fact, nothing much happened until the scientific discovery of astrology, which altered the course of dating by enabling single men to introduce themselves by asking: "What's your sign?"

The next momentous event in dating history is credited to Cleopatra, the Queen of Egypt. After her boyfriend, Caesar, was assassinated, Cleo began fooling around with Marcus Antonius, her best friend's husband. Thus, Cleopatra became the first woman in recorded history to date a married man. Like many such relationships, this one ended badly. Cleopatra committed suicide at age thirty-nine.

Centuries passed and dating took a back seat to lots and lots of wars—at least until the French Revolution, when things picked up, thanks to Marie Antoinette. A genuine boy toy, Marie liked to mix heavy necking and whipped cream, a combination that greatly aroused Louis XVI and, more importantly, was the method by which the couple inadvertently invented French kissing. Unbeknownst to Louis, Marie demonstrated their discovery to almost every garçon at Versailles, which is probably why dating enjoyed a healthy revival in the late 1700s.

During the 1800s, several technological advances radically altered the course of dating. In 1824, the process of binding rubber to cloth was first patented. This seemingly innocuous event would subsequently lead to the invention of the girdle, a garment that almost single-handedly wiped dating off the face of the earth.

In 1865, George Pullman built his first railway sleeping car, thereby creating a reason to take a date along on a business trip. It wasn't long before people began making out in other moving vehicles as well. In fact, Pullman's early efforts probably account for the popularity of airplane bathrooms among today's traveling singles (hence the advertising slogan, "Fly United!").

In 1871, the typewriter was invented, which didn't directly affect dating per se but did permit me to write this sentence without using quill and ink.

In 1907, the Model T Ford was mass-produced for the first time, enabling everyone to own a car. This was important, because how else could people get to the drive-in?

No one would dispute that the most momentous—and time-saving—contribution to dating took place in 1915 with the invention of the zipper.

What is disputed, however, is the exact moment in history when the word "relationship" crept into our dating vocabulary. Attempting to discover the origin of this term, researchers have studied hundreds of tapes of the *Dating Game*, but all to no avail.

Scholars have noted, coincidentally, that their inability to determine when a "date" became a "relationship" is the same dilemma that confuses most single men today.

•

Yet no discussion of dating would be complete without evaluating, in some detail, the seminal singles book of our century, *Sex and the Single Girl*, which was published in May 1963 and, almost instantly, became one of the most talked about books of its time. Reviewed extensively, the intrinsic intellectual value of this book was perhaps best described by Miss Joan Crawford who stated: "It [this book] should be on every man's bed table—when he's free, that is." (For further information about how Helen Gurley Brown boosted the social life of the unavailable man, see chapter on "Dating Married Men.")

As proof of its relevance to modern-day society, *Sex and the Single Girl* was made into a movie starring Tony Curtis and Natalie Wood.

In the following paragraph from her book, Mrs. Brown displays a remarkable talent for deep psychological insight into the inner workings of the male psyche.

"When a man thinks of a single woman," writes Mrs. Brown, "he pictures her alone in her apartment, smooth legs sheathed in pink silk Capri pants, lying tantalizingly among dozens of satin cushions, trying to read but not very successfully, for *he* is in that room—filling her thoughts, her dreams, her life."

While parts of *Sex and the Single Girl* have become somewhat dated (Who can afford to live alone anymore? Who has smooth legs?), a great deal of the book, particularly Mrs. Brown's sound advice, has remained, surprisingly, as refreshingly and frankly applicable to today's single gal as it was for the swinging sixties gal of long ago. Take, for instance, the following examples of Helen Gurley Brown's wisdom:

- There are three kinds of people you absolutely must have in your single life: a really good butcher, a crack car mechanic, and a rich and powerful married couple.

- Demand and inspire expensive gifts from your dates. These are the rewards of single life.

- If he asks to go Dutch treat on your date, don't stand on ceremony. Dump him immediately.

As for me, my favorite piece of advice from *Sex and the Single Girl* involves not sex, but office politics. Over and over, Mrs. Brown stresses the importance of having a solid career and competing in the market-place on an equal footing with men. In this way, perhaps Mrs. Brown could be considered a forerunner of *Ms.* magazine. Take, for example, the following piece of advice, which most certainly helped Gloria Steinem (and others like her) catapult up the corporate ladder. "About every six weeks several girls from my office and I round up all our clothes that need altering, and we gossip and sew for the evening. Isn't that jolly?"

While this idea strikes me as a wonderful way to finally get those loose buttons fixed on my raincoat, the other female executives in my office were not very receptive to the suggestion. So far, no one seems interested in a jolly evening of sewing and girl talk.

The decline in the popularity of sewing circles among female co-workers is, perhaps, not the only difference in the social life of a single woman in the days of *Sex and the Single Girl* and today. If someone were writing a late 1980s version of Helen Gurley Brown's opus (and I'm applying for the job), she might have to title the book *Sex and the Significant Other.* (Actually, in writing about my social life, the more appropriate title might be *Sex and the Insignificant Other,* but that's another story altogether.) . . .

Women born in the baby-boom years had the misfortune of entering their early to mid-twenties at a very critical moment in American history. Specifically, these women came of marriageable age during the first broadcasts of *The Mary Tyler Moore Show.* The enormous popularity of the show encouraged these women to stay home on Saturday night and watch television instead of going out on blind dates, thus greatly decreasing their chances of snagging a husband. In addition, these women were brainwashed by the blatant propaganda promoted by the show, namely that it was okay to be single, as long as you were real skinny and had funny neighbors. It wasn't until these baby boomers hit their late thirties and early forties that it dawned on them that Mary Tyler Moore, in real life, was married to a successful Jewish doctor sixteen years her junior. Many women have never fully recovered from this crushing revelation.

Today's single women are a breed apart from the single women of Helen Gurley Brown's generation. No longer labeled a Jolly Spinster, the modern single gal is likely to own her own co-op or condo and to have learned not to feel out of place with her married friends and relatives. These women usually have a good relationship with children, either of their friends or siblings. Often they have challenging jobs and many social advantages. Their lives are wholly successful even though the vast majority of them are unbelievably depressed most of the time.

In order to get a first-hand account of the dating scene and how it affects the modern woman, this reporter recently attended a gathering of single women who congregated at the Dew Drop Inn in Massapequa, New York, to discuss their social lives with the media. The room was filled to capacity with unmarried women, all of whom wore T-shirts that read: "I'd rather be married, or at least dating someone special." In the crowded room, this reporter noted that the ticking of biological clocks was almost deafening.

When asked about the problems of their social life, most of the women sounded confused and bitter.

"What can I say? It's the pits," claimed Tiffany Detroit, a thirty-four-year-old kindergarten teacher from Brooklyn. "I never meet any guys over five years old."

"At least they're single," countered a twenty-nine-year-old hairdresser who asked to remain anonymous. "You sound like you're in a great location to meet unmarried guys. The only men I meet on the job are the ones with better makeup than me."

Women at this meeting acknowledged that the holidays and the weekends were the hardest times for them. Several women reported working on Sunday in order to avoid seeing all the couples and married families having brunch or walking on the street.

"I like to spend time pampering myself on the weekends," claimed another single woman who also asked that her name be withheld. "I get into a hot bathtub on Friday night and I don't get out again until I have to go to work on Monday morning."

"Aren't you as wrinkled as an old prune by then, Betty Martin?" this reporter inquired.

"You bitch!" Betty screamed. "I told you not to mention my name!"

With a few exceptions, most of the women at the bar expressed regret that they would probably not have children of their own. "I'll never be able to manipulate a child the way Mom manipulated me," sighed one lady who'd consumed fifteen banana daiquiris and was laid out on top of the bar. "That's why I drink," she explained before passing out.

This reporter left the Dew Drop Inn with a greater understanding of the plight of the single woman and a bar tab like you wouldn't believe.

But these observations are not a reason for single women to despair; they are the reason for them to persevere.

From Adam's first "date" with Eve to the courtship of Madonna and Sean, dating has always been a test of personal endurance. And it always will be because, as the sign above the bar at the Dew Drop Inn read: If God meant life to be easy for singles, why did He create New Year's Eve?

•

THE WOMAN WHO MISTOOK HER BLIND DATE
FOR A POTENTIAL HUSBAND

Everyone knows that the best policy is to not expect miracles from life. "I didn't want to be rich," Kate (Mrs. Zero) Mostel once claimed, "I just wanted enough to get the couch reupholstered."

Still, when you go out on a blind date, it's hard not to entertain the following fantasy:

The doorbell rings. You get up from your dressing table, take one last lingering look at yourself in the mirror, and nod with approval. You open the front door.

He stands in the doorway, but you can barely see his face behind all of those enormous yellow roses he's holding in his hands. He presents you with the bouquet.

He is incredibly tall and looks like a cross between William Hurt, Tom Cruise, and the guy you loved madly in sixth grade.

His crooked smile reveals his vulnerability, a great set of real white teeth, and a neat dimple in his left cheek.

He is rendered speechless by your beauty and falls instantly in love with you.

The next day, you discover he is a millionaire brain surgeon/criminal lawyer who pilots his own Lear jet and owns an oceanfront summer house in Southampton.

Say hello to your dream blind date.

Say good-bye to reality.

The blind date is genuine proof that truth is stranger than fiction. The facts speak for themselves:

A perfect stranger calls you up. You have an extremely uncomfortable conversation, which you both pretend to enjoy. He asks you to see a movie that you have no interest in seeing. You worry about what to wear, what he'll look like, and whether you'll have anything to talk to him about.

In your heart of hearts, you know you will have a terrible time, the date will be a total washout. But, still, you have an anxiety attack if your hair frizzes while you are getting ready for him to arrive.

Your tendency during this initial stage of anxiety is to curse the friend or relative responsible for arranging the date. Try to avoid hating this person.

It is best to remember that the people who set you up on a blind date have the best of intentions, really they do. You need to keep this in mind, because the truth is you can never, never believe what anyone tells you when they describe the person you are being fixed up with.

If you're told, for instance, that your blind date looks like a movie star, you're not told that the movie star is Meat Loaf.

If you're told that your blind date is a great catch, you're not told that his wife's alimony lawyer has been trying to catch the guy for months.

If you're told this is a match made in heaven, you're not told it was on an off-day.

If you're told your blind date is an old-fashioned guy, you're not told that this applies mainly to his clothes.

But, hey! You're single, and although your phone rings constantly, it's always your mother calling you.

It is a well-known fact, by the way, that the worst blind dates, bar none, are those arranged by your mother. It doesn't matter whether the guy is a district attorney, a genius, a best-selling writer. If your mother found him, he's a geek.

Regardless, you want to take advantage of every opportunity, so you accept blind date after blind date. Eventually, however, your inner psyche begins to rebel.

Your cousin Rhonda offers to fix you up with her brother's accountant, but instead you choose to stay home and watch *St. Elsewhere*.

Your best friend meets a great new guy and you forget to ask: Does he have any single friends?

You make a firm decision that blind dating is not for you. You begin to consider the alternatives: celibacy or surrogate dating.

AN ALTERNATIVE TO BLIND DATES: SURROGATE DATING

Until recently (March 16, 1986, to be specific), single people didn't have much of an alternative to blind dating. A blind date was something you suffered through in order to tell yourself you were doing everything possible to enhance your social life. As we all know, everything changed with the advent of surrogate dating.

Surrogate dating, the practice of hiring a substitute person to date for you, was inadvertently invented by Mindy Wonger, a thirty-nine-year-old stenographer from Pasadena, California. Mindy, single and sorry, answered the phone one day and found herself accepting a blind date from Dave, an acquaintance of Mindy's Al-Anon qualifier.

After hanging up the phone, Mindy realized she'd rather walk barefoot on a bed of glass than go on another blind date, yet she was afraid to cancel the date with Dave. Except for her nightly Al-Anon meetings, Mindy hadn't gone out in three months, and, as every single woman

knows, opportunity doesn't knock all that often after you've been diagnosed as a Woman Who Loves Too Much.

Mindy solved her problem by hiring her roommate, Carla, to date
Dave. In exchange for not having to clean the bathroom for two weeks,
Carla agreed to masquerade as Mindy and to have dinner with Dave.
Carla wore a wig and Mindy's Liz Claiborne jumpsuit. Carla also prom-
ised not to fall in love and to return Dave to Mindy in the event he
proved to be marriage material.

Thus, the first surrogate dating arrangement was made.

Today, surrogate dating is a bit more complex, since not everyone
has a roommate who looks good in Liz Claiborne. Agencies such as The
Next Best Thing in Atlanta have been established to match clients and
surrogate dates. Prospective clients can select surrogates with the same
hair color and body type. Just Like You in Jacksonville, Florida, organ-
izes their employee surrogate pool into nine basic personality categories.
Clients can decide for themselves which "type" best matches their
personality and can choose from the following classifications: Princess,
Workaholic, Hippie, Easily Addicted, Punk, Sex Symbol, Homebody,
Artist, and Adaptable.

Fees up to two thousand dollars have been paid, especially when
the date has been arranged through the parents of either of the parties
involved. And, because money is now involved, written contracts are
not uncommon.

Surrogate contracts specify such contingencies as additional bonus
payments to rehire the surrogate for the couple's first fight or for their
first "totally honest" discussion about previous sexual encounters,
whichever comes first.

Surrogate dating has drastically reduced blind dating and, up until
recently, was considered a boon for the singles market. In late 1986,
Club Med established a Club Surrogate on St. Luigi's Island where guys
and gals who were too shy to travel alone could hire a surrogate to
vacation for them while they stayed home and watched television. An
episode of *Family Ties* features Michael J. Fox on a surrogate date. *People*
magazine interviewed five surrogate singles for their September 23, 1986,
issue. In late fall of the same year, Tama Janowitz published a hip novel
about the New York surrogate dating scene.

Then, suddenly, surrogate dating was nearly brought to a screeching halt
by Mary Beth Whiteface and Elysse Sterp in their now legendary lawsuit,
Sterp v. *Whiteface*.

The shocking case began in April of 1986, when Mary Beth Whiteface was hired by Elysse Sterp to date Marvin Slavin, a nephew of Ms. Sterp's mother's canasta partner. Mary Beth was paid ten thousand dollars, full combat pay, because the date involved not only Ms. Sterp's mother but her mother's canasta partner, who was also a second cousin and a bigmouth like you wouldn't believe.

Although Mary Beth claimed she only took the job out of pity for the dateless Elysse, lawyers for Ms. Sterp maintained it was no coincidence that in March of 1986, Mary Beth suffered a serious shopping attack in Bloomingdale's, specifically in the Giorgio Armani department, and desperately needed the cash.

Whatever her motives, and much to her surprise, Mary Beth enjoyed her date with Marvin. In fact, she had such a good time, she decided to keep Marvin all to herself.

In complete violation of her contract with Elysse, Mary Beth introduced Marvin to her parents.

In testimony to the court, Mary Beth later explained, "Your Honor, it was just one of those things, one of those crazy flings."

"A trip to the moon on gossamer wings?" prompted Ms. Whiteface's lawyer.

"Just one of those things," sighed Mary Beth, choking back her tears.

"One of those bells that now and then rings, I suppose," scoffed Elysse Sterp.

The most damaging argument the clever district attorney used against Mary Beth was the fact she'd neglected to tell Elysse that, on their first date, Mary Beth and Marvin engaged in a long walk by the ocean while Marvin recited his favorite lines from Woody Allen movies. (Beach walks are absolutely forbidden during surrogate dating. In fact, the rules of surrogate dating discourage encounters near any body of water, including lakes, streams, rivers, indoor pools, and Jacuzzis. Especially Jacuzzis.)

Almost as damning, Mary Beth and Marvin ran off for the weekend to the mountains. From Ye Olde Country Inn in Connecticut, Mary Beth called Elysse and pleaded to be released from her contract. When Elysse refused, Mary Beth threatened to tell Marvin that Elysse had herpes.

After a long and arduous court battle, the judge decided in favor of Elysse Sterp, requiring Mary Beth Whiteface to honor her contractual obligation and to release Marvin Slavin from the Whiteface cellar. The judge further instructed Mary Beth to return Marvin's ID bracelet.

In Mary Beth's favor, the judge ruled that Marvin and Mary Beth could maintain non-weekend visitation rights, but only if they went Dutch treat.

The Whiteface/Sterp case has, of course, raised many complex questions about the moral and ethical basis for surrogate dating.

- Even though we have the technology to provide everyone with a surrogate date, do we have any moral obligation to be truthful with the people we date?

- Does Mary Beth Whiteface have the right to fall in love and abandon her contractual obligations?

- Does Elysse Sterp really have herpes?

The adverse publicity of the Whiteface/Sterp case has greatly decreased the practice of surrogate dating. Always controversial, surrogate dating is now even more opposed by conservatives, born-agains, krishnas, and most married people in general. The only groups still supporting surrogate dating are lawyers and a splinter group of radical feminists who feel women should have the legal right to do anything.

In spite of any opposition, however, surrogate dating is unlikely to go away. Anyone who has ever accepted a blind date because they needed to meet someone new knows that no price is too high to pay when contemplating the pain and agony of opening the front door on a complete stranger who, in all probability, has dandruff.

HOW TO CALL A MAN FOR A DATE

Unfortunately, women like myself (broadly speaking, all females over the age of eighteen) are at a great disadvantage in today's dating marketplace. In our day (specifically the 1950s, 1960s, and even parts of the 1970s), only the guys had the privilege of choosing a prospective date and doing the asking. For girls, there was only one method for getting a date. You waited by your telephone for a guy to call. If he didn't call, you washed your hair.

Okay, so maybe it wasn't the most dynamic way to build a social life. In our defense, it was all we knew, never having been properly trained in the guerrilla dating tactics of today. (This is not our fault. Like most things that go wrong in our lives, we can blame our mothers for not adequately advising us.) Also, we didn't have Princess Stephanie or Cyndi Lauper as role models. Those of us who grew up with Annette,

Sonny and Cher, or Mary Tyler Moore may not have dated very much, but we had our dignity, our self-respect, our pride, and, for sure, we had clean hair.

Well, times have changed. Calling a guy for a date is as common today as Korean salad bars. Girls no longer stand on ceremony, and we older women need to adapt to these new ways. The 1980s demand aggression, guts, and lots of attitude. Women today must toss themselves into the dating pool, whether or not they wear a life preserver. Dating in the 1980s means: Sink or Swim!

The advantages of asking a man for a date are twofold. By making that call, you are taking control of your social life while at the same time gaining a unique opportunity to experience the heady power that comes from freedom of choice.

Calling a man for a date is a lot like learning how to insert a diaphragm; the first time is really embarrassing, but once you get used to the mess, you'll find the long-range advantages outweigh your initial repulsion.

If you are nervous about calling that cute guy you met in the Xerox shop, here are some useful suggestions to help build up your confidence.

You begin by convincing yourself to make that call. Stand in front of your bathroom mirror and tell yourself that you *will* call him. Persuade yourself that you actually *want* to call him, you *need* to call him. Concentrate on your image in the mirror. Remind yourself that this is not the face of a coward. Stare long and hard at yourself. (Warning: Do not get sidetracked into attacking any facial blemishes or bleaching some section of hair above your shoulders.)

If you are particularly nervous, it sometimes helps if you prepare for the worst-case scenario. A technique I often use when confronted with a difficult situation is to ask myself: *What's the worst possible thing that could happen?*

When I decided to call Darrell, a handsome man I'd taken home from a party one gloriously naughty evening, I asked myself this: What will happen if I call him?

I came up with the following list of possibilities:

a) He'll say yes.
b) He'll say no, but thank me for calling.
c) He'll say no, he can't go out with me because he forgot to mention he was attached to his wife, someone else's wife, a girlfriend, or a really weird pet.
d) He'll tell me to never call him again.

I prepared myself for each of the above contingencies. Whatever answer he gave, I was ready with a witty reply. I felt confident enough to make that phone call.

Just like a man, Darrell defied my list of possibilities, coming up with a scenario that was far beyond my imagination: Darrell didn't remember who I was. "I don't think I ever got your name," was the way Darrell explained his reaction.

My therapist artfully tried to comfort me. "At least you know the reason *why* Darrell hasn't called," Dr. Yesandno said, not unkindly.

"Yeah," I mumbled, "I suppose it's hard to call someone when you don't know their last name."

"Or their first name," my therapist, a real stickler for details, pointed out.

I waited six months before I called another male, other than Dr. Yesandno, of course.

I did, however, use the time productively by practicing my dialing skills. Every day I made at least two phony phone calls, pretending each time that I was calling Darrell. My therapist wondered why I wasn't arrested for public obscenity, even though I explained that most of the men I called seemed to actually enjoy my profanities.

Those phony phone calls taught me that practice was essential in order to "give good phone." Telephone technique is an acquired skill. By the time I was ready to call another man for a date, I had the confidence to forge ahead.

Since those early years, I have established a working routine that helps me overcome my shyness.

If you feel insecure about calling that special guy, try the following Nine Step Program that I have developed. It works for me, maybe it'll work for you!

1. Drink a glass of wine, quickly.
2. Clutch teddy bear to your chest.
3. Practice what you are going to say by talking to your teddy bear.
4. Pick up the phone and place it in your lap. Take several deep breaths.
5. Carry phone and teddy bear to dining room table.
6. Crawl under table.
7. Grit teeth, hold breath, squeeze eyes shut, and pray.
8. Dial.
9. When a woman answers the phone, hang up.

While this routine works really well for me, there are several other methods that I have also tried, with varying degrees of success. If you are not comfortable calling him from your home, call him from a party or during another date. Make sure there is plenty of noise in the background. Pretend you are so busy this was the only free moment you had to call him.

Call him in the middle of the night. If you wake him from a deep sleep, you may catch him at a weak moment when he's likely to say yes to just about anything.

Whichever method you choose, try not to panic during those excruciating moments after dialing but before the phone is answered, when "rrringg!" is the loneliest sound that you'll ever hear.

Keep an airsickness bag handy if you tend to panic under pressure.

These moments will be among the longest and most stressful of your life. Your instinct will be to hang up, which you will probably do a few times before you are steady enough to allow him time to answer the phone.

The standard procedure, if you've called and then hung up, is to wait fifteen minutes before attempting to call again.

If, however, you've called, he's answered, and then you've hung up, the standard procedure is call back immediately and say that your phone is broken.

Between attempts to reach him, boost your own morale by reminding yourself how brave you are and what a good thing you are doing. With a little bit of initiative, he will answer, say he's busy for the next six months, and you will be well on your way to your next major heartbreak.

Calling a man for a date is a real life experience; one that all women should try at least once.

So, get out there with your File-O-Fax phone sections and call him for a date!

If you can't do it for yourself, then do it for the cause.

As women, we need to fight for the right to determine our dating destiny. What our feminist forepersons achieved for us in the boardrooms, we will now achieve in the bedroom.

As we move closer and closer to a nonsexist world, women will have as equal an opportunity as men to be rejected, embarrassed, and humiliated beyond consolation.

May Swenson (1919-1989)

~ஜ ஜ~

Southbound on the Freeway

A tourist came in from Orbitville,
parked in the air, and said:

The creatures of this star
are made of metal and glass.

Through the transparent parts
you can see their guts.

Their feet are round and roll
on diagrams—or long

measuring tapes—dark
with white lines.

They have four eyes.
The two in the back are red.

Sometimes you can see a 5-eyed
one, with a red eye turning

on the top of his head.
He must be special—

the others respect him,
and go slow,

when he passes, winding
among them from behind.

They all hiss as they glide,
like inches, down the marked

tapes. Those soft shapes,
shadowy inside

the hard bodies—are they
their guts or their brains?

Judy Syfers (contemporary)

I Want a Wife

I belong to that classification of people known as wives. I am A Wife. And, not altogether incidentally, I am a mother.

Not too long ago a male friend of mine appeared on the scene fresh from a recent divorce. He had one child, who is, of course, with his ex-wife. He is looking for another wife. As I thought about him while I was ironing one evening, it suddenly occurred to me that I, too, would like to have a wife. Why do I want a wife?

I would like to go back to school so that I can become economically independent, support myself, and, if need be, support those dependent upon me. I want a wife who will work and send me to school. And while I am going to school I want a wife to take care of my children. I want a wife to keep track of the children's doctor and dentist appointments. And to keep track of mine, too. I want a wife to make sure my children eat properly and are kept clean. I want a wife who will wash the children's clothes and keep them mended. I want a wife who is a good nurturant attendant to my children, who arranges for their schooling, makes sure that they have an adequate social life with their peers, takes them to the park, the zoo, etc. I want a wife who takes care of the children when they are sick, a wife who arranges to be around when the children need special care, because, of course, I cannot miss classes at school. My wife must arrange to lose time at work and not lose the job. It may mean a small cut in my wife's income from time to time, but I guess I can tolerate that. Needless to say, my wife will arrange and pay for the care of the children while my wife is working.

I want a wife who will take care of *my* physical needs. I want a wife who will keep my house clean. A wife who will pick up after my children, a wife who will pick up after me. I want a wife who will keep my clothes clean, ironed, mended, replaced when need be, and who will see to it that my personal things are kept in their proper place so that I can find what I need the minute I need it. I want a wife who cooks the meals, a wife who is a *good* cook. I want a wife who will plan the menus, do the necessary grocery shopping, prepare the meals, serve them pleasantly, and then do the cleaning up while I do my studying. I want a wife who will care for me when I am sick and sympathize with my pain and loss of time from school. I want a wife to go along when our family takes a vacation so that someone can continue to care for me and my children when I need a rest and change of scene.

I want a wife who will not bother me with rambling complaints about a wife's duties. But I want a wife who will listen to me when I feel the need to explain a rather difficult point I have come across in my course of studies. And I want a wife who will type my papers for me when I have written them.

I want a wife who will take care of the details of my social life. When my wife and I are invited out by my friends, I want a wife who will take care of the babysitting arrangements. When I meet people at school that I like and want to entertain, I want a wife who will have the house clean, will prepare a special meal, serve it to me and my friends and not interrupt when I talk about things that interest me and my friends. I want a wife who will have arranged that the children are fed and ready for bed before my guests arrive so that the children do not bother us. I want a wife who takes care of the needs of my guests so that they feel comfortable, who makes sure that they have an ashtray, that they are passed the hors d'oeuvres, that they are offered a second helping of the food, that their wine glasses are replenished when necessary, that their coffee is served to them as they like it. And I want a wife who knows that sometimes I need a night out by myself.

I want a wife who is sensitive to my sexual needs, a wife who makes love passionately and eagerly when I feel like it, a wife who makes sure that I am satisfied. And, of course, I want a wife who will not demand sexual attention when I am not in the mood for it. I want a wife who assumes the complete responsibility for birth control, because I do not want more children. I want a wife who will remain sexually faithful to me so that I do not have to clutter up my intellectual life with jealousies. And I want a wife who understands that *my* sexual needs may entail more than strict adherence to monogamy. I must, after all, be able to relate to people as fully as possible.

If, by chance, I find another person more suitable as a wife than the wife I already have, I want the liberty to replace my present wife with another one. Naturally, I will expect a fresh, new life; my wife will take the children and be solely responsible for them so that I am left free.

When I am through with school and have a job, I want my wife to quit working and remain at home so that my wife can more fully and completely take care of a wife's duties.

My God, who *wouldn't* want a wife?

Judy Tenuta (contemporary)

~℘ ℘~

FROM *The Power of Judyism*

My mother [is] very religious. On special holidays she will still drive to have the cardinal bless the groceries.

•

Once I was riding my bike and my mom was waving to me from the window. She said, "Judy, soon your body will change."

I said, "I know—puberty."

She said, "No, that Good Humor truck."

•

One day, when I was six years old, a mere prepubescent demigoddess, my mom chained me to the high chair while my baby sister Blambo was still in it. Nice. I'm flattening my kid sister while Mom is obsessively perm-rodding me. Within two hours I was transformed into a mini Bride of Frankenstein. Imagine this frizzy-topped freak the night before my very first day of school. Perfect timing; thanks for making me into a goon, Mommy Sassoon. That morning I sat in the front yard crying my baby eyes out and Eddie Crader delivered the *Oakleaves* newspaper into my hair. At lunchtime the kids in my class hung me from my feet and whacked my hornet's head with a bat while shouting, "Where's our presents, piñata-head?"

•

And it wasn't just me she was hair-raising. Once a month, during her cycle, she'd line my six brothers up on the basement floor and trim them with the Toro. They looked like skinheads but not as happy. Nice scalping skills, Mom. Just to curtail their wailing, I'd let them play with my Tressy doll. They'd take turns brushing her long, blonde ponytail and watching it grow while screaming, "We hate you, you hair-teasing bitch!" That very same day, my mom took us to Sears for the family portrait. Between me, the maxipermed princess, and my Hari Krishna brothers, we looked like the Tree of Knowledge and the six gnomes with chrome domes.

•

"Judy, you don't know nothin' about the South. You don't even know the difference between the North and the South."

I said, "Oh yes I do. In the North, there's a cut-off age for sleeping with your parents."

•

All the great love stories are based on some poor pining plankton who can't pounce on the petite princess of his dreams. Look at *Wuthering Heights*. Do you think for one minute that if Cathy surrendered to Heathcliff he would be half as crazy about her? No way. He was in love with his fantasy of that floozie. Even after Cathy marries some society squid that she doesn't love, Heathcliff pursues her and says, "Cathy, nothing can come between our love; not even you." What a great line. Women the world over dream about such passionate prose from some pumped-up parasite.

Cathy says, "Heathcliff, I'm married. Why did you come after me?" He says, "Because you willed it." Could you hemorrhage, heifers? Heathcliff repeats, "I'm here because you willed it, Cathy." How could she not melt? I'm yelling, "Cathy, you fool, lay down already, loosen your lovesick loins." But Cathy is no fool, she knows that as a true romantic, giving in to love would be the death of lust. So she spurns Heathcliff again and he is even more mental about possessing her.

Why can't we petite flowers in the real world find a passionate love puppy like Heathcliff? Because they do not exist. Neither do Romeos or Othellos. These guys can afford to be passionate about their Juliets and Desdemonas because they don't have to earn a living like every other mortal toad.

Marlo Thomas (1943–   )

On Ruthlessness

A man has to be Joe McCarthy to be called ruthless. All a woman has to do is put you on hold.

Lily Tomlin (1939-   )

On Doctors

If you have a psychotic fixation and you go to the doctor and you want these two fingers amputated, he will not cut them off. But he *will* remove your genitals. I have more trouble getting a prescription for Valium than I do having my uterus lowered and made into a penis.

Emily Toth (contemporary)

FROM *Forbidden Jokes and Naughty Ladies*

Women writers rarely violate what I call the Humane Humor Rule— that is, Thou shalt not make fun of something that a person cannot change.

Frances Trollope (1779-1863)

FROM *The Domestic Manners of the Americans*

RELIGION

I had often heard it observed before I visited America, that one of the great blessings of its constitution was the absence of a national religion, the country being thus exonerated from all obligation of supporting the clergy; those only contributing to do so whose principles led them to it. My residence in the country has shewn me that a religious tyranny may be exerted very effectually without the aid of the government,[1] in a way much more oppressive than the paying of tithe, and without obtaining any of the salutary decorum, which I presume no one will deny is the result of an established mode of worship.

As it was impossible to remain many weeks in the country without being struck with the strange anomalies produced by its religious system, my early notes contain many observations on the subject; but as nearly the same scenes recurred in every part of the country, I state them here, not as belonging to the west alone, but to the whole Union, the same cause producing the same effect every where.

The whole people appear to be divided into an almost endless variety of religious factions, and I was told, that to be well received in society, it was necessary to declare yourself as belonging to some one of these. Let your acknowledged belief be what it may, you are said to be *not a Christian*, unless you attach yourself to a particular congregation. Besides the broad and well-known distinctions of Episcopalian, Catholic, Presbyterian, Calvinist, Baptist, Quaker, Swedenborgian, Universalist, Dunker, etc. etc. etc.; there are innumerable others springing out of these, each of which assumed a church government of its own; of this,

---

[1] I shall not expect to escape the charge of impossible exaggeration if I describe the species of petty persecution that I have seen exercised on religious subjects in America. The whole people appear to be divided into an almost endless variety of religious factions; I was told in Cincinnati that to be well received in society it was indispensably necessary to declare that you belonged to some one of these factions—it did not much matter which—as far as I could make out, the Methodists were considered as the most pious, the Presbyterians as the most powerful, the Episcopalians and the Catholics as the most genteel, the Universalists as the most liberal, the Swedenborgians as the most musical, the Unitarians as the most enlightened, the Quakers the most amiable, the dancing Shakers the most amusing, and the Jews as the most interesting. Besides these there are dozens more of fancy religions whose designations I cannot remember, but declaring yourself to belong to any one of them as far as I could learn was sufficient to constitute you a respectable member of society. Having thus declared yourself, your next submission must be that of unqualified obedience to the will and pleasure of your elected pastor, or you will run a great risk of being "passed out of the church." This was a phrase that I perpetually heard, and upon enquiry I found that it did not mean being passed neck and heels out of the building at the discretion of the sexton, but a sort of congregational excommunication which infallibly betides those who venture to [do] any thing that their pastor and master disapproves. I once heard a lady say "I must not wear high bows on my bonnet, or I shall be passed out of our church" and another "I must not go to see the dancing at the theatre or I shall be passed out of our church" and another "I must not confess that I visit Mrs. J. or I shall be passed out of our church, for they say that she does not belong to any church in the town." I think I am tolerant not only in religion but of all opinions that differ from my own, but this does not prevent my seeing that the end of a true and rational religion is better obtained when the government of the church is confided to the hands of those who act in conformity & obedience to it. [Trollope's note]

the most intriguing and factious individual is invariably the head; and in order, as it should seem, to shew a reason for this separation, each congregation invests itself with some queer variety of external observance that has the melancholy effect of exposing *all* religious ceremonies to contempt.

It is impossible, in witnessing all these unseemly vagaries, not to recognize the advantages of an an established church as a sort of headquarters for quiet unpresuming Christians, who are contented to serve faithfully, without insisting upon having each a little separate banner, embroidered with a device of their own imagining.

The Catholics alone appear exempt from the fury of division and sub-division that has seized every other persuasion. Having the Pope for their common head, regulates, I presume, their movements, and prevents the outrageous display of individual whim which every other sect is permitted.

I had the pleasure of being introduced to the Catholic bishop of Cincinnati, and have never known in any country a priest of a character and bearing more truly apostolic. He was an American, but I should never have discovered it from his pronunciation or manner. He received his education partly in England, and partly in France. His manners were highly polished; his piety active and sincere, and infinitely more mild and tolerant than that of the factious Sectarians who form the great majority of the American priesthood.

I believe I am sufficiently tolerant; but this does not prevent my seeing that the object of all religious observances is better obtained, when the government of the church is confided to the wisdom and experience of the most venerated among the people, than when it is placed in the hands of every tinker and tailor who chooses to claim a share in it. Nor is this the only evil attending the want of a national religion, supported by the State. As there is no legal and fixed provision for the clergy, it is hardly surprising that their services are confined to those who can pay them. The vehement expressions of insane or hypocritical zeal, such as were exhibited during "the Revival," can but ill atone for the want of village worship, any more than the eternal talk of the admirable and unequalled government, can atone for the continual contempt of social order. Church and State hobble along, side by side, notwithstanding their boasted independence. Almost every man you meet will tell you, that he is occupied in labors most abundant for the good of his country; and almost every woman will tell you, that besides those things that are within (her house) she has coming upon her daily the care of all the churches. Yet spite of this universal attention to the government, its laws are half asleep; and spite of the old women and their Dorcas societies, atheism is awake and thriving.

In the smaller cities and towns prayer-meetings take the place of almost all other amusements; but as the thinly scattered population of most villages can give no parties, and pay no priests, they contrive to marry, christen, and bury without them. A stranger taking up his residence in any city in America must think the natives the most religious people upon earth; but if chance lead him among her western villages, he will rarely find either churches or chapels, prayer or preacher; except, indeed, at that most terrific saturnalia, "a camp-meeting." I was much struck with the answer of a poor woman, whom I saw ironing on a Sunday. "Do you make no difference in your occupations on a Sunday?" I said, "I beant a Christian, Ma'am; we have got no opportunity," was the reply. It occurred to me, that in a country where "all men are equal," the government would be guilty of no great crime, did it so far interfere as to give them all *an opportunity* of becoming Christians if they wished it. But should the federal government dare to propose building a church, and endowing it, in some village that has never heard "the bringing home of bell and burial," it is perfectly certain that not only the sovereign state where such an abomination was proposed, would rush into the Congress to resent the odious interference, but that all the other states would join the clamor, and such an intermeddling administration would run great risk of impeachment and degradation.

Where there is a church-government so constituted as to deserve human respect, I believe it will always be found to receive it, even from those who may not assent to the dogma of its creed, and where such respect exists, it produces a decorum in manners and language often found wanting where it does not. Sectarians will not venture to rhapsodize, nor infidels to scoff, in the common intercourse of society. Both are injurious to the cause of rational religion, and to check both must be advantageous.

It is certainly possible that some of the fanciful variations upon the ancient creeds of the Christian Church, with which transatlantic religionists amuse themselves, might inspire morbid imaginations in Europe as well as in America; but before they can disturb the solemn harmony *here*, they must prelude by a defiance, not only to common sense, but what is infinitely more appalling, to common usage. They must at once rank themselves with the low and illiterate, for only such prefer the eloquence of the tub to that of the pulpit. The aristocracy must ever, as a body, belong to the established Church, and it is but a small proportion of the influential classes who would be willing to allow that they do not belong to the aristocracy. That such feelings influence the professions of men it were ignorance or hypocrisy to deny; and that nation is wise who knows how to turn even such feelings into a wholesome stream of popular influence.

As a specimen of the tone in which religion is mixed in the ordinary intercourse of society, I will transcribe the notes I took of a conversation, at which I was present, at Cincinnati; I wrote them immediately after the conversation took place.

DR. A.: "I wish, Mrs. M., that you would explain to me what a revival is. I hear it talked of all over the city, and I know it means something about Jesus Christ and religion; but that is all I know, will you instruct me farther?

MRS. M.: "I expect, Dr. A., that you want to laugh at me. But that makes no difference. I am firm in my principles, and I fear no one's laughter."

DR. A.: "Well, but what is a revival?"

MRS. M.: "It is difficult, very difficult, to make those see who have no light; to make those understand whose souls are darkened. A revival means just an elegant kindling of the spirit; it is brought about to the Lord's people by the hands of the saints, and it means salvation in the highest."

DR. A.: "But what is it the people mean by talking of feeling the revival? and waiting in spirit for the revival? and the extacy of the revival?"

MRS. M.: "Oh Doctor! I am afraid that you are too far gone astray to understand all that. It is a glorious assurance, a whispering of the everlasting covenant, it is the bleating of the lamb, it is the welcome of the shepherd, it is the essence of love, it is the fullness of glory, it is being in Jesus, it is Jesus being in us, it is taking the Holy Ghost into our bosoms, it is sitting ourselves down by God, it is being called to the high places, it is eating, and drinking, and sleeping in the Lord, it is becoming a lion in that faith, it is being lowly and meek, and kissing the hand that smites, it is being mighty and powerful, and scorning reproof, it is—"

DR. A.: "Thank you, Mrs. M., I feel quite satisfied, and I think I understand a revival now almost as well as you do yourself."

MRS. A.: "My! Where can you have learnt all that stuff, Mrs. M.?"

MRS. M.: "How benighted you are! From the holy book, from the Word of the Lord, from the Holy Ghost, and Jesus Christ themselves."

MRS. A.:   "It does seem so droll to me, to hear you talk of 'the Word of the Lord.' Why, I have been brought up to look upon the Bible as nothing better than an old newspaper."

MRS. O.:   "Surely you only say this for the sake of hearing what Mrs. M. will say in return—you do not mean it?"

MRS. A.:   "La, yes! to be sure I do."

DR. A.:   "I profess that I by no means wish my wife to read all she might find there.—What says the Colonel, Mrs. M.?"

MRS. M.:   "As to that, I never stop to ask him. I tell him every day that I believe in Father, Son, and Holy Ghost, and that it is his duty to believe in them too, and then my conscience is clear, and I don't care what he believes. Really, I have no notion of one's husband interfering in such matters."

DR. A.:   "You are quite right. I am sure I give my wife leave to believe just what she likes; but she is a good woman, and does not abuse the liberty; for she believes nothing."

It was not once, nor twice, nor thrice, but many many times, during my residence in America, that I was present when subjects which custom as well as principle had taught me to consider as fitter for the closet than the tea-table, were thus lightly discussed. I hardly know whether I was more startled at first hearing, in little dainty namby pamby tones, a profession of Atheism over a teacup, or at having my attention called from a Johnny cake, to a rhapsody on election and the second birth.

But, notwithstanding this revolting license, persecution exists to a degree unknown, I believe, in our well-ordered land since the days of Cromwell. I had the following anecdote from a gentleman perfectly well acquainted with the circumstances. A tailor sold a suit of clothes to a sailor a few moments before he sailed, which was on a Sunday morning. The corporation of New York prosecuted the tailor, and he was convicted, and sentenced to a fine greatly beyond his means to pay. Mr. F., a lawyer of New York, defended him with much eloquence, but in vain. His powerful speech, however, was not without effect, for it raised him such a host of Presbyterian enemies as sufficed to destroy his practice. Nor was this all: his nephew was at the time preparing for the bar, and soon after the above circumstance occurred his certificates were presented, and refused, with this declaration, "that no man of the name and family of F. should be admitted." I have met this young man in society; he is a person of very considerable talent, and being thus cruelly robbed of his profession, has become the editor of a newspaper.

Catharine Trotter (1679-1749)

⫷⫸

FROM *Love at a Loss*

MIRANDA: O! The men's love is not so easily starved as surfeited. 'Twill live upon the lightest airy hope, tho' soon destroy'd with fondness. We lose lovers by over care, than neglect, Lucilia.

•

BONSOT: Let it be what it will, I am never of honour's side. It's good for nothing but to make people uneasy, and I would have everybody please themselves, whether they can or no.

Sojourner Truth (1797-1883)

⫷⫸

FROM *Ain't I a Woman?*

Well, children, where there is so much racket there must be something out of kilter. I think that 'twixt the negroes of the South and the women at the North, all talking about rights, the white men will be in a fix pretty soon. But what's all this here talking about?

That man over there says that women need to be helped into carriages, and lifted over ditches, and to have the best place everywhere. Nobody ever helps me into carriages, or over mud-puddles, or gives me any best place! And ain't I a woman? Look at me! Look at my arm! I have ploughed and planted, and gathered into barns, and no man could head me! And ain't I a woman? I could work as much and eat as much as a man—when I could get it—and bear the lash as well! And ain't I a woman? I have borne thirteen children, and seen them most all sold off to slavery, and when I cried out with my mother's grief, none but Jesus heard me! And ain't I a woman?

Then they talk about this thing in the head; what's this they call it?

[Intellect, someone whispers.] That's it, honey. What's that got to do with women's rights or negro's rights? If my cup won't hold but a pint, and yours holds a quart, wouldn't you be mean not to let me have my little half-measure full?

Then that little man in black there, he says women can't have as much rights as men, 'cause Christ wasn't a woman! Where did your Christ come from? Where did your Christ come from? From God and a woman! Man had nothing to do with Him.

If the first woman God ever made was strong enough to turn the world upside down all alone, these women together ought to be able to turn it back, and get it right side up again! And now they is asking to do it, the men better let them.

Obliged to you for hearing me, and now old Sojourner ain't got nothing more to say.

Anne Tyler (1941-)

━❦ ❧━

FROM *The Clock Winder*

There were people crammed on both sidewalks, mothers with babies and little children, fathers with children on their shoulders. And suddenly I was so *surprised* by them. Isn't it amazing how hard people work to raise their children? Human beings are born so helpless, and stay helpless so long. For every grownup you see, you know there must have been at least one person who had the patience to lug them around, and feed them, and walk them nights and keep them out of danger for years and years without a break. Teaching them how to fit into civilization and how to talk back and forth with other people, taking them to zoos and parades and educational events, telling them all those nursery rhymes and word-of-mouth fairy tales. Isn't that surprising? People you wouldn't trust your purse with five minutes, maybe, but still they put in years and years of time tending their children along and they don't even make a fuss about it. Even if it's a criminal they turn out, or some other kind of failure—still, he managed to get grown, didn't he? Isn't that something?

·

FROM *Dinner at the Homesick Restaurant*

"Oh Jenny," her mother said sadly. "Do you have to see everything as a joke?"

"It's not my fault if funny things happen," Jenny said.

"It most certainly is," said her mother, but instead of explaining herself, she all at once grew brisk and requested the return of her vacuum cleaner. . . .

Robin Tyler (contemporary)

On the Mind and the Prick

The mind is much more powerful than the prick—and the mind doesn't go down in two minutes.

Judith Viorst (1936-   )

Self-Improvement Program

I've finished six pillows in Needlepoint,
And I'm reading Jane Austen and Kant,
And I'm up to the pork with black beans in Advanced Chinese Cooking.
I don't have to struggle to find myself
For I already know what I want.
I want to be healthy and wise and extremely good-looking.

I'm learning new glazes in Pottery Class,
And I'm playing new chords in Guitar,
And in Yoga I'm starting to master the lotus position.
I don't have to ponder priorities
For I already know what they are:

To be good-looking, healthy, and wise,
And adored in addition.

I'm improving my serve with a tennis pro,
And I'm practicing verb forms in Greek,
And in Primal Scream Therapy all my frustrations are vented.
I don't have to ask what I'm searching for
Since I already know that I seek
To be good-looking, healthy, and wise,
And adored.
And contented.

I've bloomed in Organic Gardening,
And in Dance I have tightened my thighs,
And in Consciousness Raising there's no one around who can top me.
And I'm working all day and I'm working all night
To be good-looking, healthy, and wise.
And adored.
And contented.
And brave.
And well-read.
And a marvelous hostess,
Fantastic in bed,
And bilingual,
Athletic,
Artistic . . .
Won't someone please stop me?

Helena Maria Viramontes (1954–)

❧ ❧

FROM *The Cariboo Cafe*

Raising a child is like building a kite. You must bend the twigs enough, but not too much, for you might break them. You must find paper that is delicate and light enough to wave on the breath of the wind, yet must withstand the ravages of a storm. You must tie the strings gently but firmly so that it may not fall apart. You must let the string go, eventually, so that the kite will stretch its ambition. It is such delicate work, Lord, being a mother.

•

FROM *Snapshots*

Since the divorce, Marge brings me balls and balls and balls of wool thread because she insists that I "take up a hobby," "keep busy as a bee," or "make the best of things" and all that other good natured advice she probably hears from old folks who answer in such a way when asked how they've managed to live so long. Honestly, I wouldn't be surprised if she walked in one day with bushels of straw for me to weave baskets.

•

This is the way I pictured it:

> His wife in the kitchen wearing a freshly ironed apron, stirring a pot of soup, whistling a whistle-while-you-work tune, and preparing frosting for some cupcakes so that when he drove home from work, tired and sweaty, he would enter his castle to find his cherub baby in a pink day suit with newly starched ribbons crawling to him and his wife looking at him with pleasing eyes and offering him a cupcake.

It was a good image I wanted him to have and everyday I almost expected him to stop, put down his lunch pail and cry at the whole scene. If it wasn't for the burnt cupcakes, my damn varicose veins, and Marge blubbering all over her day suit, it would have made a perfect snapshot.

•

I turn around and catch two youngsters on a porch swing, their mouths open, their lips chewing and chewing as if they were sharing a piece of three day old liver.

Jane Wagner (1935–   )

〜✺ ✺〜

FROM *The Search for Signs of Intelligent
Life in the Universe*

AT THE DOCTOR'S

You're sure, Doctor?
Preme*n*strual syndrome?
I mean, I'm getting divorced.
My mother's getting divorced.
I'm raising twin boys.
I have a lot of job pressure—
I've got to find one.
The ERA didn't pass,
not long ago I lost a very dear friend, and . . . and
my husband is involved . . .
not just involved, but in love, I'm afraid . . . with this
woman . . .
who's quite a bit younger than I am.

And you *think* it's my *period*
and *not* my life?

•

About a month ago, I was shown some products designed to improve
the sex lives of suburban housewives. I got so excited,
I just had to come on public access and tell you about it. To look at
me, you'd *never suspect* I was a semi-nonorgasmic woman. This means it
was *possible* for me to have an orgasm but highly unlikely.

•

I worry sometimes,
maybe Bob has gotten too much in touch with his feminine side. Last
night, I'm pretty sure, he faked an orgasm.

Alice Walker (1944-   )

~e~

Never Offer Your Heart to Someone Who Eats Hearts

Never offer your heart
to someone who eats hearts
who finds heartmeat
delicious
but not rare
who sucks the juices
drop by drop
and bloody-chinned
grins
like a God.

Never offer your heart
to a heart gravy lover.
Your stewed, overseasoned
heart consumed
he will sop up your grief
with bread
and send it shuttling
from side to side
in his mouth
like bubblegum.

If you find yourself
in love
with a person
who eats hearts
these things
you must do:

Freeze your heart
immediately.
Let him—next time

he examines your chest—
find your heart cold
flinty and unappetizing.

Refrain from kissing
lest he in revenge
dampen the spark
in your soul.

Now,
sail away to Africa
where holy women
await you
on the shore—
long having practiced the art
of replacing hearts
with God
and Song.

Margaret Walker (1915-   )

Street Demonstration

Hurry up Lucille or we won't get arrested with our group.
                              An eight-year-old demonstrator, 1963

We're hoping to be arrested
And hoping to go to jail
We'll sing and shout and pray
For Freedom and for Justice
And for Human Dignity
The Fighting may be long
And some of us will die
But Liberty is costly
And ROME they say to me
Was not built in one day.

Hurry up, Lucille. Hurry up
We're Going to Miss Our Chance to go to Jail.

Wendy Wasserstein (1950-   )

FROM *The Heidi Chronicles*

PETER: "Do you, Scoop Rosenbaum, take Lisa Friedlander to be your bride?" "Well, I feel ambivalent about her. But I am blocked emotionally, and she went to good schools, comes from a very good family, and is not particularly threatening. So, yeah, I do. Anyway, it's time for me to get married." "And do you, Lisa, take Scoop?" *Speaks her answer with Lisa's Southern accent.* "Rabbi, ever since I was a little girl I've been wanting to matriculate with an M.R.S. degree. I idolize Scoop because he is as brilliant and will be as rich as my daddy, whom I also idolize. And I am a slight masochist. Although I do come from the best Jewish family in Memphis. So, yes, Rabbi, I do take Scoop." "And now under the eyes of God and the Pierre Hotel, I pronounce you man and M.R.S. degree."

•

SUSAN: Are you writing?
HEIDI: A little. "Women and Art." "Women and Madness." "Women and Bran." The usual.

•

On Getting Out of Gym

I figured out that one of the ways I could get out of gym was if I wrote something called the Mother-Daughter Fashion Show. I know very little about fashion, but they used to have this Mother-Daughter Fashion Show once a year at the Plaza Hotel, and you got to leave school for the fashion show. But if you wrote [the show] you didn't have to go to gym for like two or three weeks, it was fantastic.

•

FROM *Bachelor Girls*

The worse the boyfriend, the more stunning your American Express bill. Since the worst boyfriends have keen and critical eyes, you have to shine for them, dress for them, coif for them, and, in California, liposuct for them. And there's nothing like primping for an uninterested party. Consider the case of the wretched Mathilde in Stendhal's *The Red and the Black*. She had her daddy, the marquis, offer her beloved Julien a fortune and a title just so he'd like her a little bit. No dice—he still preferred Madame de Rênal. But, of course, Mathilde was an extremist. She buried the head of her worst boyfriend.

•

I start giggling as I recall my favorite family-gathering story. It's the one about my friend Cindy's aunt Minah, who fell through the floor at her daughter's wedding. The Alley Cat got the better of her.

•

Being a grown-up means assuming responsibility for yourself, for your children, and—here's the big curve—for your parents. In other words, you do get to stay up later, but you want to go to sleep earlier.

•

. . . somewhere in me is the belief that losing forty pounds would herald a clean slate, a new beginning, a chance for redemption. The physical would lead the spiritual. In other words, liking myself means liking diet Jell-O.

•

There are days when I can't help thinking about Geraldine. I think about the moment she accepted her nomination. I think about where I was, who I was with, and why it made me cry. It was very simple: Finally, one of *us* was there. Whatever had happened in all of our lives—careers, babies, marriage, no careers, no babies, no marriage—was all on a much larger scale of significance. Geraldine, up there, meant there'd been some changes made.

•

Anyone who is considered funny will tell you, sometimes without your even asking, that deep inside they are very serious, neurotic, introspective people. In other words, Eddie Murphy has the heart of Hannah Arendt and Joan Rivers is really J. Robert Oppenheimer.

Personally I don't spend much time thinking about being funny. For me it's always been just a way to get by, a way to be likable yet to remain removed. When I speak up, it's not because I have any particular answers; rather, I have a desire to puncture the pretentiousness of those who seem so certain they do.

•

WINNER TAKE ALL

I dreamed I accepted the Tony Award wearing a CAMP EUGENE O'NEILL sweatshirt. It was an odd dream for two reasons. First, because my friend William Ivey Long, the costume designer, had made me a dress for the occasion; and, second, because until 1989 the only thing I'd ever won was a babka cake at a bakery on Whalley Avenue in New Haven.

My world view has always been from the vantage point of the slighted. I am the underachiever who convinces herself that it's a source of pride *not* to make the honor roll. Still, for the rest of my life I will remember the name of all those people who *did*. I am a walking Where Are They Now column. I'm perpetually curious as to what happened to all those supposed prodigies who were singled out while I and my coterie of far more interesting malcontents passed on.

As a child, on the eve of any school evaluation, I would inform my parents which of my teachers "hated me." In retrospect, it seems doubtful that I was offensive enough to evoke my teachers' animosity, but I certainly wasn't diligent enough in my schoolwork to earn their admiration, either. So, having fashioned a life based on anticipated exclusion—my date left with the blond; they gave the prize to the boy; the woman in the Anne Klein suit and the legs got the job—it came as a genuine surprise, a shock, when, for the first time ever, the winner was me.

On a gray March afternoon, I'm sitting in my bed, looking at my typewriter and thinking about how my life hasn't changed significantly since I was sixteen. I'm working up to a frothy, self-recriminating how-have-I-gone-wrong when the phone rings. On days when I'm building up to substantial negativity, I usually don't pick up the receiver but instead just listen as the messages are recorded. This time, though, the voice belongs to Marc Thibodeau, the press agent for my play *The Heidi Chronicles*, and I like him, so I pick up.

"Wendy, you just won the Pulitzer Prize."

And you, Mr. Thibodeau, are the king of Rumania.

"It's a rumor, Marc. It's just a rumor!" I begin hyperventilating. I am a woman in her thirties wearing a quilted bathrobe, half working, half lying in bed in a room cluttered with assorted stuffed animals. I am not a Pulitzer Prize winner. Edward Albee is a Pulitzer Prize winner.

Mr. Thibodeau informs me that I should call a reporter from the Associated Press. Also, I must call my mother. I begin to dial gingerly. It's possible I am having delusions of grandeur. It's possible I might shortly be calling the *Times* as Eleanor of Aquitaine. Michael Kuchwara, the AP reporter, accepts my call, however, and validates the story. Suddenly I remember sitting in our living room with my mother and watching an episode of the TV series "The Millionaire." I recall how my mother knocked on the television screen to encourage a delivery to our Brooklyn address. "Mother," I want now to shout, "Michael Anthony called me. John Beresford Tipton is giving me the Pulitzer Prize!"

Immediately, *everything* changes. The phone rings with the constancy of the American Stock Exchange. Flowers and champagne arrive in competitive quantities. (Since that day I have, in fact, become an expert on the comparative floral arrangements of Surroundings, Twigs, and the Sutton East Gardens.) My doormen are more than taken aback by the flow of deliveries to my apartment. One of them asks me when I'm getting married; another expresses amazement that so many of my friends have remembered my birthday. Eventually, my sister telephones to say that not only has my mother called my aunts to inform them that I've won the Nobel Prize, but my cousins have already begun asking when I'm going to Stockholm.

I will never forget that day. Although I consider myself a professional malcontent, I can't deny at least this one experience of pure, unadulterated happiness. I take a cab to the theater to see the cast of my play, and the whole process of creating the production flashes in front of me. I remember rewriting scenes between bites of cheeseburger as I sat alone at a coffee shop on Forty-second Street. There's something soothing about such inauspicious beginnings. If I concentrate on the coffee shop, I convince myself, I will not be overwhelmed by what is happening to me.

Joan Allen, our leading lady, suggests that I come onstage at the end of the performance. I tell her it's impossible, I'm much too shy. I've never taken a curtain call. I want an *Act One* experience. I want to be watching from the back of the theater.

At intermission, however, I find myself in the lobby face to face with Edward Albee. We know each other from the Dramatists Guild and have friends in common. He embraces me and asks me whether I'll be taking a curtain call. I shake my head. I giggle. Edward then tells me to be a person, to take off my coat and seize the moment.

Walking out onto the stage at the Plymouth Theater I become a character in someone else's script. A part of me imagines that I'm Carol Channing—I want to enter with my arm stretched to the ceiling, shouting, "Dolly will never go away again!" Another part of me has no idea what to do onstage while the audience is applauding. I begin to kiss every actor in my play. As long as I'm moving, I won't have to speak or, heaven forbid, curtsy. That night the audience gives us a standing ovation.

Nineteen eighty-nine was my favorite year so far. Perhaps it is all attributable to the astral plane, Libra in orbit, or Maggie Smith's inability to open as scheduled in *Lettice & Lovage* (which freed the Plymouth Theater for *The Heidi Chronicles*). For whatever reason, I spent the greater part of the spring of 1989 winning awards, as if to counteract on a massive front any remnants of ironic negativity. At the Outer Critics Circle Awards, my escort, the actress Caroline Aaron, whispered to me toward the end of the evening, "Wendy, it's just you and Baryshnikov left." Frankly, I would never have suspected that the two of us might be on a double bill.

Of course, there's also the down side. Will anything this wonderful ever happen to me again? How many people are now going to hate me? Where do I take all these things to be framed? Is it gauche to put them up on the walls in my apartment? What happens if Werner Kulovitz at Barbara Matera's, a theatrical costume shop, has stopped importing that feather-light apparatus to "lift and separate" when I need my next formal? And the nagging "Can *I* ever do it again?"

I haven't actually counted the awards, but I'm sure that if I did I could psych myself into some new form of anxiety over them. In the past I've given my parents every diploma or certificate I've received for them to display in their den. But this time I've been selfish—the awards are still resting in a corner of my study. Some days I ignore them in a concerted effort to get back to my life and work, to return to the point of view of the slighted. But, truthfully, there are times when I wander in and take a surreptitious peek at that corner. Nothing is quite as gratifying as recognition for work one is truly proud of.

As for next year, I will be very hurt if I don't win the Heisman Trophy.

•

FROM *Uncommon Women and Others*

SAMANTHA

SAMANTHA: Robert Cabe. I met him last night and I thought, this is the one I want. He's handsome and talented, and he's better than me and he'll love me. You'll see. I want to be his audience, and have my picture, behind him, in my long tartan kilt, in the *New York Times* Arts and Leisure section.

•

RITA, *over singing*: Know what? I think when we're twenty-five we're going to be pretty fucking incredible. All right, I'll give us another five years for emotional and career development. When we're thirty we're going to be pretty fucking amazing.

•

My parents used to call me three times a week at seven A.M. to ask me, "Are you thin, are you married to a root-canal man, are *you* a root canal man?" and I'd hang up and wonder how much longer I was going to be in "transition." I guess since college I've missed the comfort and acceptance I felt with all of you. And I thought that I didn't need that anymore, so I didn't see you.

Mary-Lou Weisman (contemporary)

✦

The Married State

Whenever two or more married couples gather together to socialize, it's not just a party, it's a masquerade. One-upmanship becomes a duet, as both husband and wife conspire, he behind his masks, she behind hers, to present in the best possible light the *third* persona they have brought to the party, their marriage. The introduction of this glittering entity is a challenge to the others, a kind of throwing down of the conjugal gauntlet. By the time all that's left of the brie is the rind, the living room rug will be strewn with gloves. What follows, and in such good humor that it is often called "having fun," is in fact a competition for "best couple."

The competition begins the moment the requisite bottle of wine passes from guest to host. Best-husband-contender No. 1 helps best-wife-contender No. 1 out of her coat and, in so doing, plants a tiny kiss on her ear lobe. The gauntlet has been thrown. All over the room wives struggle to remember the last time their husbands planted a kiss on their ear lobes, and they cannot.

Contending couple No. 2 have just returned from a vacation in the Caribbean where they celebrated their twentieth anniversary. The sun shone brightly upon them every day. They went scuba diving. They took a course together before they left. You should, too. Before you go next time.

They discovered a fabulous restaurant on the French side of the island that hardly any tourists know about. Really romantic. It was a second honeymoon. No, really, it was. On the way over, they persuaded the captain of the cruise ship to marry them—a wonderful way to celebrate a twentieth anniversary, don't you think?

All over the room husbands and wives recall nonstop, $250-a-day, American-plan rain, the ignominy of having to snorkel with minnows while couples who *do* things together, like take courses, cavorted with schools of purple fish in deep coral reefs. They didn't even know the island *had* a French side, or what it was they did to celebrate their twentieth anniversaries. They cannot remember. The brilliance of the other couple's presentation of happiness blinds them to their own. They can only remember that they did not get remarried.

Contending couple No. 3 cannot wait to get home. She pops canapés into his waiting mouth. He pats her bottom suggestively. She whispers hoarsely, "Is it too early to leave yet?" He whispers back, "Soon."

All over the room, couples whose sex lives are commercially interrupted by Bernadette Castro and Sy Syms die a little as they imagine couple No. 3 in passionate disarray ten minutes from now in the driveway.

The winner of the best-marriage competition will be declared later that evening in the privacy of each couple's bedroom, when the votes are tallied. While she climbs out of her panty hose and he hangs up his tie, they will talk about the other couples at the party and who seemed to be the happiest. They may not talk about it directly, but talk they will. "Sounds like The Twos had a terrific vacation." Or, "Did you notice The Ones? It's nice the way he kissed her ear." Or, "Maybe we should take a course." The sign of a particularly successful party is when each couple votes another couple happiest, and all couples receive one vote.

The Saturday-night masquerade, heady in the enactment, carries with it as its price a heavy aftermath of self-doubt, sometimes called Sunday.

It is the sickening green sense that everybody is having a better marriage than you are. It is the same fantasy that tempts people to believe that everybody else's Thanksgiving dinner was catered by Norman Rockwell, and that only you have a father who can't carve, a mother who can't cook, a divorced sister, a daughter who decided to spend Thanksgiving with her boyfriend's family, an uncle who won't shut up about his EST sessions and no dog Spot. It is the same ultimately self-abusing urge that makes people cling to the fantasy—against all contrary evidence—that other people who are thin eat as much as they want. Only you have to diet.

Why do we put ourselves through this perpetual torture? Why this endless game of "Keep It Up," passing our marriages overhead like volleyballs bounced from finger tips to finger tips, while our arms ache? Why doesn't somebody call for a time out?

Sometimes I think that couples have a peculiarly mutual flair for theater, a perception of husband and wife as dramatic roles, a keen sense of romantic comedy and a genuine desire to make beautiful music together. Should one or another forget the lines, there is even a mutual proclivity to fake it.

At other times, I suspect biology. I become convinced that we carry this sadomasochistic behavior in our genes, stamped on our chromosomes. There's nothing we can do about it. Peacocks preen, apes pound their chests and couples too must strut their stuff. Maybe it has survival value for the species.

And sometimes I think our couple behavior is economically determined. It seems we are so essentially a capitalistic society that we can't even refrain from trying to sell one another our marriages, or at least we can't resist advertising them. We are after all a highly competitive society. We compete at work, at school, in sports and on television game shows. All of these are but pale imitations of the competitions that are played on Saturday nights on a field of hors d'oeuvres.

Somewhere, mercifully, in the deepest and most sane recesses of their minds, everybody at the party knows that since they were putting their best marriage forward, it is likely that everybody else was doing the same.

But can they be perfectly sure? There is always the awful possibility, however slight, that at least one of the marriages at the party was so naturally, so dazzlingly ideal that it dared to come unmasked.

There is also the possibility, statistically a lot more likely, that one of the couples at the party will be divorced within the week.

With a little luck, it'll turn out to be the couple who couldn't keep their hands off one another.

Fay Weldon (1931-)

❧ ❧

FROM *Down Among the Women*

Reminds me of the story of Royalty visiting the maternity hospital. Royalty inclines towards young mother. "What lovely red hair baby has, mother. Does he take after his father?" Answer: "Don't know, ma'am, he never took his hat off."

•

A good woman knows that nature is her enemy. Look at what it does to her. Give her a packet of frozen fish fingers any day, and a spoonful of instant mashed potato, and a commercial on the telly to tell her it's good. We swallow the lot, we mothers, and laugh.

•

Hey, you over there! Man! Come to bed. Handsome, young, rich, powerful, or otherwise fortunate—is that you? Excellent? Come inside. Because what I know and perhaps you don't is that by some mysterious but certain process of osmosis I will thereupon draw something of these qualities into myself. Don't run away—I need you! I must have you. I must sap your good fortune, drawing it into myself through the walls of my vagina, gaining my pleasure through your loss. Sex is not for procreation, it is for the sharing of privilege.

You over there! Poor old man. Ugly, tired, crippled, half-witted—come along, hurry, quickly, inside, out of the cold! I've something to give you; I am generosity itself: I will share my stolen goods with you; I will redistribute good fortune through the media of my generative organs; I will make the world a fairer, better place, gaining my own pleasure through degradation, falling into a final shudder of wonder, down there at the slimy roots of the world.

•

FROM *The President's Child*

Hope once got stuck halfway up the oak tree in the communal garden. She was trying to rescue a kitten. Hope wept: the kitten wailed: the fire engine arrived. Ivor the alcoholic fell hopelessly in love with Hope, for at least a month, and Ivor's wife baked bread furiously, in the hope that her proper domestic worth and value would become apparent to him—which indeed it always was, but what has love to do with just deserts? Those who don't deserve it receive it. Those who most need it seldom have it. To those who hath, Jesus once observed, to the shock and dismay of all around, shall be given, and to those who hath not, even that small portion that they hath shall be taken away.

•

"Just because you think people are persecuting you, it doesn't mean they aren't."

•

FROM *Darcy's Utopia*

She had always remarked upon and lamented how little consideration wives were granted in adulterous relationships. They took on the role of the mother on a family outing—the nuisance and the spoilsport, the one who says "don't go too near the edge," "those apples aren't ripe," "shouldn't we get home before the fog sets in?"

•

In Darcy's Utopia it will be accepted that museums will be very boring places indeed. If you want to subdue the children you only have to take them on a visit to a museum, and they will behave at once, for fear of being taken there again.

FROM *Praxis*

I like to see men out of control, I really do. It's the peripheral bits of sex, not the sex itself, that women go for.

•

Booksellers, dentists, and whores, she had read, have the most trouble in exacting money from clients. It seemed a modest expectation of life to have free books, painless teeth and love freely offered, and she sympathised.

•

FROM *The Heart of the Country*

She was the kind of wife, who looks out of her front door in the morning and, if it's raining, apologizes.

•

She should have written to aunts who sent her birthday cards. She'd thought herself too good for too many people, said "I prefer the company of men" once too often. Pride comes before a fall; a sense of sisterhood with sad experience.

•

I like the dry-cleaners. I like the sense of refreshment and renewal. I like the way dirty old torn clothes are dumped, to be returned clean and wholesome in their slippery transparent cases. Better than confession any day. Here there is a true sense of rebirth, redemption, salvation.

•

Unlike virtue, courage is not its own reward. It has results.

•

FROM *The Shrapnel Academy*

Reader, what is etched in your [erotic consciousness]? What collar-bone, what little patch of textured skin, what dangling pendant? Think! Remember! Keep back the glacier of age by the sheer warmth, the sheer force of sexual recollections, wild imaginings! It can be done: it is worth the doing.

•

Reader, do not skip. I know you want to. So do I.

•

Now, gentle reader, shall we return . . .
    Gentle reader! What have I said! You are no more gentle than I am! I apologize for insulting you. You are as ferocious as anyone else. The notion that the reader is gentle is very bad for both readers and writers—and the latter do tend to encourage the former in this belief. We all believe ourselves to be, more or less, well intentioned, nice goodies in fact, whether we're the greengrocer or the Shah of Shahs. But we can't possibly be, or how would the world have got into the state it's in? Who else but ourselves are doing this to ourselves? We simply don't know our own natures.

•

Bella wore a plain black dress. Muffin was wearing rather a lot of pink flounces. She hated herself.

FROM *Remember Me*

Listen now, carefully, to their conversation. Madeleine and Hilary talk in riddles, as families do, even families as small and circumscribed as this one, using the everyday objects of their lives as symbols of their discontent:

1. Hilary: Mum, I can't find my shoes again.
2. Madeleine (looking): They'll be where you took them off. (Finding) Here they are.
3. Hilary: Not those old brown things. My new red ones.

Which, being translated, is:

1. Hilary: Why is this place always such a mess?
2. Madeleine: Why are you such a baby?
3. Hilary: You know nothing about me.

•

Death makes a firm dividing line between the present and the past. Then they were, and now they aren't, and the knife slides firmly into the home-baked cake, dividing. This side, that side, then and now. There, see, isn't that real enough for you? And you were beginning to think, weren't you, that experience slipped along in some kind of continual stream, more or less under your control, at your behest? That'll teach you. Before death, after death. Now you see them, now you don't. Life's still one long lesson, it turns out, with a slap and a cuff every now and then to help you keep your wits about you.

•

FROM *The Fat Woman's Joke*

A woman has all too much substance in a man's eyes at the best of times. That is why men like women to be slim. Her lack of flesh negates her. The less of her there is, the less notice he need take of her. The more like a male she appears to be, the safer he feels.

•

Running a house is not a sensible occupation for a grown woman. Dusting and sweeping, cooking and washing up—it is work for the sake of work, an eternal circle which lasts from the day you get married until the day you die, or are put into an old folks' home because you are too feeble to pick up some man's dirty clothes and wash them any more.

•

"It's time you got married."

She looked at him, instant hope mingling in her brain like instant coffee in boiling milk, but he shook his head at her and went back to his wife.

•

FROM *Female Friends*

"One doesn't choose friends. One acquires them. They are as much duty as pleasure."

•

The rest of us fear poverty, deprivation, abandonment, separation, death. Grace fears the lack of a good hairdresser.

•

He didn't see women as sex-objects, rather himself as one.

•

Patrick Bates has the mature ladies of the village in an erotic ferment and the young girls giddy with love.

•

First babies are all blows, make no mistake about it. Duck when you see one coming. The child-wife becomes a mother. The status-wife becomes a messy cowering helpless thing. Listen to her. Listen to the chorus. Help me, look after me, cosset me, she cries. Me and baby. What precious vulnerable things are we, and yes, I must have a blue ceiling for baby to stare at, you beast. Paint it when you get home from work and can't you get home earlier? LOOK AFTER ME, you bastard! Of course we can't go to the party, what about my milk supply. No, you can't go by yourself.

•

Chloe finds she is laughing, not hysterically, or miserably, but really quite lightly and merrily; and worse, not with Oliver, but at him, and in this she is, at last, in tune with the rest of the universe.

•

FROM *The Life and Loves of a She-Devil*

I am quite sure at some time or other Bobbo would have said, in the manner of husbands, "I love her. I love her but I'm not in love with her: not the way I'm in love with you. Do you understand?" And Mary Fisher would have nodded, understanding very well.

•

I make puff pastry for the chicken vol-au-vents, and when I have finished circling out the dough with the brim of a wine-glass, making wafer rounds, I take the thin curved strips the cutter left behind and mold them into a shape much like the shape of Mary Fisher, and turn the oven, high, high, and crisp the figure in it until such a stench fills the kitchen that even the fan cannot remove it. Good.

•

Little women can look up to men. But women of six feet two have trouble doing so.

•

"What about me?" asked Ruth, and words sped out into the universe, to join myriad other "what about me"s uttered by myriad other women, abandoned that very day by their husbands. Women in Korea and Buenos Aires and Stockholm and Detroit and Dubai and Tashkent, but seldom in China, where it is a punishable offense. Sound waves do not die out. They travel forever and forever. All our sentences are immortal. Our useless bleatings circle the universe for all eternity.

•

She laughed and said she was taking up arms against God Himself. Lucifer had tried and failed, but he was male. She thought she might do better, being female.

•

"I thought all that [the world of business, of money and profit and loss] was supposed to be very boring," said Nurse Hopkins.

"That is just a tale put about by men to keep the women out of it," said Ruth.

•

FROM *Letters to Alice: On First Reading Jane Austen*

It's always wonderful to find out that there is a view of the world, not just the world: a pattern to experience, not just experience—and whether you agree with the view offered, or like the pattern, is neither here nor there. Views are possible, patterns discernible—it is exciting and exhilarating and enriching to know it.

•

And it is why, I think, increasingly, any seminar on Women and Writing, or Women Writers, or the New Female Culture, or whatever, is instantly booked up—by men as well as by women. . . .

•

. . . we are not alone in the oddity of our beliefs. Our neighbour, whom we never thought would laugh when we laughed, actually does.

•

Well, the writers, I do believe, who get the best and most lasting response from readers are the writers who offer a happy ending through moral development. By a happy ending I do not mean mere fortunate events—a marriage, or a last-minute rescue from death—but some kind of spiritual reassessment or moral reconciliation, even with the self, even at death.

•

FROM *Little Sisters*

We all have friends who are richer than ourselves and they, you may be sure, have richer friends of their own. We are most of us within spitting distance of millionaires.

Spit away—if that's what you feel like.

•

I know that self-knowledge is painful. I know that to think you are a princess and find you are a beggar-girl is very disagreeable. I know that to look at a prince and find he is a toad is quite shocking. I also know, and you will probably never have the opportunity to find out, that to think you are a beggar-girl and end up a princess is perfectly dreadful.

•

Had you never noticed the way the secret world sends our signs and symbols into the ordinary world? It delivers our messages in the form of coincidences: Letters crossing in the post, unfamiliar tunes heard three times in one day, the way that blows of fate descend upon the same bowed shoulders, and beams of good fortune glow perpetually upon the blessed. Fairy tales, as I said, are lived out daily. There is far more going on in the world than we ever imagine.

•

Beware of gratitude, Elsa. Young girls so easily feel grateful, and it always leads them into trouble. Remember always that your good fortune is yours by right; you do not have to feel obliged to those who are the mere catalysts of your fate.

•

Wives bring cups of tea to torturers, chiefs of police and army generals. It is expected of them, in the name of marriage, to pass no moral judgments, let alone take any positive action to disassociate themselves from behaviour which in any other man but a husband would appear monstrous. Mind you, they usually starve if they open their mouths—and the children too.

Carolyn Wells (1862–1942)

To a Milkmaid

I hail thee, O milkmaid!
Goddess of the gaudy morn, hail!
Across the mead tripping,
Invariably across the mead tripping,
The merry mead with cowslips blooming,
With daisies blooming,
The milkmaid also more or less blooming!
I hail thee, O milkmaid!
I recognise the value of thy pail in literature and art.
What were a pastoral poet without thee?
Oh, I know thee, milkmaid!
I hail thy jaunty juvenescence.
I know thy eighteen summers and thy eternal springs.
Ay, I know thy trials!
I know how thou art outspread over pastoral poetry.
Rampant, ubiquitous, inevitable, thy riotings in pastoral poetry,
And in masterpieces of pastoral art!
How oft have I seen thee sitting;
On a tri-legged stool sitting;
On the wrong side of the cow sitting;
Garbed in all thy preposterous paraphernalia.
I know thy paraphernalia—
Yea, even thy impossible milkpail and thy improbable bodice.
Short-skirted siren!
Big-hatted beauty!
What were the gentle spring without thee!
I hail thee!
I hail thy vernality, and I rejoice in thy hackneyed ubiquitousness.
I hail the superiority of thy inferiorness, and
I lay at thy feet this garland of gratuitous
Hails!

Mae West (1893–1980)

~&~

One-liners

Is that a pistol in your pocket or are you just happy to see me?

•

. . . Why don't you come up and see me sometime? Come up on Wednesday, that's amateur night. . . .
Trust me, hundreds already have.

•

When women go wrong, men go right after them.

•

A hard man is good to find.

•

He who hesitates is last.

•

Give a man a free hand and he'll run it all over you.

•

Why should I be good when I'm packing them in by being bad?

•

FROM *Pleasure Man*

Dolores is learning the meaning of the word repentance. It is how you feel when you get caught.

•

Nellie knows people are divided into the goods and the bads. The thing is not to be caught with the goods.

•

Poor Mary Ann! She gave the guy an inch and now he thinks he's a ruler.

•

FROM *The Constant Sinner*

When Babe Gordon had told the Bearcat she had been to church, it never occurred to her that she was lying. That is, it had no moral significance for her. To Babe, a lie was simply something one told to gain an advantage, to get what one wanted by the shortest route. . . . Bearcat was now convinced that she was a good girl, had character; and now, no matter what Charlie said against her, if she were careful Bearcat would always believe in her.

Babe was the living example of all that is immoral, when viewed through conventional eyes. But she herself was unmoral. For her, morals did not exist. She would not have known what a moral was if it could be made to dance naked in front of her.

•

A distinguished looking tall man, with snow-white hair and well-groomed body, got into the cab with a dame who was highly rouged and expensively attired from shoes to the beautiful summer fur-piece about her shoulders. He caught snatches of their conversation.

"But I don't want to stop at the Plaza for tea," the man was saying, irritably. "You just want to show off that new fur I bought you."

"Please, honey," the girl begged.

"No, no. I'd be bored stiff. Let's go up to the apartment."

"But I don't want to go up there yet. It's too early."

"What has the time got to do with it? We can't get anything to drink at the Plaza." . . .

"All right, then," the girl said. "If you don't take me to the Plaza, I won't be nice to you the way you like, any more."

"Oh, I say now, Zelda," the man argued. "That's not sporting, after I've given you so much."

"Well, I don't care," said the girl. "I just won't be nice that way any more, that's all."

"Oh, good lord!" the man exclaimed, anxiously. "Well, all right." He rapped on the taxi window with his stick. "I say, my man."

"Yeah?" the Bearcat answered as he choked down the speed of the car.

"Drive us to the Plaza—the Plaza!"

"Oh, you darling!" cried the girl.

•

FROM *A Bio-Bibliography*

I like movies about strong women. I was the first liberated woman, y' know. No guy was gonna get the best of me, that's what I wrote all my scripts about.

•

You must be good and tired.
West: No, just tired.

•

I'm not a little girl from a little town making good in a big town. I'm a big girl from a big town making good in a little town.

•

Hatcheck girl: Goodness, what lovely diamonds.
West: Goodness had nothing to do with it, dearie.

•

It takes two to get one in trouble.

•

I've been things and seen places.

•

When I'm good, I'm very good, but when I'm bad, I'm better.

•

I used to be Snow White but I drifted.

•

It's not the men in my life, but the life in my men that counts.

•

Too much of a good thing can be wonderful.

•

Keep cool and collect.

•

Between two evils I always pick the one I never tried before.

•

I always say keep a diary and one day it will keep you.

•

I generally avoid temptation. Unless I can't resist it.

•

If young girls knew more about love and didn't take it so seriously, it would be better for them.

•

I have never minded foreign films, but who needs dirty foreign films? We can do better dirty films ourselves.

•

Some mousy women have more oomph in their hip pocket than a lot of beautiful women have in their whole bodies.

•

Politics? I keep up with what's going on. Although I'm not much for politics myself. But I always know a good party man when I see one. . . .

Rebecca West (1892–1983)

❧ ✦ ❧

One-liners

If there is to be any romance in marriage woman must be given every chance to earn a decent living at other occupations. Otherwise no man can be sure that he is loved for himself alone, and that his wife did not come to the Registry Office because she had no luck at the Labor Exchange.

•

People call me a feminist whenever I express sentiments that differentiate me from a doormat or a prostitute.

Edith Wharton (1862–1937)

❧ ✦ ❧

FROM *The House of Mirth*

"Ah, there's the difference—a girl must [marry], a man may if he chooses." She surveyed him critically. "Your coat's a little shabby—but who cares? It doesn't keep people from asking you to dine. If I were shabby no one would have me: a woman is asked out as much for her clothes as for herself. The clothes are the background, the frame, if you like: they don't make success, but they are a part of it. Who wants a dingy woman? We are expected to be pretty and well-dressed till we drop—and if we can't keep it up alone, we have to go into partnership."

•

It amused her to think that any one as rich as Mr. Percy Gryce should be shy; but she was gifted with treasures of indulgence for such idiosyncrasies, and besides, his timidity might serve her purpose better than too much assurance. She had the art of giving self-confidence to the embarrassed, but she was not equally sure of being able to embarrass the self-confident.

She waited till the train had emerged from the tunnel and was racing between the ragged edges of the northern suburbs. Then, as it lowered its speed near Yonkers, she rose from her seat and drifted slowly down the carriage. As she passed Mr. Gryce, the train gave a lurch, and he was aware of a slender hand gripping the back of his chair. He rose with a start, his ingenuous face looking as though it had been dipped in crimson: even the reddish tint in his beard seemed to deepen.

The train swayed again, almost flinging Miss Bart into his arms. She steadied herself with a laugh and drew back; but he was enveloped in the scent of her dress, and his shoulder had felt her fugitive touch.

"Oh, Mr. Gryce, is it you? I'm so sorry—I was trying to find the porter and get some tea."

She held out her hand as the train resumed its level rush, and they stood exchanging a few words in the aisle. Yes—he was going to Bellomont. He had heard she was to be of the party—he blushed again as he admitted it. And was he to be there for a whole week? How delightful!

But at this point one or two belated passengers from the last station forced their way into the carriage, and Lily had to retreat to her seat.

"The chair next to mine is empty—do take it," she said over her shoulder; and Mr. Gryce, with considerable embarrassment, succeeded in effecting an exchange which enabled him to transport himself and his bags to her side.

"Ah—and here is the porter, and perhaps we can have some tea."

She signalled to that official, and in a moment, with the ease that seemed to attend the fulfilment of all her wishes, a little table had been set up between the seats, and she had helped Mr. Gryce to bestow his encumbering properties beneath it.

When the tea came he watched her in silent fascination while her hands flitted above the tray, looking miraculously fine and slender in contrast to the coarse china and lumpy bread. It seemed wonderful to him that any one should perform with such careless ease the difficult task of making tea in public in a lurching train. He would never have dared to order it for himself, lest he should attract the notice of his fellow-passengers; but, secure in the shelter of her conspicuousness, he sipped the inky draught with a delicious sense of exhilaration.

Lily, with the flavour of Selden's caravan tea on her lips, had no great fancy to drown it in the railway brew which seemed such nectar to her companion; but, rightly judging that one of the charms of tea is the fact of drinking it together, she proceeded to give the last touch to Mr. Gryce's enjoyment by smiling at him across her lifted cup.

"Is it quite right—I haven't made it too strong?" she asked solicitously; and he replied with conviction that he had never tasted better tea.

"I daresay it is true," she reflected; and her imagination was fired by the thought that Mr. Gryce, who might have sounded the depths of the most complex self-indulgence, was perhaps actually taking his first journey alone with a pretty woman.

It struck her as providential that she should be the instrument of his initiation. Some girls would not have known how to manage him. They would have over-emphasized the novelty of the adventure, trying to make him feel in it the zest of an escapade. But Lily's methods were more delicate. She remembered that her cousin Jack Stepney had once defined Mr. Gryce as the young man who had promised his mother never to go out in the rain without his overshoes; and acting on this hint, she resolved to impart a gently domestic air to the scene, in the hope that her companion, instead of feeling that he was doing something reckless or unusual, would merely be led to dwell on the advantage of always having a companion to make one's tea in the train.

But in spite of her efforts, conversation flagged after the tray had been removed, and she was driven to take a fresh measurement of Mr. Gryce's limitations. It was not, after all, opportunity but imagination that he lacked: he had a mental palate which would never learn to distinguish between railway tea and nectar. There was, however, one topic she could rely on: one spring that she had only to touch to set his simple machinery in motion. She had refrained from touching it because it was a last resource, and she had relied on other arts to stimulate other sensations; but as a settled look of dullness began to creep over his candid features, she saw that extreme measures were necessary.

"And how," she said, leaning forward, "are you getting on with your Americana?"

His eye became a degree less opaque: it was as though an incipient film had been removed from it, and she felt the pride of a skillful operator.

"I've got a few new things," he said, suffused with pleasure, but lowering his voice as though he feared his fellow-passengers might be in league to despoil him.

She returned a sympathetic enquiry, and gradually he was drawn on to talk of his latest purchases. It was the one subject which enabled him to forget himself, or allowed him, rather, to remember himself without constraint, because he was at home in it, and could assert a superiority that there were few to dispute. Hardly any of his acquaintances cared for Americana, or knew anything about them; and the consciousness of this ignorance threw Mr. Gryce's knowledge into agreeable relief. The only difficulty was to introduce the topic and to keep it to the front; most people showed no desire to have their ignorance dispelled, and Mr. Gryce was like a merchant whose warehouses are crammed with an unmarketable commodity.

But Miss Bart, it appeared, really did want to know about Americana; and moreover, she was already sufficiently informed to make the task of farther instruction as easy as it was agreeable. She questioned him intelligently, she heard him submissively; and, prepared for the look of lassitude which usually crept over his listeners' faces, he grew eloquent under her receptive gaze. The "points" she had had the presence of mind to glean from Selden, in anticipation of this very contingency, were serving her to such good purpose that she began to think her visit to him had been the luckiest incident of the day. She had once more shown her talent for profiting by the unexpected, and dangerous theories as to the advisability of yielding to impulse were germinating under the surface of smiling attention which she continued to present to her companion.

Mr. Gryce's sensations, if less definite, were equally agreeable. He felt his confused titillation with which the lower organisms welcome the gratification of their needs, and all his senses floundered in a vague well-being, through which Miss Bart's personality was dimly but pleasantly perceptible.

Mr. Gryce's interest in Americana had not originated with himself: it was impossible to think of him as evolving any taste of his own. An uncle had left him a collection already noted among bibliophiles; the existence of the collection was the only fact that had ever shed glory on the name of Gryce, and the nephew took as much pride in his inheritance as though it had been his own work. Indeed, he gradually came to regard it as such, and to feel a sense of personal complacency when he chanced on any reference to the Gryce Americana. Anxious as he was to avoid personal notice, he took, in the printed mention of his name, a pleasure so exquisite and excessive that it seemed a compensation for his shrinking from publicity.

To enjoy the sensation as often as possible, he subscribed to all the reviews dealing with book-collecting in general, and American history in particular, and as allusions to his library abounded in the pages of these journals, which formed his only reading, he came to regard himself as figuring prominently in the public eye, and to enjoy the thought of the interest which would be excited if the persons he met in the street, or sat among in travelling, were suddenly to be told that he was the possessor of the Gryce Americana.

Most timidities have such secret compensations, and Miss Bart was discerning enough to know that the inner vanity is generally in proportion to the outer self-deprecation. With a more confident person she would not have dared to dwell so long on one topic, or to show such exaggerated interest in it; but she had rightly guessed that Mr. Gryce's egoism was a thirsty soil, requiring constant nurture from without. Miss Bart had the gift of following an undercurrent of thought while she appeared to be sailing on the surface of conversation; and in this case her mental excursion took the form of a rapid survey of Mr. Percy Gryce's future as combined with her own. The Gryces were from Albany, and but lately introduced to the metropolis, where the mother and son had come, after old Jefferson Gryce's death, to take possession of his house in Madison Avenue—an appalling house, all brown stone without and black walnut within, with the Gryce library in a fire-proof annex that looked like a mausoleum. Lily, however, knew all about them: young Mr. Gryce's arrival had fluttered the maternal breasts of New York, and when a girl has no mother to palpitate for her she must needs be on the alert for herself. Lily, therefore, had not only contrived to put herself in the young man's way, but had made the acquaintance of Mrs. Gryce, a monumental woman with the voice of a pulpit orator and a mind preoccupied with the iniquities of her servants, who came sometimes to sit with Mrs. Peniston and learn from that lady how she managed to prevent the kitchen-maid's smuggling groceries out of the house. Mrs. Gryce had a kind of impersonal benevolence: cases of individual need she regarded with suspicion, but she subscribed to Institutions when their annual reports showed an impressive surplus. Her domestic duties were manifold, for they extended from furtive inspections of the servants' bedrooms to unannounced descents to the cellar; but she had never allowed herself many pleasures. Once, however, she had had a special edition of the Sarum Rule printed in rubric and presented to every clergyman in the diocese; and the gilt album in which their letters of thanks were pasted formed the chief ornament of her drawing-room table.

Percy had been brought up in the principles which so excellent a woman was sure to inculcate. Every form of prudence and suspicion had been grafted on a nature originally reluctant and cautious, with the result that it would have seemed hardly needful for Mrs. Gryce to extract his promise about the overshoes, so little likely was he to hazard himself abroad in the rain. After attaining his majority, and coming into the fortune which the late Mr. Gryce had made out of a patent device for excluding fresh air from hotels, the young man continued to live with his mother in Albany; but on Jefferson Gryce's death, when another large property passed into her son's hands, Mrs. Gryce thought that what she called his "interests" demanded his presence in New York. She accordingly installed herself in the Madison Avenue house, and Percy, whose sense of duty was not inferior to his mother's, spent all his week days in the handsome Broad Street office where a batch of pale men on small salaries had grown grey in the management of the Gryce estate, and where he was initiated with becoming reverence into every detail of the art of accumulation.

As far as Lily could learn, this had hitherto been Mr. Gryce's only occupation, and she might have been pardoned for thinking it not too hard a task to interest a young man who had been kept on such low diet. At any rate, she felt herself so completely in command of the situation that she yielded to a sense of security in which all fear of Mr. Rosedale, and of the difficulties on which that fear was contingent, vanished beyond the edge of thought.

The stopping of the train at Garrisons would not have distracted her from these thoughts, had she not caught a sudden look of distress in her companion's eye. His seat faced toward the door, and she guessed that he had been perturbed by the approach of an acquaintance; a fact confirmed by the turning of heads and general sense of commotion which her own entrance into a railway-carriage was apt to produce.

She knew the symptoms at once, and was not surprised to be hailed by the high notes of a pretty woman, who entered the train accompanied by a maid, a bull-terrier, and a footman staggering under a load of bags and dressing-cases.

"Oh, Lily—are you going to Bellomont? Then you can't let me have your seat, I suppose? But I *must* have a seat in this carriage—porter, you must find me a place at once. Can't some one be put somewhere else? I want to be with my friends. Oh, how do you do, Mr. Gryce? Do please make him understand that I must have a seat next to you and Lily."

Mrs. George Dorset, regardless of the mild efforts of a traveller with a carpet-bag, who was doing his best to make room for her by getting out of the train, stood in the middle of the aisle, diffusing about her that general sense of exasperation which a pretty woman on her travels not infrequently creates.

She was smaller and thinner than Lily Bart, with a restless pliability of pose, as if she could have been crumpled up and run through a ring, like the sinuous draperies she affected. Her small pale face seemed the mere setting of a pair of dark exaggerated eyes, of which the visionary gaze contrasted curiously with her self-assertive tone and gestures; so that, as one of her friends observed, she was like a disembodied spirit who took up a great deal of room.

Having finally discovered that the seat adjoining Miss Bart's was at her disposal, she possessed herself of it with a farther displacement of her surroundings, explaining meanwhile that she had come across from Mount Kisco in her motor-car that morning, and had been kicking her heels for an hour at Garrisons, without even the alleviation of a cigarette, her brute of a husband having neglected to replenish her case before they parted that morning.

"And at this hour of the day I don't suppose you've a single one left, have you, Lily?" she plaintively concluded.

Miss Bart caught the startled glance of Mr. Percy Gryce, whose own lips were never defiled by tobacco.

"What an absurd question, Bertha!" she exclaimed, blushing at the thought of the store she had laid in at Lawrence Selden's.

"Why, don't you smoke? Since when have you given it up? What—you never— And you don't either, Mr. Gryce? Ah, of course —how stupid of me—I understand."

And Mrs. Dorset leaned back against her travelling cushions with a smile which made Lily wish there had been no vacant seat beside her own.

•

Bridge at Bellomont usually lasted till the small hours; and when Lily went to bed that night she had played too long for her own good.

Feeling no desire for the self-communion which awaited her in her room, she lingered on the broad stairway, looking down into the hall below, where the last card-players were grouped about the tray of tall glasses and silver-collared decanters which the butler had just placed on a low table near the fire.

The hall was arcaded, with a gallery supported on columns of pale yellow marble. Tall clumps of flowering plants were grouped against a background of dark foliage in the angles of the walls. On the crimson carpet a deer-hound and two or three spaniels dozed luxuriously before the fire, and the light from the great central lantern overhead shed a brightness on the women's hair and struck sparks from their jewels as they moved.

There were moments when such scenes delighted Lily, when they gratified her sense of beauty and her craving for the external finish of life; there were others when they gave a sharper edge to the meagerness of her own opportunities. This was one of the moments when the sense of contrast was uppermost, and she turned away impatiently as Mrs. George Dorset, glittering in serpentine spangles, drew Percy Gryce in her wake to a confidential nook beneath the gallery.

It was not that Miss Bart was afraid of losing her newly acquired hold over Mr. Gryce. Mrs. Dorset might startle or dazzle him, but she had neither the skill nor the patience to effect his capture. She was too self-engrossed to penetrate the recesses of his shyness, and besides, why should she care to give herself the trouble? At most it might amuse her to make sport of his simplicity for an evening—after that he would be merely a burden to her, and knowing this, she was far too experienced to encourage him. But the mere thought of that other woman who could take a man up and toss him aside as she willed, without having to regard him as a possible factor in her plans, filled Lily Bart with envy. She had been bored all the afternoon by Percy Gryce—the mere thought seemed to waken an echo of his droning voice—but she could not ignore him on the morrow, she must follow up her success, must submit to more boredom, must be ready with fresh compliances and adaptabilities, and all on the bare chance that he might ultimately decide to do her the honor of boring her for life.

•

FROM *The Custom of the Country*

Mrs. Fairford made no tactless allusions to her being a newcomer in New York—there was nothing as bitter to the girl as that—but her questions as to what pictures had interested Undine at the various exhibitions of the moment, and which of the new books she had read, were almost as open to suspicion, since they had to be answered in the negative. Undine did not even know that there were any pictures to be seen, much less that "people" went to see them; and she had read no new book but "When The Kissing Had to Stop," of which Mrs. Fairford seemed not to have heard. On the theater they were equally at odds, for while Undine had seen "Oolaloo" fourteen times, and was "wild" about Ned Norris in "The Soda-Water Fountain," she had not heard of the famous Berlin comedians who were performing Shakespeare at the German Theatre, and knew only by name the clever American actress who was trying to give "repertory" plays with a good stock company. The conversation was revived for a moment by her recalling that she had seen Sarah Bernhardt in a play she called "Leg-long," and another which she pronounced "Fade"; but even this did not carry them far, as she had forgotten what both plays were about and had found the actress a good deal older than she expected.

·

His mother and sister of course wanted him to marry. They had the usual theory that he was "made" for conjugal bliss: women always thought that of a fellow who didn't get drunk and have low tastes. Ralph smiled at the idea as he sat crouched among his secret treasures. Marry —but whom, in the name of light and freedom? The daughters of his own race sold themselves to the Invaders; the daughters of the Invaders bought their husbands as they bought an opera-box. It ought all to have been transacted on the Stock Exchange. His mother, he knew, had no such ambitions for him: she would have liked him to fancy a "nice girl" like Harriet Ray. Harriet Ray was neither vulgar nor ambitious. She regarded Washington Square as the birthplace of Society, knew by heart all the cousinships of early New York, hated motor-cars, could not make herself understood on the telephone, and was determined, if she married, never to receive a divorced woman. As Mrs. Marvell often said, such girls as Harriet were growing rare. Ralph was not sure about this. He was inclined to think that, certain modifications allowed for, there would always be plenty of Harriet Rays for unworldly mothers to commend to their sons; and he had no desire to diminish their number by removing one from the ranks of the marriageable.

·

She had read in the "Boudoir Chat" of one of the Sunday papers that the smartest women were using the new pigeon-blood notepaper with white ink; and rather against her mother's advice she had ordered a large supply, with her monogram in silver. It was a disappointment, therefore, to find that Mrs. Fairford wrote on the old-fashioned white sheet, without even a monogram—simply her address and telephone number. It gave Undine rather a poor opinion of Mrs. Fairford's social standing, and for a moment she thought with considerable satisfaction of answering the note on her pigeon-blood paper. Then she remembered Mrs. Heeny's emphatic commendation of Mrs. Fairford, and her pen wavered. What if white paper were really newer than pigeon-blood? It might be more stylish, anyhow. Well, she didn't care if Mrs. Fairford didn't like red paper—*she* did!

Frances Miriam Whitcher (1814-1852)

～❦ ❦～

FROM *The Widow Bedott Papers*

He was a wonderful hand to moralize, husband was, specially after he begun to enjoy poor health. He made an observation once, when he was in one of his poor turns, that I shall never forget the longest day I live.

He says to me one winter evenin as we was a-settin by the fire— I was a-knittin. I was always a great knitter—and he was smokin, though the doctor used to tell him he'd be better off to leave tobacco alone. When he was well, he used to take his pipe and smoke a spell after he'd got the chores done up, and when he warn't well, he used to smoke the biggest part of the time.

Well, he took his pipe out of his mouth and turned toward me, and I knowed somethin was comin, for he had a particular way of lookin round when he was a-goin to say anything uncommon. Well, he says to me, "Silly,"—my name was Prisilly, naturally, but he generally called me "Silly" because 'twas handier, you know—well, he says to me, "Silly," and he looked pretty solemn, I tell you! He had a solemn countenance, and after he got to be deacon 'twas more so, but since he'd lost his health he looked solemner than ever, and certainly you wouldn't wonder at it if you knew how much he underwent. He was troubled with a pain in his chest and mazin weakness in the spine of his back, besides the pleurisy in his side, and bein broke of his rest of nights because he was put to it for breath when he laid down. Why, it's an unaccountable fact that when that man died he hadn't seen a well day in fifteen year, though when he was married and for five or six year after, I shouldn't desire to see a ruggeder man than he was. But the time I'm a-speakin of, he'd been out of health nigh upon ten year, and, oh dear sakes! How he had altered since the first time I ever see him! That was to a quiltin to Squire Smith's a spell before Sally was married. I'd no idea *then* that Sal Smith was a-goin to be married to Sam Pendergrass. She'd been keepin company with Mose Hewlitt for better'n a year, and everybody said that was a settled thing, and lo and behold! All of a sudden she up and took Sam Pendergrass. Well, that was the first time I ever see my husband, and if anybody'd a-told me then that I should ever marry him, I should a-said—

But lawful sakes! I was a-goin to tell you what he said to me that evenin, and when a body begins to tell a thing I believe in finishin on it some time or other. Some folks have a way of talkin round and round and round for evermore. Now there's Miss Jenkins, she that was Poll Bingham before she was married—but what husband said to me was this. He says to me, "Silly."

Says I, "What?" I didn't say, "What, Hezekiah?" for I didn't like his name. The first time I ever heard it I near killed myself a-laughin. "Hezekiah Bedott!" says I. "Well, I would give up if I had such a name!" But then, you know, I had no more idea of marryin the feller than you have this minute of marryin the governor. I suppose you think it's curious we should name our oldest son Hezekiah. Well, we done it to please Father and Mother Bedott. It's his name, and he and Mother Bedott both used to think that names had ought to go down from generation to generation. But we always called him Kiah, you know. That boy is a blessin! I ain't the only one that thinks so, I guess. Now, don't you ever tell anybody that I said so, but between you and me, I rather guess that if Kesiah Winkel thinks she's a-goin to catch Kiah Bedott, she is a little out of her reckonin!

Well, husband he says to me, "Silly." And says I, "What?" though I'd no idea what he was a-goin to say, didn't know but what it was somethin about his sufferins, though he warn't apt to complain, but used to say that he wouldn't wish his worst enemy to suffer one minute as he did all the time, but that can't be called grumblin—think it can? Why, I've seen him when you'd a-thought no mortal could a-helped grumblin, but he didn't. He and me went once in the dead of winter in a one-hoss sleigh out to see a sister of his. You know the snow is deep in this section of the country. Well, the hoss got stuck in one of them snow banks, and there we set, unable to stir, and to cap it all, husband was took with a dreadful crick in his back. Now that is what I call a predicament!

Most men would a-swore, but husband didn't. We might a-been settin there to this day, far as I know, if there hadn't a-happened to come along a mess of men in a double team, and they pulled us out.

But husband says to me—I could see by the light of the fire, for there didn't happen to be any candle burnin, if I don't disremember, though my memory is sometimes rather forgetful, but I know we weren't apt to burn candles exceptin when we had company—I could see by the light of the fire that his mind was uncommon solemnized. Says to he me, "Silly."

I says to him, "What?"

He says to me, says he, "We're all poor creatures."

Paulette Childress White (contemporary)

~≈ ❧ ❧ ≈~

FROM *Mothers and Daughters*

If you were a woman or a girl over twelve, walking this block—even on the safe side—could be painful. They usually hollered at you and never mind what they said. Today, because it was hot and early, we made it by with only one weak *Hey baby* from a drunk sitting in the poolroom door.

"Hey baby yourself," I said but not too loudly, pushing my flat chest out and stabbing my eyes in his direction.

"Minerva girl, you better watch your mouth with grown men like that," Momma said, her eyes catching me up in real warning though I could see that she was holding down a smile.

Katharine Whitehorn (c. 1928–   )

~≈ ❧ ❧ ≈~

On Fat and Thin, Big and Small

Outside every thin girl there's a fat man trying to get in.

•

Female size, especially brain size, has always been held to explain their unfitness for this or that; whole nineteenth-century theories were based

on the smaller size of the brain of women and "inferior races"—until
it was found that elephants' brains were even larger than men's.

Isabella Whitney (16th century)
~❦ ❧~

The Maner of Her Wyll, & What She Left
to London: And to All Those in it:
At Her Departing

I whole in body and in minde,
but very weake in Purse:
Do make, and write my Testament
for feare it wyll be wurse.
And fyrst I wholy doo commend,
my Soule and Body eke:
To God The Father and the Son,
so long as I can speake.
And after speach: my Soule to hym,
And Body to the Grave:
Tyll time that all shall rise agayne,
their Judgement for to have.

And now let mee dispose such things,
as I shal leave behinde:
That those which shall receave the same,
may know my wylling minde.
I first of all to London leave
because I there was bred:
Brave buildyings rare, of Churches store,
and Pauls to the head.
Betweene the same: fayre streats there bee,
and people goodly store:
Because their keeping craveth cost,
I yet wil leave him more.
First for their foode, I Butchers leave,
that every day shall kyll:

By Thames you shal have Brewers store,
and Bakers at your wyll.
And such as orders doo observe,
and eat fish thrice a weeke:
I leave two Streets, full fraught therwith
they neede not farre to seeke.

For Women shall you Taylors have,
by Bow, the chiefest dwel:
In every Lane you some shall finde,
can doo indifferent well.
And for the men, few Streetes or Lanes,
but Bodymakers bee:
And such as make the sweeping cloakes,
with Gardes beneth the knee.

Now when thy folke are fed and clad
with such as I have namde:
For daynty mouthes, and stomachs weake
some Junckets must be framde.
Wherfore I Poticaries leave,
with Banquets in their Shop:
Phisicians also for the sicke,
Diseases for to stop.

If they that keepe what I you leave,
aske Mony: when they sell it:
At Mint there is such store, it is
unpossible to tell it.

Now for the people in thee left,
I have done as I may:
And that the poore, when I am gone,
have cause for me to pray.
I wyll to prisons portions leave,
what though but very small:
Yet that they may remember me,
occasion be it shall:

Now London have I (for thy sake)
within thee, and without:
As coms into my memory,
dispearsed round about

Such needfull thinges, as they should have
herre left now unto thee,
When I am gon, with conscience
let them dispearsed bee.
And though I nothing named have,
to bury mee withall:
Consider that above the ground,
annoyance bee I shall.

Rejoice in God that I am gon,
out of this vale so vile.
And that of ech thing, left such store,
as may your wants exile,
I make thee sole executor, because
I lov'de thee best.
And thee I put in trust, to geve
the goodes unto the rest.

And (though I am perswade) that I
shall never more thee see:
Yet to the last, I shal not cease
to wish much good to thee.
This xx, of October,
in ANNO DOMINI
A thousand: v hundred seventy three
as Alminacks descry.
Did write this Wyll with mine owne hand
and it to London gave:

In witnes of the standers by,
whose names yf you wyll have,
Paper, pen and Standish were:
at that same present by:
With Time, who promised to reveale,
so fast as she could hye
The same: least of my nearer kyn,
for any thing should vary:
So finally I make an end
no longer can I tary.

Thyra Samter Winslow (1893-1927)

~☙ ❧~

FROM *Semi-professional Astrology*

Now, when's your birthday? The exact hour you were born. . . . Are you sure about that? Who told you? . . . Oh, your mother. Well, it ought to be about right, then, don't you think? Now the year. . . . Not nineteen-five? You'll have to talk a little louder. I'm a little deaf. Now wait until I look it up. . . .

Have you ever tried to do anything in the artistic line? I think you'd make a good dancer. . . . Yes, you do seem a little heavy for a dancer, that's right. Have you ever tried dancing? Have you ever tried anything else artistic? . . . Oh, you paint. That's very nice, I'm sure. You see, I knew there was something artistic there the minute I looked at your horoscope. . . .

Your husband's got very good aspects, now. I'd keep him. If you do leave him you'll get another husband and it wouldn't be any different. You're the kind of woman that marries and marries, but the husbands are all just about alike, and this is about the best husband you'd get. Now about your first husband. He didn't marry again, did he? . . . Oh, he did marry again? He has a peculiar disposition. You better keep the husband you have. . . . Oh, you intend to. Well, that's a wise idea. He is as good as you'll do. If you marry again—but then I can't tell you that because I haven't got the birthday of your third husband. . . . Oh, you don't intend ever to marry again. Well, I think you're doing the wise thing to put up with your second husband.

Liz Winstead (contemporary)

~∾ ❧ ᔕ~

I think, therefore I'm single.

Virginia Woolf (1882-1941)

~∾ ❧ ᔕ~

FROM *A Room of One's Own*

. . . And then I went on very warily, on the very tips of my toes (so cowardly am I, so afraid of the lash that was once almost laid on my own shoulders), to murmur that she should also learn to laugh, without bitterness, at the vanities—say rather at the peculiarities, for it is a less offensive word—of the other sex. For there is a spot the size of a shilling at the back of the head which one can never see for oneself. It is one of the good offices that sex can discharge for sex—to describe that spot the size of a shilling at the back of the head. Think how much women have profited by the comments of Juvenal; by the criticism of Strindberg. Think with what humanity and brilliancy men, from the earliest ages, have pointed out to women that dark place at the back of the head! And if Mary were very brave and very honest, she would go behind the other sex and tell us what she found there. A true picture of man as a whole can never be painted until a woman has described that spot the size of a shilling. Mr. Woodhouse and Mr. Casaubon are spots of that size and nature. Not of course that any one in their senses would counsel her to hold up to scorn and ridicule of set purpose—literature shows the futility of what is written in that spirit. Be truthful, one would say, and the result is bound to be amazingly interesting. Comedy is bound to be enriched. New facts are bound to be discovered.

•

FROM *The Voyage Out*

William Pepper . . . he knew about a great many things—about mathematics, history, Greek, zoology, economics, and the Icelandic Sagas. He had turned Persian poetry into English prose, and English prose into Greek iambics; he was an authority upon coins, and—one other thing —oh yes, she thought it was vehicular traffic.

•

She had begun her meditations with a shout of laughter, caused by the following translation from *Tristan*:

> In shrinking trepidation
> His shame he seems to hide
> While to the king his relation
> He brings the corpse-like Bride.
> Seems it so senseless what I say?

She cried that it did, and threw down the book.

•

Her mind was in the state of an intelligent man's in the beginning of the reign of Queen Elizabeth.

•

She knew that scholars married any one—girls they met in farms on reading parties; or little suburban women who said disagreeably, "Of course I know it's my husband you want; not *me.*"

•

"Jane Austen? I don't like Jane Austen," said Rachel.

"You monster!" Clarissa exclaimed. "I can only just forgive you. Tell me why?"

"She's so—so—well, like a tight plait," Rachel floundered.

•

She thought that there must be something wrong in this confusion between politics and kissing politicians, and that an elder person ought to be able to help.

•

"Seeing life" was the phrase they used for their habit of strolling through the town after dark.

•

Hirst . . . observed, "Oh, but we're all agreed by this time that nature's a mistake. She's either very ugly, appallingly uncomfortable, or absolutely terrifying. I don't know which alarms me most—a cow or a tree. I once

met a cow in a field by night. The creature looked at me. I assure you
it turned my hair grey. It's a disgrace that the animals should be allowed
to go at large."

•

"This is the dance for people who don't know how to dance!" she cried.
The tune changed to a minuet; St. John hopped with incredible swiftness
first on his left leg, then on his right; the tune flowed melodiously;
Hewet, swaying his arms and holding out the tails of his coat, swam
down the room in imitation of the voluptuous dreamy dance of an
Indian maiden dancing before her Rajah. The tune marched; and Miss
Allan advanced with skirts extended and bowed profoundly to the engaged pair. Once their feet fell in with the rhythm they showed a complete lack of self-consciousness. From Mozart Rachel passed without
stopping to old English hunting songs, carols, and hymn tunes, for, as
she had observed, any good tune, with a little management, became a
tune one could dance to. By degrees every person in the room was
tripping and turning in pairs or alone. Mr. Pepper executed an ingenious
pointed step derived from figure-skating, for which he once held some
local championship; while Mrs. Thornbury tried to recall an old country
dance which she had seen danced by her father's tenants in Dorsetshire
in the old days. As for Mr. and Mrs. Elliot, they gallopaded round and
round the room with such impetuosity that the other dancers shivered
at their approach. Some people were heard to criticize the performance
as a romp; to others it was the most enjoyable part of the evening.

"Now for the great round dance!" Hewet shouted. Instantly a gi-
gantic circle was formed, the dancers holding hands and shouting out,
"D'you ken John Peel," as they swung faster and faster and faster, until
the strain was too great, and one link of the chain—Mrs. Thornbury—
gave way, and the rest went flying across the room in all directions, to
land upon the floor or the chairs or in each other's arms as seemed most
convenient.

•

To come to a decision was very difficult to her, because she had a natural
dislike of anything final and done with; she liked to go on and on—
always on and on.

•

FROM *Orlando*

With some of the guineas left from the sale of the tenth pearl of her
string, Orlando had bought herself a complete outfit of such clothes as

women then wore, and it was in the dress of a young Englishwoman of rank that she now sat on the deck of the *Enamoured Lady*. It is a strange fact, but a true one that up to this moment she had scarcely given her sex a thought. Perhaps the Turkish trousers, which she had hitherto worn had done something to distract her thoughts; and the gipsy women, except in one or two important particulars, differ very little from the gipsy men. At any rate, it was not until she felt the coil of skirts about her legs and the Captain offered, with the greatest politeness, to have an awning spread for her on deck that she realized, with a start the penalties and the privileges of her position. But that start was not of the kind that might have been expected.

It was not caused, that is to say, simply and solely by the thought of her chastity and how she could preserve it. In normal circumstances a lovely young woman alone would have thought of nothing else; the whole edifice of female government is based on that foundation stone; chastity is their jewel, their center piece, which they run mad to protect, and die when ravished of. But if one has been a man for thirty years or so, and an Ambassador into the bargain, if one has held a Queen in one's arms and one or two other ladies, if report be true, of less exalted rank, if one has married a Rosina Pepita, and so on, one does not perhaps give such a very great start about that. Orlando's start was of a very complicated kind, and not to be summed up in a trice. Nobody, indeed, ever accused her of being one of those quick wits, who run to the end of things in a minute. It took her the entire length of the voyage to moralize out the meaning of her start, and so, at her own pace, we will follow her.

"Lord," she thought, when she had recovered from her start, stretching herself out at length under her awning, "this is a pleasant, lazy way of life, to be sure. But," she thought, giving her legs a kick, "these skirts are plaguey things to have about one's heels. Yet the stuff (flowered paduasoy) is the loveliest in the world. Never have I seen my own skin (here she laid her hand on her knee) look to such advantage as now. Could I, however, leap overboard and swim in clothes like these? No! Therefore, I should have to trust to the protection of a blue-jacket. Do I object to that? Now do I?" she wondered, her encountering the first knot in the smooth skein of her argument.

Dinner came before she had untied it, and then it was the Captain himself—Captain Nicholas Benedict Bartolus, a sea-captain of distinguished aspect, who did it for her as he helped her to a slice of corned beef.

"A little of the fat, Ma'am?" he asked. "Let me cut you just the tiniest little slice the size of your finger nail." At those words, a delicious tremor ran through her frame. Birds sang; the torrents rushed. It recalled the feeling of indescribable pleasure with which she had first seen Sasha, hundreds of years ago. Then she had pursued, now she fled. Which is the greater ecstasy? The man's or the woman's? And are they not perhaps the same? No, she thought, this is the most delicious (thanking the Captain but refusing) to refuse, and see him frown. Well, she would, if he wished it, have the very thinnest, smallest shiver in the world. This was the most delicious, to yield and see him smile. "For nothing," she thought, regaining her couch on deck, and continuing the argument, "is more heavenly than to resist and to yield; to yield and to resist. Surely it throws the spirit into such a rapture that nothing else can. So that I'm not sure," she continued, "that I won't throw myself overboard, for the mere pleasure of being rescued by a blue-jacket after all."

(It must be remembered that she was like a child, entering into possession of a pleasaunce or toycupboard; her arguments would not commend themselves to mature women, who have had the run of it all their lives.)

"But what used we young fellows in the cockpit of the *Marie Rose* to say about a woman who threw herself overboard for the pleasure of being rescued by a blue-jacket?" she said. "We had a word for them. Ah! I have it. . . ." (But we must omit the word; it was disrespectful in the extreme and passing strange on a lady's lips.) "Lord! Lord!" she cried again at the conclusion of her thoughts, "must I then begin to respect the opinion of the other sex, however monstrous I think it? If I wear skirts, if I can swim, if I have to be rescued by a blue-jacket, by God!" she cried, "I must!" Upon which, a gloom fell over her. Candid by nature, and averse to all kinds of equivocation, to tell lies bored her. It seemed to her a roundabout way of going to work. Yet, she reflected, the flowered paduasoy—the pleasure of being rescued by a blue-jacket —if these were only to be obtained by roundabout ways, roundabout one must go, she supposed. She remembered how, as a young man, she had insisted that women must be obedient, chaste, scented, and exquisitely apparelled. "Now I shall have to pay in my own person for those desires," she reflected; "for women are not (judging by my own short experience of the sex) obedient, chaste, scented, and exquisitely apparelled by nature. They can only attain these graces, without which they may enjoy none of the delights of life, by the most tedious discipline. There's the hairdressing," she thought, "that alone will take an hour of my morning; there's looking in the looking-glass, another hour; there's staying and lacing; there's washing and powdering; there's changing from silk to lace and from lace to paduasoy; and there's being chaste year in year out. . . ." Here she tossed her foot impatiently, and showed an inch or two of calf. A sailor on the mast, who happened to look down at the moment, started so violently that he missed his footing and only saved himself by the skin of his teeth. "If the sight of my ankles means death to an honest fellow who, no doubt, has a wife and family to support, I must, in all humanity, keep them covered," Orlando thought. Yet her legs were among her chiefest beauties. And she fell to thinking what an odd pass we have come to when all a woman's beauty has to be kept covered, lest a sailor may fall from a mast-head. "A pox on them!" she said, realizing for the first time, what, in other circumstances, she would have been taught as a child, that is to say, the sacred responsibilities of womanhood.

"And that's the last oath I shall ever be able to swear," she thought; "once I set foot on English soil. And I shall never be able to crack a man over the head, or tell him he lies in his teeth, or draw my sword and run him through the body, or sit among my peers, or wear a coronet, or walk in procession, or sentence a man to death, or lead an army, or prance down Whitehall on a charger, or wear seventy-two different medals on my breast. All I can do, once I set foot on English soil, is to pour out tea, and ask my lords how they like it. D'you take sugar? D'you take cream?" And mincing out the words, she was horrified to perceive how low an opinion she was forming of the other sex, the manly, to which it had once been her pride to belong. "To fall from a mast-head," she thought, "because you see a woman's ankles; to dress up like a Guy Fawkes and parade the streets, so that women may praise you; to deny a woman teaching lest she may laugh at you; to be the slave of the frailest chit in petticoats, and yet to go about as if you were the Lords of creation.—Heavens!" she thought, "what fools they make of us— what fools we are!"

•

FROM *Three Guineas*

It would seem to follow then as an indisputable fact that "we"—meaning by "we" a whole made up of body, brain and spirit, influenced by memory and tradition—must still differ in some essential respects from "you," whose body, brain and spirit have been so differently trained and are so differently influenced by memory and tradition. Though we see the same world, we see it through different eyes.

•

. . . Shall I ask them to rebuild the college on the old lines? Or shall I ask them to rebuild it, but differently? Or shall I ask them to buy rags and petrol and Bryant & May's matches and burn the college to the ground?

.

. . . It must be built not of carved stone and stained glass, but of some cheap, easily combustible material which does not hoard dust and per-petrate traditions. Do not have chapels. Do not have museums and li-braries with chained books and first editions under glass cases. Let the pictures and the books be new and always changing. Let it be decorated afresh by each generation with their own hands cheaply. The work of the living is cheap; often they will give it for the sake of being allowed to do it.

.

. . . Therefore the guinea should be earmarked "Rags. Petrol. Matches." And this note should be attached to it. "Take this guinea and with it burn the college to the ground. Set fire the old hypocrisies. Let the light of the burning building scare the nightingales and incarnadine the wil-lows. And let the daughters of educated men dance round the fire and heap armful upon armful of dead leaves upon the flames. And let their mothers lean from the upper windows and cry, 'Let it blaze! Let it blaze! For we have done with this "education"!' "

.

. . . Therefore this guinea, which is to help you to help women to enter the professions, has this condition as a first condition attached to it. You shall swear that you will do all in your power to insist that any woman who enters any profession shall in no way hinder any other human being, whether man or woman, white or black, provided that he or she is qualified to enter that profession, from entering it; but shall do all in her power to help them."

.

. . . Take this guinea then and use it, not to burn the house down, but to make its windows blaze. And let the daughters of uneducated women dance round the new house, the poor house, the house that stands in a narrow street where omnibuses pass and the street hawkers cry their wares, and let them sing, 'We have done with war! We have done with tyranny.' And their mothers will laugh from their graves, 'It was for this that we suffered obloquy and contempt! Light up the windows of the new house, daughters! Let them blaze!'

.

But that chastity, whether real or imposed, was an immense power, whether good or bad, it is impossible to doubt. Even today it is probable that a woman has to fight a psychological battle of some severity with the ghost of St. Paul, before she can have intercourse with a man other than her husband.

•

Even at a time of great political stress like the present it is remarkable how much criticism is still bestowed upon women. The announcement, "A shrewd, witty and provocative study of modern woman," appears on an average three times yearly in publishers' lists. The author, often a doctor of letters, is invariably of the male sex; and "to mere man," as the blurb puts it (see *Times Lit. Sup.*, March 12th, 1938), "this book will be an eye-opener." Presumably the need for a scapegoat is largely responsible, and the role is traditionally a woman's. (See Genesis.)

•

FROM *The Mark on the Wall*

There was a crash. A slate had fallen down the chimney. The great log had snapped in two. Flakes of plaster fell from the shield above the fireplace.

"Falling," old Miss Rashleigh chuckled. "Falling."

"And who," said Miss Antonia, looking at the flakes on the carpet, "who's to pay?"

Crowing like old babies, indifferent, reckless, they laughed; crossed to the fireplace, and sipped the sherry by the wood ashes and the plaster, until each glass held only one drop of wine, reddish purple, at the bottom. And this the old women did not wish to part with, so it seemed; for they fingered their glasses, as they sat side by side by the ashes; but they never raised them to their lips.

•

FROM *Night and Day*

. . . Mrs. Hilbery would have been perfectly well able to sustain herself if the world had been what the world is not. She was beautifully adapted for life in another planet. But the natural genius she had for conducting affairs there was of no real use to her here. Her watch, for example, was a constant source of surprise to her, and at the age of sixty-five she was still amazed at the ascendancy which rules and reasons exerted over the lives of other people. She had never learnt her lesson, and had constantly to be punished for her ignorance. But as that ignorance was combined with a fine natural insight which saw deep whenever it saw at all, it was not possible to write Mrs. Hilbery off among the dunces; on the contrary, she had a way of seeming the wisest person in the room. But, on the whole, she found it very necessary to seek support in her daughter.

Katharine, thus, was a member of a very great profession which has, as yet, no title and very little recognition, although the labor of mill and factory is, perhaps, no more severe and the results of less benefit to the world. She lived at home. She did it very well, too. Any one coming to the house in Cheyne Walk felt that here was an orderly place, shapely, controlled—a place where life had been trained to show to the best advantage—and, though composed of different elements, made to appear harmonious and with a character of its own. Perhaps it was the chief triumph of Katharine's art that Mrs. Hilbery's character predominated. She and Mr. Hilbery appeared to be a rich background for her mother's more striking qualities.

Silence being, thus, both natural to her and imposed upon her, the only other remark that her mother's friends were in the habit of making about it was that it was neither a stupid silence nor an indifferent silence. But to what quality it owed its character, since character of some sort it had, no one troubled themselves to inquire. It was understood that she was helping her mother to produce a great book. She was known to manage the household. She was certainly beautiful. That accounted for her satisfactorily. But it would have been a surprise, not only to other people but to Katharine herself, if some magic watch could have taken count of the moments spent in an entirely different occupation for her ostensible one. Sitting with faded papers before her, she took part in a series of scenes such as the taming of wild ponies upon the American prairies, or the conduct of a vast ship in a hurricane round a black promontory of rock, or in others more peaceful, but marked by her complete emancipation from her present surroundings and, needless to say, by her surpassing ability in her new vocation. When she was rid of the pretense of paper and pen, phrase-making and biography, she turned her attention in a more legitimate direction, though, strangely enough, she would rather have confessed her wildest dreams of hurricane and prairie than the fact that, upstairs, alone in her room, she rose early in the morning or sat up late at night to . . . work at mathematics. No force on earth would have made her confess that. Her actions when thus engaged were furtive and secretive, like those of some nocturnal animal. Steps had only to sound on the staircase, and she slipped her paper between the leaves of a great Greek dictionary which she had purloined from her father's room for this purpose. It was only at night, indeed, that she felt secure enough from surprise to concentrate her mind to the utmost.

Perhaps the unwomanly nature of the science made her instinctively wish to conceal her love of it. But the more profound reason was that in her mind mathematics were directly opposed to literature. She would not have cared to confess how infinitely she preferred the exactitude, the star-like impersonality, of figures to the confusion, agitation, and vagueness of the finest prose. There was something a little unseemly in thus opposing the tradition of her family; something that made her feel wrong-headed, and thus more than ever disposed to shut her desires away from view and cherish them with extraordinary fondness. Again and again she was thinking of some problem when she should have been thinking of her grandfather. Waking from these trances, she would see that her mother, too, had lapsed into some dream almost as visionary as her own, for the people who played their parts in it had long been numbered among the dead. But, seeing her own state mirrored in her mother's face, Katharine would shake herself awake with a sense of irritation. Her mother was the last person she wished to resemble, much though she admired her. Her common sense would assert itself almost brutally, and Mrs. Hilbery, looking at her with her odd sidelong glance, that was half malicious and half tender, would liken her to "your wicked old Uncle Judge Peter, who used to be heard delivering sentence of death in the bathroom. Thank Heaven, Katharine, I've not a drop of *him* in me!"

"It's very dull that you can only marry one husband, certainly," Mrs. Hilbery reflected. "I always wish that you could marry everybody who wants to marry you. Perhaps they'll come to that in time, but meanwhile I confess that dear William——" But here Mr. Hilbery came in, and the more solid part of the evening began. This consisted in the reading aloud by Katharine from some prose work or other, while her mother knitted scarves intermittently on a little circular frame, and her father read the newspaper, not so attentively but that he could comment humorously now and again upon the fortunes of the hero and the heroine. The Hilberys subscribed to a library, which delivered books on Tuesdays and Fridays, and Katharine did her best to interest her parents in the works of living and highly respectable authors; but Mrs. Hilbery was perturbed by the very look of the light, gold-wreathed volumes, and would make little faces as if she tasted something bitter as the reading went on; while Mr. Hilbery would treat the moderns with a curious elaborate banter such as one might apply to the antics of a promising child. So this evening, after five pages or so of one of these masters,

Mrs. Hilbery protested that it was all too clever and cheap and nasty for words.

"Please, Katharine, read us something *real*."

•

. . . She liked getting hold of some book which neither her father or mother had read, and keeping it to herself, and gnawing its contents in privacy, and pondering the meaning without sharing her thoughts with any one, or having to decide whether the book was a good one or a bad one. This evening she had twisted the words of Dostoevsky to suit her mood—a fatalistic mood—to proclaim that the process of discovery was life, and that, presumably, the nature of one's goal mattered not at all.

•

. . . [She listened] chiefly with a view to confirming herself in the belief that to be engaged to marry some one with whom you are not in love is an inevitable step in a world where the existence of passion is only a traveller's story brought from the heart of deep forests and told so rarely that wise people doubt whether the story can be true.

•

. . . she had come half to believe in her joke, which was, she said, at least as good as other people's facts.

•

The sight, unfortunately, was so comically apt in its illustration of the picture in her mind, the ruse was so transparent, that Katharine was seized with laughter. She laughed uncontrollably. William flushed red. No display of anger could have hurt his feelings more profoundly. It was not only that she was laughing at him; the detachment of the sound was horrible.

Hannah Woolley (1623–1675)

On Female Education

The right Education of the Female Sex, as it is in a manner everywhere neglected, so it ought to be generally lamented. Most in this depraved later Age think a Woman learned and wise enough if she can distinguish her Husbands Bed from anothers.

Author Biographies

Mary Alcock (1742–98), English poet whose work *The Confined Debtor: A Fragment from a Prison* resulted in the release of numerous debtors from Ilchester and Newgate. *The Air-Balloon* was published in 1784. *Poems*, published posthumously in 1799, was edited and contained a short memoir by her niece, Joanna Hughes, one of the many nieces of an orphan family for whom Alcock provided.

Louisa May Alcott (1832–88), American novelist known primarily as a children's writer and the author of *Little Women* (1868), *Little Men* (1871), and *Jo's Boys* (1886). Alcott also wrote numerous adult novels, including *Work* (1873) and *Transcendental Wild Oats* (1872), and sensational stories, many published pseudonymously under the name A. M. Barnard. Alcott's ambidexterity, a skill she developed in her later years to allow her to keep up with the demands of her readers and publishers, is an ironic reflection of the two distinctive genres she worked in.

Maria Allen (c. 1750–?), friend and correspondent of Frances Burney.

Lisa Alther (1944–), American novelist whose work includes *Original Sins* (1981), *Other Women* (1985), *Bedrock* (1991), and *Five Minutes in Heaven* (1995). On *Kinflicks* (1975), Alther's first novel, Doris Lessing remarks: "a strong, salty, original talent . . . she had me laughing at four in the morning. . . . It made me wonder what *Tom Jones* would be like written now."

Margaret Atwood (1939–), Canadian poet, novelist, children's and nonfiction writer. Her poetry includes *Double Persephone* (1961), *Procedures for Underground* (1970), and *Morning in the Burned House* (1995); novels include *The Edible Woman* (1969), *Surfacing* (1972), *Lady Oracle* (1979), and *The Handmaid's Tale* (1985). She has also published literary criticism and short fiction. As she herself quotes from Jessamyn West, in an epitaph to *Robber Bride* (1993), "A rattlesnake that doesn't bite teaches you nothing."

Jane Austen (1775–1817), English novelist who published four novels during her lifetime: *Sense and Sensibility* (1811), *Pride and Prejudice* (1813), *Mansfield Park* (1814), and *Emma* (1816). Two more novels, *Northanger Abbey* and *Persuasion*, were published posthumously in 1818. *Lady Susan, Sanditon,* and *The Watsons* were published in 1923, 1925, and 1927 respectively.

Sheila Ballantyne, contemporary American novelist, short-fiction writer, and professor at Mills College. Her work includes *Norma Jean the Termite Queen* (1975) and *Life on Earth: Stories* (1988). In *Imaginary Crimes* (1982), Ballantyne's main character remarks that she "had been in labor fifteen hours when Alex pulled the cold pastrami sandwich from his pocket and sat down on the vacant bed in the now empty labor room and began to eat in front of me. I should have considered how long he had held off, but didn't."

Tallulah Bankhead (1902–68), American actress who starred in *The Little Foxes* (1939) and *Skin of Our Teeth* (1943). Her autobiography, *Tallulah*, was published in 1952.

Mary Barber (1690–1757). In the same year that her *Poems on Several Occasions* (1734, in quarto), was published, Barber was arrested for smuggling the manuscripts of Jonathan Swift (one of her strongest supporters). Other publications include *The Widows Address* (Dublin, 1725), *A Tale, Being an Addition to Mr. Gay's Fables* (1728), and additional copies of *Poems on Several Occasions* (1735, in octavo; reissued in 1736). The 1755 edition of *Poems by Eminent Ladies* contained a sizable number of her poems.

Djuna Barnes (1892–1982), American-born playwright, novelist, short-fiction writer, and illustrator. Her work includes *A Book* (1923), *Ryder* (1928), and *Nightwood* (1936), the novel for which she is best remembered; it is located in Paris and New York City, and evokes a nightmare, neo-gothic world.

Lynda Barry (1956–   ), American cartoonist and novelist whose work includes *The Good Times Are Killing Me* (1988), *Down the Street* (1988), *Come Over, Come Over* (1990), and *Girls and Boys* (1993). Barry's comics appear in *The Village Voice, Esquire,* and more than 40 national newsweeklies. She describes country music as "music that is played so precisely and quickly it's like hitting the gas and the brakes at the same time but in a gorgeous way."

Anne Beatts (1947–   ), American humorist, editor, and comedy writer who won two Emmy Awards, in 1976 and 1977, for her work on the TV show *Saturday Night Live*. She created and produced the TV comedy series *Square Pegs* (1982–83). She was the editor of *National Lampoon*, 1970–74, and co-editor (with Deanne Stillman and Judith Jacklin) of *Titters: The First Collection of Humor by Women* (1976), *The Mom Book* (1983), and *Titters 101* (1984).

Joy Behar, contemporary American comedian, actress, and radio personality. She describes her voice (which the *New York Times* once called "a decent paint remover") as "distinctive yet annoying."

Aphra Behn (1649–89), prolific English playwright, poet, novelist, and translator. Her plays include *The Forc'd Marriage* (1671), *The Dutch Lover* (1673), *The Rover* (1677), *Sir Patient* (1678), *The Feign'd Curtizans* (1679), *The Roundheads* (1682), *The Lucky Chance*, and *The History of the Nun* (1689). Her novels include *Oroonoko* (1678), *Love-Letters between a Nobleman and His Sister* (1684–87), and *The Fair Jilt* (1688).

Jennifer Berman, contemporary Chicago-based cartoonist whose work appears in over fifty publications. Berman has a nationally distributed line of postcards, Humerus Cartoons, where many of her cartoons first appear. Her books include *Why Dogs Are Better than Men* and *Adult Children of Normal Parents* (1994).

Shirley Temple Black (1928–), American child actress, politician, and U.S. ambassador, who observes in *Child Star: An Autobiography* (1988) that "anyone three feet tall has a problem with people six feet tall. In a group of standing adults, my vision necessarily centered on belt buckles, tie clasps, and handbags. Of course a lot can be learned from this angle."

Naomi Bliven (1925–), American writer, editor, and critic whose book reviews have appeared in *The New Yorker* since 1958. She has worked as an editor for *The New Republic* and Random House, and has written for the *New York Times* as well as many other publications.

Erma Bombeck (1927–), American syndicated columnist, humorist, and political activist whose work includes *At Wit's End* (1965), *The Grass Is Always Greener Over the Septic Tank* (1976), and *Motherhood: The Second Oldest Profession* (1984). She campaigned for the Equal Rights Amendment, served on the President's Advisory Committee for Women, and has been awarded honorary degrees from numerous universities and colleges.

Elayne Boosler (1953–), American stand-up comedian and author who, it is observed in *Current Biography*, "is noted for her easy manner and lack of self-deprecation."

Elizabeth Bowen (1899–1973), Anglo-Irish novelist and critic whose phraseology in describing Jane Austen's novels as "life with the lid on" has been used by critics to praise her own descriptive work. Her novels include *The Hotel* (1928), *The Last September* (1929), *To the North* (1933), *The House in Paris* (1936), *The Death of the Heart* (1939), *The Heat of the Day* (1949), *A World of Love* (1955), and *Eva Trout* (1969). Her *Collected Stories* was published in 1980.

Blanche McCrary Boyd (1945–   ), American author of *The Revolution of Little Girls* and *The Redneck Way of Knowledge*, teaches writing at Connecticut College.

Julia A. Boyd, contemporary African-American psychotherapist. Her work includes *In the Company of My Sisters: Black Women and Self-Esteem* (1993), which looks at the necessity for both individual and collective healing for black women's self-images.

Peg Bracken (1918–   ), American humorist whose work includes *The I Hate to Cook Book* (1960), *I Didn't Come Here to Argue* (1970), *But I Wouldn't Have Missed It for the World* (1970), and *A Window Over the Sink* (1981). Bracken's work subverts that aspect of American culture which still demands women be bound to their homes and housework as if to their highest calling.

Anne Bradstreet (c. 1612–72), English-born American poet. A collection of her work, *The Tenth Muse Lately Sprung Up in America* was published, without her knowledge, in London in 1650. To add insult to injury, the preface, written by her brother-in-law, reassured the reader that though he might doubt that a member of "the inferior sex" could actually have written the poems, they were indeed penned by a woman. In 1678, after her death, a second edition, with her own additions and corrections, was published in Boston.

Clare Bretecher, contemporary French cartoonist.

Anne Brontë (1820–49), English novelist. Her work includes *Agnes Grey* (1847) and *The Tenant of Wildfell Hall* (1848), both originally published under the pseudonym Acton Bell. *Wildfell Hall* has been described as the first sustained feminist novel. Like her sisters, Emily and Charlotte, Anne also wrote a great deal of poetry and, with Emily, invented Gondal, an imaginary world in which much of their poetry is set.

Charlotte Brontë (1816–55), English novelist once described in a letter by Matthew Arnold as one whose mind contained "hunger, rebellion and rage." Her work (all of it published under the pseudonym Currer Bell) includes *Jane Eyre* (1847), *Shirley* (1849), *Villette* (1853), and *The Professor* (1857), as well as a great deal of poetry and juvenilia.

Emily Brontë (1818–48), a prolific poet first published in *Poems* (1846), a small volume containing her work and that of her sisters, Anne and

Charlotte, under their pseudonyms Acton, Ellis, and Currer Bell. Her one novel, *Wuthering Heights* (1847), virtually ignored during her lifetime, has since been recognized as one of the great books of English literature.

Gwendolyn Brooks (1917–   ), African-American poet, novelist, children's writer, nonfiction writer, autobiographer, and political activist. She was the 1950 recipient of the Pulitzer Prize for poetry for *Annie Allen*. Her books include *Maud Martha* (1953), *The Bean Eaters* (1960), *In the Mecca* (1968), and *Blacks* (1987), a collected volume of her works. The twenty-ninth Consultant in Poetry to the Library of Congress, Brooks has declared that her goals in life are "to be clean of heart, clear of mind, and claiming of what is right and just."

Helen Gurley Brown (1922–   ), American writer and thirty-year editor of *Cosmopolitan*, whose work includes *Sex and the Single Girl* (1962), *Having It All!: Love, Success, Sex, Money, Even If You're Starting with Nothing* (1982), and *The Late Show: A Semiwild but Practical Survival Plan for Women over 50* (1993).

Rita Mae Brown (1944–   ), American poet and novelist. Her fiction includes *Songs to a Handsome Woman* (1973), *Southern Discomfort* (1982), *Sudden Death* (1983), and *Dolley: A Novel of Dolley Madison in Love and War* (1994). Her first novel, *Rubyfruit Jungle* (1973), a "classic American success story" with a lesbian heroine, was initially rejected by mainstream publishers for fear of its limited appeal. After proving its appeal was not quite so limited by selling well when published by a small press, it was picked up by a mainstream publisher and finally sold more than a million copies.

Elizabeth Barrett Browning (1806–61), English poet and translator who felt that poets were "the only truth-tellers still left to God" and that "they must speak against tyranny, against unjust wars, against the exploitation of women and children, against want and slavery, against complacency and ignorance." Her work includes *The Battle of Marathon* (1820), *An Essay on Mind* (1826), *The Seraphim and Other Poems* (1838), *Poems* (1844), *Casa Guidi Windows* (1851), *Aurora Leigh* (1857), *Poems Before Congress* (1860), and *Last Poems* (1862).

Frances (Fanny) Burney (1752–1840), English comic novelist, diarist, editor, and second keeper of the robes to Queen Charlotte (1786). She is most famous for her first novel, *Evelina* (1778), which deftly juxtaposes hilarious comedy with moral gravity. Other works include *Cecilia* (1782), *Camilla* (1796), and *The Wanderer* (1814).

Brett Butler, contemporary American writer, comedian, and star of the television series, *Grace Under Fire*.

Liz Carpenter (1920–   ), American journalist and biographer whose work includes *Ruffles and Flourishes: The Warm and Tender Story of a Simple Girl Who Found Adventure in the White House* (1970) and *Getting Better All the Time* (1987).

Rosario Castellanos (1925–74), Mexican poet, playwright, essayist, and short-fiction writer. Her work includes *The Nine Guardians* (1959), *Convidados de Agusto* (1977), *Album de Familia, Another Way to Be* (1990), and *City of Kings* (1993), originally published in Spanish as *Ciudad Real* (1960). She was part of the "Generation of 1950," and one of Mexico's leading feminist writers. Her work has been collected in *A Rosario Castellanos Reader* (1986).

Charlotte Charke (1713–c. 1760), English playwright, autobiographer, actress, sausage maker, publican, grocer, and more. She was a talented (though unlucky) and versatile woman who would, and could, turn her hand to nearly anything to support herself and her daughter. Her work includes *The Art of Management; or, Tragedy Expell'd* (1735), *The Mercer; or, Fatal Extravagance* (1756), *The History of Henry Dumont, Esq.; and Miss Charlotte Evelyn* (1755), and *A Narrative of the Life of Mrs. Charlotte Charke* (1755).

Ilka Chase (1903–1978), American writer and actress.

Roz Chast (1954–   ), American cartoonist whose collected work includes *The Four Elements* (1984), *Parallel Universes* (1984), and *Proof of Life on Earth*. Her work often appears in *The New Yorker* and *Mother Jones*. She collaborated with authors Jane Read Martin and Patricia Marx to produce *Now Everybody Really Hates Me* (1994), a highly acclaimed children's book.

Margaret Cho, contemporary American stand-up comic who often discusses being Asian-American.

Lady Mary Chudleigh (1656–1710), English essayist and poet. Her publications include *The Ladies Defence* (1701), published in response to a sermon advocating the virtual slavery of women to their husbands, *Poems on Several Occasions* (1703), and *Essays upon Several Subjects* (1710).

Caryl Churchill (1938–   ), English-born playwright, radio and television writer. Her work includes *Owners* (1972), *Light Shining in Buckinghamshire* (1977), *Cloud Nine* (1979), *Softcops* (1984) and *Top Girls* (1988).

Ina Claire (1895–1985), American actress.

Ellen Cleghorn, contemporary American writer and comedian who has been a cast member of *Saturday Night Live* for several years.

(Thelma) Lucille Clifton (1936–   ), African-American poet and prose and children's writer who, when she "began to find her own voice" at

Freedonia State Teachers College in 1955, realized "what I was writing was not like the poems I'd been reading." Her collections include *Good Times* (1969), *Don't You Remember* (1973), *An Ordinary Woman* (1974), *Two-Headed Woman* (1980), *Next* (1987), *Generations: A Memoir* (1976), and *Good Woman: Poems and a Memoir 1969–1980* (1987). She was awarded the Juniper Prize in 1980.

Kate Clinton, contemporary feminist activist, lesbian comic, and author whose groundbreaking work on women's humor, written since the 1970s, continues to influence scholars and critics.

Jane Collier (1710–55), English essayist and novelist. Her work includes *Essay on the Art of Ingeniously Tormenting* (1753), published anonymously, and *The Cry* (1754), an allegorical tale written with Sarah Fielding.

Patricia Collinge (1894–?), Irish actress and short-fiction writer. Her work includes *The B.O.W.S.* (1945) and *Small Mosaics of Mr. and Mrs. Engel* (1959).

Julie Connelly, contemporary American financial expert and senior editor of *Fortune*, as well as veteran writer for *Time, Money*, and *Institutional Investor*.

Lucha Corpi (1945–   ), Chicana novelist. Her work includes *Delia's Song* (1989), *Eulogy for a Brown Angel: A Mystery Novel* (1992), and a book of poetry, *Variations on a Storm* (1990).

Elena Tajena Creef, contemporary Japanese-American writer whose interests include Russian Blue cats, Asian-American women's history, and unpopular culture.

Amanda Cross (Carolyn G. Heilbrun) (1926–   ), American mystery writer whose work includes *No Word from Winifred* (1986), *A Trap for Fools* (1989), and *The Players Come Again* (1990). She was the winner of the 1981 Nero Wolfe Award for mystery fiction for *Death in a Tenured Position*.

Ellen Currie, contemporary American novelist and short-fiction writer whose work has appeared in *The New Yorker* and in O. Henry collections and numerous other anthologies. Her books include *Available Light* (1986) and *Moses Supposes* (1994).

Mary Daly (1928–   ), American feminist theorist and theologian whose work includes *Gyn/Ecology: The Metaethics of Radical Feminism* (1978), *Pure Lust* (1984), and *Websters' First New Intergalactic Wickedary of the English Language* (1987). Her definition of phallosophy: "inflated foolosophy: 'wisdom' loaded with seminal ideas and disseminated by means of thrusting arguments." Daly teaches at Boston College.

Josephine Daskam (1876–1961), American author of short stories, novels, articles, and poems. She also compiled the *Girl Scout National*

Handbook (1920). Work includes *Smith College Stories* (1900), *Kathy* (1934), and *Domestic Adventures* (1907).

Emily Dickinson (1830–86), American poet who wrote nearly two thousand poems, though only seven were published during her lifetime. She has been credited as the inventor of modern American poetry. Critic Suzanne Juhasz describes her work as that which "on closer reading . . . become[s] more, not less, complicated; but in that complexity lies the richness of Dickinson. A Dickinson poem cannot be skimmed: it must be entered, and the reader must be prepared for an extended visit." One of the most satisfactory collections of her work is *The Complete Poems of Emily Dickinson* (1955), edited by Thomas H. Johnson.

Annie Dillard (1945–), American poet, prose writer, and novelist whose work includes *Pilgrim at Tinker Creek* (1974), *Tickets for a Prayer Wheel* (1974), *Living by Fiction* (1982), *The Writing Life* (1989), and *The Living* (1978). In *Teaching a Stone to Talk* (1982), Dillard notes that "the island where I live is peopled with cranks like myself."

Phyllis Diller (1917–), American comedian and writer. Her work includes *Housekeeping Hints* (1966), *Phyllis Diller's Marriage Manual* (1967), and *The Joys of Aging—and how to avoid them* (1981).

Sarah Dixon (1672–1765), English poet. Her publications include the originally anonymous *Poems on Several Occasions* (Canterbury, 1740). Additional poems transcribed on pages at the back of the British Library copy once owned by her niece, Mrs. Eliza Bunce, include "The Expedition to Swinfield Minnis" (1745), and, pasted on a flyleaf, "The Ruins of St. Austin's, Canterbury" (1774).

Margaret Drabble (1939–), English novelist, playwright, critic, and biographer whose work includes *The Waterfall* (1969), *The Middleground* (1980), and *A Natural Curiosity* (1989).

Lady Dorothea Dubois (1728–74), poet and novelist. Her publications include *Poems on Several Occasions* (Dublin, 1764), *The Case of Ann Countess of Anglesey . . . and of Her Three Surviving Daughters* (1766), *Theodora*, a novel published in 1770, *The Divorce* (1771), and *The Lady's Polite Secretary, Or, New Female Letter Writer* (1771).

Maria Edgeworth (1767–1849), Anglo-Irish essayist, novelist, and children's writer. Her nonfiction includes *Letters to Literary Ladies* (1795) and *Practical Education* (1798), which she co-authored with her father. Her fiction includes *Castle Rackrent* (1800), *Leonora* (1806), *The Absentee* (1812), *Patronage* (1814), *Ormand* (1817), and *Helen* (1834). *Belinda* (1801) was praised in *Northanger Abbey* by Jane Austen, who sent Edgeworth a copy of *Emma* in 1816.

Sarah Egerton (1670–1723), English poet who wrote *The Female Ad-*

vocate (1686), an answer to a misogynist satire, at the age of fourteen. Her *Poems on Several Occasions* (1703) appeared the same year she was embroiled in a divorce suit (which never came through). As a result of public scandal, she was the object of several poetic satires. Egerton continued to write poetry throughout her life, including a piece on Dryden's death, *Luctus Britannici; or the Tears of the British Muses* (1700).

George Eliot (Mary Ann Evans) (1819–80), English novelist, poet, and essayist. Her work includes *Adam Bede* (1859), *The Mill on the Floss* (1860), *Silas Marner* (1861), *Romola* (1863), *Felix Holt, the Radical* (1866), *The Spanish Gypsy* (1868), *Middlemarch* (1871–72), *Daniel Deronda* (1876), and a collection of essays, *Impressions of Theophrastus Such* (1879).

Mary Ellmann teaches English at Long Beach City College. Her work includes *Thinking About Women* (1968).

Nora Ephron (1941–   ), American journalist, novelist, and screenwriter. Her work includes *Wallflower at the Orgy* (1970, interviews), *Crazy Salad* (1975), the semiautobiographical *Heartburn* (1983), *Silkwood* (a screenplay co-authored with Alice Arlen, 1983), and the 1989 script for *When Harry Met Sally*. Ephron's parents, Phoebe and Henry Ephron, both screenplay writers, based one of their own works on their daughter's letters home from college.

Fanny Fern (Sara Payson [Willis] Parton) (1811–72), American essayist, novelist, columnist, and co-founder, with Jane Croly, in 1868, of New York City's "pioneering women's club, Sorosis." Her publications include *Fern Leaves from Fanny's Port-folio* (1854), *Gingersnaps* (1870), *Ruth Hall* (1886), and *Rose Clark* (1856).

Geraldine Ferraro (1935–   ), American vice-presidential candidate, New York congressperson, and autobiographer whose concise August 1984 answer to Mississippi Agriculture Commissioner Jim Buck Ross's penetrating question "Can you bake a blueberry muffin?" is recorded in *Ferraro: My Story*: "I sure can, can you?"

Anne Finch (1661–1720), English poet. Her verse was included in Charles Giddon's *New Collection of Poems on Several Occasions* (1701) and Delariviere Manley's *Secret Memoirs . . . from the New Atlantis* (1709), and her prefatory poems in Pope's collected *Works* (1717) and his *Poems on Several Occasions* (1717).

Mary (1865–1963) and **Jane** (1866–1946) **Findlater**, Scottish novelists and short-fiction writers who both collaborated and wrote separately, as did their mother, Sarah, on religious works. Publications include *Songs and Sonnets* (1895), *The Green Graves of Balgowerie* (1896) (as children, the girls' religious education included visits to deathbeds), and *Crossriggs* (1908).

Fannie Flagg, contemporary American actress, screenwriter, director, comedian, and novelist who was expelled from school in the fifth grade for producing, directing, and starring in "The Whoopee Girls," a three-act comedy containing the word "martini." Her work includes *Coming Attractions* (1981) and *Fried Green Tomatoes at the Whistle Stop Cafe* (1987).

Diane Ford, contemporary American stand-up comic who deals with gender issues and talks a great deal about growing up in Minnesota. She makes frequent appearances on HBO.

Margaret Fuller (1810–50), American social reformer, journalist, critic, and editor of *The Dial*. Her work includes *Summer on the Lake* (1843) and *Women in the 19th Century and Kindred Papers relating to the Sphere, Condition and Duties of Woman* (1855).

Zsa Zsa Gabor (1918?–   ), Hungarian-born actress and autobiographer whose work includes *Zsa Zsa Gabor: My Story* (1960) and *One Lifetime Is Not Enough* (1991), in which she remarks, "Ankara electrified me, enthralled me with its winding streets, golden cupolas, exotic food, and erotic aura of Eastern promise. My new husband, however, was not so promising."

Elizabeth Gaskell (1810–1865), English novelist and biographer. Her work includes *Mary Barton* (1848), *Ruth* (1853), *Cranford* (1853), and *North and South* (1855), as well as *The Life of Charlotte Brontë* (1857), commissioned by Brontë's father. Her biographer, Winifred Gérin, described Gaskell as having "a special quality of radiance."

Stella Gibbons (1902–1989), English novelist and poet whose work includes *The Priestess and Other Poems* (1924), *Christmas at Cold Comfort Farm* (1932), and *The Woods in Winter* (1970). It was as a reviewer of novels for the English magazine *Lady* that, Gibbons claimed, her talent for satire was roused.

Charlotte Perkins Gilman (1869–1935), American novelist, short-fiction writer, poet, and polemicist whose semiautobiographical master-piece, "The Yellow Wallpaper," was originally rejected by an editor at *The Atlantic Monthly*, who claimed he "could not forgive myself if I made others as miserable as I have made myself [in reading your story]!" Other works include *Women and Economics* (1898), *What Diantha Did* (1910), and *Herland* (1915).

Nikki Giovanni (1943–   ), African-American poet, essayist, and autobiographer. Her work includes *Gemini: An Extended Autobiographical Statement on My First Twenty-Five Years of Being a Black Poet* (1971), *Sacred Cows and Other Edibles* (1988), and *Racism 101* (1994). Giovanni claims that "the new black poetry is in fact just a manifestation of our collective needs."

Whoopi Goldberg (1950–   ), American stand-up comedian, writer, and actress whose films include *The Color Purple, Corinna Corinna, Jumpin Jack Flash,* and *Boys on the Side.*

Ellen Goodman (1941–   ), American syndicated columnist and commentator. Her works include the Pulitzer Prize–winning *Close to Home* (1979), *At Large* (1981), *Keeping in Touch* (1985), and *Making Sense* (1989).

Serena Gray, contemporary American essayist whose work has appeared in *Cosmopolitan* and *Women's Own.* Her work includes *The Slags Almanac* and *Beached on the Shores of Love* (1989).

Germaine Greer (1939–   ), Australian-born feminist, critic, and journalist. Her work includes *The Female Eunuch* (1970), a feminist milestone, which was translated into twelve languages, *The Obstacle Race* (1979), published under the pseudonym "Rose Blight," *Sex and Destiny: The Politics of Human Fertility* (1984), and *The Madwoman's Underclothes* (1987).

Nicole Gregory, contemporary American magazine writer and editor. She is the co-author, with **Judith Stone,** of *Heeling Your Inner Dog: A Self-Welp Book* (1993), and *The Top Ten Almanac* (1992).

Sarah Moore Grimké (1792–1873), American essayist and Quaker minister. She and her sister, as members of the New York Anti-Slavery Society, were, in 1836, the first American women to address mixed audiences. Her work includes *Epistle to the Clergy of the Southern States* (1836) and *Letters on the Equality of the Sexes and the Condition of Women* (1838).

Cathy Guisewite, contemporary American cartoonist and creator of the widely syndicated "Cathy" comic strip. Her work includes *Dancing Through Life on a Pair of Broken Heels: Extremely Short Stories for the Totally Stressed* (1993), which she co-authored with her sister, Mickey Guisewite.

Modine Gunch, contemporary American columnist and regular contributor to *New Orleans Magazine.* Gunch believes that anyone willing to wear the recently reintroduced body shirts, "a cruel item . . . which buttons underneath the crotch to achieve maximum tightness . . . needs to reevaluate their priorities." Her work includes *Never Heave Your Bosom in a Front-Hook Bra* (1987).

Margaret Halsey (1910–   ), American novelist, social critic, humorist, and autobiographer whose work includes *With Malice Toward Some* (1938), *Some of My Best Friends Are Soldiers* (1944), *This Demi-Paradise: A Westchester Diary* (1960), and *No Laughing Matter: The Autobiography of a WASP* (1977). Halsey's work, which focuses on a wide range of political and social issues, foresaw the Nixon administration debacle in *The Pseudo-Ethic* in 1963.

Eliza Haywood (c. 1693–1756), English playwright, novelist, editor, and actress. Her work includes *Love in Excess* (1719), *The Fair Captive* (1721), the periodical *The Female Spectator* (1744), *The History of Miss Betty Thoughtless* (1751), and *Jenny and Jeremy Jessamy* (1752). Her *Memoirs of a Certain Island Adjacent to Utopia* (1724) and her *Secret History of the Present Intrigues of the Court of Caramania* (1727) resulted in Pope's savage attack in *The Female Dunciad* (1728), in which he called her a "shameless scribbler" and claimed she was the mother of two "love-children."

Cynthia Heimel (1947–   ), American humorist whose work includes *Sex Tips for Girls* (1983) and *But Enough About You* (1986). In her *Get Your Tongue Out of My Mouth, I'm Kissing You Good-bye* (1993), she notes that " 'Slut' used to mean a slovenly woman. Now it means a woman who will go to bed with everyone. This is considered a bad thing in a woman, although perfectly fabulous in a man. 'Bitch' means a woman who will go to bed with everyone but you."

Nicole Hollander, contemporary American humorist and cartoonist whose work includes *The Whole Enchilada* (1976), *That Woman Must Be on Drugs: A Collection of Sylvia* (1981), and *Mercy, It's the Revolution and I'm Still in My Bathrobe* (1992). Her character Sylvia is syndicated in 60 newspapers.

Marietta Holley (1836–1926), American essayist, poet, and humorist. Her work, which confronts a wide range of political issues, such as imperialism, racism, women's rights, prostitution, and temperance, includes *My Opinions and Betsey Bobbet's* (1873), *Sweet Cicely* (1885), *Samantha at Saratoga: or Racin' After Fashion* (1887), and *The Widder Doodle's Courtship* (1896).

Judy Holliday (1922–65), American actress who won an Oscar in 1950 for her role in *Born Yesterday*. She was compared to Charlie Chaplin by critics and directors. Her films include *Adam's Rib* (1949), *The Marrying Kind* (1952), and *Phfft* (1954). Holliday was partially blacklisted after appearing before the Senate Internal Security Subcommittee in 1952.

Marie Jenney Howe (c. 1871–1934), a one-time Unitarian minister who organized a successful theatrical company in Manhattan's Twenty-fifth Assembly District of the Woman Suffrage Party; it toured in and around New York. Howe was inspired by the nineteenth-century French woman writer George Sand. She was Sand's biographer and editor of *The Intimate Journal of George Sand* (1929).

Josephine Humphreys, contemporary American novelist whose *Dreams of Sleep* (1985) won the Ernest Hemingway Foundation Award from PEN for a first work of fiction. Her second novel is *Rich in Love* (1987).

Zora Neale Hurston (1909–60), African-American novelist, folklorist, and anthropologist. Her works include her autobiography, *Dust Tracks on a Road* (1942), and the novels *Jonah's Gourd Vine* (1934) and *Their Eyes Were Watching God* (1937). In the 1920s and '30s Hurston was one of only a handful of eminent women engaged in the African-American cultural movement now referred to as the Harlem Renaissance.

Ann E. Imbrie, contemporary nonfiction writer and English professor at Vassar College. Her work includes *Spoken in Darkness: Small-Town Murder and a Friendship Beyond Death* (1993), a book that tells the story of her childhood best friend, a young woman who fell victim to a serial killer.

Elizabeth Inchbald (1753–1821), English novelist, dramatist, editor, and actress. Her plays include *The Mogul Tale* (1784), *I'll Tell You What* (1795), *Lover's Vows* (1798), and *To Marry or Not to Marry* (1805); novels include *A Simple Story* (1791) and *Nature and Art* (1796). She edited *The British Theatre* (1806–09), a 25-volume collection of plays. On her confessor's advice, she unfortunately destroyed most of 50 years' worth of her letters and journals. James Boaden attempted to reconstruct her life from what was left, in *Memoirs of Mrs. Inchbald* (1833).

Molly Ivins (1944–   ), American journalist and humorist who writes frequently for the *Texas Observer* and the *New York Times*, is also a contributor to the *NewsHour with Jim Lehrer*. She was the recipient of the 1991 Carey McWilliams Award, given by the American Political Science Association. Her work includes *Molly Ivins Can't Say That, Can She?* (1991) and *Nothin' but Good Times Ahead* (1993).

Elaine Jackson, contemporary African-American playwright whose work includes *Toe Jam* (1971), *Cockfight* (1978), and *Paper Dolls* (1983), was the 1978–79 winner of the Rockefeller Award for playwriting, the 1979 winner of the Langston Hughes Playwriting Award, and the 1983 winner of the NEA Award for playwriting.

Shirley Jackson (1919–65), American novelist, short-fiction and children's book writer, screenwriter, essayist, and humorist, whose work, critic Ihab Hassan claims, "moves on the invisible shadow line between fantasy and verisimilitude; it also hovers between innocence and dark knowledge." Her fiction includes *The Road through the Wall* (1948), "The Lottery," which appeared in *The New Yorker* in 1948, *Life Among the Savages* (1953), *The Haunting of Hill House* (1959), and *Come Along with Me* (1968).

Bonnie Januszewski-Ytuarte (1957–   ) is an educator who grew up on Long Island. Using theater and other innovative methods, she has pioneered programs in AIDS education, sexuality awareness, and is presently working with autistic children.

Jenny Jones, contemporary stand-up comic and columnist.

Erica Jong (1942–   ), American poet and novelist. Her work includes *Half-Lives* (1973), *At the Edge of the Body* (1979), *Fear of Flying* (1974), and *Fear of Fifty* (1994), a "mid-life memoir" that explores the changing ideals of womanhood and the mind-bending Doris Day/Gloria Steinem/ Madonna syndrome.

Judith Katz, contemporary American novelist whose work includes *Running Fiercely Toward a High Thin Sound* (1992), has been the recipient of both the Bush Foundation Creative Writing Award and an NEA Fellowship.

Pamela Katz, contemporary American filmmaker, screenwriter, and author. She has written numerous screenplays, including an adaptation of Fay Weldon's story *Angel, All Innocence*.

Florynce Kennedy (1916–   ), American feminist essayist and lawyer and author of *Color Me Flo* (1976).

Jean Kerr (1923–   ), American playwright and humorist whose mainly autobiographical work includes *The Snake Has All the Lines* (1960), *Please Don't Eat the Daisies* (1957) (the movie version starred Doris Day), *How I Got to Be Perfect* (1978), and *Lunch Hour* (1982).

Laura Kightlinger, contemporary American comedian and essayist whose work has appeared in *New Perspectives on Women and Comedy* (1992). She joined the cast of *Saturday Night Live* in 1994.

Florence King (1936–   ), American writer and critic. Her work includes *He, an Irreverent Look at the American Male* (1978), *Confessions of a Failed Southern Lady* (1985), *Reflections in a Jaundiced Eye* (1989), and *Lump It or Leave It* (1990).

Maxine Hong Kingston (1940–   ), Chinese-American autobiographer and novelist. Her works include *The Woman Warrior: Memoirs of a Girlhood Among Ghosts* (1976), *China Men* (1980), and *Tripmaster Monkey: His Fake Book* (1988). About those who criticize the nontraditional use of myth in her work, Kingston says, "They don't understand that myths have to change, be useful or be forgotten."

Sarah Kemble Knight (1666–1727), early American diarist whose *Journal of Madam Knight* (1825) humorously records her unescorted round-trip journey between Boston and New York in 1704. A businesswoman with sharp skills of observation and an even sharper pen, she is said to have at one time included the young Ben Franklin among the neighborhood children she taught to read and write in her Boston neighborhood.

Nella Larsen (c. 1891–1964), American novelist whose work was much praised for its portrayal of black middle-class life. Her early work appeared in the children's magazine *The Brownies Book*. *Quicksand* (1928) won the Harmon Foundation's Bronze award for literature. Her work has been collected in *An Intimation of Things Distant: The Collected Fiction of Nella Larsen* (1992). David Thadious's biography, *Nella Larsen, Novelist of the Harlem Renaissance: A Woman's Life Unveiled*, was published in 1994.

Mary Leapor (1722–46), English poet. Her works, published posthumously, include *Poems Upon Several Occasions* (1748), edited and reprinted in 1751 by Samuel Richardson and Isaac Hawkins Brown. Employed as a cookmaid, she is said to have neglected her duties for her writing. Much of her work was concerned with the plight of women.

Fran Lebowitz (1951?–), American columnist, critic, and essayist whose work includes *Metropolitan Life* (1978) and *Social Studies* (1981). Her humor has been described by Cathleen Schine, in *Vogue*, as "pedagogical satire." Her hero is Oscar Wilde.

Carol Leifer, contemporary American comedian whose recent television work includes "Carol Leifer: Gaudy, Bawdy and Blue."

Charlotte Lennox (1729–1804), English playwright, novelist, and critic. Her plays include *The Sister* (1769) and *Old City Manners* (1775); novels include *The Life of Harriet Stuart* (1751), *The Female Quixote* (1752), *Henrietta* (1758), *The History of Harriet and Sophia* (1760–61), and *Euphemia* (1790). Her *Shakespeare Illustrated* (1753–54) was the first work of literary criticism to trace Shakespeare's sources.

Baird Leonard, (c. 1890–?) American humorist whose 1920s *New Yorker* series, "Metropolitan Monotypes," satirizes (among other things) the stereotype of the impossibly perfect wife.

Doris Lessing (1919–), Persian-born English novelist, essayist, and short-fiction writer. Her works include *The Grass Is Singing* (1950), the "Children of Violence" quintet (1952–69), *The Golden Notebook* (1962), the "Canopus in Argus: Archives" sequence (1979–1983), *The Diary of a Good Neighbor*, as *The Diaries of Jane Somers* (1984), *The Good Terrorist* (1985), and *Doris Lessing Conversations* (1994). In *African Laughter: Four Visits to Zimbabwe* (1992), Lessing records the following exchange: "What is the most dangerous job in Zimbabwe?" "Minister for Internal Affairs: your conscience will kill you."

Esther Lewis (fl. 1747–89), English poet whose verse appeared in the *Bath Journal* in 1749 under the name "Sylvia," and was ocassionally reprinted in London periodicals such as the *Gentleman's Magazine*. Dr. Samuel Bowden included her work in his *Poems on Various Subjects* in 1754; she herself published *Poems Moral and Entertaining* in Bath in 1778.

Judy Little, contemporary author of *Comedy and the Woman Writer:*

Woolf, Spark, and Feminism (1983). She teaches literature and women's studies at Southern Illinois University, Carbondale.

Anita Loos (1893–1981), American playwright, screenwriter, and autobiographer. Her work on more than 200 films and plays includes *The Whole Town's Talking* (1923), *The Fall of Eve* (1925), and *Gentlemen Prefer Blondes* (1925). Her two autobiographical works are *A Girl Like I* (1966) and *Kiss Hollywood Goodby* (1974). Loos, who began writing movie scripts at age twelve, was greatly admired by Aldous Huxley, H. G. Wells, and philosopher George Santayana.

Jackey "Moms" Mabley (1894–1975), African-American singer and comedian who performed at the famous Apollo Theatre and Cotton Club in Harlem in their heyday. Her motion picture roles include *Boarding House Blues* (1929), *Emperor Jones* (1939), and *Amazing Grace* (1974).

Betty MacDonald (Anne Elizabeth Campbell Bard) (1908–1958), American novelist. Her work includes *The Egg and I* (1945), *The Plague and I* (1948), *Anybody Can Do Anything* (1950), and *Onions in the Stew* (1955). Her autobiographical works reveal the false illusions and ridiculous assumptions under which married women were expected to cheerily operate (and still are—see Regina Barreca's *Perfect Husbands and Other Fairy Tales* [1994]).

Patricia Mainard, contemporary American optimist concerning men's sharing of household chores. She is one of the founding members of Redstockings, an art historian who teaches at the City University of New York, and author of *Art and Politics of the Second Empire* (1987).

Mary Delariviere Manley (1663–1724), English playwright, editor, and essayist. Her work includes *The Secret History of Queen Zarah* (1705), *Secret Memoirs and Manners of Several Persons of Quality of Both Sexes* (1709), *Memoirs of Europe* (1710), and *The Adventures of Rivella* (1714).

Katherine Mansfield (1888–1923), New Zealand-born short-fiction writer who spent most of her adult life in England and in Europe. Her works include *In a German Pension* (1926), *Bliss and Other Stories* (1921), and *The Garden Party and Other Stories* (1923). Her original and experimental work was greatly influenced by Chekhov, whom she admired immensely.

Merrill Markoe, contemporary American humorist, scriptwriter, and recipient of the Writers Guild and Ace awards for *Not Necessarily the News*. Markoe is also the creator of "Stupid Pet Tricks," and a four-time Emmy Award winner as head writer for *Late Night with David Letterman*. Her work includes *What the Dogs Have Taught Me and Other Amazing Things I've Learned* (1992) and *How to Be Hap-Hap-Happy Like Me* (1994).

Penny Marshall, contemporary film producer, actress, and director. She directed *A League of Their Own.*

Judith Martin (1938–   ), American film critic and humorist, essayist, novelist, and syndicated television writer. Her work includes *The Name on the White House Floor* (1972), *Gilbert: A Comedy of Manners* (1982), and *Miss Manners' Guide to Excruciatingly Correct Behavior* (1983).

Harriet Martineau (1802–76), remarkably prolific English essayist, novelist, journalist, autobiographer, travel and children's writer who claims, "There was something that I wanted to say, and I said it. That was all." Some of her numerous works include *The Hampdens* (1880), *Life in the Sick-Room* (1844), and *Deerbrook* (1839).

Bobbie Ann Mason (1942–   ), American short-fiction writer whose collections include *Shiloh and Other Stories* (1982), *Love Life* (1989), and *Feather Crowns* (1993). She is also the author of *The Girl Sleuth: A Feminist Guide to the Bobbsey Twins, Nancy Drew, and Their Sisters* (1975), a book that explores the popular fiction avidly read by many female children, including Mason herself.

Phyllis McGinley (1905–78), American poet, essayist, and children's writer whose work includes *A Pocketful of Wry* (1940), *Stones from a Glass House* (1946), and *A Short Walk from the Station* (1951). McGinley defended women's traditional roles in two books of essays, *The Province of the Heart* (1959) and *Sixpence in Her Shoe* (1964).

Terry McMillan (1951–   ), African-American novelist and critic whose work includes *Mama* (1987), *Disappearing Acts* (1989), and *Fife for Five: The Films of Spike Lee* (1991). About *Waiting to Exhale* (1992), Spike Lee comments: "No doubt the author will hear . . . the cries that the Black man has been wronged, the Black man has been dogged. I disagree: Terry McMillan has crafted a well-written, truthful and funny story. . . ."

Beverly Mickins, contemporary African-American actress and comedian. She became interested in comedy after realizing how limited were the number of roles for black women actresses.

Edna St. Vincent Millay (1892–1950), American poet. Her works include *Renascence and Other Poems* (1917), *A Few Figs from Thistles* (1920), and *Collected Poems* (1956). The publication of "Renascence" in *Lyric Year* occasioned controversy over the gender of the author. In 1923 Millay received the first Pulitzer Prize in poetry awarded to a woman.

Alice Duer Miller (1874–1942), American novelist, poet, short-fiction writer, and newspaper columnist. Her work includes *The Charm School* (1919), *Manslaughter* (1921), *Gowns by Roberta* (1933), and *The White Cliffs* (1944), a romance written in verse. In response to the unfair firing of a woman boiler attendant ("for her own good"), Miller wrote the satiric "The Gallant Sex," a poem which explores the reality of the gallantry behind the dismissal. She ends the poem with "Prithee rest,— or starve or rob—/Only let me have your job."

Carol Mitchell, contemporary American writer whose work has appeared in *Western Folklore*. She is a professor of English at Colorado State University.

Lady Mary Wortley Montagu (1689–1762), poet and letter writer whose first collection of poetry, *Court Poems* (1716) was published without her permission. She accompanied her husband to Turkey where he was ambassador, and recorded her impressions in letters about Turkish culture and life. In 1737–1738, she published a series of articles, *The Nonsense of Common Sense*, in response to the Opposition journal, *Common Sense*.

Marianne Moore (1887–1972), American poet, translator, and essayist whose work includes *Observations* (1924), *Predilictions* (1955), and *Unfinished Poems* (1972). Her *Collected Poems* (1951) won the National Book Award for poetry, the Bollingen Prize in poetry, and the Pulitzer Prize. One of the major voices of the new order of literature, along with fellow student H. D., Moore once remarked about poetry, "I, too, dislike it . . . there are things that are important beyond all this fiddle."

Toni Morrison (1931–   ), African-American novelist and professor. Her works include *The Bluest Eye* (1969), *Sula* (1973), *Song of Solomon* (1977), *Tar Baby* (1981), *Beloved* (1987), which won the Pulitzer Prize, and *Jazz* (1992). Morrison claims that the best art is "irrevocably beautiful and unquestionably political at the same time."

Judith Sargent Murray (1751–1820), American poet, essayist, and playwright whose radical "Essay on the Equality of the Sexes," written in 1779, published in 1790, preceded Mary Wollstonecraft's germinal *Vindication of the Rights of Woman* by two years. Additional works include *The Gleaner* (1792), *The Medium, or Virtue Triumphant* (1795, the first American play staged in Boston), and *The Traveller Returned* (1798).

Gloria Naylor (1950–   ), African-American novelist who claims she found both the assurance and her own authority for the written word after reading Toni Morrison's *The Bluest Eye*. Her work includes *The Women of Brewster Place* (1982), *Linden Hills* (1985), *Mama Day* (1988), and *Bailey's Cafe* (1992).

Itabari Njeri, contemporary African-American award-winning journalist. Njeri's many hats include arts critic, essayist, autobiographer, reporter, and producer for NPR in Boston, as well as singer and actress. Her work has appeared in the *Los Angeles Times*, the *Miami Herald*, and the *Greenville News*. Her autobiography is *Every Good-bye Ain't Gone: Family Portraits and Personal Escapades* (1990).

Sheryl Noethe, contemporary American poet whose work includes *The Descent of Heaven Over the Lake* (1984). She worked as a mime while traveling through Europe and Greece.

Edna O'Brien (1932–   ), Anglo-Irish short-fiction writer and novelist. Her work includes *The Country Girls* (1960), *The Lonely Girl* (1962), *Girls in Their Married Bliss* (1964), *A Scandalous Woman* (1974), and *The House of Splendid Isolation* (1994). In the prologue to *Time & Tide: A Novel* (1992), she writes, "That is the thing with words. You cannot wash them and wipe them the way you wipe dishes."

Flannery O'Connor (1925–64), American short-fiction writer and novelist. Her work includes *Wise Blood* (1952), *The Violent Bear It Away* (1960), and *The Complete Stories* (1971). In a letter written during a serious illness to Caroline Gordon Tate, O'Connor reported that "the doctor says I can't do any work. But he says it's all right for me to write a little fiction."

Jane O'Reilly, contemporary American journalist who contributes frequently to *Gentleman's Quarterly*, *The Nation*, the *New York Times Book Review*, *Ms.*, and *Glamour*. Her work includes *The Girl I Left Behind* (1980).

Dorothy Osborne (1627–94), British writer whose private correspondence with her lover contains astute observations about her surroundings, literature, and culture.

Grace Paley (1922–   ), American short-fiction writer whose work has appeared in *The New Yorker*, *The Atlantic Monthly*, and *Esquire*. She became interested in women and children living apart from men when she herself lived in army camps with other soldiers' wives in the early years of her marriage to soldier Jess Paley. Collections of her works include *The Little Disturbances of Man* (1959), *Enormous Changes at the Last Minute* (1974), *Shenandoah* (1976), and *Later the Same Day* (1985).

Gail Parent, contemporary American novelist, script and screenplay writer who, with Kenny Solms, wrote *The Carol Burnett Show* for four years. Other work includes *Shelia Levine Is Dead and Living in New York* (1972), *A Little Bit Married* (1984), and *A Sign of the Eighties* (1987).

Dorothy Parker (1893–1967), American poet, playwright, short-fiction writer, and critic who was blacklisted, as was her husband and partner, Alan Campbell, for their political views in the Hollywood of the 1940s. Her work can be found in *Collected Stories of Dorothy Parker* (1942), *Collected Poetry of Dorothy Parker* (1944), and *The Portable Dorothy Parker* (1944).

Cathie Pelletier, contemporary American novelist, poet, and short-ficton writer who was raised in Maine. Her work includes *The Funeral Makers* (1986), *The Weight of Winter: A Novel* (1991), and *A Marriage Made at Woodstock* (1994). She is an active friend to stray dogs and cats and animals of all kinds, as well as an eager bird-watcher.

Ann Petry (Lane) (1908–   ), African-American novelist, journalist, short-fiction and children's writer, who says, "Because I was born black and female I write for survivors (especially when I write for children)." Her work includes *The Country Place* (1947), *The Narrows* (1953), and *Miss Muriel and Other Stories* (1971).

Fiona Pitt-Kethley (1954–   ), British author whose work includes *Sky Ray Lolly* (1986) and *The Literary Companion to Sex: An Anthology of Prose and Poetry* (1992).

Sylvia Plath (1932–63), American poet and novelist. Her poetry (much of it published posthumously) appears in *The Colossus* (1960), *Ariel* (1966), *Crossing the Water* (1971), *Winter Trees* (1971), and *Collected Poems* (1981). *Johnny Panic and the Bible of Dreams*, a collection of prose pieces, appeared in 1977; her only novel, *The Bell Jar*, was published one month before her suicide. In a 1953 journal entry Plath remarked that she couldn't "be satisfied with the colossal job of merely living. Oh, no, I must order life in sonnets and sestinas and provide a verbal reflector for my 60-watt lighted head."

Letty Cottin Pogrebin (1939–   ), American writer, one of the founding editors of *Ms.*, and co-developer, with Marlo Thomas, of the books *Free to Be You and Me* (1974) and *Free to Be a Family* (1987). Her work includes *Family Politics: Love and Power* (1983) and *Deborah, Golda, and Me: Being Jewish and Female in America* (1991).

Mimi Pond, contemporary American humorist whose work includes *Shoes Never Lie* (1985) and *A Groom of One's Own and Other Bridal Necessities* (1991). Her comic strip, "Mimi's Page," appears monthly in *Seventeen*.

Paula Poundstone, contemporary American comedian, foster parent, and regular contributor to *Mother Jones*, who, although she wishes to "be like Gandhi," realizes her "efforts are much smaller. He liberated India. I let people in in traffic."

Barbara Pym (1913–80), English novelist whose works include *Excellent Women* (1952), *A Glass of Blessings* (1959), and *Quartet in Autumn* (1977). As *The British Women Writer's Reference Guide* notes, while Pym's "world may on the surface be a cosy one . . . the implications it suggests are bleak."

Gilda Radner (1946–89), American comedian, actress, and writer. She was the first woman to join the cast of the original *Saturday Night Live*; later she appeared on Broadway and in movies. Her work includes *It's Always Something* (1989), a book about her struggle with ovarian cancer.

Libby Reid, contemporary American cartoonist whose work includes *Do You Hate Your Hips More than Nuclear War* and *You Don't Have to Pet to be Popular* (1989). Former careers included cheese hostess and radio announcer.

Agnes Repplier (1855–1950), American essayist, lecturer, biographer, and autobiographer. Her work includes *Books and Men* (1888), *Points of View* (1891), *Essays in Miniature* (1892), and *Counter-Currents* (1916).

Joan Rivers (1939?–), American comedian whose books include *The Life and Hard Times of Heidi Abromowitz* (1985), *Enter Talking* (1986), and *Still Talking* (1991).

Roseanne (1952–), American stand-up comic, writer, actress, and creator of the popular television program bearing her name.

Helen Rowland (1875–1950), American columnist and essayist. Her works are collected in *The Digressions of Polly* (1905), *The Widow* (1908), *Reflections of a Bachelor Girl* (1909), *The Sayings of Mrs. Solomon* (1913), *A Guide to Men* (1922), and *This Married Life* (1927). Rowland wrote satirically, and sometimes cynically, about the inequality inherent in the institution of marriage.

Jill Ruckelshaus (1937?–), American politician and lecturer.

Rita Rudner, contemporary American comedian, humorist, and winner of the 1990 American Comedy Award for Funniest Female Stand-Up. Her work includes *Friendly Advice* (1990) and *Naked Beneath My Clothes: Tales of a Revealing Nature* (1992).

Muriel Rukeyser (1913–80), American social activist, teacher, screenwriter, poet, translator, biographer, and author of books for children. Her work includes *Theory of Flight* (1935), *The Speed of Darkness* (1968), and *The Gates* (1976). Her commitment to political, economic, racial, and gender issues, combined with her later interest in mythic and historical female figures, has produced a significant body of innovative work.

Joanna Russ (1937–), American critic, short-fiction and science-fiction writer. Her work includes *The Female Man* (1975), *The Two of Them* (1978) and a book of feminist criticism, *How to Suppress Women's Writing* (1983). Russ turned to science fiction and fantasy writing when she realized in college that, being female, her life experience was not considered legitimate material for literature.

Mary Russo, contemporary American literary critic, editor, and professor of humanities at Hampshire College in Amherst, Massachusetts.

Her work includes "Notes on Post-Feminism: Proceedings of the Essex Conference on the Sociology of Literature" (1982) and "Female Grotesques: Carnival and Theory" (1986).

Dorothy L. Sayers (1893–1957), modern British novelist, playwright, and translator of Dante's *Divine Comedy*. Her detective fiction includes *Murder Must Advertise* (1933) and *The Nine Tailors* (1934). Sayers was the first woman ever to receive an Oxford degree, in the field of medieval linguistics.

Florence Guy Seabury (1881–1951), American writer and social commentator whose book, *The Delicatessen Husband and Other Essays* (1926), confronts the changing of relations between the genders. She was a socialist who served as editor for *The Woman Voter* and contributed articles to numerous magazines, including *Harper's*, *McCall's*, and *The New Republic*.

Anne Sexton (1928–74), American poet whose first book of poetry, *To Bedlam and Part Way Back* (1960), chronicled her experience with and recovery from mental illness. Other works include the Pulitzer Prize–winning *Live or Die* (1966).

Ntozake Shange (1948–   ), African-American playwright, novelist, and essayist whose work includes *For Colored Girls Who Have Considered Suicide, When the Rainbow Is Enuf* (1975), *Sassafras, Cypress, and Indigo* (1982), *Betsey Brown* (1985), *See No Evil: Prefaces, Essays, and Accounts* (1984). Shange's work courageously explores the double difficulties which face African-American girls and women.

Joane Sharpe, seventeenth-century author who protested against misogynistic images of women.

May Sinclair (1863–1946), English poet, critic, philosopher, short-fiction writer, and novelist. Her work includes *The Three Sisters* (1914), *Mary Olivier* (1919), *Life and Death of Harriet Frean* (1920), and *Mr. Waddington of Wyck* (1921). Sinclair was an early advocate of modernist literary efforts attempting to break with standard Victorian conventions.

Betty Smith (1896–1972), American novelist and playwright who published over 70 works, including *A Tree Grows in Brooklyn* (1943), *Tomorrow Will be Better* (1948), and *Joy in the Morning* (1963). Although Smith left school at a young age in order to support her family, she eventually returned, studying playwrighting at Yale and holding a fellowship at the University of North Carolina.

Stevie Smith (1902–71), English poet and novelist. Her works include *Novel on Yellow Paper* (1936), *The Holiday* (1949), *A Good Time Was Had by All* (1937), and *Not Waving but Drowning* (1957). The poet Robert Lowell noted that she sounded "a unique and cheerfully gruesome voice."

Carrie Snow, contemporary writer and comedian.

Muriel Spark (1918–   ), Scottish novelist, short-fiction writer, playwright, and poet. Her work includes *The Comforters* (1957), *The Prime of Miss Jean Brodie* (1961), *Loitering with Intent* (1981), and *Curriculum Vitae*, a memoir (1992), as well as collections of poetry and plays. Spark's conversion to Catholicism at the age of thirty-six provided her with a great deal of problematic and ironic material.

Elizabeth Cady Stanton (1815–1902), American co-author, with Susan B. Anthony and Matilda Joslyn Gage, of the three-volume *History of Woman's Suffrage* (1881–1922). Other books include *The Woman's Bible* (1895, 1898), and her autobiography, *Eighty Years and More* (1898). She was co-founder, with Anthony, of the National Woman Suffrage Association, as well as its president and major spokesperson for twenty-one years.

Linda Stasi, contemporary American writer whose work includes *Simply Beautiful* (1983) and *A Field Guide to Impossible Men* (1987). Her "Hot Copy" column appears in the New York *Daily News*. She is also the creator and host of "Good Looks," a daily "Dial-it" program for the telephone company, the creator of "Seventeen at School" for *Seventeen*, and the Beauty and Fashion Editor of *Weight Watchers Magazine*.

Abby Stein, contemporary American stand-up comic and former president of the Professional Comedians Association in New York City, who discovered her affinity for comedy through a $30 course on how to be a stand-up comic.

Gertrude Stein (1874–1946), American-born poet, novelist, autobiographer, and patron of the arts who spent most of her adult life in Paris. Her work includes *Three Lives* (1909), *Tender Buttons* (1914), and *The Autobiography of Alice B. Toklas* (1933). Stein remarks, in *Geographical History of America* (1936), that "in this epoch the important literary thinking is done by a woman."

Gloria Steinem (1934–   ), American essayist, political activist, and ground-breaking feminist, whose work includes *Outrageous Acts and Everyday Rebellions* (1983), *Marilyn: Norma Jean* (1986), *Revolution from Within: A Book of Self-Esteem* (1992), and *Moving Beyond Words* (1994). Steinem became a founding editor of *Ms.* in response to the prevalent sexist content and policies she found while working as a freelance writer and consultant to *The Ladies' Home Journal*, *Esquire*, and *Cosmopolitan*.

Eliza "Mother" Stewart (1816–1908), American temperance leader whose work includes *Memories of the Crusade* (1889).

Deanne Stillman, contemporary American playwright, journalist, and critic whose work includes *Play for Surf*, one of the two winners at the 1991 Theatre Works Festival at the University of Colorado. She and

Anne Beatts co-edited *Titters: The First Collection of Humor by Women* (1976).

Catharine R. Stimpson (1936–), American novelist and founding editor of *Signs*. Her work includes *Class Notes: A Novel* (1979) and *Where the Meanings Are: Feminism and Cultural Spaces* (1988). She is the co-editor, with Ethel Person, of *Women—Sex and Sexuality* (1980), and the dean of Graduate Studies at Rutgers University.

Judith Stone (1946–), contemporary American magazine writer, editor, and co-author, with **Nicole Gregory**, of *Heeling Your Inner Dog: A Self-Welp Book* (1993). Stone is a contributing editor to both *Discover* and *Glamour*. Other works include *Light Elements* (1991).

Pam Stone, contemporary American actress and stand-up comic who appears on the ABC situation comedy *Coach* as basketball coach Judy Watkins.

Harriet Beecher Stowe (1811–96), American novelist, essayist, and short-fiction writer. Her work includes *Uncle Tom's Cabin* (1852), *The Minister's Wooing* (1859), and *Pogamic People* (1878). Stowe's sense of the moral power of women was strongly influenced by her older sister, Catherine Beecher, who believed women could both reform and redeem American culture through adherence to Christian behavior.

Linda Sunshine, contemporary American humorist whose work includes *Women Who Date Too Much (And Those Who Should Be So Lucky)* (1988) and *Lovers* (1992). Her work frequently appears in *Victoria*, *Omni*, *Harper's Bazaar*, and *Glamour*.

May Swenson (1919–89), American poet who claimed she typographically shaped her verse in order "to make an existence in space, as well as time, for the poem." Her collections include *Another Animal* (1954), *To Mix with Time: New and Selected Poems* (1963), and *Iconographs* (1970).

Judy Syfers (Brady), contemporary American feminist writer.

Judy Tenuta, contemporary American comedian whose alter-ego, "the goddess," is a "Prom Queen from Hell." Her work includes *The Power of Judyism* (1991).

Marlo Thomas (1943–), American actress and co-developer, with Letty Cottin Pogrebin, of the books and television shows *Free to Be You and Me* (1974) and *Free to Be a Family* (1987).

Lily Tomlin (1939–), American actress and comedian who starred in the television show *Laugh-in*, and the movies *Nashville* (1975), *9 to 5* (1980), and *Short Cuts* (1994).

Emily Toth, contemporary American critic. She is the author of *Inside Peyton Place: The Life of Grace Metalious* (1981) and *Kate Chopin* (1990), and the editor of *Regionalism and the Female Imagination* (1985).

Frances Milton Trollope (1779–1863), English writer. Her work includes *The Refugee in America* (1832), *Domestic Manners of the Americans* (1832), *Paris and the Parisians* (1835), *Jonathan Jefferson Whitlow* (1836), and *A Visit to Italy* (1842).

Catharine Trotter (1679–1749), English playwright, essayist, and poet whose work includes *The Fatal Friendship: A Tragedy* (1698), *The Revolution in Sweden* (1706), and *Remarks upon the Principles and Reasonings of Dr. Rutherford's Essay on the Nature and Obligation of Virtue* (1747). In "A Letter of Advice to my Son," she urges her son to respect women and treat them fairly rather than barbarously and unjustly as "often practiced towards them, under the specious names of love and gallantry."

Sojourner Truth (1797–1883), former slave who escaped to freedom in 1827. Her speeches were originally recorded by Elizabeth Cady Stanton in *History of Woman Suffrage* (1881–86), but have since been modernized in Miriam Schneir's *Feminism: The Essential Historical Writings* (1972). It has been claimed Truth bared a breast at a women's rights convention in response to allegations that she was a man.

Anne Tyler (1941–), American novelist whose work includes *Dinner at the Homesick Restaurant* (1982), *The Accidental Tourist* (1985), and *Breathing Lessons* (1988). Among her favorite authors are Gabriel García Márquez, Joyce Carol Oates, and Eudora Welty.

Robin Tyler, contemporary American comedian included in the 1992 film about female comedians, *Wisecracks*, about which reviewer Charles Leerhsen wrote, "What the filmmaker, and some of the female comics, seem to miss is that funniness cures all social ills."

Judith Viorst (1936–), American humorist and poet who describes her verse as "aggravation recollected in tranquillity." Collections of her work include *The Village Square* (1965), *People and Other Aggravations* (1971), *Love & Guilt & The Meaning of Life, Etc.* (1979), and *Necessary Losses* (1986).

Helena Maria Viramontes (1954–), Chicana short-fiction writer, editor, and coordinator of the Los Angeles Latino Writers Association. Published collections include *The Moths and Other Stories* (1985). In her work, Viramontes often examines the complex relationship between the personal and the collective identity.

Jane Wagner (1935–), American humorist and writer whose work includes *The Search for Signs of Intelligent Life in the Universe* (1985), and *Edith Ann: My Life So Far* (1994).

Alice Walker (1944–), African-American poet, novelist, short-fiction and children's writer, and essayist. Her work includes *The Third Life of Grange Copeland* (1970), *Revolutionary Petunias* (1973), *The Color Purple*

(1982), and *In Search of Our Mothers' Gardens: Womanist Prose* (1983). Says Walker, "Books are by-products of our lives. If art doesn't make us better, then what on earth is it for?"

Margaret Walker (1915–), African-American poet, critic, and historical novelist whose verse often employs jazz rhythms and blues meters to convey the spirit of her characters. Her work includes *For My People* (1942), *Jubilee* (1966), and *October Journey* (1973).

Wendy Wasserstein (1950–), American playwright whose work includes *Uncommon Women and Others* (1975), *Isn't It Romantic* (1984), *The Heidi Chronicles* (1988), and *The Sisters Rosensweig* (1993). As Andre Bishop writes, "It seems to me that Wendy's plays are plays of *ideas* that happen to be written as comedies."

Mary-Lou Weisman, contemporary American journalist and freelance writer whose work includes the memoir *Intensive Care: A Family Love Story* (1982). Weisman's work has appeared in the *New York Times*, *The New Republic*, and *The Atlantic*.

Fay Weldon (1931–), New Zealand-born novelist, essayist, and television playwright who wrote the first television script for *Upstairs, Downstairs*. Her work includes *The Fat Woman's Joke* (1967), *Praxis* (1978), *The Life and Loves of a She-Devil* (1983), and *Trouble* (1993). Weldon was the winner of the 1989 *Los Angeles Times* Fiction Award for *The Heart of the Country*.

Carolyn Wells (1862–1942), American children's, mystery, detective, and humor writer who produced more than 170 books. Her work includes *At the Sign of the Sphinx* (1896), *The Jungle Book* (1899), *Idle Idyles* (1900), *A Nonsense Anthology* (1902), and *The Rest of My Life* (1926).

Mae West (1893–1980), American actress, screenwriter, autobiographer, and novelist. Her work includes *Diamond Lil* (1928), *The Constant Sinner* (1931), and *Go West Young Man* (1936). West's first play, *Sex* (1926), was considered so shocking that it was closed down and she was jailed for obscenity.

Rebecca West (Cicily Isabel Fairfield) (1892–1983), English novelist, critic, biographer, journalist, and travel writer. Her works include *The Judge* (1922), *The Return of the Soldier* (1918), and the anti-Nazi travel book *Black Lamb and Grey Falcon* (1941). West took her chosen name from Ibsen's *Romersholm* (1886), a play whose central character, Rebecca West, was a feminist radical.

Edith Wharton (1862–1937), American short-fiction writer, poet, autobiographer, and novelist. Her work includes *The House of Mirth* (1905), *Ethan Frome* (1911), and *The Age of Innocence* (1920). In *A Backward Glance* (1934), Wharton poignantly, but ironically, remarked that "none of my relations ever spoke to me of my books, either to praise or blame—they simply ignored them. . . . The subject was avoided as if it were a kind of family disgrace."

Frances Miriam Berry Whitcher (1814–1852), American humorist who satirized life in a small New York town. Her work includes *The Widow Bedott Papers* (1856) and *Widow Spriggins, Mary Elmer, and Other Sketches* (1867).

Paulette Childress White, contemporary African-American poet. Her work includes *Love Poem to a Black Junkie* (1975) and *The Watermelon Dress* (1984).

Katharine Whitehorn (Katherine Elizabeth Lyall) (1928?–), English fashion editor and columnist whose work includes *Cooking in a Bedsitter* (1960), *Social Survival* (1968), and *View from a Column* (1981).

Isabella Whitney (sixteenth century) was the first Englishwoman to publish a book of poetry. Her work includes *Copy of a Letter . . . in Meeter by a Young Gentilwoman to Her Unconstant Lover* (1567?) and *A Sweet Nosegay, or Pleasant Posye Contaynning a Hundred and Ten Phylosophicall Flowers* (1573).

Thyra Samter Winslow (1893–1927), American short fiction writer, critic, journalist, screenwriter, and novelist. Her work includes *Picture Frames* (1923), *Show Business* (1926), and *My Own, My Native Land*, which was originally published as a series of sketches in *The New Yorker*. Her brief experience as a member of a chorus line exposed her to the more sordid side of the theater and provided material for some of her later work.

Liz Winstead, contemporary writer and comedian, who has appeared in a variety of television specials on women's comedy.

Virginia Woolf (1882–1941), English essayist, short-fiction writer, literary critic, and novelist. Her work includes *The Voyage Out* (1915), *Mrs. Dalloway* (1925), *To the Lighthouse* (1927), and *A Room of One's Own* (1929), in which Woolf wittily and wonderfully portrays the all-important relationship between economic and intellectual freedom.

Hannah Woolley (1623–75), English governess and writer of advice and cookbooks.

654

FOR THE BEST IN PAPERBACKS, LOOK FOR THE

In every corner of the world, on every subject under the sun, Penguin represents quality and variety—the very best in publishing today.

For complete information about books available from Penguin—including Puffins, Penguin Classics, and Arkana—and how to order them, write to us at the appropriate address below. Please note that for copyright reasons the selection of books varies from country to country.

In the United Kingdom: Please write to *Dept. JC, Penguin Books Ltd, FREEPOST, West Drayton, Middlesex UB7 0BR.*

If you have any difficulty in obtaining a title, please send your order with the correct money, plus ten percent for postage and packaging, to *P.O. Box No. 11, West Drayton, Middlesex UB7 0BR*

In the United States: Please write to *Consumer Sales, Penguin USA, P.O. Box 999, Dept. 17109, Bergenfield, New Jersey 07621-0120.* VISA and MasterCard holders call 1-800-253-6476 to order all Penguin titles

In Canada: Please write to *Penguin Books Canada Ltd, 10 Alcorn Avenue, Suite 300, Toronto, Ontario M4V 3B2*

In Australia: Please write to *Penguin Books Australia Ltd, P.O. Box 257, Ringwood, Victoria 3134*

In New Zealand: Please write to *Penguin Books (NZ) Ltd, Private Bag 102902, North Shore Mail Centre, Auckland 10*

In India: Please write to *Penguin Books India Pvt Ltd, 706 Eros Apartments, 56 Nehru Place, New Delhi 110 019*

In the Netherlands: Please write to *Penguin Books Netherlands bv, Postbus 3507, NL-1001 AH Amsterdam*

In Germany: Please write to *Penguin Books Deutschland GmbH, Metzlerstrasse 26, 60594 Frankfurt am Main*

In Spain: Please write to *Penguin Books S.A., Bravo Murillo 19, 1° B, 28015 Madrid*

In Italy: Please write to *Penguin Italia s.r.l., Via Felice Casati 20, I-20124 Milano*

In France: Please write to *Penguin France S.A., 17 rue Lejeune, F-31000 Toulouse*

In Japan: Please write to *Penguin Books Japan, Ishikiribashi Building, 2-5-4, Suido, Bunkyo-ku, Tokyo 112*

In Greece: Please write to *Penguin Hellas Ltd, Dimocritou 3, GR-106 71 Athens*

In South Africa: Please write to *Longman Penguin Southern Africa (Pty) Ltd, Private Bag X08, Bertsham 2013*